Corrections in America

An Introduction

Fifth Edition

Harry E. Allen, Ph.D.
San Jose State University

Clifford E. Simonsen, Ph.D.
Central Washington University

Macmillan Publishing Company
NEW YORK

Macmillan Publishing Company
866 Third Avenue, New York, New York 10022

Collier Macmillan Canada, Inc.

LIBRARY OF CONGRESS CATALOGING-IN-PUBLICATION DATA
    Allen, Harry E.
        Corrections in America.
        Includes bibliographies and index.
        1. Corrections — United States.   I. Simonsen,
    Clifford E. II. Title.
    HV9304.A63 1989   364.6′0973   88-12386
    ISBN 0-02-301710-4

Printing: 4   5   6   7   Year: 0   1   2   3   4   5

This edition is dedicated to Cleo, a spark that we will sorely miss, and to Fran, a spark we're both glad to have in our lives.

Foreword

From 2,000 B.C. to the final discussions of future trends—the fifth edition of *Corrections in America: An Introduction* by Harry E. Allen and Clifford E. Simonsen is a virtual "thesaurus of corrections." Their careful and logical addition of over *seventy* new topics into what was already, in its earlier editions, a truly mind-boggling amount of practical information in a single volume is laudatory.

The graphics and threefold increase in photographs give this edition an appeal that extends beyond the classroom. Several audiences will find particular value and substance in this text: the neophyte to corrections and criminal justice; the student of criminal justice and corrections; the correctional professional; correctional administrators and managers; and even the interested citizen.

The neophyte—including researchers, journalists, legislative staffers, and others—can quickly gain a historical perspective on how society has treated its lawbreakers over the years, tracing changing correctional philosophies over time.

The student of criminal justice and corrections is concisely introduced to a literal "dictionary" of correctional terms, phrases, processes, and concepts. Presented in clearly articulated narrative, backed up by clearly presented descriptive charts, statistics, and photographs, is a thorough and complete framework of correctional history, present-day programs, and descriptions of fads, trends, and issues.

The correctional professional will find the text both thought-provoking as well as providing a concise blending of all the separate parts into a whole. The methodical detailing of all of the parts of the system allows the professional to synthesize those parts, regardless of his or her jurisdiction.

The correctional manager and administrator, frequently tasked with responding to the media, giving speeches to public groups, and writing comprehensive reports to executives and legislators, will find this text to be of invaluable use as a desk reference and ready reminder of the key issues. The all-encompassing scope, and the breadth of relevant information available make this edition stand above all other correctional texts.

The interested citizen will find this an excellent "coffee table" book for reference to those items that appear so often on the evening news in regard to detention and corrections. The clear and concise writing style, combined with excellent graphics and special descriptions and definitions contained in reference "boxes," make it incredibly easy for anyone to gain a grasp of the issues and to gain facts instead of conjecture.

Overall, this fifth edition of an already successful textbook has clearly developed into a generic corrections handbook — without losing its value in the academic world — and remains easy to read and useful to all on the criminal justice continuum as well as to others who might have interest in this fascinating field.

Chase Riveland
Secretary
Department of Corrections
Washington State

Preface

Corrections in America: An Introduction, in its fifth edition, remains a text for use at the introductory level, exploring the broad spectrum of systems, processes, and people that constitute the field of corrections. The corrections concept covers a wide range of activity. This text will attempt to review where corrections in America originated, where it is today, where it seems to be going from here, and what issues need to be resolved to get there. The reader will soon appreciate that there are no easy answers to the question, "What is corrections?" It will become apparent in the course of reading this text that corrections programs are a poorly articulated series of nearly independent operations, sometimes with conflicting goals, all trying to effect some kind of change in the offender. This knowledge should stimulate readers to seek appropriate reforms in their chosen sectors of criminal justice.

We have attempted to give a clear overview of each of the categories that comprise this field. We have not attempted to explore particular subjects in great depth at the sacrifice of others of which it is important for the introductory student to be aware. We offer this text to the student in the firm belief that it will provide an enjoyable as well as educational experience. To the educator, we offer a text that has been organized and written with the goal of making the teaching and learning experiences as effective and interesting as possible while covering the essentials of the subject.

The fifth edition of *Corrections in America* builds on the strengths of the previous four editions. We have, however, completely revamped the presentation of the material, with many more photographs, more graphs and charts, and a generally more attractive look. The body of the text has been updated completely with new data, concepts, and issues in corrections. We have continued to place footnotes at the end of each chapter, but have moved even more reference "boxes" into the body of the text, to minimize the need for the student to constantly refer to lengthy footnotes.

These efforts, along with the necessary updating of statistical and topical information, result in a book that is still the same in regard to readability and effectiveness as a teaching tool, but is at the same time new and fresh.

Organization of the Text

This text remains divided into eight parts and twenty-seven chapters which have been updated, revised, and consolidated to meet the many changes that have taken place since the fourth edition was written. Part I, "History and Evolution of Corrections," examines the past and present status of the handling of prisoners and the emergence of a system of correctional institutions, philosophies, and processes to deal with this segment of the criminal justice system. Chapter 1 examines early history from tribalism to the Age of Enlightenment. Chapter 2 examines the emergence of imprisonment as a form of punishment and atonement for crime. Chapter 3 looks at the development and spread of the industrial prisons in America and the problems that beset the "Age of Prisons." Chapter 4 studies the problems of a society faced with modern problems and nineteenth-century facilities in which men and women are faced with enforced idleness. Chapter 5 wraps up the section by examining the various ideologies associated with the treatment and processing of society's prisoners and their cyclical swings between hard and soft orientations.

Part II, "Law and the Correctional Process," deals with the offender in the arms of the judicial system and the options available. Chapter 6 looks at the two basic types of offenses that bring the offender into the system — the misdemeanor and the felony. Chapter 7 studies the various alternatives that are available to the courts and the funneling process that precedes incarceration for the few. Chapter 8 examines the currently difficult issue of sentencing and the range of choices between "flat" and "indeterminate." The last chapter in this part, Chapter 9, deals with the logjam that has developed in the appeals system and the changes expected in the United States Supreme Court.

Part III, "The Correctional Process," examines the three major subsystems of the larger process called corrections. Chapter 10 deals with probation — the option that is available before incarceration — and its derivation and practice. Chapter 11 is the major chapter focusing on the process of imprisonment, studying the ranges of control and process in this part of corrections. Chapter 12 examines a system under attack — the concept of early release under parole supervision.

Part IV, "The Rights of the Convicted Criminal," is concerned with some of the major issues in this regard. Chapter 13, "Prisoners' Rights in Confinement," examines in detail inmate rights and current problems. Chapter 14 is a complete update and reexamination of the problems surrounding the issue of capital punishment in light of the rapidly changing legal scene. Chapter 15 delves into the key issues that affect the offender attempting to reenter society, especially those dealing with a chance for a job and reentry into society.

Part V, "The Correctional Client," is a review of the different kinds of persons who are processed by the various systems. Chapter 16 combines previous chapters that looked at male and female inmates separately into a chapter called "Adult Offenders." The differences in facilities and programs between male and female systems are covered inside this new and comprehensive chapter. Chapter 17 has been restructured to reflect some of the critical issues facing the juvenile justice system and the treatment of juvenile offenders. Chapter 18 deals with those categories that are at the "fringes" of the correctional system and that pose problems for all of the programs. This chapter examines in detail elderly inmates and the problems that surround them.

Part VI, "Correctional Administration," has been restructured to reflect more management theory and applications in corrections. Chapter 19 presents management concepts and how they can apply to corrections. Chapters 20 and 21 deal with the problems that exist between the two missions of custody and treatment, plus detailing ways that these problems have been addressed and prescriptions for remedy of these rifts.

Part VII, "Correctional Systems," looks at the present systems at the federal, state, and local levels, as well as at the field of community corrections. Chapter 22 examines the county jails and local detention facilities, describing the new incentives to improve them physically and operationally. Chapter 23 reviews correctional systems at the state level. The Federal Bureau of Prisons—its benefits and its problems—is covered from a historical and operational standpoint in Chapter 24. Chapter 25 is an updated view of the emerging hope of community corrections and the impact of these programs on the critical overcrowding at the institutional level.

Part VIII, "Summary and Overview," is composed of two new chapters that address the hopes and fears of the 1990s for corrections and the correctional process. Chapter 26 deals with the massive changes in the issues that impact on modern corrections, from a clientele and programmic standpoint. Chapter 27 deals with similar kinds of emerging issues and problems from more of a physical plant, major dangers (drugs and AIDS), and legalistic standpoint, and then attempts to sum up the future state of corrections at the beginning of the twenty-first century.

A glossary of terms for the criminal justice professional is included in Appendix A, along with a complete index to persons, topics, and terminology. Another, and new, topic in Appendix B is provided to show the currently ratified and approved national policies for corrections that have come out of the massive efforts by the American Correctional Association and the National Conference on Correctional Policy in 1986. Finally, a comprehensive index is provided for the sake of easily finding specific persons and events described in the text.

Acknowledgments _____

As we finish our work on the fifth edition, we would like to acknowledge our debt to those who encouraged us to write this text initially, to those whose wide use of the text has required second, third, fourth, and now fifth editions, and to those who advised and critiqued these efforts. We are flattered and pleased that the text continues to be used and reused by our colleagues. The efforts of the Bureau of Justice Statistics in producing current and topical research, publications, monographs, and other material must be congratulated. These materials allow a writer to have the broadest possible perspective at hand in the preparation of a text such as this one.

The Federal Bureau of Prisons, the American Correctional Association, the National Sheriff's Association, and the American Jail Association were especially helpful in providing historical and current material, as well as most of the photographs used in this text. The publications of the National Advisory Commission on Criminal Justice Standards and Goals also provided exceptional material and made it possible for us not only to describe the correctional milieu, but also to prescribe in many areas possible cures for its problems.

It is virtually impossible to acknowledge all of the other colleagues and professionals who assisted and encouraged us in this endeavor. To delineate a list of those who did would result in the certainty of omission of some of them. You all know who you are, so we hereby acknowledge each of you with deep gratitude. Chris Cardone, our Senior Editor at Macmillan, deserves a special thanks for her gentle but persistent nagging at two busy, and sometimes lazy, authors, and it finally got the job done! We must also thank Barbara A. Chernow and her dedicated crew for sorting out our cryptic and sometimes illegible revisions. Copy editors always make us proud of what "we" wrote. Their efforts, including the prodding of sometimes bullheaded authors, have made this edition a readable effort. The outstanding physical appearance of this edition is largely a result of the cooperative effort between John Sollami of the Macmillan production staff, augmented by the understanding tolerance of Barbara A. Chernow and Chris Cardone, with the tolerant support and consistent approval of Tony English. Last, but not least, we thank our families and friends—all of whom saw little of us during this process.

H.E.A.
C.E.S.

Contents

Chapter 21   **Treatment**   **504**

PART VII   CORRECTIONAL SYSTEMS

Chapter 22   **Jails and Detention Facilities**   **527**

PART VIII   SUMMARY AND OVERVIEW

Corrections
in America

History and Evolution of Corrections

1

Early History
(2000 B.C.–A.D. 1700)

The descent to hell is easy. The gates stand open
day and night. But to reclimb the slope and escape
to the upper air: this is labor. . . .
—VIRGIL, *Aeneid*, *Book 6*

This text is not intended to be a history of corrections or a dissertation on its legal aspects. It is helpful, however, to know at least a little of the historical background—legal and social—to gain an improved understanding of the concepts that we will discuss later. In describing this background, we have tried to avoid technical jargon to keep misunderstanding to a minimum. Where appropriate, specific individuals and events that have influenced the history of corrections are detailed in the text for easy reference.

We shall begin by tracing the roots of corrections back to the early beginnings of civilization.

Behavior as a Continuum

Behavior in social groups, whether they be primitive tribes or complex modern nations, can be regarded as points on a simple continuum, as shown in Figure 1-1. In all societies, certain acts or groups of acts have been universally forbidden, or *proscribed*. Such acts include murder, rape, kidnapping, and treason (or some form of rebellion against the group authority). By contrast, most societies have encouraged, or *prescribed,* such other behaviors as having children, marrying, hunting, growing food, and other actions that benefit the common welfare.

Behavior that is situated toward the center of the continuum (Figure 1-1) is usually controlled by a set of social rules called *folkways*. These rules are enforced by means of mild disapproval (the raising of an eyebrow, staring, or a look of shock) or by mild encouragement (applause or a smile). Actions farther out on the continuum, which serve either to perpetuate or to threaten the group's existence, are controlled by a stronger

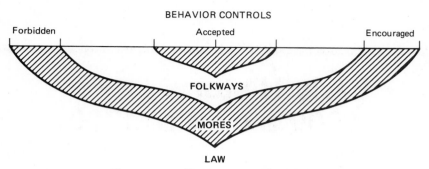

BEHAVIOR CONTROLS

Figure 1-1 Continuum of Behavior

set of rules called *mores.* Long ago, mores were enforced by means of strong social disapproval (verbal abuse, beatings, temporary ostracism, or even death) or strong encouragement (dowries, secure social or financial status, or fertility rites), and these informal controls still protect certain mores today. But as societies became more complex, they devised more structured sanctions to prevent violation of those mores that were essential to the group's survival. These sanctions have been codified in the form of written rules, or *laws,* and the reward for obeying these laws is simply the ability to function as a respected and productive member of society.

Redress of Wrongs _____

Retaliation

The earliest remedy for wrongs done to one's person or property was simply to retaliate against the wrongdoer. In early primitive societies this personal retaliation was accepted and even encouraged by members of the tribal group. This ancient concept of personal revenge could hardly be considered "law." Yet it has influenced the development of most legal systems, especially English criminal law, from which most American criminal law derives.

The practice of personal retaliation was later augmented by the "blood feud," in which the victim's family or tribe took revenge on the offender's family or tribe. Because this form of retaliation could easily escalate and result in an endless vendetta between the injured factions, some method of control had to be devised to make these blood feuds less costly and damaging.

The practice of retaliation usually begins to develop into a system of criminal law when it becomes customary for the victim of the wrongdoing to accept money or property in place of blood vengeance. This custom, when established, is usually dictated by tribal tradition and the relative power of the injured party and the wrongdoer. Custom has always exerted great force among primitive societies. The acceptance of vengeance in the form of a payment (such as cattle, food, or personal services) was usually not compulsory, and victims were still free to take whatever vengeance they wished. Legal historians Albert Kocourek and John Wigmore described this pressure to retaliate:

> It must not be forgotten that the right of personal revenge was also in many cases a duty. A man was bound by all the force of religion to avenge the death of his kinsman. This duty was by universal practice imposed upon the nearest male relative—the avenger of blood, as he is called in the Scripture accounts.[1]

The custom of atonement for wrongs by payment to appease the victim's family or tribe became known as *lex salica*[2] (or *wergeld,*[3] in Europe). It is still in effect in many Middle Eastern and Far Eastern countries, with the amount of payment based on the injured person's rank and position.

Fines and Punishments

How did these simple, voluntary programs become part of an official system of fines and punishments? As tribal leaders, elders, and (later) kings came into power, they began to exert their authority on the negotiations. Wrongdoers could choose to stay away from the proceedings; this was their right. But if they refused to abide by the sentence imposed, they were declared to be outside the law of the tribe (nation, family), or an *outlaw*. There is little doubt that outlawry, or exile, was the first punishment imposed by society,[4] and it heralded the beginning of criminal law as we now know it.

Criminal law, even primitive criminal law, requires an element of public action against the wrongdoer—as in a pronouncement of outlawry. Before this element of public action, the backgrounds of criminal law and sanctions seem to have been parallel in all legal systems. The subsequent creation of legal codes and sanctions for different crimes either stressed or refined the vengeance factor, according to the particular society's values.

Early Codes _____

Babylonian and Sumerian Codes

Even primitive ethics demanded that a society express its vengeance within a system of regulations and rules. Moses was advised to follow the "eye for eye, and tooth for tooth" doctrine stated in Exodus 21:24, but this concept *(lex talionis)* is far older than the Bible; it appears in the Sumerian codes and in the code of King Hammurabi of Babylon,[5] compiled over five hundred years before the Book of the Covenant.

As early societies developed language and writing skills, they began to record the laws of their nations. The Hammurabic Code is viewed by most historians as the first comprehensive attempt at codifying social interaction. The Sumerian codes[6] preceded it by about a century, and the principle of *lex talionis* was evident in both. The punishments under these codes were harsh and based on vengeance (or *talion*), in many cases inflicted by the injured party. In the Babylonian code, over two dozen offenses called for the penalty of death. Both codes also prescribed mutilation, whipping, or forced labor as punishments for numerous crimes. The following excerpt illustrates the vengeance principle:

> If either a slave or slave-girl has received anything from the hand of a married woman, the nose and the ears of the slave or slave-girl shall be cut off, the stolen property shall be requited; the man shall cut off his wife's ears. Or if the man has let his wife go free [and] has not cut off her ears, [the nose and ears] of the slave or slave-girl shall not be cut off and [the theft of] the stolen property shall not be requited.[7]

The kinds of punishment applied to slaves and bond servants have been cited by many scholars[8] as the origin of the punishments that in later law applied to all offenders. As historian Gustav Radbruch stated:

> Applied earlier almost exclusively to slaves, [the mutilating penalties] became used more and more on freemen during the Carolingian period [A.D. 640–1012] and specially for offenses which betokened a base and servile mentality. Up to the end of the Carolingian era, punishments "to hide and hair" were overwhelmingly reserved for slaves. Even death penalties occurred as slave punishments and account for the growing popularity of such penalties in Carolingian times. The aggravated death penalties, combining corporal and capital punishments, have their roots in the penal law governing slaves.[9]

The early punishments were considered synonymous with slavery; those punished even had their heads shaved, indicating the "mark of the slave."[10] In Roman days, the extensive use of penal servitude was spurred by the need for workers to perform hard labor in the great public works. The sentence to penal servitude was reserved for the lower classes; it usually meant life in chains working in the mines or galleys or building the public works planned by the government. These sentences carried with them the complete loss of citizenship and liberty and were classed, along with exile and death, as capital punishment. Penal servitude, or *civil death,* meant that the offender's property was confiscated in the name of the state and that his wife was declared a widow, eligible to remarry. To society, the criminal was, in effect, "dead."

Crime and Sin

Punishment of the individual in the name of the state also included the concept of superstitious revenge. Here crime was entangled with sin, and punishment in the form of *wergeld* (payment to the victim) or *friedensgeld*[11] (payment to the state) was not sufficient. If society believed the crime might have offended a divinity, the accused had to undergo a long period of progressively harsher punishment in order to appease the gods. The zone between church law and state law became more and more blurred, and the concept of personal responsibility for one's act was combined with the need to "get right with God."[12] The early codes, even the Ten Commandments, were designed to make the offender's punishment acceptable to both society and God.

Roman and Greek Codes

In the sixth century A.D., Emperor Justinian of Rome wrote his code of laws, one of the most ambitious early efforts to match a desirable amount of punishment to all possible crimes. Roman art of the period depicts the "scales of justice," a metaphor that demanded that the punishment balance with the crime. Justinian's effort, as might be expected, bogged down in the morass of administrative details that were required to enforce it.[13] The Code of Justinian did not survive the fall of the Roman Empire, but it left the foundation on which most of the Western world's legal codes were built.

In Greece, the harsh Code of Draco[14] provided the same penalties for both citizens and slaves, incorporating many of the concepts used in primitive societies (for example, vengeance, outlawry, and blood feuds). The Greeks were the first society to allow any citizen to prosecute the offender in the name of the injured party. This clearly illustrates that during this period, the public interest and protection of the social order were becoming more important than individual injury and individual vengeance.

The Middle Ages

The Middle Ages were a period of general disorder. Vast changes in the social structure and the growing influence of the church on everyday life resulted in a divided system of justice. Reformation was viewed as a process of religious, not secular, redemption. As in early civilizations, the sinner had to pay two debts, one to society and another to God. The "ordeal" was the church's substitute for a trial, until the practice was abolished in A.D. 1215. In trials by ordeal, guilt or innocence was determined by subjecting the accused to dangerous or painful tests, in the belief that the innocent would emerge unscathed, whereas the guilty would suffer agonies and die. The brutality of most trials by ordeal ensured a very high percentage of convictions.

The church expanded the concept of crime to include some new areas, still reflected in modern codes. During the Middle Ages, sexual activity was seen as especially sinful. Sex offenses usually involved either public or "unnatural" acts, and they provoked horrible punishments, as did heresy and witchcraft. The church justified cruel reprisals as a means of saving the unfortunate sinner from the devil. The zealous movement to stamp out heresy brought on the Inquisition[15] and its use of the most vicious tortures imaginable to gain "confessions" and "repentance" from alleged heretics. Thousands of persons died at the hands of the inquisitioners in Spain and Holland, where these methods were the most extensively used. Punishment was not viewed as an end in itself, but as the offender's only hope of pacifying a wrathful God.

The main contribution of the medieval church to our study of corrections is the concept of *free will*. This idea assumes that individuals choose their actions, good or bad, and thus can be held fully responsible for them. The religious doctrines of eternal punishment, atonement, and spiritual conversion rest on the assumption that individuals who commit sins could have acted differently if they had chosen to do so.

These early codes and their administration were usually based on the belief that punishment was necessary to avenge the victim. In early small tribal groups and less complex societies, direct compensation to the victim was used in place of revenge to prevent disintegration of the social structure through extended blood feuds. When these groups concentrated their power in a king or similar ruler, the concept of crime as an offense against the victim gave way to the idea that crime—however lowly the victim—was an offense against the state. In the process, *wergeld* was replaced by *friedensgeld,* and the administration of punishment became the responsibility of the king. Concentrating this power also led to a tendency to ignore victims and their losses, while concentrating on the crime and the criminal.

Punishment

Capital and Corporal Punishment

The most common forms of state punishment over the centuries have been death, torture, mutilation, branding, public humiliation, fines, forfeits of property, banishment, transportation, and imprisonment.[16] These acts, and numerous variations on them, have always symbolized retribution for crimes. (Imprisonment and transportation are relatively modern penal practices; these will be discussed in later chapters.)

The death penalty was the most universal form of punishment among early societies. There was very little knowledge of behavior modification and other modern techniques to control violent persons, and often the feared offenders were condemned to death by hanging, crucifixion, burning at the stake, drowning, and any other cruel and unusual method the human mind could conceive. As technology advanced, methods for killing offenders became more sophisticated. In the belief that punishment, especially capital punishment, would act as a deterrent to others, societies carried out executions and lesser punishments in public.

Torture, mutilation, and branding fall in the general category of corporal punishment. Many tortures were used to extract a "confession" from the accused, often resulting in the death penalty for an innocent person. Mutilation was often done in an attempt to match the crime with an "appropriate" punishment. (A liar's tongue was ripped out, a rapist's genitals were removed, a thief's hands were cut off, and so on.) Branding was still practiced as late as the nineteenth century in many countries, including the United States. Corporal punishment was considered a deterrent to other potential offenders.

The public humiliation of offenders was a popular practice in early America, utilizing such devices as the stocks, the pillory, ducking stools, and branding. The most significant aspect of these punishments was their public nature. Offenders were placed in the stocks (sitting down, hands and feet fastened into a locked frame) or in the pillory (standing, with head and hands fastened into a locked frame) and were flogged, spat upon, heaped with garbage, and reviled by all who passed by.

The ducking stool and the brank were used as common public punishments for gossips. The ducking stool was a chair or platform placed at the end of a long lever, allowing the operator on the bank of a stream to dunk the victim. The brank was a birdcage-like instrument placed over the offender's head, containing a plate of iron with sharp spikes in it that extended into the subject's mouth. Any movement of the mouth or tongue would result in painful injury.

Flogging (or whipping) has been a common punishment in almost all Western civilizations. The method was used particularly to preserve discipline in domestic, military, and academic settings. It was usually administered by a short lash at the end of a solid handle about three feet long or by a whip made of nine knotted lines or cords fastened to a handle (the famed "cat-o'-nine-tails"), sometimes with sharp spikes worked into the knots. Flogging was a popular method of inducing "confessions" at heresy trials, as few victims could stand up long under the tongue of the lash.

Deterrence

The extensive use of capital and corporal punishment during the Middle Ages reflected, in part, a belief that public punishment would deter potential wrongdoers — a belief that the passing years have refuted: "It is plain that, however futile it may be, social revenge is the only honest, straightforward, and logical justification for punishing criminals. The claim for deterrence is belied by both history and logic."[17] No matter how society tried to "beat the devil" out of offenders, the only criminal deterred was the one tortured to death. Later, enlightened thinkers began to seek more rational deterrents for crime by investigating its cause.

Emergence of Secular Law

The problem of drawing up a set of laws that applied to the actions of men and women in earthly communities was compounded by Christian philosophers who insisted that law was made in heaven. In the fourth century A.D., St. Augustine recognized the need for justice, but only as decreed by God. The issue was somewhat clarified by Thomas Aquinas in the thirteenth century, when he distinguished among three laws: eternal law *(lex eterna),* natural law *(lex naturalis),* and human law *(lex humana),* all intended for the common good.[18] The last was considered valid only if it did not conflict with the other two.

As time passed and the secular leaders, (kings and other monarchs) became more powerful, rulers wanted to detach themselves from the divine legal order and its restrictions on their power. In the early fourteenth century, many scholars advocated the independence of the monarchy from the pope. Dante, the Italian poet and philosopher, proposed the establishment of a world state, completely under the rule of secular power.

England's lord chancellor, Sir Thomas More, opposed the forces advocating the unification of church and state and died on the executioner's block as a result. He refused to bend ecclesiastical law to suit the marital whims of his king, the fickle Henry VIII. More was out of line with his day in another sense as well: as an advocate of the seemingly radical theory that punishment could not prevent crime, he was one of the first to see that prevention might require a close look at the conditions that gave rise to crime. In the sixteenth century, unfortunately, this line of thought was too far ahead of its time, but More's ideas persisted and eventually contributed much to the foundation of modern theories in criminology and penology.

This early background of law and punishment points up the significance of social revenge as a justification for individual or societal punishment against an offender. This rationale allowed the development of penal slavery and civil death as retaliation for wrongs against the Crown. The idea of correcting an offender was entirely incidental to punishment. Imprisonment served purely for detention. Offenders condemned to the galleys or the sulfur mines suffered a form of social vengeance, often including the lash and other physical abuse, far more painful than was the loss of freedom alone. The offender was placed in dungeons, galleys, or mines to *receive* punishment, not as punishment.

This idea of punishment to repay society and expiate one's transgressions against God explains in part why most punishments were cruel and barbarous. Presumably, the hardships of physical torture, social degradation,

Early Use of the Pillory (Courtesy Federal Bureau of Prisons)

exile, or financial loss (the four fundamental types of punishment[19]) would be rewarded by eternal joy in heaven. Ironically, these punishments did little to halt the spread of crime: "Even in the era when extremely severe punishment was imposed for crimes of minor importance, no evidence can be found to support the view that punitive measures materially curtailed the volume of crime."[20]

Early Prisons

What kinds of facilities for imprisonment existed during earlier ages? It is important to examine some aspects of these first institutions that relate to later correctional practices. Some form of detention for offenders, whether temporary or permanent, has been a social institution from the earliest times. Offenders were, of course, detained against their will, but the concept of imprisonment as a punishment in itself is a fairly recent one. Formerly, imprisonment was primarily a means of holding the accused until the authorities had decided on his or her real punishment, chosen from the variety described above. Those condemned to penal servitude in the Roman public works must surely have been kept in some special place at night. Unfortunately, little is known about this form of imprisonment. Most places of confinement were basically cages. Later, stone quarries and similar places designed for other purposes were used to house prisoners. The only early Roman place of confinement we know much about is the Mamertine Prison, a vast system of primitive dungeons built under the main sewer of Rome in 64 B.C.[21]

In the Middle Ages, after the fall of Rome, fortresses, castles, bridge abutments, and town gates were strongly and securely built to defend against roving bands of raiders. With the advent of gunpowder, these fortress cities lost much of their deterrent power, and the massive structures were then used as places of confinement. Many became famous as places to house political prisoners.[22] Not until the twelfth century were prison chambers specifically included in castle plans.

The Christian church had followed the custom of sanctuary or asylum[23] since the time of Constantine, placing the wrongdoer in seclusion to create an atmosphere conducive to penitence. This form of imprisonment was modified into more formalized places of punishment within the walls of monasteries and abbeys. Long periods in solitary confinement for alleged transgressions against canon law were common. The prisons built during the Inquisition were similar in concept, if not in operation, to later cellular prisons in America. The idea of reformation through isolation and prayer had some influence on our first penitentiaries, but in general, the impact of these practices remains hard to evaluate.

Workhouses

Bridewell, a workhouse built for the employment and housing of London's "riffraff" in 1557, was based on the work ethic[24] that followed the breakup of feudalism and the increased movement of the population to urban areas. The workhouse was so successful that by 1576 Parliament required the construction of a "bridewell" in every county in England. The same unsettled social conditions prevailed in Holland, and the Dutch began building workhouses in 1596, which were soon copied all over Europe.

Early Congregate Confinement (Courtesy Federal Bureau of Prisons)

Unfortunately, workhouses did not typify the places of confinement used for minor offenders and other prisoners in the seventeenth and eighteenth centuries. Most cities had to make prisons out of buildings erected for some other purpose. No attempt was made to keep the young from the old, the well from the sick, or even the males from the females. No food was provided for those without money, and sanitary conditions were usually deplorable. Exploitation of inmates by other inmates and jailers resulted in the most vicious acts of violence. "Jail fever" (typhus), which was bred in these conditions, spread easily to surrounding cities and seemed to be the main method of keeping the country's population down. By the beginning of the eighteenth century, workhouses, prisons, and houses of correction in England and the rest of Europe had deteriorated into shocking condition. Forcing criminals to exist in such miserable prisons became perhaps the most ruthless—if abstract—social revenge of all the punishments thus far described. "Out of sight, out of mind" was the watchword of that period, with the public seldom aware of what happened behind the walls.

Summary

    In this chapter, we have seen the principle of punishment pass from an individual's response to a wrong, to a blood feud that involved the family, to an abstract action taken by some bureaucracy in the name of the state. This approach to justice and punishment allowed the places of confinement to become human cesspools. It took the brilliant and dedicated reformers of the eighteenth century to establish the basis for modern penal philosophy, and their works will be examined in the next chapter.

Review Questions

1. What are the differences among folkways, mores, and laws?
2. At what point in a society's development does retaliation begin to become criminal law?
3. What effect did the kings' increasing power have on punishment?
4. What was the first punishment imposed by society?
5. What is meant by civil death?
6. What is meant by free will?
7. What form of punishment has been most widely used?
8. What is meant by "deterrence as a result of punishment"?
9. What were some of the earliest forms of imprisonment?
10. From what does most American law derive?

Key Terms

1. vendetta (p. 4)
2. *wergeld* (p. 5)
3. outlawry (p. 5)
4. *lex talionis* (p. 5)
5. *friedensgeld* (p. 7)
6. heresy (p. 8)
7. Inquisition (p. 8)
8. corporal punishment (p. 8)
9. sanctuary (p. 12)
10. Bridewell (p. 12)

Notes

1. Albert Kocourek and John Wigmore, *Evolution of Law, Vol. II: Punitive and Ancient Legal Institutions* (Boston: Little Brown, 1915), p. 124.
2. *Lex salica* was the fine paid for homicide, and it varied according to the rank, sex, and age of the murdered person. In general, *lex salica* refers to a payment for death or injury.
3. *Wergeld,* which means "man-money," originally referred to the death of an individual and the individual's supposed value to his or her family. It later referred to personal injury as well.
4. Kocourek and Wigmore, *Evolution of Law, Vol. II,* p. 126.

5. The Code of Hammurabi is estimated to have been written about 1750 B.C.
6. The Sumerian codes were those of Kings Lipit-Ishtar and Eshnunna and are estimated to date from about 1860 B.C.
7. G. R. Driver and John C. Mills, *The Assyrian Laws* (Oxford, England: Clarendon Press, 1935), p. 383.
8. Thorsten Sellin, "A Look at Prison History," *Federal Probation* (September 1967): 18.
9. Gustav Radbruch, *Elegantiae Juris Criminalis,* 2d ed. (Basel, Switzerland: Verlag für Recht and Gesellshaft A. G., 1950), p. 5.
10. Slaves were also marked by branding on the forehead or by metal collars that could not easily be removed.
11. *Friedensgeld* was the practice of paying restitution to the Crown, in addition to individuals, for crimes. It later replaced payment to individuals and became the system of fines paid to the state. With fines, the victim disappeared from the criminal justice system, becoming the ignored component of the crime.
12. This religious requirement brought the two issues of sin and crime into the same arena and broadened the scope of the church courts. The offender was obligated to make retribution to both God and the state.
13. Emperor Justinian I (A.D. 483–565) was a great preserver of Roman law who collected all imperial statutes, issued a digest of all writings of Roman jurists, and wrote a revised code and a textbook for students. His *Corpus Juris Civilis* became the foundation of law in most of continental Europe.
14. Draco, ruler of Greece in 621 B.C., drew up a very harsh and cruel code that used corporal punishment so extensively that it was said to be written not in ink but in blood.
15. The Inquisition was a tribunal established by the Catholic church in the Middle Ages with very wide powers for the suppression of heresy. The tribunal searched out heretics and other offenders rather than waiting for charges to be brought forward (somewhat in the manner of Senator Joseph McCarthy, who rooted out "Communists" in the early 1950s). Emperor Frederick II made the Inquisition a formal institution in 1224, and it came to an end in 1834.
16. Walter C. Reckless, *The Crime Problem,* 4th ed. (New York: Appleton-Century-Crofts, 1969), p. 497.
17. Harry Elmer Barnes and Negley K. Teeters, *New Horizons in Criminology,* 3d ed. (Englewood Cliffs, N.J.: Prentice-Hall, 1959), p. 286.
18. Stephen Schafer, *Theories in Criminology* (New York: Random House, 1969), p. 25.
19. Edwin H. Sutherland, *Criminology* (Philadelphia: Lippincott, 1924), p. 317.
20. Reckless, *The Crime Problem,* p. 504. There is no evidence that increased use of incarceration will lead to lower levels of crime. See David Biles, "Crime and the Use of Prisons," *Federal Probation* (June 1979): 39–43.
21. Norman Johnston, *The Human Cage: A Brief History of Prison Architecture* (Washington, D.C.: American Foundation, 1973), p. 5.
22. Johnston, *The Human Cage,* p. 6.
23. The practice of granting a criminal sanctuary from punishment was generally reserved for holy places. It was abandoned in England in the seventeenth century.
24. Work ethic refers to the generally held belief in the Judeo-Christian world that hard work is good for both the soul and society.

CHAPTER 2

A Century of Change (1700–1800)

The vilest deeds like poison weeds
Bloom well in prison air;
It is only what is good in man
That wastes and withers there.
Pale anguish keeps the heavy gate
And the warder is Despair.
—OSCAR WILDE, *"The Ballad of Reading Gaol"*

As Chapter 1 suggests, the underlying principle of public revenge for private wrongs invariably tipped the scales of justice in favor of the state. Corporal and capital punishment were the rule; executioners in sixteenth- and seventeenth-century Europe had at least thirty different methods from which to choose. These ranged from hanging and burning at the stake to the prisoner on the "rack." Public punishment and degradation were commonly prescribed for even minor offenses. Imprisonment served only as a preface to some gory punishment, carried out in the name of justice. With over two hundred crimes in England punishable by death, that nation witnessed some eight hundred public executions a year. As the seventeenth century drew to a close, the concept of retributive punishment by the state (with its implication that pity and justice are forever locked in opposition) was firmly entrenched in the laws of England and other European countries.

Age of Enlightenment and Reform

The events of the eighteenth century are especially important to the student of corrections. For it was during this period—later known as the Age of Enlightenment—that some of the most brilliant philosophers of our history recognized humanity's essential dignity and imperfection. The movement for reform was led by such giants as Charles Montesquieu, Voltaire, Cesare Beccaria, Jeremy Bentham, John Howard, and William Penn. The impact of their work, though not confined to any one area, was

> **Charles Louis Secondat, Baron de la Brede et de Montesquieu** (1689–1755) was a French historian and philosopher who analyzed law as an expression of justice. He believed that harsh punishment would undermine morality and that appealing to moral sentiment was a better means of preventing crime.

> **Voltaire (Francois Marie Arouet)** (1694–1778) was the most versatile of the eighteenth-century philosophers, believing that the fear of shame was a deterrent to crime. He fought the legally sanctioned practice of torture, winning reversals—even after convicted felons had been executed—on convictions so obtained under the old code. He was imprisoned in the Bastille in 1726 and released on the condition that he leave France.

> **Denis Diderot** (1713–1784) was a French encyclopedist and philosopher who was thrown into prison in 1749 for his work *Lettre sur les Aveugles* ("Letter on the Blind"), a strong attack on orthodox religion. He worked for twenty years on his twenty-eight volume *Encyclopedia*, along with Voltaire, Montesquieu, and other great thinkers of the time. His *Encyclopedia* became a force in the fight for change in the eighteenth century.

particularly constructive with regard to the treatment of criminals. Let us consider the contribution made by each.

Montesquieu and Voltaire, the French Humanists

The French thinkers Montesquieu and Voltaire, along with Denis Diderot, epitomized the Enlightenment's concern for the rights of humanity. In his essay *Persian Letters*,[1] Montesquieu used his mighty pen to bring the abuses of criminal law into public view. Voltaire became involved in a number of trials that challenged the old ideas of legalized torture, criminal responsibility, and justice. The humanitarian efforts of these men paralleled the work of the most influential criminal law reformer of the era, Cesare Beccaria.

Beccaria, Founder of the "Classical" School

The best-known work of Cesare Beccaria is *An Essay on Crimes and Punishment*—a primary influence in the transition from punishment to corrections. It established these principles:

1. The basis of all social action must be the utilitarian conception of the greatest happiness for the greatest number.

2. Crime must be considered an injury to society, and the only rational measure of crime is the extent of that injury.

3. Prevention of crime is more important than punishment for crimes; indeed punishment is justifiable only on the supposition that it helps to prevent criminal conduct. In preventing crime it is necessary to improve and publish the laws, so that the nation can understand and support them; to reward virtue; and to improve the public's education both in regard to legislation and to life.

4. In criminal procedure secret accusations and torture should be abolished. There should be speedy trials. The accused should be treated humanely before trial and must have every right and facility to bring forward evidence in his or her behalf. Turning state's evidence should be done away with, as it amounts to no more than the public authorization of treachery.

5. The purpose of punishment is to deter persons from the commission of crime and not to provide social revenge. Not severity, but certainty and swiftness in punishment best secure this result. Punishment must be sure and swift and penalties determined strictly in accordance with the social damage wrought by the crime. Crimes against property should be punished solely by fines, or by imprisonment when the person is unable to pay the fine. Banishment is an excellent punishment for crimes against the state. There should be no capital punishment. Life imprisonment is a better deterrent. Capital punishment is irreparable and hence makes no provision for possible mistakes and the desirability of later rectification.

6. Imprisonment should be more widely employed but its mode of application should be greatly improved through providing better physical quarters and by separating and classifying the prisoners as to age, sex, and degree of criminality.[2]

When the essay was first published, Beccaria attempted to remain anonymous so as to "defend the truth without becoming her martyr."[3] After two hard years of writing, he felt he had made enough of a contribution, and

---

Cesare Bonesana, Marchese di Beccaria (1738–1794) wrote *An Essay on Crimes and Punishment*, which was published anonymously in 1764—the most exciting essay on law of the eighteenth century. It proposed a reorientation of criminal law toward humanistic goals. Beccaria suggested that judges should not interpret the law but, rather, that the law should be made more specific, as he believed that the real measure of crime was its harm to society. He is regarded as the founder of the classical school of criminology.

UTILITARIANISM

This is a doctrine in which the aim of all action should be the greatest pleasure for the largest number of citizens. Hence the law should be used to inflict enough pain on offenders that they will cease crime (the "good" to be achieved).

he did his best to avoid persecution for his sharp criticism of the conditions of the time. But it was soon evident that he was not to be persecuted but hailed as a genius, and when his identity was disclosed he was promptly invited to Paris by Domenico Morellet.[4] He did not want to leave Italy and his young wife, however, and, when he finally made the trip, he had a miserable time. The great philosophers who came to Paris found the brilliant and fiery writer to be a shy, withdrawn, and slightly disturbed young man of twenty-six. He refused to debate with anyone and soon returned to Milan, never to journey away again. In later years he even refused an invitation from Catherine II of Russia to be her legislative adviser at court.

Although Beccaria himself did not seek or receive great personal fame, his small volume was praised as one of the most significant books produced by the Age of Enlightenment. Four of his newer ideas were incorporated into the French Code of Criminal Procedure in 1808 and into the French Penal Code of 1810:

1. An individual should be regarded as innocent until proven guilty.
2. An individual should not be forced to testify against himself or herself.
3. An individual should have the right to employ counsel and to cross-examine the state's witnesses.
4. An individual should have the right to a prompt and public trial and, in most cases, a trial by jury.

Among the philosophers inspired by Beccaria's ideas were the authors of the U.S. Constitution. It seems we owe a great deal to this shy Italian writer of the eighteenth century.

Bentham and the "Hedonistic Calculus"

Jeremy Bentham was the leading reformer of the British criminal law system during the late eighteenth and early nineteenth centuries. He strongly advocated a system of graduated penalties to tie more closely the punishment to the crime. As political equality became a dominant philosophy, new penal policies were required to accommodate this change in emphasis. Thorsten Sellin stated:

> Older penal law had reflected the views dominant in societies where slavery or serfdom flourished, political inequality was the rule, and sovereignty was assumed to be resting in absolute monarchs. Now the most objectionable features of that law, which had favored the upper classes and had provided often arbitrary, brutal and revolting corporal and capital punishments for the lower classes, were to be removed and equality before the law established. Judicial torture for the purpose of extracting evidence was to be abolished, other than penal measures used to control some conduct previously punished as crime, and punishments made only severe enough to outweigh the gains expected by the criminal from his crime. This meant a more humane law,

no doubt, applied without discrimination to all citizens alike in harmony with the new democratic ideas.[5]

Bentham believed that an individual's conduct could be influenced in a more scientific manner. Asserting that the main objective of an intelligent person is to achieve the most pleasure while receiving the least amount of pain, he developed his "hedonistic calculus,"[6] which he applied to all his efforts to reform the criminal law. He, like Beccaria, believed that punishment could act as a deterrent, but only if it were made appropriate to the crime. This line of thought, adopted by active reformers Samuel Romilly and Robert Peel in the early nineteenth century, has been instrumental in the development of the modern prison.

DETERRENT
Punishment or program designed to discourage commission of a criminal act.

Jeremy Bentham (1748–1832) was the greatest leader in the reform of English criminal law. He believed that if punishments were designed to negate whatever pleasure or gain the criminal derived from crime, the crime rate would go down. He wrote prodigiously on all aspects of criminal justice. Something of a crackpot in his later years, he devised his ultimate prison: the Panopticon. This monstrosity was never constructed, but debate over it slowed progress in English penology.

Sir Samuel Romilly (1757–1818), a follower of Bentham, was an able lawyer and the most effective leader in direct and persistent agitation for reform of the English criminal code. He pressed for construction of the first modern English prison, Millbank, in 1816. This prison idea was taken up by Romilly's followers, Sir James Mackintosh (1765–1832) and Sir Thomas Fowell Buxton (1786–1845).

Sir Robert Peel (1788–1850) was the leader in the English legislature for reform of the criminal code, pushing through programs devised by Bentham, Romilly, and others. He established the Irish constabulary, called the "Peelers" after the founder. In 1829, he started the London metropolitan police known as "Bobbies," also after Sir Robert. He was active in all phases of criminal justice.

John Howard

John Howard gave little thought to prisons or prison reform until he was appointed sheriff of Bedfordshire in 1773. This appointment opened

John Howard, Early Jail Reformer (Courtesy Federal Bureau of Prisons)

his eyes to horrors he never dreamed could have existed. He was appalled by the conditions he found in the hulks[7] and gaols[8] and pressed for legislation to alleviate some of the abuses and improve sanitary conditions. He also traveled extensively on the European continent to examine prisons in other countries. He saw similarly deplorable conditions in most areas but was most impressed by some of the institutions in France and Italy. In 1777, he described these conditions and suggested reforms in his *State of Prisons*. In 1779, Parliament passed the Penitentiary Act, providing four principles for reform: secure and sanitary structures, systematic inspection, abolition of fees, and a reformatory regime.[9]

HULKS
Decrepit transport or former warships used to house prisoners in eighteenth and nineteenth century England.

GAOL (JAIL)
Pretrial detention facilities operated by the English sheriffs in England during the eighteenth century.

> **John Howard** (1726–1790), shocked by the conditions he found in the English prison while serving as high sheriff of Bedfordshire in 1773, devoted his life and fortune to prison reform. His monumental study, *The State of Prisons in England and Wales* (1777), led Parliament to correct many abuses.

This act resulted in the first penitentiary, located at Wyndomham in Norfolk, England, and operated by Sir Thomas Beever, the sheriff of Wyndomham. As will be seen, the principles contained in the act, though lofty in concept, were hard to implement in the prevailing atmosphere of indifference. It is ironic that this great advocate for better prison conditions did himself die of jail fever (typhus) in the Russian Ukraine in 1790. John Howard's name has become synonymous with prison reform, and the John Howard Society has carried his ideas forward to this day.[10]

William Penn and the "Great Law"

The American colonies were governed by the British under codes established by the Duke of York in 1676 and part of the older Hampshire code established in 1664. These codes were similar to those followed in England, and the use of capital and corporal punishment was the rule of the day. Branding, flogging, the stocks, the pillory, and the brank were also in vogue.

The concept of more humanitarian treatment of offenders was brought to America by William Penn, the founder of Pennsylvania and leader of the Quakers. The Quaker movement was the touchstone of penal reform, not only in America, but also in Italy and England through its influence on such advocates as Beccaria and Howard. Compared with the harsh colonial codes in force at the time, the "Great Law" of the Quakers was quite humane. This body of laws envisioned hard labor as a more effective punishment than death for serious crimes, and capital punishment was eliminated from the original codes. Later, in supplementary acts, murder and manslaughter were included as social crimes. Only premeditated murder was punishable by death; other acts were treated according to the circumstances.

It is interesting to note that the Quakers' Great Law did away with most religious offenses and stuck to strictly criminal jurisprudence. This was a departure from the codes of other colonies and the earlier European codes. Under the Great Law, a "house of corrections" was established where most punishment was meted out in the form of hard labor. This was the first time that correctional confinement at hard labor was used as a punishment for serious crimes, and not merely as a preface to punishment scheduled for a later date. This Quaker code of 1682 was in force until 1718, when it was repealed, ironically, just one day after the death of

William Penn (1644–1718), an English Quaker, fought for religious freedom and individual rights. In 1681, he obtained a charter from King Charles II and founded the Quaker settlement of Pennsylvania.

William Penn. The Great Law was replaced by the English Anglican code, and the mild Quaker philosophy gave way to harsh punishments. This new code was even worse than the previous codes of the Duke of York. Capital punishment was prescribed for thirteen offenses,[11] and mutilation, branding, and other corporal punishments were restored for many others.

The influence of Montesquieu, Voltaire, Beccaria, Bentham, Howard, and Penn was felt throughout colonial America. Much of the idealism embodied in the U.S. Constitution reflects the writings of these progressive eighteenth-century leaders. With their philosophies in mind, we can consider some of the major developments in correctional practice in that era of reform.

Houses of Correction, Workhouses, and Gaols _____

The proliferation of Bridewell-style houses of correction in England was originally intended as a humanitarian move, and in 1576, Parliament ordered that each county in England construct such an institution. These were not merely extensions of almshouses or poorhouses but were actually penal institutions for all sorts of misdemeanants. Although the bloody penalties for major offenses were growing in number, not even the most callous would advocate harsh physical punishment for all offenders. All sorts of rogues, from idlers to whores, were put into these bridewells, where they were compelled to work under strict discipline at the direction of hard taskmasters. Today, the house of correction and the workhouse are regarded as synonymous. Actually, the workhouse was not intended as a penal institution but as a place for the training and care of the poor. In practice, however, the two soon became indistinguishable, first in England and later in America. Conditions and practices in these institutions were no better than in the gaols (jails) by the turn of the eighteenth century.

The use of gaols to detain prisoners has a grim and unsavory history. As the eighteenth century began, gaol administration was usually left up to the whim of the gaoler, who was usually under the control of the sheriff. Gaols were often used to extort huge fines from those who had the means, by holding these people indefinitely in pretrial confinement until they gave in and paid. The lot of the common "gaolbird"[12] was surely not a happy one, and many of the prisoners perished long before their trial date. The squalid and unhealthy conditions gave rise to epidemics of gaol fever that spread to all levels of English life. John Howard claimed that more people died from this malady between 1773 and 1774 than were executed by the Crown.[13] Ironically, prisoners, and not prison conditions, were blamed for the spread of this deadly disease, and even more sanguinary penalties for offenses were devised. Robert Caldwell describes the typical English gaol:

> Devoid of privacy and restrictions, its contaminated air heavy with the stench of unwashed bodies, human excrement, and the discharge of loathsome sores, the gaol bred the basest thoughts and the foulest deeds. The inmates made their own rules, and the weak and the innocent were exposed to the tyranny of the strong and the vicious. Prostitutes plied their trade with ease, often with the connivance and support of the gaolers, who thus sought to supplement their fees. Even virtuous women sold themselves to obtain food and clothing, and frequently the worst elements of the town used the gaol as they would a brothel. Thus, idleness, vice, perversion, profligacy, shameless exploitation, and ruthless cruelty were compounded in hotbeds of infection and cesspools of corruption. These were the common gaols of England.[14]

It is depressing to think that John Howard, shocked into humanitarian reform efforts when he found himself responsible for one of these human cesspools, was the only sheriff to undertake action against such institutions.

Transportation Systems _____

Deportation to the Colonies and Australia

One of the earliest forms of social vengeance was banishment. In primitive societies the offender was cast out into the wilderness, usually to be eaten by wild beasts or to succumb to the elements. As we have seen, imprisonment and capital punishment were later substituted for banishment. Banishment to penal servitude was, in effect, civil death. Banishment to the gaols, however, more often than not ended in physical death.

The wandering and jobless lower classes, in the period following the breakup of feudalism, were concentrated mostly in high-crime slums in the major cities. As economic conditions worsened, the number of imprisonable crimes was increased to the point that the available prisons were filled. In England, from 1596 to 1776, the pressure was partially relieved by the deportation or transportation of malefactors to the colonies in America. Estimates vary greatly of how many American settlers arrived in chains. Margaret Wilson estimated between three and four hundred annually;[15] other authorities put the figure as high as two thousand a year. The use of convict labor was widespread before the adoption of slavery in the colonies. And even though the entering flow of dangerous felons

> **TRANSPORTATION**
> Banishment by deportation to a distant location or other colonies by a national court system.

was somewhat slowed by the introduction of slavery, the poor and the misdemeanant continued to come in great numbers.

Transportation to America was brought to an abrupt halt in 1776 by the Revolution. But England still needed to send somewhere the criminals overloading its crowded institutions. Captain James Cook had discovered Australia in 1770, and soon the system of transportation was transferred to that continent. It was planned that the criminals would help tame that new and wild land. Over 135,000 felons were sent to Australia between 1787 and 1875, when the British finally abandoned the system.

The ships in which felons were transported have been described as "floating hells"[16]—an understatement. The conditions below decks were worse than those of the gaols. Many died on the long voyages, but enough survived to make it a profitable venture for the shipowners, who fitted out ships specifically for this purpose. Other nations turned to transportation in the nineteenth century, as we shall see later.

Hulks: A Sordid Episode

From 1776 until 1875, even with limited transportation to Australia, the increased prisoner loads wreaked havoc in England's few available facilities. The immediate solution to that problem created one of the most odious episodes in the history of penology and corrections: the use of old "hulks," abandoned or unusable transport ships anchored in rivers and harbors throughout the British Isles, to confine criminal offenders. The brutal and degrading conditions found in the gaols, houses of correction, and workhouses paled in comparison with that which was found in these fetid and rotting human garbage dumps.

Those responsible for the hulks made no attempt to segregate young from old, hardened criminals from poor misdemeanants, or even men from women. Brutal flogging and degrading labor soon bred moral degeneration in both inmates and keepers. The hulks were originally intended only as a temporary solution to a problem, but they were not completely abandoned until eighty years later, in 1858. (Hulks were used in California in the nineteenth century, and one state, Washington, considered the use of decommissioned U.S. Navy warships in 1976. New York tried using old ferries and barges as recently as 1987–88.) This episode in penal history becomes especially relevant when the problems of overcrowding in our maximum security prisons are examined.

Convict Hulk, Nineteenth-Century England (Courtesy Federal Bureau of Prisons)

Early Cellular Prisons

The Maison de Force at Ghent and the Hospice of San Michele

In his travels on the Continent, John Howard was most impressed by Jean Jacques Vilain's Maison de Force (stronghouse) at Ghent, Belgium, and by the Hospice (hospital) of San Michele in Rome. Although these institutions had developed along entirely different lines, both made lasting impressions on Howard. Both served as workhouses, but otherwise they had little in common: their differences were more important than their similarities.

Predecessors of the Belgian workhouses were those in neighboring Amsterdam, constructed around 1596. Most were intended to make a profit, not to exemplify humanitarian ideals, and were seen as a place to put rogues and able-bodied beggars to work. The workhouses were modeled after the Bridewell institution in England and followed a similar pattern of hard work and cruel punishment. By the eighteenth century, Belgium, too, was faced with increasing numbers of beggars and vagrants, and the government called on administrator and disciplinarian Jean Jacques Vilain for help. His solution—the Maison de Force built in Ghent in 1773—

followed the basic workhouse pattern established in Holland and England, but in many respects it was far more just and humane.

Vilain's efforts at improving the administration of the workhouse earned him an honored place in penal history. He was one of the first to develop a system of classification to separate women and children from hardened criminals, and felons from minor offenders. Although he was a stern disciplinarian, he was opposed to life imprisonment or cruel punishment. Rather, he defined discipline by the biblical rule, "If any man will not work, neither let him eat." Vilain's use of individual cells and a system of silence while working resembled the procedures observed at the Hospice of San Michele in Rome. His far-reaching concepts of fair and just treatment, when viewed against the harsh backdrop of that era, mark Vilain as a true visionary in the correctional field.

The Hospice of San Michele was built in 1704 by Pope Clement XI. The pope himself placed an inscription over the door that remains to this day: "It is insufficient to restrain the wicked by punishment unless you render them virtuous by corrective discipline."

The Hospice of San Michele was designed for incorrigible boys and youths under twenty. As such it is recognized as one of the first institutions to handle juvenile offenders exclusively. Prisoners were administered massive doses of Scripture and hard work in hopes that this regime would reform them. The rule of strict silence was enforced through the flogging of violators. The use of separate cells for sleeping and a large central hall for working became the model for penal institutions in the nineteenth century. This concept of expiation and penance, as applied to corrections, was new and exciting to John Howard, and his Puritan ethic enabled him to see the value of repentance and hard work as demonstrated by the program at San Michele. Under somewhat different policies, the Hospice of San Michele is still used today as a reformatory for delinquent boys.

The main concepts that carried over from these early cellular institutions were the monastic regime of silence and expiation, the central community work area, and individual cells for sleeping. The philosophy of penitence and monastic contemplation of past wrongs espoused by these institutions was reflected in the Quakers' early prison efforts in America.

The Walnut Street Jail

As we have seen, the world of the eighteenth century had prisons, but they were generally used as places of detention for minor offenders and for pretrial confinement. One of the earliest American attempts to operate a state prison for felons was located in an abandoned copper mine in Simsbury, Connecticut.[17] This underground prison began operation in 1773 and quickly became the site of America's first prison riots, in 1774. Although some have called it the first state prison, it was really not much more than a throwback to the sulfur pits of ancient Rome, and it did

---

PENITENTIARY

Originally, a place where offenders reflected on their crimes and repented (changed). Now a major adult facility where felons are incarcerated as punishment.

---

nothing to advance the state of American corrections. The prisoners were housed in long mine shafts, and the administration buildings were placed near the entrances. Underground "mine shaft" prisons constituted one of several American attempts to provide a special place in which to house and work convicted felons. The establishment of such a special facility was finally accomplished in Pennsylvania in 1790.

It is hard to imagine a time when there were no long-term penitentiaries for felons, but before 1790 that was the case. Ironically, in that year the first penitentiary in America, the prototype of the modern prison system, was born in the same city that spawned the fledgling United States as a nation. Philadelphia, Pennsylvania, the home of the Declaration of Independence, is also—thanks to the Quakers—the home of the Walnut Street Jail,[18] the first true correctional institution in America.

Despite earlier efforts at prison reform, the Quakers had been thwarted in their humanistic goals by the repeal of Penn's Great Law in 1718. In 1776, the first American Penitentiary Act was passed, but its implementation was delayed because of the War of Independence. In 1790, with the Rev-

The Walnut Street Jail, Philadelphia, 1790 (Courtesy Federal Bureau of Prisons)

olution behind them, the Quakers reasserted their concern with the treatment of convicted criminals.[19] After much prodding, they convinced the Pennsylvania legislature to declare a wing of the Walnut Street Jail a penitentiary house for all convicted felons except those sentenced to death.[20] Thus, although prisons, gaols, dungeons, and workhouses had existed before, this wing was the first to be used exclusively for the correction of convicted felons.

Some of the concepts embodied in the Walnut Street Jail had their antecedents in the charter of William Penn in 1682. Those provisions, repressed by the harsh Anglican code, were that

1. All prisoners were to be bailable.
2. Those wrongfully imprisoned could recover double damages.
3. Prisons were to be free as to fees, food, and lodging.
4. The lands and goods of felons were to be liable for confiscation and double restitution to injured parties.
5. All counties were to provide houses to replace the pillory, stocks, and the like.[21]

Although not all of these idealistic reforms were adopted, the direction of change had been established. The system of prison discipline developed at the Walnut Street Jail became known as the "Pennsylvania system." The Pennsylvania system was developed through the ideas and efforts of such reformers as Benjamin Franklin and Benjamin Rush, building on the humanitarian ideals of Howard, Bentham, Beccaria, and Montesquieu. Patriot and war hero William Bradford, who drafted the codes that implemented the system, praised the European reformers in the state legislature.

As originally conceived, the basic element of the Pennsylvania system called for solitary confinement without work. It was assumed that this method would result in quicker reformations. Offenders could reflect on their crimes all day and would soon repent so that they might rejoin humanity. The terrible effects of such isolation—physical and psychological—soon became apparent. Some kind of work had to be provided, as well as moral and religious instruction, to maintain the prisoners' mental and bodily health. The work schedule thus was from eight to ten hours a day, and the prisoner worked in isolation, usually on piecework or handicrafts.

More and more convicts were sent to the new state prison, and overcrowding shattered early hopes for its success. Even the original system of separate areas for women and children broke down with the flood of inmates. But despite the ultimate failure of the Walnut Street program, it represented a major breakthrough. New prisons were soon in demand throughout America, and the Walnut Street Jail was copied extensively, in at least ten states and many foreign countries.[22]

> **Benjamin Franklin** (1706–1790) founded the American Philosophical Society in Philadelphia in 1743. He served as Pennsylvania's appointed agent to England and as a member of the second Continental Congress (1777) to draft the Declaration of Independence, which he signed. He was plenipotentiary to France and negotiated to obtain that country's help in the Revolution. He was also a statesman, scientist, and philosopher.

> **Benjamin Rush** (1745–1813), physician and political leader, was a member of both Continental Congresses (1776, 1777) and a signer of the Declaration of Independence. He established the first free dispensary in the United States (1786) and was an advocate of prison reform and humane treatment.

> **William Bradford** (1721–1791), the "Patriot Printer of 1776," was one of the early advocates of a Continental Congress. He was a member of the Sons of Liberty, a political rival of Benjamin Franklin, and an active reformer of the harsh British codes. As a major in the army, he became a hero of the Revolution.

Bentham's Panopticon

Jeremy Bentham was more than a philosopher and an idealist; he was also a practical man and an architect. The tragic situation of the hulks on the rivers and in the harbors of England created a stir in the British Parliament, and its members saw the need for some alternative to these horrors for the housing of convicted felons and other offenders. A national penitentiary system was considered a viable solution. Bentham had been working on the design of a national penitentiary in line with John Howard's four principles: secure and sanitary conditions, systematic inspection, abolition of fees, and a reformatory regime. Parliament had passed a bill in 1779 to erect one or more national institutions but never provided the funds. In 1799, that bill was superseded by a contract with Bentham to furnish the design of a building that he called a Panopticon (inspection-house). Even though this monstrosity was never actually constructed, some of the principles Bentham followed in designing it are worth discussing.

Essentially, the Panopticon plan called for a huge structure covered by a glass roof. A central cupola allowed the guards to see into all the cells, which were arranged around it in a circular arrangement like spokes on a wheel. It was Bentham's belief that the visibility of the cells would make it easier for the custodians to manage the inmates. There was a great deal of controversy over this radically new concept, and in the end, Bentham spent almost all of his time and his family fortune in vain attempts to get the structure built.

Although the British government was not convinced of the Panopticon's worth, many U.S. prisons were based on that principle. Perhaps the Western Penitentiary in Pennsylvania came closest to Bentham's plans. Certainly, the radiating spoke design, constructed on a large scale, characterized many of the massive institutions built in the nineteenth century.

Summary

As the eighteenth century drew to a close, the move for prison reform was sparked by a new feeling of vigor and energy. The decade after the Walnut Street Jail opened was full of hope for the concepts embodied there, however imperfectly. It would be an oversimplification to say that the Walnut Street Jail was the world's first real attempt at a prison for convicted felons. The eighteenth century produced many such attempts, both in Europe and in America. Some of the principles behind the Walnut Street Jail, however, had a permanent influence on the development of correctional institutions throughout the world. Connecticut's abortive attempt to establish a state prison at Simsbury failed because the mine shafts could not be made habitable and because there was little public enthusiasm for the project. The Quakers' compassionate efforts, though much more humane, were doomed to failure by the lack of public and political support, incompetent personnel, and enforced idleness. With the industrial age came overcrowded prisons, which forced the new administrators to consider much larger and more productive kinds of institutions. As America entered the nineteenth century, it also entered an age of expansion. The prison movement adopted this growth-oriented philosophy, and as we shall see in the next chapter, the nineteenth and early twentieth centuries became the age of prisons.

Review Questions

1. What was Beccaria's main contribution to corrections?
2. What were John Howard's four principles for a penitentiary system?
3. Many reformers tried to improve prison conditions in the eighteenth century. Name at least three and describe their major contributions.

Key Terms

1. hulks (p. 21)
2. gaols (p. 21)
3. workhorse (p. 23)
4. jail fever (p. 24)
5. transportation (p. 25)
6. Maison de Force (p. 26)
7. penitentiary (p. 28)
8. Walnut Street Jail (p. 28)
9. Anglican code (p.29)
10. Panopticon (p. 30)

Notes _____

1. The *Persian Letters* was a satirical essay by Montesquieu on the abuses of current criminal law. The essay greatly influenced Beccaria. This, along with Voltaire's activities, led Beccaria to write his *Crimes and Punishment.*

2. Harry Elmer Barnes and Negley K. Teeters, *New Horizons in Criminology,* 3d ed. (Englewood Cliffs, N.J.: Prentice-Hall, 1959), p. 322.

3. Cesare Beccaria, *An Essay on Crimes and Punishment* (Philadelphia: P. H. Nicklin, 1819).

4. Domenico Morellet (1727–1819) was a French philosopher who worked with Diderot on the *Encyclopedia.*

5. Thorsten Sellin, "A Look at Prison History," *Federal Probation* (September 1967): 20.

6. *Hedonistic calculus* was a term devised by Jeremy Bentham to describe the idea that "to achieve the most pleasure and the least pain is the main objective of an intelligent man."

7. Convict hulks were among the earliest examples of imprisonment used as a method of dealing with criminals. The hulks, sometimes called "hell holes," were broken-down war vessels, stripped and anchored on bays and rivers around England. They were unsanitary, full of vermin, and unventilated. Disease ran rampant and often wiped out the whole prisoner population, and sometimes the crew and neighboring citizens as well. The last European hulk was still maintained at Gibraltar as late as 1875.

8. Gaols (jails) were used primarily as places of detention. Some prisoners waited to be tried, others could not pay their fines, and still others awaited execution. No attempt was made to segregate prisoners by age, sex, or crime. Food was often sold by the sheriff at inflated prices, and those who could not pay or have food brought in starved. Early efforts of reformers like John Howard helped clean up the gaols, but even today jails are usually the worst disgrace of the criminal justice system.

9. Barnes and Teeters, *New Horizons in Criminology,* p. 335. See also John Freeman, *Prisons Past and Present* (London: Heinemann, 1978), for an excellent set of papers celebrating Howard's contributions to prison reform.

10. The John Howard Society is a nonprofit organization supported by contributions. It provides casework service to inmates and their families, and it also works to promote community understanding of prison problems and offers technical assistance to correctional agencies. (608 South Dearborn Street, Chicago, Illinois 60605)

11. Only larceny was exempt from capital punishment. All other major crimes were punishable by death.

12. Gaolbird (jailbird) was coined because of the large cagelike cells used to confine the prisoners in unsegregated bunches, like "birds in a cage."

13. John Howard, *The State of Prisons* (New York: Dutton, 1929).

14. Robert G. Caldwell, *Criminology* (New York: Ronald Press, 1965), p. 494.

15. Margaret Wilson, *The Crime of Punishment* (New York: Harcourt, Brace and World, 1931), p. 224.

16. Transportation ships are described in Harry Elmer Barnes, *The Story of Punishment,* 2d ed. (Montclair, N.J.: Patterson Smith, 1972), p. 74:

Hired transports were employed to convey the convicts from England to New South Wales. Contractors received between £20 and £30 per head. The more convicts carried the greater the profit would be, thus as many were usually crammed on board as the ships would hold. As a result of such a state of confinement the most loathsome disease was common and the death rate was extremely high. Out of 502 who were placed on the "Neptune" in 1790 for conveyance to Australia, 158, and in 1799, 95 out of the 300 on board the "Hillsborough" died on the voyage. Those who did arrive were so near dead that they could not stand, and it was necessary to sling them like goods and hoist them out of the ships, and when first landed they died at the rate of ten or twelve a day. The government attempted in 1802 to correct these evils by sending convicts twice a year in ships specially fitted out for the purpose, and placed under the direction of a transport board and commanded by naval officers. Although the transports continued to be crowded, health conditions apparently had greatly improved as it was reported in 1819 by Sir T. B. Martin, the head of the transport board, that within the past three years only 53 out of 6,409, or at the rate of 1 in 112, had died. Out of the 10 transports which had recently sailed only one or two had died. See also Robert Hughes, *The Fatal Shore: The Epic of Australia's Founding* (New York: Knopf, 1987).

17. For a short history of this facility, see Charles W. Dean, "The Story of Newgate," *Federal Probation* (June 1797): 8–14.

18. The Walnut Street Jail, until the innovation of solitary confinement for felons, was typical of colonial jails. These are described in David J. Rothman, *Discovery of the Asylum* (Boston: Little, Brown, 1971), p. 55:

    Jails in fact closely resembled the household in structure and routine. They lacked a distinct architecture and special procedures. When the Virginia burgess required that county prisons be "good, strong, and substantial," and explicitly recommended that they follow "after the form of Virginia housing," results were in keeping with these directions. The doors were perhaps somewhat sturdier, the locks slightly more impressive, but the general design of the jail was the same as for an ordinary residence. True to the household model, the keeper and his family resided in the jail, occupying one of its rooms; the prisoners lived several together in the others, with little to differentiate the keeper's quarters from their own. They wore no special clothing or uniforms and usually neither cuffs nor chains restrained their movements. They walked—not marched—about the jail. The workhouse model was so irrelevant that nowhere were they required to perform the slightest labor.

19. Barnes and Teeters, *New Horizons in Criminology,* p. 336.

20. Negley K. Teeters, *The Cradle of the Penitentiary* (Philadelphia: Pennsylvania Prison Society, 1955).

21. Donald R. Taft, *Criminology,* 3d ed. (New York: Macmillan, 1956), p. 478.

22. Barnes, *The Story of Punishment,* p. 128.

The Age of Prisons (1800–1960)

To the builders of this nitemare
Though you may never get to read these words I pity you;
For the cruelty of your minds have designed this Hell;
If men's buildings are a reflection of what they are,
This one portraits the ugliness of all humanity.
IF ONLY YOU HAD SOME COMPASSION
—*on a prison wall*

The Pennsylvania System

With the advent of the nineteenth century and the social upheaval produced by the Industrial Revolution, the citizens of Pennsylvania began to lead the way in developing a penitentiary system. The Walnut Street Jail had been fairly effective for a decade, and that Pennsylvania system was copied extensively in both architectural design and administration (Table 3.1). But when the Philadelphia Society for the Alleviation of the Miseries of Public Prisons[1] observed the many emerging problems at the Walnut Street Jail, a radically new prison was proposed for the state. It was proposed that solitary confinement without labor continue to be used as the sole reformatory process. As mentioned in the previous chapter, the rationale here was that complete isolation would work as a quick reformer.

TABLE 3.1 American Prisons before Auburn

Pennsylvania	Walnut St. Jail, Philadelphia	1790
New York	Newgate Prison, New York City	1797
New Jersey	State Penitentiary, Lamberton	1798
Kentucky	State Penitentiary, Frankfort	1800
Virginia	State Penitentiary, Richmond	1800
Massachusetts	State Prison, Charlestown	1805
Vermont	State Prison, Windsor	1809
Maryland	State Penitentiary, Baltimore	1812
New Hampshire	State Prison, Concord	1812
Ohio	State Penitentiary, Columbus	1816
Georgia	State Penitentiary, Milledgeville	1817

Eastern State Penitentiary, Philadelphia (Courtesy Federal Bureau of Prisons)

The Western Penitentiary at Pittsburgh, built in 1826, was based on the cellular isolation wing of the Walnut Street Jail. Essentially, the Western Penitentiary amounted to a poor imitation of Bentham's Panopticon, an octagonal monstrosity which originally provided for solitary confinement and no labor. The legislature amended the program in 1829, maintaining solitary confinement but adding the provision that inmates perform some labor in their cells. In 1833, the small, dark cells were torn down, and larger outside cells were built. These efforts influenced the development of the Eastern Penitentiary, located in Philadelphia.

The Eastern Penitentiary became the model and primary exponent of the Pennsylvania or "separate" system. This prison was built somewhat like a square wheel, with the cell blocks arranged like spokes around the hub, or central rotunda. The routine at Eastern—solitary confinement, silence, and labor in "outside"[2] cells—clearly stressed the separation of each inmate from the others (Figure 3-1a).

Although the Pennsylvania system aroused great interest among other nations, it was adopted by only two other states. The New Jersey State Penitentiary in Trenton began operations in 1837 along the lines of the separate system—soon abandoned, however, in favor of that used at Auburn, New York. Rhode Island followed the same pattern as New Jersey. Its first prison, built in 1838 along the lines of the Eastern Penitentiary, abandoned the separate system by 1852. By contrast, many European countries wholeheartedly adopted the Pennsylvania model.[3]

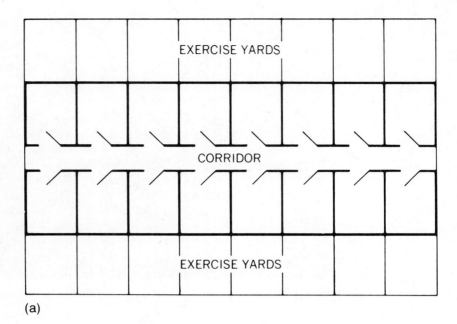

(a)

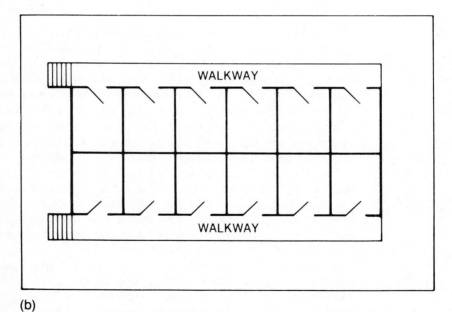

(b)

Figure 3-1 Cell Designs: (a) "Outside" Cell Design; (b) "Inside" Cell Design

The Auburn System _____

The major evils of the jails and other confinement facilities before 1800 were indiscriminate congregate confinement and enforced idleness. The rapid debasement of the prisoners when kept in filthy conditions, with men, women, and children thrown together under a regime of neglect and brutality, appalled the early reformers. The long-term prisons established in the last decade of the eighteenth century were not just a substitute for capital and corporal punishment; they were total administrative and custodial systems intended to remedy the evils of the old methods. In the first quarter of the nineteenth century, administrators experimented with many new systems. The leading contenders for the world's attention were the Eastern Penitentiary and the New York State Prison at Auburn, opened in 1819.

The Auburn prison administrators developed a system that was almost the opposite of that used at the Eastern Penitentiary. The building itself was based on a new "inside" cell design (Figure 3-1b),[4] and the cells were small when compared with those at Eastern. These small cells were designed just for sleeping, not for work. In addition, a new style of discipline was inaugurated at Auburn, which became known as the Auburn or "congregate" system.

In the early years of the Auburn prison, administrators tried an experiment to test the efficacy of the Pennsylvania system. They selected eighty

A Typical "Inside" Cell Block (Courtesy of American Correctional Association)

of the most hardened convicts, placing them in solitary confinement and enforced idleness from Christmas 1821 through Christmas 1823. So many of these men succumbed to sickness and insanity that the experiment was discontinued. The Auburn administration thus claimed failure for solitary confinement when the method included idleness. Given the small inside cells at Auburn, their claim was no doubt a valid one. However, the Auburn experiment cannot be considered a fair test of the Pennsylvania system, because the latter system used large outside cells and provided for handicraft and other labor in the cells.

Discipline at Auburn

An unfortunate by-product of the badly planned Auburn experiment was the use of solitary confinement as a means of punishment within the prison. The discipline regimen at Auburn also included congregate work in the shops during the day, separation of prisoners into small individual cells at night, silence at all times, lockstep marching formations, and a congregate mess at which the prisoners sat face-to-back.[5] There was great emphasis on silence. In the belief that verbal exchange between prisoners was contaminating, conversation was prevented by liberal use of the whip.

Cleaning the "Slop Jars," Early Auburn-Style Prison (Courtesy Federal Bureau of Prisons)

An excellent description of the Auburn system in its early stages is contained in the classic *The Story of Punishment* by the great criminologist and historian Harry Elmer Barnes, appearing in the form of a letter from Louis Dwight:

At Auburn we have a more beautiful example still of what may be done by proper discipline, in a prison well constructed. It is not possible to describe the pleasure which we feel in contemplating this noble institution, after wading through the fraud, and the material and moral filth of many prisons. We regard it as a model worthy of the world's imitation. We do not mean that there is nothing in this institution which admits of improvement; for there have been a few cases of unjustifiable severity in punishments; but, upon the whole, the institution is immensely elevated above the old penitentiaries.

The whole establishment, from the gate to the sewer, is a specimen of neatness. The unremitted industry, the entire subordination and subdued feelings of the convicts, has probably no parallel among an equal number of criminals. In their solitary cells they spend the night, with no other book but the Bible, and at sunrise they proceed, in military order, under the eye of the turnkeys, in solid columns, with the lock march, to their workshops; thence, in the same order at the hour of breakfast, to the common hall, where they partake of their wholesome and frugal meal in silence. Not even a whisper is heard; though the silence is such that a whisper might be heard through the whole apartment. The convicts are seated, in single file, at narrow tables, with their backs towards the center, so that there can be no interchange of signs. If one has more food than he wants, he raises his left hand; and if another has less, he raises his right hand, and the waiter changes it. When they have done eating, at the ringing of a little bell, of the softest sound, they rise from the table, form the solid columns, and return, under the eye of the turnkeys, to the workshops. From one end of the shops to the other, it is the testimony of many witnesses, that they have passed more than three hundred convicts, without seeing one leave his work, or turn his head to gaze at them. There is the most perfect attention to business from morning till night, interrupted only by the time necessary to dine, and never by the fact that the whole body of prisoners have done their tasks, and the time is now their own, and they can do as they please. At the close of the day, a little before sunset, the work is all laid aside at once, and the convicts return, in military order, to the solitary cells, where they partake of the frugal meal, which they were permitted to take from the kitchen, where it was furnished for them as they returned from the shops. After supper, they can, if they choose, read Scripture undisturbed and then reflect in silence on the errors of their lives. They must not disturb their fellow prisoners by even a whisper.[6]

Harry Elmer Barnes (1889–1968) was a great American educator and sociologist, who coauthored many books on penology, punishment, and criminology.

> **Louis Dwight** (1793–1854) organized the Prison Discipline Society of Boston. He was originally trained for the ministry but injured his lungs and could not preach. In 1824, he rode through the countryside distributing Bibles to prisoners. He was the most vocal advocate of the Auburn system and, as director of the Prison Discipline Society of Boston from 1825 to 1854, was the best source of information on this era of American prisons.

A Model for Other Prisons

The Auburn system became the pattern for over thirty state prisons in the next half century (see Table 3.2). Sing Sing Prison in New York followed the Auburn pattern in 1825. Wethersford Prison in Connecticut copied the Auburn system but used a more moderate form of the brutal punishment employed at Auburn and Sing Sing. Later prisons modeled their disciplinary systems after Wethersford, in preference to the earlier New York systems.

Auburn's structural design—inside cells and wings composed of cell tiers (cell blocks)—became the model for most prisons built in the following 150 years. Variations on the Auburn concept are shown in Figure 3-2. The most popular of these types, first constructed in 1898 at Fresnes, France, became known as the "telephone pole" design. Regardless of the cell block arrangement, the inside-cell design became the most common model in America.

TABLE 3.2 American Prisoners after Auburn (through 1869)

New York (Sing Sing)	1825	Kentucky	1842
Pennsylvania (Pittsburgh)	1826	Indiana (Jeffersonville)	1842
Connecticut (Wethersford)	1827	Mississippi (Jackson)	1842
Massachusetts (a wing)	1829	Maine (Thomaston)	1845
Vermont	1831	New York (Clinton)	1845
Tennessee (Nashville)	1831	Texas (Huntsville)	1848
New Hampshire	1832	Minnesota (Stillwater)	1851
Illinois (Alton)	1833	California (San Quentin)	1852
Ohio (Columbus)	1834	Wisconsin (Waupun)	1852
Louisiana (Baton Rouge)	1835	Illinois (Joliet)	1858
Pennsylvania (Philadelphia)	1835	Indiana (Michigan City)	1860
Missouri (Jefferson City)	1836	Idaho (Boise)	1863
New Jersey (Trenton)	1837	Kansas (Lansing)	1864
Rhode Island (Providence)	1838	Nevada (Carson City)	1864
Michigan (Jackson)	1838	South Carolina (Columbia)	1865
Iowa (Ft. Madison)	1840	W. Virginia (Moundsville)	1866
Alabama (Wetumpka)	1841	Nebraska (Lincoln)	1869
Georgia	1841		

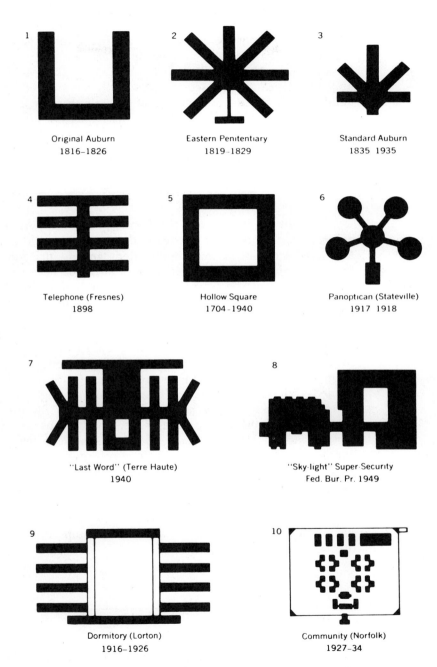

Figure 3-2 Types of Prison Structure (through 1960) (© Howard B. Gill, 1960. Reproduction permitted by Institute of Correctional Administration, Boston, Mass.)

One of the more important, but less noted, aspects of early prison architecture was the grand scale and sheer size of these institutions. "Bigger is better" (and cheaper) was the watchword of early prison builders. Huge, gothic-style structures achieved an effect similar to that of the cathedrals of Europe in the Middle Ages ... making the people inside seem small and insignificant. This feeling was further enhanced by the stern discipline employed in these huge castles of despair. Size will be discussed again in later chapters, but we should note here that the size of these early prisons gave rise to a subtle pressure to keep them filled with society's castoffs.

Prison Discipline

The main theme in both the Pennsylvania and Auburn systems was the belief that a regimen of silence and penitence would prevent cross-infection and encourage behavior improvement in the prisoner. Supporters of the Pennsylvania system claimed it was superior because the system made it easier to control the prisoners, gave more consideration to their individual needs, prevented contamination by the complete separation of prisoners from one another, and provided more opportunity for meditation and repentance. Another advantage they cited was that prisoners could leave that system with their background known only to a few administrators because they did not come in contact with other prisoners.

On the other hand, supporters of the Auburn, or congregate, system argued that it was cheaper to construct and get started, offered better vocational training, and produced more money for the state.[7] The persuasive power of economics finally decided the battle, and the congregate system was adopted in almost all other American prisons, even in Pennsylvania. The Western Penitentiary was converted in 1869 and, finally in 1913, the Eastern Penitentiary changed its system. The capitulation of the Pennsylvania system followed many long years of fierce controversy between the two systems. "The only gratifying feature of the controversy was that both systems were so greatly superior to the unspeakable ... system which they displaced that their competition inevitably worked for the betterment of penal conditions."[8]

Rules

As mentioned in Chapter 1, the prisons can be viewed as yet another method to implement social vengeance for wrongs against society. Europeans examining the Auburn and Pennsylvania systems made a keen observation on the American society and its prisons:

It must be acknowledged that the penitentiary system in America is severe. While society in the United States gives the example of the most extended liberty, the prisons of the same country offer the spectacle of the most complete despotism.[9]

In this context, the individual citizen's sense of guilt when he or she inflicts brutal or cruel punishment on another is diffused by the need for revenge on criminal offenders as a class and for the protection of society. The "out of sight, out of mind" principle was especially evident in the early nineteenth-century prisons. Most of them were located far out in the countryside, free from either interference or inspection by the communities that supplied the prisoners. It is not too hard to understand why rules and procedures emphasized the smooth and undisturbed operation of the prison rather than the modification of the individual prisoner's behavior. Administrators were judged by the prison's production record and the number of escapes, not by the number of successful rehabilitations. Because of this, rules were designed to keep prisoners under total control. It is these early and well-established prison practices that have been the most difficult to overcome.

These practices, sometimes called the "old prison discipline," were outlined by the penalogist Howard B. Gill:

> *Hard labor.* Through productive work from "making little ones out of big ones" (smashing boulders into gravel) to constructive prison industries, or through nonproductive punitive labor such as the tread-mill and the carrying of cannon shot from one end of the prison yard to the other.
> *Deprivation.* Of everything except the bare essentials of existence.
> *Monotony.* Of diet and drab daily routine.
> *Uniformity.* The warden's proudest boast: "We treat every prisoner alike."
> *Mass movement.* Mass living in cell blocks, mass eating, mass recreation, even mass bathing. In this monolithic type of program the loss of individual personality was characteristic. One watched the dull gray line with its prison shuffle where the faces of men were as if shellacked with a single mask.
> *Degradation.* To complete the loss of identity, prisoners became numbers. Housed in monkey cages, dressed in shoddy nondescript clothing, denied civil contacts even with guards like the one who snarled: "Who the hell are you to wish me a Merry Christmas?" Degradation became complete.
> *Subservience.* To rules, rules, rules—the petty whims of petty men.
> *Corporal punishment.* Brutality and force prevailed. In Tennessee the paddle, in Colorado the whip, in Florida the sweat box, etc.
> *Noncommunication.* Silence or solitary confinement; limited news, letters, visits, or contacts of any normal kind.
> *Recreation.* At first none; later a desultory or perfunctory daily hour in the yard.
> *No responsibility.* "No prisoner is going to tell me how to run my prison." Actually prisoners were relieved of every social, civic, domestic, economic, or even personal responsibility for the simplest daily routines.

Isolation. Often sixteen hours a day. Psychologically the admonition to "do your own time" with no thought for the other fellow only increased the egocentricity of the lone wolves.

No "fraternization" with the guards. The rule found in many prisons that guards must not talk with prisoners about their personal problems or their crimes prevented any attempt at solving the criminal problem.

Reform by exhortation. Now that psychology has come of age, we know that such a discipline denied every normal, basic need of the human personality and its corresponding opposite essential to a healthy and normal life. These included love and a proper comprehension of its opposite, hate; independence and the right kind of dependence; constructive use of imagination and truth; achievement and learning how to meet failure; identity and a decent humility which recognized the dignity of the individual; intimacy and its opposite — discrimination; creativity and constructive criticism; integration and concentration.

These sixteen human needs are recognized today as basic in the making of a healthy personality. Yet the prison discipline which was current for one-hundred years prior to 1925 denied every one of these basic needs. More than this, such a discipline fostered every pathology which results from a malfunctioning of these needs, namely, rejection, doubt, guilt, inferiority, inadequacy, diffusion, self-absorption, apathy, despair. Is it any wonder that men left prison worse than when they entered?[10]

Elam Lynds, warden of Auburn and later of Sing Sing (which he built), was one of the most influential persons in the development of early prison discipline in America. He is described as having been a strict disciplinarian who believed that all convicts were cowards who could not be reformed until their spirit was broken. To this end he devised a system of brutal punishments and degrading procedures, many of which remained as accepted practice until very recent times.

Lockstep and Prison Stripes (Courtesy of American Correctional Association)

As mentioned, the imposition of silence was seen as the most important part of the discipline program. The rule of absolute silence and noncommunication was maintained and enforced by the immediate use of the lash for the slightest infraction. Flogging was advocated by Lynds as the most effective way to maintain order. He sometimes used a "cat" made of wire strands, but more often a rawhide whip. One remembers the stereotyped ex-con from the movies of the 1930s and 1940s who was always shown talking out of the side of his mouth; this technique actually developed earlier, in the "silent" prisons, to get around the silence rules.

Another bizarre form of discipline that was developed at Auburn was the lockstep formation. Prisoners were required to line up in close formation with their hands on the shoulders or under the arms of the prisoner in front. The line then moved rapidly toward its destination as the prisoners shuffled their feet in unison, without lifting them from the ground. Because this nonstop shuffle was "encouraged" by the use of the lash, any prisoner who fell out of lockstep risked a broken ankle or other serious injury from the steadily moving formation. Breaking the rule of silence during formation was considered especially objectionable and was punished viciously.

The use of degrading prison garb was also initiated at Auburn and Sing Sing. Early prisoners were allowed to wear the same clothing as the free society did. At Auburn and Sing Sing different colors were used for the first-time offenders and for repeaters. Bizarre outfits served to reveal the prisoners' classification at a glance, to institutionalize them further, and to facilitate identification of escapees. The famous "prison stripes" came into being in 1815 in New York. Only very recently were the stripes abandoned in most prisons.

The methods used to prevent conversation or communication during meals were also humiliating. As mentioned earlier, prisoners were required to sit face-to-back. They were given their meager, and usually bland and unsavory, meal to eat in silence. If they wanted more food, they would raise one hand; if they had too much they raised the other. Any infraction of the rule of silence resulted in a flogging and the loss of a meal. This kind of entrenched procedure, very resistant to modern reforms, has been the source of many prison riots.

One of the earliest and most well-known forms of prison discipline was the "prison-within-a-prison," or solitary confinement, used as punishment

---

PRISON STRIPES

A development of the various forms of attire used to degrade and identify prisoners. Wide alternating black-and-white horizontal bands were placed on the loose-fitting heavy cotton garments. Stripes were still in use in the South as late as the 1940s and 1950s. They have been generally replaced in most security prisons by blue denims or whites.

> ### THE HOLE, OR SOLITARY CONFINEMENT
> This was usually located in the lower levels of the prison. Most were small four-by-eight cells, with no light, and solid walls and doors, usually painted black. Time in the hole was usually accompanied by reduced rations and the loss of all privileges. Today solitary confinement is used for administrative or disciplinary segregation, usually in cells similar to all others except for their single occupancy.

for violation of institutional rules. Although the early experiment with total solitary confinement at Auburn showed that it could not serve as the basis of a permanent prison system, the administrators saw its possibilities as a punishment for infractions of prison rules. Most of the prisons designed along the Auburn model, therefore, had a block of cells somewhere inside the walls, often referred to as the "hole." Usually, a sentence to solitary confinement was accompanied by reduced rations as well, consisting often of only bread and water. Solitary confinement is frequently used to discipline prisoners even today, although under more humane conditions.

Although many new prisons appeared in the century after the Eastern Penitentiary and the Auburn Prison were built, they made few, if any, contributions to the development of penology or corrections. The two greatest innovations, which persist today, were prison industries and the massive structures using the interior cell block. Enforced silence was finally seen as a failure and has been abandoned. Cruel and barbaric punishments, though publicly decried, are still sometimes used—largely because most prisons are isolated from society and its controls. The development of corrections between 1800 and 1870, branching into procedures and philosophies that were unjust, still produced better methods than did the universally accepted capital and corporal punishment that preceded it. And in the following era the swing toward a more realistic and humanistic correctional approach began.

Beginnings of Prison Industry _____

The introduction of handicrafts into the solitary Eastern Penitentiary cells represented the origin of prison industries in America. In continental Europe and England, the infamous efforts to provide labor in the workhouses and bridewells had resulted in such fruitless activities as the treadmill. The modern pressure to provide vocational training or earnings for inmates did not concern early American prison administrators; rather, they wanted to make the prisons self-sustaining. Toward this goal, the prison workshops were merely extensions of the early factory workshops. When the factory production system was introduced into prisons and they began

The "Hole" (Courtesy of American Correctional Association)

THE TREADMILL

This was devised to provide an exercise outlet for prisoners in the workhouses in England. They were actually human-powered squirrel cages, and although sometimes used to power some mills and factory tools, their primary function was to keep prisoners busy. The lack of activity in the Walnut Street Jail caused the treadmill to be introduced in the early 1800s. The term "on the treadmill" refers to motion without going anywhere, like the prisoners on the great wheels of the treadmills.

---

to show actual profits from their output, legislators were quickly convinced that prison industries were a sound operation. The Auburn system held out over the less efficient Pennsylvania system because it paid better returns on the taxpayer's investment. By the 1860s, the system of absolute silence had begun to fall apart because of the necessity for communication in the industrial shops. Production became the paramount goal of prisons. As a report of that period stated, "There is not a state prison in America in which the reformation of the convict is the supreme object of the discipline."[11] Early prison industries, in effect, exploited the available free labor for the sole purpose of perpetuating the institution itself. Some leaders in the field, however, saw that a change in emphasis could make the industries an important factor in prisoner rehabilitation.

Maconochie and Crofton: A New Approach _____

The reformatory system in America owes a great deal to the work of an Englishman, Captain Alexander Maconochie, and an Irishman, Sir Walter Crofton. Together they laid the foundation for reformative rather than purely punitive programs for the treatment of criminals.

Maconochie and the Indeterminate Sentence

In 1840, Captain Maconochie was put in charge of the British penal colony on Norfolk Island, about a thousand miles off the coast of Australia. To this island were sent the criminals who were "twice condemned": they had been shipped to Australia from England and then from Australia to Norfolk. Conditions were so bad at Norfolk that men reprieved from the death penalty wept, and those who were to die thanked God.[12] This was the kind of hell that Maconochie inherited.

The first thing Maconochie did was to eliminate the flat sentence,[13] a system that had allowed no hope of release until the full time had been served. Then he developed a "mark system" whereby a convict could earn freedom by hard work and good behavior. This put the burden of release on the convict. As Maconochie said, "When a man keeps the key of his own prison, he is soon persuaded to fit it into the lock." The system had five principles:

1. Release should not be based on the completing of a sentence for a set period of time, but on the completion of a determined and specified quantity of labor. In brief, time sentences should be abolished, and task sentences substituted.
2. The quantity of labor a prisoner must perform should be expressed in a number of "marks" which he must earn, by improvement of conduct, frugality of living, and habits of industry, before he can be released.
3. While in prison he should earn everything he receives. All sustenance and indulgences should be added to his debt of marks.
4. When qualified by discipline to do so, he should work in association with a small number of other prisoners, forming a group of six or seven, and the whole group should be answerable for the conduct and labor of each member.
5. In the final stage, a prisoner, while still obliged to earn his daily tally of marks, should be given a proprietary interest in his own labor and be subject to a less rigorous discipline, to prepare him for release into society.[14]

It is a sorry fact that Maconochie's visionary efforts toward rehabilitation were not appreciated or supported by the unenlightened bureaucrats above him. His results thus were disclaimed, and the colony fell back into its former brutalized routine almost as soon as he left it.

Crofton and the Irish System

Fortunately, Maconochie's ideas did reach beyond the shores of Norfolk Island. His successful use of the indeterminate sentence[15] showed that imprisonment could be used to prepare a convict for eventual return to the community. If this were true, then the length of sentence should not be an arbitrary period of time but should be related to the rehabilitation of the offender. Sir Walter Crofton of Ireland used this concept in developing what he called the "indeterminate system," which came to be known as the "Irish system." He reasoned that if penitentiaries are places where offenders think about their crimes and can decide to stop their criminal misbehavior ("repent"), then there must be a mechanism to determine that this decision has in fact been made, as well as a mechanism for getting the inmate out when penitence has been done. The indeterminate sentence was believed to be the best mechanism.

The system Crofton devised—like Maconochie's—consisted of a series of stages, each bringing the convict closer to the free society. The first stage was composed of solitary confinement and monotonous work. The second stage was assignment to public works and a progression through various grades, each grade shortening the length of stay. The last stage was assignment to an intermediate prison where the prisoner worked without supervision and moved in and out of the free community. If the prisoner's conduct continued to be good and if he or she were able to find employment, then the offender returned to the community on a conditional pardon or "ticket-of-leave." This ticket could be revoked at any time within the span of the original fixed sentence if the prisoner's conduct was not up to standards established by those who supervised the conditional pardon. Crofton's plan was the first effort to establish a system of conditional liberty in the community, the system we know today as *parole*.

The Reformatory Era (1870–1910) _____

Leaders in U.S. penology and prison administration met at the American Prison Congress of 1870[16] to discuss the direction that corrections practices should take. They were especially concerned about overcrowding, and they discussed what new kinds of prisons should be built to alleviate it. Many urged that Maconochie's and Crofton's plans be adopted in America. This idea was endorsed by the members, and the reformatory era in American corrections was born.

The first reformatory in America, built in Elmira, New York, in 1876, became the model for all those that followed. Zebulon Brockway, the first superintendent, had introduced some new educational methods at the Detroit House of Corrections, and he expanded on this concept at Elmira. Elmira was originally built for adult felons, but it was used instead for youths from sixteen to thirty years of age who were serving their first

Elmira Reformatory Prisoner Regiment (Courtesy Federal Bureau of Prisons)

term in prison. One observer cited the following characteristics as the standards for Elmira, and many of these reappeared in its imitators:

1. The material structural establishment itself. The general plan and arrangements should be those of the Auburn system, modified and modernized; and 10 percent of the cells might well be constructed like those of the Pennsylvania system. The whole should be supplied with suitable modern sanitary appliances and with abundance of natural and artificial light.

2. Clothing — not degradingly distinctive, but uniform, ... fitly representing the respective grades or standing of the prisoners.... Scrupulous cleanliness should be maintained and the prisoners appropriately groomed.

3. A liberal prison diet designed to promote vigor. Deprivation of food, by a general regulation, is deprecated....

4. All the modern appliances for scientific physical culture; a gymnasium completely equipped with baths and apparatus; and facilities for field athletics.

5. Facilities for manual training sufficient for about one-third of the population.... This special manual training covers, in addition to other exercises in other departments, mechanical and freehand drawing; sloyd [manual training] in wood and metals; cardboard constructive form work; clay modeling; cabinet making; clipping and filing; and iron molding.

6. Trade instruction based on the needs and capacities of individual prisoners. (Where a thousand prisoners are involved, thirty-six trades may be usefully taught.)

7. A regimental military organization with a band of music, swords for officers, and dummy guns for the rank and file of prisoners.

8. School of letters with a curriculum that reaches from an adaptation of the kindergarten ... up to the usual high school course; and, in addition, special classes in college subjects....

9. A well-selected library for circulation, consultation, and for occasional semi-social use.

10. The weekly institutional newspaper, in lieu of all outside newspapers, edited and printed by the prisoners under due censorship.

11. Recreating and diverting entertainments for the mass of the population, provided in the great auditorium; not any vaudeville or minstrel shows, but entertainments of such a class as the middle cultured people of a community would enjoy....

12. Religious opportunities ... adapted to the hereditary [and] habitual ... denominational predilection of the individual prisoners.

13. Definitely planned, carefully directed, emotional occasions; not summoned, primarily, for either instruction, diversion, nor, specifically, for a common religious impression, but, figuratively, for a kind of irrigation.[17]

The only real differences between the programs at Elmira and those at the adult prisons were the emphasis on reforming youth, increased academic education, and more extensive trade training. Two outstanding features were adopted for the reformatories, though: the indeterminate sentence and a grading system based on marks that could lead to parole.

> **Zebulon Reed Brockway** (1827–1920), along with Enoch C. Wines and Franklin Benjamin Sanborn, was the third member of the "big three" of penology in 1870. He served on many commissions to improve prisons and even founded the U.S. Army Disciplinary Barracks at Fort Leavenworth. Later, he was the first superintendent at the Elmira Reformatory, where he used military organization and discipline to govern the prisoners. His book *Fifty Years of Prison Service* (1912) is a classic.

Elmira was copied, in one form or another, by seventeen states between 1876 and 1913 (Table 3-3). Brockway's leadership produced the first attempt to offer programs of education and reformation to all inmates, adult or youth. Trade training, academic education, and the military type of discipline utilized at Elmira undoubtedly also influenced the programs of many of the older prisoners. Some aspects of the indeterminate sentence and parole concepts were finally extended to the state prisons. It is not surprising that in an era when public education was considered to be the answer to so many problems in the outside world, it was viewed as the answer to crime, as well. But because the same physical environment and the same underpaid and poorly qualified personnel found in prisons were also found in reformatories, these institutions were soon reduced to junior prisons with the usual routine. The old "prison discipline" was still the most dominant factor in any penal program.

Although the two main contributions of the reformatory era were the indeterminate sentence and parole, the seeds of education, vocational training, and individual rehabilitation had been sown. Even though these radical ideas could not flourish in the barren and hostile environment of that period, they took root and grew to fruition in later years.

Post-Civil War Prisons

The sixteen states that built prisons between 1870 and 1900 were almost all in the northern or western part of the country (Table 3.4). Their only

TABLE 3.3 Early Reformatories

New York (Elmira)	1876	Ind. (Jeffersonville)	1897
Michigan (Ionia)	1877	Wis. (Green Bay)	1898
Mass. (Concord)	1884	New Jersey (Rahway)	1901
Pa. (Huntingdon)	1889	Washington (Monroe)	1908–1909
Minnesota (St. Cloud)	1889	Oklahoma (Granite)	1910–1911
Colorado (Buena Vista)	1890	Maine (S. Windham)	1912–1919
Illinois (Pontiac)	1891	Wyoming (Worland)	1912
Kansas (Hutchinson)	1895	Nebraska (Lincoln)	1912–1913
Ohio (Mansfield)	1896	Conn. (Cheshire)	1913

TABLE 3.4 Post-Civil War Prisons

Oregon (Salem)	1871	Kentucky (Eddyville)	1883
Iowa (Anamosa)	1873	New Mexico (Santa Fe)	1884
Arizona (Yuma)	1875	Washington (Walla Walla)	1886
N. Carolina (Raleigh)	1889	Montana (Deer Lodge)	1889
Colorado (Canon City)	1876	Michigan (Marquette)	1889
Illinois (Menard)	1878	S. Dakota (Sioux Falls)	1891
California (Folsom)	1880	Tennessee (Brushy Mt.)	1895
N. Dakota (Bismarck)	1883	Utah (Salt Lake City)	1896

claim to improvement was the introduction of plumbing and running water. All were of the Auburn type, and the only modifications in the older prison routine were the abandonment of the silent system and the use of the indeterminate sentence and parole.

In the South, devastated by the Civil War, the penitentiary system had been virtually wiped out. Some states attempted to solve their prison problems by leasing out their entire convict population to contractors.[18] Others took in contract work or devised combinations of both leasing out prisoners and taking in contracts. The freed blacks were thus replaced by yet another group of slaves: the convicted felons. The South was unique in that it ignored the Auburn and reformatory systems. The South's agrarian economy made exploitation of cheap labor both easy and desirable. A large portion of the prison population in the South was composed of plantation blacks who had no influence or resources, and they were treated with no mercy. Leasing was eventually replaced by prison farms in most Southern states, but the practice was not completely erased until the mid-1920s. This sordid period in penal history, brought to light again in the 1960s in Arkansas,[19] simply confirms the depths to which even "civilized" people can sink in the treatment of their castoffs. The correctional experience in the South made only a negative contribution regarding both procedure and discipline.

The Twentieth Century and the Industrial Prison _____

From the beginning of the twentieth century until 1940, the number of inmates in United States prisons increased by 174 percent.[20] Ten new Auburn-style prisons and one based on Bentham's Panopticon were built during this period—often referred to as the industrial era for prisons in America—that reached its zenith in 1935. These new prisons were considered "as cold and hard and abnormal as the prisoners whom they were intended to persuade toward better things."[21]

The industrial prison really had its origins in the profits turned by the

A Typical Industrial Prison: Still Around in the 1980s (Courtesy Department of Adult Corrections, State of Washington)

first state prisons. Early in the nineteenth century, however, mechanics and cabinetmakers began to complain about the unfair competition they faced from the virtually free labor force available to prisons. The use of lease and contract systems aggravated this problem and led to a series of investigations that reached national prominence in 1886. The emergence of the labor union movement, coupled with abuses of the contract and lease systems of prison labor, eliminated these systems in the northern prisons by the end of the nineteenth century. They were replaced by piece-price[22] and state-account[23] systems. Opposition to prison industries resulted in enforced idleness among the increasing inmate population. This forced the adult prisons to adopt reformatory methods in some measure but made self-sustaining institutions a thing of the past.

The story of the prison industry's battle with organized labor is a history in itself and will not be covered here. The beginning of the end for large-scale prison industries, which kept inmates employed in some kind of work, was the enactment of two federal laws controlling the character of prison products. The Hawes-Cooper Act, passed in 1929, required that prison products be subject to the laws of any state to which they were shipped. The Ashurst-Sumners Act, passed in 1935, essentially stopped the interstate transport of prison products, by requiring that all prison products shipped out of the state be labeled with the prison name and by prohibit-

---

HAWES-COOPER ACT, CHAP. 79

Be it enacted by the Senate and House of Representatives of the United States of America in Congress assembled, That all goods, wares, and merchandise manufactured, produced, or mined, wholly or in part, by convicts or prisoners, except convicts or prisoners on parole or probation, or in any penal and/or reformatory institutions, except commodities manufactured in Federal penal and correctional institutions for use by the Federal Government, transported into any State or Territory of the United States and remaining therein for use, consumption, sale, or storage, shall upon arrival and delivery in such State or Territory be subject to the operation and effect of the laws of such State or Territory to the same extent and in the same manner as though such goods, wares, and merchandise had been manufactured, produced, or mined in such State or Territory, and shall not be exempt therefrom by reason of being introduced in the original package or otherwise.

SEC. 2. This act shall take effect five years after the date of its approval. Approved, January 19, 1929.

A Prison Farm of the 1950s (Courtesy of the Ohio Department of Rehabilitation and Corrections)

ASHURST-SUMNERS ACT, CHAP. 412

Be it enacted by the Senate and House of Representatives of the United States of America in Congress assembled, That it shall be unlawful for any person knowingly to transport or cause to be transported, in any manner or by any means whatsoever, or aid or assist in obtaining transportation for or in transporting any goods, wares, and merchandise manufactured, produced, or mined wholly or in part by convicts or prisoners (except convicts or prisoners on parole or probation), or in any penal or reformatory institution, from one State, Territory, Puerto Rico, Virgin Islands, or District of the United States, or place noncontiguous but subject to the jurisdiction thereof, or from any foreign country, into any State, Territory, Puerto Rico, Virgin Islands, or District of the United States, or place noncontiguous but subject to the jurisdiction thereof, where said goods, wares, and merchandise are intended by any person interested therein to be received, possessed, sold, or in any manner used, either in the original package or otherwise in violation of any law of such State, Territory, Puerto Rico, Virgin Islands, or District of the United States, or place noncontiguous but subject to the jurisdiction thereof. Nothing herein shall apply to commodities manufactured in Federal penal and correctional institutions for use by the Federal Government.

SEC. 2. All packages containing any goods, wares, and merchandise manufactured, produced, or mined wholly or in part by convicts or prisoners, except convicts or prisoners on parole or probation, or in any penal or reformatory institution, when shipped or transported in interstate or foreign commerce shall be plainly and clearly marked, so that the name and address of the shipper, the name and address of the consignee, the nature of the contents, and the name and location of the penal or reformatory institution where produced wholly or in part may be readily ascertained on an inspection of the outside of such package   SEC. 3. Any person violating any provision of this Act shall for each offense, upon conviction thereof, be punished by a fine of not more than $1,000, and such goods, wares, and merchandise shall be forfeited to the United States, and may be seized and condemned by like proceedings as those provided by law for the seizure and forfeiture of property imported into the United States contrary to law.

SEC. 4. Any violation of this Act shall be prosecuted in any court having jurisdiction of crime within the district in which said violation was committed, or from, or into which any such goods, wares, or merchandise may have been carried or transported, or in any Territory, Puerto Rico, Virgin Islands, or the District of Columbia, contrary to the provisions of this Act. Approved, July 24, 1935.

---

ing interstate shipment where state laws forbade it. In 1940, the Ashurst-Sumners Act was amended to prohibit fully the interstate shipment of prison products.

The economic strains of the Great Depression, beginning with the Wall Street stock market crash in 1929 and spanning the period from 1929 to 1940, led thirty-three states to pass laws that prohibited the sale of prison products on the open market. These statutes tolled the death knell for the

> **Sanford Bates** (1884–1972), a legendary figure in American corrections, was president of the American Correctional Association in 1926. He became the first superintendent of federal prisons in 1929 and the first director of the United States Bureau of Prisons in 1930. In 1937 he became the executive director of the Boys' Clubs of America. Later he served as commissioner of the New York State Board of Parole and commissioner of the New Jersey Department of Institutions and Agencies. He was also an active consultant and writer.

industrial prison. With the exception of a few license plate and state furniture shops, most state prisons took a giant step backward to their original purposes: punishment and custody. Fortunately, another model was emerging at the same time: the "new penology" of the 1930s and the rising star of the U.S. Bureau of Prisons under the leadership of Sanford Bates.

The Period of Transition (1935–1960)

The quarter century between 1935 and 1960 was one of great turmoil in the prisons. Administrators, stuck with the huge fortresses of the previous century, were now deprived of the ability to provide meaningful work for inmates. The depression and the criminal excesses of the 1920s and 1930s hardened the public's attitude toward convict rehabilitation at a time when behavioral scientists were just beginning to propose hopeful reforms in prisoner treatment. J. Edgar Hoover, director of the Federal Bureau of Investigation (FBI), led the battle against "hoity-toity professors"

Alacatraz: The Supermaximum Prison (Courtesy Federal Bureau of Prisons)

ALCATRAZ

A twelve-acre island in San Francisco Bay. Starting in 1859, it was the site of an army disciplinary barracks, which was replaced in 1909 by a military prison. In 1934 the military prison was converted to a federal prison that was considered virtually escape-proof. It was closed in 1963. It is now a National Park that receives thousands of visitors each year.

John Herbert Dillinger (1902–1934) was an infamous American gangster and bank robber. He deserted the navy in 1923, and in 1924 was imprisoned for nine years following an assault to rob a grocery. He committed his first bank robbery in 1933. Another famous gangster, "Baby Face" Nelson, was part of his gang. Dillinger robbed and killed across the Midwest until he was killed by the FBI outside the Biograph Cinema in Chicago. Anna Sage, a madame and friend of Dillinger's, betrayed him for the reward.

Bonnie Parker (?–1934) **and** Clyde Barrow (1910–1934) were the leaders of the Barrow gang, which terrorized the Midwest in 1933 and 1934. They were gunned down in a Ford V-8 during a famous ambush in 1934. Clyde's dead hands clutched a shotgun with seven notches on the stock, Bonnie's a pistol with three. Bonnie had sent a song, "The Story of Bonnie and Clyde," to a music publisher to be released after her death. It caught the imagination of the country and was a hit, making pseudoheroes of these cheap killers (who were restored to fame again in the 1967 movie glorifying their exploits).

Kate Clark ("Ma") Barker (1872–1935) was the coleader of another infamous gang in the 1933–1934 era of crime waves in the Midwest. Her husband and four sons made up the nucleus of the gang. Alvin Karpis was also a member. They robbed banks and plundered around the St. Paul, Minnesota, area. In early 1935, "Ma" Barker and her husband, Fred, were surrounded and killed in a cabin on Lake Weir, Florida. She was found with a submachine gun in her hands.

---

and the "cream-puff school of criminology." His war on crime helped give the world the supermaximum prison, Alcatraz. Located on an island in San Francisco Bay, Alcatraz was constructed to house the hardest criminals in America. When it was built in 1934, it was seen as the answer to the outrages of such desperate criminals as John Dillinger, Bonnie and Clyde, and Ma Barker. Eventually, the U.S. Bureau of Prisons abandoned this idea as another failure, and Alcatraz was closed in 1963.

Early efforts toward diagnostic classification and casework were

---

LOCK PSYCHOSIS

The unreasonable fear by prison administrators that leads them to lock prisoners behind several layers of barred doors and other barricades. The huge ring of keys carried by most prison personnel is an outward manifestation of this psychosis. Counts are usually conducted several times a day to ensure that all prisoners are locked up.

CONVICT BOGEY

Society's exaggerated fear of the convict and ex-convict, which is usually far out of proportion to the real danger they present. The tough escaped convicts shown in the movies and on television are a contributing factor to this unreasonable fear of convicts as a group.

---

pioneered by such notables as Bernard Glueck at Sing Sing between 1915 and 1920, Edgar Doll and W. G. Ellis in New Jersey in 1925, and A. W. Stearns in Massachusetts in 1930. Sanford Bates introduced procedures into the U.S. Bureau of Prisons in 1934. Although sometimes "borrowing" principles from states across the nation, the U.S. Bureau of Prisons gradually emerged as the national leader in corrections, introducing many new concepts that have been copied by state systems. Two major contributions were diagnosis and classification and the use of professional personnel such as psychiatrists and psychologists to help rehabilitate inmates. The federal system also led the way to more humane treatment and better living conditions. But no matter how they were cleaned up, prisons remained monuments to idleness, monotony, frustration, and repression. Despite attempts to tear down the massive walls around some prisons, the forces of "lock psychosis" continued to hold out. Prison inmates were feared as the "convict bogey," who could be dealt with only by locking and relocking, counting and recounting.

It is not too surprising that the long hours of idleness, forbidding architecture, growing populations, and unnecessarily repressive controls created unbearable tensions among the inmates. The first riots in this country, as noted earlier, were at the mine-shaft prison in Simsbury, Connecticut. Riots at the Walnut Street Jail were reported in the early 1800s as well. The mid-nineteenth century, when prison industries provided extensive work for convicts, was a time of few riots. Presumably, the inmates were either too tired to riot, or the control was too strict. As the prison industries died out, riots began to take place more regularly, adding evidence to the theory that enforced idleness causes restlessness and discontent among prisoners. There was a wave of riots in the prisons between 1929 and 1932. During World War II there were few problems, but in 1946 there was even a riot in Alcatraz, the superprison.

Whether the Alcatraz publicity offered an incentive or whether the rising prosperity of the 1950s simply presented too sharp a contrast with the bleak life on the inside, there was an explosion of prison discontent during that decade. Over one hundred riots or other major disturbances troubled American prisons between 1950 and 1966. The American Correctional Association investigated the riots and reported what appeared to be the main causes:

- Inadequate financial support and official and public indifference,
- Substandard personnel,
- Enforced idleness,
- Lack of professional leadership and professional programs,
- Excessive size and overcrowding of institutions,
- Political domination and motivation of management, and
- Unwise sentencing and parole practices.[24]

The period of transition saw a movement toward drastic measures, inside and outside the walls of America's prisons, to get across the point that mass-treatment prisons had failed. The giant fortresses to futility, built to house prisoners in silence and hard labor, were still being used for inmates no longer silent and forbidden to compete with outside labor. These prisons were becoming the "hulks" of the twentieth century.

With a few exceptions, the principles established at the first prison congress in 1870—untried and untested to this day—were crushed by the administrators' need to maintain custody and control at any cost. As America entered the 1960s, the emphasis turned slowly toward the individual prisoner's needs, and some of the technology and ability that led us into the atomic age was finally focused on the problems of corrections.

Summary _____

The period following the emergence of the penitentiary as a social tool for the reintegration of the offender back into society was filled with hope. The Industrial Revolution provided a method for using the "captive" work force in productive, if not always totally effective, enterprises. The growth of industrial prisons, however, also resulted in the use of thousands of prisoners as slave labor. This brought opposition from labor organizations, do-gooders, and even penal administrators. Although the prison industries were shut down for understandable reasons, the resulting inactivity in the massive fortress prisons became a devastating factor in the development of corrections through the 1960s. Riots and unrest became a way of life in the huge monuments to the ideas of the nineteenth century.

The entry into corrections of psychologists, psychiatrists, and educators resulted in attempts to solve the problems of the idleness imposed on inmates in industrial prisons through methods predicated on the "medical model." Institutionalization soon took precedence over treatment, however, resulting in more obsession with "locks and clocks" and less support for a treatment model. This lack of consensus as to the proper model for prisons to follow continued into the 1960s, and good intentions to reform the system continued to pave the road to chaos in America's prisons. It is said that a leopard cannot change its spots, and so removing the stripes from prisoners and calling them "residents" changed very little in American prisons. Without the commitment to total change in fortress prisons, true reform can never take place.

Review Questions

1. What effect did the Industrial Revolution have on prisons and prison discipline?
2. Which of the two early nineteenth-century prison systems won out in America? Why?
3. What were the major differences between prisons and reformatories?

Key Terms

1. outside cells (p. 35)
2. Auburn system (p. 37)
3. inside cells (p. 37)
4. congregate system (p. 37)
5. penitence (p. 42)
6. lockstep (p. 45)
7. stripes (p. 45)
8. the hole (p. 46)
9. mark system (p. 48)
10. ticket of leave (p. 50)
11. conditional release (p. 50)
12. lease system (p. 54)
13. state-account system (p. 54)
14. Great Depression (p. 56)
15. Alcatraz (p. 58)

Notes

1. The Philadelphia Society for the Alleviation of the Miseries of Public Prisons was originally formed by a group of concerned citizens in 1787. Because of their continued efforts, the law of 1790 was passed, and the Walnut Street Jail was remodeled to accommodate felons in solitary confinement. The Society is now the Pennsylvania Prison Society (Social Service Building, 311 S. Juniper Street, Philadelphia, PA 19107).
2. Outside cells were each about six feet wide, eight feet deep, and nine feet high, with a central corridor extending the length of the building in between. Some of them had individual yards added on the outside, with high walls between.
3. That system, in modified form, is used to this day in Belgium, France, and West Germany.
4. Inside cells are built back-to-back in tiers within a hollow building. Doors

open onto galleries or runs that are eight to ten feet from the outside wall; cells are small and intended only for sleeping. The interior cell block has become characteristic of American prisons.

5. Walter C. Reckless, *The Crime Problem,* 4th ed. (New York: Appleton-Century-Crofts, 1969), p. 548.
6. Harry Elmer Barnes, *The Story of Punishment,* 2d ed. (Montclair, N.J.: Patterson Smith, 1972), p. 136.
7. Robert G. Caldwell, *Criminology,* 2d ed. (New York: Ronald Press, 1965), p. 506.
8. Barnes, *The Story of Punishment,* p. 140.
9. G. de Beaumont and A. de Tocqueville, *On the Penitentiary System in the United States and Its Application in France* (Philadelphia: Francis Lieber, 1833).
10. Howard B. Gill, "A New Prison Discipline: Implementing the Declaration of Principles of 1870," *Federal Probation* (June 1970): 29–30.
11. George C. Killinger and Paul F. Cromwell, Jr., *Penology* (St. Paul: West Publishing, 1973), p. 40.
12. John V. Barry, "Captain Alexander Maconochie," *Victorian Historical Magazine* 27 (June 1957): 5.
13. Flat sentence refers to a specific period of time (for example, five years, ten years) in confinement for an offense, with no time off for any reason.
14. Harry Elmer Barnes and Negley K. Teeters, *New Horizons in Criminology,* 3d ed. (Englewood Cliffs, N.J.: Prentice-Hall, 1959), p. 419.
15. An indeterminate sentence usually has broad beginning and end figures (three to five years, one to ten years, and so on), instead of a certain fixed period. Prisoners are allowed to earn their freedom by means of good conduct.
16. Progressive penologists of the era met in Cincinnati, Ohio, on October 12, 1870, to plan the ideal prison system. Two earlier attempts to gather had failed, but this meeting of the American Prison Congress developed into the National Prison Association, later the American Correctional Association. (4321 Hartwick Road, College Park, Md. 20740)
17. Barnes and Teeters, *New Horizons in Criminology,* p. 426.
18. Georgia, Florida, Mississippi, Louisiana, and Arkansas, in particular, followed this procedure.
19. Tom Murton and Joe Hyams, *Accomplices to the Crime: The Arkansas Prison Scandal* (New York: Grove Press, 1967).
20. Margaret Calahan, *Historical Corrections Statistics in the United States: 1850–1984,* (Washington, D.C.: U.S. Department of Justice, 1986): p. 36.
21. Wayne Morse, *The Attorney General's Survey of Release Procedures* (Washington, D.C.: U.S. Government Printing Office, 1940).
22. Under the piece-price system, a variation of the contract system, the contractor supplied the raw material and paid a price for each finished product delivered. Thailand currently uses this system.
23. In the state-account or public-account system, all employment and activity are under the direction of the state, and products are sold on the open market. The prisoner receives a very small wage, and the profit goes to the state. Usually binder twine, rope, and hempsacks were produced this way; it provided a lot of work for prisoners, but little training. See American Correctional Association, *A Study of Prison Industry: History, Components, and Goals,* (Washington, D.C.: U.S. Department of Justice, 1986).
24. Barnes and Teeters, *New Horizons in Criminology,* p. 385.

4

The Modern Era (1960–1980)

The failures within our correctional institutions
are part of our larger failures throughout society.
A simultaneous war against poverty and racism
must accompany the war against crime.
—HON. A. LEON HIGGINBOTHAM, JR.,
United States District Judge

The modern era of corrections began about 1960, and it was characterized by a pattern of change that was to highlight the next decade. The 1960s in the United States were noted for turbulent and violent confrontations at almost every level of activity affecting human rights. The forces for change at work in the overall society were also reflected in great pressures for change in corrections. The dramatic reinterpretations of criminal law, the civil rights movement, violent and nonviolent demonstrations in the streets, the assassinations of a popular president and two other important national figures, the longest and most unpopular war in American history—all these outside pressures were also felt inside the walls of the nation's prisons. Reaction took the form of periodic violent prison riots and disorders. The Supreme Court of the United States emerged as the primary external agent for the enforced recognition of the basic rights of those swept up in the criminal justice system. This external pressure was generated by a long series of significant judicial interpretations. In addition, leadership and funding by the federal government were given to corrections administrators and planners at the state and local levels, enabling them to create, implement, and evaluate new policies and practices. Unfortunately, aspiring politicians and the media[1] have collectively generated and nurtured inaccurate stereotypes about offenders, blunting correctional gains and giving rise to more intractable problems. The turmoil continues.

Internally Sought Reform

Early prisons were less secure than modern ones are, and escape was far more common. It was easier to "disappear" into early American society, with a new name and a new start. Inmate security and control, improved in recent years, have made escape from prisons difficult. And systems of identification and control, including computer banks of data on each of us, have made escape into society almost impossible.

When the prisons became so secure that escape was cut off, the inmates' frustration and agitation turned inward. Prisoners in this "total institution"[2] used disturbances and riots to express their desire for reforms and changes in rules and conditions. Disturbances also served to resolve power struggles between inmate groups. The early disturbances were characterized by disorganization and rapid dispersion; inmates used these methods to settle old grudges, refusing to fall in line behind any kind of leadership. In the 1950s and 1960s, disturbances were commonplace in most large state systems, reflecting the usual grievances: crowded living conditions, harsh rules, poor food, excessive punishment, and guard brutality. Even the highly respected Federal Prison System was rocked in 1987 by large-scale hostage-taking by Cuban inmates who feared being deported to Cuba. The growing awareness of individual rights on the outside that began in the 1960s led inmates to seek the same rights in prison.

Beginning about 1966, the nature of the demands changed from those involving basic conditions to those concerning basic rights. In that year the Maryland Penitentiary in Baltimore was the scene of a riot involving over one thousand inmates. The warden claimed the disturbance was caused by heat waves and overcrowding, but "the riot had to have social overtones," said Joseph Bullock, a member of the State House of Delegates. "If they don't stop telling these people [blacks] about their rights," Bullock went on, "things will get worse."[3] Rioting and violence spilled over from the streets into the prisons of America. The "political prisoner" label, particularly for blacks and Chicanos, offered a more acceptable way for minority groups to state their feelings of deprivation. They struck out at a system that they perceived gave them an unequal start in life and then jailed them for failing to live up to the rules of that system.[4] Clearly, outside social behavior and conditions do carry over into prison. Little that is new in society starts in prison.

Of the dozen or so large prison riots that broke out after 1966, many had racial overtones. A riot at the California State Penitentiary in San Quentin, in 1967, stemmed from conflict between Black Muslim and white inmates.[5] On July 4, 1970, while Bob Hope, Billy Graham, and 350,000 people were celebrating Honor America Day[6] in Washington, D.C., a major riot took place at Holmesburg Prison in Philadelphia. Ninety percent of the 1,300 inmates at Holmesburg were black. Superintendent Hendricks

---

RIOT

A violent, tumultuous disturbance within a prison or other correctional institution involving three or more inmates assembled together and acting in a common cause.

placed the blame for this riot, which left 80 prisoners and 25 guards injured, on "hard-core black militants."[7] Statements on civil rights and political liberation for blacks, made at Soledad and San Quentin prisons in 1971, contributed to the tense atmosphere that produced shootings and riots in several prisons.[8]

In September 1971, a tense situation at the New York State Penitentiary at Attica erupted and made nationwide newspaper headlines. At the final count, thirty-two prisoners and eleven guards were killed in this terrible prison riot. The governor of New York appointed a commission to study the reasons for the Attica tragedy and to search for ways to prevent a recurrence. The results of this study showed that riot leaders were using Attica as an arena to highlight the despair and inhumane treatment of "political prisoners."[9] Winston E. Moore, executive director of the Cook County Department of Corrections, an outspoken prison reformer and himself black, said that although the civil rights movement had helped cut down racial discrimination and similar abuses outside prison walls, practically nothing had changed inside. Thus, he found that "the recent killings in Attica and other prisons [such as New Mexico in 1980] have served notice that racist practices will no longer be tolerated by the inmates."[10]

Change, though often temporary, does come about as a result of prison riots. More often today, new voices can help shape prison policies—through an inmate council, grievance procedures, conflict resolution, or inmates serving on regular prison committees, following a collaborative model. Some systems also use an *ombudsman* as a link between the prisoner and the establishment. These methods are thought to be effective, and their continued use appears to be the trend for the future. Inmate self-government, tried in the 1800s at Elmira Reformatory in New York and more recently at the Washington State Penitentiary in Walla Walla, does not appear to offer the same promise as does selected individual representation.[11]

The expansion of community-based corrections will not eliminate the prison riot from the scene, however. Paradoxically, prison riots may pose a great threat in the fewer and smaller maximum security prisons envisioned for the future. As more and more offenders are treated in the community, the "hard core" that must be kept in institutions will require careful supervision to avoid problems in control and treatment. The prison riot has not been the most effective tool for the expression of inmate grievances, but it has helped focus public attention on prison problems. Increasingly, inmates are turning to the federal courts to redress their grievances.

OMBUDSMAN

An appointed official who receives and investigates inmates' complaints against correctional practices, reports findings, and recommends corrective action . . . without the inmate having fear of reprisal.

Changing the internal administration of prisons is another, although less sensational, method of reform. In the Arkansas system, prison administrator Tom Murton (given great national attention in the movie *Brubaker,* 1980, starring film idol Robert Redford), was appointed to act in the role of "reformer" by Governor Winthrop Rockefeller and managed to unearth various scandals (and human skeletons) in the state prison system, thereby achieving temporary reform.[12] The threat of institutionalization is real to the staff as well as to the inmate, however. The routine of the standard prison is one that leads to staff burnout in a relatively short time.[13] Internally initiated reform by the staff is, therefore, often short-lived; either the old routine returns, or the reforms settle into a new but equally sterile routine. Unless real reform occurs at all levels of the correctional system, there is little incentive for continuing new programs. The most lasting reforms appear to be those accomplished either as a result of outside pressure or with the knowledge and support of the outside community and public leaders. How are these external pressures brought to bear?

Externally Induced Reform

Corrections, as a social system, is above all a political unit established by an authorizing mandate, supported by tax revenues, and subject to political influences. It reflects both the system of justice and the overall sociocultural environment. The latter is the source of externally induced reform. In externally induced reform, changes are effected by individuals or groups outside the correctional system.[14]

At the state and local levels, correctional reform is usually accomplished through legislative or executive action. Examples of reform by legislation range from the complete revision of a state's criminal code to passage of simple amendments to bills, allowing such benefits as educational and home furloughs. The executive branch of government can also exert a direct effect on correctional reform through executive orders. These orders can accomplish small but important changes, such as the abolition of mail censorship,[15] the appointment of a task force of involved citizens to seek correctional reform,[16] and the withholding of support for clearly unsound correctional programs.[17]

At the federal level, the most active agent for external reform has been the courts—particularly the U.S. Supreme Court, which has traditionally upheld the principle of individual rights in the face of government power. Major court cases that produced prison reforms include *Gideon* v. *Wainwright* (regarding right to counsel), *Johnson* v. *Avery* (regarding jailhouse lawyers), and *Furman* v. *Georgia* (regarding the death penalty). Some details on these and other cases are supplied in the section that follows.

Reform by the Courts

Between 1960 and 1972, American criminal law passed from a state of evolution to a state of revolution.[18] The step-by-step extension to the states of the various federal constitutional guarantees of individual rights was clearly the goal of the courts' quiet but effective revolution. The decisions of the much-maligned—or -revered—Warren Court are more readily understood when viewed from this perspective. During the 1960s, nearly all the guarantees of the Fourth, Fifth, Sixth, and Eighth Amendments of the Constitution were made binding on the states.

The Fourteenth Amendment (due process clause) provided the primary leverage in these landmark decisions, described in the cases that follow. The extension of constitutional guarantees to all persons accused in state proceedings has produced dramatic and significant changes in criminal law and criminal procedures and important effects on corrections.

Mapp v. Ohio. The case of *Mapp* v. *Ohio* (exclusionary rule), 367 U.S. 643 (1960), opened a Pandora's box of Fourteenth Amendment rulings. A crack in the armor of state proceedings, it paved the way for the flood of cases heard by the Court during the next decade, in reference not only to illegally obtained evidence but also to all areas of individual rights. The basic finding in *Mapp* v. *Ohio* is that evidence obtained during an

---

SELECTED AMENDMENTS
TO THE UNITED STATES CONSTITUTION

FOURTH AMENDMENT: The right of the people to be secure in their persons, houses, papers, and effects, against unreasonable searches and seizures, shall not be violated, and no warrants shall issue, but upon probable cause, supported by oath or affirmation, and particularly describing the place to be searched, and the person or things to be seized.

FIFTH AMENDMENT: No person shall be held to answer for a capital, or otherwise infamous crime, unless a presentment or indictment of a Grand Jury, except in cases arising in the land or naval forces, or the Militia, when in actual service in time of War or public danger; nor shall any person be subject for the same offense to twice be put in jeopardy of life or limb; nor shall be compelled in any criminal case to be a witness against himself, nor be deprived of life, liberty, or property, without due process of law; nor shall private property be taken for public use, without just compensation.

SIXTH AMENDMENT: In all criminal prosecutions, the accused shall enjoy the right to a speedy and public trail, by an impartial jury of the state or district wherein the crime shall have been committed, which district shall have been previously ascertained by law, and to be informed of the nature and cause of the accusation; to be confronted with the witness in his favor, and to have the Assistance of Counsel for his defense.

EIGHTH AMENDMENT: Excessive bail shall not be required, nor excessive fines imposed, nor cruel and unusual punishment inflicted.

> **SELECTED AMENDMENTS**
> **TO THE UNITED STATES CONSTITUTION (cont.)**
> **FOURTEENTH AMENDMENT**: All persons born and naturalized in the United States, and subject to the jurisdiction thereof, are citizens of the United States and of the State wherein they reside. No State shall make or enforce any law which shall abridge the privileges or immunities of citizens of the United States; nor shall any State deprive any person of life, liberty, or property, without due process of law; nor deny any person within its jurisdiction the equal protection of the laws.

illegal search or seizure is "fruit of the poisoned tree" and therefore inadmissible in both federal and state courts. *Mapp* v. *Ohio* dealt primarily with illegally obtained evidence and as such had little effect on corrections. Its primary interest here lies in the Court's use of the Fourteenth Amendment to support its decision.

Robinson v. California. In the California case of *Robinson* v. *California* (cruel and unusual punishment), 370 U.S. 660 (1961), the Eighth Amendment's clause forbidding cruel and unusual punishment was made binding on state proceedings. The case involved the arrest of the subject on the charge of being a drug addict, even though he had neither used drugs in the state nor was in any way guilty of irregular behavior. The majority opinion stated that a law that imprisons a person for being sick inflicts a cruel and unusual punishment in violation of the Eighth Amendment and due process under the Fourteenth Amendment.[19] Although several issues raised by the cruel and unusual punishment clause have been considered since that time, the Eighth Amendment has repeatedly come under scrutiny in recent decisions regarding the death penalty.

Furman v. Georgia. In *Furman* v. *Georgia,* 408 U.S. 238 (1972), the issue of cruel and unusual punishment as applied to the death penalty was raised in a petition by several states for clarification of this long-standing dilemma. In June 1972, the U.S. Supreme Court held that any statute that permits a jury to demand the death penalty is unconstitutional. The majority stated that the death penalty, left to the discretion of the jury, violates the Eighth Amendment—not because it is inherently intolerable, but because it is applied "so wantonly and freakishly" that it serves no deterrent purpose and therefore constitutes cruel and unusual punishment.[20] States sought to get around the *Furman* decision by making mandatory death penalty laws. Several of these laws were declared unconstitutional by the Supreme Court in a series of decisions in 1976, notably *Roberts* v. *Louisiana* and *Woodson* v. *North Carolina*. Large numbers of prisoners had their death penalties rescinded (265 in 1976 alone). However, three other cases at the same time gave the Court the opportunity to state that the death penalty was not inherently unconstitutional and that the statutes that set forth specific guidelines to assist the sentencing authority, in a separate sentencing procedure, in considering mitigating or aggravated circumstances, were constitutionally sound. Thus, the Court determined for the first time, that the punishment of death was not cruel and unusual punishment per se. Despite the lifting of the restrictions on administering the death penalty, the small (but growing) number that have been executed under the new guidelines indicates continuing resistance, hesitation, and confusion in the use of this ultimate sanction (see Chapter 14).

Gideon v. Wainwright. In the crucial decision of *Gideon* v. *Wainwright* (right to counsel), 372 U.S. 335 (1963), the Court held that defendants in noncapital cases are entitled to assistance of counsel at trial as a matter of right. This right was extended to state proceedings, again under the provisions of the Fourteenth Amendment. This decision opened the door to a number of subsequent decisions involving not only the right to counsel under the Sixth Amendment but also the protection against self-incrimination under the Fifth Amendment. *Morrissey* v. *Brewer,* 408 U.S. 471 (1972) also provided the right to counsel at parole board revocation hearings, and *Gagnon* v. *Scarpelli*, 411 U.S. 778 (1973) guaranteed that right at the probation revocation hearing.

Johnson v. Avery. A significant 1969 decision provided prisoners in state penal institutions with legal assistance in preparing habeas corpus proceedings. In *Johnson* v. *Avery,* 393 U.S. 483, the Court held that states not providing adequate legal assistance would have to put up with "jailhouse lawyers"[21] — prisoners determined to research and conduct their own and others' appeals. Some states, although not in a position to provide the vast number of lawyers required, have accommodated the prisoners through the use of law students and trained lay persons. Law libraries were set up in many state correctional institutions, with the help of the Law Enforcement Assistance Administration.[22] Right to counsel has been firmly established, and the responsibility for maintaining this right lies squarely on the shoulders of correctional administrators. On April 27, 1977, the Supreme Court reinforced this right with the decision that law libraries must be made available to prisoners who seek legal assistance.[23] Jailhouse lawyering remains constitutionally protected.

Miranda v. Arizona. As noted earlier, the application of the Fifth Amendment protections against self-incrimination was influenced by the *Gideon* decision. An interim decision was rendered in 1964 by the Supreme

---

JAILHOUSE LAWYERS
Inmates claiming to have some legal knowledge, who counsel and assist other inmates in the preparation of legal documents.

MIRANDA WARNINGS

* You have the right to remain silent.
* Any statement you make may be used as evidence against you in a criminal trial.
* You have the right to consult with counsel and to have counsel present with you during questioning.
* You may retain counsel at your own expense or counsel will be appointed for you at no expense to you.
* Even if you decide to answer questions now, without having counsel present, you may stop answering questions at any time.
* Also, you may request counsel at any time during questioning.

Court in *Escobedo* v. *Illinois,* 378 U.S. 478, which required certain procedural safeguards against self-incrimination during an interrogation at the station house. Confusion as to the nature of procedures and the time at which they should be applied resulted in the Court's most controversial decision of the criminal justice revolution. For the first time, in the 1966 decision of *Miranda* v. *Arizona,* 384 U.S. 436, a set of specific and detailed police warnings to the arrested person were required, through the due process clause, at specific and distinct points in the criminal process.

The *Miranda* decision stated that the privilege against self-incrimination "is available outside of criminal court proceedings and serves to protect persons in all settings in which their freedom of action is curtailed in any significant way on being compelled to incriminate themselves." Although some law enforcement officers have claimed to be "handcuffed" by the *Miranda* warnings, the safeguards appear to be effective and have not materially hindered the securing of confessions.[24] Although court decisions made in 1976 through 1984 have tempered the conditions necessitating the *Miranda* warnings, they are still the law of the land and have established an important procedural precedent.[25]

It should be pointed out that in addition to these particular cases, in the 1960s and 1970s, the Supreme Court entertained cases concerning the civil rights of inmates, calling on the Civil Rights Act of 1871. As we enter the mid-eighties, many prisons in most states are under court orders or are facing constitutional challenges under Chapter 42, U.S. Code Section

---

CHAPTER 42 OF THE UNITED STATES CODE, SECTION 1983

Every person, who under the color of any statute, ordinance, regulation, custom, or usage of any State or Territory, subjects or causes to be subjected, any citizen of the United States or other person within the jurisdiction thereof to the deprivation of rights, privileges, or immunities secured by the Constitution or laws, shall be liable to the party injured in the action at law, suit in equity, or other proper proceding for redress.

1983.[26] Many states are being sued, and federal masters have been appointed to oversee the conditions in state prisons.

In summary, the student can see how external pressure from the U.S. Supreme Court has modified and clarified the criminal law and offered basic constitutional guarantees to all persons, including those incarcerated in state and federal prisons. Such pressures, especially in the area of juvenile corrections, can be expected to continue, marching under the banner of the Fourteenth Amendment until all other federal constitutional protection provisions are also imposed on the states.

This effort to return the control over prison conditions to the courts has resulted in over four thousand court decisions in the past two decades. The return of the power of the courts over correctional administration is a hopeful sign for the modern era. The erosion of this power, which had its gradual beginning in 1970, and the subsequent assumption of power by the executive branch have been at the core of many of the problems noted at the beginning of this chapter.[27]

External pressure is also brought to bear by private organizations and some groups composed of former prisoners. The John Howard Association,[28] the American Correctional Association,[29] and the National Council on Crime and Delinquency[30] seek reform through prison certification visits and suggestions to correctional administrators. These efforts help keep the major problem areas in corrections before the public view. Organizations of ex-offenders who work with prisoners, such as the Seventh Step Foundation,[31] Man-to-Man,[32] and the Fortune Society,[33] also seek correctional reform.

Reform by Legislation

Passage of meaningful reform legislation, especially in the corrections area, has been painfully slow. Even more difficult has been the provision of adequate funding to accomplish reform. The turbulence of the early 1960s prompted federal enactment of the Law Enforcement Assistance Act of 1965. That act, designed to test the value of granting federal funds to assist local law enforcement, was a symbol of things to come. After the release of the findings of President Lyndon Johnson's criminal justice commission, entitled *The Challenge of Crime in a Free Society* (1967), legislation was introduced to expand the Law Enforcement Assistance Act, with direct grants to state and local governments focusing on causation research, prevention, and control of crime. But the U.S. Senate moved slowly; the bill was deadlocked in committee when Congress was shocked from its apathy by the assassination of presidential aspirant Senator Robert Kennedy. This dramatic demonstration of the nation's need for more effective crime control prompted its quick passage.

The final version of the bill, known as the Omnibus Crime Control and Safe Streets Act of 1968, replaced direct grants to local governments with block grants to the states but was otherwise passed substantially as sub-mitted. This far-reaching act, implemented by the Law Enforcement Assis-tance Administration (LEAA), provided billions of dollars to states for action programs, research, education, evaluation, training, and administra-tion of the criminal justice system. Amendments in 1970 created a category of funds especially earmarked for corrections. As part of LEAA, the Law Enforcement Education Program funneled more than $260 million to at least 300,000 criminal justice students from 1968 to 1981.

The policy change embodied in this act was a reaction to overemphasis on police needs in previous years, and it reflected a new awareness of the realities of local political structures. The criminal justice system, however loosely structured it may be, is still subject to the rules of any social system. When too much effort was expended on improving the police ability to catch criminals, judicial and correctional sectors were overwhelmed by the impact of their success. Most experts now recognize that corrections also must improve, or we will simply continue to recycle indefinitely the same or similar people through the system. As Chief Justice Warren Burger stated in 1967, "the total process is a deadly serious business that begins with an arrest, proceeds through a trial, and is followed by a judgment and a sentence to a term of confinement in a prison or other institution. The administration of criminal justice in any civilized country must embrace the idea of rehabilitation of the guilty person as well as the protection of society."[34]

The LEAA finally came to an end under the early Reagan administration and may be viewed in later years as a "New Society" idea initiated under the Johnson years. Its legacy has yet to be determined, but initial evaluations of the impact of LEAA programs on the states seems to be favorable.[35]

Reform by Executive Order

Not since 1929, when President Herbert Hoover established the National Commission on Law Observance and Enforcement (commonly known as the Wickersham Commission), had the executive office undertaken an in-depth examination of crime in America. The Great Depression, World War II, the Korean War, and subsequent adjustments to peace all led a series of presidents to assign a low priority to criminal justice reforms.

The outbreak of violence on the streets of America in the early 1960s changed all that. From the embattled ghettos of Los Angeles and Detroit to the assassination of President Kennedy in Dallas, such events highlight-ed the problems of crime and violence across the nation. On July 23, 1965, President Lyndon B. Johnson established the Commission on Law Enforce-ment and Administration of Justice with a mandate to examine every area of the American criminal justice system. The commission's report, *The Challenge of Crime in a Free Society,* and its more detailed papers have become the basic reference points for progress on all fronts of the criminal justice system.

The President's Commission confirmed in many respects the earlier Wickersham report. Many recommendations were found to be as pertinent in 1967 as they had been in 1929. At that time, the three thousand federal and state prisons, reformatories, workhouses, and county and city jails were cited for deficiencies in prisoner classification, employment, education, parole, and probation. They were characterized by outdated physical facilities, untrained and inadequate staffs, and inmates beset by idleness. Identical problems, with few exceptions, were found in the massive study of corrections in America completed in 1967. The president's involvement, through his commission, pushed such issues as crime on the streets, corrections, and judicial processes to the top of the list for legislative proposals and action. Finally spurred to action, Congress provided federal funds to the states, through LEAA, to work on the problems.

Disturbed by the problems in their own states, a number of governors also began examining, evaluating, and improving the conditions of their criminal justice systems, especially the corrections sector (see box). Using

---

EXPANDING CORRECTIONS: ONE GOVERNOR'S PERSPECTIVE

When I became governor in 1977, Delaware was committing about 3 percent of its State budget to corrections. Like all new officeholders, I had a list of things I wanted to improve during my administration. And corrections seemed to me to be the one thing that certainly needed improvement. I wanted to cut its demands on tax revenues, which I felt we more urgently needed in other areas. We were, I concluded, pouring too much money into our prisons and jails. . . .

This year corrections will account for more than 7 percent of the total State budget, which means that there is still more pressure on the other vital services that State must provide. Indeed, in real dollar terms, our State's corrections budget has grown over 300 percent in just 7 years. This makes it by far the most inflated budget in State government since I took over.

. . . [T]here are answers to the correctional dilemma . . . the proposals that are under active consideration in Delaware are no mere "quick fixes" or exercises in political legerdemain.

Instead, what I propose will require a major overhaul of the corrections system and the establishment of a more flexible and effective sentencing structure. This will require public understanding and acceptance at a time when the criminal justice system is under considerable pressure for not being rigid enough in dealing with criminals.

Balanced against these considerations are the problems of doing nothing at all. The costs in terms of money, of public dismay at growing criminality, and the waste of human effort are too appalling to permit this to be a viable option.

Source: Pierre S. du Pont IV, *Expanding Sentencing Options: A Governor's Perspective* (Washington, D.C.: U.S. Department of Justice, 1985):1–2.

the citizens' task force concept as a model, they searched for ways to reform prison operations. Federal funding enabled them to implement many key suggestions from their state task forces. This was particularly important when a needed reform required more than state funds or a simple executive order. Notable among the citizens' task forces were those in Ohio and Wisconsin.

Contemporary Corrections

The need for correctional reforms and structured plans to achieve them was documented by the Wickersham Commission, President Johnson's Task Force on Corrections, and the various state task forces. The early 1960s emerged as a period of seeking alternative methods, programs, treatment procedures, and designs for facilities—all in line with the new emphasis on correcting offenders. This search took place through hundreds of feasibility studies and test programs throughout the nation. As a result of these evaluations and programs, many of the treasured beliefs of the public and correctional administrators and practitioners were shown to be inaccurate, if not totally false. The most astonishing and significant findings included the following:

1. Long sentences are self-defeating in regard to rehabilitation.
2. Most offenders—perhaps as many as 85 percent—do not need to be incarcerated and could function better back in the community under supervision.
3. Most inmates derive maximum benefit from incarceration during their first two years; after that period, it becomes less and less likely that they could function as productive citizens if returned to society.
4. Community-based corrections are more realistic, less expensive, and at least as effective as incarceration is.
5. Corrections, as a system, must encompass all aspects of rehabilitative service, including mental health, employment services, education, and social services.
6. Some offenders—because of their dangerousness—will require extensive incarceration and treatment programs especially designed and implemented in secure institutions. The staff in these institutions must be extensive and of high quality.
7. Most inmates are not mentally ill but suffer from a variety of educational, medical, psychological, maturational, economic, and interpersonal handicaps that are seldom reduced or resolved in contemporary correctional systems.
8. Inmates must be given the opportunity and capability to earn a living wage so as to compensate their victims and support their own

families, keeping them off public assistance rolls.

9. The pay for inmates presently incarcerated is too low to be regarded as wages. Thus the rates of pay must be increased to at least the minimum wage on the outside for similar labor.

10. Laws that prohibit the meaningful development of prison industries must be replaced. The private economic sector must be sought out and used to provide both training and work programs that will produce employable workers at the end of the corrections cycle.

Despite the evidence, three important developments in corrections have occurred over the last fifteen years. These are (1) the abandonment of the ideological basis for postadjudication handling of convicted offenders, commonly referred to as the *medical model;* (2) the shift to determinate sentencing, which places limits on the judge's power to determine how long the offender might serve in prison; and, (3) a search for punishments that would be more effective than court-ordered probation and less severe than long-term incarceration, the so-called *intermediate punishments.*

The medical-model perspective views the criminal offender as "sick," and the role of corrections is to make the criminal "well." This process would entail diagnosing the cause of the criminal act, and planning a treatment program that would remove the criminal tendencies that led the offender to commit the act. There would be some way to detect when the "patient" was well enough to be released back into the community, on "aftercare" by some qualified authority (parole board) that would turn the offender over to community supervision until he or she fully "recuperated."

The medical model ceased to be the predominant rationale for corrections for many reasons not yet fully clear. Certainly the public's growing fear of and impatience with crime, fueled by self-serving demagogues and a media eager to exploit the issue, contributed to this model's demise. Other factors include inmate dissatisfaction with parole board release policies, the emergence of "get tough" legislation, a "hardening of the attitudes" by the citizenry, studies that seemed to show that "nothing works" in corrections, and the post-World War II baby boomers that placed massive numbers of persons into the high crime-risk ages (19–29). For whatever reasons, the medical model has been largely abandoned in American corrections.

In the place of the medical model has arisen the *punishment ideology,*[36] a rebirth of the neoclassical answers to the questions of, "Who are criminals and what should society do about them?" Offenders are seen as rational but evil humans, making calculated judgments to commit crimes because the personal benefit and minor risks are favorable to them. With the perceived failure of the medical model, the choices as to the correct responses to such offenders have boiled down to giving them the punishment they obviously deserved ("doing justice"), and changing the sentencing system to place more offenders in prison, where they would serve longer

A Modern Control Center at Wyoming Correctional Facility, Attica, New York. (Courtesy of American Correctional Association, photo by CRSS Constructers, Inc.)

sentences. By 1987, the majority of the states embraced determinate sentencing, abolishing parole in at least nineteen states, and imposing mandatory add-on time for use of a gun in crimes, sale of narcotics, and some especially brutal crimes. The reemergence of retribution in contemporary corrections has in part led to seriously overcrowded prisons, a deluge of lawsuits by prisoners seeking better conditions in incarceration, and intense search for new alternatives to imprisonment that would still provide public safety and constitutionally viable conditions for prisoners.

The intermediate punishments that have emerged are new for American corrections; some even apply contemporary "high-tech" concepts to controlling offenders. These concepts will be explored later in the text, but it is necessary at least to introduce the reader to the most common of the new alternatives. These include restitution programs, intensive supervised probation, house arrest, electronic monitoring, and home incarceration (see box).

We must mention a final note about contemporary developments in the modern era. American corrections has undertaken an enormous construction program, in what may be a futile effort to build enough cells to relieve overcrowding in prisons, penitentiaries, reformatories, corrections centers, and other facilities for incarceration. Imprisonment, generally acknowledged to cost the taxpayer about $15,000 per inmate annually, requires a larger and larger portion of the generally shrinking resources of government at all levels. Financing of prison construction, costing up to as much as $150,000 per bed, is borrowing against the future and flirting with bankruptcy for governmental jurisdictions. Corrections has become so expensive that private entrepreneurs have provided correctional

A Modern Tower, Using Electronic Sensing and Razor Wire (Courtesy of American Correctional Association, photo by CRSS Constructers, Inc.)

INTERMEDIATE PUNISHMENTS

RESTITUTION: Usually a cash payment by the offender to the victim of an amount considered to offset the loss incurred by the victim or community. The amount of payment may be scaled down to the offender's earning capacity, and/or payment may be made in installments. Sometimes services directly or indirectly benefiting the victim may be substituted for cash payment.

INTENSIVE SUPERVISED PROBATION: A court-ordered program of community supervision by probation officers working with very small caseloads to provide intensive supervision. Such programs are usually linked to impromptu drug testing, curfews, restitution, volunteer sponsors, probation fees, and other punitive intrusions. Sometimes (as in Georgia) two officers will share a caseload of up to forty probationers.

HOUSE ARREST: A more intensive program that requires the offender to remain secluded in his or her home except for work, grocery shopping, community restitution service, or other minor exceptions. Frequently, house arrest may be intensified by requiring the offender to wear an electronic devise that signals a computer monitor that the offender is present at home.

ELECTRONIC MONITORING OF OFFENDERS: This program requires an offender to wear a bracelet or anklet that will emit an electronic signal, confirming via a telephone contact that the offender is located at a specific, required location. Some monitoring systems have the capability of emitting signals that can be picked up by cellular listing posts within a community, to signal to a computer monitor that the offender is moving within the community (not at home). Frequently, the electronic monitoring system is buttressed by scheduled probation officer visits, drug testing, and other surveillance options.

---

services at local jurisdictions, and have proposed to provide correctional services for entire state systems at less cost and with greater effectiveness.

Corrections in America is at a "crossroad," a crisis unparalleled in the past two hundred years. The remainder of this text will describe current developments and practices in corrections, innovations, proposed solutions, and ways to ease the crisis and improve the effectiveness of the system. To understand these recent developments, we need to explore the correctional ideologies detailed in the next chapter.

Summary

_____

The explosion predicted from the conditions created by overcrowding, idleness, and lack of public concern erupted at Attica in the fall of 1971. The modern era became a period of seeking ways to prevent more such events: community-based corrections became the watchword for reform in corrections, and the "correctional funnel," (discussed in Chapter 7) was supplied with more outlets for diverting inmates from seething, overcrowded prisons. Supreme Court decisions created further pressure for reform. The result, at least until the end of the 1970s, was a state of uneasy status quo. The status quo was broken in the beginning of the 1980s by riots at the New Mexico prison, which resulted in numerous brutal deaths and public outrage.

It appears now that some of the programs designed to relieve the problems in the overcrowded fortress prisons have in fact contributed to many of the conditions and made them even more ripe for violence. With many nondangerous offenders being diverted to more humane processes, the remaining populations of American prisons have become increasingly hardcore. These inmates represent the principal problem for the administrator of the 1980s. The fortress prisons are still here, they are even more overcrowded, and their clients are now the bottom of the barrel in regard to behavioral problems. This has caused a movement away from the medical model and toward a model emphasizing custody and control over all else in a futile effort to keep peace in the institutions and "protect society." The problem of selecting a philosophy of ideology that is effective and reflective of society's mood is a problem that administrators will have to confront in the next decade.

Review Questions

1. Which has the most lasting effect, prison riots or internal administrative changes?
2. What has been the most effective outside force for prison reform? Why?
3. What amendment to the Constitution has had the most effect on reform in criminal justice? Explain the reason for its effect.
4. What contradicting trends exist in contemporary corrections?
5. How has the U.S. Supreme Court made federally guaranteed rights apply to state prisoners?

Key Terms

1. racism (p. 64)
2. chicano (p. 64)
3. riot (p. 64)
4. Soledad (p. 65)
5. Attica (p. 65)
6. ombudsman (p. 65)
7. jailhouse lawyers (p. 69)
8. due process clause (p. 67)
9. *Miranda* warnings (p. 706)
10. LEAA (p. 72)
11. task force model (p. 74)
12. restitution (p. 78)
13. intensive supervised probation (p. 78)
14. house arrest (p. 78)

Notes _____

1. John Irwin and James Austin, *It's About Time* (San Francisco: National Council on Crime and Delinquency, 1987), pp. 13–19.
2. Irving Goffman, "On the Characteristics of Total Institutions: Staff-Inmate Relations," in D. R. Cressey, ed., *The Prison* (New York: Holt, Rinehart & Winston, 1966), pp. 16–22. This concept refers to the sum of conditions created by a large number of people living around the clock within a close space, with tightly scheduled sequences of activity coordinated by a central authority.
3. *New York Times,* July 9, 1966, p. 9, col. 2.
4. James W. L. Park, "What Is a Political Prisoner? The Politics of Predators," *American Journal of Corrections* 34 (November–December 1972): 22–23. See also Robert Leger and Harvey Barnes, "Black Attitudes in Prison: A Sociological Analysis," *Journal of Criminal Justice* 14 (1986): 105–122.
5. *New York Times,* January 19, 1968, p. 69, col. 8. Currently, the three major prison gangs in California are blacks, Chicanos, and Aryans (racist whites). For data on national prison gangs, see George Camp and Camille Camp, *Prison Gangs* (Washington, D.C.: U.S. Department of Justice, 1985).
6. Honor America Day was conducted to try to bolster a sagging spirit in the nation following the riots of 1968 and 1969 on the streets and the continued escalation of the Vietnam War. Top entertainers donated their time for a nationally televised live show on the mall in Washington, D.C. Bob Hope was the chairman.
7. Law Enforcement Assistance Administration, *Outside Looking In: A Series of Monographs Assessing the Effectiveness of Corrections* (Washington, D.C.: U.S. Department of Justice, 1970), p. 7.
8. Statements attributed to George Jackson, San Quentin Prison, June 11, 1971.
9. *McKay Commission Report* (New York: September 1972). A "must" reading for serious students of penology.
10. Winston E. Moore, "My Cure for Prison Riots: End Prison Racism," *Ebony* (December 1971): 85–95.
11. Prison self-government systems in a total institution are subject to the pressures of the inmate subculture, making it very difficult to achieve the goals of true inmate representation.
12. Tom Murton and Joe Hyans, *Accomplices to the Crime: The Arkansas Prison Scandal* (New York: Grove Press, 1967).
13. Staff burnout refers to the development of a pattern that takes place after a staff member has worked for a certain period of time in a total institution. Innovative ideas and concern for the inmate give way to routine and concern for the institution.
14. H. E. Allen, "The Task Force Model As a Vehicle for Correctional Change: Liability or Asset?" Paper presented at the Interamerican Congress of the American Society of Criminology and the Interamerican Association of Criminology, Caracas, Venezuela, November 20, 1972.
15. J. J. Gilligan, Governor, Ohio, Administrative Orders 814, 814A, 814B, August 5, 1971.

16. For example, Ohio Citizens' Task Force on Corrections, February 1971; Wisconsin Citizens' Study Committee on Offender Rehabilitation, May 1971.

17. An example of such withdrawal is the abolition of prison farm programs throughout the nation. Farming has ceased to be a relevant vocational training vehicle for primarily urban offenders, and in most states, the programs are too expensive to operate.

18. Editors of *Criminal Law Reporter, The Criminal Law Revolution and Its Aftermath, 1960–71* (Washington, D.C.: BNA Books, 1972).

19. The Court declared that sickness may not be made a crime, nor may sick people be punished for being sick. Because narcotics addiction is a sickness, a state cannot make it a punishable offense any more than it can put a man in jail "for the 'crime' of having a common cold."

20. All nine members of the Court delivered separate opinions; Justices Douglas, Brennan, Stewart, White, and Marshall writing concurring remarks, with Chief Justice Burger and Justices Blackman, Powell, and Rehnquist writing dissenting opinions.

21. Mr. Justice Abe Fortas, who wrote the majority opinion, acknowledged that the state has an interest in preservation of prison discipline. However, he emphasized that interest "must yield to a prisoner's habeas corpus rights."

22. Illinois, for example, has established law libraries at each of its adult institutions.

23. "Court Rules on Prison Law Libraries," *Corrections Digest* 8 (May 11, 1977): 3–4.

24. Actually, the Miranda warnings have caused the police to upgrade the quality of their investigative activity. This originally created some problems, but the long-term effect has been better cases and a better police image.

25. Larry E. Holtz, "*Miranda* in a Juvenile Setting: A Child's Right to Silence," *Journal of Criminal Law and Criminology* 78 (Fall 1987): 534–536. See also Alfredo Garcia, *Miranda* Revisited: The Erosion of a Clear Standard," *Journal of Contemporary Criminal Justice* 3 (August 1987): 19–29.

26. Richard Allison, "Thirty-Two States Involved in Prison Litigation," *Criminal Justice Newsletter* 10 (July 30, 1979): 4–5. See also "Illinois Forced Release Restricted," *Criminal Justice Newsletter* 14 (August 1983): 1–2, and Joseph Pellicciotti, "42 U.S. Code Section 1983 and Correctional Officials' Liability: A Look at the New Century," *Journal of Contemporary Criminal Justice* 3 (August 1987): 1–9.

27. Howard K. Gill, based on comments before the Philadelphia Bar Association and in *William and Mary Law Review* 5 (1964): 30–45.

28. The John Howard Association, named after the famous prison reformer, seeks reform by visits and inspections to prison systems. (537 South Dearborn Street, Chicago, Ill. 60605)

29. The American Correctional Association, the major professional organization of practicing penologists, was founded in 1870. It publishes the *American Journal of Corrections*. (4321 Hartwick Road, College Park, Md. 20740)

30. The National Council on Crime and Delinquency is a voluntary citizens' organization that operates a clearing house for criminal justice information and attempts to develop innovations in corrections and influence legislation. (NCCD Center, 77 Maiden Lane, Fourth Floor, San Francisco, Calif. 94108)

31. Seventh Step Foundation is an ex-offender organization formed by Bill Sands, who wrote the book *My Shadow Ran Fast*. This organization works inside and

outside prisons in a manner similar to that of Alcoholics Anonymous. (136 East Maple, Independence, Mo. 64058)

32. Man-to-Man Associates, Inc., is a volunteer organization that contacts pro-grammed release prisoners six months prior to their actual release and starts their adjustment. Members meet prisoners on their release day and provide help wherever needed. (935 East Broad Street, Columbus, Ohio 43215).

33. Fortune Society is an ex-offender organization with the goal of helping former inmates back into society by providing limited shelter and help in finding a job. (1545 Broadway, New York, N.Y. 10036)

34. "Paradoxes in the Administration of Criminal Justice," *Journal of Criminal Law, Corrections and Police Science* (1967): 428. Based on a commencement address delivered at Ripon College, May 21, 1967.

35. John Hudzik, *Federal Aid to Criminal Justice: Rhetoric, Results, Lessons* (Washington, D.C.: National Criminal Justice Associates, 1984).

36. Alexis Durham, "Correctional Privatization and the Justice Model: The Collision of Justice and Utility," *Journal of Contemporary Criminal Justice* 3 (May 1987): 57–69.

5

Correctional Ideologies: The Pendulum Swings

The mood and temper of the public with regard to the treatment of crime and criminals is one of the most unfailing tests of the civilization of any country.
— *SIR WINSTON CHURCHILL*

Conflicting Correctional Ideologies

Underlying the field of corrections are three basic ideologies regarding the societal response to illegal behavior and the offender. The ideologies attempt to answer the questions as to who are offenders and what we should do with (to?) them. In order to understand the current state of corrections, its problems and issues, and its possible futures, we shall turn first to a discussion of ideologies. An *ideology*, according to Webster's, is "a systematic body of concepts, especially about human life or culture." A *correctional ideology*, then, refers to a body of ideas and practices that pertain to the treatment of offenders. Obviously, the actions of various correctional authorities and organizational units are shaped in large part by the particular ideologies to which they subscribe. In the history of treatment and punishment of offenders, the ideologies of different societies have supplied both the basis and the rationalization for the broad range of efforts—vengeful to semihumane—aimed at getting criminals off the streets. When a given effort is clearly a failure, the ideology eventually shifts to justify a different approach.

In modern times, a strong belief in the efficacy of one correctional ideology or another has sometimes led administrators to commit vast sums to an unproven approach, thus causing themselves to be shackled to a possibly worthless plan for an indefinite period. By the same token, if the administrator's ideology happens to conflict with the approach favored by the society he or she serves, the administrator may try to resolve the conflict in one of two ways: by working out a compromise or by trying to sabotage

---

IDEOLOGIES

Ideologies serve three basic functions for believers. First, they help us understand the past. Second, they help us interpret the present. Finally, they allow us to make predictions about the future. To understand how ideologies work, let us look at small-town Alabama during the 1960s, at the hypothetical town of Amels. There, an eleven-man board of education was responsible for allocating funds to the school system, kindergarten through twelfth grade. But Amels was a segregated town and had not one, but two separate school systems: one for whites and one for *coloreds*.

The eleven-man board unamiously held *racist* ideologies. They believed that blacks had not evolved culturally as had whites. Further, because blacks were considered to be biologically inferior, they were regarded as less able to learn, were thought incapable of mastering complex ideas and concepts, and were considered uninterested in attaining the best education possible. Whites, on the other hand, were believed to have just the opposite qualities: capabilities, motivation, interest, competence, and superiority.

Based on these beliefs, which were commonly accepted, the board consistently allocated more support to the white school system, in terms of books, number of teachers, audio-visuals, office equipment, food, heating, lights, and maintenance. In fact, used texts from the white system were the only available books for blacks. This system allowed the board to save money by not having to purchase new texts for blacks. The white students benefited from lower teacher-student ratios, textbooks, supplies, and all other items on the budget. They also received college preparatory courses, higher mathematics, humanities, and languages.

Near the end of the school year, all students—white and black alike—were required to take standardized tests to measure the mastery of content from their studies. White students consistently outscored the black students, which is no surprise in light of the opportunities and resources available to the white students.

When the scores arrived at the board of education, there was back slapping at the success of the white students and clucking of tongues at the lower scores earned by black students. The scores served to reinforce what the board members "always knew." Blacks were biologically inferior, could not learn as fast as whites, were disinterested in education, and would not be motivated adequately. In short, educating blacks was a waste of taxpayers' money. Never did the board ever ask if the results they observed were caused by their own ideology.

Again, an ideology allows us to understand the past, interpret the present, and predict the future.

---

the system. If the superintendent of a juvenile institution feels that society is trying to liberalize rules so rapidly that it threatens personal security, he or she may encourage or even trigger frequent escapes and walk-aways from the institution. In correction, the backgrounds and ideologies of the keepers and the kept often diverge sharply, so it is difficult to convince both groups that they can work toward a mutual goal.

Most of the ideologies applied to correctional actions over the years fall in one of three categories: *punishment, treatment,* or *prevention.* These often overlap, of course—punishment and treatment are usually justified as means to prevention, rather than as ends in themselves—but the division is useful for the purpose of this analysis.

The Punishment Ideology

Retribution. Since the first system of laws was developed, punishment has been officially sanctioned as a means of regulating criminal behavior. The punishment ideology holds that the criminal is an enemy of society who deserves severe punishment, including banishment or death, for willfully breaking its rules. This philosophy has its roots in a societal need for retribution. As noted in Chapter 1, punishment once was administered in the form of immmediate and personal retribution, by either the victim or the victim's family. Society's authorization of punishment can be traced to this individual need for retaliation and vengeance. There are many theories as to the reason for the transfer of the vengeance motive from the individual to the state:

> Philosophers have debated the reasons for this transfer to government of the victim's desire to strike back at the offender. Heinrich Oppenheimer lists several theories. Three of them are as follows: (1) In the *theological* view, retaliation fulfills a religious mission to punish the criminal. (2) In the *aesthetic* view, punishment resolves the social discord created by the offense and

---

RETRIBUTION

Philosophically, this term generally means "getting even" with the perpetrator. Social revenge suggests that individuals cannot exact punishment, but that the state will do so in their name.

Retribution assumes that the offenders willfully chose to commit the evil acts, are responsible for their own behavior, are likely to commit similar acts again, and should receive the punishment they richly deserve.

The *just deserts* movement in sentencing reflects the retribution philosophy. For many, it provides a justifiable rationale for support of the death penalty.

Many students of corrections, and penologists, have considerable difficulty with the concept of retribution, because it requires the state to make an offender suffer for the sake of suffering. To many, this idea runs counter to the Eighth Amendment's prohibition against cruel and unusual punishment. One respected criminologist has proposed that correctional punishments include electroshock in lieu of incarceration, as it can be calibrated, leaves less long-term emotional damage, is cheaper to administer, and would allow the victim the opportunity to witness the retribution. Is it possible that televising the electroshock sessions might act as a deterrent to other potential malefactors?

reestablishes a sense of harmony through requital. (3) In the *expiatory* view, guilt must be washed away through suffering. Ledger Wood advances a fourth explanation, a *utilitarian* theory. Punishment is considered to be a means of achieving beneficial and social consequences through application of a specific form and degree of punishment deemed most appropriate to the particular offender after careful individualized study of the offender [emphasis added].[1]

Deterrence.   Yet another reason for punishment of criminals is the belief that such actions have a deterrent effect, specifically on the offender or generally on others who might consider a similar act.[2] For punishment to serve as a deterrent, it must be swift, perceived, closely linked to the forbidden action so that it discourages future recurrences of that crime, certain, and categorical (all persons committing a certain crime will receive the same punishment).[3] Furthermore, the state and its representatives must uphold superior values and conforming behavior to serve as irreproachable examples of good citizenship. Finally, after punishment, offenders must be allowed to resume their prior positions in society, without stigma or disability.

The failure of early penologists to recognize that uniform punishment was not as effective as was selective and specialized punishment contributed to the failure of prisons that were based on the punishment ideology. Overpunishment has little deterrent effect as well, because when the compliance point has been passed and the punishment continues, the offender ceases to care about the crime. For example, even after an offender has successfully completed a punishment-oriented correctional process, the stigma of conviction and imprisonment is carried for the rest of the ex-offender's life.[4] Finding it almost impossible to get a job because of a criminal past, the ex-offender decides, "If I'm going to have the name, I might as well play the game." At that point, neither the punishment nor the stigma is an effective deterrent, and the offender is likely to return to crime.

Incapacitation.   A third reason to punish the offender derives from the concept of incapacitation. This theory asserts that there is no hope for the individual as far as rehabilitation is concerned and that the only solution is temporarily to isolate, remove, or cripple such persons in some way. This approach is sometimes referred to as the "theory of disablement," a euphemism for death, banishment, or mutilation. Ideally, the disablement should relate to the crime (for example, in some countries castration has been used to punish sex criminals). One variation of the isolation rationale of incapacitation is the selective incapacitation movement. Greenwood argued that prison overcrowding and the scarcity of beds in prisons require a policy of sending only repetitive or violent offenders to prison; especially recommended prison for those who commit armed robbery.[5] Selective incapacitation would thus result in better uses of correctional resources and more effective crime prevention, he believed. Miller and others[6] contended

A Prisoner Heads for His Judgement (Photo by R. Simonsen)

that if certain offenders committing repetitive criminal acts were categorically incarcerated and incapacitated for a mandatory period (three or even five years), significantly fewer crimes would have been committed in Columbus, Ohio in 1975.

SELECTIVE INCAPACITATION

This doctrine of isolating the offender, or causing "social disablement," proposes adopting a policy of incarcerating those whose criminal behavior is so damaging or probable that nothing short of isolation will prevent recidivism. This "nothing-else-works" approach would require correctly identifying those offenders who would be eligible for longer-term imprisonment and diverting others into correctional alternatives. Thus we would be able to make maximum effective use of prison cells, a scarce resource, to protect society from the depredations of such dangerous and repetitive offenders.

Current correctional technology does not permit our correctly identifying those who require incapacitation. Rather, the evidence is that we would probably incarcerate numerous noneligibles (a "false positive" problem) and release to lesser confinement many of those eligible (a "false negative" problem). Whatever benefits might accrue to this sentencing doctrine have thus far eluded corrections.

This was further spotlighted in the *Report to the Nation on Crime and Justice*:

Career Criminals, though Few in Number, Account for Most Crime Even though chronic repeat offenders (those with five or more arrests by age 18) make up a relatively small proportion of all offenders, they commit a very high proportion of all crimes. The evidence includes data for juveniles and adults, males, and females, and for urban and rural areas. In Wolfgang's Philadelphia study, chronic offenders accounted for 23% of all male offenders in the study, but they had committed 61% of all the crimes. Of all crimes by all members of the group studied, chronic offenders committed:

61% of all homicides
76% of all rapes
73% of all robberies
65% of all aggravated assaults.[7]

The Effect of Punishment. It is recognized that some punishment can be effective when applied in the right amounts and at the right time. But when the ideology of punishment is applied in a correctional institution, the result is usually negative for both the punished and the punisher. Correctional personnel tend to watch for minor rule infringements or non-conformism so that the punishment can be administered, and they overlook any positive actions by offenders. Often the rules that are prepared for a punishment-oriented environment surround the offender with a wall of "do nots," leaving almost no leeway to *do* anything. As evidenced by a high crime rate, punishment by the law does not seem to create much respect for the law, even in jurisdictions where punishment may actually be swift, harsh, and certain. Overuse of punishment in a society that claims to be open and free creates a situation in which the punished can characterize their punishers as persecutors of the poor and helpless. The accusation turns attention away from crimes and gives rise to the concept of the "political prisoner." Thus, minority group members are likely to blame their incarceration on repression by the rich, on political persecution, or on attempted genocide. Punishments are then made more and more severe, in a hopeless effort to compensate for their ineffectiveness. Often such punishment motivates offenders to become more sophisticated criminals (rather than noncriminals) in the belief (no doubt valid) that the more skilled one is at a trade, the less likely one is to be caught. The offenders become hardened to the punishment, and the administrators learn to dole it out automatically as their only means of control. Both parties are degraded in the process.

The argument that the use of punishment can halt crime is refuted by both history and science:

Punitiveness is a complex of attitudes about social revenge having as component parts strong sanctions and retribution through a severe system of penalties and punishment. Institutionalization is a critical variable in punitiveness. It should also be noted that older age and maturation, in conjunction with incarceration, produce less punitive attitudes. These two findings, in particular, suggest that it may be the type and degree of legal treatment relative to the *mala acta* that calls forth maximum efficacy in the alteration of attitudes.

Durkheim stated, when he wrote of the function of crime in society, that the group must victimize offenders in order that nonoffenders may be reinforced in law-abiding behavior. This victimization with attendant punitiveness is intended to insure conformity to norms.

If the behavior of those whom society punishes is frequently unaltered by such treatment, perhaps it is time to seek more satisfactory and effective techniques of rehabilitation; this can and must be done within the framework of a system which punishes violations, since the general public seems unwilling to forgo its almost blind faith in punitiveness as the principal vehicle of social control.[8]

Many factors contribute to make punishment the least effective means of reducing crime:

1. The use of punishment for deterrence must avoid the over-severity of application which arouses public sympathy for the offender.
2. Those persons most likely to be imprisoned are already accustomed to experience deprivations and frustration of personal goals routinely in daily life.
3. It is impossible to fashion a practical legal "slide rule" which will determine exact degrees of retribution appropriate for a list of crimes ranging from handkerchief theft to murder.
4. The simple application of naked coercion does not guarantee that the subjects of its force will alter their behavior to conform to new legal norms or to improve their conformity with norms previously violated.
5. The possibility of deterrence varies with the chances of keeping the particular type of crime secret and consequently of avoiding social reprobation.[9]

It must be understood that the significance of punishment as an ideology in correctional practice lies in the viewpoint of the punished offenders. If they see the punishment as an unjust imposition of the will and power of the establishment, and if they are reinforced in this belief by their peers (other offenders), their punishment will only encourage them to maintain negative behavior patterns. By contrast, if offenders feel that their punishment is both deserved and just, and their social group agrees, the punishment may have a startlingly different and more positive result. If a prosocial criminal (one who is not totally committed to a life of crime) is justly treated, this offender may abandon crime; but excessive punishment may push the offender over the edge and destroy every chance of reform. The punished and stigmatized offenders turn to those who are most like them for support and values. If they are embittered by the punishment they have received, they are likely to reject the very values the punishment was intended to reinforce.[10]

The punishment ideology is particularly attractive to those with a strong hostile urge just below the surface—although these people may appear to be upright and productive citizens. Thus, justifications for the punishment ideology have been found in theories on theology, aesthetics, and utility, the idea being that the offender's suffering and expiation serve to cleanse and reestablish accord throughout the society as a whole. Although all kinds of logical arguments for punishment can be devised, it has been an obvious failure when set up as a uniform and inflexible response to negative behavior. The routine use of punishment in institutions designed to correct offenders can be viewed as more degrading to society than are the offenses themselves in many cases.

The punishment ideology soon becomes a punishment procedure that is applied without regard to the individual nature of those being punished. Because of this, prisons become places where inmates look to one another for support and values, and the agents of the law become the enemy. This is one of the main reasons that many authorities on corrections refer to prisons as "schools of crime." The punishment ideology is a major factor in correctional programs. For a while it gave way to the therapeutic ideology, but around 1975 punitiveness became fashionable once again. Punitiveness has led legislatures to change sentencing from an indeterminate structure in which parole boards share the process of determining minimum and maximum sentence lengths. The new legislative initiatives abandon parole as an early release mechanism, install determinate/presumptive sentencing, and result in overcrowding of prisons. Punitiveness has led to a "brick and mortar" solution for the prison overcrowding situation: the building of more and more prisons is seen as the only answer. Finally, this change in attitude has led to a painful search for alternatives to probation (regarded as *no punishment)* and imprisonment (regarded as *too expensive* a form of punishment). The emerging alternatives—known as intermediate punishments—promise relief from the pressures of prison overcrowding. In addition, the new wave of punitiveness has contributed to selective incapacitation, an important and effective tool for correctional administrators, but only if it is designed to suit an individual offender and an individual situation. General and uniform punishment is still the rule rather than the exception, however, and the movement toward a treatment or preventive model is slow.

The Treatment Ideology

A major trend in corrections is to approach the offender much as one would the mentally ill, the neglected, or the underprivileged. This more humane ideology, reflected in the *treatment model,* sees the criminal behavior as just another manifestation of pathology that can be handled by some form of therapeutic activity. Although the criminal may be referred to as "sick," the treatment ideology is not analogous to a medical approach.

DETERMINATE SENTENCING

A fixed period of incarceration imposed on the offender by the sentencing court. The ideology underlying detrminate sentencing is retribution, just deserts, or incapacitation.

A presumptive sentence is a term of imprisonment suggested by a policy-setting governmental agency, such as the State Legislature or a sentencing council. The sentencing judge is *expected* to impose the indicated sentence, unless certain circumstances proven in court would require a different (longer or shorter) period of imprisonment.

The closest comparison with physical illness lies in the need for offenders to recognize the danger and undesirability of their criminal behavior and then to make significant efforts to rid themselves of that behavior. The treatment model does not "remove" criminal behavior, as one might remove an infected limb; rather, the "patient" (inmate) is made to see the rewards of positive behavior and is encouraged and equipped to adopt it as a model.

The treatment ideology does not encourage inmates to be coddled and allowed to do as they please within the institution. It is a fairly common belief among many elements of the criminal justice system that any program that is not punitive or restrictive is being "soft" or akin to "running a country club." In fact, some form of treatment ideology can be applied in even the most restrictive and security-oriented institution. The main difference between the treatment and punishment ideologies is that in the former, offenders are assigned to the institution for a correctional program intended to prepare them for readjustment to or reintegration into the community, not just for punishment and confinement. There is room for punishment and security in the treatment approach, but little room for treatment in the punitive approach. The more humane treatment methods are intended to be used in conjunction with the employment of authority in a constructive and positive manner, but inmates must be allowed to try, even if they fail. Authoritarian procedures, used alone, only give the offender more ammunition to support a self-image as an oppressed and impotent pawn of the power structure.

It must be recalled that the field of corrections, especially in its early history in America, underwent significant change as innovators again sought the answers to those same two questions, "Who are offenders and what should we do with them?" The treatment ideology contains four separate answers to those questions, commonly referred to as "treatment doctrines."

The Quaker reform movement, arising in 1790, held that offenders were out of touch with God. The corresponding treatment approach was isolation. Prisoner were supplied with a Bible for reading and doing penitence. The doctrine for the Quakers was to help offenders find their way back to God; it was believed that once God was found, crime would cease.

The reformatory movement solutions, after 1890, provided somewhat different answers. Offenders were seen as disadvantaged, "unfortunate," persons whose education, training, and discipline had been inadequate. The *educational doctrine* answer was to provide education at a functional level, emphasis on vocational and occupational skills, and a regime of discipline that was aimed at the internalization of controls to prevent reoccurence of criminal behavior when the prisoner was released.

The *medical model* that developed in the late 1920s and early 1930s, under the leadership of Stanford Bates and the U.S. Bureau of Prisons, saw the answers as lying within the individual. It then became necessary to diagnose the individual problem, develop a treatment program that might remedy it, and then apply treatment. When the "patient" was found to be well, he or she would be released to a program of aftercare in the community under the supervision of therapeutic parole officers who would continue casework therapy until the offender was "rehabilitated." The medical model offered hope of rehabilitation. It was the responsibility of corrections to "make the ill well." The "ill" would thus be passive recipients of beneficent therapy like patients in a hospital.

The fourth doctrine emerged in the late 1960s. It is fashionable to use either 1965 or 1969 as the date of origin, but whichever date is used, the form of treatment has been a significant trend throughout the 1980s. Known as the *reintegration model*, the form of treatment made differing assumptions about the cause and solutions to crime and the criminal. The community was seen as the basic etiological factor, and the offender was considered to be the product of a local community that excluded, failed to provide for, or discriminated against the offender. Because the basic cause is regarded as community-related, proponents thought it best to address the problem using community resources that correctional personnel are able to marshal or develop. The offender's role requires active participation in the effort to resolve the difficulty; correctional personnel serve as brokers for services. Ideally, a community management approach is used, wherein several officers can specialize to maximize the delivery of opportunities to the offender, who is eager to reintegrate and become part of the community. All four doctrines require treatment, and coexist in the correctional ideology called *treatment*.

Treatment procedures are almost as varied as are the imaginations of the treatment staff that designs them. When one thinks of the therapeutic approach to treatment, the most common conception is the psychiatrist and his or her efforts to assist the offender to adjust. Actually, the use of classic psychiatric treatment techniques in the correctional institution is relatively rare. A more common approach is the use of group therapy programs, which include staff members as well as offenders. These are more in tune with the belief that most criminal behavior is learned from and encouraged by the offender's associates. Group therapy programs are intended to transfer the offender's allegiance from the values and activities of the criminal group to those of the noncriminal group. If that group can be labeled as desirable in terms of future associations, the offender will develop a new behavior model that will represent status and security. Groups conducted in a routine manner, as just another duty that inmates and personnel must perform, have little chance for success. Rather, the leader must be a skilled and dedicated therapist, with the ability to stimulate intense exchanges and help participants — offenders and staff — understand what they are learning about themselves.

The main purpose of the treatment approach in corrections is to offer a means by which the individual who has some kind of a defect¹or problem can hope to overcome it. The offender is placed into a correctional environment to identify and treat this problem, not to be punished for criminal actions without regard for the underlying causes.

Treatment in the correctional field is still fraught with problems. The needs of the institution often take precedence over the needs of the individual, and treatment programs may be temporarily suspended because of institutional activity or disciplinary actions. For example, inmates who violate institutional rules may be placed in a disciplinary cell (or isolation) for a period of time without books or materials. If they are enrolled in an academic program, such disruptions may cause them to fall so far behind the rest of their class that they will have to drop out until the next class starts. In many cases, it may be six months before they can resume their education. Similarly, encounter groups and other treatments can be broken up when the needs of the institution are paramount, causing them to lose their effect.

Despite this handicap, however, group therapy is becoming increasingly popular as a form of institutional treatment. Group programs that involve correctional personnel can benefit not only the offenders but the staff members as well. Regular interaction between staff and inmates tends to break down barriers between them and provide insights into the problems of both sides.

The administrator who wants to instill a treatment atmosphere in a formerly punishment-oriented institution faces many difficulties. The security staff, generally believed to be indoctrinated to the punitive model, will resist change as a threat to institutional order. Because treatment programs are usually much more expensive than are control models, legislators are slow to assign the necessary funds. The public, like the staff, exhibits an unreasonable fear of crime and presses for more punishment when treatment alternatives are proposed; and politicians often bow to the wishes of the voters, even in the face of evidence that a treatment model is more effective. Criminal activities come to the public's attention via the media more vividly today than ever before, and it is difficult to convince average citizens that prisoners deserve expensive treatment when they have seen the Attica riots on television, live and in color. Like their colleagues in law enforcement, correctional administrators seem to make the headlines only during times of crisis or adversity. The real hope for the acceptance of the treatment ideology in corrections is to ensure sufficient security and control so that the successes are not drowned out by failure headlines. Punishment can be part of a treatment program so long as it is a disciplinary procedure, not the focus of the program.

Punishment, therapy, and reintegration are geared to deal with offenders after they have been convicted of an offense. The more recent trend is to anticipate offenders before they enter the criminal justice system, in hopes of preventing future offenses entirely.

The Prevention Ideology

As mentioned earlier, the problem of crime cannot be divided from the individual offender. In a sense, the problem can be temporarily removed from the community when the offender is sent off to prison. Almost all offenders are eventually released, however, and the problem returns unless it has been effectively treated while the offender is in the prison. Because of the minimal success of present correctional programs (recidivism rates range from 40 to 70 percent),[11] many communities and governmental agencies are turning to crime prevention as a possible solution. Prevention methods have a dual focus: on the individual and on the environment in which he or she lives. Much crime-prevention activity is designed to steer potential delinquents away from a life of trouble. Such programs generally begin at the school level, where truancy and dropping out are often the precursors of criminal activity. These early programs, for the most part, attempt to identify the first signs of criminal behavior.

Prediction is a complex process, even when it is carefully controlled. The famous studies by Sheldon and Eleanor Glueck illustrate the problems inherent in most prediction efforts.[12] Prevention programs in schools today aim to treat the problem child by providing specialized classes, vocational education, and counseling;[13] they do not aim to force the juvenile out of the picture by expulsion from school. The prevention ideology recognizes that problem children must have supportive help, or they are very likely to use crime as an outlet for unhappiness and insecurity.

Those who advocate the prevention ideology are well aware that total prevention of crime is probably impossible. Emile Durkheim believed that crime in some form was an inevitable accompaniment to human society and that if serious crime were prevented, authorities would focus their attention on minor offenses.[14] Essentially, the prevention ideology holds that crime may at least be reduced through an attack on the social and emotional problems that encourage a child's criminal inclinations.

The individual's environment is recognized as a crucial focus in the prevention of crime; the prevention ideology emphasizes the need to structure the environment so that criminal opportunity is minimized. As an example, it has been said that the greatest crime-prevention device ever invented was the street light. The movement toward crime prevention through environmental design is one that has great promise for the future. The object of such an approach is not only to provide barriers to crime (such as bars on windows, fences, locks, and airport security checks)[15] but also to enhance the existing features that tend to discourage crime (for example, providing more lighting around homes and apartment buildings, more windows in dark hallways, and community projects aimed at getting people to know their neighbors). The conditions that produce a high or low crime rate in a given area are not all physical, however; the environment includes the people, activities, pressures, and ideas to which an individual is exposed every day. The prevention ideology advocates the maximum use of resources in areas that have special problems such as poverty and overcrowding—funds should be allocated for crime·prevention rather than for prison construction.[16]

In community corrections, the prevention ideology is combined with treatment. The emphasis is on the identification and treatment of the problems that have caused past criminal behavior, to prevent its recurrence. Even-

Officer Friendly Program in Seattle Teaches Youngsters to Respect the Police (Courtesy the Seattle Police Department)

tually, the emphasis may lead to a closer, more interdependent relationship between the agencies now involved in crime prevention and those that provide community services. As they presently operate, criminal justice agencies actually tend to create more problems for minor offenders, instead of treating the problems that got these people into trouble.[17] If schools, churches, service agencies, and similar organizations could become more involved, before persons become involved in the criminal justice system, many criminal careers could be prevented before they start. Diversion and nonjudicial approaches to offenders are seen as potentially valuable alternatives to a more formal, punishment-oriented reaction to the problem of crime. A combination of prevention and treatment ideologies would be the most promising and humane organization of corrections beliefs and practices.

The Pendulum Swings _____

Since 1976, when crime took a temporary downturn, the high crime rates have caused the forces of society to lean again toward the punishment ideology. As the populations of the country's jails and prisons have grown to almost unmanageable proportions, administrators and legislatures have been more willing to accept this turn backward in order to have at least some way to cope with the growing and more violent criminal populations. The following chapters will discuss the problems faced by harried and underfunded administrators trying to deal with institutions that are beyond bursting at the seams. Budgets are stripped of "frills" such as treatment and must be used to add beds, food, and custody staff to house and feed inmates and protect society. The trend toward determinate sentences and "get tough" laws at all levels exacerbates the situation. At best, treatment is difficult to carry out in a security institution. At worst, treatment is all but impossible to find. This pessimistic situation has been the trend of the 1980s. Criticisms, in the mid-1970s, by Martinson[18] and a growing contingent of those who are disenchanted with the treatment model,[19] has made it harder for people to defend that model, from either a theoretical or a pragmatic viewpoint. The correctional "nonsystem" will stagger through the 1990s in a continuing state of indecision as to what to embrace as its core ideology.[20] The signs seem clear, however, and the hope for treatment that dominated in the 1960s and 1970s seems lost now that the cry for "hard time" for offenders, poor economic conditions, and continued overcrowding exist at levels unprecedented in the short history of corrections in America. As we shall see, however, the decisions being made now will affect our prisons and jails for many decades to come. The pendulum has swung far to the right, and it will take major changes in the future for it to begin to move back toward the center. The task ahead for today's student will be both important and difficult.

Summary _____

Only when American society decides which ideology or combination of ideologies most deserves its support will the problems facing the correctional administrator be properly addressed. It may be that some combination will be the only possible answer, given the wide variety of problems and offenders. Offenders may respond only to a punitive ideology, at least until we are able to develop treatment techniques that offer greater potential for success and that are constitutionally acceptable. The offender who can respond to treatment, however, must be given a chance to receive it—without being totally free of control, as the protection of society remains the paramount concern. The prevention ideology offers great promise, but it seems too idealistic to suffice in and of itself. As prison populations become increasingly unmanageable, it may become necessary to introduce ex-offenders into the prison environment, as leavening and change agents working with the correctional administration. This is becoming more acceptable in the fields of probation and parole. These ideas will undoubtedly lead to the development of other alternatives to incarceration, and some possibilities will be outlined in later sections. To comprehend the current issues in corrections, one must examine the decision process and options available to the prosecution, judiciary, and releasing authorities. This process and these options will be described in the next chapter.

Review Questions _____

1. What basic ideologies have determined the handling of offenders over the years? Which is the oldest?
2. What criteria must be met if punishment is to act as a deterrent?
3. How does the treatment ideology differ from punishment? Are they necessarily exclusive of each other?
4. What are some of the changes presently taking place in the clientele of the correctional system?

Key Terms _____

1. ideology (p. 83)
2. retribution (p. 85)
3. theological (p. 85)
4. aesthetic (p. 85)
5. expiation (p. 86)
6. utilitarian (p. 86)
7. selective punishment (p. 86)
8. disablement (p. 86)
9. selective incapacitation (p. 87)
10. genocide (p. 88)
11. therapeutic approach (p. 92)
12. criminal opportunity (p. 94)

Notes _____

1. Elmer H. Johnson, *Crime, Correction, and Society* (Homewood, Ill.: Dorsey Press, 1974), p. 173.
2. Norman Carlson, "A More Balanced Correctional Philosophy," *FBI Law Enforcement Bulletin* 46 (January 1977): 22–25. See also Jerry Parker and H. G. Grasmick, "Linking Actual and Perceived Certainty of Punishment," *Criminology* 17 (November 1979): 366–379.
3. See Raymond Paternoster for a review of the evidence on the deterrent effects of punishment, "The Deterrent Effect of the Perceived Certainty and Severity of Punishment: A Review of the Evidence and Issues," *Justice Quartery* 4 (June 1987): 173–217.
4. John Irwin and James Austin, *It's About Time* (San Francisco, National Council on Crime and Delinquency, 1987), pp 12–14.
5. Peter B. Greenwood, *Selective Incapacitation* (Santa Monica, Calif.: Rand Corporation, 1983). M. Gottfredson and T. Hirschi, "The True Value of Lambda Would Appear to Be Zero: An Essay on Criminal Careers, Selective Incapacitation, Cohort Studies, and Related Topics," *Criminology* 24 (May 1986): 213–233. Scott Decker and Barbara Salert, "Predicting the Career Criminal: An Empirical Test of the Greenwood Scale," *Journal of Criminal Law and Criminology* 77 (1986): 215–236.
6. Stuart Miller, Simon Dinitz, and John Conrad, *Careers of the Violent* (Lexington, Mass.: Lexington Books, 1982).
7. Marianne W. Zawitz, ed., *Report to the Nation on Crime and Justice* (Washington D.C.: U.S. Department of Justice, Bureau of Justice Statistics, U.S. Government Printing Office, 1983), p. 35.
8. Christine G. Schultz and Harry E. Allen, "Inmate and Non-Inmate Attitudes Toward Punitiveness," *Criminologica* 5 (August 1967): 40–45. See also Robert Langworthy and John Whitehead, "Liberalism and Fear as Explanations of Punitiveness," *Criminology* 24 (1986): 575–591.
9. Johnson, *Crime, Correction and Society,* pp. 361–365. A European view of punishment can be found in Andrew von Hirsch, "'Neoclassicism', Proportionality and the Rationale for Punishment: Thoughts on the Scandinavian Debate," *Crime and Delinquency* 29 (January 1983): 52–70.
10. There is a current rebirth of the punishment ideology, described in detail by Donal E. J. MacNamara, "The Medical Model in Corrections: *Requiescat in Pace,*" *Criminology* 14 (February 1977): 439–448. For a counterargument, see Daniel Glaser, "The Counterproductivity of Conservative Thinking About Crime," in E. Sagarin, ed., *Criminology: New Concerns* (Beverly Hills, Calif.: Sage Publications, 1979), pp. 89–104.
11. The effectiveness of correctional programs is under scrutiny and criticism. See Robert Martinson, "What Works?—Questions and Answers About Prison Reform," *Public Interest* 35 (Spring 1974): 22–55. In an unusual shift, after arguing that little in the area of correctional treatment has any demonstrable effect on recidivism, Martinson contended that recidivism rates are considerably lower than previously estimated—in the less-than-one-third rate area. See "New Martinson/Wilks Analysis Shows That Recidivism is Much Lower Than Previously

Believed—and Dropping," *Criminal Justice Newsletter* 7 (October 25, 1976): 1–2. See also the more recent evaluation by Paul Gendreau and Bob Ross, "Effective Correctional Treatment: Bibliotherapy for Cynics," *Crime and Delinquency* 25 (October 1979): 463–489.

12. Eleanor and Sheldon Glueck conducted a number of large research projects in the 1930s, 1940s, and 1950s to develop predictive instruments. The reliability and efficacy of these instruments are still in question.

13. June Andrew, "Violence and Poor Reading," *Criminology* 17 (November 1979): 361–365.

14. Emile Durkheim, *Division of Labor in Society,* trans. George Simpson (Glencoe, Ill: Free Press, 1947).

15. William Minor, "Skyjacking Crime Control Models," *Journal of Criminal Law and Criminology* 66 (March 1975): 94–105.

16. C. Ray Jeffery, *Crime Prevention Through Environmental Design,* 2d ed. (Beverly Hills, Calif.: Sage Publications, 1977).

17. Scott Decker, "A Systematic Analysis of Diversion: Net Widening and Beyond," *Journal of Criminal Justice* 13 (1985): 207–216

18. Martinson, What Works?—Questions and Answers About Prison Reform."

19. See MacNamara, "The Medical Model in Corrections," for a list of the most important of these writers.

20. Harry E. Allen and Edward Latessa, "Corrections in America: 2000 A.D.," *Journal of Contemporary Criminal Justice* 1 (1980): 1–3.

Recommended Readings ————————————————————————————————

Allen, Harry E., and Nancy Beran. *Reform in Corrections.* New York: Praeger, 1977.

Alpert, Geoffrey. *Legal Rights of Prisoners.* Lexington, Mass.: Heath, 1978.

Bagdikian, Ben H. *The Shame of Prisons.* New York: Pocket Books, 1972.

Baiamonte, John. *Spirit of Vengance: Nativism and Louisiana Justice, 1921–1924.* Baton Rouge: Louisiana State University Press, 1986.

Barnes, Harry Elmer. *The Story of Punishment.* 2d ed. Montclair, N.J.: Patterson Smith, 1972.

Barnes, Harry Elmer, and Negley K. Teeters. *New Horizons in Criminology.* 2d ed. Englewood Cliffs, N.J.: Prentice-Hall, 1959.

Baunach, Phyllis, Jo. *Mothers in Prison.* New Brunswick, N.J.: Transaction Books, 1985.

Brockway, Zebulon Reed. *Fifty Years of Prison Service.* Montclair, N.J.: Patterson Smith, 1969.

Carter, Robert M., Daniel Glaser, and Leslie T. Wilkins. *Correctional Institutions.* New York: Lippincott, 1972.

Cohen, Albert, George Cole, and Robert Bailey. *Prison Violence.* Lexington, Mass.: Heath, 1976.

Criminology: An Interdisciplinary Journal 14 (February 1977): 4. Special issue devoted to incarceration.

Cullen, Francis, and Karen Gilbert. *Reaffirming Rehabilitation.* Cincinnati: Anderson Publishing, 1982.

Greenwood, Peter, and Susan Turner. *Selective Incapacitation Revisited: Why the High-Rate Offenders Are Hard to Predict.* Santa Monica, Calif.: Rand Corporation, 1987.

Irwin, John, and James Austin. *It's About Time.* San Francisco: National Council on Crime and Deliquency, 1987.

Jeffery, C. R., ed. *Biology and Crime.* Beverly Hills, Calif.: Sage Publications, 1979.

Johnston, Norman. *The Human Cage: A Brief History of Prison Architecture.* New York: Walker, 1973.

Joint Commission on Correctional Manpower and Training. *Perspectives on Correctional Manpower and Training.* Lebanon, Pa.: Sowers Printing, 1970.

McCarthy, Belinda, ed. *Intermediate Punishment.* Monsey, N.Y.: Willow Tree Press, 1987.

Nagel, William. *The New Red Barn.* New York: Walker, 1973.

National Advisory Commission on Criminal Justice Standards and Goals. *Corrections.* Washington, D.C.: U.S. Department of Justice, 1973.

Petersilia, Joan. *The Influence of Criminal Justice Research.* Santa Monica, Calif.: The Rand Corporation, 1987.

Petersilia, Joan. *Racial Disparities in the Criminal Justice System.* Santa Monica, Calif.: The Rand Corporation, 1983.

President's Commission on Law Enforcement and Administration of Justice. *Task Force Report: Corrections.* Washington, D.C.: U.S. Government Printing Office, 1967.

Rothman, David J. *The Discovery of the Asylum.* Boston: Little, Brown, 1971.

Sagarin, Edward, ed. *Criminology: New Concerns.* Beverly Hills, Calif.: Sage Publications, 1979.

Scacco, Anthony. *Rape in Prison.* Springfield, Ill.: Chas. C. Thomas, 1975.

Wilbanks, William. *The Myth of a Racist Criminal Justice System.* Monterey, Calif.: Brookes-Cole, 1986.

Law and the
Correctional Process

6

Misdemeanants and Felons: A Dual System

Crime is normal because a society exempt from it
is utterly impossible.
—EMILE DURKHEIM

Common-Law Origins of Crime

Most crimes fall into one of two categories, *felonies* or *misdemeanors*. Felonies are a group of offenses considered in most societies serious enough to deserve severe punishment or even death. Although they vary somewhat in their specific names, the major felony crimes are remarkably similar for all jurisdictions. In the United States, we have come to define most "common-law" crimes as felonies, because we inherited many of their designations from the English common-law statutes. Under the common law, which developed by history and precedent, there were three categories of crime: treason, felony, and misdemeanor.[1] Originally, the distinction between felonies and misdemeanors was based on the fact that all felonies were capital offenses, also involving forfeiture of all lands and property of the perpetrator, whereas misdemeanors called for lesser penalties. Even though the United States adopted many aspects of English common law, the severity of felony punishment was modified to reflect the American way of life.

The distinction between a felony and a misdemeanor in America is generally based either on the type of institution in which the offender would be incarcerated or the length of the sentence imposed. Most felony convictions require a sentence of at least one year in a state prison. This guideline is not infallible, but it serves as a good rule of thumb in determining which crimes are generally considered felonies. Most legal agencies tend to lump the various kinds of felonies into categories that pertain to the social harm involved: offenses against the person, offenses against the habitation, offenses against property, offenses against morality and decency, and so on (See Table 6.1). We now shall look at these categories and the correctional clients they produce.

> **FELONY**
> A criminal offense punishable by death or by incarceration in a state or federal confinement for a period of which the lower limit is prescribed by statute in a given jurisdiction, typically one year or more.
> **MISDEMEANOR**
> An offense usually punishable by incarceration in a local facility for a period of which the upper limit is prescribed by statute in a given jurisdiction, typically limited to a year or less.

Felonies

Crimes Against the Person

Four of the eight major or "index" offenses cited in the Federal Bureau of Investigation's *Uniform Crime Reports* are usually labeled *crimes against the person*.[2] These four crime categories (murder and nonnegligent manslaughter, aggravated assault, forcible rape, and robbery) are "headline crimes," which create public fear and promote support for "get tough" laws and stronger law enforcement. Despite their shock effect, these four offenses accounted for only 11.2 percent of the index crimes reported in 1986 (1,488,140 out of 13,210,800).[3] The emphasis placed on these crimes is demonstrated by the higher percentage that is cleared by arrest: it is only logical that the principal resources of our law enforcement agencies should be marshaled to solve those crimes that the public fears most. An average of 44 percent of the crimes in these four categories are cleared by arrest, compared with only 17 percent in crimes against property. Murder and nonnegligent manslaughter lead with a clearance rate of 70 percent; aggravated assault follows with 59 percent; forcible rape has a 52 percent rate of clearance; and robbery has only a 25 percent rate.[4]

A nationwide survey of 191,400 prisoners in custody of state correctional authorities in 1974 revealed the following offenses for which they were currently incarcerated (instant offense):

An estimated 61 percent of the offenders in custody had been incarcerated at least once before.[5] (See Table 6-1 for a list of offenses committed by offenders sentenced to state prisons in 1982.)

Crimes against the person have the most severe penalties for the convicted offender. All of these offenses either are, or have been, capital offenses in the United States. A recent example of the seriousness of these offenses is found in the sentences and penalties attached to them in the Ohio Criminal Code:[6]

TABLE 6.1 Offenses of State Prisoners, 1986

Offense	Percent:
All Offenses	100.0 %
Violent, Total	54.6 %
Murder	11.2
Negligent Manslaughter	3.2
Kidnapping	1.7
Rape	4.2
Other Sexual Assault	4.5
Robbery	20.9
Assault	8.0
Other Violent	.8
Property Offenses:	31.0 %
Burglary	16.5
Larceny/Theft	6.0
Motor Vehicle Theft	1.4
Arson	.8
Fraud	3.8
Stolen Property	2.0
Other Property	.5
Drug Offenses:	8.6 %
Possession	2.9
Trafficking	5.4
Other Drug	.3
Public-order Offenses:	5.2 %
Weapons	1.4
Other Public-order	3.7
Other Offenses:	.7 %

Source: Christopher Innes, *Profile of State Prison Inmates: 1986* (Washington, D.C.: U.S. Department of Justice, 1988), p. 3.

CRIMES AGAINST THE PERSON

Criminal Homicide, which refers to murder and nonnegligent manslaughter, is the willful (nonnegligent) killing of one human being by another.

Forcible Rape is the carnal knowledge of a female forcibly and against her will. Assaults or attempts to commit forcible rape by force or threat of force are also included; however, statutory rape (without force) and other sex offenses are not included in this category.

Robbery is the taking or attempting to take anything of value from the care, custody, or control of a person or persons by force or threat of force and violence and/or putting the victim in fear.

Aggravated Assault is an unlawful attack by one person upon another for the purpose of inflicting severe or aggravated bodily injury. This type of assault is usually accompanied by the use of a weapon or by means likely to produce death or great bodily harm. Attempts are also included because it is not necessary that an injury result when a gun, knife, or other weapon is used that could and probably would result in a serious injury if the crime were successfully completed.

1. Murder: death penalty or life imprisonment
2. Forcible rape: 4 to 25 years (life imprisonment if victim was under 13 years of age)
3. Aggravated assault: 4 to 25 years
4. Robbery: 4 to 25 years

At one time or another, murder has been a capital offense on the statutes of nearly all countries in the Western world. An attempt to understand the correctional client who commits crimes against the person might well begin with the murderer, as described in the *Uniform Crime Reports* for 1986. Because murder is usually considered the most completely reported, cleared and resolved crime, it is a good vehicle for examining the offender who commits crimes against the person. First, one cannot fail to observe that a disproportionate number of blacks are the victims of murder (44 percent) and the offenders arrested for murder (36 percent). It is also notable that over 41 percent of the persons arrested for murder in 1986 were under twenty-five years old. Those between eighteen and twenty-four, in fact, accounted for one in three of the arrests for murder. The 1986 report showed that 55 percent of the adults arrested for murder were prosecuted during that year and that 54 of these were found guilty as charged. Of the remaining 46 percent, 14 percent were convicted of some lesser charge, and the remainder were either acquitted or dismissed. It is clear from the analysis of the processing of murder cases that they are considered important and get more thorough attention than do less publicized crimes.

The American murderer is often a young male who kills his victim during an argument or over a family problem. The profile of the circumstances under which murder occurs is shown in Table 6.2.

TABLE 6.2 Murder Circumstances, 1966–1986 (Percent Distribution)

Year	Total Number	Romantic Triangle and Lovers' Quarrels	Other Arguments	Known Felony Type	Suspected Felony Type
1966	10,950	8.5%	40.9%	14.8%	7.0%
1969	14,640	7.0	41.3	19.3	7.2
1972	18,520	7.1	41.2	22.1	5.3
1975	20,510	7.3	37.9	23.0	9.4
1978	18,714	2.7	42.8	16.7	5.6
1979	20,591	2.4	42.9	16.9	5.3
1980	21,860	2.3	44.6	17.7	6.7
1981	20,053	2.5	42.2	17.2	5.5
1986	20,613	2.8	45.6	25.0	4.8

Source: Federal Bureau of Investigation, *Uniform Crime Reports,* 1981, 1986 (Washington, D.C.: U.S. Department of Justice, 1982, 1987). 1981 data, page 37; 1986 data, page 39.

Although there is serious public alarm and concern about murderers, as prisoners they are usually the least problematic of all offenders. They are frequently given "honor" status and work in the warden's quarters as domestics.

The rates of prosecution and conviction for aggravated assault and forcible rape are very similar to those for murder. Although a major study by the Law Enforcement Assistance Administration suggests that the actual crime rate may be as much as three to five times the reported crime rate,[7] this probability does not change the fact that many of the persons convicted and sentenced to state prisons are young and aggressive and have committed prior violent offenses.

Crimes Against Property

Of the estimated 2.7 million individuals who are under correctional supervision in America each day, the majority are placed there for offenses against property. Even with the low clearance by arrest percentages, the sheer volume of the property crimes tends to keep our prisons full. Reported incidents of burglary, for example, totaled 3,241,410 in 1986,[8] and the clearance by arrest rate for burglary was 14 percent. Similar figures apply to both larceny (20 percent) and auto theft (15 percent), with convictions for all three of these offenses totaling over one million clients for the correctional system.

The offender against property is usually young. The number of auto theft cases alone that must be referred to juvenile authorities is over 20 percent of the total for those offenses. The same is true for 23 percent of the larceny and 21 percent of the burglary cases reported. Persons under twenty-one accounted for 46 percent of the larcenies and 58 percent of the auto thefts; persons under twenty-five accounted for 55 percent of the burglaries.[9] Crimes against the person may account for the longer sentences, but crimes against property contribute most to the volume in the correctional pipelines.

Burglary is usually considered a crime against the habitation and is the most common crime reported in the crime index. There were over three million burglaries reported in 1986, a decrease from 1978. Because 66 percent of these burglaries are committed in dwellings, it is a crime that alarms the citizens. There is a great amount of fear, sometimes resulting in overreaction by the victim, that forcible entry into one's home necessarily implies violence against one's person. The homeowner's zeal for self-preservation results in a number of tragic accidents each year, even though burglary offenders are seldom aggressive. It has been estimated that property worth billions of dollars each year is taken to obtain money for drugs, but this claim has been seriously challenged.[10] Drug abuse may be one of the reasons that daytime burglaries are on the increase, however, especially with the increased chance of absence of both adults in a family, as more women take jobs. Because the crime of burglary requires stealth and cunning, offenders are seldom caught at the scene. Most often, they are arrested when they attempt to sell the stolen goods. Although the clearance by arrest rate was only 21 percent in 1986, this is a deceptive figure.[11] Some burglaries are perpetrated by more than one offender, but in other cases one person may be responsible for numerous offenses. Unless arrested offenders choose to confess to more than the offense for which they were caught, many thousands of burglaries will go unsolved.

Crimes Against Morality and Decency

Crimes that may get even more publicity than murder receives are those that have a sexual connotation. The child molester, for example, excites widespread public alarm' and high interest on the part of the media. (They sell papers!) This individual also assumes the lowest position in the inmate social system in most prisons; other bizarre sex crimes, with the possible exception of rape, are also considered repulsive by the inmate subculture. Rape is at least vaguely linked to manhood and is sometimes, in a perverse way, viewed as an accomplishment of some note. Although homosexuals are looked upon as "weirdos" in prisons, they can also be welcome to other inmates, although they create dissension and trouble for correctional administrators. Many of the so-called "acts between consenting adults" are being removed from the criminal codes, leaving only the forcible assaultive homosexuals to be sent to prison. This may aggravate an already growing problem in the control of the prison population.

Rape is possibly the most underreported crime in America. It has been argued that the stigma and prosecution problems for the victim in this type of case are often more damaging than the penalty for the offender. There were 90,434 forcible rapes reported in 1986, but some experts believe that there were actually as many as five times that number. Although the victim has good reason to remember her assailant, only 52 percent of forcible rapes were cleared by arrest in 1986—a trend that continues.

Forcible rape continues to be the most underreported of the index crimes against persons. In the case of rape, usually the only witness is the victim. In the absence of physical or other testimonial evidence, the rapist thus often goes free. The greatest number of rapists were found in the sixteen- to twenty-nine-year-old group, and the white-black percentages were 52 to

---

CONSENTING ADULTS

Acts between consenting adults are generally defined as sexual activity that does not involve coercion or force and that takes place in private. These are generally considered not the law's business and represent previously criminal acts that have been decriminalized.

47. The rapist, then, is young, probably from an urban area, and represents another aggressive problem for the correctional administrator.[12] Many states have made the crime of rape, as well as many other crimes against morality and decency, a nonprobational offense.[13] This means that most of these offenders will spend some time — and frequently a long time — in prison before they can hope to be back on the streets. Sex crimes that involve extremely peculiar acts or psychopathic personalities are discussed in Chapter 19.

Domestic Crimes

Two more major crimes deserve attention before we turn to misdemeanors: domestic violence and sexual abuse of children. Both fall within the "domestic crimes" category, but the Uniform Crime Reports do not permit collecting detailed information for these types of offenses. Both are viewed with considerable disdain by the public, which holds strong opinions on what should be done, and opinions based on misinformed underestimates about the volume of these crimes.

Spouse Abuse. Domestic violence, a catch-all term for "battering" and "spouse abuse," consists of serious, repetitive and harmful crimes that can continue across many generations as children unfortunately learn that "this is the way husbands and wives ought to act." Domestic violence refers to assaultive behavior between adults who are married, cohabiting, or who have either an ongoing or a former existing interpersonal relationship. About nineteen women are battered for every one male.[14]

The lethal consequences of spouse battering are detailed by the Federal Bureau of Investigation, which reported that 30 percent of all females murdered were slain by either their boyfriends or husbands.[15] Rarely is spouse abuse a single incident; a battered woman faces a high probability of being attacked again, especially if she does not call the police. Battering tends to escalate both in severity and frequency over time.

Law enforcement officers called to the scene of a domestic disturbance have generally (until the last decade) been wary of intervening, not only because of the danger to the officers themselves[16] but also because there

---

CHANGING THE BATTERER

The judge told him, in no uncertain terms, that the law doesn't allow him to assault me just because I'm his wife. He said that he'll send him to jail if he's brought back for another offense. Right there in the courtroom ... you should have seen the look on his face. I think he knew the judge wasn't kidding, and that's when he decided to do something about it.

—a former battered wife

> ### POLICE RESPONSE TO SPOUSE ABUSE
> Police departments throughout the country are beginning to educate officers about the dynamics of domestic violence, and are adopting official policies encouraging or requiring officers to arrest suspects in domestic violence incidents. State laws are expanding officers' legal authority to arrest in these cases: in most states, officers are now permitted — or in some states [such as California], required — to arrest suspects in misdemeanor domestic violence incidents without attaining a warrant even if they did not witness the crime, provided that they have probable cause to believe that a crime has been committed by the person being arrested.
>
> *Source:* Gail Goolkasian, *Confronting Domestic Violence: The Role of Criminal Court Judges* (Washington, D.C.: U.S. Department of Justice, 1986), p. 3.

was no general policy that required a formal action. Thus the earlier police responses were to physically separate and calm both persons, and make referrals to social service agencies. Often the officers would have to return to the same address in a short time, to repeat the generally ineffective nonintervention. Now there is a growing consensus across the nation that the best policy is to arrest the batterer, and for prosecutors and judges to use criminal sanctions to force a cessation of the battering as well as to provide treatment for batterers. Court-ordered counseling and education programs can stop domestic abuse, if court orders contain enforcement sanctions and compliance is monitored. Yet much remains to be done to initiate safe havens for the battered spouse, train counselors, find community funding, educate justice personnel, and intervene successfully with the battered spouse syndrome.

Sexual Abuse of Children. At least 72,000 children a year are mistreated by a parent or household member in child sexual abuse cases. Acts involve sexual behavior with an inappropriate person too young or too closely related by blood, kinship, or marriage.[17]

Long-term psychological damage, twisted lives, children growing into adults unable to love or be loved, delinquent behavior, and other damages result from sexual abuse of children. The actual number of victims is unknown but is undoubtedly many times the actual number of victims that come to the attention of authorities.

Sexual abusers of children are most frequently related to their victims — such as fathers, stepfathers, uncles, aunts, or other relatives — although a small percentage of these offenders are strangers. Most offenders misuse their positions of intimate relationship by engaging in sexual-oriented and intrusive behaviors with their children, wards, and loved ones.

These sexual abusers seldom are committed to prison, where they would occupy despised positions on the inmate social system and would themselves be targeted for assault by other inmates. Instead, little is done to protect abused children in this country. For example, some 90 percent[18] of the relatively few cases brought to the attention of authorities do not go forward to prosecution, thus allowing abusers to escape any deterrent penalty and continue further abuse of their original victims or other children.

Young children are often believed to have little capability to report an incident accurately. Furthermore, adults the child trusts may believe the report to be a fabrication, fantasy, or lie. Even if the child is believed, parents and health professionals are reluctant to carry the case to law enforcement authorities, primarily for fear that legal proceedings will have a greater negative impact on the victim than the initial act may have. Prosecutors face an inability to prove that the crime occurred, much less to gather sufficient evidence to secure conviction. The rules of evidence, preventing hearsay, are predicated on the belief that children are unreliable, incompetent, or not creditable as witnesses. Even a sensitive prosecutor, trained in special techniques for prosecuting cases of child sexual abuse, has some reluctance about exposing a child to the grinding impact of an adversarial court trial.

If sexually abused children are to be protected effectively, states will have to reform their statutes to abolish the special competency requirements for children (which some twenty states have already done), and legislatures will need to create special hearsay exceptions that would meet constitutional muster. Each prosecutor's office should have at least one attorney specially trained in child abuse cases, and both community health and child development professionals should be tapped for assistance at trial, as well as for interviewing the abused child. Finally, judges should also be specially trained and, if necessary, should permit closed circuit televised testimony and videotaped depositions.[19] Child sexual abuse is widespread and these victims suffer in silence, largely unprotected by the justice or correctional systems.

Misdemeanors

The Statistics

Although the number of arrests for index crimes reported in 1986 reached a total of 2,167,071, the total number of arrests was 12,500,000.[20] By the time that many of the arrests reported are bargained down and finally resolved, a huge number of misdemeanants are being handled by local detention facilities and jails. It is obvious that this problem touches all of the related subsystems of the criminal justice system, affecting plans, work loads, and personnel.

A misdemeanor conviction usually brings a sentence of less than one year, usually served at a jail or workhouse rather than a state prison. A misdemeanor can also be punished by the assessment of a fine. This broad definition varies from jurisdiction to jurisdiction, but the standard of less than one year's imprisonment is fairly common.

Alcoholics and the Revolving Door

In some parts of the country, one can stagger down the sidewalk in drunken splendor and seldom run afoul of the law.[21] In most areas, however, the "common drunk" is the most typical client for the misdemeanor facilities. Over 50 percent of misdemeanor arrests are for drunkenness or offenses directly related to drinking. One study found that 43 percent of the states' imprisoned male felons were drinking at the time they committed their crimes, and one in three were under the influence of an illegal drug. It is estimated that over two million arrests are made each year for public drunkenness alone.[22] Of course, this creates several problems for the police, not the least of which is the need for great numbers of personnel to handle these drunks. The second area to feel the crunch in this huge volume is the lower-court system. The packed dockets are not able to cope with the numbers and tend to dish out "assembly-line justice" in order to function at all. It is estimated that approximately 50 percent of the convicted jail population could be treated in facilities other than jails, if such facilities were available.

Alcoholism is a major problem in America. In terms of numbers, it is our leading drug abuse problem. It is estimated that there are at least

The Public Drunk: Criminal or Nuisance? (Photo by R. Simonsen)

> **SKID ROWS**
> Skid rows were used in logging work in the Pacific Northwest as a route through the underbrush and timber for dragging logs to the rivers. The most famous of these skid rows ended up in Puget Sound in Seattle, Washington, near what is now called Pioneer Square. The poorer sections of the city were situated along the course of the skid row, and thus it became associated with being down on one's luck or "being on the skids."

twelve million alcoholics in the United States, most of whom do not recognize their problem. The skid rows[23] of America are populated with the derelicts and dregs of a society that treats the drinking problem as a criminal offense. Most of the offenders arrested for public drunkenness are chronic, having been arrested many times before. The conditions in most jails allow for little more than a drying-out period, followed by the inevitable return of the offender to the streets and the bottle. This situation was evaluated by Austin MacCormick,[24] former president of the American Correctional Association, as follows:

> The appallingly poor quality of most of the county jails in the United States is so well known that it is probably not necessary to discuss this point at any great length. The fact that the majority of all convicted alcoholics go to these institutions, however, makes it imperative that the public, and particularly those thoughtful citizens who are interested in the treatment of alcoholics, never be allowed to forget that our county jails are a disgrace to the country . . . and that they have a destructive rather than a beneficial effect not only on alcoholics who are committed to them but also on those others who are convicted of the most petty offenses.[25]

The alcoholic is neither deterred nor cured by frequent trips to jail. All that is accomplished is the provision of a brief period of sobriety and removal from public view. The system of misdemeanant corrections is unable to deal with the alcoholic, either medically or from a social standpoint, and jail is usually the only available local response.

In several court cases, petitioners have attempted to draw an analogy between public drunkenness for an alcoholic and the logic of *Robinson* v. *California*. In that 1961 California case, the U.S. Supreme Court found that an individual could not be punished simply for being a drug addict. The argument for applying this logic to the alcoholic was finally reviewed in 1968 by the Supreme Court in the case of *Powell* v. *Texas*. The Court found that being drunk in public was not a compulsion symptomatic of the disease; therefore, arrest and confinement for it did not constitute cruel and unusual punishment. As stated by Justice Thurgood Marshall:

[A]ppellant was convicted, not for being a chronic alcoholic, but for being in public while drunk on a particular occasion. Texas thus has not sought to punish a mere status, as California did in _Robinson;_ nor has it attempted to regulate appellant's behavior in the privacy of his own home. Rather, it has imposed upon appellant a criminal sanction for public behavior which may create substantial health and safety hazards, both for appellant and . . . the general public, and which offends the moral and aesthetic sensibilities of a large segment of the community. This seems a far cry from convicting one for being an addict, being a chronic alcoholic, being mentally ill or a leper."

Robinson so viewed brings this Court but a very small way into the substantive criminal law. And unless _Robinson_ is so viewed it is difficult to see any limiting principle that would serve to prevent this Court from becoming, under the aegis of the cruel and unusual punishment clause, the ultimate arbiter of the standards of criminal responsibility, in diverse areas of the criminal law, throughout the country. . . . The entire thrust of _Robinson's_ interpretation of the cruel and unusual punishment clause is that criminal penalties may be inflicted only if the accused has committed some act, has engaged in some behavior, which society has an interest in preventing, or perhaps in historical common law terms, has committed some _actus reus._ It thus does not deal with the question of whether certain conduct cannot constitutionally be punished because it is, in some sense, "involuntary" or "occasioned by a compulsion."[26]

This decision was a setback for those attempting to decriminalize the drunkenness laws, but the Court has not completely barred the door to alternative constitutional approaches to the problem.

The sheer volume of drunkenness cases makes it imperative to discover alternatives to the automatic jailing of the chronic drunk. One study of only six chronic offenders in Washington, D.C., found that the group had amassed a total of 1,409 arrests for drunkenness and had spent, all together, over 125 years behind bars.[27] The increasing use of alternatives to incarceration for alcoholics and drunkenness offenders suggests that these other methods are proving somewhat effective in rehabilitating chronic offenders, especially compared with more conventional techniques. The most popular form of diverting alcoholics from the criminal justice system is the _detoxification center,_ now being used in numerous jurisdictions.

The detoxification center is a civil, treatment-oriented alternative to the police station as the processing point for offenders whose only crime is drunkenness. Offenders are retained there until they have been restored to a stable and sober condition. The option of treatment beyond the initial drying-out period[28] is usually left up to the individual and, in most detoxification centers, the majority elect to stay for more treatment. Detoxification centers are usually staffed with medical and other professional personnel to determine the exact needs of each individual. In the case of serious complications, the patient can be transferred to a public hospital for more extensive care. An example of the concept in practice is the

Dayton, Ohio, "Pilot Cities" program, sponsored by the U.S. Department of Health, Education and Welfare (now the Department of Health and Human Services). The structure and goals of the project are outlined in the HEW evaluation report:

> A screening and detoxification center, located in the City Mission, is designated to diagnose medical problems and provide medical treatment to persons suffering from the physical symptoms associated with drinking. Persons coming to the center may be referred from a variety of sources: police, courts, probation department, hospitals, social agencies, the correctional farm, and volunteer admissions. Disposition of persons from the screening centers can occur in a variety of ways: (1) persons with acute medical problems will be sent to local hospitals; (2) persons progressing in the reduction of medical problems will be sent to a halfway house; (3) persons not having a serious or chronic drinking problem will be returned to society; (4) persons may elect another rehabilitation program such as the one at the City Mission. The planned procedure to bring persons to the screening center by the police merits special comment. Instead of arresting persons for public drunkenness, police are to bring such persons to the screening center unless the offender refuses or exhibits violent behavior, in which case he is arrested. However, there is no legal compulsion imposed on an individual to participate in the program. He may terminate his individual involvement at any time without suffering legal consequences.[29]

The removal of over two million such "customers" from the work load of the country's law enforcement agencies, permitting the agencies to concentrate on more serious threats, would be no small step toward the reduction of major crime in America.[30] One model for a comprehensive system for the diversion of the public drunk is shown in Figure 6.1.

Trends Not Favoring Misdemeanants

An estimated 256,615 persons were confined in the nation's local jails on June 30, 1985. This is an increase of over 22 percent from the figures reported in June 30, 1982. Although this trend follows the same alarmingly higher rate as that for U.S. prisons, jail inmates are especially difficult to manage in the local communities' restricted environs. In the twelve months ending on June 30, 1985, over 16 million persons had passed through the nation's jails. Although a substantial portion of these were repeaters, if each of them had been first-timers, then 7 percent of the population of the United States would have gone to jail in that twelve-month period alone![31]

Even though the public drunk has been afforded a special status and, to some extent, has been removed from the jail population, the public has begun to "get tough" on the drinking driver and has replaced the drunk with the person arrested for "Driving While Intoxicated" (DWI).[32] From

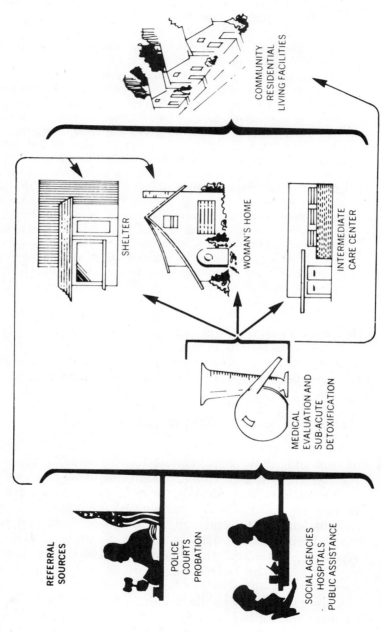

Figure 6-1 Comprehensive Public Inebriate Diversionary Program (National Institute of Law Enforcement and Criminal Justice, *Diversion of the Public Inebriate from the Criminal Justice System* [Washington, D.C.: U.S. Department of Justice, 1973], p. 7)

1972 to 1986, the number of persons arrested for drunkenness declined from 1,080,899 to 777,866, whereas those arrested for DWI increased over 100 percent, from 468,753 to 1,458,531.[33] In a system already overloaded, the efforts to crack down on the DWI with stiffer and longer sentences has only begun to be felt. As organizations such as MADD[34] try to slow the carnage on American highways, this problem may become in the next decade the most significant administrative issue to face managers of local jails.

JAILING DRUNK DRIVERS

Drunk driving is one of the most serious public health and safety problems facing the American people and their policymakers. In a 2-year period, 50,000 Americans die as a result of drunk driving—almost as many American lives as were lost in the entire 10 years of the Vietnam War. Conservative estimates place the annual economic loss from drunk-driving accidents at $21 billion to $24 billion for property damage alone.

In the past, state laws dealing with drunk driving ran the gamut of sanctions from release with warning, through moderate to heavy fines, to suspension and revocation of licenses, and—rarely—to incarceration. Enforcement, too, varies considerably from one jurisdiction to the next.

In the last few years, a growing awareness of the magnitude of the problem, coupled with the actions of citizen groups, has led many states to reform both their laws and their enforcement. Since 1981, more than 30 states have enacted legislation directed at drunk-driving control, most often by prescribing more severe sanctions such as mandatory confinement. When researchers examined the effects of mandatory confinement for drunk drivers . . . the findings revealed:

- When mandatory confinement is introduced and well publicized, drunk driver arrests usually increase.
- The introduction of mandatory confinement imposes new and heavy demands on courts, incarceration facilities, and probation services.
- The adoption of mandatory confinement is frequently accompanied by increased public concern about drunk driving and is associated with a decline in traffic fatalities.
- Mandatory confinement can be imposed either through legislation or through judicial policy.
- The implementation of mandatory confinement often requires additional resources for the criminal justice system.
- Appropriate systemwide planning can minimize dysfunction and substantially reduce the impact of mandatory confinement on criminal justice operations.
- Publicity is crucial to enhance the deterrent effects.
- Special attention for repeat offenders and scofflaws will require a mechanism to identify scofflaws incorporated into the routine screening of license renewal and registration applications at the motor vehicle department.

Source: Jailing Drunk Drivers (Washington, D.C.: U.S. Department of Justice, 1984), p. 1–2.

Misdemeanor or Felony: Offender or Offense? _____

Does the misdemeanor offender graduate to more serious crime, or is he or she usually a felon to begin with, who has plea bargained down a charge? The answer seems to be yes to both questions. It is a common practice to plea bargain a felony charge down to a misdemeanor, especially in the case of a first offense. But some studies show that misdemeanants (excluding the drunkenness offenders) tend to repeat their acts and eventually are convicted of a felony. How, then, do we go about drawing a line between a misdemeanor and a felony?

The definition of a misdemeanor, as mentioned earlier, varies from state to state. The legal definition is usually rooted in the statutes, according to how severe the penalty is for the act, the level of government at which the offender is tried, or some specific list of offenses. In many cases, the term is a catchall, with any crime not specifically listed as a felony automatically considered a misdemeanor. The gray area between a misdemeanor and a felony is even further confounded in some jurisdictions that attempt to differentiate between "high" or "gross" misdemeanors and the regular garden variety. In general, however, the term *misdemeanor* applies to such offenses as drunkenness, vagrancy, disorderly conduct, breach of the peace, minor assaults, larcenies of small amounts, small-scale gambling and other forms of "vice," shoplifting, and other minor offenses.

Most felonies also contain the elements of some misdemeanor. If they have a weak felony case, prosecutors will often try to persuade the defendant to plead guilty to a lesser, included offense. This usually saves the state time and money if the accused accepts the deal. It also gives the offender one more opportunity to remain free of a felony record. Almost nothing is known about the empirical disposition of misdemeanor offenders in America, and so any attempt to state the frequency with which prosecutors use this form of plea bargaining would be mere conjecture. Plea bargaining is discussed in more detail in Chapter 7.

Many felonies and misdemeanors are similar. The main difference, as noted earlier, lies in the kind of treatment that offenders can expect, depending on whether they are handled as felons or as misdemeanants. The convicted felon can expect to receive, in the majority of cases, a better chance for probation services, institutional programs, and parole services when released. On the other hand, as the system now works, those advantages are more than offset by the loss of civil rights and later employment problems that make a felony conviction a serious and permanent handicap. Although there are efforts under way to adopt licensing standards and restore civil rights for ex-offenders, movement in this area is extremely slow. For this reason, many offenders avoid the stigma of a felony conviction by the expedient of a misdemeanor guilty plea. The correctional system must be adapted to offer similar services to all convicted offenders, whether

A Typical Nineteenth-Century State Institution for Housing Felons (Courtesy of the Ohio Department of Rehabilitation and Corrections)

or not they are felons. A false distinction between the offenses does not change the basic problems that led the offender to commit the act in the first place. When correctional treatment can be placed on a sensible continuum, so that procedures are related to the needs of the individual offender, the stigma of being called a "felon" will be reduced, and real corrections can be made.

Summary

The problem of treating different levels of crimes in different ways is one of the basic tenets of the medical model for rehabilitation. This model assumes that laws can be devised to make "the punishment fit the crime," a noble premise but one that eluded both the Emperor Justinian and Gilbert and Sullivan's Mikado. The process of treating the criminal and causing real behavioral change has proved to be so costly and difficult that it seems doomed to total eclipse over the next decade. Also, although the legal differentiation between a misdemeanor and a felony is convenient in the criminal justice process, it holds little significance for the true classification, treatment, and behavioral control of individual offenders. Those who commit (or who are at least convicted for) misdemeanors can turn out to have worse or better custody and/or treatment problems than those who are labeled as felons. Perhaps the future will see a more effective utilization of the medical model, but it is doubtful that change will take place over the next few years.

Review Questions

1. What are the four main crimes against the person?
2. Explain why the clearance-by-arrest rate is higher for crimes against the person than for other crimes.
3. Explain why the drunken driver represents a serious problem in the correctional system.
4. Explain the difference between a felony and a misdemeanor.
5. What are spouse batterers, and what can be done to lessen the battering problem?
6. Define child sexual abuse. Why are so few cases brought into court?
7. What problems does the drunk driver pose for society? What possible solutions are there to this problem?

Key Terms

1. felony (p. 105)
2. misdemeanor (p. 105)
3. index crime (p. 105)
4. crimes against person (p. 106)
5. burglary (p. 109)
6. forcible rape (p. 106)
7. domestic crimes (p. 111)
8. spouse abuse (p. 111)
9. common drunk (p. 114)
10. skid row (p. 115)
11. alcoholism (p. 115)
12. detoxification (p. 116)
13. DWI (p. 118)

Notes

1. Rollin M. Perkins, *Criminal Law and Procedure,* 4th ed. (Mineola, N.Y.: Foundation Press, 1972), p. 4.
2. Crimes against the person are defined in the *Uniform Crime Reports* of the Federal Bureau of Investigation, issued annually.
3. William H. Webster, *Uniform Crime Reports* (Washington, D.C.: U.S. Department of Justice, 1987), p. 41.
4. Ibid., p. 155.
5. Lawrence Greenfield, *Examining Recidivism* (Washington, D.C.: U.S. Department of Justice, 1985).

6. Ohio House Bill 511, which went into effect on January 1, 1974. See James Wright, *The Armed Criminal in America* (Washington, D.C.: U.S. Department of Justice, 1986); see also Carole Wolf Harlow, *Robbery Victims* (Washington, D.C.: U.S. Department of Justice, 1987).

7. Law Enforcement Assistance Administration, *National Crime Panel: Preliminary Report* (Washington, D.C.: U.S. Department of Justice, 1973), pp. 4–9.

8. Webster, *Uniform Crime Reports,* p. 124.

9. Ibid., pp. 174–75.

10. The Drug Abuse Foundation, *Heroin Addiction: The Issues* (Washington, D.C.: Drug Abuse Foundation, 1973).

11. Webster, *Uniform Crime Reports,* p. 125.

12. Webster, *Uniform Crime Reports,* pp. 14–15. See also Patsy Kalus and Marshall DeBerry, *The Crime of Rape* (Washington, D.C.: U.S. Department of Justice, 1985).

13. In Ohio this can apply generally to any repeat or dangerous offenders. The court must consider the likelihood that the offender will commit another offense; the nature and circumstance of the offense; and the history, character, and condition of the offender. Those who fall into the nonprobationable category generally serve much longer prison terms. For a discussion of prediction in justice, see Norval Morris and Marc Miller, *Predictions of Dangerousness in the Criminal Law* (Washington, D.C.: U.S. Department of Justice, 1987).

14. Gail Gooklasian, *Confronting Domestic Violence: The Rule of Criminal Court Judges* (Washington, D.C., U.S. Department of Justice, 1986).

15. William Webster, *Uniform Crime Report—1985* (Washington, D.C.: Federal Bureau of Investigation, 1986), p. 11. Two particularly useful reports are by Patrick Langan and Christopher Innes, *Preventing Domestic Violence Against Women* (Washington, D.C.: U.S. Department of Justice, 1986), and Anita Timrots and Michael Rand, *Violent Crime by Strangers and Nonstrangers* (Washington, D.C.: U.S. Department of Justice, 1987).

16. Robert Menzies, "Psychiatrists in Blue: Police Apprehension of Mental Disorder and Dangerousness," *Criminology* 25 (1987): 429–454.

17. Debra Whitcomb, *Prosecution of Child Sexual Abuse: Innovations in Practice* (Washington, D.C.: U.S. Department of Justice, 1985), p. 1.

18. James Stewart, "From the Director," in Whitcomb, Note 17, p. 1.

19. David McCord, "Expert Psychological Testimony About Child Complaints in Sexual Abuse Prosecutions: A Foray Into the Admissibility of Novel Psychological Evidence," *Journal of Criminal Law and Criminology* 77 (1986): 1–68. See also Catherine Whitaker, *Teenage Victims* (Washington, D.C.: U.S. Department of Justice, 1986), and Ellen Gray, *Child Abuse: Prelude to Delinquency* (Washington, D.C.: U.S. Department of Justice, 1986).

20. Webster, *Uniform Crime Reports to 1986,* p. 163.

21. President's Commission on Law Enforcement and Administration of Justice, *The Challenge of Crime in a Free Society* (Washington, D.C.: U.S. Government Printing Office, 1967), p. 234.

22. President's Commission, *The Challenge of Crime in a Free Society,* p. 233.

23. See David Whitford, "The Skid Row Merry-Go-Round," *Corrections Magazine* 9 (1983): 29–36.

24. Austin MacCormick (1893–1979) was born in Georgetown, Ontario, Canada. He graduated in 1915 from Bowdoin College where he became interested in

prison reform. His studies of penal institutions in the United States led to his writing the *Handbook of American Prisons* (1926), *Handbook of American Prisons and Reformatories* (1929), and *Education of Adult Prisoners* (1931). MacCormick was assistant director of the U.S. Bureau of Prisons (1929–1933) and Commissioner of Corrections in New York (1934–1940). In 1946 he became executive director of the Osborne Association, a leading penological research and welfare organization. He was appointed professor of criminology at the University of California (Berkeley) in 1951.

25. President's Commission, *The Challenge of Crime in a Free Society,* p. 234.
26. *Powell* v. *Texas,* 392 U.S. 514, 88 S. Ct., 2145, 20 L. Ed. 2d 1254 (1968).
27. President's Commission, *The Challenge of Crime in a Free Society,* p. 233.
28. Drying out refers to the period required for the alcoholic's body to readjust to a lowered level of alcohol. This often presents a very severe shock to the system, resulting in withdrawal symptoms like those experienced by the drug user who goes "cold turkey."
29. Community Research, Inc., *Evaluation of the Alcoholic Rehabilitation Program, Dayton-Montgomery County Pilot Cities Program* (Dayton, Ohio: CRI, 1972), pp. 6–70.
30. John Snortum, Ragnar Hauge, and Dale Berger, "Deterring Alcohol-Impaired Driving: A Comparative Analysis of Compliance in Norway and the United States," *Justice Quarterly* 3 (1986): 139–165.
31. Bureau of Justice Statistics, *Jail Inmates 1985* (Washington, D.C.: U.S. Department of Justice, 1987), p. 1.
32. DWI is the term used for persons arrested for driving while under the influence. Though generally related to alcohol, this category includes driving while under the influence of drugs and other substances, whether obtained legally or by prescription.
33. Webster, *Uniform Crime Reports,* 1986, p. 165.
34. MADD stands for "Mothers Against Drunk Drivers," a group formed by the mothers of the victims of accidents that had caused the death or serious injury of their children.

7

The Correctional Funnel

In the halls of justice the only justice
is in the halls.
—LENNY BRUCE

The first requirement for any correctional process is a *client* (otherwise known as an inmate, resident, or felon). Whether one examines the largest maximum security prison in the world[1] or a rural jail, the common denominator is always some individual who has been placed there for detention, punishment, or rehabilitation. Why was one person incarcerated while another was freed or placed under some other kind of supervision in his or her home community? American corrections is a diversified mix of facilities, theories, techniques, programs, and practices. This amalgam is also part of a poorly articulated combination of police, courts, juvenile authorities, probation, prisons, and parole that is somewhat simplistically referred to as our criminal justice system.

The nonsystematic nature of criminal justice in America can be better understood by examining the prevailing sentiments and goals at the two extremes of the process: police and corrections. The police, in their law-and-order role, are working hard to get offenders off the streets and out of the community. If offenders are locked up, no matter how temporarily, they are no longer a police problem. In this role, police are often viewed by the public as agents of banishment. In the course of their work, the police see offenders at their worst, often while they are committing the offense. It is therefore understandable that the police's reaction to offenders sometimes leans toward the ideologies of retribution and punishment rather than reintegration and rehabilitation.

Correctional personnel, on the other hand, are attempting to get the offender out of prison and reintegrated into society. Accomplishing this involves taking calculated risks and releasing some offenders who might return to crime. Usually, only the worst risks fail to abide by the law; unfortunately, these failures are the only examples of "corrected" felons who come in contact with the police. Thus, the police—already overworked and saddled with an often thankless job—view attempts to reintegrate former felons into their communities as a threat and an extra work burden.

The offender, if caught, passes through most of the different stages of the criminal justice (non)system on the way to prison. Many do not pass through every procedural step but fall out of the system at different stations along the way. Therefore, it is essential to examine this screening process, called the *correctional funnel,* to determine at what point and for what reasons certain offenders are dropped from the system.

The Elements of the Criminal Justice System _____

The popular myth that our criminal justice system provides fair and uniform treatment of offenders was exploded by our own Department of Justice:

> A substantial obstacle to development of effective corrections lies in its relationship to police and courts, the other subsystems of the criminal justice system. Corrections inherits any inefficiency, inequity, and improper discrimination that may have occurred in any earlier step of the criminal justice process. Its clients come to it from the other subsystems; it is the consistent heir to their defects.
>
> The contemporary view is to consider society's institutionalized response to crime as the criminal justice system and its activities as the criminal justice process. This model envisions interdependent and interrelated agencies and programs that will provide a coordinated and consistent response to crime. The model, however, remains a model—it does not exist in fact. Although cooperation between the various components has improved noticeably in some localities, it cannot be said that a criminal justice "system" really exists.[2]

The American criminal justice system is, in fact, many separate systems of institutions and procedures. The thousands of American villages, towns, cities, counties, states—and even the federal government—all have criminal justice "systems" of sorts. Though they may appear similar in that all function to apprehend, prosecute, convict, and sentence lawbreakers, no two are exactly alike.

A diagrammatic representation of the flow of offenders through police, prosecution courts, and corrections is shown in Figure 7-1. This diagram emphasizes the points at which the "typical" criminal justice system provides alternative courses of action, so that many suspects may be processed out of the system before they even come close to a correctional institution.

The criminal justice system is composed of three separate subsystems— police, courts, and corrections—each with its own tasks. These subsystems are by no means mutually exclusive of one another, however, and what is done in one has a direct effect on another. Courts receive their raw material from the police; the corrections sector receives clients from the courts; and the cycle goes on when the released offenders are again arrested by the police. Any increased success by the police affects the courts and corrections by overloading already heavy work schedules. Also, if correc-

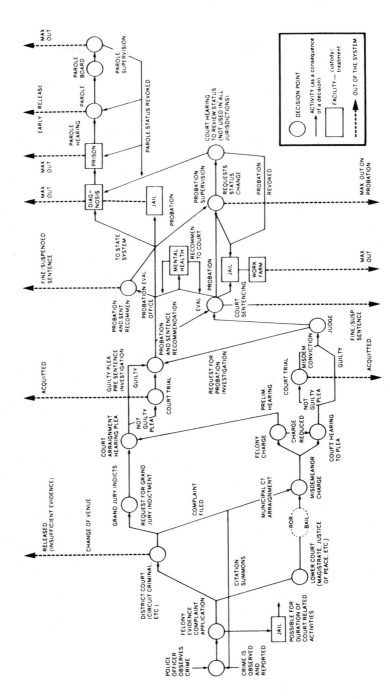

Figure 7-1 Criminal Justice System (National Clearinghouse for Correctional Programming and Architecture, *Correctional Environments* [Washington, D.C.: U.S. Department of Justice, 1973], p. 46)

tions cannot succeed in its reintegration efforts, the police are overloaded with repeat offenders (*recidivists*). This circular process is the focal point for much controversy among the three parts. We shall examine each subsystem and its effect on the correctional funnel.

Discretion and the Police

In the criminal justice subsystem, particularly corrections, there has been an increasing focus on those situations and circumstances in which guidelines, operating policies, and procedures are missing, contradictory, or unwritten. The potential abuse of discretionary power has become an area for considerable concern and angry debate. This concern, evident in all subsystems, may be illustrated by the police sector.

Decision making in most administrative agencies is usually the responsibility of an organization's top executive. This individual is probably the highest paid, best educated, most experienced, and most mature individual in the organization. The executive is given a staff to marshal the information needed to make decisions and usually is given sufficient time to deliberate on them.

The police system, it can be argued, appears to be just the opposite. The decision to arrest or not to arrest, to shoot or not to shoot is usually made in a split second and often by young, inexperienced officers at the bottom of the organizational ladder. In most cases they are also in the lowest pay bracket, with little education, experience, or maturity. They have no staff to give them data but must make decisions based on whatever training they do have and how they perceive the situation at the moment. It is small wonder that the use of this broad discretionary power at the lowest levels tends to arouse a general distrust of police statistics that show an increasing crime rate and to create hostility among the subsystems.

The principal document used to determine the crime rates in America is the Federal Bureau of Investigation's *Uniform Crime Reports*,[3] although increasing emphasis is being placed on victimization studies. This report is an accumulation of crimes known to the police from over fifteen thousand police agencies in America. The agencies that contribute data to the *Uniform Crime Reports* do so on a voluntary basis. The report was started in 1930 by the Committee on Uniform Crime Records of the International Association of the Chiefs of Police. Since that time, its statistical coverage has extended to 97 percent of the population in America. The expression "crimes known to the police" was explained in the *Uniform Crime Reports* for 1986:

> Law enforcement does not purport to know the total volume of crime because of the many criminal actions which are not reported to official sources. Estimates as to the level of unreported crime can be developed through costly victim surveys but this does not eliminate the reluctance of the victim to

---

NATIONAL CRIME STATISTICS

The **Uniform Crime Reports** (UCR) program is the product of a voluntary cooperative law enforcement effort to produce national crime statistics. Approximately 15,000 law enforcement agencies, covering some 97 percent of the U.S. population, submit monthly and annual reports to the Federal Bureau of Investigation so that information can be assembled to depict the current crime problem. This program is entirely voluntary on the part of the law enforcement agencies.

In addition to this entirely voluntary source of crime data, national crime surveys (NCS) are conducted by the Bureau of the Census and the Bureau of Justice Statistics. The NCS data indicate that the UCR vastly underestimates the volume of crime. With the exception of homicide and motor vehicle theft, there are from two to five times more Type I offenses (serious crimes) reported annually by the NCS than are reported by the UCR.

Yet the **UCR**, in recent years, indicates that crime has increased recently (up 6.3 percent in 1986 over 1985), while the NCS data strongly state that crime has decreased approximately 14 percent since 1978. Since the NCS data are more comprehensive and are less sensitive to political factors, one can cautiously conclude that crime is decreasing in the United States.

---

report all criminal actions to law enforcement agencies. In light of this situation, the best source for obtaining usable crime counts is the next logical universe, which is the offenses known to the police. The crimes used in the crime index are those considered to be most constantly reported and proved the capability to compute meaningful crime trends and crime rates.[4]

Over 13,210,800 crime index offenses were reported by law enforcement agencies in 1986. During this same period 283,200 individuals were admitted to prisons in America.[5] Where did the remaining 13,000,000 disappear to? This situation shows the correctional funnel in action.

First of all, most crimes known to the police are never solved. The rate of *clearance by arrest* for various crimes varies greatly, from 70 percent for murder to 15 percent for motor vehicle theft and burglary.[6] The aggregate number of serious (index) crimes cleared by arrest[7] in 1982 was only 21 percent, with 44 percent clearance for violent crimes and 17 percent for property crimes. Of course, this means that 79 percent (four out of five index crimes) did not result in an offender's entering the criminal justice system. Even if one assumes that any one criminal may be responsible for many offenses, there is a great narrowing of the funnel at the entry point, leaving us with only about 2.1 million offenses cleared by arrest in 1986.

The Prosecutor's Decision

The next step in the flow of criminals is the prosecutor's office. It is here that prosecutors implement their broad discretionary power to dismiss

---

PLEA BARGAINING
Plea bargaining refers to the prosecutor's practice of permitting the defendant to plead to a lesser charge than the one he or she was arrested for, usually because the prosecutor does not feel the case is strong enough on the more serious charge or because the prosecutor hopes to persuade the defendant to provide information about other crimes or offenders. Plea bargaining may lead to the prosecutor's agreeing to dismiss multiple charges, reduce charges, or recommend a light sentence. The gains that offenders are alleged to secure by plea bargaining may be less than anticipated, if not ephemeral in many cases.

---

the charges or reduce them to charges for which the defendant will plead guilty. Recent studies indicate that as many as 50 to 90 percent of the felony cases initiated by the police are dismissed by prosecutors. A high percentage of charges not dismissed are reduced through *plea bargaining* to a less serious charge to which the defendant agrees to plead guilty. The usual explanation for this further narrowing of the correctional funnel is that high caseloads and limited resources force prosecutors to dispense with much of their caseload as quickly as possible in order to avoid overwhelming the courts. The time factor does not explain, however, why some cases are prosecuted and others dismissed. Here, the wide discretionary power given to prosecutors becomes a crucial issue, and prosecutors consider such factors as the case's strength, evenhandedness, harm done to the victim, and the attorneys' personal attributes.

The prosecutors' effectiveness is usually measured by the number of convictions they get while in office. Because their political survival depends on their success in securing convictions, it is not too surprising that they will dismiss or bargain away those cases that show little promise of conviction. They may even bargain for probation without prosecution ("deferred prosecution") in cases they cannot possibly win. The general public is seldom concerned with the prosecutors' methods of obtaining convictions, as long as they get them:[8]

When a case finally reaches the trial court, the prosecutor earnestly prepares for a real battle, not for justice, but for a conviction. His professional reputation is at stake. He must resort to all the oratory and psychological trickery he can mobilize. He is ethically no better and no worse than the defense lawyer in this judicial bout. The average trial, unfortunately, becomes more a show or contest than a struggle for justice. The judge acts as referee—to see that there is something like fair play. The jury sits in amazement, at times flattered at the compliments paid them by the lawyers, and at times incensed at the threats and insults exchanged by the lawyers in reckless fashion. During the court recess the two lawyers may often be seen slapping each other on the back in perfect amity. Here is a basic American institution in action, with tragic implications that most Americans do not grasp.[9]

The prosecutor's discretion to dismiss or bargain further helps explain the gap between the number of reported crimes and the number of actual imprisonments.

Because this part of the decision process is so critical to the offenders, it will be helpful to review it in detail. The decision to charge an offender occurs after the police have made their arrest and presented their information to the prosecuting attorney. Except in those few police departments with legal advisers on call twenty-four hours a day, the prosecutors are the first legally trained individuals to examine the facts. It is their job to decide whether to charge the suspect or to dismiss ("no paper" or *Nolle Prosequi*[10]) the case.

The legal decision to proceed will be made only if the alleged crime displays certain elements."[11] There must be a narrowly defined unlawful act and the presence of criminal intent. The offender must have intended to commit the unlawful act, or the case is on shaky legal ground. Many crimes may include a number of lesser crimes within their definition. Alternatives to the charge of first-degree murder, which is very difficult to prove, might be unpremeditated murder (manslaughter), aggravated assault, assault with intent to kill, and so on. With a bit of imagination, good prosecutors can make the intent and the acts match up well enough to ensure a fairly strong case for conviction. If they think they can get a defendant to plead guilty to a lesser charge (and accept a lesser penalty), they may well bargain for it. Often, if the defendant will not accept the lesser charge, the case is dropped because of its low potential for conviction if pursued (thereby maintaining the good track record the prosecutor needs for reelection or advancement). At least 90 percent of the defendants convicted will have pled guilty (or "no contest") to a charge.

Aside from the "legal sufficiency" issue, the prosecutor will also consider a complaint from an extralegal standpoint. Often the most important extralegal considerations are determined by the matter of equity or by department policy. Age, sex, race, prior convictions, and similar factors have no bearing on guilt, but they are obviously taken into account in the charging decision.[12] If established department policy diverts all first offenders or all those under eighteen years of age to nonjudicial programs, the prosecutor will act accordingly. By the same token, a tough departmental position on certain offenses means that almost everyone who commits such an offense will be charged and processed through the courts.

The initial screening by the prosecuting attorney is the most important step in the criminal justice system for most suspects. Although more statis-

---

NOLLE PROSEQUI
The cessation of adjudication of a criminal charge against a defendant by the decision of the prosecutor not to continue the case. In some jurisdictions, termination of adjudication requires court approval.

A Deal Is Struck and "Justice" Is Done (Courtesy National Clearinghouse for Correctional Programming and Architecture)

tics are being gathered on this critical process, it is still a cloudy area. As early as 1933, criminologist N. Baker wrote as follows:

> How much more significant would it be to have figures on the situations arising behind closed doors in the prosecutor's office! Court statistics are enlightening to such an extent that it is now almost commonplace to designate the prosecutor as the most powerful official in local government. If we had some means of checking the decisions of the prosecutor when the question "to prosecute or not to prosecute?" arises, such figures would go much farther to substantiate such a statement.[13]

Plea bargaining has been studied since Alaska abolished it in 1975. Generally, these studies have found that the plea has little impact on the length of the prison sentence and that the alleged process of the police's overcharging on multiple crimes is not as widespread as was previously assumed. Defendants may not necessarily benefit from plea negotiations. Jack Call, David England, and Susette Talarico reviewed these evaluations and concluded that plea bargaining by judges and prosecutors can be effectively controlled, that abolishing plea bargaining will result in more trials but that the system can accommodate them, and that its reduction or elimination will not result in either significantly longer or more severe sentences. Plea bargaining has been eliminated not only in Alaska but also in Detroit and Denver, among other jurisdictions. In the military services, neither the air force nor the coast guard allows plea bargaining.[14]

The Court's Dilemma

The criminal court is at the core of the American criminal justice system. The courts are highly structured, deeply venerated, and circumscribed by law and tradition. The rest of the system is dependent on and responsible to the courts.[15] The police and their procedures are molded and restricted by the courts' decisions; prosecutors must weigh the legal and extralegal issues surrounding the cases before them in light of the court that will try them; and the correctional system is dependent on the court for its work load. The formal processes that take place in the courtroom are not merely symbolic but are often crucial for the protection of the individual suspect and society.[16]

Judges are either elected or appointed to office. In either case, they can be put in a position in which they owe a political debt to their backers. Because of the corrupt practices of a very few judges, it is often felt that judges in general are responsive only to pressure groups and will dismiss cases if told to do so by those in power. Actually, the discretion of a judge in a criminal court is quite limited.

Dean Wigmore[17] is credited with the "sporting theory" of justice as a description of a court trial.[18] The trial can boil down to a legal contest between two highly skilled lawyers, with the judge playing the role of a referee. Our adversary system of justice pits two lawyers against each other in an attempt to prove the suspect's technical guilt or innocence. The judge, who may be considerably less skilled at law than either the prosecutor or the defense attorney is, simply determines the outcome of various procedural disputes. If the judge makes one wrong decision, the offender may question it on appeal, and that alone can suffice to overturn the conviction. It is a basic concept of the American system of justice to permit many guilty persons to go free rather than risk convicting one innocent person because the procedures that protect his or her rights were not observed to the letter.

The courts, like the prosecutor, may work in several ways to narrow the correctional funnel. Cases may be dismissed at the early stages of the trial because the court finds there was a mistake in either the charges or the facts. The court itself may allow damaging or false evidence to be admitted, which would cause the case to be reversed later by an appellate court. Also, both the prosecutor and the court may divert the offender into

> **PROBATION**
>
> Probation is a sentence imposed by the court that does not involve confinement and imposes conditions to restrain the offender's actions in the community. The court retains authority to modify the conditions of sentence or to resentence the offender if he or she violates the conditions.
>
> Shock probation is a deterrence-based sentence to prison, designed to give the offender a taste of incarceration in the belief that this will deter future criminal activity. The sentencing court can later recall the offender and place him or her on probation with conditions, similar to regular probation.

treatment systems that are alternatives to the state's correctional institutions. Thus, many potential correctional clients who enter the court process do not actually end up in prison.

Although prosecuting attorneys may have good cause to believe that a certain suspect committed a particular offense, cause to charge that suspect, and cause to bring the suspect to trial, they sometimes make errors. These errors are usually brought to the court's attention by the defense attorney during the suspect's preliminary appearance before the judge. A judge who is convinced at this point that the charges are in error can dismiss the case. He or she will usually accompany this dismissal with a few unkind words to the prosecutor for presenting such a poor case. It is this kind of problem that the ambitious prosecutor seeks to avoid at all costs.

Sometimes, though seldom as often as television might lead one to think, the case against a suspect falls apart during the trial. The defense lawyers make critical motions in attempts to suppress evidence or restrict certain testimony. The judges must rule on these crucial issues, knowing that their ruling might be reversed on appeal. If they make a decision that later is appealed and overruled, their reputation may suffer. On the other hand, they may agree with the motions and dismiss the case at that point, saving the state the expense and bother of a long string of appeals. In either case, yet another client may fall out of the correctional funnel.

In earlier days, the choices for a judge were relatively simple. The suspect would be found guilty and sentenced to prison, or innocent and then released. A few were found not guilty by reason of insanity, but most of those convicted were sentenced to the prisons of early nineteenth- and twentieth-century America. Today, a guilty finding means the judge must choose among a broad range of alternative paths. A few of these are mentioned below, and many will be covered in detail later.

Probation has become by far the most popular alternative to incarceration in state prisons. Judges have seen this approach as an opportunity to allow guilty individuals who present little or no danger to society to continue a productive life, on condition of good behavior. Probation is used in as many as 60 percent of the cases in some states. A variation on probation, called "shock probation," has been initiated in at least fourteen states, including Ohio, Kentucky, and Indiana. In this system the offender is given the maximum sentence for a crime, then released after a short taste of prison life (up to ninety days) and returned to the community on regular probation. Judges find this system a desirable way to punish offenders whose crimes are slightly more serious than those for which regular probation is clearly an effective and appropriate remedy.[19]

Another method of diverting clients from the corrections system is, instead, to place them in the mental health system. Many states have psychopathic-offender or habitual-offender statutes[20] that allow the court to have offenders examined and committed after conviction but before sentencing. Still other states have systems that offer this path before conviction. The pleas of "incompetency to stand trial" and "not guilty by reason of insanity"[21] are also available to the defendant in most jurisdictions. In addition, about 40 percent of the states have passed laws that would allow a person who might plead "not guilty by reason of insanity" to be convicted as "guilty but mentally ill," requiring the commitment to prison and, usually, later treatment for mental illness.

All of these procedures provide a temporary or permanent escape from the corrections system and further accelerate the funneling process. One result of this process, it appears, is that the offenders who are eventually incarcerated are significantly different in composition from all those who are arrested.

Even those offenders who are found guilty and sentenced to the corrections system are often destined for units other than prisons. A broad range of community correctional programs[22] has sprung up across the nation. Some (such as halfway houses) are designed to provide housing and treatment while the offender attempts to maintain family and job ties in the community. The sharply increased emphasis on and use of these programs herald the beginning of the end of treatment methods predicated on the fortress prisons of the past. Judges are more inclined to choose a treatment option that provides a measure of humanity and hope. The community-based correctional programs are believed to offer great promise in this regard.

MENTAL ILLNESS AND THE CRIMINAL COURTS

"Incompetent to stand trial" means that the defendant's mental or physical condition is such that he or she cannot assist counsel in their own defense. Specific statutes vary across jurisdictions.

The expression "not guilty by reason of insanity" generally refers to the M'Naghten test, established in England in 1843. To establish a defense on the grounds of insanity, it must be clearly proved that, when the crime was committed, the offender's mind was so unsound that the offender did not know what he or she was doing, did not realize that the act was wrong, or was unable to choose between right and wrong.

> ## HALFWAY HOUSES
> Halfway houses are nonconfining residential facilities for adjudicated adults or juveniles, or those subject to criminal or juvenile proceedings. They are intended as an alternative to confinement for persons not suited for probation or who need a period of readjustment to the community after imprisonment.
>
> It is common to refer to halfway houses providing services for probationers as "quarter-way houses." For those servicing parolees, the term would be "halfway" houses. For those providing assistance to persons who are assigned to halfway houses as an intensive alternative to prison commitment, the term would be "three-quarter" houses.
>
> There are many more halfway houses providing services for juveniles than for adults, and some houses specialize by client or treatment modality: women only, prerelease federal furloughees, alcohol abusers, narcotics abusers, developmentally disabled, etc.

Although these are the most widespread options for judges in their sentencing decisions, others are available as well. In several jurisdictions, for minor crimes, a fine or restitution to the victim may be required in place of a prison sentence. Public service has also been used as a substitute for prison. Weekend or evening imprisonment, community work-orders, and attendance centers have also been used instead of full-time incarceration. All recognize the importance of allowing offenders to remain in the community and hold their jobs while paying for their crimes in some reasonable way. (A more detailed discussion of these programs is found in Chapter 25.)

Sometimes the criminal justice process at times may seem unwieldy and inefficient. This very lack of efficiency reflects our American concern for justice, as suggested by President Johnson's crime commission:

> [T]he basic procedures of the criminal court must conform to concepts of "due process" that have grown from English common law seeds. A defendant must be formally notified of the charge against him and must have an opportunity to confront witnesses, to present evidence in his own defense, and to have this proof weighed by an impartial jury under the supervision of an impartial judge. In addition, due process has come to incorporate the right of a defendant to be represented by an attorney. Unquestionably adherence to due process complicates, and in many instances handicaps, the work of the courts. They could be more efficient — in the sense that the likelihood and speed of conviction would be greater — if the constitutional requirements of due process were not so demanding. But the law rightly values due process over efficient process. And by permitting the accused to challenge its fairness and legality at every stage of his prosecution, the system provides the occasion for the law to develop in accordance with changes in society and society's ideals.[23]

This system allows many clients to slip through the correctional funnel, but it also provides a safeguard for defendants in cases of doubtful merit.

Another Look at Crime Statistics _____

The reader can now see that the extent of the crime picture in America depends on where a person is in the system with respect to the correctional funnel (see Figure 7-2). Statistics are helpful, as they keep us informed about how many people have been arrested, prosecuted, convicted, acquitted, committed, and placed on probation or parole. But they can also be deceptive, because so many cases fall out of the process along the way. It

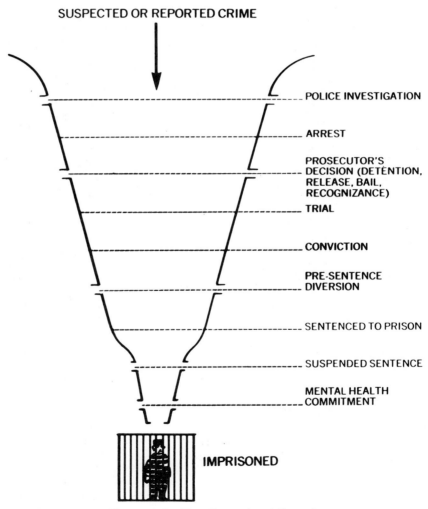

SUSPECTED OR REPORTED CRIME

POLICE INVESTIGATION

ARREST

PROSECUTOR'S DECISION (DETENTION, RELEASE, BAIL, RECOGNIZANCE)

TRIAL

CONVICTION

PRE-SENTENCE DIVERSION

SENTENCED TO PRISON

SUSPENDED SENTENCE

MENTAL HEALTH COMMITMENT

IMPRISONED

Figure 7-2 The Correctional Funnel

is far too easy for the beginning student of corrections or criminal justice to assume that the number of prisoners in our correctional institutions reflects an accurate picture of the crime problem. The preceding description of the screening process, with its limiting effect on the number of offenders actually incarcerated, suggests the error of this assumption. There is a great discrepancy between the number of actual crimes (reported and un-reported) and the number of incarcerated felons.

For the student to understand the correctional funnel better, a concrete example of the California funnel can be found in Table 7.1. Here the reader will see that there were 469,982 arrests for the 911,697 index crimes in California in 1986. During that year, a total of 257,832 arrested persons were processed through the funnel and 42.7 percent of the arrestees were not incarcerated. Those not incarcerated received release at the stationhouse or at first review of case by the prosecutor, were dismissed by prosecutor (later) or court, or were found not guilty at trial.

Stated somewhat differently, of every 100 persons arrested for an index crime in California in 1986, slightly over 57 were found guilty and sentenced. Most of the sentenced offenders received a combination of jail time

TABLE 7.1 The Correctional Funnel in California, 1986

Funnel Phase		Outcome
Total Index Crimes, 1984		911,697
Total Arrests for Index Crime		469,982
Dispositions of Arrest Persons:		257,832
Stationhouse Release	8.8	
Prosecutorial Denial of Complaint	18.5	
Complaint Filed by Prosecutor	72.7	27.3% funnelled out
	100.0%	
Dispositions of Filed Complaints:		
Dismissed by Court, Prosecutor	14.9	
Found Not Guilty at Trial	.5	
Guilty and Sentenced	57.3	15.4% funnelled out
	72.7%	
Sentence Dispositions:		
Probation	8.3	
Probation and Jail	34.5	
Jail	4.8	
Imprisoned	9.7	
	57.3%	

Source: John Van de Kamp, *Crime and Delinquency in California, 1986* (Sacramento: California Department of Justice, 1987). Does not total 100% due to rounding error.

followed by probation. Slightly over 8 received straight probation, and almost 10 were sent to prison. Lest the significance of this finding be lost, we repeat: *For every 100 persons arrested for felonies in California, ten were imprisoned.* (The impact of this rate of incarceration will be explored in more detail in Chapters 11 and 23.)

When the reader considers that most of the early studies on crime were conducted in regard to incarcerated offenders in adult prisons, it is small wonder that some of our theories are unsound. There is no doubt that statistics can help us in deciding new procedures or processes, but statistics regarding criminal justice have some strange characteristics that must be taken into consideration. Law professor Thorsten Sellin, discussing the problems of analyzing crime records, stated as his "second principle": "The value of criminal statistics as a basis for the measurement of criminality in geographic areas decreases as the procedure takes us farther away from the offense itself."[24] Because prisons usually represent the farthest possible point from the offense, clearly one must be skeptical about drawing conclusions from statistics that originate from prison populations.

Summary

The correctional funnel offers us both a problem and an advantage. The problem is that the number of incarcerated felons is quite different from the number of crimes known to the police or from arrest figures shown in the *Uniform Crime Reports*. This means that those programs aimed at the small sample of criminals who actually end up in prison are attacking only the tip of the iceberg. The advantage that this knowledge gives the criminal justice administrators is the recognition that their efforts must be redirected toward the real crime problems. Without a thorough knowledge of the funneling process, much effort could be wasted on a very small part of the problem.

In the following chapters and discussions about law and the correctional process, we shall examine the practices and alternatives available. While following these discussions, you should keep in mind the drastic effect the correctional funnel exerts on those who cannot manage to avoid imprisonment. One recalls the famous line from George Orwell's political satire, *Animal Farm:* "All pigs are equal, but some are more equal than others."[25]

Review Questions

1. What are the main elements of the criminal justice system?
2. What are the *Uniform Crime Reports?*

3. What effect does the correctional funnel have on crime statistics?
4. What are the National Crime Surveys, and what do they suggest about crime in the United States?
5. Define the correctional funnel and indicate how the accused escape from the funnel.
6. How are arrested persons (the suspected) different from those imprisoned at the end of the correctional funnel?
7. What does the defendant gain by plea bargaining? the prosecutor?

Key Terms

1. discretion (p. 128)
2. cleared by arrest (p. 129)
3. UCR (p. 129)
4. plea bargaining (p. 130)
5. elements of system (p. 130)
6. *Nolle Prosequi* (p. 131)
7. no contest (p. 131)
8. no paper (p. 131)
9. shock probation (p. 134)
10. incompetency (p. 135)
11. insanity (p. 135)
12. not guilty by reason of insanity (p. 135)
13. halfway houses (p. 135)

Notes

1. The largest prison in the Western world is the State Prison of California at Folsom. It was built in 1947 and currently has a prison population of almost 5,600 inmates but was built to house only 3,796. See Ann Bancroft, San Quentin Gets New Warden, Reform," *San Francisco Chronicle,* November 2, 1983, p. 6.
2. National Advisory Commission on Criminal Justice Standards and Goals, *Corrections* (Washington, D.C.: U.S. Department of Justice, 1973), pp. 5–6.
3. See Edwin Zedlewsdki, "Deterrence Findings and Data Sources: A Comparison of the Uniform Crime Reports and the National Crime Surveys," *Journal of Research in Crime and Delinquency* 20 (July 1983): 262–276.
4. William Webster, *Crime in the United States: 1986 (Uniform Crime Reports)* (Washington, D.C.: U.S. Government Printing Office, 1987), p. 2.
5. William Webster, Uniform Crime Reports: 1986 (Washington, D.C.: Federal Bureau of Investigation, 1987): 41. Data on prison admissions are from George and Camille Camp, *The Corrections Yearbook: 1987* (South Salem, NY: Criminal Justice Institute, 1987): 11.
6. William H. Webster, *Uniform Crime Reports for the United States* (Washington, D.C.: Department of Justice, 1987), p. 151.
7. In the *Uniform Crime Reports* program, police clear a crime when they have identified the offender, have sufficient evidence to charge the offender, and actually take the offender into custody.
8. Joseph Sanborn, "A Historical Sketch of Plea Bargaining," *Justice Quarterly* 3 (1986): 111–38. See also Douglas Smith, "The Plea Bargaining Controversy, *Journal of Criminal Law and Criminology* 77 (1986): 949–967: Jack Call, David

England, and Susette Talarico, "Abolition of Plea Bargaining in the Coast Guard," *Journal of Criminal Justice* 11 (1983): 351–358.

9. Harry Elmer Barnes and Negley T. Teeters, *New Horizons in Criminology,* 3d ed. (Englewood Cliffs, N.J.: Prentice-Hall, 1959), p. 242.

10. A no-paper action generally means that the prosecutor has decided there is not enough likelihood of conviction to warrant filing an information.

11. The expression *elements of a crime* refers to specific and precise statutory conditions of fact that must exist in order for that crime to have taken place. (For example, it must be dark for "burglary in the night season" to take place.)

12. Josephine McDonough, "Gender Differences in Informal Processing: A Look at Charge Bargaining and Sentence Reduction in Washington, D.C.," *Journal of Research in Crime and Delinquency* 77 (1986): 949–967. See also Cassia Spohn, John Gruhl, and Susan Welch, "The Impact of the Ethnicity and Gender of Defendants on the Decision to Reject or Dismiss Felony Charges," *Criminology* 25 (1987): 175–190.

13. N. Baker, "The Prosecutor—Initiation of Prosecution," *Journal of Criminal Law, Criminology and Police Science* 23 (1933): 771.

14. See Call et al., "Abolition of Plea Bargaining." Considerable interest in plea bargaining has developed in the last ten years, and the process has become more open to the public. In Indiana, for example, prosecutors are required to inform victims of plea bargains before they may be finalized. See Robert Davis, "Victim/Witness Noncooperation: A Second Look at a Persistent Phenomenon," *Journal of Criminal Justice* 11 (1983): 287–299. See also Edwin Villmoare and Virginia Neto, *Victim Appearances at Sentencing Under California's Victims' Bill of Rights* (Washington, D.C.: U.S. Department of Justice, 1987).

15. Mary Lee Luskin and Robert C. Luskin, "Why So Fast, Why So Slow: Explaining Case Processing Time," *Journal of Criminal Law and Criminology* 77 (1986): 190–214.

16. For an intense discussion of the legal system and plea bargaining, see Ralph Adam Fine, *Escape of the Guilty* (New York: Dodd-Mead, 1986).

17. John Henry Wigmore (1863–1943) was probably the world's foremost authority on the law of evidence. His *Treatise on the Anglo-American System of Evidence Trials at Common Law,* written in 1904–1905, is generally regarded as one of the world's greatest law books. He had great influence on the reform of evidentiary law.

18. Roscoe Pound, *Criminal Justice in America* (New York: Holt, Rinehart & Winston, 1929), p. 163.

19. On the other hand, shock probation may work to expose the offender to the least desirable elements of both probation and incarceration, an argument used by many opponents of the plan. See David Petersen and Paul Friday, "Shock of Imprisonment: Short-Term Incarceration as a Treatment Technique," *International Journal of Criminology and Penology* 1 (November 1973): 319–326. The most sophisticated analysis of shock probation to date is by Gennaro Vito and Harry E. Allen, "Shock Probation in Ohio: A Comparison of Outcomes," *International Journal of Offender Therapy and Comparative Criminology* 25 (1981): 70–75. These researchers found that incarceration may be the main factor that increases recidivism among shock probationers.

20. Psychopathic-offender and habitual-offender statutes received a great impetus in the late 1930s and early 1940s. Their main function is to permit an exami-

nation to determine if the offender is psychopathic or an habitual criminal, as a basis for possible commitment.

21. Pleading NGRI may not be quite as advantageous for defendants as was once commonly believed. See Jeraldine Branff, Thomas Arvanites, and Henry Steadman, "Detention Patterns of Successful and Unsuccessful Insanity Defendants," *Criminology* 21 (August 1983): 439–448.

22. Community corrections generally refers to programs that take place in the community or draw heavily on community resources in their operation.

23. President's Commission on Law Enforcement and Administration of Justice, *The Challenge of Crime in a Free Society* (Washington, D.C.: U.S. Government Printing Office, 1967), p. 125.

24. Thorsten Sellin, "The Signficance of Records of Crime," *Law Quarterly Review* 67 (October 1951): 498.

25. George Orwell, *Animal Farm* (New York: Harcourt, Brace and World, 1954).

Sentencing

My object all sublime
I shall achieve in time—
To let the punishment fit the crime,
The punishment fit the crime.
—WILLIAM S. GILBERT, *The Mikado*

The Sentencing Decision

Defendants who reach the sentencing stage of the criminal proceeding are those who have not escaped the correctional funnel. At this point they have either pled guilty to or been found guilty of a crime. The court must now decide how to dispose of them. To make a sentencing decision is often the most complicated and difficult task for the sentencing judge.

Rapid Change in Sentencing

By 1930, most states and federal courts were operating under the indeterminate sentencing structure: the judge would impose a prison sentence with both a minimum and a maximum term, such as two to five or three to ten years. The wide range of sentence lengths reflected the dominant rehabilitation goal of the correctional system and its belief that once the offender had been rehabilitated, the parole board would detect the change and then order his or her release. Parole boards actually determined the length of the sentence served, using their authority of discretionary release.

Following the long era (1930–1974) of relative inactivity, both American sentencing laws and practices underwent a rapid change, a fundamental restructuring of the sentencing process. The causes have been identified as[1]

1. Prison uprisings (such as at Attica in New York, and others in New Mexico, Oklahoma, California, and Florida) indicated that inmates were particularly discontented with the rhetoric of rehabilitation and the reality of the prison environment.
2. The abuse of discretion caused concerns about individual rights, as prosecutors, judges, and parole boards were immune from review and some practiced arbitrary uses of discretion.

SENTENCING DISPARITY

Divergence in the type and lengths of sentences imposed for the same crimes, with no evident reason for the differences.

---

3. Court orders and decisions led to a movement that demanded account-ability in official decision making and outcomes.
4. The rehabilitation ideal was challenged, both empirically and ideolog-ically, which undermined the rationale of the indeterminate sentence's "parole after rehabilitation" corollary.
5. Experimental and statistical studies of judicial sentencing found sub-stantial disparity and both racial and class discrimination.[2] Such in-consistencies and disparities fostered the conclusion that sentencing practices were unfair.
6. Crime control and corrections became a political football,[3] useful for those seeking election to public office. Such political opportunists led the general public to believe that lenient judges and parole boards were releasing dangerous offenders back into the community, with little concern for public safety.

New Goals

Although corrections in the 1970s generally reflected the utilitarian goal of rehabilitation, the dialogue and arguments from the reform movement brought other primary goals to the forefront in the 1980s, such as the incapacitation of persons likely to commit future crimes and its variant of selective incapacitation, in which the highest-risk offenders would receive much longer sentences in order to prevent any more criminal activity.[4] The specific deterrence of sentenced offenders—and the general deterrence of those contemplating committing a crime—was legitimized as a social policy goal. In addition, the retributivist goal became attractive, inasmuch as it would impose deserved punishment. (Such a "just-desserts" goal looks backward to the offender's personal culpability, focuses on the nature of the act, and considers the harm done.)[5]

Reform Options

As a result of the reform movement, sentencing practices were changed, in the belief that such practices would limit disparity and discretion, and establish more detailed criteria for sentencing or new sentencing institu-tions. These contradictory options included (1) abolishing plea bargaining, (2) establishing plea-bargaining rules and guidelines, (3) setting mandatory minimum sentences, (4) establishing statutory determinate sentencing, (5) setting voluntary or descriptive sentencing guidelines or presumptive or prescriptive sentencing guidelines, (6) creating sentencing councils, (7) requiring judges to provide reasons for their sentences, (8) setting parole guidelines to limit parole board discretion, (9) abolishing parole, (10) adopting or modifying good-time procedures, and (11) routinizing appellate review of sentences.[6] These options represent only the principal steps designed to limit unbridled discretion, lessen discrimination, make sentencing more fair, and enhance justice.

Reform Effects

In less than a decade, these dramatic changes in sentencing structures and practices became evident. Release by a parole board was abolished in at least ten states, and parole sentencing guidelines had been established in eight others. More than ten states used determinate sentencing (with a known release date), and at least 43 states established mandatory minimum sentences for at least one crime. Several states adopted statewide sentencing councils, and at least fifty jurisdictions drew up local sentencing guidelines. It is against this background of concern and change that we shall look at the sentencing decision (see Figure 8.1).

Predicting Behavior

If the sentence had no purpose except to punish the offender, as was the case until fairly recently, the judge's job would be easily prescribed by statute. In modern times, however, the sentence is also intended to be the cornerstone for reintegration. These broadly divergent objectives create a paradox that may force judges to choose between equally unwise alternatives based on the offense rather than the offender. This choice is often further complicated by subtle pressures from police, prosecutors, and the public to incarcerate certain offenders for long periods of time.

One of the main problems with the sentencing decision is that it requires that judges predict human behavior. As judges ask themselves if specific offenders will respond to prison positively or perhaps benefit more from psychiatric help while on probation, they have little factual information to guide them. In the final analysis, most judges must rely on a presentence investigation and their own intuition, experience, and imagination to produce the best decision.

The Presentence Investigation _____

Only about one-fourth of the states make a presentence report mandatory for offenses for which imprisonment can be more than one year. It is estimated that over 85 percent of the states do prepare some kind of

KEY

V Violent crime
H Habitual offender
N Narcotic/drug law violation
G Handgun/Firearm

	V	H	N	G		V	H	N	G
Federal system	—	—	—	—	Montana	V	—	N	G
District of Columbia	—	—	N	G	Nebraska	V	H	—	—
					Nevada	V	H	N	G
Alabama	V	H	N	—	New Hampshire	V	—	—	G
Alaska	V	H	N	G	New Jersey	V	—	—	G
Arizona	V	H	N	G					
Arkansas	V	H	—	G	New Mexico	V	H	—	G
California	V	H	N	G	New York	V	H	N	G
Colorado	V	H	—	—	North Carolina	V	—	N	G
Connecticut	V	—	N	G	North Dakota	V	—	—	G
Delaware	V	H	N	G	Ohio	V	H	N	G
Florida	V	—	N	G					
Georgia	V	H	N	G	Oklahoma	—	H	N	—
					Oregon	V	—	—	G
Hawaii	V	H	N	—	Pennsylvania	V	H	—	G
Idaho	V	H	N	G	Rhode Island	—	H	N	G
Illinois	V	H	N	G	South Carolina	V	H	N	—
Indiana	V	H	N	G					
Iowa	V	—	N	G	South Dakota	V	—	N	—
					Tennessee	V	H	N	—
Kansas	—	—	—	G	Texas	V	H	—	—
Kentucky	—	H	—	G	Utah	—	—	—	—
Louisiana	V	H	N	G	Vermont	—	—	—	—
Maine	V	—	—	G					
Maryland	V	H	—	G	Virginia	—	—	—	G
					Washington	V	—	N	G
Massachusetts	V	H	N	G	West Virginia	V	H	—	G
Michigan	V	—	N	G	Wisconsin	V	—	—	—
Minnesota	V	—	—	G	Wyoming	V	H	N	—
Mississippi	V	H	—	G					
Missouri	V	—	N	G					

Figure 8-1 Mandatory Prison Term Statutes Now Exist in Most Jurisdictions, Particularly for Certain Violent Offenses (Bureau of Justice Statistics, *Setting Prison Terms* [Washington, D.C.: U.S. Department of Justice, August 1983], p. 3)

presentence report on felony cases, although there may be extreme variation in the report's usefulness and quality. The presentence report, if properly researched and prepared, can be a valuable document for trial judges in their sentence decisions.

The presentence investigation is usually prepared by the court's probation officer or by any available staff of social workers. The defense attorney usually reviews, and may challenge, points in the presentence report in order to help the judge make a sentencing decision based on information from all sources.[7] Walter C. Reckless pointed out the essential elements of a workable presentence investigation report:[8]

A presentence investigation report, when written up and presented to the judge, should include in summary form such information as: present offense (including the person's attitudes toward it and his role in it); previous criminal record,[9] family situation (including tensions and discord and the factors affecting his happiness); neighborhood environment; school and educational history; employment history (especially the skills and the efficiency and stability as a worker); associates and participation; habits (including alcohol, gambling, promiscuity, and so forth); physical and mental health (as reported by various sources and by special examinations); summary and recommendations. Although most presentence investigations will emphasize such objective facts in a case as age, grade reached in school, number of children, and so on, it is important that the investigating officer capture as much subjective content as possible, especially how the defendant looks at things and the meaning of various plights and difficulties to him. The defendant's perspective on life and the way he approaches it, as well as his attitudes toward the objects and the relationships of his milieu, are the most crucial items in a presentence investigation, just as they are in more elaborate case studies. Subjective data,[10] in short, give the more revealing clues as to what has shaped the destiny of the defendant so far and what the possibilities of his future are.

In 1982, there were 3,303 agencies engaged in probation services, and most (2,540) prepared presentence investigation reports for sentencing courts. Over 1 million presentence reports were prepared in 1985.[11]

A Modern Courtroom (Courtesy National Clearinghouse for Correctional Programming and Architecture)

The presentence investigation report gives the judge a comprehensive and factual overview of the offender, his or her crime, nature, history, habits, personality, problems, needs, and risks. It also usually contains a recommendation to the court of an appropriate disposition for the case. Judges tend to accept the presentence recommendation at a rate of about 83 percent for probation and at about 87 percent for imprisonment.[12]

The presentence report serves many functions. Not only is it of immediate use in determining an appropriate sentence, but it also is used by correctional agencies or institutions for classification and program activities assignments. It will aid the probation officer in handling the case, if probation is the sentence imposed. It will also follow the offender to parole, at which time it will be used by the parole officer in supervising the case. Appellate review courts use the document when considering an appeal of sentence, and the presentence investigation reports also offer a database from which to conduct research on convicted offenders, case flows, and court management.[13]

Judicial Versus Administrative Sentencing _____

Traditionally, the sentencing process has involved a judicial determination of the appropriate punishment for a specific crime. There have been extensive changes in judicial power in the last century, however, particularly over the last decade. In the early days, when a judge sentenced an offender to ten years in prison, it was almost a certainty that the offender would serve ten years to the day. As administrative forms of sentence shortening (involving such matters as good time, pardon, parole, and clemency) became more common, the correlation between the judge's sentence and the time the offender served largely disappeared. In practice, courts using indeterminate sentencing can establish minimum and maximum sentences within the sentencing statutes, but the actual length of the sentence is often left up to the administrators of the correctional system—to the executive rather than the judicial branch of government.

A comparison of the judicial and administrative styles of decision making in sentencing reveals some similar criteria:

1. [A] determination of how much time is right for the kind of crime at issue, with the decision-maker's own sense of values and expectations usually (but not always) heavily influenced by the pressures of his environment and what he perceives to be the norms of his colleagues;[14]
2. classification within that crime category of the offender's particular act as mitigated, average, or aggravated;
3. his past criminal record (slight, average, or aggravated);
4. the extent of his repentance, his attitude toward available "treatment," and the official prognosis of his reformability; or

5. the anticipated public (usually meaning law enforcement) reaction to a proposed disposition.

Not all of these criteria are used or even relevant in every case and many other variables may be raised because of the existence of particular facts (such as strong middle-class background and allegiance) or the peculiarities or hangups of an individual decisionmaker. Something approximating the basic list given, however, appears to comprise the critical factors in most sentence-fixing. Presumably, very similar criteria are involved in prosecutorial sentence-bargaining at the prearraignment stage.[15]

Practical Problems in Sentencing _____

As we have seen previously, a flowchart of the criminal justice process reveals at every step along the way an imbalance of input to output (number of arrests versus number of incarcerations). Many cases are winnowed out in the early stages, and it is a highly select group of prisoners who end up in the Atticas and San Quentins of America. In a statistical sense, the negative selection process that admits the offender to prison may be considered more discriminating than the positive one that admits students to Ivy League colleges. But for the practical need to spread limited resources over an overwhelming number of cases, scores of additional offenders would join each of the relatively small proportion of offenders who do end up in prison.

The state and federal correctional systems are finite in size. The sentencing decision must take into account the decisions at the other end of the funnel process, which determine release rates. The system can become blocked if sentences do not approximately balance releases, and dangerous overcrowding can result. Worst, prison overcrowding can contribute to judicial overuse of probation for offenders whose risk level is too high. This can result in overworked probation officers and unacceptably high probation failure rates by offenders who continue to commit serious crime and are revoked from probation to be resentenced to imprisonment in state institutions.[16] Sentencing, therefore, must reflect both the number of prisoners in the institutions and the limited resources for handling them.

Problems in Setting Prison Terms _____

In the past, the determination of prison terms has been left largely to the courts. Decisions were made within the broad parameters of plea bargaining and statutory limitations. The courts generally established maximum sentences and parole boards determined the actual lengths of confinement

---

GRANTING FELONS PROBATION

A high percentage of felony offenders in California were committed to prison in 1986; about one in three persons convicted of felony offenses were imprisoned in California compared to one in ten in 1970. This has resulted in a critically overcrowded prison system holding over 64,000 inmates and that will hold an estimated 100,000 inmates by 1991.

To find an answer to the crisis, California has embarked on a "bricks-and-mortar" attempt to construct enough prison cells to accommodate the overcapacity problem (the prisons are operating at 80 percent over their rated capacities). California opened four new prisons in 1986 (about 2600 new beds) and plans to open 12 new facilities in the immediate future. Even this effort is not likely to produce sufficient beds to accommodate the projected population.

Judges in California, faced with the problem of having to sentence felons and acutely aware of the prison overcrowding crisis, have responded by sentencing adults convicted of felony crimes to probation. Over one-third of the probationers in California are **felony probationers**.

Joan Petersilia and others studied the probation outcomes of felons granted probation and found that, over a 40-month period, 65 percent of the study group were arrested, 51 percent were reconvicted (new crime), and one in three were incarcerated. Some three out of four (75 percent) of the new charges filed against the study group were for major crimes directly threatening public safety: robbery, theft, burglary and other violent crimes.

Sentencing judges' decisions are made in a social context that includes prison-bed availability. When this is a scarce commodity, sentencing dispositions will need to include alternatives to incarceration. In this California example, the option cited above had deleterious implications for public safety. The legislature in this state is now considering providing more alternatives for sentencing judges in their important decisions.

Outcome figures for this Box are from Joan Petersilia et al., *Granting Felons Probation* (Santa Monica, Calif.: Rand Corp. 1985)

---

according to limits established by the court and by law. In the past decade, however, control over the sentencing process has become more of a concern to state legislatures. Concerns about disparate sentences and other abuses or perceived abuses of the system have resulted in six basic strategies to formalize legislative control over the sentencing process:

- *Determinate sentencing*—sentencing systems under which parole boards no longer may release prisoners before their sentences (minus good time) have expired;
- *Mandatory prison terms*—statutes through which legislatures require a prison term always to be imposed for convictions for certain offenses or offenders;
- *Sentencing guidelines*—procedures designed to structure sentencing decisions based on measures of offense severity and criminal history;

- *Parole guidelines*—procedures designed to structure parole release decisions based on measurable offender criteria;
- *Good-time policies*—statutes that allow for reducing a prison term based on an offender's behavior in prison; and
- *Emergency crowding provisions*—policies that relieve prison crowding by systematically making inmates eligible for release sooner.[17]

Prison populations are increasing in almost every state. Policies for setting prison terms influence the size of prison populations by both the number that are sentenced and the length of time that they stay in prison. As a result, many states have attempted to find ways to modify prison terms and reduce population pressures. These methods include the following:

- sentencing guidelines[18] that use available prison capacity as a consideration in setting the length of terms (such as those in Minnesota);[19]

PRESUMPTIVE SENTENCING

One alternative to limit sentencing disparity is the presumptive sentencing system, in which the state legislature sets minimum, average, and maximum terms, allowing the judge to select a term based on the characteristics of the offender and aggravating circumstances. The sentence imposed will be the time served, less any credits against the sentence that the offender earns (such as credit for time served in jail, good behavior in prison, program participation, and so on). California has a presumptive sentencing structure that provides three options to the sentencing judge, as seen in the crime of "burglary":

1. Aggravating Circumstances   7
2. Presumptive (Average) Sentence   5
3. Mitigating Circumstances   3

Ordinarily, the judge would decide if the offender were to be placed on probation or sentenced to prison (the "in-out" decision). Assuming imprisonment to be the answer, the judge would impose the average sentence of 5 years, *unless* mitigating circumstances were present at the time of the offense (for example, if the offender were under the influence of a controlled substance, a weak personality easily led into committing a crime for peer approval, and so on). If mitigating circumstances were proven, the judge would impose the least sentence (3 years). However, if aggravating circumstances were proven, the judge must impose the highest sentence (7 years).

Some examples of aggravating circumstances are gross bodily harm to victim, prior incarceration in prison, vulnerability of victim (over 60 years of age, blind, paraplegic, etc.).

Such a sentencing structure limits judicial imperialism in sentencing, as the legislature heavily influences the sentence length. Whether there are unforeseen problems in presumptive sentencing remains to be proven, but California's prison population problems may well be due to a corollary of presumptive sentencing: abolition of parole board early release authority to control prison overcrowding.

- mechanisms for accelerating good time; and
- direct release of certain prisoners—usually those already close to their release date—under administrative provisions (such as the emergency crowding law in Michigan, the use of commutation in Georgia, and the early-release program in Illinois and Washington).[20]

Figure 8-2 demonstrates the amount of discretion in sentencing between jurisdictions. The determinate sentencing states—California, Colorado, Connecticut, Illinois, Indiana, Maine, Minnesota, New Mexico, and North Carolina and to be joined later by Washington—tend to afford the least amount of discretion. Offenders usually receive fixed sentences and they are served in full, minus good time credits. Generally in these states, parole boards continue to handle revocations and good time-decisions.

Mandatory prison-term statutes exist in 43 states. These statutes apply for certain crimes of violence and for habitual criminals, and the court's

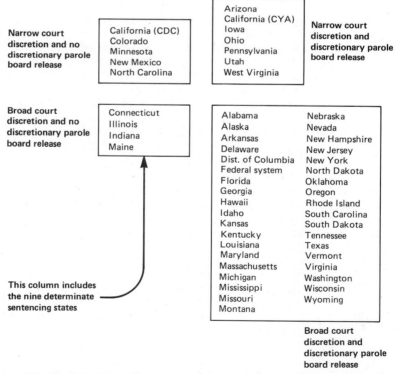

Figure 8-2 Control Over the Length of Time a Person Serves in Prison Varies Among Jurisdictions (Bureau of Justice Statistics, *Setting Prison Terms* [Washington, D.C.: U.S. Department of Justice, August 1983], p. 3)

SENTENCING GUIDELINES

In an attempt to limit if not remove sentencing disparity, many jurisdictions have implemented a set of guidelines to help judges decide what sentence ought to be imposed, given the seriousness of the offense and characteristics of the offender. Guidelines are based on past experience of a large number of sentencing judges, and represent average sentences imposed by his or her peers in similar cases. And obviously since these are guidelines, judges are not *required* to impose the recommended sentence (but must state in writing the reasons for ignoring the guidelines).

One such guideline to determine sentence length is from Minnesota. Across the top of the guideline grid is a score for the characteristics the offender brings to the sentencing hearing: number of prior juvenile adjudications, adult misdemeanor and felony convictions: number of times the offender has been previously incarcerated; employment status or educational attainment; whether the offender escaped, or was on probation or parole at the time of the instant offense, and so on. Obviously, the higher the score, the worse the criminal history (and the longer the recommended sentence).

The severity of the offense is found on the left side of the grid, ranked from least severe to highest (murder in the second degree) offense. After the judge calculates the criminal history score, she or he locates the offense category and reads across to see what other judges have given in terms of sentence length. The sentencing judge then imposes a sanction within the range suggested.

Although this procedure may appear to be a mechanical and impersonal manner of determining sentence length, it will remove much of the disparity in sentencing. Obviously, guidelines of this sort must be periodically updated so they reflect the most recent practices. Minnesota has reduced sentencing disparity through the effective use of guidelines. For more information, see Herbert Koppel, *"Sentencing Practices in 13 States"* (Washington, D.C.: U.S. Department of Justice, 1983).

---

discretion in these cases (regarding, for example, probation, fines, and suspended sentences) has been eliminated by statute.

In some states the imposition of a prison term is constrained by sentencing guidelines, such as those shown in Figure 8-3. Guidelines are usually set by a governor's commission, including a cross section of the state population. As noted by a recent study:

A sentencing commission in each state monitors the use of the guidelines and departures from the recommended sentences by the judiciary. Written explanations are required from judges who depart from guideline ranges. The Minnesota Sentencing Guidelines Commission states that "while the sentencing guidelines are advisory to the sentencing judge, departures from the presumptive sentences established in the guidelines should be made only when substantial and compelling circumstances exist." Pennsylvania sentencing guidelines stipulate that court failure to explain sentences deviating from the

Sentencing guidelines are written into state statutes	Minnesota (1980) Pennsylvania (1982)

Sentencing guidelines are system-wide policy but are not written into state statutes	Utah (1979)

Sentencing guidelines may be applied in selected jurisdictions or on an experimental basis	Maryland (1981) Massachusetts (1980) Rhode Island (1980) Vermont (1982) Washington (1979) Wisconsin (1981)

Figure 8-3 Three States Have System-Wide Sentencing Guidelines (Bureau of Justice Statistics, *Setting Prison Terms* [Washington, D.C.: U.S. Department of Justice, August 1983], p. 3)

Severity levels of conviction offense		Criminal History Score						
		0	1	2	3	4	5	6 or more
Unauthorized use of motor vehicle Possession of marijuana	I	12	12	12	15	18	21	24 *23-25*
Theft-related crimes ($150–$2500) Sale of marijuana	II	12	12	14	17	20	23	27 *25-29*
Theft crimes ($150–$2500)	III	12	13	16	19	22 *21-23*	27 *25-29*	32 *30-34*
Burglary—felony intent Receiving stolen goods ($150–$2500)	IV	12	15	18	21	25 *24-26*	32 *30-34*	41 *37-45*
Simple robbery	V	18	23	27	30 *29-31*	38 *36-40*	46 *43-49*	54 *50-58*
Assault, 2d degree	VI	21	26	30	34 *33-35*	44 *42-46*	54 *50-58*	65 *60-70*
Aggravated robbery	VII	24 *23-25*	32 *30-34*	41 *38-44*	49 *45-53*	65 *60-70*	81 *75-87*	97 *90-104*
Assault, 1st degree Criminal sexual conduct, 1st degree	VIII	43 *41-45*	54 *50-58*	65 *60-70*	76 *71-81*	95 *89-101*	113 *106-120*	132 *124-140*
Murder, 3d degree	IX	97 *94-100*	119 *116-122*	127 *124-130*	149 *143-155*	176 *168-184*	205 *195-215*	230 *218-242*
Murder, 2d degree	X	116 *111-121*	140 *133-147*	162 *153-171*	203 *192-214*	243 *231-255*	284 *270-298*	324 *309-339*

Italicized numbers within the grid denote the range within which a judge may sentence without the sentence's being deemed a departure. First-degree murder is excluded from the guidelines by law and is punished by life imprisonment.

Figure 8-4 Minnesota Sentencing Guidelines Grid (presumptive sentence length in months)

recommendations "shall be grounds for vacating the sentence and resentencing the defendant." Furthermore, if the court does not consider the guidelines or inaccurately or inappropriately applies them, an imposed sentence may be vacated upon appeal to a higher court by either the defense or the prosecution.[21]

The range and particular format for sentencing guidelines can include such things as specifically worded statutes and grids with a range of judicial options. Parole guidelines are sometimes closely prescribed, and sometimes wide discretion is afforded to the parole board. The amount of flexibility in these decisions can directly enhance or detract from the efforts to relieve crowded prison conditions. (See Figures 8-4 and 8-5.) In the early 1970s, thousands of inmates were paroled from Florida prisons to make room for a backlog of inmates whose petitions for parole were flatly turned down by Director of Corrections Louis Wainwright. Because most parole decisions are not made on time but on "risk to the community," tighter and tighter criteria make it difficult to manage populations by these types of decisions.

Good-time policies are another way to control behavior in the institutions and to control population pressures as well. The threat of losing up to one-third of their sentence by poor conduct does act as a control over some inmates' behavior. The states that use good time and programming time (sometime called *earned time*) to reduce the length of a prison sentence are listed in Figure 8-6. All of the practices listed are aids to the proper and safe management of prison populations by corrections administrators and other members of the criminal justice system.

Guidelines for paroling decisions are written into statutes	Federal system (1973) Florida (1978) New York (1977)
Guidelines for paroling decisions are system-wide policy but are not written into statutes	Alaska (1981) California (CYA, 1978) Dist. of Columbia (1982) Georgia (1980) Maryland (1979) Missouri (1982) New Jersey (1980) Oklahoma (1980) Oregon (1979) Pennsylvania (1980) Utah (1979) Washington (1979)
Guidelines for paroling decisions are selectively applied	California (CDC, 1977) Minnesota (1976)

Figure 8-5 Fifteen Jurisdictions Have System-Wide Parole Guidelines As of January 1983 (Bureau of Justice Statistics, *Setting Prison Terms* [Washington, D.C.: U.S. Department of Justice, August, 1983], p. 4)

KEY

B Reductions for good behavior
P Reductions for program participation

	B	P		B	P
Federal system	B	P	Montana	B	P
District of Columbia	B	—	Nebraska	B	P
			Nevada	B	P
Alabama	B	P	New Hampshire	B	P
Alaska	B	—	New Jersey	B	P
Arizona	B	—			
Arkansas	—	P	New Mexico	B	P
California	—	P	New York	B	—
			North Carolina	B	P
Colorado	B	P	North Dakota	B	P
Connecticut	B	P	Ohio	B	—
Delaware	B	P			
Florida	B	P	Oklahoma	—	P
Georgia	B	—	Oregon	B	P
			Pennsylvania	—	—
Hawaii	—	—	Rhode Island	B	P
Idaho	B	P	South Carolina	B	P
Illinois	B	P			
Indiana	B	—	South Dakota	B	—
Iowa	B	P	Tennessee	—	—
			Texas	B	P
Kansas	B	P	Utah	—	—
Kentucky	B	P	Vermont	B	P
Louisiana	—	P			
Maine	B	P	Virginia	B	P
Maryland	B	P	Washington	B	—
			West Virginia	B	P
Massachusetts	B	P	Wisconsin	B	P
Michigan	B	P	Wyoming	B	P
Minnesota	B	—			
Mississippi	B	P			
Missouri	B	P			

Figure 8-6 All But Four Jurisdictions Have Provisions for the Administrative Reduction of the Length of Time Spent in Prison (as of January 1985) (Bureau of Justice Statistics, *Setting Prison Terms* [Washington, D.C.: U.S. Department of Justice, August 1983], p. 6)

Our review of the changes in sentencing practices and their consequences in the last decade clearly shows the shifts that have taken place. Although discretion in determining sentence length has been somewhat removed from the sentencing judge and parole board, it was reduced by legislatures through their enactment of new sentencing structures. In turn, in many jurisdictions, the prosecutor's discretion was increased. The prison populations will continue to climb as more and more offenders are committed and serve longer and longer sentences. American corrections appears to be on a collision course with the standard of human decency: the Eighth Amendment to the U.S. Constitution, which forbids cruel and unusual punishment. To understand the situation, it is necessary to look at the problems with the penal codes.

Problems with Penal Codes _____

The penal codes of most jurisdictions are a potpourri of social thinking from past eras. Most of the earlier penal codes were devised in response to a specific event or set of events, often after a particularly heinous crime or repugnant act. Such acts bring public pressure on legislators, and if that pressure is persistent enough, a new law is created, with a formula for punishment attached. Unfortunately, these laws, with punishments that are often irrationally severe, remain on the books for decades after the incident and the legislators have long been forgotten.

Many states are in the process of updating and revising their entire criminal codes. This is a long and arduous task, however, and there is a great temptation to use the old as a model for the new. It is felt by many that sentence fixing should not be part of penal legislation. The obvious failure of the early penal codes, designed to mete out specific punishments for specific offenses, has reinforced the belief that legislators and judges should be excluded from the sentence-fixing process. One alternative that was advocated is the use of professional psychologists, trained to understand human behavior, as a replacement for legislators and jurists in fixing the penalties for crimes.

In 1967 President Johnson's Crime Commission reported that "a common characteristic of American penal codes is the severity of sentence available for almost all felony offenses.[22]" This background of severity has inhibited meaningful change in penal codes. In examining sentencing practices, one must review both the system of criminal justice and the erratic quality of justice dispensed by that system. Failure to observe the difference between justice in the law and justice before the law can result in unfair criticism of the judge.

The Model Penal Code[23] drafted by the American Law Institute addresses the problems of severity and inconsistency of present penal codes with regard to sentencing. Imprisonment is seen as a last resort, to be used only when

1. there is undue risk that during the period of suspended sentence or probation the defendant will commit another crime; or
2. the defendant is in need of correctional treatment that can be provided most effectively by commitment to an institution; or
3. a lesser sentence will depreciate the seriousness of the defendant's crime.[24]

These criteria are intended as a guide for extreme cases only. The model code envisions that every alternative to imprisonment will be explored in a given case before the criteria are applied. The Model Penal Code of the

American Law Institute would reduce all crimes to five grades, three for felonies and two for misdemeanors. A maximum penalty would be assigned to each grade, shorter in most cases than those now used by the states. Minimums would be set at one year for most felonies and at three years for only the very serious felonies. If the offense were especially dangerous, the judge would be able to extend the maximum. Judges would be granted the flexibility they need to fit the sentence to the particular case. Although the Model Penal Code has great appeal to the practitioners in the field of corrections, it has had slow acceptance in legislatures, which must choose between a humane and workable code and the outcry of an enraged citizenry when the harsh law-and-order codes are struck down.

The main problem with penal code revision is the need to make codes conform to modern-day standards and capabilities. The American Bar Association outlined some general principles for statutory structure:

1. All crimes should be classified for the purpose of sentencing into categories which reflect substantial differences in gravity. The categories should be very few in number. Each should specify the sentencing alternatives available for offenses which fall within it. The penal codes of each jurisdiction should be revised where necessary to accomplish this result.
2. The sentencing court should be provided in all cases with a wide range of alternatives, with gradations of supervisory, supportive, and custodial facilities at its disposal so as to permit a sentence appropriate for each individual case.
3. The legislature should not specify a mandatory sentence for any sentencing category or for any particular offense.
4. It should be recognized that in many instances in this country the prison sentences which are now authorized, and sometimes required, are significantly higher than are needed in the vast majority of cases in order adequately to protect the interests of the public. Except for a very few particularly serious offenses, and except under the circumstances set forth (in the section dealing with special terms for certain types of offenders), the maximum authorized prison term ought to be five years and only rarely ten.[25]

Another issue in penal code revision is the disparity of sentencing for the same or similar offenses. The emphasis today is on reintegration, but prisoners who feel that they have been unfairly treated in sentencing may well reject all efforts to reintegrate them. This kind of disparity also destroys public confidence in the criminal justice system. The elimination or revision of antiquated statutes and the adoption of principles that are widely accepted by both the judiciary and correctional administrators will go a long way toward encouraging consistent and appropriate sentencing.

Models for Sentencing _____

How should the jurist arrive at the proper length of sentence for an offender? The present system, sometimes referred to as the "hunch" system,[26] results in discriminatory sentences by the same judge, and between different judges, for the same offenses. Over a quarter of a century ago, reformers felt that it should be no great task to set up a diagnostic clinic for administration of persons sentenced. In this clinic, impartial, disinterested scientists would function under conditions that never exist in the courts.[27] Diagnostic clinics have been very slow in coming, but at least the presentence clinic is in wider use than before.

At the 1971 National Conference on Corrections in Williamsburg, Virginia, eight points were made in regard to more appropriate sentencing:

1. It should be mandatory that trial judges have presentence reports in all felony cases. These reports should be prepared by qualified probation or corrections officers. The report should also be made a part of the record for any sentence appeal which may be permitted.
2. Diagnostic facilities should be made available to all judges.
3. Jury sentencing should be abolished.
4. Sentencing judges should be required to record the reasons for each sentence. These reasons are to be made known to the defendant, with

copies to the corrections personnel involved and to the appellate courts in those instances in which the sentences are appealed.

5. Sentencing judges should educate their communities on the philosophy of sentencing.

6. Defense counsel and the prosecutor should be consulted by the judge before imposing sentence.

7. Probation officers and judges should receive instructions in sentencing, perhaps attend sentencing institutes.

8. Trial judges should be elected or appointed in as nonpolitical a way as possible.[28]

Another approach to sentencing reform has been devised by David Fogel, the executive director of the Illinois Law Enforcement Commission. In his "justice model," which groups crimes into five categories, each category would have a flat sentence of from two to twenty-five years, depending on the offense. Sentencing judges would be allowed a 20 percent leeway in either direction under this legislative plan, but each circumstance that might affect the severity of the sentence would be spelled out in detail.[29]

A discussion of sentencing would be incomplete without mentioning the policy implications of the increasing demand for deterrence. Some writers now argue that those states that imprison more of the offender population (rather than use community corrections) would have lower crime rates if the proportion of persons sentenced to prison were to increase. Though this may appeal to conservatives who believe that the criminal justice system can affect the rates of crime and serve as a deterrent, the data on the effects of higher imprisonment rates do not bear out the presumed effects. In both the United States and Canada, the rates of crime do not go down with increased imprisonment. Instead, the rates of crime go up when the proportion of offenders per 100,000 who are sentenced to prison is raised. We thus need to think about the use of imprisonment to deter others from committing crime, when studies show that it has just the opposite effect![30]

Summary _____

The past fifteen years represent a revolution in sentencing in the United States. Among the changes imposed are the abolition of the parole board's authority to release offenders at their discretion and the adoption of sentencing guidelines for judges. Changes also include shifting to mandatory prison sentences for specified crimes, adoption of presumptive sentences, and other efforts to limit discretion and disparity in sentencing and length of time served in prison. So widespread have the changes been that only three states (North Dakota, Virginia, and Wyoming) have left unchanged their sentencing laws.[31]

In addition to the sentencing law changes, sharp increases have occurred in the number of persons incarcerated. Never in the history of the United States have we had so many and such a large proportion of the public incarcerated in prisons. Why the sudden increase is not exactly understood; it is obvious that corrections is once again in crisis and on a collision course with the Eighth Amendment's prohibition against cruel and unusual punishment. The next chapter examines some of the legal issues.

Review Questions _____

1. What is the principal reason for the judge's diminished sentencing power?
2. What are some of the aids available to help the judge decide what sentence to impose?
3. What factors have led to the rapid changes in the sentencing structures in the United States?
4. Identify the basic policy goals of sentencing, and define each.
5. What roles can the presentence investigation report play in corrections?
6. How does a legislature influence sentencing?
7. In what ways can a prosecutor influence sentence length?
8. Why are prison populations increasing?
9. Cite the advantages and disadvantages of the indeterminate sentence.
10. What problems can arise when adult felony offenders are placed on probation?
11. What are some implications of overcrowded prisons for the sentencing decision?

Key Terms _____

1. sentencing disparity (p. 144)
2. just-desserts (p. 144)
3. presentence report (p. 146)
4. administrative sentencing (p. 148)
5. felony probation (p. 150)
6. determinate sentencing (p. 150)
7. sentencing guidelines (p. 150)
8. good-time policies (p. 151)
9. presumptive sentencing (p. 151)
10. Model Penal Code (p. 157)
11. justice model (p. 160)
12. deterrence by sentencing (p. 160)

Notes

1. National Institute of Corrections, *Research on Sentencing: The Search for Reform* (Washington, D.C.: U.S. Department of Justice, December 1983).
2. For an examination of how the offender's race biases sentence length, see R. D. Peterson and J. Hagan, "Changing Conceptions of Race and Sentencing Outcomes," *American Sociological Review* 49 (1984): 56–70. See also Christopher Turk and Neal Shover, "Research Note: The Origin of Sentencing Reforms," *Justice Quarterly* 3 (1986): 329–342; Leo Carroll and Claire Cornell, "Racial Composition, Sentencing Reforms, and Rates of Incarceration," *Justice Quarterly* 2 (1985): 473–490; and Marjorie Zatz, "The Changing Forms of Racial/Ethnic Biases in Sentencing," *Journal of Research in Crime and Delinquency* 24 (1987): 69–92.
3. John Irwin and James Austin, *It's About Time* (San Francisco, Calif.: National Council on Crime and Delinquency, 1987), p. 15.
4. John Blackman and J. Welsh, "Selective Incapacitation: Sentencing According to Risk," *Crime and Delinquency* 29 (1983): 504–528. See also Peter Greenwood and Susan Turner, *Selective Incapacitation Revisited: Why the High-Rate Offenders Are Hard to Predict* (Santa Monica, Calif.: Rand Corporation, 1987).
5. For a discussion of the federal "just-desserts" juvenile code, see Craig Fischer, "As Model Code Nears Completion, Practitioners Ask 'What Code?'" *Criminal Justice Newsletter* 17 (October 15, 1986): 5–7.
6. Sandra Shane-Dubow, Alice Brown, and Erik Olsen, *Sentencing Reform in the United States: History, Content, and Effect* (Washington, D.C.: U.S. Department of Justice, 1985). See also Turk and Shover, note 2.
7. Walter Dickey, "The Lawyer and Accuracy of the Presentence Report," *Federal Probation* 43 (June 1979): 28–39. See also David Roberts, "Effects of Court Officials on Sentence Severity: Do Judges Make a Difference?" *Criminology* 22 (February 1984): 135–138.
8. Walter C. Reckless, *The Crime Problem*, 4th ed. (New York: Appleton-Century-Crofts, 1967), pp. 673–674.
9. Susan Welch and Cassia Spohn, "Evaluating the Impact of Prior Record on Judges' Sentencing Decisions: A Seven-City Comparison," *Justice Quarterly* 3 (1986): 389–408; Cassia Spohn and Susan Welch, "The Effect of Prior Record in Sentencing Research: An Examination of the Assumption That Any Measure Is Adequate," *Justice Quarterly* 4 (1987): 287–302; and Alexis Durham, "Justice In Sentencing: The Role of Prior Record of Criminal Involvement," *Journal of Criminal Law and Criminology* 78 (1987): 614–643.
10. John Rosencranz, "Extralegal Factors and Probation Presentence Reports," *Journal of Contemporary Criminal Justice* 3 (1987): 38–56.
11. Bureau of Justice Statistics, *Probation and Parole 1982* (Washington, D.C.: U.S. Department of Justice, 1983).
12. The degree of agreement may also depend on the report preparer's knowing the negotiated plea and proposed sentence to which the prosecutor and defense counsel have agreed.
13. See J. M. Schmolesky and T. K. Thorson, "The Importance of the Presentence Investigation Report *After* Sentencing," *Criminal Law Bulletin* 18 (1982): 406–441.

14. Peter Brimelow, "Judicial Imperialism," *Forbes Magazine* (June 1, 1987): 109–112.

15. Caleb Foote, "The Sentencing Function," in Roscoe Pound, ed., *A Program for Prison Reform* (Cambridge, Mass.: American Trial Lawyers Foundation, 1973), p. 30.

16. Lawrence Greenfield, *Probation and Parole* 1984 (Washington, D.C.: U.S. Department of Justice, 1986), pp. 2–3.

17. Bureau of Justice Statistics, *Setting Prison Terms* (Washington, D.C.: U.S. Department of Justice, 1983).

18. Harvey Silets and Susan Brenner, "Commentary on the Preliminary Draft of the Sentencing Guidelines Issued by the United States Sentencing Commission in September 1986," *Journal of Criminal Law and Criminology* 77 (1986): 1069–1111. See also Michael Block and William Rhodes, "The Impact of the Federal Sentencing Guidelines," *NIJ Reports* (1987): 2–13.

19. Herbert Koppel, *Sentencing Practices in 13 States* (Washington, D.C.: U.S. Department of Justice, 1984): 5.

20. Bureau of Justice Statistics, *Setting Prison Terms*. See also Herbert Koppel, *Time Served in Prison* (Washington, D.C.: U.S. Department of Justice, 1984); Mark Cunniff, *Felony Sentencing in 18 Local Jurisdictions* (Washington, D.C.: U.S. Department of Justice, 1985); and Alexander Smith, Harriet Pollack, and F. Warren Benton, "Sentencing Problems: A Pragmatic View," *Federal Probation LI* (1987): 67–74.

21. President's Commission on Law Enforcement and Administration of Justice, *The Challenge of Crime in a Free Society* (Washington, D.C.: U.S. Government Printing Office, 1967), p. 142.

22. Ibid.

23. American Law Institute, *Model Penal Code, Proposed Official Draft* (Philadelphia: ALI, 1962).

24. American Law Institute, *Model Penal Code.*

25. American Bar Association, *Standards Relating to Sentencing Alternatives and Procedures* (New York: Office of the Criminal Justice Project, 1968).

26. Harry Elmer Barnes and Negley Teeters, *New Horizons in Criminology,* 3d ed. (Englewood Cliffs, N.J.: Prentice-Hall, 1959), p. 264.

27. Barnes and Teeters, *New Horizons in Criminology,* p. 264.

28. *National Conference on Corrections, Williamsburg, Virginia* (Washington, D.C.: U.S. Government Printing Office, 1971), pp. 2–3.

29. Michael Serrill, "Critics of Corrections Speak Out," *Corrections Magazine* (March 1976): 23.

30. David Biles, "Crime and the Use of Prisons," *Federal Probation* 43 (June 1979): 39–43. For a discussion of using prisons to incapacitate offenders, see Todd Clear and O. Barry, "Some Conceptual Issues in Incapacitating Offenders," *Crime and Delinquency* (October 1983): 529–545. Edmund McGarrell and Timothy Flanagan, "Measuring and Explaining Legislator Crime Control Ideology," *Journal of Research in Crime and Delinquency* 24 (1987): 102–118.

31. Link and Shover, p. 330.

9

Appellate Review

The openness of courts to entertain prisoner suits
and readiness to intrude deeply into prison operations has created problems of both volume and
substance.
—SAMUEL JAN BRAKEN (1987)

The Issue of Due Process

A basic tenet of the criminal justice process in America is that every
defendant is presumed innocent until proven guilty. Not only does our
system demand proof of guilt, but it also requires that this proof be obtained fairly and legally, and the process of appellate review helps ensure
that it will be. In effect, the appellate review acts as a shield for the
defendant caught up in the processes of criminal trial, incarceration, or
supervision in the community. The state has considerable resources to
prosecute those it considers offenders, and the Constitution protects us
from the kind of government "railroading" that could deprive us of life,
liberty, or property without the benefit of due process of law. Due process
has been a constitutional right for all Americans under federal law since
the passage of the Fourteenth Amendment in 1868. It was not until the
"criminal law revolution" (see Chapter 4) of the 1960s, however, that the
due process clause of the Fourteenth Amendment was also made binding
on all the states through a series of Supreme Court decisions (see Chapter
4). In the field of corrections, like every other segment of criminal justice,
these decisions have created a climate of great challenge and rapid change.

RAILROADED

The term *railroaded* has become part of American slang. Its origins lie in
the practice by early state prisons of having a train pick up prisoners at various
points, jails, and counties along the way, and drop them at the prison. Sometimes local undesirables were put on the prison train to end up in prison under
less than due process conditions.

> **FOURTEENTH AMENDMENT**
>
> All persons born and naturalized in the United States, and subject to the jurisdiction thereof, are citizens of the United States and of the State wherein they reside. No State shall make or enforce any law which shall abridge the privileges or immunities of citizens of the United States: nor shall any State deprive any person of life, liberty, or property, without due process of law, nor deny to any person within its jurisdiction the equal protection of the law.

This chapter includes a brief examination of the appeal process and procedure, a glance at several significant cases, and an analysis of trends that appear to be emerging in pending appeals.

One of the problems with due process of law is not that it is *due*—that is, something we are entitled to—but rather determining how much of it is due.[1] Only a few decades ago, very few criminal cases were appealed. Since the case of *Gideon* v. *Wainwright*, however, the picture has radically changed. The securing of the right to counsel for all defendants, stemming from that landmark decision, has opened the floodgates in the review courts across America. In some jurisdictions the rate of appeals is as high as 90 percent of all convictions (see Figure 9-1). Collateral attack,[2] or the filing of an appeal in the federal system while the state case is still undecided—almost unknown before the 1960s—is now routine in most state courts. The result of this overload in the review system has been a monumental increase in the work load for state and federal judges.[3] It has also created extended periods of litigation, often stretched out over several years, that have eroded any lingering belief that a conviction for a criminal offense must be considered final. The review procedure has as many as eleven steps in some state systems, and it is not unusual for a defendant to explore at least four or five. The eleven steps are

1. New trial motion filed in court where conviction was imposed;
2. Appeal to state intermediate appellate court (in states where there is no intermediate appellate court this step would not be available);
3. Appeal to state supreme court;
4. Petition to U.S. Supreme Court to review state court decision on appeal;
5. Postconviction proceeding in state trial court;
6. Appeal of postconviction proceeding to state intermediate appellate court;
7. Appeal to state supreme court;
8. Petition to U.S. Supreme Court to review state court decision on appeal from postconviction proceeding;
9. Habeas corpus petition in federal district court;
10. Appeal to U.S. Court of Appeals; and
11. Petition to U.S. Supreme Court to review court of appeals decision on habeas corpus petition.[4]

APPEALS

An appeal occurs when the defendant in a criminal case requests that a court with appellate jurisdiction rule on a decision that has been made at a trial court. In making its final disposition of the case, an appellate court may do one of the following:

- *Affirm* or uphold the lower court rulling;
- *Modify* the lower court ruling by changing it in part, but not totally reversing it;
- *Reverse* or set aside the lower court ruling and not require any further court action;
- *Reverse and remand* the case by overturning the lower court ruling that may range from conducting a new trial to entering a proper judgement; or
- *Remand* all or part of the case by sending it back to the lower court without overturning the lower court's ruling but with instructions for further proceedings that may range from conducting a new trial to entering a proper judgement.

Bureau of Justice Statistics, Washington, D.C.: U.S. Department of Justice *The Growth of Appeals*, (1985), p. 3.

It is easy to see why the review process can take so long, especially when some steps may be used several times in a single appeal, with reviews of the same case taking place simultaneously in different court systems. Thus due process may be a long and complicated procedure and, when appeal is part of the scheme, it can become a seemingly endless cycle.

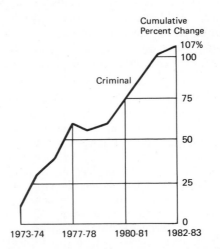

Figure 9-1 Cumulative Growth in Appeals Filed, 1973–1983 (Bureau of Justice Statistics, *The Growth of Appeals* [Washington, D.C.: U.S. Department of Justice, 1985], p. 2)

The Path of a Criminal Case _____

There are so many points in the criminal proceeding to which appellate actions can be directed that it is worthwhile to reexamine the steps in which the courts become participants (see Figure 9-2). The first point at which most defendants come into contact with the criminal justice system is at the time of their *arrest*, usually by a police officer. Even at this early step, the potential for a later appeal is great. It is all too true that the "guilty often go free because the constable blundered." A suspect's Fourth and Fifth Amendment rights have been clearly established by decisions such as *Mapp* v. *Ohio* and *Miranda* v. *Arizona*. The failure of law enforcement officers to comply with the procedural safeguards established as a result of these landmark cases can mean an overturned conviction in a review court later on.

The next stage of the criminal justice process is usually the *initial appearance* before a judge. Often the court where this appearance takes place may not actually have the jurisdiction to try the defendant, but the defendant has the right to state his or her case before a court as soon as possible after arrest.[5] This initial appearance is usually accompanied by the presentation of a complaint by the prosecution. The judge at the initial appearance has several tasks to perform, and the failure to perform them correctly can result—as with the arresting officer—in a successful appeal at a later time. The defendant must be made aware of the charges against him or her and warned against making any self-incriminating statements. If the accused is to be assigned an attorney at state expense, this procedure is initiated. When the initial court does not have the jurisdiction to try a particular case, a decision must be made as to the continued detention of the accused (in the case of dangerous persons), or some arrangement must be made for the accused's release prior to trial before the court of primary jurisdiction. The defendant can be released on his or her own recognizance[6] or may be required to post bail. In the first instance, the judge believes that the defendant will appear in court as required because he or she has nothing to gain—and a reputation to lose—by running away. In the second, the defendant "posts" a certain sum of money that is forfeited if he or she fails to appear. In both cases, the object is to encourage the defendant's appearance at further proceedings on the case.

RECOGNIZANCE

Release on recognizance means that the court accepts that the defendant will be available for trial and that it does not need to exact a financial penalty ("surety bond") for nonappearance. In a sense, it means "release on the defendant's word of honor."

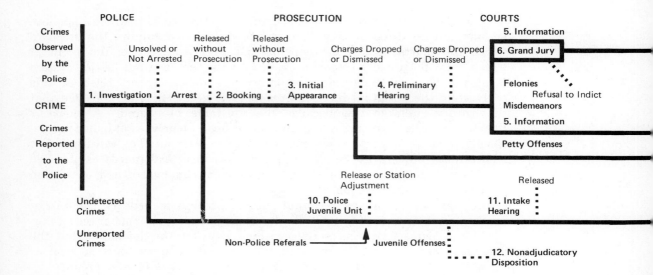

1. **Investigation.** May continue until trial.

2. **Booking.** Administrative record of arrest. First step at which temporary release on bail may be available.

3. **Initial Appearance.** Before magistrate, commissioner, or justice of peace. Formal notice of charge, advice of rights. Bail set. Summary trials for petty offenses usually conducted here without further processing.

4. **Preliminary Hearing.** Preliminary testing of evidence against defendant. Charge may be reduced. No separate preliminary hearing for misdemeanors in some systems.

5. **Information.** Charge filed by prosecutor on basis of information submitted by police or citizens. Alternative to grand jury indictment; often used in felonies, almost always in misdemeanors.

6. **Grand Jury.** Reviews whether government evidence sufficient to justify trial. some states have no grand jury system; others seldom use it.

Figure 9-2 General Flow of the Criminal Justice System

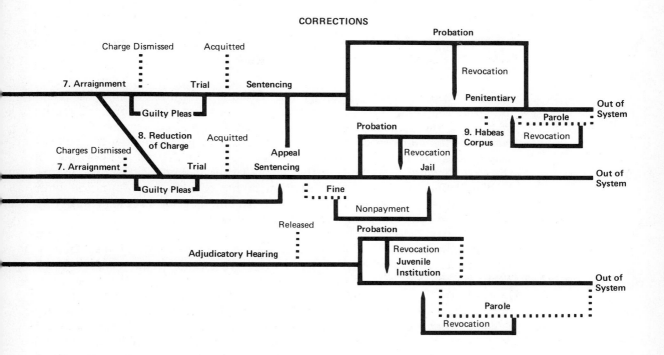

7. **Arraignment.** Appearance for plea; defendant elects trial by judge or jury (if available); counsel for indigent usually appointed here in felonies. Often not at all in other cases.

8. **Reduction of Charge.** Charge may be reduced at any time prior to trial in return for plea of guilty or for other reasons.

9. **Habeas Corpus.** Challenge on constitutional grounds to legality of detention. May be sought at any point in process.

10 **Police Juvenile Unit.** Police often hold informal hearings, dismiss or adjust many cases without further processing.

11. **Intake Hearing.** Probation officer decides desirability of further court action.

12. **Nonadjudicatory Disposition.** Welfare agency, social services, counselling, medical care, etc., for cases where adjudicatory handling not needed.

BAIL

A guarantee backed by security (cash, bond, or property pledged to court) that the accused will appear in court for trial as required.

If the case does not fall under the initial court's jurisdiction, the defendant has the right to request a *preliminary hearing*, to examine the merits of binding the case over to a higher court. The preliminary hearing gives both defense and prosecution the opportunity to gather evidence and witnesses and present them informally. It constitutes a sort of "preview" of the case for both sides and for the judge. To the defendant, the preliminary hearing offers an informal evaluation of his or her chances in the later trial. It is at this point that many defendants decide to plead guilty to their charge or to negotiate a plea to a lesser charge.[7]

The next step is the filing of a *formal criminal charge* in the court that will try the case. If a federal crime punishable by death, imprisonment, hard labor, or loss of civil or political privileges has been committed, the filing of charges may be preceded by another review of the facts by a grand jury. If the grand jury agrees there is probable cause that the offense has occurred and the defendant might have done it, a document is issued that constitutes the formal charging of the accused. This document is called an *indictment*. A defendant has a right to participate in the preliminary hearing but is not usually allowed to appear before the grand jury unless special permission is obtained.

The federal government permits the waiver of a grand jury in noncapital cases, and the grand jury has been used less and less in recent years (Watergate was one instance in which a grand jury was considered necessary.) If the grand jury inquiry is not required, the prosecutor simply files a document called an *information*, which contains the formal criminal charge. Many challenges are made in regard to this portion of the process. Some of the challenges must be made at this time, or they cannot be used as grounds for later appeal. In fact, the resolution of issues raised at this point—in regard to search and seizure, police interrogation techniques, and other questions as to the admissibility of evidence—may consume more court time than the actual trial does.

The next critical point is the *arraignment,* the offender's first formal appearance before the trial court. At this point the defendant is asked how he or she will plead. If the defendant chooses to stand mute, a plea of "not guilty" is entered automatically. It is when the defendant pleads guilty at this point (in about 90 percent of the cases) that the judge must be careful about procedural errors that might result in an appeal. The defendant who pleads guilty must understand the nature of the charges and the consequences of a guilty plea. The judge should have some basis for accepting the plea, usually evidence from the prosecutor that indicates or establishes guilt. Although there usually is little error on this last

---

GRAND JURY

A grand jury is a body of citizens selected from a local jurisdiction according to law and frequently totaling 23 or more persons. Their primary duties are to hear the initial evidence against the accused to determine if it were sufficient to charge the suspect and bring the accused to trial. Grand juries may also investigate criminal activity within their jurisdiction as well as the conduct and behavior of elected, appointed, and other officials and agencies.

If the grand jury decides the evidence is sufficient to charge, a formal document called an indictment is returned against the accused. (Prosecutors may also initiate a formal charge by issuing a bill of information.) The grand jury does not determine guilt, as the process is left to a *petit jury*.

---

point, probably because those who plead guilty seldom appeal, it is another legal basis for appeals.

The *trial*, so memorably dramatized on television and in the movies, appears to be the main target for the appellate procedure. It is the trial that best illustrates the impact of our adversary system[8] on the process of criminal justice. Grounds for appeal abound in the trial, from the selection of the jury to the finding of guilt or innocence. The burden of proof of guilt is on the prosecution throughout. Many defense motions[9] are made only to establish grounds for later efforts at appeal. After a determination of guilt or innocence, the trial is completed. The effect of most appeals is to require that a new trial be held—not to ensure an overturned conviction for the accused.

The last step in the court process is *sentencing* by the court. The judge usually prescribes the sentence, but the procedure can be done by a jury in some jurisdictions. In the case of a guilty plea, the sentencing usually follows the completion of a pretrial or presentencing investigation of the defendant, who has become the convicted offender. The sentencing process has not generated many appeal actions, probably because sentences are usually determined by specific statutes rather than by the judge's discretion. Excessive or cruel sentencing practices do come under appeal, however, and the indeterminate sentence has been attacked many times.

The Mechanics of an Appeal _____

Now that we have seen the points at which appealable errors are most likely to occur, the effects of some of the major cases, and the potential of future appeals, it is important to know how one makes an appeal following a criminal conviction. The process is highly fragmented and cumbersome, but there is a basic scheme that applies to most jurisdictions. Although there are many alternatives to this basic model, it covers most of the avenues for appeals.

Who Makes the Appeal?

The entire process stems, of course, from a conviction of guilt by some court system at the municipal, county, state, or federal level. In each case, the procedure for appeal is determined by the court of record for that case. These appeals, known as postconviction remedies, were not generally available until after the seventeenth century. They are usually made by the defendant. The state is unlikely to appeal a decision, regardless of the outcome: if the accused is convicted, that is the result the state was after, and if the accused is declared innocent, the state cannot appeal—the Constitution guarantees that someone who is found innocent cannot be placed in *double jeopardy* (subjected to a second trial). The effect of an appropriately introduced appeal is a stay in the execution of the original sentence until the appeal is decided. As soon as possible, if not immediately after the sentence is pronounced, the defendant's counsel must either move for a new trial or make an appeal on some reasonable grounds, as appellate courts usually make short work of "frivolous" appeals. But as long ago as 1933, the significance of the appeal process was firmly established:

Appellate courts ... do not reverse decisions simply because they disagree with them. Reversal must proceed from error of law and such error must be substantial. But if this account is to be veracious I must call attention to a

	STATE COURT SYSTEM	FEDERAL COURT SYSTEM
Level 4	COURT OF LAST RESORT "Supreme Court" "Court of Criminal Appeals" "Supreme Court of Appeals" "Supreme Judicial Court," etc.	COURT OF LAST RESORT U.S. Supreme Court
Level 3	INTERMEDIATE APPELLATE COURTS "Superior Court" "District Court of Appeals" "Appellate Court" "Supreme Court," etc.	INTERMEDIATE APPELLATE COURTS U.S. Courts of Appeals
Level 2	TRIAL COURTS (COURTS OF GENERAL JURISDICTION) "Circuit Court" "District Court" "State Court" "County Court," etc.	TRIAL COURTS U.S. District Courts
Level 1	LOWER COURTS (COURTS OF LIMITED JURISDICTION) "Municipal Court" "Justice of the Peace" "Small Claims Court" "Traffic Court" "Magistrate's Court," etc.	LOWER COURTS U.S. Magistrates and Specialized Courts

Figure 9-3 Parallels Between State Court Systems and the Federal Court System

The Rehnquist Court (Photo courtesy the United States Supreme Court Historical Society) (Warren Burger has been replaced by Antonin Scalia; Lewis Powell by Anthony Kennedy)

fact familiar to every experienced lawyer, yet not apparent in the classical literature of the law, and probably not consciously admitted even to themselves by most appellate judges. Practically every decision of a lower court *can* be reversed. By that I mean practically every record contains some erroneous rulings [and] they can nearly always find some error if they want grounds for reversal.[10]

Each state has an appellate tribunal that serves as the "court of last resort." The titles vary (as shown by Figure 9-3) but, no matter what the title, a pathway for appeal is open to all in the American judicial system.

The Courts of Appeal

Table 9.1 illustrates the court of appeal of each state, by level of jurisdiction. The level immediately above the trial court is usually called the *court of appeals*. In some states, and in the federal system, there is more than one level of appeal. In these cases, the highest level of appellate court is generally called the *supreme court*. The Supreme Court of the United States is the court of last resort; cases decided there are considered final. The U.S. Supreme Court will usually hear cases from the state

TABLE 9.1   Courts of Appeal by Level of Jurisdiction and Organization, by State

State	Courts of Last Resort	Courts of Intermediate Appeals
Alabama	Supreme court	Court of civil appeals
		Court of criminal appeals
Alaska	Supreme court	None
Arizona	Supreme court	Court of appeals (two departments)
Arkansas	Supreme court	None
California	Supreme court	Court of appeals (five districts)
Colorado	Supreme court	Court of appeals
Connecticut	Supreme court	None
Delaware	Supreme court	None
District of Columbia	Court of appeals	None
Florida	Supreme court	Court of appeals (four districts)
Georgia	Supreme court	Court of appeals
Hawaii	Supreme court	None
Idaho	Supreme court	None
Illinois	Supreme court	Appellate court (five districts)
Indiana	Supreme court	Court of appeals
Iowa	Supreme court	None
Kansas	Supreme court	None
Kentucky	Court of appeals	None
Louisiana	Supreme court	Court of appeals (four circuits)
Maine	Supreme judicial court	None
Maryland	Court of appeals	Court of special appeals
Massachusetts	Supreme judicial court	None
Michigan	Supreme court	Court of appeals
Minnesota	Supreme court	None
Mississippi	Supreme court	None
Missouri	Supreme court	Court of appeals (three districts)
Montana	Supreme court	None
Nebraska	Supreme court	None
Nevada	Supreme court	None
New Hampshire	Supreme court	None
New Jersey	Supreme court	Appellate division of superior court
New Mexico	Supreme court	Court of appeals
New York	Court of appeals	Appellate division of supreme court (four departments)
North Carolina	Supreme court	Court of appeals
North Dakota	Supreme court	None
Ohio	Supreme court	Court of appeals (eleven districts)
Oklahoma	Supreme court	
	Court of criminal appeals (three districts)	Court of appeals
Oregon	Supreme court	Court of appeals

TABLE 9.1   *Continued*

Pennsylvania	Supreme court	Superior court
		Commonwealth court
Rhode Island	Supreme court	None
South Carolina	Supreme court	None
South Dakota	Supreme court	None
Tennessee	Supreme court	Court of appeals
		Court of criminal appeals
Texas	Supreme court	Court of civil appeals
	Court of criminal appeals	(fourteen districts)
Utah	Supreme court	None
Vermont	Supreme court	None
Virginia	Supreme court of appeals	None
Washington	Supreme court	Court of appeals (three divisions)
West Virginia	Supreme court of appeals	None
Wisconsin	Supreme court	None
Wyoming	Supreme court	None

Source: National Survey of Court Organization (Washington, D.C.: U.S. Department of Justice, 1971), p. 4.

systems only after the defendant has exhausted all state remedies and the case has been finally adjudicated.

In most state systems, the court of appeals reviews the trial court's decisions for judicial error. The facts in the case are not in question, and the trial court's decisions on that aspect of the case are binding on the appellate court. Because of this aspect of appellate review, evidence on the facts of the case is not presented to the court of appeals; rather, the review is based on the trial record. An appellate court cannot reverse the factual findings of the trial court unless they are totally erroneous. In states that have a second level of review, the trial record and the intermediary court's decision are examined. Usually, the refusal to hear an appeal over a lower appellate court's ruling is the same as upholding the decision, and the case stops there, unless an appeal is filed separately in a federal court of appeals on some constitutional issue.

The federal court system currently includes ninety-four trial courts (federal district courts) and thirteen intermediary review courts (courts of appeal) between the state trial courts and the U.S. Supreme Court. The federal courts of appeal are spread across the country in "circuits" to facilitate servicing the ninety-four trial courts. Federal courts are restricted in their powers to

> . . . cases arising under the Constitution, federal laws, or treaties, all cases affecting ambassadors, public ministers, and consuls, admiralty and maritime cases, controversies where the United States is a party, controversies between states, between a state and a citizen of another state, between citizens of the same state claiming lands under grants from different states, and in cases between a state or citizens of a state and foreign states, citizens, or subjects.[11]

The federal courts of appeals are similar to the state courts of appeals in that they review for error the cases tried by the federal district courts:

> The Supreme Court is the ultimate interpreter of the Constitution and federal statutes. It reviews the decisions of the courts of appeals, and some direct appeals from district courts. The Supreme Court also reviews the decisions of state courts involving matters of federal constitutional rights where the case has been finally adjudicated in the state court system. Besides its appellate function, the Court has original jurisdiction in suits where a state is a party and in controversies involving ambassadors, ministers and consuls.[12]

Appeals from Behind the Walls

In the early twentieth century, most appeals were based on the issues in the trial. In the 1960s, appeals began to move toward issues related to individual rights under the U.S. Constitution.[13] Using the Fourteenth Amendment as a lever, the Supreme Court affirmed these rights to individuals in the separate states on a piecemeal basis. Under the "hands off" doctrine established by Chief Justice Felix Frankfurter, the Court had restricted its early decisions to the actions of judges. Later, abandoning the Frankfurter policy, the Court began to impose procedural guidelines on law enforcement, corrections, and every other element of the criminal justice system. Constitutional rights of prisoners (to be discussed in Part 4) were more sharply defined by the appellate courts' decisions. Many of these appeals came from desperate people behind prison walls, and these appeals increased 131% between 1973 and 1983.[14]

No prison is without its share of jailhouse lawyers, prisoners who have become familiar with the substance of the law and courtroom procedures from firsthand experience. In the days when the indigent (poor) suspect's right to an attorney—in court or in prison—had not been established, these jailhouse lawyers helped other inmates assemble cases for appellate review. With time on their hands and great personal interest in their causes, these inmates paved the way for appeals by the prisoners of today. Probably the most famous early appeal was that of Clarence Earl Gideon, an indigent prisoner in Florida's Raiford Prison:

> Gideon was a fifty-one-year-old white man who had been in and out of prisons much of his life. He had served time for four previous felonies, and he bore the physical marks of a destitute life: a wrinkled, prematurely aged face, a voice and hands that trembled, a frail body, white hair. He had never been a professional criminal or a man of violence; he just could not seem to settle down to work, and so he had made his way by gambling and occasional thefts. Those who had known him, even the men who had arrested him and those who were now his jailers, considered Gideon a perfectly harmless human

being, rather likeable, but one tossed aside by life. Anyone meeting him for
the first time would be likely to regard him as the most wretched of men.
And yet a flame still burned in Clarence Earl Gideon. He had not given up
caring about life or freedom; he had not lost his sense of injustice. Right
now he had a passionate—some thought almost irrational—feeling of having
been wronged by the state of Florida, and he had the determination to try
to do something about it.[15]

His petition, submitted to the U.S. Supreme Court, was done as a pauper
(in forma pauperis) under a special federal statute. This statute makes
great allowances for those unable to afford the expense of counsel and
unable to meet administrative technicalities. As an example, the court
usually requires forty typewritten copies of a petition; Gideon submitted
one, handwritten in pencil on lined yellow sheets.[16] Although Gideon did
not have counsel for his trial in 1961 when he was accused of breaking
into a pool hall, when his petition was heard before the Supreme Court
in the 1962–1963 term he was magnificently represented—for free. Abe
Fortas,[17] one of Washington's most successful lawyers, who later became
a Supreme Court justice, was appointed by the Court as Gideon's attorney
for this case. The Court's decision was unanimous (as opposed to an awkward five to four split,[18] which might have lessened its impact):

> In deciding as it did—that appointment of counsel is not a fundamental right,
> essential to a fair trial"—the Court in *Betts* . . . made an abrupt break with
> its own well-considered precedents. In returning to these old precedents, sounder
> we believe than the new, we but restore constitutional principles established
> to achieve a fair system of justice. Not only these precedents but also reason
> and reflection require us to recognize that in our adversary system of criminal
> justice, any person summoned into court, who is too poor to hire a lawyer,
> cannot be assured a fair trial unless counsel is provided for him.[19]

As if to emphasize the Court's finding, when Gideon was finally retried
with counsel, he was acquitted. Subsequently, in decision after decision
the Supreme Court has ruled in favor of the right to counsel at a "critical
stage" in the defendant's case. This "critical stage" has been extended from
the initial police contact to the preparation of a brief for appeal and even
for assistance in the preparation of transcripts of the trial. It is easy to
see how this case signaled an avalanche of appellate cases that has not
yet abated.

A flood of appeals made with the help of court-appointed lawyers filled
the dockets of the appeals courts in the 1960s. As rights were established
in the obvious areas outside prison walls (arrest, search and seizure, privacy and intrusion, cruel and unusual punishment), they were eventually
tested with regard to events inside the walls as well. The autonomous and
discretionary control over inmates was finally lifted, as the right to counsel
moved into the prison as well as the courtroom. A milestone case was

decided in the 1967–1968 Supreme Court term, when *Mempa* v. *Rhay*[20] extended the right to counsel to state probation revocation hearings, previously considered an essentially administrative action. The Court held that the application of a deferred sentence was a "critical point" in the proceeding.

The right to counsel for defendants both inside and outside the walls of America's prisons has strained the entire criminal justice system. As more and more aspects of the criminal justice system are challenged, often by court-appointed lawyers, the real problem becomes the need for a routine way to reduce the flow of frivolous cases into the system.

Breaking the Appellate Logjam

The criminal courts have been forced to become almost administrative in nature because of the overload of cases. Because as many as 90 percent of trial convictions are appealed, the review courts are equally inundated. (See Table 9.2 for the latest available data.) The National Advisory Commission on Criminal Justice Standards and Goals expended much effort in trying to find ways to reduce the court caseload. The first recommendations that were made included a number of alternatives.

Screening

One of the methods suggested was to place more stress on *screening*, as the guidelines for screening offenders vary greatly from jurisdiction to jurisdiction. To help in drawing up criteria for screening suspected offenders out of the process, the following suggestions were made by the commission:

An accused should be screened out of the criminal justice system if there is not a reasonable likelihood that the evidence admissible against him would

---

INMATE LITIGATION

Over the decade, in the States for which statistics are available, 379,000 civil appeals were filed compared with 296,000 criminal appeals. Criminal cases accounted for 43 to 46% of total appellate volume. Criminal appeals had composed only 10 to 15% of the total appeals until the 1960's, when a rapid increase in criminal filings occurred, probably because of the 1963 U.S. Supreme Court ruling in *Douglas* v. *California* that provided indigent defendants with counsel on appeal, as well as other Court decisions establishing "new rights" that could then be the basis of appeals.

Source: Thomas Marvel and Sue Lindgren *The Growth of Appeals* (Washington, D.C.: U.S. Department of Justice, 1985); p. 2.

TABLE 9.2 Percent Change in Appeals Filed, by State, 1973–1983

State	Total Appeals	Criminal Appeals	Civil Appeals
Alaska	305	914	91
Connecticut	265	454	227
Oregon	212	253	181
Hawaii	201	483	103
Montana	187	217	180
Florida	186	—	—
Kentucky	186	200	180
Minnesota	172	219	160
Michigan	167	157	180
Maine	161	39	343
Nevada	159	203	131
South Dakota	156	—	—
Alabama	156	137	182
Massachusetts	154	191	138
Arizona	145	273	70
New Hampshire	144	178	133
Texas	140	147	132
Louisiana	139	454	94
Vermont	137	170	126
Illinois	129	80	184
Utah	116	69	130
Rhode Island	110	41	135
Colorado	108	88	118
Kansas	108	214	81
Wyoming	103	196	74
Missouri	97	80	105
Washington	96.	148	74
Ohio	95	—	—
Pennsylvania	94	—	—
California	89	66	120
New York	87	—	—
New Mexico	86	50	111
Oklahoma	85	16	122
Idaho	72	125	53
Iowa	68	35	91
Nebraska	68	23	109
Delaware	67	81	59
New Jersey	62	72	55
Tennessee	62	48	74
Dist. of Columbia	57	40	80
Virginia	60	39	99
Maryland	53	52	55
Mississippi	38	51	31

Source: Thomas Marvel and Sue Lindgren, *The Growth of Appeals* (Washington, D.C.: U.S. Department of Justice, 1985), p. 2.

be sufficient to obtain a conviction and sustain it on appeal. In screening on this basis, the prosecutor should consider the value of a conviction in reducing future offenses, as well as the probability of conviction and affirmance of that conviction on appeal.

An accused should be screened out of the criminal justice system when the benefits to be derived from prosecution or diversion would be outweighed by the costs of such action.[21]

Narrowing the correctional funnel at this point would result in a great work load reduction throughout the rest of the criminal justice system.

Many of the lawsuits filed by inmates that allege violations of constitutional and civil rights are with merit, and much has been done to improve the quality of life in prison settings.[22] Yet there are undoubtedly many, perhaps a large proportion, of suits that are spurious and frivolous litigations. The American Correctional Association has suggested that such suits can be discouraged by the following actions:

- Having the incarcerated complainant pay fees to the court when cases are filed and resolved;
- Limiting the number of lawsuits an inmate may file annually;
- Requiring the complainant to certify that the claims being raised have not been adjudicated before; and
- Having the judiciary require that court permission be secured before filing additional claims.[23]

Diversion

Another effort in the drive to reduce the number of cases brought to trial is the *diversion* of offenders before conviction. Diversion is quite different from screening, as it assumes that the individual will participate in some treatment program in return for removal from the criminal justice process before trial. In screening, the individual is dropped out of the process before it really begins, with no threat of continued prosecution or promise of special programs for his or her cooperation. Diversion programs may be run by agencies within the criminal justice system or by private and public agencies entirely outside it. The primary benefit from both screening and diversion programs is their ability to offer services to offenders without placing the stigma of further criminalization on them. Overcriminalization, usually a result of too many antiquated laws remaining on the books, is one of the reasons that so many cases sit on dockets. The commission also suggested guidelines for when diversion should take place:

In appropriate cases offenders should be diverted into noncriminal programs before formal trial or conviction.

> Such diversion is appropriate where there is a substantial likelihood that conviction could be obtained and the benefits to society from channeling an offender into an available noncriminal diversion program outweigh any harm done to society by abandoning criminal prosecution.[24]

Diversion programs are another recognition of the situational nature of many crimes. By expanding the base of available services and keeping the offender out of the damaging stages of the criminal justice process, society gives the offender a much better chance to adjust in the community.

Where Are the Next Areas of Appeal? _____

As has been shown, the appellate system[25] has brought rights and reform to the criminal justice system, as a whole, and to the sector known as corrections, in particular. If the stone walls that surround our American fortress prisons cannot be torn down, then at least the basic rights available to those outside must be brought in. This process has only begun, but thanks to the efforts of inmates like Clarence Gideon, attorneys like Abe Fortas, and many other prisoners and lawyers, the courts are whittling down the dictatorial powers formerly held by prison administrators.

The basic rights granted to citizens under most of the constitutional amendments have been extended to the inmates in our prisons. In the years to come, the peripheral issues will be examined. Two of the most controversial issues will be the *right to treatment* and its corollary — the *right to refuse treatment*. These issues stem from the widespread use of the treatment model in most of our adult correctional systems. Lack of prison industries and enforced idleness have encouraged the development of treatment programs to fill time.[26] The long-term value of such programs is questionable at best, and they are coming under attack.

Following an interim decision in *Wyatt* v. *Stickney*,[27] in which the United States District Court held that the states had to provide adequate treatment for patients involuntarily confined in mental institutions, the United States Supreme Court also ruled on this issue in *O'Connor* v. *Donaldson*.[28] The decision in this case leaves little question that civilly committed mentally ill persons have a right to treatment. The Court stated that every person has a constitutional right to liberty. It also concluded that

> A state cannot constitutionally confine . . . a nondangerous individual who is capable of surviving safely in freedom by himself or with the help of willing and responsible family members or friends. Since the jury found, upon ample evidence, that O'Connor, as an agent of the State, knowingly did so confine Donaldson, it properly concluded that O'Connor violated Donaldson's constitutional right to freedom.[29]

Because the justification for the indefinite commitment of mentally disturbed offenders (that is, the "incompetent to stand trial," the "not guilty by reason of insanity," and, by some court interpretations, those adjudicated psychopathic offenders) is a need for treatment,[30] the right might easily be extended to this class of residents of mental health institutions.

As in the right to treatment for the mentally ill, cases supporting the right to rehabilitation have been argued on both statutory and constitutional grounds. For instance, if state statutes clearly define the purpose of confinement as rehabilitation, the major responsibility of the administering organization could easily be conceived of as providing rehabilitation opportunities. A number of states include in their criminal codes some reference to the rehabilitative goals of incarceration. Ohio, for example, even changed the name of its state department responsible for incarcerating offenders to the Department of Rehabilitation and Correction. Although these statutes state rehabilitative purposes, the enforcement of rights based on these statutes has been delayed because societal values emphasize other goals and because corrections appears to lack knowledge of proven rehabilitative methods.

Arguments for a constitutional right to treatment derived from the Eighth Amendment prohibition of cruel and unusual punishment were made applicable to state actions in 1962.[31] Since that time, federal courts have increasingly intervened in prison administration, making decisions on the right-to-treatment issue. Some decisions uphold the view that governmental entities have no constitutional duty to rehabilitate prisoners.[32] Others withhold constitutional affirmation of the right to rehabilitation but conclude that the absence of rehabilitation programs, in conjunction with other prison conditions, may result in the definition of a specific prison's setting as cruel and unusual punishment.

The courts have yet to define specifically a right to rehabilitation, but many feel that the constitutional identification is inevitable, if not imminent. The right to treatment for the mentally ill has progressed slowly through the courts. The impediment of defensive and punitive public opinion has delayed implementation of the humanitarian philosophy of a right to treatment for prisoners, but this right should not be ignored. The indications are numerous and strong that the time for such recognition is near and that collateral consequences will be substantial. In addition to the signs from the judiciary, a Harris poll conducted in 1981 reported that 49 percent of Americans felt the main emphasis in prisons should be on rehabilitation,[33] and 59 percent of a sample of Seattle citizens believed the goal of punishment should be rehabilitation.[34] Practitioners in the field of corrections thus would do well to anticipate and prepare for the likely effects of this new emphasis.

Obviously, the resolution of this problem could decide whether the future of corrections lies in real correction efforts or a return to old-fashioned imprisonment. Unless some highly effective treatments for criminal behavior are found, backed by solid evaluation, the treatment programs are in serious trouble.

A final area of future appeals will relate to treatment programs directed at an offender's motivation, rather than the specific actions that brought him or her to prison. One such program involves *behavior modification.* In a 1973 case, *Mackey* v. *Procunier,*[35] the Ninth Circuit Court raised the issue of "impermissible tinkering with the mental processes." Later the same year, in the case of *Kaimowitz* v. *Michigan Department of Mental Health*[36] (which pertained to lobotomy operations), such tinkering was labeled a violation of the First Amendment by the Michigan Circuit Court.

Appeals will continue until inmates behind prison walls are granted the same constitutionally guaranteed protections accorded to their counterparts in the free world, except those obviously denied by incarceration such as the right to privacy, to choose one's associates, and freedom of movement.[37] When appeals do fail; however, convicted and sentenced offenders must pay a debt to society in the correctional process—the subject of the next part of this text.

The Aging Court

The last half of the 1980s has seen major changes in the makeup of the Supreme Court. As shown by the data in Table 9.3, the average age of the Supreme Court members was sixty-seven, with the relatively junior members (Scalia and Kennedy) figured in, and some will soon retire. This will continue to change the complexion of the Court as the older members retire or die. As the Court's attitudes continue to match the "get tough" public attitudes of the late 1980s, the liberal complexion of the Warren Court will move more toward the conservative side of the scale. The Court is usually a decade behind the public in its decisions, a factor that tends

TABLE 9.3   The Aging Supreme Court

Justice	Year of Birth	Age (1988)
William J. Brennan, Jr.	1906	82
Byron R. White	1917	71
Thurgood Marshall	1908	80
Harry A. Blackmun	1908	80
William H. Rehnquist	1924	64
John Paul Stevens	1920	68
Sandra Day O'Connor	1930	58
Antonin Scalia	1936	52
Anthony M. Kennedy	1936	52
	Average Age	67

to do away with short and erratic swings in the trend of its decisions. It will no doubt be a long time before the sweeping changes of the 1950s and 1960s can be reversed, but it seems clear that the pendulum has begun to swing back to the right.

Perhaps the most significant change in recent years was the appointment of the first female jurist to the highest court in the United States. On September 21, 1981, the Senate unanimously confirmed Sandra Day O'Connor, an Arizona State Court of Appeals judge, as an associate justice of the Supreme Court. But it is more important to note the conservative orientation of Justice O'Connor and not to focus on the fact that she is a female jurist in what had been the exclusive domain of the "Brotherhood." Time will tell if other highly qualified minorities will be appointed to the aging Court.

The mere cost of judicial action will also begin to have an impact in the next few years. The seemingly bottomless pit of funds for all kinds of services for inmates and others in the criminal justice system has begun to find a bottom in times of economic stress. The Court's short-term movement may not be affected by the economics of justice, but the long term may see a reexamination of some of the so-called rights provided by public funds. This will be the challenge of the next decade: to preserve rights and still find ways to fund them.

Summary

As the decade of the 1980s draws to a close, the aging of the United States Supreme Court figures directly into the future of corrections in America. The strong showing of President Reagan's conservative campaign in 1984 presaged a shift to the right in the makeup of the Court. Three sitting justices are into their eighties, and the replacements selected by Reagan have begun to swing the Court back to a law-and-order conservatism. Indeed, the spate of 5-to-4 decisions over the past years seems to indicate a delicate balance in the Court which, with just one or two appointments, may shift further in direction. Of course, the sweeping decisions of the 1950s and 1960s will not be reversed in a wholesale manner, but there seems to be a hardening of some conservative attitudes in America and the pendulum of public opinion seems to be moving to the right. Recently, the Court has also recognized the need to modernize its procedures in order to break through the logjam of appeals that has brought a portion of the judicial process almost to a halt. Proposals have been made to speed up the review of the death penalty appeals, and to refuse to review more and more "frivolous" appeals. The changes that the Court decides upon will have a direct effect on the corrections field, and they are a matter for a close scrutiny by the students and serious professionals in that field.

Review Questions ——————————————————————————————

1. Explain the difference between a court of appeals and a supreme court.
2. Who was Clarence Gideon? Explain the actions he took to make his appeal.
3. Why is there such a logjam in the appellate system? What are some suggestions for easing the pressure?
4. What rights does an inmate have? What rights does he or she not have?
5. Explain why the rights of inmates began to be extensively defined since the 1960s.
6. What are appeals and what options are available to appeal courts when a decision is made?
7. What might be done to cut down on frivolous appeals?

Key Terms ——————————————————————————————————

1. **due process (p. 164)**
2. **affirm (p. 166)**
3. **modify (p. 166)**
4. **reverse (p. 166)**
5. **remand (p. 166)**
6. **recognizance (p. 167)**
7. **initial appearance (p. 167)**
8. **preliminary appearance (p. 170)**
9. **indictment (p. 170)**
10. **grand jury (p. 171)**
11. **court of last resort (p. 172)**
12. **double jeopardy (p. 172)**
13. *Gideon* **-vs-** *Wainwright* **(p. 176)**
14. **screening (p. 179)**
15. **diversion (p. 180)**

Notes ————————————————————————————————————

1. For an excellent discussion of the amount of process due offenders, see John Conrad, "The Rights of Wrongdoers," *Criminal Justice Research Bulletin* 3 (1987).
2. National Advisory Commission on Criminal Justice Standards and Goals, *Courts* (Washington, D.C.: U.S. Government Printing Office, 1973), p. 113. For an excellent review of legal trends and issues in corrections, see Rolando del Carmen, "Legal Issues and Liabilities in Community Corrections," paper presented at the annual meeting of the Academy of Criminal Justice Sciences, Chicago, 1984. See also William C. Collins, *Correctional Law* 1986 (Olympia, Wash.: Collins, 1986).
3. While the number of criminal trials in the United States increased relatively little from 1973–1983, the number of appeals increased 107 percent. See also Daniel Gillis, *The Federal Civil Justice System.* (Washington, D.C.: U.S. Department of Justice, 1987).
4. National Advisory Commission, *Courts*, p. 113.
5. This is what is generally called the right to habeas corpus.
6. See Chris Eskridge, *Pretrial Release Programming* (New York: Clark Boardman, 1983), pp. 33–59.
7. This is a classic example of plea bargaining (see Chapter 7). See also Terance Miethe, "Charging and Plea Bargaining Practices Under Determinate Sentenc-

ing: An Investigation of the Hydraulic Effect of Discretion." *Journal of Criminal Law and Criminology* 78 (1987): 155–176.

8. The adversary system refers to the battle between the prosecution and defense attorneys during a trial when each cross-examines and attacks the witnesses and facts presented by the other. See Gary Goodpaster, "On the Theory of American Adversary Criminal Trial," *Journal of Criminal Law and Criminology* 78 (1987); 118–154. See also Stephen Schulhofer, "The Future of the Adversary System," *Justice Quarterly* 3 (1986): 83–93.

9. Such motions usually concern the admissibility of evidence and are aimed to suppress the presentation of evidence that might hurt the defense attorney's case.

10. Joseph N. Ulman, *The Judge Takes the Stand* (New York: Knopf, 1933), pp. 265–266.

11. U.S. Constitution, Article III, Section 2.

12. John Palmer, *Constitutional Rights for Prisoners* (Cincinnati, Ohio: Anderson, 1973), p. 10.

13. Thomas Marvel and Sue Lindgren, *The Growth of Appeals* (Washington, D.C.: U.S. Department of Justice, 1985): p. 2.

14. Ibid., p. 3. See also Samuel Jan Braken, "Prison Reform Litigation: Has the Revolution Gone Too Far?" *Corrections Today* 49 (1987): 160–168.

15. Anthony Lewis, *Gideon's Trumpet* (New York: Vintage Books, 1966), pp. 5–6.

16. Ibid, p. 4.

17. Abe Fortas (1910–1982) was Lyndon Johnson's first appointee to the Supreme Court, on July 29, 1965. A close adviser to President Johnson, he represented "Bobby" Baker in the scandal over Baker's business activities. Fortas left the Supreme Court in 1969.

18. For a discussion of the effects of a "close vote," see Craig Fischer, "Supreme Court, Short a Justice, Takes Up Criminal Law Issues," *Criminal Justice Newsletter* 18 (November 2, 1987): 2–4.

19. Editors, *The Criminal Law Reporter, The Criminal Law Revolution and Its Aftermath 1960–1971* (Washington, D.C.: BNA Books, 1972), p. 25.

20. *Mempa* v. *Rhay,* 389 U.S. 128, 2d Cir. 3023 (1968). A petitioner filed a habeas corpus claiming a denial of the right to counsel at the probation revocation and sentencing proceedings. The Supreme Court of the State of Washington denied the petition. The U.S. Supreme Court reversed the previous decision, asserting the necessity that counsel be present at such a hearing.

21. National Advisory Commission, *Courts,* p. 20.

22. Steven Nay, "Constitutional Compliance: Avoiding Inmate Litigation," *Corrections Today* 49 (1987): 186–191. See also Jim Thomas, Devin Keeler, and Kathy Harris, "Issues and Misconceptions in Prisoner Litigation: A Critical View," *Criminology* 24 (1986): 775–797.

23. Debra Anderson, *Curbing the Abuses of Inmate Litigation* (College Park, Md.: American Correctional Association, 1987).

24. National Advisory Commission *Courts,* p. 32.

25. Peter Brimelow, "Judicial Imperialism," *Forbes* (June 1, 1987): 109–112.

26. Under a consent decree, South Carolina has agreed to establish full-time programming for general population inmates in its 28 institutions, as well as for those in protective custody. See Nay, "Institutional Compliance," p. 190.

27. *Wyatt* v. *Stickney,* 325 F. Supp. 781 (M.D. Ala. 1971), 344 F. Supp. 373, and 374 F. Supp. 387 (1972). See also *Wyatt* v. *Aderholt,* 503 F. 2d 1305 (1974).
28. *O'Connor* v. *Donaldson,* 43 L.W. 4929 (1975).
29. *O'Connor* v. *Donaldson* at 4933.
30. Issues over inadequate mental health and medical service abound, and court orders in these areas are frequent. See, in particular, *Cody* v. *Hillard,* 599 F. Supp. 1015 (D.S.D. 1984), and the consent decree of 1985 for *Ruiz* v. *Estelle* 670 F.2d 1115 (1982).
31. *Robinson* v. *California,* 370 U.S. 660 (1962).
32. See *McLaramore* v. *State,* 257 S.C. 413 (1972).
33. Reported in U.S. Department of Justice, *Sourcebook of Criminal Justice Statistics, 1981,* (Washington, D.C.: U.S. Government Printing Office, 1982), p. 208.
34. Mark Warr and Mark Stafford, "Public Goals of Punishment and Support for the Death Penalty," *Journal of Research in Crime and Delinquency* 21 (1984): 95–111.
35. *Mackey* v. *Procunier,* 477 F. 2d (9th Circuit, 1973).
36. *Kaimowitz* v. *Michigan Department of Mental Health*, 42 U.S. L.W. 2063 (Michigan Cir. Ct., 1973).
37. Conrad, p. 3.

Recommended Readings _____

Blumstein, Alfred, Jacqueline Cohen, Jeffery Roth, and Christy Visher. *Criminal Careers and "Career Criminals"* (Washington, D.C.: National Academy Press, 1986).

Dennis, Anthony. "Fifth Amendment: Due Process Rights At Sentencing," *Journal of Criminal Law and Criminology* 77 (1986): 646–665.

Ennis, Phillip. *Criminal Victimization in the United States: A Report of a National Survey.* Washington, D.C.: U.S. Government Printing Office, 1967.

Eskridge, Chris W. *Pretrial Release Programming: Issues and Trends* (New York: Clark Boardman, 1983).

Fairchild, Erika, and V. J. Webb. *The Politics of Crime and Criminal Justice* (Beverly Hills, Calif.: Sage, 1985.).

Early, Barbara and Stephen Early. *Prisoners' Rights in America* (Chicago: Nelson Hall, 1986).

Kobayashi, Glenn. "Fourteenth Amendment: Reexamining Judicial Vindictiveness." *Journal of Criminal Law and Criminology* 77 (1986): 867–893.

Morris, Norval, and Gordon Hawkins. *The Honest Politician's Guide to Crime Control.* Chicago: University of Chicago Press, 1970.

National Advisory Commission on Criminal Justice Standards and Goals. *Courts.* Washington, D.C.: U.S. Department of Justice, 1973.

Packer, Herbert L. *The Limits of the Criminal Sanction.* Stanford, Calif.: Stanford University Press, 1968.

Pastroff, Sanford. "Eighth Amendment: The Constitutional Rights of the Insane on Death Row." *Journal of Criminal Law and Criminology* 77 (1986): 844–866.

Petersilia, Joan. *The Influence of Criminal Justice Research* (Santa Monica, Calif.: Rand Corporation, 1987).

Shover, Neal. *Aging Criminals* (Beverly Hills, Calif.: Sage, 1985).

PART III

The Correctional Process

CHAPTER
10

Probation and Intermediate Punishments

Humane treatment may raise up one in whom the
divine image has long been obscured. It is with
the unfortunate, above all, that humane conduct
is necessary.
—DOSTOEVSKI

The Sanctuary and Suspended Sentence

Following a determination of guilt, the courts have a number of options
for dealing with the offender. These include fines, probation, house arrest,
restitution, community work orders, incarceration in jail, shock probation,
imprisonment in state penal facilities, halfway house treatment, or combination of many of these. In recent times, the option most often selected
is probation; approximately 60 percent of convicted felons are placed on
probation in a given year, yielding a probation rate of 1,178 per 100,000
adults in the United States (1987). There were 1,968,712 adults on probation in 1986, over 65 percent of those adults under correctional supervision.[1]

Probation is a derivative of the suspended sentence, handed down to us
somewhat indirectly by way of past judicial procedures. Both the suspended
sentence and probation mitigate the punishment for an offender through
a judicial procedure, and their earliest antecedent is found in the *right of
sanctuary*,[2] frequently cited in the Bible. In many cultures, holy places
and certain cities were traditionally set aside as places for sanctuary.

The right of sanctuary was written into Mosaic law.[3] To escape the blood
vengeance of a victim's family, a killer could go to certain specified cities
and find refuge. During the Middle Ages, many churches were able to
offer sanctuary for those hiding from harsh secular law. The practice of
sanctuary disappeared in England in the seventeenth century and was
replaced with *benefit of clergy*. This practice, originally reserved for clerics,
was eventually extended to those who could pass the Psalm 51 test—a

> **PROBATION**
>
> A sentence not involving confinement that imposes conditions. The sentencing court retains authority to supervise, modify the conditions, and resentence the offender if conditions are violated.
>
> Probation is increasingly being linked with a short sentence to jail, followed by a period of probation. In California (1986), such a sentence combination was the dominant sentence for felony offenders.

test of the offender's ability to read the verse that begins "Have mercy upon me." The result was a form of suspended sentence that allowed the offender to move about in society.

The suspended sentence differs from probation, though the terms are sometimes used interchangeably. The suspended sentence does not require supervision and usually does not prescribe a specified set of goals for the offender to work toward. It is merely a form of quasi-freedom that can be revoked, with a prison sentence imposed at the instruction of the court. Sentence can be suspended in two ways:

1. The sentence is imposed, but its execution is suspended.
2. Both the imposition and execution of the sentence are suspended.

Of these two, the second is the more desirable because of the reduced stigma. However, the practice of suspending sentences, like sanctuary, has generally been replaced in America with supervised probation. Sentences may be vacated by the sentencing judge, and the offender may be placed at liberty in the community, but this is a relatively infrequent occurrence.

Under the European model of suspended sentence, or *sursis* (surcease), the offender has satisfactorily fulfilled the conditions if no further offense is committed during the period established. Little control or supervision is provided, with the result that most offenders with suspended sentences are denied the specialized or therapeutic services needed to prevent further criminal involvement.[4]

> **STIGMA**
>
> A mark of shame and disgrace assigned to an offender by virtue of his or her having committed the offense or conviction. Stigma also means the person is disvalued (from a previous status), and the social reaction is generally to avoid, punish, or isolate the disvalued person. Societal reaction is believed to create additional difficulties for ex-offenders who desire to become nonoffenders or to "go straight."

The History of Probation _____

Probation has undergone a number of changes since its first informal beginnings in the nineteenth century. Let us take a brief look at just how this concept was born.

The Birth of Probation

John Augustus,[5] a Boston shoemaker, is credited with being the "father" of probation. He liked to spend his spare moments observing what transpired in the courts, and he was disturbed by the fact that common drunks were often forced to remain in jail because they had no money with which to pay their fines. He convinced the authorities to allow him to pay their fines and offered them friendly supervision. Between 1841 and 1858 he bailed out almost two thousand men, women, and children. He was sharply criticized for his "strange" ideas, which were described by criminologist Sheldon Glueck:[6]

> His method was to bail the offender after conviction, to utilize this favor as an entering wedge to the convict's confidence and friendship, and through such evidence of friendliness as helping the offender to obtain a job and aiding his family in various ways, to drive the wedge home. When the defendant was later brought into court for sentence, Augustus would report on his progress toward reformation, and the judge would usually fine the convict one cent and costs, instead of committing him to an institution.[7]

Augustus's efforts encouraged his home state of Massachusetts to pass the first probation statute in 1878. Four more states had followed suit by 1900.[8] Probation was established as a legitimate alternative to incarceration, and a strong impetus to employ it came with the creation of the first juvenile court in 1899:[9] the need to supervise young offenders and keep them out of adult prisons.

John Augustus (1785–1859). Augustus, the "father of probation," was a Boston shoemaker interested particularly in the temperance crusade in the 1840s. As a member of the Washington Total Abstinence Society, he worked at getting men to give up alcohol. Part of his voluntary service in Boston was to visit courts and request temporary suspensions or postponements of sentence for those whom he judged were ready to quit liquor. During the next brief few weeks, Augustus would work with the bailed person, and return to court to encourage a fine (usually one penny and court costs) for the men he felt would remain sober and law abiding. He bailed almost 2,000 men, women and children and, of the first 1,100, only one forfeited a bond. He died almost penniless, after having established a new way of dealing with offenders: probation.

The Spread of Probation

Juvenile probation service developed with the growing movement for juvenile courts. By 1910, thirty-seven states and the District of Columbia had passed a children's court act, and forty had established some kind of probation service for juveniles. Every state had enacted juvenile probation service in some measure by 1927, as the practice became firmly entrenched.

Not until 1956, however, was probation available for adult offenders in every state. The variations in the organization and operation of probation services make it difficult to compare them by state, but the growth in the number of registered probation officers attests to the rapid acceptance of this area of corrections. In 1907, the first directory of probation officers identified 795 volunteers, welfare workers, court personnel, and part-time personnel serving as officers. Most of these were in the juvenile system. By 1937 the figure had grown to over 3,800, of which 80 percent were in full-time service. By 1970, probation and parole officers were listed together and numbered over 25,000. In 1976, 1,929 agencies reported adult probation services as one of their functions, with a total of 923,064 clients being supervised through an average client caseload of 107 probationers (see Figure 10-1 for 1985 data). Probation is seen as one of the brightest hopes in the field of corrections, and the number of probation officers continues to grow.

What Is Probation Today?

Probation, often confused with the suspended sentence, is actually a form of sentence in itself. The American Bar Association defines probation as

a sentence not involving confinement which imposes conditions and retains authority in the sentencing court to modify the conditions of sentence or to resentence the offender if he [or she] violates the conditions. Such a sentence should not involve or require suspension of the imposition or execution of any other sentence.... A sentence to probation should be treated as a final judgment for purposes of appeal and similar procedural purposes.[10]

TABLE 10.1 **Percent of Adult Population Under Correctional Control (January 1, 1986)**

	Correctional Population	Percent Adults in Nation
Probation	1,870,132	1.06%
Jail	254,094	.14
Prison	503,315	.29
Parole	277,438	.16
Total	2,904,979	1.65%

Source: Lawrence Greenfield, *Probation and Parole* 1986 (Washington, D.C.: U.S. Department of Justice, 1987); p. 4.

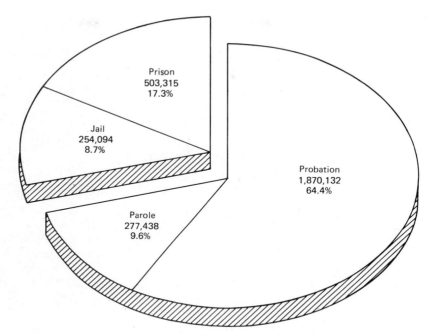

Figure 10-1 Adults Under Correctional Supervision, January 1, 1986 (Lawrence Greenfield, *Probation and Parole, 1985* [Washington, D.C.: U.S. Department of Justice, 1987]

Across the nation, probation is administered by hundreds of separate agencies, with a wide variety of rules and structures within the states. Whereas one agency may be required to serve juvenile, misdemeanant, and felony offenders, another agency may handle only one type of offender. The term *probation* has multiple meanings within the multiple areas of corrections.

As a *disposition*, probation was first seen as a new type of suspended sentence. If convicted offenders could meet certain conditions established by the court, they were allowed to remain in their communities under limited freedom. These conditions vary greatly from jurisdiction to jurisdiction and judge to judge, but they usually include prohibitions regarding drinking, travel, association with undesirable persons, restitution, community work orders, house arrest, electronic monitoring, and intensively supervised probation. These are discussed below. Currently, probation is a sentence in its own right.

As a *status*, probation has many advantages for offenders. Although their freedom is somewhat limited, their status is considered better than that of confined offenders. They are neither completely free nor totally restricted; they can work, keep their families off welfare, avoid the stigma of incarceration, and make restitution to their victims.

Some People Think Probation Is Too "Soft" on Criminals . . . Others Feel It Is the Only Hope for the Future (Courtesy of American Correctional Association)

As a *subsystem* of the criminal justice system, probation has many different structures and organizations. In this context, it refers to the administrative agency that offers the probation service to juvenile or adult offenders.

The set of functions, activities, and services that probation performs for its administrative agency and the offender is the probation *process*. The process model for probation service is usually seen as a series of interlinking activities among the courts, the offender, and the offender's community and its resources. The process includes the offender's *reporting* regularly to a probation officer; the *servicing* of the offender's needs through treatment, counseling, and so on; and the officer's *supervision* of the probationer to ensure that the rules of the probation order are observed.

Hence, probation today is a process that gives the judge an alternative disposition, which results in an improved status for the offender within a subsystem of the criminal justice system.

Organization and Administration

The problems associated with a lack of organization in the criminal justice system are exemplified in probation services. Under the original concept, the judges themselves were to administer the probation services.

For small jurisdictions this may still be the case in some instances, and these judges may be the best-informed decision makers in the criminal justice system. Most states, however, administer probation through a wide range of organizational and operational systems that are often unresponsive to one another's goals or efforts. The most common plan offers probation service at the state level.[11] Even in those states that have attempted to form a state-administered probation system,[12] county participation has sometimes been maintained at the discretion of local officials. This concept of local autonomy is an American tradition, but it has hampered efforts to develop integrated probation services on a state-wide basis.

Although the issue of state versus local probation administration is controversial, the state system does have some advantages:

> A state-administered system can more easily organize around the needs of a particular locality or region without having to consider local political impediments. It also can recommend new programs and implement them without requiring additional approval by local political bodies.
>
> A state-administered system provides greater assurance that goals and objectives can be met and that uniform policies and procedures can be developed. Also, more efficiency in the disposition of resources is assured because all staff members are state employees and a larger agency can make more flexible use of manpower, funds, and other resources.[13]

Some state administrators have tried to encourage local probation systems to comply with state standards, by assisting them with either personnel or subsidies. In Michigan, for example, parole officers on the state payroll are assigned to work alongside local officers. In New York, where local communities are reimbursed up to 50 percent of probation service costs if they meet state standards, the number of probation officers in-

---

PROBATION SUBSIDY

A probation subsidy is a program run by a state. The subsidy provides money to counties and local jurisdictions for *not* committing offenders to prisons. The intents of subsidies are to bolster local probation services, encourage expansion of probation services, develop innovative probation strategies, and lessen the prison overcrowding problem.

Probation subsidies originated in California and, for a period before the resurgence of neoclassical ideology forced sharp changes in an otherwise enlightened environment, reduced the proportion of felon offenders sentenced to California penal institutions. Increasing probation service strength also saved the California prison system millions of dollars in the interim. Coupled with intermediate punishments, particularly intensive supervised probation, such subsidies could form the backbone of a correctional reform in many states suffering from prison overcrowding.

creased by over 28 percent from 1965 to 1972.[14] Washington and California adopted a novel and promising approach:

> These states attempt to resolve a problem that is inherent when probation is a local function; namely, that financing probation is a local responsibility. However, when juveniles or adults are sent to correctional institutions, these are usually administered and financed by the state. A consequence often is the shifting of financial responsibility from the local government to the state government by sentences of incarceration rather than probation.
>
> California and Washington have developed probation subsidy programs in which counties are reimbursed in proportion to the number of individuals that remain in the community rather than being sent to state institutions. The subsidy program in California was developed as a result of a study that indicated that some individuals eligible for commitment to state correctional institutions could safely be retained on probation and that with good probation supervision, they could make a satisfactory adjustment. It was estimated that at least 25 percent of the new admissions to state correctional institutions could remain in the community with good probation supervision.
>
> The state of Washington has had a similar experience with the probation subsidy program begun in January 1970. Its purpose was to reduce the number of commitments to institutions from county juvenile courts. In the two years the program has been in operation, there has been a marked reduction in the number of children and youth sent to state institutions.[15]

The means of administering probation programs are as varied as the types of organizations. Many are administered by judges, some by social workers, and a few by persons trained in public administration. In some states (such as Florida), the Salvation Army provides presentence investigation services, as well as probation case supervision for select offenders. The need for public administration training for probation personnel has been expressed in at least two major studies.[16] Because the methods of most probation officers reflect the background and training of their administrators, there is little uniformity in approaches. Different perspectives at different levels within the same agency can result in poorly defined goals

---

NEGATIVE SUBSIDY

In addition to the policy option of subsidizing probation services in counties that commit fewer than expected offenders to prison every year, or for meeting state requirements and standards, some states have decided that certain types of offenders ought to be kept in their local community under probation control. To encourage such retention, Oregon charges each county $3,000 for every committed offender whose crime falls in the "least severe" category. This means that a check for $3,000 must accompany the commitment papers when the least risky case offender is transported to prison. This is a "negative" subsidy, designed to encourage local communities to accept responsibility for providing correctional care and control for their own residents.

and policies within the organization. The deeply rooted tradition of placing and keeping probation under court supervision, combined with rapid expansion of services, has undermined those agencies' effectiveness. This problem is especially critical in states that have not made an effort to train their administrators, especially at the executive and middle-management levels. Training probation officers in the field is a highly commendable goal, but change must begin at the management level to ensure maximum benefit from the officers' increased skills.[17]

Probation Services _____

The average probation officer suffers from the problem of serving two masters. The officer is usually required to meet with probationers to discuss their progress and troubles (casework)[18] and to give the court their reports and recommendations. The idea that the probation officer must often act as a social worker has had a profound effect on the development of probation services. Earlier, overemphasis on casework and the medical model of the probation officer as a "therapist" resulted in a narrow focus on the relationship between probationer and officer. As a result, many officers overlooked the social factors that might have contributed to the offender's criminal behavior, such as poverty, unemployment, poor housing, racism, poor health, and lack of education. The undesirability of the casework emphasis was expressed in a report by the National Advisory Commission on Criminal Justice Standards and Goals:

CASEWORK

Casework generally refers to the social-work model of offering services to the client based on an analysis of the case, diagnosis of client needs and problems, and designing a treatment plan to rehabilitate the offender. This approach reflects a "medical model" of corrections that raises the two questions of "Who are offenders and what shall we do with them?" The answers are: "They are sick, and corrections should heal them and make them well."

Faced with the realities that most federal probation officers are not well prepared to provide casework and that most clients do not require this approach, the Federal Probation Service has shifted emphases to a Community Resource Management Team model. Basically, this approach argues that the offender should be reintegrated in the community, using existing community resources. Team members, usually specializing in one aspect of client needs (such as employment, drug abuse problems, emotional counseling), serve as "brokers," referring clients to local facilities and services. This team approach is believed to be a more effective reintegration approach than an officer would provide through conducting classical casework therapy.

The social task in corrections seems to call for social workers rather than for caseworkers or group workers. All social workers in corrections work with individuals, groups, and communities, with less emphasis on the use of one method than is characteristic of many social work jobs.[19]

One inherent drawback in the casework model is the likelihood that the officer will try to exceed the limited function assigned to probation. Placing probationers in foster homes, operating shelters for them, and attempting to deal with such extreme problems as alcoholism, drug addiction, and mental illness should properly be the concern of the appropriate community agency, not the probation officer. Probation officers do not usually have the background required to handle all the problems of their probationers. But probation officers are expected to account for their probationers if they get into trouble again. One of the first questions asked by the court in this circumstance is usually "When did you last see your client?" In a system that demands accountability of this kind, probation officers often over-extend themselves in an effort to prevent or justify their clients' failure.

Large caseloads have been the probation officer's most common excuse for failure and a traditional reason for expanding probation staffs. A standard load of fifty cases per officer was considered desirable as early as 1917, but no research was conducted to validate whether this figure was achieved. The San Francisco Project,[20] a 1969 study of the relationship between recidivism and probation caseloads, shattered many of these long-held beliefs:

> Four levels of workloads were established: (1) ideal (50 cases); (2) intensive (25, i.e., half the ideal); (3) normal (100, twice the ideal); and (4) minimum supervision (with a ceiling of 250 cases). Persons in minimum supervision caseloads were required only to submit a monthly written report; no contacts occurred except when requested by the probationer. It was found that offenders in minimum caseloads performed as well as those under normal supervision. The minimum and ideal caseloads had almost identical violation rates. In the intensive caseloads, the violation rate did not decline, but technical violations increased.
>
> The study indicated that the number of contacts between probationer and staff appeared to have little relationship to success or failure on probation. The conclusion was that the concept of a caseload is meaningless without some type of classification and matching of offender type, service to be offered, and staff.[21]

A probation officer supervised an average of 104 probationers in 1986. The concept of an optimum, or ideal, caseload (such as thirty-five cases) is handy when calculating rough estimates of resources. The danger is that these figures seem to translate into the "standard" caseload that each officer should carry, even though different probationers require different kinds and degrees of service. A frequent response to the pressures resulting

Probation Counseling Helps Judicial Decisions (Courtesy of American Correctional Association)

from these highly mixed caseloads is the establishment of a standardized procedure for all cases, regardless of their complexity. A broad system of different treatments, assigning specific kinds of cases to specific types of probation officers, is a crucial need. Methods of providing the probation service are undergoing rapid change.

Restrictions and Conditions _____

Restrictions on and conditions of probation are usually a result of statutory requirements and the opinion of the sentencing court regarding the offender. Most states have a number of statutory restrictions for felony cases, usually related to the type of offense. Probation will often be denied to an offender with a prior record or one convicted of murder or sex crimes. Murder and rape are the most universally recognized offenses that do not permit probation. Otherwise, restrictive offenses and standards vary greatly among states. The most important aid in deciding to deny or grant probation is giving detailed and accurate presentencing information to the judge. It is also important to ensure that the decision-making process focuses on the offender, not the offense, insofar as the statutes will allow.

This is difficult when statutory limitations are extensive. Although many states are moving toward eliminating these mandatory exclusions, others are expanding their list of exclusions.

Rules or conditions for probation cannot be formulated as a set of standard operating procedures. The conditions for continuing probation should be tailored to the needs of the individual offender. Unfortunately, the court's frequent delegation of rule-making power to probation officers puts them in the almost impossible position of being lawmakers, enforcers, and confidants. The most effective way to ensure that rules are not established arbitrarily is to have them carefully reviewed by the court. In a situation in which probation officers are devising too many rules, their violations will soon overload the court.

It is generally conceded that probation rules should not extend to every kind of conduct. A number of courts require the probation officer who makes the presentence investigation to recommend the conditions for the offender's probation, which are usually based on the officer's expectations regarding where the offender will be living, how he or she will make a living, and so on. The terms are discussed by the judge with the probation candidate, his or her counsel, and the probation officer. Decisions made in this manner will usually result in a few important restrictions, giving the probationer a clear idea of what constitutes acceptable behavior.

Even when probationers have a clear picture of what conditions are expected, many cannot conform to these due to multiple problems, drug dependency, rebelliousness, and sense of "having gotten away with it" because the judge did not sentence them to a prison term. Under these conditions, judges increasingly engage in "tournaquet sentencing": tightening the conditions of probation until the offender begins to constrain his or her behavior to avoid more punitive conditions. This is particularly seen in the intermediate punishments: those sentencing dispositions that fall between probation and long-term incarceration. These include victim restitution, community work orders, house arrest, electronic monitoring, and intensive supervised probation.

Restitution Programs

A common condition for probation is the requirement that victims be compensated for their losses or injury. The emphasis given to the study of victimology in the last few years has resulted in some state compensation of crime victims by payment of medical costs and other financial reimbursement. Through the system of probation, however, the victim is often repaid by the offender. It is important that probation authorities link the amount of payment to the offender's ability to pay. Installment payment is usually the most realistic approach. In some cases a partial restitution may be all that is reasonably possible (for example, in the case of an arsonist who burns down a multimillion-dollar building). There are many reasons offered

---

VICTIMOLOGY

A subspecialty of criminology, victimology is the study of the offender-victim relationship, including victim-precipitated crime, victim compensation, victimization (particularly surveys of victims to determine the extent of crime), costs of crime to victims, victim cooperation within the justice system, and crime prevention. Efforts are directed toward high-risk victim candidates and the focus is on state compensation programs and restitution made by the offender to the victim.

---

to support restitution programs. Obviously, restitution offsets the victim's loss when property is stolen; restitution can even be ordered for the deductible amount an insurance company might require an insured victim to pay before the insurance coverage would become effective. Time lost from work, while being a witness in court, and being hospitalized are subject to offender restitution. It appears that restitution may be ordered for any injury caused by the offense for which the offender was convicted. Other rationales are that restitution forces the offender to accept personal responsibility for the crime; restitution can lead to reconciliation of offender and victim; and, finally, it provides one way that the victim can become part of the otherwise impersonal processing of victims within the justice system. It appears that restitution programs are more numerous in the juvenile justice system than in the adult system.[22]

Community Work Orders

Community work orders represent court-ordered voluntary work for specified numbers of hours that offenders perform, usually in the form of free labor to some charitable organization or in public service such as serving as a volunteer hospital orderly, doing street cleaning, maintenance, or repair of public housing, or providing service to indigent groups. Some

---

RESTITUTION

A court-ordered condition of probation that requires the offender to repair the financial, emotional, or physical damage done (a reparative sentence) by making financial payment of money to the victim or, alternatively, to a fund to provide services to victims. In addition, restitution programs are frequently ordered in the absence of a sentence to probation.

Almost every state has restitution programs in operation, although Florida, Minnesota, and Michigan appear to be leaders in the development of American restitution programs. (Restitution programs have been extensively implemented and evaluated in Great Britain.) In Minnesota, parolees may also be required to reside in a residential center and pay part of their wages to victims. Other jurisdictions require victim-offender conferences to establish the amount of financial compensation to be given the victim.

---

examples of the latter would be a dentist sentenced to perform one hundred hours of free dental service to welfare recipients, or a physician performing fifty hours of free medical attention to jail inmates on Saturdays.

Both community work orders and restitution programs have their critics. Some argue that offenders committing crimes of violence should not be allowed a penalty less than incarceration for their offenses, and that the physical and psychological costs to victims of crimes of violence are almost impossible to calculate. There also seems to be some uncertainty over whether an offender sentenced to perform community work or restitution ought to be resentenced to incarceration for noncompliance. Despite the criticism, there appears to be consensus that offenders should repay their victims for losses, even if the repayment is as symbolic as community work. Both sentencing options provide punishment that falls between "traditional" probation and incarceration.[23]

Intensive Supervised Probation

Another alternative punishment program is intensive supervised probation, designed to provide increased surveillance of offenders deemed to be too serious for "routine" probation. The program is also a management strategy for probation services, which might need to increase the level of surveillance for individuals who were not adjusting on probation.

Persons placed on intensive supervised probation (ISP) usually have more frequent contacts with probation officers who are carrying smaller caseloads. In Georgia, for example, two officers might share a caseload of twenty-five probationers, or a team of three officers might supervise forty probationers.[24] ISP probationers typically make restitution payments, perform community work, work at legal employment, pay probation fees,[25] and undergo random alcohol- and drug-use testing. The Georgia program described in the box on page 205 provides an excellent example of an ISP program.

ISP has emerged as the most popular program to prevent prison overcrowding. Programs that have this effect are known as "front-end" solutions to the overpopulation crisis, and ISP represents attractive objectives. It serves to

1. Heighten supervision of participants and increase their contacts with respectable members of the community;
2. Make participants more accountable for their behavior by requiring victim restitution, community service, and reimbursement of supervision cost through payment of probation fees;
3. Lessen recidivism by limiting criminal opportunity via curfew and constructive use of free time by participants;
4. Reinforce reintegration objectives by increased use of community resources, counseling services, mandated employment, and decreased reliance on chemical substances.[26]

**GEORGIA'S EXPERIENCE WITH INTENSIVE
PROBATION SUPERVISION (IPS)**

While probation programs with varying degrees of supervision have been implemented throughout the country, Georgia's IPS is widely regarded as one of the most stringent in the Nation. Standards include:

• Five face-to-face contacts per week;
• 132 hours of mandatory community service;
• Mandatory curfew;
• Weekly check of local arrest records;
• Automatic notification of arrest elsewhere via the State Crime Information Network listing; and
• Routine and unannounced alcohol and drug testing.

The supervision standards are enforced by a team consisting of a Probation Officer and a Surveillance Officer. The team supervises 25 probationers. In some jurisdictions, a team of one Probation Officer and two Surveillance Officers supervises 40 probationers. The standards are designed to provide sufficient surveillance to control risk to the community and give a framework to treatment-oriented counseling. The counseling is designed to help the offender direct his energies toward productive activities, to assume responsibilities, and to become a law-abiding citizen. Most offenders chosen for the IPS pilot program were already sentenced to prison, presented an acceptable risk to the community, and had not committed a violent offense. A risk assessment instrument was used to screen select offenders. While the majority of those selected fell into the category of nonviolent property offenders, a large number of individuals convicted of drug- and alcohol-related offenses were included as the program developed. Some of these offenses also involved personal violence.

Of the 2,322 people in the program between 1982 and 1985, 370 (or 16 percent) absconded or had their probation revoked. The remaining 1,952 were successfully diverted from prison: many were still under some form of probationary supervision. Some have successfully completed their sentence.

Source: Billie Erwin and Lawrence Bennett, *New Dimensions in Probation* (Washington, D.C.: U.S. Department of Justice, 1987), p. 2.

ISP programs have been implemented in at least forty states, including Ohio, California, Washington, and Georgia, to name a few. Initial evaluations and implications are favorable.[27] Intensive supervision can also be a part of parole service,[28] or it can be used with shock probationers[29] as will be seen later.

House Arrest and Electronic Monitoring

House arrest is a court-ordered sentence confining offenders to their households for the duration of sentence. The sentence may be in conjunction with probation, but usually is imposed by the court as a separate punishment. Arrestees may leave their residences for such legitimate purposes

---

SOLUTIONS TO PRISON OVERCROWDING

Due to the prison population crisis across the Nation, many states are exploring strategies to reduce the overcrowding. The basic three strategies can be described as "bricks and mortar" (see Chapter 9), "front-end solutions," and "back-end" solutions.

"Bricks and mortar" refers to attempts to construct new or renovate existing facilities to expand available beds. Even though there are literally billions of dollars in construction, renovation, expansion, and retrofitting ongoing, no one with any understanding of the comprehensive nature of the problem holds out much hope that the nation can build enough prisons to accommodate the influx of inmates.

"Front-end solutions" refers to those alternative sentences and intermediate punishments that would control offenders without penal commitment. These would include, among others, probation, house arrest, deferred prosecution, electronic monitoring, shock probation, intensive supervised probation, intermittent jail incarceration, and other programs.

"Back-end solutions" refers to ways used to reduce prison populations after the offender arrives in prison. These can be viewed as "early-out" or "extended limits" options: parole, shock parole, emergency release (usually court-ordered), expanded good time credits to count against the minimum sentence, work and educational furlough, prerelease to halfway houses (used extensively by the U.S. Bureau of Prisons, the Federal prison system), and other programs.

At the end of 1988, there were at least 600,000 inmates in the prisons of the 52 jurisdictions of the nation, another all-time high.

---

as employment, food shopping, medical attention, performance of community service, or observation of religious services. Otherwise, the curfew lasts twenty-four hours a day.

Participants may be required to make victim compensation, perform community work service, pay probation fees, undergo drug and alcohol testing, and, in some instances, wear electronic monitoring equipment to verify their presence in residence. (In some jurisdictions, house arrest is used on a pretrial basis, as an isolated sentence, in conjunction with probation or parole, or with a prerelease status such as education or work furlough. House arrest is a punitive sentence and was designed in most cases to relieve institutional overcrowding. For many offenders, it is their "last chance" to escape from being committed to prison.[30]

In addition to enabling control of the offender, house arrest is viewed as a cost-avoidance program, a "front-end" solution to prison overcrowding, and as a flexible alternative for certain offenders (such as a pregnant offender until time of delivery).[31] The use of telemonitoring devices, usually in conjunction with house arrest, can significantly increase the correctional surveillance of offenders.

Electronic monitoring typically requires that the house arrestee wear a device on the leg or wrist that emits a radio signal into a special device mounted on a telephone and activated by a computer. The computer automatically dials the telephone number of the arrestee's residence, randomly at any hour of the day or night. The offender must then insert the leg or wrist device into the telephone receiver, sending a confirming radio signal to the computer. Arrestees who do not respond by confirmation are subject to arrest and incarceration. Some one in three community control arrestees are fitted with the wristlet or bracelet.[32] The effectiveness of the house arrest plus the telemonitoring approach is not yet firmly established, but Lilly et al. report a 5.7 percent recidivism rate among Kentucky participants[33] and Petersilia reports a 22 percent recidivism rate among Florida arrestees.[34] In conjunction, both approaches appear to be punitive, controlling, effective, and cost-saving.[35]

Shock Probation

In 1965, the Ohio legislature passed a law permitting sentencing judges to incarcerate offenders in State prisons for short periods of time, and then recall the inmate to probation within the community. The assumption was that a short period of incarceration (90 to 130 days), followed by a period of probation, would "shock" the offender into abandoning criminal activity and into pursuit of law-abiding behavior. Clearly, this program is based on a "specific deterrence" model, and was designed for a segment of the offender population for whom probation was insufficient punishment but long-term imprisonment was not necessary. The method would be used not for first-time offenders but for persons not yet committed to giving up predatory behavior.

This option, now adopted by at least fourteen states,[36] puts decision-making power squarely in the hands of the judiciary. The sentencing judge is allowed to reconsider the original sentence to prison and, upon motion, to recall the inmate and place him or her on probation, under conditions deemed appropriate.

Evaluations of the effectiveness of shock probation in preventing recidivism and cost avoidance have focused on Ohio, Texas, and Kentucky. Vito[37] has conducted the most sophisticated evaluations and has concluded as follows:

1. The shock experience should not be limited to first-time offenders; eligibility should properly include those with prior records, as deemed eligible by the judge.
2. The length of incarceration necessary to secure the deterrent effect could be much shorter, probably 30 days or less.
3. Reincarceration rates have never exceeded 26 percent and, in Ohio, have been as low as 10 percent. The level of these rates clearly indicates that the program has potential for reintegration.
4. Shock probation has considerable potential to reduce institutional overcrowding characteristic of contemporary corrections.[38]

Shock probation can be seen as an alternative disposition for sentencing judges who wish to control probationer behavior through tourniquet sentencing. It is the "last ditch" program of prison avoidance available to judges faced with the difficult decision of how best to protect the public while maximizing offender reintegration.

Probation Continues to be a Mainstay of Corrections

Although probation is similar to parole in its practice, it occurs at a point in the process that tends to minimize the damage that incarceration inflicts on the first-time or relatively non-violent offender. Whereas some states do use probation as a method for community supervision after an offender's short incarceration in jail or prison, the most common form of probation comes directly from the court. Probation is basically a judicial function that can be granted and terminated by the courts. Although many states administer both probation and parole by a single agency, the majority have separate agencies for those two purposes. During 1986, the population of probationers rose by over 227,000 to a total of 1,968,712 (an 13.0 percent increase over 1985). Over 1,265,748 offenders entered into probation supervision. The probation rate per 100,000 adults for 1986 was 1,178. Rates were lowest in West Virginia (281) and highest in the District of Columbia (2,522). The whole picture across America is shown in Table 10.2. It seems that the use of probation and intermediate punishments will continue to grow as the nation's prisons continue to deal with an increasingly crowded and unmanageable population. Increasingly, courts are using their discretion to link probation to a term of incarceration. Some of the possible combinations are listed below:

- *Split sentences* — where the court specifies a period of incarceration to be followed by a period of probation.
- *Modification of sentence* — where the original sentencing court may reconsider an offender's prison sentence within a limited time and change it to probation.
- *Shock probation* — where an offender sentenced to incarceration is released after a period of time in confinement (the shock) and resentenced to probation.
- *Intermittent incarceration* — where an offender on probation may spend weekends or nights in jail.[39]

Summary _____

Probation is clearly an important function in corrections. It is generally conceded, however, that the full potential of this alternative to imprisonment cannot be reached without some effort to fulfill two needs: (1) to

TABLE 10.2 Adults on Probation, 1986

Regions and Jurisdictions	Probation Population 1/1/86	1986 Entries	1986 Exits	Probation Population 12/31/86	Percent Change in Probation Population 1985–86	1986 Probationers per 100,000 Adult Residents
U.S. Total	1,968,712	1,265,748	1,140,055	2,094,405	6.4%	1,178
Federal	55,378	25,797	22,005	59,170	6.8	
State	1,913,334	1,239,951	1,118,050	2,035,235	6.4	1,145
Northeast	366,040	203,996	175,653	394,383	7.7	1,040
Connecticut	36,805	30,237	25,168	41,874	13.8	1,723
Maine	4,451	4,661	4,492	4,620	3.8	530
Massachusetts	86,597	50,925	46,359	91,163	5.3	2,030
New Hampshire	3,096	2,477	1,955	3,618	16.9	472
New Jersey	47,483	28,077	22,530	53,030	11.7	916
New York	99,183	41,168	32,794	107,557	8.4	803
Pennsylvania	75,591	39,183	35,789	78,985	4.5	874
Rhode Island	7,536	4,416	3,778	8,174	8.5	1,093
Vermont	5,298	2,852	2,788	5,362	1.2	1,337
Midwest	408,880	312,341	284,600	436,621	6.8	1,003
Illinois	74,156	46,992	44,945	76,203	2.8	897
Indiana	42,800	45,345	38,880	49,265	15.1	1,224
Iowa	12,063	12,108	11,587	12,584	4.3	598
Kansas	16,204	9,093	9,344	15,953	- 1.5	879
Michigan	99,365	77,732	72,235	104,862	5.5	1,571
Minnesota	32,986	28,332	26,091	35,227	6.8	1,135
Missouri	26,081	20,474	15,633	30,922	18.6	823
Nebraska	10,720	12,264	11,719	11,265	5.1	963
North Dakota	1,569	802	827	1,544	- 1.6	316
Ohio	66,810	43,975	38,863	71,922	7.7	911
South Dakota	2,249	3,967	3,990	2,226	- 1.0	436
Wisconsin	23,877	11,257	10,486	24,648	3.2	701
South	789,702	511,433	464,817	836,318	5.9	1,377
Alabama	16,520	5,400	4,895	17,025	3.1	579
Arkansas	9,268	2,526	1,659	10,135	9.4	587
Delaware	7,139	4,624	3,778	7,985	11.9	1,688
Dist. of Columbia	11,777	10,253	9,723	12,307	4.5	2,522
Florida	130,399	152,522	142,672	140,249	7.6	1,551
Georgia	94,461	57,738	51,636	100,563	6.5	2,290
Kentucky	6,594	4,916	4,669	6,841	3.8	252
Louisiana	26,638	11,767	10,728	27,677	3.9	877
Maryland	67,138	40,648	38,652	69,134	3.0	2,062
Mississippi	6,636	3,018	3,196	6,458	2.7	354
North Carolina	56,207	32,123	29,686	58,644	4.3	1,245
Oklahoma	21,480	11,237	9,726	22,991	7.0	956
South Carolina	17,979	10,210	9,948	18,241	1.5	748
Tennessee	26,205	16,399	16,313	26,291	.3	740
Texas	269,909	139,033	118,868	290,074	7.5	2,468
Virginia	17,447	6,730	6,448	17,729	1.6	408
West Virginia	3,905	2,289	2,220	3,974	1.8	281

TABLE 10.2 *Continued*

West	348,712	212,181	192,980	367,913	5.5	1,034
Alaska	2,606	1,308	1,029	2,885	10.7	797
Arizona	18,068	9,241	7,026	20,283	12.3	842
California	210,449	126,155	115,862	220,742	4.9	1,111
Colorado	17,612	10,585	10,980	17,217	- 2.2	717
Hawaii	7,986	5,102	4,684	8,404	5.2	1,082
Idaho	3,414	2,130	1,774	3,770	10.4	546
Montana	2,637	1,277	971	2,943	11.6	501
Nevada[d]	5,365	2,593	2,440	5,518	2.9	762
New Mexico	4,130	3,831	3,786	4,175	1.1	403
Oregon	23,000	13,589	13,934	22,655	- 1.5	1,126
Utah	6,330	3,559	3,511	6,378	.8	610
Washington	45,399	31,630	25,873	51,156	12.7	1,547
Wyoming	1,716	1,181	1,110	1,787	4.1	506

Source: Thomas Hester, *Probation and Parole 1986* (Washington, D.C.: U.S. Department of Justice, 1987), p. 2.

provide an effective system to determine which offenders should receive probation and (2) to offer support and services for the probationers in the community, to allow them to live independently in a socially accepted way. To achieve these goals, probation services must be better organized, staffed, and funded. The shifting of money and resources to the efforts of community-based projects is necessary to make probation a viable alternative. The National Advisory Commission on Criminal Justice Standards and Goals has recommended that the nation use probation as the preferred disposition. It has also recommended that probation, which started as a volunteer service, seek out even more volunteers to serve in all capacities.

The persuasive arguments favoring probation over imprisonment focus on reduced stigma, community help, and other advantages to the offender. Perhaps one of the most telling arguments, from the public's point of view, is that probation is so much cheaper than imprisonment. The taxpayer can easily appreciate the fact that whereas it costs about $17,500 a year (excluding capital costs) to keep the average adult offender in prison, probation runs about one-tenth that figure.

Probation has established itself as the main component of corrections. It appears that the emphasis on probation as the preferred disposition will keep it in the forefront of correctional reform. If the costs of prison and probation are compared, the taxpayer will rule in favor of probation. As the population grows, the number of offenders and variations on probation strategies will surely increase as well. Students of probation concur that the practice is approximately 75 percent effective on a national basis;[40] some states, particularly Nebraska, report a 90 percent success rate. An alternative to imprisonment that is about one-tenth as costly (and at least as effective) has great appeal and clearly answers the need for a sound and economical approach to corrections.

Review Questions _____

1. Explain the purpose of probation, and describe the methods by which it is usually administered.
2. What organizational system is best suited for probation? Why?
3. What are some of the restrictions often applied to probation? What kinds of offenders are usually denied probation?
4. Discuss the effectiveness of probation as compared with imprisonment.
5. Identify and define five "front-end" solutions to prison overcrowding.
6. What role conflicts are inherent in the nation's probation service, and how can these be reduced?

Key Terms _____

1. **right of sanctuary (p. 191)**
2. **benefit of clergy (p. 191)**
3. **stigma (p. 192)**
4. **probation subsidy (p. 197)**
5. **negative subsidy (p. 198)**
6. **casework (p. 199)**
7. **restrictions (p. 201)**
8. **conditions (p. 202)**
9. **restitution (p. 202)**
10. **ISP (p. 204)**
11. **house arrest (p. 205)**
12. **electronic monitoring (p. 206)**
13. **shock probation (p. 206)**
14. **split sentences (p. 208)**

Notes _____

1. For a summary of probation and parole trends, see Lawrence Greenfield, *Probation and Parole 1986* (Washington, D.C.: U.S. Department of Justice, 1987).
2. Norman Johnston, *The Human Cage: A Brief History of Prison Architecture* (New York: Walker, 1973), p. 8: "The concept of imprisonment as a substitute for death or mutilation of the body was derived in part from a custom of the early Church of granting asylum or sanctuary to fugitives and criminals."
3. See Numbers 35:6 and Joshua 20:2–6.
4. David Fogel, "Nordic Approaches to Crime and Justice," *CJ International* 3 (January–February 1987): 8–21.
5. Alexander Smith and Louis Berlin, *Introduction to Probation and Parole* (St. Paul: West, 1976): pp. 76–78.
6. Sheldon Glueck (1896–1980) was an American criminologist noted for his extensive long-range research on criminal careers. These studies followed the history of many groups of young people; Glueck aimed to predict who might become delinquent. Glueck wrote many books with his wife, Eleanor, who was an equally famous criminologist and educator.

7. Harry Elmer Barnes and Negley K. Teeters, *New Horizons in Criminology,* 3d ed. (Englewood Cliffs, N.J.: Prentice-Hall, 1959), p. 554.

8. Missouri (1897), Rhode Island (1899), New Jersey (1900), Vermont (1900).

9. The first juvenile court in the United States was established in Chicago in 1899. See Harry Allen, Chris Eskridge, Edward Latessa, and Gennaro Vito, *Probation and Parole in America* (New York: Free Press, 1985): 36–62.

10. American Bar Association Project on Standards for Criminal Justice, *Standards Relating to Probation* (New York: Institute of Judicial Administration, 1970), p. 9.

11. Harry E. Allen et al., *Critical Issues in Adult Probation: Summary Report* (Washington, D.C.: U.S. Department of Justice, 1979), p. 43.

12. New Jersey, California, Michigan, and Washington.

13. National Advisory Commission on Criminal Justice Standards and Goals, *Corrections* (Washington, D.C.: U.S. Department of Justice, 1973), p. 315.

14. Ibid., p. 315.

15. Ibid., p. 315.

16. The two studies are Joint Commission on Correctional Manpower and Training, *Corrections 1968: A Climate for Change* (Washington, D.C.: JCCMT, 1968), p. 30; and Herman Piven and Abraham Alcabes, *The Crisis of Qualified Manpower for Criminal Justice: An Analytic Assessment with Guidelines for New Policy,* Vol. 1 (Washington, D.C.: U.S. Government Printing Office, 1969).

17. See John Whitehead, "Probation Mission Reform," *Criminal Justice Review* 9 (1984): 15–21: and "Job Burnout and Job Satisfaction Among Probation Managers," *Journal of Criminal Justice* 14 (1985): 29–40.

18. John Dierna, "Counseling in Federal Probation," *Federal Probation* LI (1987): 4–16; and Eric Assur, Gerald Jackson and Teresa Muncy, "Probation Counselors and the Adult Children of Alcoholics," *Federal Probation* LI (1987): 41–46.

19. National Advisory Commission, *Corrections,* p. 318.

20. James Robinson et al., *The San Francisco Project,* Research Report No. 14 (Berkeley: University of California School of Criminology, 1969), pp. 48–57.

21. National Advisory Commission, *Corrections,* p. 319. See also R. Adams and H. J. Vetter, Probation Caseload Size and Recidivism Rate," *British Journal of Criminology and Deviant Behavior 11* (1974). On classification, see the July 1987 issue of *Crime and Delinquency* 32 (1986): 251–390.

22. Jean Warner and Vincent Burke, *National Directory of Juvenile Restitution Programs 1987* (Washington, D.C.: U.S. Department of Justice, 1987). See also Anne Schneider, "Restitution and Recidivism Rates of Juvenile Offenders: Results From Four Experimental Studies," *Criminology* 24 (1986): 533–552: Richard Boalt, "Restitution, Criminal Law and the Ideology of Individuality," *Journal of Criminal Law and Criminology* 77 (1986): 969–1022.

23. Richard Meyer and Henry Dufour, "Experimenting with Community Service: A Punitive Alternative to Incarceration," *Federal Probation* 51 (1987): 22–27.

24. Bille Erwin and Lawrence Bennett, *New Dimensions in Probation: Georgia's Experience with Intensive Probation Supervision (IPS)* (Washington, D.C.: U.S. Department of Justice, 1987).

25. Christopher Baird, Douglas Holien, and Audrey Bakke, *Fees for Probation Services* (Madison, Wis.: National Council on Crime and Delinquency, 1986).

26. Extracted from Joan Petersilia, *Expanding Options for Criminal Sentencing* (Santa Monica, Calif.: Rand Corporation, 1987): 11.

27. Erwin and Bennett, p. 7.

28. Informal communication with Frank Pearson, director of the evaluation program for New Jersey's intensive supervision program (November 19, 1987).

29. Edward Latessa and Gennaro Vito, "The Effects of Intensive Supervision on Shock Probationers." Paper presented at the annual meeting of the Academy of Criminal Justice Sciences, San Francisco, March 29, 1984. See also Edward Latessa, *An Evaluation of the Intensive Treatment Supervision Program of the Montgomery County Common Pleas Court General Division Adult Probation Department* (Cincinnati: University of Cincinnati, 1986). See the cautionary note by Edward Latessa, "The Cost Effectiveness of Intensive Probation Supervision," *Federal Probation* 50 (1986): 70–74.

30. For a historical view of telemonitoring, see Ralph Kirland Gable, "Application of Personal Telemonitoring to Current Problems in Corrections," *Journal of Criminal Justice* 14 (1986): 173–182.

31. Petersilia, p. 33.

32. Ibid, p. 37.

33. J. Robert Lilly, Richard Ball, and Jennifer Wright, "Home Incarceration with Electronic Monitoring in Kenton County, Kentucky: An Evaluation," in Belinda McCarthy (ed.), *Intermediate Punishments* (Monsey, New York: Criminal Justice Press) pp. 189–203. See also J. Robert Lilly, Richard Ball and Robert Lotz, "Electronic Jail Revisited," *Justice Quarterly* 3 (1986): 353–361.

34. Petersilia, p. 34.

35. Lilly et al., 196.

36. Gennaro Vito and Harry Allen, "Shock Probation in Ohio: A Comparison of Outcomes," *International Journal of Offender Therapy and Comparative Criminology* 25 (1981): 70–77.

37. Gennaro Vito, "Development in Shock Probation: A Review of Research Findings and Policy Implication," *Federal Probation* 50 (1985): 22–27.

38. Ibid.: 23–25.

39. *U.S. Bureau of Census Supplementary Report P-25, No. 930* (U.S. Department of Justice, Washington, D.C., U.S. Govt. Printing Office, 1983).

40. Allen et al., *Critical Issues in Adult Probation,* pp. 30–37.

11

Imprisonment

As he went through Cold-Bath Fields he saw
A solitary cell;
And the Devil was pleased, for it gave him a hint
For improving his prisons in Hell.
—SAMUEL TAYLOR COLERIDGE

The History of Imprisonment

Organized society has dealt with criminal offenders in a variety of ways. As we saw in Part 1, when victims were responsible for dealing with offenders, their approach was motivated by revenge or compensation for loss. When the state began to intervene and act in the name of the victim, retribution became the basic motive. The death penalty was the most common form of retribution for criminal acts. Death or mutilation by the state, in the name of justice, were common practices by the end of the sixteenth century. In most societies, the purpose of confinement was only to detain offenders until some more severe form of punishment could be imposed.

The Church was evidently the first social institution to use confinement as a form of punishment. In *The Human Cage,* Norman Johnston described how the philosophy of imprisonment as a punishment evolved:

The concept of imprisonment as a substitute for death or mutilation of the body was derived in part from a custom of the early Church of granting asylum or sanctuary to fugitives and criminals. Begun largely during the reign of Constantine, this ancient right existed earlier among Assyrians, Hebrews, and others. The Church at that time had under its aegis a large number of clergy, clerks, functionaries, monks, and serfs, and, except the latter, most of these fell under the jurisdiction of the church courts. Traditionally forbidden to shed blood and drawing on the Christian theme of purification through suffering, these canon courts came to subject the wrongdoer to reclusion and even solitary cellular confinement, not as punishment alone, but as a way of providing conditions under which penitence would most likely occur.

> **PRISON**
> A state or federal confinement facility having custodial authority over adults sentenced to confinement for more than a year.

. . . Some of the monastic quarters provided totally separate facilities for each monk so that it was a simple matter to lock up an errant brother for brief periods.

As "mother houses" of monastic orders had satellite houses often located in less desirable places, it was also the practice to transfer monks for periods of time to such locations. There is some evidence that some of these satellites came to be regarded as punitive facilities.[1]

The Church built several kinds of prisons. In monastic prisons, offenders lived in solitary confinement, supervised by monks, for long periods of time. The Inquisition used underground cells for the lifetime imprisonment of heretics, witches, sorcerers, and others spared the death penalty. The Church also organized workhouses to keep deviants and the unemployed off the streets while teaching them the work ethic.

Men in Cages in the 1930s (Courtesy Washington State Department of Corrections)

As noted in Part 1, the penitentiary was basically an American idea. From the creation of a few solitary cells in the Walnut Street Jail to the four new institutions opened in California in 1986,[2] prisons are characteristically American in philosophy and construction. Conceived at a time when the new nation was breaking away from all the old ties with Europe, the American prison has come to represent both a monument and an obstruction to the development of corrections. Prisons in America quickly outgrew the function originally conceived by the early reformers—serving as another example of a good idea poorly implemented and oversold. Today, with most judges well aware that prisons tend, at best, to be badly run, prison sentences are often a last resort.

This chapter will examine the background and current state of imprisonment practices in America, focusing on the institutions for the adult male felons and their effect on inmates. Institutions for juveniles[3] and women are discussed in Part 5.

A basic philosophical tenet underlying the use of imprisonment in America appears to be a belief in the perfectability of people. The Revolution inspired a great zeal for reform. Hated codes from the past were struck down, and incarceration became the American substitute for England's indiscriminate use of the death penalty. A rational system of corrections, with punishment certain but humane, was expected to deter offenders from a life of crime. Early American efforts to reform the penal codes were strongly influenced by Cesare Beccaria's comments on laws relating to punishment:

> If we glance at the pages of history, we will find that laws, which surely are, or ought to be, compacts of free men, have been, for the most part, a mere tool of the passions of some.... The severity of punishment of itself emboldens men to commit the very wrongs it is supposed to prevent.... They are driven to commit additional crimes to avoid the punishment for a single one. The countries and times most notorious for severity of penalties have always been those in which the bloodiest and most inhumane of deeds were committed.... The certainty of a punishment, even if it be moderate, will always make a stronger impression than the fear of another which is more terrible but combined with the hope of impunity.... Do you want to prevent crimes? See to it that the laws are clear and simple and that the entire force of a nation is united in their defense.[4]

The passage of "clear" laws was seen as the most important aspect in the deterrence of deviant behavior. If the old British codes had encouraged crime, the new American codes would, it was believed, soon end the problem. Actually, it was the general reaction against the cruel practices of the British penal codes rather than faith in the penitentiary system that encouraged this belief. Unfortunately, this emphasis on law rather than on the lawbreaker drew attention away from the prisons and prison conditions. The fact of imprisonment, not the internal routine within the prison, became the chief concern. David J. Rothman pointed out that as the emphasis moved away from the legal system, systematic change occurred in the prisons:

> The focus shifted to the deviant and the penitentiary, away from the legal system. Men intently scrutinized the life history of the criminal and methodically arranged the institution to house him. Part of the cause for this change was the obvious failure of the first campaign. The faith of the 1790s now seemed misplaced; more rational codes had not decreased crime. The roots of deviancy went deeper than the certainty of a punishment. Nor were the institutions fulfilling the elementary task of protecting society, since escapes and riots were commonplace occurrences. More important, the second generation of Americans confronted new challenges and shared fresh ideas. Communities had undergone many critical changes between 1790 and 1830, and so had men's thinking. Citizens found cause for deep despair and yet incredible optimism. The safety and security of their social order seemed to them in far greater danger than that of their fathers, yet they hoped to eradicate crime from the new world.[5]

America embraced prisons with its typical zeal for humanitarian advances and built the fortresses of the late nineteenth and early twentieth centuries on the theory of reformation by confinement. "Lock 'em up" may have become the American replacement for "Off with their heads." Even after over a century and a half of failure, imprisonment is still practiced as the ultimate response to criminal behavior. (See Table 11.1 for data on incarceration rates for the United States.)

TABLE 11.1 Prisoners under the Jurisdiction of State and Federal Correctional Authorities, by Region and State, Yearend 1985 and 1986

	Total			Sentenced to More Than 1 Year			
Region and State	Advance 1986	Final 1985	Percent Change 1985–86	Advance 1986	Final 1985	Percent Change 1985–86	Incarceration Rate 1986
U.S. Total	546,659	503,271	8.6%	523,922	481,393	8.8%	216
Federal	44,408	40,223	10.4	36,531	32,695	11.7	15
State	502,251	463,048	8.5	487,391	448,698	8.6	201
Northeast	82,388	75,706	8.8%	79,071	72,656	8.8%	158
Connecticut	6,905	6,149	12.3	4,043	4,326	7.0	135
Maine	1,316	1,226	7.3	1,165	967	20.5	99
Massachusetts	5,678	5,390	5.3	5,678	5,390	5.3	97
New Hampshire	782	683	14.5	782	683	14.5	76
New Jersey	12,020	11,335	6.0	12,020	11,335	6.0	157
New York	38,449	34,712	10.8	38,449	34,712	10.8	216
Pennsylvania	15,201	14,227	6.8	15,165	14,119	7.4	128
Rhode Island	1,361	1,307	4.1	1,010	964	4.8	103
Vermont	676	677	- 0.1	476	443	7.4	88

TABLE 11.1 *Continued*

Midwest	103,101	95,704	7.7%	102,689	95,245	7.8%	173
Illinois	19,456	18,634	4.4	19,456	18,634	4.4	168
Indiana	10,175	9,904	2.7	9,963	9,615	3.6	181
Iowa	2,777	2,832	- 1.9	2,777	2,832	- 1.9	98
Kansas	5,425	4,732	14.6	5,425	4,732	14.6	220
Michigan	20,742	17,755	16.8	20,742	17,755	16.8	227
Minnesota	2,462	2,343	5.1	2,462	2,343	5.1	58
Missouri	10,485	9,915	5.7	10,485	9,915	5.7	206
Nebraska	1,953	1,814	7.7	1,863	1,733	7.5	116
North Dakota	421	422	- 0.2	361	375	- 3.7	53
Ohio	22,463	20,864	7.7	22,463	20,864	7.7	209
South Dakota	1,045	1,047	- 0.2	1,014	1,035	- 2.0	143
Wisconsin	5,697	5,442	4.7	5,678	5,412	4.9	119
South	215,713	202,926	6.3%	208,374	195,868	6.4%	249
Alabama	11,710	11,015	6.3	11,504	10,749	7.0	283
Arkansas	4,701	4,611	2.0	4,701	4,611	2.0	198
Delaware	2,828	2,553	10.8	2,026	1,759	15.2	324
Dist. of Columbia	6,746	6,404	5.3	4,786	4,604	4.0	753
Florida	32,228	28,600	12.7	32,219	28,482	13.1	272
Georgia	17,363	16,014	8.4	16,291	15,115	7.8	265
Kentucky	6,322	5,801	9.0	6,322	5,801	9.0	169
Louisiana	14,580	13,890	5.0	14,580	13,890	5.0	322
Maryland	13,326	13,005	2.5	12,559	12,303	2.1	280
Mississippi	6,747	6,392	5.6	6,565	6,208	5.8	249
North Carolina	17,762	17,344	2.4	16,460	16,007	2.8	258
Oklahoma	9,596	8,330	15.2	9,596	8,330	15.2	288
South Carolina	11,676	10,510	11.1	11,022	9,908	11.2	324
Tennessee	7,182	7,127	0.8	7,182	7,127	0.8	149
Texas	38,534	37,532	2.7	38,534	37,532	2.7	228
Virginia	12,930	12,073	7.1	12,545	11,717	7.1	215
West Virginia	1,482	1,725	-14.1	1,482	1,725	-14.1	77
West	101,049	88,712	13.9%	97,257	84,929	14.5%	198
Alaska	2,460	2,329	5.6	1,666	1,530	8.9	306
Arizona	9,434	8,531	10.6	9,038	8,273	9.2	268
California	59,484	50,111	18.7	57,725	48,279	19.6	212
Colorado	3,673	3,369	9.0	3,673	3,369	9.0	111
Hawaii	2,180	2,111	3.3	1,521	1,428	6.5	142
Idaho	1,451	1,294	12.1	1,451	1,294	12.1	144
Montana	1,111	1,129	- 1.6	1,111	1,129	- 1.6	135
Nevada	4,505	3,771	19.5	4,505	3,771	19.5	462
New Mexico	2,701	2,313	16.8	2,545	2,112	20.5	170
Oregon	4,737	4,454	6.4	4,737	4,454	6.4	175
Utah	1,845	1,633	13.0	1,817	1,623	12.0	108
Washington	6,603	6,909	- 4.4	6,603	6,909	- 4.4	147
Wyoming	865	758	14.1	865	758	14.1	170

Source: Lawrence Greenfield, *Prisoners in 1986* (Washington, D.C.: U.S. Department of Justice, 1987), p. 2.

As can be seen from the data in Table 11.1, the United States imprisons more people per capita than does any other large country in the Western World except for the Soviet Union and South Africa. And the trends of

---

IMPRISONMENT IN FOUR COUNTRIES

Comparisons have consistently shown that the United States has a higher proportion of its population incarcerated for criminal offenses than the other Western democracies. This has led many to conclude that the United States is considerably more punitive in its treatment of criminals. This trend might account for the larger number of prison inmates.

Yet the data below on three major crimes indicates that the number of arrestees going to prison per 100 crimes is about the same in the four countries studied.

Estimated Percent of Arrested Adults Incarcerated After Conviction

Offense	USA	Canada	England	Germany (FRG)
Robbery	49%	52%	48%	23–58%*
Burglary	35	23	30	***
Theft	18	14	14	4–9

*estimated

A major explanation for the higher number of American prisoners is the number of offenders; we have more criminals per 100,000 population. An alternative explanation is that we sentence offenders to longer prison terms. Most likely, it is a combination of the latter two explanations.

Data drawn from James Lynch, *Imprisonment in Four Countries* (Washington, D.C.: U.S. Department of Justice, 1987) p. 2.

---

the few years indicate that we are willing and ready to build more and more prisons and incarcerate an even larger percentage of the population. Some 131 new facilities or additions to existing institutions are under construction in 34 jurisdictions (state and federal). These will add more than 56,000 new beds to our prisons, at a direct cost in excess of $2.5 billion. The Federal Bureau of Prisons and 40 States also have another 60,000 beds in the planning stages.[6] Efforts for prison improvement fly in the face of get-tough legislation, the population's epidemic fear of crime, and sentencing laws and procedures that put even more persons behind bars (see Chapter 8). Some of the ambivalence of the American public regarding prisons and imprisonment relate to a lack of clear understanding and mutual acceptance of the purpose for confinement.

These can be divided into five security levels: Maximum (13 percent); High/Close (11 percent); Medium (33 percent); Minimum (22 percent); and Community Facilities (20 percent).[7] We turn first. . . .

Maximum Security Prisons _____

The purposes of confinement are punishment, deterrence, quarantine, rehabilitation, and, more recently, integration into the community.[8] The

> **MAXIMUM SECURITY PRISON**
> A facility designed, built, and managed so as to minimize escape, disturbance, and violence, while maximizing control over the inmate population. Custody and security are the primary concerns in a maximum security prison.

specific goals and the settings for their achievement are dictated by the particular society's dominant orientation, whether toward individual rights or collective security. Because both orientations command a strong following in America, neither one has entirely superseded the other. The scales have tipped in favor of security more often than equity, however, and the battle continues. We are currently witnessing a swing toward using incarceration for purposes of punishment and deterrence.

The Gothic Monoliths

Prisons were originally built as places that stressed maximum security above all other concerns. Typically, they are surrounded by a wall, usually thirty to fifty feet high and several feet thick, equipped with towers, manned by armed guards trained and prepared to prevent possible escapes or riots, lit by floodlights after dark, and sometimes bounded by electrified wire fences to further discourage escape attempts. These stone fortresses are usually placed far out in the countryside, away from the mainstream of American life.

The walled prison was so popular that it was not until 1926 that the first unwalled prison appeared in the United States.[9] It is clear when one approaches a typical maximum security prison that they are designed for punishment. The fearsome and forbidding atmosphere of the Auburn style of prison exemplifies the penal philosophy that prisoners must not only do time for their misdeeds but must also do so in an environment that emphasizes rejection, doubt, guilt, inferiority, diffusion, self-absorption, apathy, and despair.[10] It is small wonder that these prisons usually release men who are emotionally less stable than they were when they entered.[11]

The Human Cage vividly describes the nineteenth-century maximum security prison:

> In 1825 prisoners arrived in leg shackles from Auburn at a site on the Hudson River, later to be known as Sing Sing, to construct a new prison. The plan was similar: tiny cells back to back on five tiers, with stairways on either end in the center of the very long range. Cell doors were iron with grillework in the upper portion, and they fastened with gang locks. Cells received small amounts of light coming through a tiny window located nine feet away in the outer wall opposite the cell door. These cells were extremely damp, dark, and poorly ventilated and, like those at Auburn, contained no toilet facilities except buckets. The East House, which alone contained 1,000

Ohio State Penitentiary, Maximum Security. Now a Reception and Medical Center (Courtesy of the Ohio Department of Rehabilitation and Corrections)

cells and continued in use until 1943, was to become the prototype for most American prison cellhouse construction, rather than the earlier Auburn prison from which the system took its name.

For the remainder of the nineteenth century in this country, the characteristic layout for nearly all prisons was to consist of a central building housing offices, mess hall, and chapel, usually flanked and joined on each side by a multitiered cell block. In the prison enclosure formed by the wall would be shops, hospital, and power plant. In 1834 Ohio opened a prison on this plan in Columbus. Five tiers of tiny cells (7 × 3½ × 7 feet) back to back were built with convict labor. Wisconsin opened a similar type of prison at Waupun in 1851. The Illinois Penitentiary at Joliet (1856–1858), the Rhode Island Penitentiary at Cranston (1873–1878), the Tennessee Penitentiary at Nashville (1895), and a number of others were on this plan. The largest prison of this sort was the Western Penitentiary at Pittsburgh (1882) with 1,100 cells on five tiers. A few such institutions were erected following the turn of the century—Cheshire, Connecticut, was opened in 1913 and Monroe, Washington, in 1908—but by that time nearly all the states had built maximum security prisons and little prison building would occur again until the 1930s.[12]

These great Gothic-style[13] monoliths had been built in the belief that this kind of architecture, as part of the total system, would aid in the restoration of prisoners. This idea was discredited by the beginning of the twentieth century, however, and both American and European penologists began to concentrate on treatment strategies. But because America was left with almost sixty of these monstrosities,[14] built before 1900 with only economy, security, and isolation in mind, the new programs had to be designed to fit the existing structures. Of course, it should have been the other way around—the physical plants should have been built to fit the programs, and although corrections philosophy has changed drastically in the past fifty years, America is still tied to the approaches of a century and a half ago by the outmoded architecture of most maximum security prisons.

Classification: A Move Toward Corrections

The demoralizing influence of the maximum security prisons and the enforced idleness they produce resulted in two movements in corrections over the last half-century. One course of action has been continually to upgrade living conditions and humanitarian treatment within the security prisons. The second action introduces classification, a concept borrowed from psychology, into the imprisonment process. Classification in prison usually refers to two actions:

1. A differentiation of the prisoner population into custodial or security groups, thus permitting a degree of planned custodial flexibility not possible previously.
2. Opening of the prisons to the teacher, psychologist, social worker, psychiatrist, and others.[15]

The advent of classification in the post-World War II era marks a substantial shift from imprisonment to correction as a goal for American prisons. The timing was fortuitous, as unionism and federal legislation of the 1930s severely restricted prison industries. The idleness that followed the restrictive federal laws would have been even more troublesome were it not for the Prison Industries Reorganization Administration. Operating between 1935 and 1940, this agency developed programs of constructive activities for prisons, contributing to the rehabilitation programs more characteristic of prisons between 1940 and 1973.

The movement toward increased use of classification was accompanied by a great amount of rhetoric about "correctional treatment." Some of the more positive aspects of this strategy were outlined by the American Correctional Association:

The offender was perceived as a person with social, intellectual, or emotional deficiencies which should be diagnosed carefully and his deficiencies "clinically" defined. Programs should be designed to correct these deficiencies to the point that would permit him to assume a productive, law-abiding place in the community. To achieve the goals of correctional treatment, it would be necessary only to maintain the pressure on the inmate for his participation in the treatment programs, to continue to humanize institutional living, to upgrade the educational level of the line officer, and to expand the complement of professional treatment and training personnel. The coordination of the variety of treatment and training programs would be assured by the establishment of a division of "classification, treatment, and training" or some similar designation, either in the central office, in the institution, or both. This model of the "progressive prison" continues to be advocated as the standard pattern of the contemporary prison.[16]

"Correctional treatment," however, defies definition, especially when attempted in a maximum security institution where the overriding emphasis is on custody. According to current convention, almost everything done to, for, with, or by the inmate is immediately covered by the umbrella categorization of correctional treatment.

Correctional treatment is generally assumed to begin with the classification process. Classification procedures are conducted in a reception unit located in the prisons or in special reception and classification centers. They are sometimes carried out by classification committees, reception-diagnostic centers, or community classification teams. The purpose of classification varies among institutions, but basically it helps in management or treatment planning.

Management classification dates back to the earliest efforts to segregate prisoners by categories. The European Standard Minimum Rules for the Treatment of Offenders is a good example of a classification scheme using segregation as a management tool:

The different categories of prisoners shall be kept in separate institutions or parts of the institution, taking account of their sex, age, criminal record, the legal reasons for their detention, and the necessities of their treatment. Thus, (a) men and women shall so far as possible be detained in separate institutions. In an institution which receives both men and women, the whole of the premises allocated to women shall be entirely separate; (b) untried prisoners shall be kept separate from convicted prisoners; (c) persons imprisoned for debt and other civil prisoners shall be kept separate from persons imprisoned by reason of criminal offense; (d) young prisoners shall be kept separate from adults.[17]

Although management categories are valuable for the correctional administrator, continuing status evaluation and reclassification are critical. If treatment in the correctional setting is to be effective, the inmate must be reclassified and different treatments designed and applied. Unfortunately, many a well-conceived treatment plan has failed because of inaccurate or nonexistent reclassification.

Management and treatment classification plans must be based on procedures that can be readily implemented within the prison environment. The 1967 report by President Johnson's task force on corrections stressed this point:

> [I]t would be of great help to have some relatively simple screening process, capable of administration in general day-to-day correctional intake procedures, that would group offenders according to their management and treatment needs. To the extent that such screening procedures could be regularized, the errors attendant upon having a wide variety of persons make decisions on the basis of different kinds of information and presumptions would be reduced.[18]

That this "simple screening process" has not appeared on the correctional horizon is readily apparent. There are many promising starts, however, and more are being developed.[19]

The general model for classification is a variation on the caseworker plan, adopted from the social work profession, which assumes that offenders are sick and therefore require help from the treatment team, whether or not they want it.[20] In most cases the goals for this kind of help are established by caseworkers and the treatment staff. This model, which has been shown to be ineffective, violates two principles of social casework: it does not recognize that the offenders may not perceive themselves as sick and therefore may lack the motivation to seek help, and it ignores the offenders' ability to establish their own goals. Thus it is a catch-22 situation for the prisoners:[21]

> In order to use them as a foundation for practice, it is necessary to assume that all offenders are sick. This is, "We know you're sick. If you deny that you're sick, you're really sick. But if you acknowledge that you're sick, then you really must be sick or you wouldn't admit it."[22]

The usual purpose for classification, from the viewpoint of the staff, is to create a plan that will "correct" the prisoners and send them back to society as changed people. The prisoners, on the other hand, see the classification process only as a way to get out. They try to determine what they are supposed to do to prove they are ready for release and then do it. Because the emphasis on what they must do tends to shift in accordance with the convenience of the administration, the composition of the treatment staff, or "suggestions for improvement" from the paroling authority, this is not an easy task. An inmate may be classified as deficient in education, for example, and so he begins day classes. But because he is a skilled baker, he is needed in the kitchen and must shift to that role to earn a "good attitude" rating. In the complex organization of the prison, institutional needs must be met, even at the expense of correcting the offenders.[23]

Classification was hailed as a revolution in corrections, moving the focus from the mass-production tactics of the past to individualized treatment. The failure of classification and advanced social work techniques lies partly in the fact that the establishment is resistant to change and partly in the poor environment for change provided in the prisons themselves. Several states have abandoned classification reception-diagnostic centers as counterproductive, as the centers raised inmate and staff aspirations above the level of possible achievement. The treatment model has a place in corrections, but not in maximum security prisons.

Inside the Walls

After classification, the offender may be transported to one of the more than 130 maximum security prisons still in operation. If he is fortunate, he will be placed in one of the smaller institutions; if not, he will enter one of the giant walled cities. He will pass through a double fence or stone wall surrounded by manned guard towers. As the large steel main gate slams shut behind him, the process of *prisonization* begins. Donald Clemmer, the originator of this concept, described it best:

Every man who enters the penitentiary undergoes prisonization to some extent. The first and most obvious integrative step concerns his status. He becomes at once an anonymous figure in a subordinate group. A number replaces a name. He wears the clothes of the other members of the subordinate group. He is questioned and admonished. He soon learns that the warden is all-powerful. He soon learns the ranks, titles, and authority of various officials. And whether he uses the prison slang and argot or not, he comes to know their meanings. Even though a new man may hold himself aloof from other inmates and remain a solitary figure, he finds himself within a few months referring to or thinking of keepers as "screws," the physician as the "croaker," and using the local nicknames to designate persons. He follows the examples already set in wearing his cap. He learns to eat in haste and in obtaining food he imitates the tricks of those near him.

After the new arrival recovers from the effects of the swallowing-up process, he assigns a new meaning to conditions he had previously taken for granted. The fact that food, shelter, clothing, and a work activity had been given him originally made no special impression. It is only after some weeks or months that there comes to him a new interpretation of these necessities of life. This new conception results from mingling with other men and it places emphasis on the fact that the environment *should* administer to him. This point is intangible and difficult to describe insofar as it is only a subtle and minute change in attitude from the taken-for-granted perception. Exhaustive questioning of hundreds of men reveals that this slight change in attitude is a fundamental step in the process we are calling prisonization.[24]

·The effort to depersonalize and routinize is seemingly without respite. The maximum security prison is geared to supervision, control, and surveillance of the inmate's every move. Every other human consideration is weighed against its possible effect on security.

The pragmatic penal leaders in the last half of the nineteenth century began to accept imprisonment as a valid end in itself, rather than as a means to reform. This attitude turned prisons into a dumping ground for America's poor and "different" masses. Immigrants, blacks, and people who did not fit the "all-American" mold were likely candidates for these remote asylums.[25] The reformers' rhetoric spoke of rehabilitation, but the actions of corrections administrators belied this emphasis. Prisons were built to keep the prisoners in, but also to keep the public out. To justify the imprisonment of such a heterogeneous group of offenders under such rigid control required a theory of uniform treatment and uniform punishment, without regard to individual differences.

The tendency in the nineteenth century to incarcerate minorities remains in the current era (see Table 11.2). Whereas almost one-half of one percent of the adult American males were incarcerated in prisons in 1982, blacks were considerably overrepresented: they formed over 2 percent of the adult male population. In 1982, adult black males in America were almost nine times more likely to be in prison than were adult white males. For females, the ratio is over eight to one. The reasons for the disparity are hotly debated.

The new inmate is reminded of this principle as he is processed into the prison. The buildings, policies, rules, regulations, and control procedures all are designed to minimize his control over his environment. No privacy is allowed in his windowless and open cell. Even the toilet is open

TABLE 11.2 The Prevalence of State Imprisonment of Adults in the United States on December 31, 1978 to 1982, Total Adult Population, by Sex, and by Sex and Race

Population Segment	Percent of Adult Population 18 and Over in State Prisons on December 31,				
	1978	1979	1980	1981	1982
Total	.175%	.179%	.186%	.204%	.227%
Male	.353	.359	.373	.411	.455
White	.204	.209	.218	.242	.266
Black	1.665	1.667	1.703	1.859	2.044
Other	.192	.202	.189	.207	.229
Female	.013	.014	.014	.016	.018
White	.007	.007	.007	.009	.010
Black	.062	.063	.062	.073	.082
Other	.011	.011	.009	.011	.012

Source: Patrick Langan, *The Prevalence of Imprisonment* (Washington, D.C.: U.S. Department of Justice, 1985), p. 3.

PRISON GANGS

Every correctional system has a common problem: prison gangs. California, for example, has many *major* gangs in prison, based on ethnicity (e.g. Aryan Nation, Nuestra Famila, Black Guerilla, Crypts, Bloods). In Illinois, the gangs are based on "turf" controlled in cities. Other states have larger concentrations of outlaw motorcycle gangs, hate groups, terrorist cells, and so on.

Inside prisons, gangs war among themselves as well as commit frequently lethal assaults on correctional officers and weaker inmates. Some traffic in drugs; others concentrate on extortion. Exploitation of the weak is rampant in some maximum security institutions; this practice includes forcing other inmates to turn over all commissary goods, as well as enter into forced sexual acts. Correctional managers and staff receive death threats, and some officers are coerced into smuggling drugs into the institution to "buy" protection for their spouses and children. Finally, many states have adopted a policy of "lock up" of prison gangs, preferring inmate lawsuits to the acts of predation. Other states segregate major prison gangs by institution, to minimize intergang war.

Increasingly, correctional officers are joining their criminal justice colleagues in intelligence sharing, preemptive arrest, shared training programs, and cooperation in securing evidence to pursue criminal conspiracy convictions. Prison gangs will remain a correctional management problem for the near future.

---

to view, and showers are taken under close supervision. Every consideration is given by the designers and operators to prevent intrusion or contact from the outside. Visits are usually closely supervised, and a visitor's contacts with the inmates are possible only by special communication devices[26] that allow conversation but no physical contact. A body search of the inmate, including all body cavities, is invariably conducted if contact has been made. Everything is locked, and all movements require short trips between locked doors.

This description offers only a rough idea of a "typical" maximum security prison on the inside. Nothing can substitute for an actual visit to or confinement in one of these monuments to society's triumph of external control over internal reform. Some of these human cages are over 150 years old, and some are relatively new, but the differences involve only minor construction refinements, not basic philosophical changes. These prisons form the backbone of corrections because they house well over 200,000 inmates[27] and because they are both expensive and durable. The national average cost per square foot of covered floor space in the United States is approximately $141 (1987 dollars).[28]

Prisons vary so greatly from state to state that generalizations are dangerous, and the comments of Alexis de Tocqueville in this regard, though made over a century ago, are still valid today.[29] He wrote in 1833 that, aside from common interests, the several states preserve their individual independence, and each of them is sovereign master to rule itself

Thirty-Foot Walls Give Way to Fences and Razor Wire (Courtesy of American Correctional Association)

according to its own pleasure. . . . By the side of one state, the penitentiaries of which might serve as a model, we find another whose prisons present the example of everything which ought to be avoided."[30]

> **MEDIUM AND MINIMUM SECURITY**
>
> Medium security institutions are prisons designed, built, and operated to prevent escape, disturbances and violence. However, they have fewer restrictions on the movement and activities of prison inmates than would be found in maximum security institutions.
>
> Minimum security prisons allow maximum inmate movement, freedom, and self-determination, while still following methods to avoid escape, violence, and disturbances. Most inmates prefer less secure settings, but usually these environments are viewed as privileges for inmates who are felt to be trustworthy or who have proven their ability to conform in less structured environments. Regular reclassification reviews will improve the match between lesser security and inmate trustworthiness.

Medium and Minimum Security Institutions _____

In the twentieth century, a broad range of experimental alternatives to the maximum security approach was launched. Much of the construction in corrections over the past half-century has been for medium security institutions, in which are now housed about one-third of all state prisoners. Early medium security prisons were hard to distinguish from maximum security institutions; control was still the dominant concern. But even though security may be almost as tight in a medium security prison, the prisoners are not made so aware that they are being watched. Also, medium security prisons are usually smaller, without the overwhelming impersonality of the maximum security monoliths, and the offender's routine is somewhat less regimented.

Some of the most recent medium security prisons are patterned after the so-called campus design, including attractive residence areas with single rooms (not cells) and dormitories for inmates. External fences and subtle features installed within buildings to maintain security and protect the inmates from one another are the only obvious signs that the prisoners are under observation. Sophisticated electronic and other surveillance equipment is used, but unobtrusively. Assisting in the effective design of these new correctional facilities are such organizations as the National Clearinghouse for Correctional Programming and Architecture.[31] If we continue to use imprisonment as a response to criminal behavior, these new medium security systems may well represent the first wave of the future for correctional prisons in America.

One of the newer trends to emerge from overreliance on prisons for correcting offenders is the so-called "bricks and mortar" solution to prison overcrowding. Basically, states are attempting to solve a policy problem by constructing new buildings or renovating older facilities. Ordinarily, construction is time-consuming and prisons are "hand-crafted" on site; the

Omaha Correctional Center: OCC (Courtesy of American Correctional Association, photo Omaha Correctional Center)

expected time from the decision to build to committing the first inmate to prison is almost five years. Innovations in prison construction have taken place in Oklahoma,[32] Florida,[33] California,[34] and Ohio.[35] These newer options in construction and financing have allowed corrections to avoid more costly and time-consuming construction approaches, and have somewhat eased prison overcrowding.

There are two other kinds of correctional institutions today: the minimum security and open institutions, designed to serve the needs of rural farm areas and public works rather than those of the offender. Prisoners with good security classifications are assigned to these programs, which range from plantation-style prison farms to small forestry and road camps.

In many ways, the minimum security and open facilities are beneficial. They rescue relatively stable inmates from the oppressive rigors of confinement and from personal danger in the large, stifling prisons. As long as we continue to give long prison terms to offenders who are little threat to themselves or the public, the open facilities are preferable to traditional prisons. On the other hand, if we develop more programs of education, work, and vocational training,[36] and treatment within the maximum and medium security institutions, those in the minimum security, work-oriented camps will miss those opportunities. Also, as community-based corrections programs begin to drain off the least dangerous and more treatable offenders, the open facilities will lose their value—they are not suited to the hard-core offenders who will remain. Professionals in the corrections field will have to resist efforts to place men into minimum security or open facilities for economic reasons, rather than placing them into community-based programs for correctional treatment reasons.

The minimum security institution is a logical compromise between the medium security prison and community-based corrections. The abandonment of the fortress-style prisons of a bygone era is a necessary step in this direction, as a few very small maximum security facilities could be built or renovated to house the estimated 15 to 20 percent of the incarcerated felons who need this kind of protection and surveillance.

Prison Populations Increase _____

Between 1962 and 1969, the prison population in America decreased from 220,000 inmates to a low of 187,000. In 1970, however, the population figure began a dramatic turnaround and, between January 1977 and January 1978, it soared to a high of 300,908. In addition to that astounding figure, another 6,476 inmates sentenced to state prisons were being held in county jails and detention facilities. Since that time, the populations have skyrocketed upward by another estimated 293,000, with the total in

---

EFFECTS OF PRISON OVERCROWDING

Despite the fact that the nation has opened or expanded over a hundred prisons in less than 5 years, the average prison space available for inmates has dropped by over 10 percent. Prison crowding is getting worse.

What effects does prison crowding have? One is that fewer programs are available for inmates on a relative basis; another is that recreational opportunities are less. But it is in the health and safety areas that the impact is felt most.

The rates of death, suicide, homicides, inmate assaults, and disturbances increase as prison population density increases (population density is measured by square feet of floor space per inmate.) This finding holds regardless of whether a prisoner is confined in maximum, medium, or minimum security.

The incidence of colds, infectious diseases, tuberculosis, sexually communicable diseases, psychological disturbances, and psychiatric crises also is related to overcrowding. The more overcrowded the institution, the higher the incidence of medical problems.

Overcrowded maximum security prisons appear to be most likely to have the worst impact on prisoner health and safety. Correctional administrators and elected officials must plan to reduce the negative impacts of imprisonment on offenders.

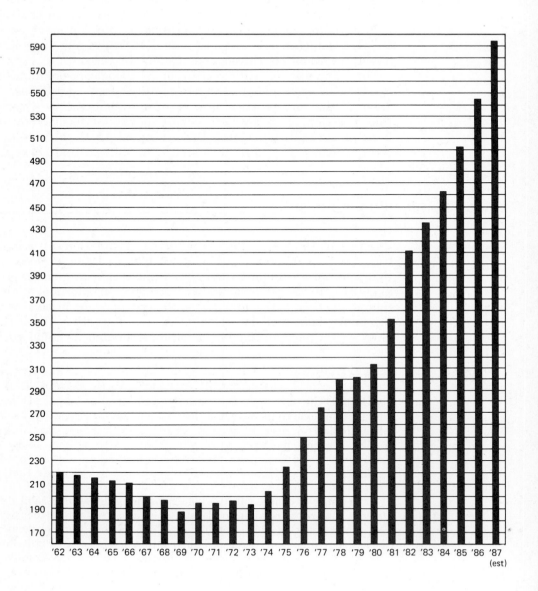

Figure 11-1 Total Population of U.S. State and Federal Prisons—1962–1979
(Figures are in thousands—as of January 1.) (LEAA figures for 1969, 1970,
and 1971 do not include certain states. Figures for 1962–1974 from LEAA;
1975–1977 figures from *Corrections Magazine*; 1978 figures from LEAA. Later
years from U.S. Department of Justice annual surveys.)

the state and federal adult prisons standing at an estimated 581,609 on December 31, 1987[37]!

The consequent overcrowding of the system means that offenders are doubled up in cells meant for one, packed into makeshift dormitories, and bunked in the basements, corridors, converted hospital facilities, tents, trailers, warehouses, and program activity areas of the nation's prisons. There are currently 216 Americans in prison for every 100,000 citizens — the highest rate for any democratic nation. If present trends continue, there will be over 725,000 Americans in prisons by 1990 (see Figure 11-1).

Although such a rapid increase in prison population is not easily explained, part of the reason for it may be traced to a hardening of public attitudes toward crime. The attitude in turn produces more and more "get tough" policies in the criminal justice system. (See Figure 11-2) The courts are under pressure to deter crime by giving longer sentences, and so they are using probation less often and are themselves pressing for better legislation in the area of probation. The legislators respond by passing more mandatory-sentencing laws, limiting the judges' latitude to grant probation or reduce the minimum time for parole consideration. Evidently, the policymakers are not aware of the evidence that an increased use of imprisonment is positively correlated with higher, rather than lower, levels of crime. Public safety is not enhanced by greater use of imprisonment.[38]

Another factor contributing to the increase of the prison population as a whole is the increase in the general population in the twenty- to thirty-year-old age group. This is seen as the population at risk, as crime is usually a young person's activity. This group is a direct result of the baby boom following World War II, which clogged the school systems of America in the 1950s and 1960s and has now affected yet another area — urban crime. This group is also the one with the highest unemployment rate and, in a time of general underemployment, will continue to commit crime out of proportion to its size.[39]

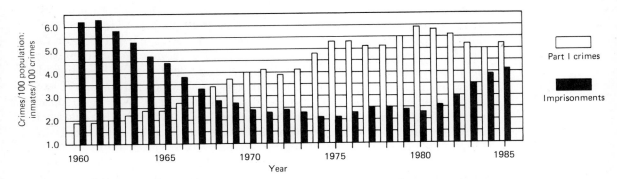

Figure 11-2 Crime Rates and Prison Risks: 1960–1985 (Edwin Zedlewski, Making Confinement Decisions [Washington, D.C.: U.S. Department of Justice, 1987], p. 5)

Currently, billions of dollars are programmed for prison construction, with many projects already under way. Until they are available or community corrections programs are expanded, prison administrators must be careful to redouble their efforts at early diagnosis, classification, and separation of different categories of offenders. The dangerous must be separated from the young and the weak, and the permanently sick from those who are able to respond to treatment. Although more staff will help, prison administrators will need to devote more time and resources to the development and maintenance of rational programming[40] and segregation of the more explosive members of the offender population.[41]

The public demands more prisons in America. There were 970 state and 49 federal adult prisons in America in 1987 — 427 more state prisons and one more federal prison than there were in 1984. The "boom" in prison construction is continuing into the last half of the 1980s, and there appears to be no end in sight.

Alternatives to Prison Overcrowding

There are basically three correctional options for reducing prison populations and overcrowding, and the reader has already encountered two: the so-called "bricks and mortar" building program and the "front end" or prison-avoidance programming. The latter includes restitution programs, intensive supervised probation, house arrest, electronic monitoring, shock probation, intermittent imprisonment, and other innovative programs of intermediate punishments. In the next chapter, dealing with parole, we encounter the "back end" alternatives: early release, parole, increased "good-time credits," home arrest under parole, halfway houses, prerelease centers, and other alternatives to prison overcrowding.

These are all viable options, but three major points need to be stressed. First, the further the offender is carried into the prison–parole cycle, the more expensive corrections will become. Second, the "bricks and mortar" solution tends to mortgage the future of corrections and taxpayers, saddling both with institutions that are not likely to be emptied in the near future. Finally, there is considerable evidence that the longer the offender remains in prison, the more likely that incapacitation will lead to recidivism.

An analysis of the nation's 1980 arrest data reveals that some 70 percent of the persons arrested for the eight most serious (Type I) offenses had prior adult arrests and about 27 percent had a prior adult incarceration. By July 1982, 40 percent of the 1980 arrestees had been arrested again.[42] Greenfield found that an estimated 61 percent of those admitted to prison in 1979 were recidivists (had been incarcerated as juvenile or adult, or both). Almost half of the prison releasees will return to prison in less than twenty years, usually by the first three years following initial release.[43] Prisons that are overcrowded do little to lower the recidivism rate.

Sex and Corrections _____

The subject of homosexuality and other sexual problems in prisons has always been highly controversial. Many states have passed legislation decriminalizing homosexual practices between "consenting adults." Yet great pains are taken to prevent such activity in an institution that is filled with sexually experienced individuals who are forced to exist in a one-sex society. The sexual drive is not one that can be turned off when the offender is placed in an institution. The standard beliefs about sex in prison are based on a number of unfounded assumptions and misleading implications:

- That the incidence of homosexual rape is high.
- That homosexual rape is the characteristic form of prison homosexuality.
- That there exist two distinct role types — an aggressor and an unwilling victim.
- That solutions would require establishing alternative outlets for the sexual drives.

Actually, recent evidence and theory suggest that none of these assumptions or implications is true. It is important, therefore, that any discussion of prison homosexuality begin by stripping away the myths and rationalizations surrounding the subject. One such approach is to focus initially on the prison context in which such behavior takes on meaning to the participants.[44]

It is estimated that there is a relationship between prior homosexual experience and the intensity of such activity in institutional custody:

The relationship between prison homosexuality and preinstitutional homosexual experience is also an issue requiring further elucidation. Working on the assumption that 40 to 50 percent of a penal population will have homosexual experience in prison, Gagnon has estimated that 5 to 10 percent will have had no prior homosexual experience, 25 to 30 percent will have had casual or intermittent prior experience, and 5 to 10 percent will have had extensive or nearly exclusive homosexual commitment in the free community. Gagnon bases his estimates in part on interview data from the Institute for Sex Research which found that in a group of 888 white prisoners, about 7 percent had homosexual experience for the first time while in prison. Based on continuing study of long-term maximum security institutions, Thomas finds 30 percent with a prior commitment to homosexual adjustment strong enough to suggest clinical fixation, while 60 percent have negligible prior experience, but undertake homosexual behavior in prison due to regression occasioned by the emotionally impoverished environment.

Even with these relatively high *incidence* figures, it seems quite clear that the *frequency* of homosexual contact is usually quite low, even among cellmates; and in no sense does it approach the rate of heterosexual or homosexual behavior of these same prisoners on the outside, except possibly for those prisoners who come into the institution with well-developed homosexual commitments and who become the "passive" partner in homosexual liaisons. In some prisons, usually those with a very low order of custody inside the walls, high rates of homosexual behavior may be achieved; however, these are not the prevalent conditions in most prison systems.[45]

AIDS IN PRISONS AND JAILS

Acquired Immune Deficiency Syndrome (AIDS) has rapidly become one of the most difficult and complex public health issues facing the United States. Since AIDS was first identified in this country in 1981, some 50,000 Americans have developed the disease, and three percent of the nation's inmates test positive.

The key terms in understanding AIDS are the following:

AIDS — Acquired Immune Deficiency Syndrome, a viral infection that destroys victims' immune systems, making them vulnerable to a wide range of other diseases.

HIV — Human Immunodeficiency Virus — the AIDS virus.

ARC — AIDS-related Complex — the preliminary symptoms of AIDS. A person with ARC has the virus and a mild form of the disease but has not been diagnosed with the opportunistic infection needed for full-blown AIDS.

Opportunistic infection — infections that do not affect people with normal immune systems. Example: PCP — pneumocystic carinii pneumonia.

Seropositivity — blood tests positive for the AIDS virus. The person has the virus and is contagious.

AIDS test — a blood test to look for antibodies produced by the body in response to the AIDS virus. The test determines whether a person has had the antibodies, indicating exposure to the disease. According to Brian James, AIDS program coordinator for the Nebraska Department of Health, 45 percent of the people who test positive go on to develop AIDS within the first six years of exposure. Scientists predict this number may reach 60 to 90 percent in ten years.

Full-blown AIDS — the last stage, brought on by another infection. It is almost always fatal.

In corrections, dealing with the problem of AIDS may pose even more difficult problems than in the free world, since inmate populations include high proportions of individuals in AIDS risk groups, particularly intraveneous drug users (more frequent in New York), and homosexual and bisexual men (more frequent in California).

Although no known cases have been reported among correctional staff (who were not already in high-risk group), AIDS in prisons has led to many correctional needs and problems. In particular, education and training of staff and inmates are vital to keeping the spread of the disease at a minimum. Currently the nation's prisons have no unified policies on AIDS testing, housing policies, treatment, precautionary measures, or legal issues, particularly in relation to the Eighth Amendment prohibition against cruel and unusual punishment and administrative isolation.

Excerpted in part from T. Hammett, *Aids in Prisons and Jails* (Washington, D.C.: U.S. Department of Justice, 1986).]

Most of this research is based on fragmentary evidence, and homosexuality is probably much less common in prison than the popular mythology leads us to believe. At least one researcher, however, believes that homosexual rape in prison is increasing and that it reflects an attempt by minority group members to "get even" with a repressive society.[46] Probably the most universal sexual outlet in prison is masturbation, a practice not unknown in the free world.

The problem of how to deal with sex in prison is a difficult one for the correctional administrator, as intervention in this area is one of the principal sources of violence in the institutional setting. Some of the administrator's problems are made clear in the following excerpt from *Homosexuality in Prisons:*

> What is clear is that it is not the sexual drive itself that makes a prison full of unrest and that as a matter of fact most males survive the deprivation of the sexual outlet and usually even survive transitory homosexual commitments to return to relatively conventional heterosexual lives on the outside. What the sexual problem in the male prison does represent is a series of land mines, some for the administration, more for the inmates. In the case of the inmates, men get into relationships which have some potential for shaping their future commitments to sexuality; relationships which leave them open to exploitation and especially for those who take the passive role, the possiblity of distortion of their self-conceptions. Further, there is some jealousy. When a relationship deteriorates or when a transfer of affection takes place, there is a distinct possibility of violence. The violence that does occur often is extreme, and at this point becomes a serious matter for prison management.
>
> The dilemma for the prison manager is that often he is not aware of the relationships until they erupt into violence. Attempts at intervention in this process through getting inmates to aid in the identification of those involved may result in serious scapegoating of these persons out of the sexual anxieties of the other prisoners. The segregation of these prisoners has also been attempted. However, one major difficulty with this measure seems to be that when the most obvious homosexuals are removed from the situation there is a tendency to co-opt other persons to take their place. This tendency is also noted when the aggressive male is removed, though the policy has usually been to remove only those men who are conventionally obvious, that is, who appear excessively effeminate.[47]

The conjugal visit has frequently been proposed to solve the problem of an institution with no heterosexual outlets. The adoption of this practice is inhibited by the American society's reluctance to accept any sexual relationship outside marriage, limiting the benefits of conjugal visits to inmates with an intact family. The practice of home furloughs, without supervision, is a more reasonable and natural response to the inmate's need for relationships outside the prison, whether sexual or otherwise. The treatment of more and more offenders in a community environment is another reasonable and viable response, as is a coeducational correctional staff.

The main cause of the sexual problems that arise in prisons is probably the prison environment itself. As the prison becomes the last resort for a small percentage of the inmate population, appropriate means for providing the residual prisoners with sexual outlets will need to be found. A society that uses sex appeal in almost every aspect of its mass media and sales promotional material should not raise an eyebrow at the news that sexually experienced and relatively normal persons cannot be deprived of this outlet for months and years, without problems. One of the issues to be resolved by future correctional administrators will be the possibility of accepting homosexual activity between consenting prisoners, when it is legally accepted in the free world.

Southern Ohio Correctional Facility, Lucasville (Courtesy of the Ohio Department of Rehabilitation and Corrections)

The Future of Imprisonment _____

It has frequently been shown that the large adult prisons operated by the state provide the least effective means to rehabilitate and reintegrate offenders. Despite findings to this effect, in the 1920s,[48] 1930s,[49] 1960s,[50] and 1970s,[51] the building and filling of maximum security prisons continued. The advent, and relative success, of community-based treatment of criminal offenders has begun to dent the armor of the diehards who advocate punitive prison as the ultimate correctional solution. It is the threat that these new programs pose to the old-line institutional staff that must be overcome before the present system, which exists primarily to perpetuate itself, can undergo any real change.

There are other reasons that the system is so slow to change, too. Long sentences are one problem: it is difficult to offer programs and promise of the future to a man who will not be released for ten years or more. Also, laws and practices that restrict the employment of ex-offenders make a mockery of the vocational training programs in many prisons. And to expect a man who has been earning $500 a day as a drug pusher to return to the same environment and work cheerfully as a janitor for the minimum wage is totally unreasonable. The street conditions that make possible such high illegal earnings cannot be controlled by the correctional staff, but the conditions do influence the results of the programs' efforts.

Summary _____

The litany of cures for correctional ills may seem to be a replay of previous efforts. The significant difference today lies in the interest and assistance of the federal government in the form of funds, technical advice, and planning assistance through the efforts of the National Institute of Justice and the National Institute of Corrections.

The kind of patchwork effort recommended by the National Advisory Commission is a good beginning. Prison problems are relentless, however, and even the most humane reformers are subtly changed by the enormous problems that face them. They become cold, callous, and finally prisonized themselves. William Nagel, in *The New Red Barn*, quotes early twentieth-century scholar and penologist Frank Tannenbaum:

> We must destroy the prison, root and branch. That will not solve our problem, but it will be a good beginning.... Let us substitute something. Almost anything will be an improvement. It cannot be worse. It cannot be more brutal and useless.[52]

Although this is a laudable goal, the realities of prison population increases and the opening of two or three new facilities a month in America will make the goal difficult to attain in the foreseeable future.

Review Questions

1. What are the main purposes of confinement?
2. Differentiate between classification for management and for treatment.
3. Describe a typical maximum security prison. Explain the main differences among maximum, medium, and minimum security institutions.
4. What are the "front end" solutions to prison overcrowding? The "bricks and mortar" solution?
5. What are the impacts of prison overcrowding?
6. Develop an argument against imprisonment of offenders from the recidivism perspective.
7. Why is the prison population so high in the nation?
8. Why are minority members overrepresented in prison?
9. What correctional problems do prison gangs pose for correctional administrators?
10. Why is homosexual behavior a problem in prison?

Key Terms

1. perfectability (p. 216)
2. maximum security prison (p. 219)
3. gothic monolith (p. 219)
4. classification (p. 222)
5. prison gangs (p. 227)
6. "bricks and mortar" (p. 229)
7. overcrowding (p. 231)
8. AIDS (p. 236)
9. conjugal visit (p. 237)
10. community-based treatment (p. 239)

Notes

1. Norman Johnston, *The Human Cage: A Brief History of Prison Architecture* (New York: Walker, 1973), p. 8.
2. In 1986, California opened four new institutions to provide 2,620 new beds at a construction cost of $182,000,000, or $69,000 per bed. Retiring construction bonds for prisons would increase the cost to $236,000 per bed (assuming 8 percent interest and 30-year bonds).
3. For an overview of institutional research in England, see Roy Walmsley, "Current Prison Research in England," paper presented at the annual meeting of the American Society of Criminology (Atlanta: October 30, 1986).

4. Cesare Beccaria, *On Crimes and Punishments,* trans. Henry Paolucci (Indianapolis: Bobbs-Merrill, 1963), pp. 8, 43–44, 58, 94.

5. David J. Rothman, *The Discovery of the Asylum* (Boston: Little Brown, 1971), p. 62. See also Raymond Paternoster, "The Deterrent Effect of the Perceived Certainty and Severity of Punishment: A Review of the Evidence and Issues," *Justice Quarterly* 4 (1987): 173–217.

6. George Camp and Camille Camp, *The Corrections Yearbook 1987* (South Salem, New York: Criminal Justice Institute, 1987), p. 24.

7. Camp and Camp, p. 21

8. William G. Nagel, *The New Red Barn: A Critical Look at the Modern American Prison* (New York: Walker, 1973), pp. 11–13.

9. The District of Columbia Reformatory, built at Lorton, Virginia, in 1926.

10. Howard B. Gill, "Correctional Philosophy and Architecture," *Journal of Criminal Law, Criminology, and Police Science* 53 (1962): 312–322. For a profile of Howard Gill, see Barbara Neff, "Celebrating 61 Years in Corrections," *Corrections Today* 49 (1987): 159–160.

11. Franco Ferracuti et al., *Mental Deterioration in Prison* (Columbus: Ohio State University Program for Study of Crime and Delinquency, 1978), p. 81.

12. Johnston, p. 40.

13. Gothic architecture was designed to overwhelm the person who entered such structures. The famous Gothic churches of Europe were known to make people feel small and insignificant.

14. Maximum security prisons in America:
    Prior to 1830 —   6
    1831 to 1870 — 17
    1871 to 1900 — 33
    1901 to 1930 — 21
    1931 to 1960 — 15
    1961 to 1975 — 21
    1976 to 1986 — 17
        Total   —130

15. Benjamin Frank, "Basic Issues in Corrections," *Perspectives on Correctional Manpower and Training* (Washington, D.C.: American Correctional Association, 1970). See also the special topic volume devoted to classification, *Crime and Delinquency* 32 (1986), p. 317.

16. American Correctional Association, *Manual of Correctional Standards,* 3d ed. (Washington, D.C.: American Correctional Association, 1966), pp. 2–3.

17. United Nations Department of Economic and Social Affairs, *Standard Minimum Rules for the Treatment of Prisoners and Related Recommendations* (New York: United Nations, 1958), p. B-16.

18. President's Commission on Law Enforcement and Administration of Justice, *Task Force Report: Corrections* (Washington, D.C.: U.S. Government Printing Office, 1967), p. 20.

19. See Thomas Kane, "The Validity of Prison Classification: An Introduction to Practical Considerations and Research Issues," *Crime and Delinquency* 32 (1987): 367–390.

20. "Help" in this context would include the full array of services available—medical, psychological, psychiatric, educational, vocational, and others.

21. "Catch-22" means that one can escape from an unpleasant situation only by

meeting certain conditions, but if one meets those conditions, one can't escape. The expression was popularized by Joseph Heller's novel of that name, about an army pilot constantly required to fly suicidal missions. He knew it was crazy to fly the missions but, according to the army, because he knew it was crazy, he was perfectly sane. And if he were sane, he could continue to fly the missions.

22. National Advisory Commission on Criminal Justice Standards and Goals, *Corrections* (Washington, D.C.: U.S. Department of Justice, 1973), p. 199.

23. Guidelines for developing, implementing and testing objective prison classification instruments can be found in Robert Buchanan, Karen Whitlow, and James Austin, "National Evaluation of Objective Prison Classification Systems: The Current State of the Art," *Crime and Delinquency* 32 (1987): 272–290.

24. Donald Clemmer, "The Process of Prisonization," in Leon Radzinowicz and Marvin Wolfgang, eds., *The Criminal in Confinement* (New York: Basic Books, 1971), pp. 92–93.

25. Minorities are vastly overrepresented in prisons. Explanations of this disparity range from system discrimination to differential involvement in crime. For the differential involvement position, see Patrick Langan, "Racism on Trial: New Evidence to Explain the Racial Composition of Prisons in the United States," *Journal of Criminal Law and Criminology* 76 (1985): 666–683. For the discrimination perspective, see Cassia Spohn, John Gruhl, and Susan Welch, "The Impact of the Ethnicity and Gender of Defendants on the Decision to Reject or Dismiss Felony Charges," *Criminology* 25 (1987): 175–191.

26. Special devices for communicating include such things as telephones on either side of bulletproof glass and booths with wire screen between.

27. National Advisory Commission, *Corrections,* p. 344.

28. Ohio Department of Rehabilitation and Correction (Columbus, Ohio), *The Communicator* 1, 12. This figure is a projection from $45 in 1973.

29. Alexis de Tocqueville was one of the French commissioners who visited America in 1833. He wrote a treatise on what he observed in the American penitentiary system. (See note 30.)

30. Gustave de Beaumont and Alexis de Tocqueville, *On the Penitentiary System in the United States and Its Application in France* (Carbondale, Ill.: Southern Illinois University Press, 1964), p. 48.

31. The National Clearinghouse for Correctional Programming and Architecture is located at the University of Illinois, Department of Architecture, Urbana, Illinois 61801. For more information on prison architecture, see Randy Atlas, "High Rise Confinement for the 'Innocent Until Proven Guilty'," *Florida Architecture* 15 (May–June 1984): 29–30: Michael Cohn, "Tomorrow's Designs Today," *Corrections Today* 49 (1987): 32–34, American Institute of Architects, *1985 Architecture for Justice Exhibition* (Washington, D.C.: American Institute of Architects, 1985); and Dale Sechrest and Shelley Price, *Correctional Facility Design and Construction Management* (Washington, D.C.: U.S. Department of Justice, 1985).

32. Charles DeWitt and Cindie Unger, *Oklahoma Prison Expansion Saves Time and Money* (Washington, D.C.: U.S. Department of Justice, 1987).

33. Charles DeWitt, *Florida Sets Example With Use of Concrete Modules* (Washington, D.C.: U.S. Department of Justice, 1986).

34. Charles DeWitt, *California Tests New Construction Concepts* (Washington, D.C.: U.S. Department of Justice, 1986).

35. Charles DeWitt, *Ohio's New Approach to Prison and Jail Financing* (Washington, D.C.: U.S. Department of Justice, 1986).

36. Gennaro Vito, "Putting Prisoners to Work: Policies and Problems," *Journal of Offender Counseling Services, and Rehabilitation* 9 (1985): 21–34.

37. *Prisoners in State and Federal Institutions on December 31, 1978: Advance Report* (Washington, D.C.: U.S. Department of Justice, 1979). The 1988 data are from Craig Fischer, "Inmate Population Sets Record for 13th Consecutive Year," *Criminal Justice Newsletter* 19 (May 2, 1988): 3.

38. David Biles, "Crime and the Use of Prisons," *Federal Probation* 43 (June 1979): 39–43.

39. Richard Allinson, "Does Recession Bode Rise in Imprisonment?" *Criminal Justice Newsletter* 10 (October 22, 1979): 5–6. But see Robert Parker and Allan Horowitz, "Unemployment, Crime and Imprisonment: A Panel Approach," *Criminology* 24 (1986): 751–773.

40. Murray Cullen, "Anger Control Programs: Good Programs Can Enhance Security," *Corrections Today* 49 (1987): 32–33, 129–31.

41. Richard McGee, George Warner, and Nora Harlow, *The Special Management Inmate* (Washington, D.C.: U.S. Department of Justice, 1985).

42. Cornelius Behan, "ROPE: Repeat Offender Program Experiment," *FBI Law Enforcement Bulletin* 56 (1987): 1–5

43. Lawrence Greenfield, *Examining Recidivism* (Washington, D.C.: U.S. Department of Justice, 1985), p. 340.

44. Peter C. Buffum, *Homosexuality in Prisons* (Washington, D.C.: U.S. Department of Justice, 1972), pp. 2–3.

45. Ibid., p. 13.

46. Anthony Scacco, Jr., *Rape in Prison* (Springfield, Ill.: Chas. C. Thomas, 1975), p. 17.

47. Buffum, pp. 28–29.

48. National Commission on Law Observance and Enforcement (Wickersham commission), U.S. Government Printing Office, Washington D.C., 1929.

49. *Attorney General's Survey of Release Procedures,* 1939.

50. President's Commission on Law Enforcement and Administration of Justice, 1967.

51. National Advisory Commission on Criminal Justice Standards and Goals, 1973.

52. Nagel, p. 148.

12

Parole

The problems of crime bring us together. Even as we join in common action, we know that there can be no instant victory. Ancient evils do not yield to easy conquest. We cannot limit our efforts to enemies we can see. We must, with equal resolve, seek out new knowledge, new techniques, and new understanding.
—LYNDON B. JOHNSON

Origins of Parole

Earlier in American history, offenders were sentenced to prison for a fixed period, and they were not released until they had "jammed their time." In the Middle Ages, the fixed period of time was often life, leaving the prisoners with little hope for release or incentive to change their ways. Beccaria's theorem of punishment bears review:

> In order for punishment not to be, in every instance, an act of violence of one or of many against a private citizen, it must be essentially public, prompt, necessary, the least possible in the given circumstances, proportionate to the crimes, dictated by the laws.[1]

This theorem, of course, was not observed by those who devised the long, excessively severe, and far-from-public punishments meted out in the early prisons. One of the great breakthroughs in the development of corrections was the *indeterminate* (sometimes called *indefinite*) sentence, preceded by a form of sentence reduction called *good-time laws*.

Good-Time Laws

The term *good time* did not refer to fun within the walls, but to taking days off the offender's sentence as a result of conduct and behavior in accordance with the institutional rules. In 1817, New York was the first state to pass a good-time law. The rules throughout the nation were firm

> ### INDETERMINATE SENTENCE
>
> An indeterminate sentence is a sentence to incarceration pronounced by a judge that sets minimum and maximum periods of incarceration of the offender (such as from one to five years). The minimum term would establish the earliest release date (adjusted for certain time credits for, as an example, jail time during pretrial detention) or the first time before the inmate could possibly be released. At the maximum term, the inmate would have to be released.
>
> Underlying the indeterminate sentence are assumptions of rehabilitation, and early release, if the offender is treated and is reformed. The minimum and maximum periods (such as a one-to-five year sentence) reflect the inability of the sentencing judge to know when the offender would be reformed.

and fairly straightforward, varying from state to state. New York's enabled the correctional administrator to reduce by one-fourth the sentence of any prisoner sentenced to imprisonment for not less than five years, upon certificate of the principal keeper and other satisfactory evidence, that such prisoner had behaved well and had acquired, in the whole, the net sum of $15 dollars or more per annum.[2] Every state in the union and the District of Columbia had passed some kind of good-time law by 1916. The U.S. Parole Commission further rewards inmates who successfully complete rehabilitation programs by shaving more time off their prison terms (called *presumptive* sentences).[3] California awarded good time in 1988 at a "1 for 2" ratio: one day of reduction for every two days of good time.

Though the good-time laws were a step forward, they were really not much better than the methods used to gain pardons for prisoners. *Pardons* were often sought to relieve offenders of oppressively heavy sentences. In some cases the juries themselves petitioned the governor to grant pardon when the only sentence the law allowed them to recommend was extremely long. The power of pardon was often used to empty out the prisons so that courts would have some place to send newly sentenced offenders. In addition, that power made weak governors succumb to pressure from rich or influential offenders. The good-time laws were a help, but they were usually bound by a fixed formula, so that many prisoners were kept long after officials had agreed that they were ready for release. By 1832 a new concept was being developed and discussed: indeterminate sentencing.

Indeterminate Sentencing

The idea of the indeterminate sentence is usually attributed to the efforts of England's Alexander Maconochie and Ireland's Sir Walter Crofton (see Chapter 3). The effectiveness of Crofton's Irish system was discussed at the meeting of the National Prison Association in 1870, at which Crofton himself presented a paper on the indeterminate sentence. Zebulon Brockway, who had encouraged the Michigan legislature to pass an indeterminate sentence act in 1867 and who used it in his position as superintendent

---

TIME CREDITS AND PAROLE

There are three major ways for inmates to earn credits of time against their sentences. These are for: (1) time incarcerated in jail prior to being transported to the prison; (2) observing institutional rules regarding appropriate behavior; and (3) participating in institutional programming.

"Jail time" is credited against the inmate's sentence, based on the number of days the offender is detained in jail prior to being admitted to prison. Some inmates are granted credit for the entire number of days in jail, such as nine months credit for a pretrial detention of 270 days. Other states (such as California) generally allow only one-half credit for time served (such as three months or 90 days credit for 180 days in jail detention). In 1984, the average amount of time spent in jail that was credited toward the offender's prison sentence was about four months. "Good time" is earned for conformity to institutional rules and regulations, for not fighting, for absence of rule infractions, for working on prison crews, and so on. Some refer to this procedure as "time off for keeping your nose clean." "Program credit" is earned in a limited number of jurisdictions for participation in treatment programming, or for completion of a particular program (such as earning a high school equivalency diploma, completion of a baking course, graduation from a drug treatment program).

In states with indeterminate sentencing, credits are generally applied against both the *minimum* and maximum sentences. Thus the first date for an inmate to have a parole hearing could be significantly truncated for those entering a prison with nine months of jail time and indeterminate sentences such as one–three years. The incoming inmate would have a parole hearing date shortly after arriving, and some percent (albeit small) of these inmates would be paroled almost immediately after prison admission.

Time credit also lessens the *maximum* time an inmate could be imprisoned. An inmate bringing nine months of jail time into a prison where good-time credits are earned at the rate of one month off for every two months of compliant behavior, and whose original sentence was "no less than one nor more than three years" would be released no later than at the end of 18 months, having completed the "time to be served."
The figures are these:

Jail time credit	9 months
Time served	18 months
Good time (1/2 × 18 months)	9 months
Total	36 months

In states with flat, determinate or presumptive sentences, credits generally are applied against the maximum time before parole. On average, offenders serve about 45 percent of the maximum length of their court-ordered sentences.

---

of the Detroit House of Corrections,[4] also advocated its widespread adoption. The indeterminate sentencing and parole ideas espoused by Brockway and Crofton in 1870 were finally put into practice at Elmira Reformatory in 1876. A form of parole was worked out at Elmira that kept the prisoner under the supervision and control of the prison authorities for an additional six months after release.

The use of a true indeterminate sentence won acceptance more slowly than the use of parole did. A genuine indeterminate sentence has no minimum and no maximum time limits; release is based entirely on the offender's willingness to conform to whatever model is used to determine 'his or her ability to return to free society. Many judges are reluctant to give up such a large part of their sentencing power. Others fear that it is dangerous to leave such a broad power over the inmate in the hands of correctional administrators, as it could result in a life sentence for a minor offense if an administrator bore a grudge against an inmate. Most indeterminate sentence laws have, therefore, been designed with some kind of a minimum and maximum time that still allows broad discretion to the administrator. In most jurisdictions, the minimum sentence is no more than half of the maximum (for example, ten to twenty, fifteen to thirty, five to ten), although the minimum can be as low as deemed necessary (for example, six months to three years, one to twenty, three to thirty).

The general consensus is that the practice of parole, though not totally dependent on the indeterminate sentence, could not have developed without it. The indeterminate sentence, sometimes attacked as too lenient, is in fact a sound alternative. It gives deserving offenders a chance to get out from under the oppressive sentencing practices of earlier judges, while offering a means of retaining the incorrigibles in custody. It can also be used by the paroling authority to reduce or eliminate disparities in sentencing.

Although more states have retained indeterminate sentences than have shifted toward alternatives, the trend in the United States is toward the determinate sentence, which does not bode well for the future of parole as a viable alternative to prisoners being released back on the streets without supervision.

Pardon and Parole: The Way Out of Prison

Most offenders who enter the prisons of America eventually end up back on the streets of the old neighborhoods. Unless prisoners die in prison (from natural causes or otherwise), almost all will come out someday. The cruelly long sentences of the nineteenth century usually meant that the few offenders who did leave the prisons were bitter, broken, or both. Today the odds are heavy that offenders will leave prison on parole, usually long before the expiration of their maximum sentences. In recent years, the

---

PAROLE

Release of an inmate from confinement prior to expiration of sentence on condition of good behavior and supervision in the community.

DEATHS IN PRISON

Although most offenders are released from prison under some program or parole, or after serving their maximum sentence, a small number die while incarcerated. Here are the 1986 data on death in prisons:

Source	Number	Percent of Total Deaths
Homicide	101	9%
Suicide	123	10
AIDS	231	19
Execution	18	2
Natural Causes (includes AIDS)	715	60
Total	1,188	100%

Source: George Camp and Camille Camp, *The Correctional Yearbook 1987* (South Salem, N.Y.: 1987), pp. 19-20

number and percentage of prisoners released on parole have climbed steadily. In 1966, the prisoners released on parole numbered 61 percent of the total, but this figure jumped to 74 percent by 1985. (see Table 12.1)[5] In some states prisoners on parole account for 100 percent of the releases.[6] The United States parole population has grown by more than 16 percent since 1983, and at the start of 1988, there were approximately 300,203 offenders on parole (see Figure 12-1).[7] The significance of parole is clear when one recognizes that the only alternatives are clemency, completion of sentence, or death.

In the days of frequent capital punishment and life sentences, death in prison was a strong possibility. The prisoner might die as a result of natural causes, an accident, or homicide inside the walls. Another way

TABLE 12.1 State Prison Releases, by Method, 1977–86

Year	Total Releases from Prisons	Percent of prison releases						
		All	Discretionary Parole	Mandatory Release	Expiration of Term	Probation	Commutation	Other
1977	115,213	100%	71.9%	5.9%	16.1%	3.6%	1.1%	1.4%
1978	119,796	100	70.4	5.8	17.0	3.3	.7	2.8
1979	128,954	100	60.2	16.9	16.3	3.3	.4	3.0
1980	136,968	100	57.4	19.5	14.9	3.6	.5	4.0
1981	142,489	100	54.6	21.4	13.9	3.7	2.4	4.0
1982	157,144	100	51.9	24.4	14.4	4.8	.3	4.2
1983	191,237	100	48.1	26.9	16.1	5.2	.5	3.2
1984	191,499	100	46.0	28.7	16.3	4.9	.5	3.6
1985	203,895	100	43.2	30.8	16.9	4.5	.4	4.1
1986	230,672	100	43.2	31.1	14.8	4.5	.3	6.0

Source: Thomas Hester, *Probation and Parole 1986* (Washington, D.C.: U.S. Department of Justice, 1987), p. 4.

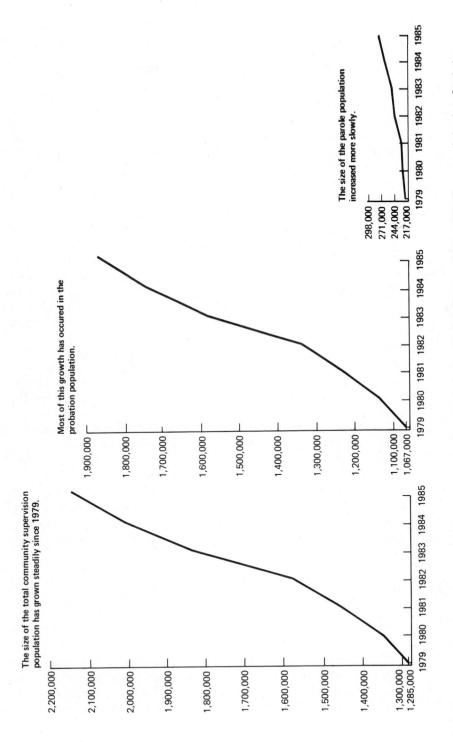

Figure 12-1 Increases in Probation and Parole Caseloads in the United States: 1979–1985 (Bureau of Justice Statistics, *Probation and Parole 1982* [Washington, D.C.: U.S. Department of Justice, 1983], p. 1; Bureau of Justice Statistics, *Probation and Parole, 1985* [Washington, D.C.: U.S. Department of Justice, 1987], p. 3)

out—sometimes not much better, from the offender's viewpoint—is to be forced to serve the entire maximum sentence before release (to "max out").

Infinitely better, but rare, is *executive clemency,* in the form of a pardon or similar action by the governor. A full pardon usually means complete exoneration of blame for the offense and relieves the prisoner of the stigma of guilt. One version of the pardon is *amnesty*, which may be granted to a group or class of offenders. The United States has a long tradition of granting amnesty to soldiers who deserted in major wars. And in countries where it is customary to imprison any and all political dissidents, the government may use mass amnesty to gain public favor. Executive power can also be used to grant a *reprieve*, usually in the case of the death penalty. (One remembers the old "B" grade movies in which the star is granted a last-minute reprieve while being strapped into the electric chair.) A reprieve does not usually result in a release, but merely a reduction in the severity of the punishment. Punishment can also be lessened by *commutation*, a shortening of the sentence by executive order. Usually the commutation is based on time already spent in jail and prison and results in almost immediate release of the petitioner. Another form of release, discussed in Chapter 9, results from some sort of appellate review action. These procedures, along with parole (and, of course, escape) cover the possible ways a prisoner can expect to leave prison.

The classic definition of parole is "release of an offender from a penal or correctional institution, after he has served a portion of his sentence, under the continued custody of the state and under conditions that permit his reincarceration in the event of misbehavior."[8] The term *parole* is attributed to Dr. S. G. Howe of Boston,[9] who used it in a letter to the Prison Association of New York in 1846. It is the amount of supervision exercised over the parolee that distinguishes American parole procedures from those of other countries. As the state parole systems developed in America, the reliance on rules and supervision became a crucial element. As the nation entered the twentieth century, parole had gained a strong foothold as a way for prisoners to return to the free world. Today, all but two states have some system of parole supervision for released offenders, even though some nineteen states are now in the process of reducing or eliminating its use.

Parole Administration

If prisoners want to be released on parole, they must be recommended and reviewed by some procedure that will select them for this option. For this reason, how parole is administered and by whom are of vital concern to the prison population, as well as to the rest of society.

The Parole Board

When parole selection procedures were first instituted, many states had a single commissioner of parole, appointed by the governor. This kind of political patronage soon led to corruption and controversy and was generally abandoned after World War II. Two models for parole recommendation have replaced it: (1) parole boards that are linked to, or actually part of, the correctional system staff, and (2) parole boards that are independent of correctional institutions and the administrators of the system. A third model, a consolidation of all correctional and parole services, incorporates the most desirable aspects of the first two models.

The correctional system model tends to perceive the parole decision as merely another in a series of decisions regarding the offender. The institutional staff feels that it is best suited, because of its close contact with the offender, to make the parole decision. This argument, however, is based on the false assumption that strict obedience to the conditions and rules that dominate prison life somehow is linked to a healthy adjustment on the outside. In other words, the kind of behavior that might lead the staff to conclude that an inmate was ready for parole could in fact cripple his or her efforts to cope on the outside. Complete subordination to rules and regulations and suppression of individuality—the desired behavior in institutions to ensure a smooth operation—are hardly the requisite skills for survival in the free world. Another potential problem with parole decisions made by the institutional staff could be a twisted use of that procedure to get rid of prison troublemakers. Institutional decision making can be buried too readily in the invisible activity behind the walls. Removed from public scrutiny or control, the parole decision soon becomes just another mechanical process that treats offenders, vitally concerned with the decision, as only incidental to the outcome.

In time, the independently authorized parole-releasing authority became the most widely used model in adult corrections. As a matter of fact, today no adult parole authority is controlled directly by the staff of a penal institution.[10] The obvious purpose of this independent authority was to remove the decision-making procedure from the atmosphere outlined in the previous paragraph. It was felt that the institutional parole authorities were too easily swayed by the subjective input of the staff.

Although an independent board may well be more objective than would the correctional bureaucracy be in making parole recommendations, it does not provide the perfect system. Board members' lack of knowledge about

---

PAROLE BOARD

Any correctional person, authority, or board that has the authority to release on parole those adults (or juveniles) committed to confinement facilities, to set conditions for behavior, to revoke from parole and to discharge from parole.

A Typical Parole Board Confrontation of the 1950s (Courtesy of the Ohio Department of Rehabilitation and Corrections)

the programs, policies, and conditions within the prisons creates an organizational gap, critics have argued, that causes unnecessary conflict between prison authorities and the boards:

> First, the claim is made that such boards tend to be insensitive to institutional programs and fail to give them the support they require. Second, independent boards are accused of basing their decisions on inappropriate considerations, such as the feelings of a local police chief. Third, their remoteness from the institutional program gives independent boards little appreciation of the dynamics in a given case; their work tends to be cursory, with the result that too often persons who should be paroled are not, and those who should not be paroled are released. Fourth, the argument is made that independent systems tend to place on parole boards persons who have little training or experience in corrections.[11]

An attempt to solve the problems that have plagued the institutional and independent systems has resulted in the newest and most popular model, the *consolidated board*. The consolidated model places the authority for parole decisions in the department of corrections but includes independent powers in the decision-making process. This arrangement reflects the general move toward the consolidation of all correctional services, such as institutional programs, community-based programs, and parole and aftercare programs, under state departments of correction. The consolidation model views the treatment of offenders as they pass through the correctional system as a continuum, rather than a series of separate, unrelated experiences. It is claimed that removal of the decision-making authority to a level above the institutions, but still within the system, tends to foster objectivity while maintaining a sensitivity to the programs and problems of the prison administrators. This approach is gaining wide acceptance, and over 60 percent of the state parole boards responsible for releasing adult offenders now function as part of an administrative structure that includes other agencies for offenders.[12] Although this system is preferable to the alternatives outlined earlier, its advocates still must struggle to maintain its autonomy through careful selection of board members and avoidance of automatic tenure, with explicit delineation of parole board tasks and responsibilities.

The Parole Selection Process

How is an offender selected for parole? This question has been asked by many researchers and, until recently, little concrete evidence was found that any reasonably objective criteria were used. These earlier studies showed that the main factor considered in the selection process was the seriousness of the crime for which the offender was originally convicted.[13] In 1979, however, a national study of parole boards determined that specific factors were considered evidence of parole readiness. The five most important factors were participation in prison programs, good prison behavior, change in attitudes, increased maturity, and development of insight.[14] Perhaps a good way to analyze this process is to follow a typical parole review and selection effort.

Most parole boards operate by assigning cases to individual board members, who review the cases in detail and then make recommendations to the board as a whole. In most cases the recommendation of the individual member is accepted, but sometimes the assembled board will request more information. At this point, the prisoner will often be asked to appear. Some states send individual board members to the institutions to interview the inmate and the prison staff; others convene the entire board at the various institutions on a regular schedule. If inmates do not meet whatever mysterious standards the board has established for parole, their sentences are continued and they are "flopped." But if they are accepted, they are

---

"FLOPPED"

"Flopped" is inmate slang for failing to meet parole board standards for release. A flop usually means that the inmate will not be eligible to be considered anew by the board until another six months or more of incarceration, treatment, or observation in the institution.

DISCRETIONARY RELEASE

Parole of an inmate from prison prior to the expiration of maximum sentence, according to the boundaries set by the sentence and the legislature. Discretionary release functions usually under the indeterminate sentence and implies that the inmate is ready to undergo community treatment and supervision.

---

prepared for turnover to the adult parole authority for a period of supervision determined by the parole board.

One problem in making parole decisions is the tendency of most boards to disregard the right of offenders to know what standards they are expected to meet (and, if they fail, the reasons for it):

> It is an essential element of justice that the role and processes for measuring parole readiness be made known to the inmate. This knowledge can greatly facilitate the earnest inmate toward his own rehabilitation. It is just as important for an inmate to know the rules and basis of the judgment upon which he will be granted or denied parole as it was important for him to know the basis of the charge against him and the evidence upon which he was convicted. One can imagine nothing more cruel, inhuman, and frustrating than serving a prison term without knowledge of what will be measured and the rules determining whether one is ready for release.... Justice can never be a product of unreasoned judgment.[15]

This criteria problem also affects the correctional staff, who should know the "rules of the game" so that they can guide inmates in the direction desired by the parole board.

Another problem facing potential parolees is the lack of an appeal process. Because criteria for granting parole and reasons for denying it are not specified, inmates—and concerned citizens—have often questioned the validity of board decisions. Future parole selection processes must include self-regulating internal appeal procedures, or the courts will be deluged with relevant cases until the Supreme Court finally establishes a basis for rules and procedures under the rubric of the Fourteenth Amendment. Some states, recognizing the handwriting on the wall, have begun to estab-

---

MANDATORY RELEASE

The required release of an inmate from incarceration because the statutes mandate the release of any inmate having served the equivalent of the maximum term. Mandatory release means the parole board refused to release the inmate prior to attainment of the equivalent of the maximum time imposed by the court. Mandatory release reflects the impacts of good-time, jail-time, and program-time credits on the actual length of time an offender can be held on a sentence of incarceration. More than 30 percent of prison releasees are by mandatory release.

A Modern, More Relaxed Parole Hearing (Courtesy Federal Bureau of Prisons)

lish criteria and develop appeal procedures before they are forced to do so by court decisions based on class action suits.

Inmates, correctional critics, scholars, parole board members, study panels, and prison writers have commented on the release decision, characterizing it as arbitrary, capricious, prejudiced, lawless, and offering no meaningful future directions for inmates who have not been released. One response to these criticisms has been the development of parole guidelines; the U.S. Parole Commission has been in the forefront of this movement, although other jurisdictions (such as Alabama and Georgia) are drawing up their own guidelines.

The federal guidelines use characteristics of the offense and the traits and previous criminal behaviors the inmate brings to the current offense to construct a matrix that specifies the amount of time (within narrow bounds) that an inmate would have to serve before release. Good-time and earned-time credits can reduce the anticipated prison sentence. Such an approach permits the offender to know immediately how long the sentence will be and what must be done to shorten it. The approach also reduces the anxiety and hostility of the "on-the-spot" decision-making process frequently found in other jurisdictions. If the parole commission deviates more than 20 percent from the guidelines, the rationale for deviation must be explained in writing, and an appeal procedure permits legal review. More states should consider this promising approach!

The rules for conditional release developed under Crofton's Irish system form the basis for most parole stipulations, even today. The conditions for parole should be related to the objectives of a parole system, as follows:

1. Release of each person from confinement at the most favorable time, with appropriate consideration to requirements of justice, expectations of subsequent behavior, and cost.
2. The largest possible number of successful parole completions.
3. The smallest possible number of new crimes committed by released offenders.
4. The smallest possible number of violent acts committed by released offenders.
5. An increase of general community confidence in parole administration.[16]

The methods by which these objectives can be carried out include the following:

1. A process for selecting persons who should be given parole and for determining the time of release.
2. A system for prerelease planning both inside the institution with the offender and outside the institution with others in the community at large.
3. A system for supervision and assistance in the community.
4. A set of policies, procedures, and guidelines for situations in which the question of reimprisonment must be decided.[17]

Designed in the belief that these conditions should be followed to the letter, and in the awareness that the public saw the paroled offender as a "convict bogey," many early programs were based on unreasonable restrictions. Many of these rules were no more than convenient techniques for ensuring the quick return of parolees to prison if they created even a slight stir for the parole supervisors. An example of such rules, in force as recently as 1962, is displayed in Figure 12-2. More recently, that rigid formula was replaced with the simple and commonsense statement presented in Figure 12-3.

One can imagine that conforming to the early rule requiring the parolee to "only associate with persons of good reputation" would be difficult for a man whose wife was a prostitute or whose father was an ex-convict. The emphasis on such rules gave parole officers great discretionary power over parolees. The parolees knew that they could be returned to prison for a technical violation of their parole conditions at almost any time the parole officer desired, a situation hardly conducive to reform and respect

1. Upon leaving the institution I will go directly to the place to which I have been paroled and will report as directed to my parole officer.

2. I will remain in the county and state to which I have been paroled unless I obtain written permission to leave through my parole officer. I will consult with my parole officer and obtain the officer's approval before changing my address or residence within the county to which I have been paroled.

3. I will submit true written reports of my activities to my parole officer as directed. A false report will constitute a violation of my parole.

4. I will reply promptly to any communication from the Adult Parole Authority or any of their officers.

5. I will report in person to such person or persons at such time and in such place and manner as may be directed by the Adult Parole Authority.

6. I will make every effort to obtain and keep satisfactory employment as is approved by my parole officer. If my employment should stop for any reason I will immediately report this fact to my parole officer. I will not voluntarily change my place or type of employment without first obtaining permission from my parole officer.

7. I will support to the best of my ability those persons for whom I am responsible.

8. I will enter into marriage only after I have received the written permission of my parole officer. Under no circumstances will I cohabit with anyone not my legal spouse.

9. I will associate and communicate only with persons of good reputation. I will avoid contact with persons who have criminal records or persons who are on probation or parole. I will not visit persons or frequent places or areas forbidden by my parole officer.

10. I will get written permission from my parole officer before purchasing, owning or operating any motor vehicle, aircraft, or powerboat, in addition to satisfying any conditions which might apply to my particular case. I understand this permission will be given only after I have a valid operator's license and such liability insurance as is approved by my parole officer.

11. I will not purchase, own, possess, use or have under my control any deadly weapon or firearm. I understand there will be no exceptions to this rule while I am on parole.

12. I will not have in my possession, use, sell, distribute or have under my control any narcotic drugs, barbiturates, marijuana, paregoric, or extracts containing them in any form or instruments for administering them except on prescription of a licensed physician.

13. I will not use intoxicants to such an excess that in the opinion of my parole officer my health or the safety or welfare of others is placed in jeopardy, or that it interferes with meeting financial obligations, employment, my family relations, or acceptable behavior.

14. I will obey all municipal ordinances, state and federal laws, and will at all times conduct myself as a respectable law-abiding citizen.

Special Conditions

In addition to agreeing to abide by the above conditions of parole, I understand and accept that while on parole I do not have the right to vote, serve on juries, or hold public office.

I further understand that if I am granted permission to be in another state or if I should be there without permission and my return to [my home state] is authorized, I hereby waive extradition to the [said] state . . . and agree not to contest efforts to effect such return.

By affixing my signature below I signify my acceptance of these conditions of parole and any other special conditions which the Adult Parole Authority might impose. I agree to abide by and follow any instructions given by the Adult Parole Authority or any of its supervisors or officers and I accept them as part of the conditions of my parole.

These conditions of parole have been explained to me and I understand them.

Witness _____   Signed _____

Date _____ [17]

Figure 12-2 Rules of Parole, 1962 (Walter C. Reckless, *The Crime Problem*, 4th ed. [New York: Appleton-Century Crofts, 1967], p. 761)

The Members of the Parole Board have agreed that you have earned the opportunity of parole and eventually a final release from your present conviction. The Parole Board is therefore ordering a Parole Release in your case.

Parole Status has a two-fold meaning: One is a trust status in which the Parole Board accepts your word you will do your best to abide by the Conditions of Parole that are set down in your case; the other, by state law, means the Adult Parole Authority has the legal duty to enforce the Conditions of Parole even to the extent of arrest and return to the institution should that become necessary.

1. Upon release from the institution, report as instructed to your Parole Officer (or any other person designated) and thereafter report as often as directed.
2. Secure written permission of the Adult Parole Authority before leaving the [said] state.
3. Obey all municipal ordinances, state and federal laws, and at all times conduct yourself as a responsible law-abiding citizen.
4. Never purchase, own, possess, use or have under your control, a deadly weapon or firearm.
5. Follow all instructions given you by your Parole Officer or other officials of the Adult Parole Authority and abide by any special conditions imposed by the Adult Authority.
6. If you feel any of the Conditions or instructions are causing problems, you may request a meeting with your Parole Officer's supervisor. The request stating your reasons for the conference should be in writing when possible.
7. Special Conditions: (as determined). I have read, or have had read to me, the foregoing Conditions of my Parole. I fully understand them and I agree to observe and abide by my Parole Conditions.

Witness _____ Parole Candidate _____

Date _____

Figure 12-3 Statement of Parole Agreement, 1973 (State of Ohio, Department of Rehabilitation and Correction, Adult Parole Authority, *Statement of Parole Agreement* [APA-271] [Columbus, Ohio: State of Ohio, 1973])

for the law. Parolees who had committed some minor violation might decide, "If I'm going to get busted for a technical violation, I might as well do something *really* wrong." The revised, nonrestrictive rules in the 1973 statement are aimed at eliminating the need for this kind of rationale.

Even with the new and simpler rules, of course, technical violations are

PAROLE VIOLATION

A parolee can be returned to prison for committing a new criminal act or failing to conform to the conditions of parole. The latter is frequently known as a technical parole violation: a rule violation that is not a criminal act but that is prohibited by the conditions of the parole agreement. The latter might include persistent consumption of alcohol, failure to observe curfew, refusal to make victims restitution, failure to file required reports, and so on. Approximately 22 percent of the males and 14 percent of the females on parole in 1984 were returned to custody for parole violation.

> ### PAROLEE RIGHTS AT REVOCATION
> Because of arbitrary procedures used in earlier parole revocation hearings, the U.S. Supreme Court in 1971 defined the basic rights of parolees at a parole revocation hearing in *Morrissey v. Brewer*, 408 U.S. 271. Parolees must be notified in writing of the charges they face, at least twenty-four hours before the preliminary hearing ("probable cause"). Revocation candidates have a right to hear the evidence against them, to cross-examine, and to refute the testimony. Furthermore, they can present their own evidence and have the right to a written report from the hearing that must be held before a neutral third party. Some states mandate legal counsel at this stage. At the second hearing, usually before a representative or member(s) of a parole board, the same rights are continued.

possible, and Ohio has taken special steps to handle them. If parolees have violated one of the simple conditions but have not committed another convictable offense, they may be sent to a community reintegration center.[18] There they are given guidance to help them deal with complete freedom in the community without the need to return to a penal institution. Ohio's reintegration centers, located in three communities, give parolees a chance to continue their employment and other community contacts while proving to the parole authorities that they can adjust to their problems without further incarceration. The centers are stlll too new to determine the extent of their effectiveness, but they represent a hopeful model for handling technical violations by parolees. A combination of rules that are easy to grasp and follow, plus an alternative to reincarceration for those who slip up occasionally, are more humane, less expensive, and less damaging solutions than is return to prison.

Innovations in Parole Supervision _____

In addition to trying the casework approach of traditional parole field supervision, many jurisdictions are developing alternative techniques for supervising clients more intensively, or providing a different parole service delivery mechanism. Some states have also begun to shift the focus of parole away from service delivery to supervision. These efforts are seen in house arrest, electronic monitoring of parolees, shock parole, and intensive supervised parole. All four of these strategies have been explored in Chapter 10, as "intermediate punishments." Our focus here is on the experiences of various jurisdictions in their efforts to manage offenders on parole.

House Arrest

House arrest can be both an effective community control tactic as well as a mechanism for reducing prison overcrowding.[19] Other advantages cited

---

FURLOUGH

Every state has enabling authorization that permits an inmate to leave the confinement of the prison for emergency family crises, usually accompanied by a correctional officer. Crises include visiting "death-bed" ill relatives, going to funerals, or seeking critical medical attention that is otherwise unavailable within the correctional system. Many states also have furlough programs, established when legislatures extended the limits of confinement from the penal institution to include not only the emergency leaves above, but also for purposes of participating in education, work, or training programs and other goals consistent with reintegration missions. These "programs of leave" are most frequently furloughs for educational and vocational training.

High-need but low-risk offenders, usually carefully selected to minimize further criminal behavior, are allowed to leave the limits of confinement under supervision. Technically, such furloughees remain prisoners, although they may not necessarily be under constant custodial supervision. Parole boards are believed to grant parole status expeditiously to furloughees who appear to be successful in their objectives. Thus furlough achieves reintegration objectives while avoiding some of the consequences of prison overcrowding.

---

are that it complements the reintegration ideology and provides a sound alternative to imprisonment, because many offenders do not need long-term incarceration. Oklahoma initiated this option in 1979, as part of the work-release mechanism, and, by 1985, over 2,400 offenders were released to house arrest supervision. Client supervision included contacts with employers, random house checks, frequent personal interviews, and field contacts, weekly meetings at a prison (host facility), and random telephone contacts and substance abuse testing. House arrestees also paid a $45/month supervision fee and made restitution. The success rate was 67 percent of all participants, and only 5 percent were returned for new crimes! There are at least ten states that utilize this approach, including Florida.[20]

Electronic Monitoring

Some jurisdictions (such as Florida) use electronic telemonitoring of parolees, particularly for those under house arrest, to increase the amount of surveillance deemed necessary due to offender risk or behavior, or to tighten the amount of control over the parolee's spare time. As with house arrest and probation,[21] computers randomly telephone the homes of parolees, who have a few seconds to insert the bracelet or anklet into the telephone unit that would send back a confirming radio signal, affirming their presence at the home. Other systems are less demanding: the anklet or bracelet continuously emits a radio signal to a receiver attached to the telephone; this receiving device would call the computer to report a broken transmission (parolee has left the premises). Absence from home without approval or "clear and compelling" reason is grounds for parole revocation and return to prison.

Shock Parole

In 1974, the Ohio legislature passed a bill that would provide for the early parole of inmates after six months of incarceration. Limited to first offenders, the theoretical underpinning is specific deterrence. The offender would be so "shocked" by the realities of the prison experience and punishment that he or she would want to avoid further incarceration after release. Shock parole also attempts to release the inmate before he or she becomes extensively prisonized and identifies with more predatory offenders. Offenders can be released from prison if the following criteria are met:

1. The offense for which the prisoner is incarcerated was not murder or aggravated assault.
2. The prisoner has not served at least 30 days for a prior felony conviction in any federal or state reformatory or prison.
3. The prisoner is not a psychopathic offender.
4. Further confinement for purposes of rehabilitation or correction is not needed.
5. There is a strong possibility that the offender will respond positively to early parole and is not likely to commit another crime.[22]

Thus this discretionary release program is vested with the parole board, which conducts hearings on eligibility in the same fashion as for other parole considerations. Early research[23] indicates less recidivism and parole violations for shock parolees than for other parolees. At least eight states have shock parole procedures. In a period of serious prison overcrowding, this innovative program can send a clear deterrent message to naive inmates, lessen overcrowding, and reduce the staggering costs of imprisonment.

Intensive Supervised Parole

Many jurisdictions are implementing intensive supervision programs to increase the surveillance of offenders, heighten service delivery, lower rates and costs of imprisonment, increase victim restitution, and lower recidivism by such clients as parolees. Perhaps the best-known of these is the New Jersey experiment in intensive supervision program (ISP). Set up as intermediate punishment program, the ISP program set out to do as follows:

1. improve the use of scarce prison beds by releasing some low-risk felons after a short (three–four month) period of incarceration, thus freeing up resources to confine the more serious felony offenders;
2. provide service at a cost-beneficial and cost-effective alternative to imprisonment;
3. prevent further recidivism by felons selected to participate in the community on ISP parole;

4. deliver appropriate intermediate punishment in the community (rather than in prison).

To select participants, a special "resentencing judge panel" screens inmate applicants to determine if they are nonviolent, first-time felony offenders who have served at least two months of their sentence and appear to meet the tests of probable employment, having a community support network willing to help offenders, and willingness to abide by these required conditions:

1. high frequency of contacts for counseling;
2. curfew;
3. weekly urinanalysis to detect drug usage;
4. community service work (minimum of sixteen hours per month);
5. frequent "eye-to-eye" contact with surveillance officers;
6. payment of restitution, fines, court costs, supervision fees, and so on; and
7. required employment as a condition of ISP parole.

Although the data available on success of the ISP are not extensive, there is encouraging evidence of lower recidivism. high program participation, low caseloads and intensive supervision (about twenty cases per ISP officer), no tolerated rules infractions, high rates of employment and payment of fees and costs, extensive participation in rehabilitative programs, and widespread community involvement to support and assist program participants. The New Jersey correctional system may have saved some $7,000 per participant per year in prison costs (over the ISP costs), and over 400 inmates have been diverted from prison, representing a savings of about 300 inmate/years in cost. It is clear that the ISP parole program is an innovation that bears further analysis, investigation, and replication in other jurisdictions.

Personnel and Caseload Problems in Parole

As one of the fast-growing parts of corrections, the field of parole offers great opportunities and challenges for professionals in criminal justice. It was estimated that over 326,752 offenders were under parole supervision in America in 1986;[24] the number of parole officers will have to increase dramatically to match further increases. It is essential that well-qualified individuals seek careers in parole supervision. In the past, a lack of such qualified personnel forced the recruitment of parole officers whose basic orientation came from other disciplines (for example, law enforcement officers, teachers, investigators, and custodial personnel from prisons). These officers often favored the "watchdog" or "control" model of parole supervision, whereby the officer's constant expectation that the parolee would fail did indeed produce such failure (a self-fulfilling prophecy).[25] The expansion of parole services in the last two decades has attracted more professionals from the social sciences, especially social workers. This trend, if it continues, will assist in the overall goal of professionalizing corrections as a whole.

Because social workers have become more prominent in the field of parole supervision, the old caseload issue has arisen as a persistent and continuing problem. As early as 1931, the government's *Report on Penal Institutions, Probation and Parole* (the Wickersham report) recommended that the caseload for parole officers average no more than fifty[26] — at a time when only a little over 50 percent of all offenders were released on parole. In 1986, the average caseload for parole officers ran from a low of 2 to a high of 117, depending on the state.[27] Even the increased number of officers today could not begin to handle the 1967 caseload on a fifty-per-officer basis, and the current load is at least 42 percent greater than it was in 1967.

Actually, research has shown that it is not the number of cases each parole officer handles that makes the biggest difference in outcome. Rather, the type of case as it relates to the background and experience of the parole officer and the agency's orientation are the keys to the officer's effectiveness. Some officers can handle as many as one hundred fairly simple, low-risk cases in which parolees require little assistance to lead a crime-free existence in the community, whereas the same officers can barely handle a caseload of ten high-risk cases. The message is clear. Administrators must emphasize a differential assignment of cases, keeping in mind such factors as the complexity of the cases, the type of offenders, and the background and ability of the parole officer. A proper assignment would match parolees who need minimal attention and reporting with officers whose background stresses enforcement and custody, and parolees whose problems are more extensive with officers who have had social work experience. Clearly, the rising number of parolees creates a fertile field for the criminal justice professional.

Emerging Issues in Parole _____

Although parole has taken its place as one of the most important areas of the correctional spectrum, it still presents some problems for administrators, and it has its share of enemies. One of the problems is the selection of parole authority personnel. It is difficult to decide between candidates from within the department, who might be hesitant to challenge a system that gave them their chance, and candidates from outside the system, who might be uninformed and politically motivated individuals willing to use the position for personal gain. Standards have been suggested for the selection of parole authority personnel, but they do not guarantee that boards will display the expertise and skills required. The only really effective way to ensure qualified boards is to make the standards part of the statutes, thus removing the selection process from the political arena. Among other considerations, these statutory measures should permit qualified ex-offenders to serve, especially as hearing examiners.[28] No one could be as sensitive as an ex-offender to an inmate's tension and uncertainty when trying to present his or her case to the parole board. In addition to the careful selection of board members based on statutory criteria, administrators must require that parole personnel undergo extensive training in recent legal decisions, advances in technology, and current correctional practices in the institutions they will serve. The government's Standards and Goals Commission has recommended that such training be provided on a national scale.[29]

The trend today is toward the determinate sentence or "just desserts" model for sentencing in more and more states. Hussey and Lagoy studied the process and impact in eight of the current nine determinate sentencing states, and a summary of the provisions in those states is shown in Table 12.2. Their conclusions have far-reaching implications for the future of parole as we know it.

> After examining the determinate sentencing schemes in the seven states reviewed ... it is difficult to escape the conclusion that they are inconsistent structurally and philosophically. It is equally clear that the parole system has been significantly altered in all seven states. Arizona is the only system

TABLE 12.2 Summary of Determinate Sentencing Provisions

	California	Indiana	Illinois	Maine	New Mexico	Colorado	Arizona
Does a parole board make the release decision?	No	No	No	No	No	No	Yes
Are aggravating/mitigating reasons articulated in the penal code?	No	Yes	Yes	No	No	No	Yes
How much good time is available?	33%	50%	50%	33%	58%	16–55%	"33%"*
Is there post-release supervision?	Yes	Yes	Yes	No	Yes	Yes	Yes
What is the likely time on parole?	1 yr	1 yr	2 yrs	None	1–2 yrs	1 yr	30–50% of sentence

*Good time does not reduce the length of stay in prison, but does reduce the maximum sentence.

Source: Frederick A. Hussey and Stephen P. Lagoy, "The Determinate Sentence and its Impact on Parole," *Criminal Law Bulletin* 19 (March–April 1983): 112.

that retains both discretionary parole release and parole supervision until the expiration of the sentence imposed.

It appears that the influence of politics can be most closely observed in the prescription of potentially severe sentence lengths (i.e., twenty to fifty years) and in the magnitude of the range of sentences within a particular crime class. This suggests that legislatures are uncomfortable with the basic tenets of just desserts—limited incarcerative terms uniformly imposed. Apparently, they perceive that the public demands that they be tough on crime and being tough does not allow for shorter prison terms, even if they are imposed more uniformly on a greater number of offenders.

The value questions that emerge most clearly from this examination are: (1) on what kind of behavior should sentence reductions be based, and (2) who ought to be making sentence-reduction decisions? We might begin to address these questions by first pointing out that determinate sentencing systems, like their indeterminate predecessors, can be seen as involving "minimum" and "maximum" terms. In all states except Maine [and Connecticut], there is a minimum below which a judge cannot go, and a maximum which he cannot exceed. Even after a judge fixes a "determinate" sentence from within the range, the idea of "minimum" and "maximum" term persists. For example, a burglar in Indiana who receives a ten-year sentence, from within a six- to- twenty-year range, has a minimum of five years—if all available good time is earned—and a maximum of ten years if no good time is earned.

The first value question, "on what kind of behavior should sentencing reductions be based?" requires a judgment as to whether inmates should be able to reduce their time through the exhibition of positive, goal-oriented, rehabilitative behavior or whether they should be able to reduce their time through the exhibition of nonaggressive, passive, or neutral behavior. If we send people to prison *as* punishment (and not *for* punishment) and we hope that they will develop skills and abilities which are helpful to them and to society once they are released, then we would conclude that time served should be reduced for exhibiting positive, goal-oriented behavior. If, on the other hand, time should be reduced for the nonoccurrence of behavior—usually the nonviolation of prison conduct standards—or for the exhibition of passive behavior, then we must conclude that society finds it acceptable for people to go to prison and to do nothing but pass the time as punishment.

The second value question is related to the first. It asks: should parole boards be making decisions about time reduction or should guards be making those decisions? One could argue that parole boards should make time-reduction decisions because there would be a small number of people reviewing a large number of cases, therefore enhancing the consistency of decisions throughout a state system. Parole boards, because of their small size, could develop criteria upon which to base their decisions. On the other hand, if guards are to make time-reduction decisions, then there will be as many decisionmakers and as many different sets of criteria for decisions as there are guards. This is not to say that guards will have the final say in denying good time; however, they will be making the basic decisions relative to the acceptability of inmate behavior that can result in good-time reduction.

Though there may yet be disagreement on the questions of why people are sent to prison, and who should make time-reduction decisions, there appears to be consensus that a released inmate can benefit from parole supervision even if, and perhaps especially if, the total supervision period is reduced. The message of determinate sentencing for parole agents is they will have to do a better job of planning for the arrival of each new client because they may not have the time they would like to work on successful reintegration.

One of the questions posed [in the introduction to this article] was whether or not determinate sentencing and parole could coexist. It is clear that at least the supervision component of the parole equation [in these jurisdictions] *is* coexisting with determinate sentencing. On the other hand, parole board release decisionmaking has been almost totally eliminated. Given, however, the apparent statutory rejection of fundamental just-desserts tenets (brevity in sentencing, in particular) which has resulted in rather large time-reduction decisions by correctional personnel, it might be possible for parole board decisionmaking to coexist with determinate sentencing as well. The use of guidelines by parole boards could, it seems, achieve the ends of determinacy without the "tyranny of parole boards" or the "tyranny of disciplinary committees."[30]

In an earlier study, Hirsch and Hanrahan asked whether parole should be abolished. Though their conclusions do not support parole as we now know it, they do seem to feel that there is a role for some form of supervision.

The theory and practice of criminal sentencing is today experiencing extensive change. One often-heard recommendation is that parole be abolished. Abolition has been advocated by persons representing a wide spectrum of political and philosophical viewpoints; parole has been eliminated or sharply curtailed in some jurisdictions, and others are contemplating similar action. This report is an effort to examine the case for and against parole.

The report concludes that parole should not be continued in its present form. The authors recommend that (1) instead of a discretionary release decision made on the basis of rehabilitative or incapacitative considerations, there should be explicit standards governing duration of confinement, and those standards should be based primarily on a "just desserts" rationale; (2) instead of deferring the release decision until well into the offender's term, the decision fixing the release date should be made early—at or shortly after sentencing; (3) instead of permitting parole revocation for releasees suspected of new criminal activity, they should be prosecuted as any other suspect; and (4) instead of routinely imposing supervision on ex-prisoners, supervision should be eliminated entirely, or if retained, should be reduced substantially in scope, sanctions for noncompliance should be decreased, and the process should be carefully examined for effectiveness and cost.

The role of the parole board as a decision-making body is a more complex question, however. Whatever its defects, the parole board has performed one essential function: it transforms lengthy judicial sentences into more realistic terms of actual confinement. The authors therefore urge caution in abolishing the parole board. The report describes ways in which the parole board could assist in carrying out the above-described reforms; and recommends that any effort to phase out parole release be undertaken gradually and with specified safeguards.[31]

It is clear that the movement toward determinate sentencing and away from the so-called treatment model presents, in more and more jurisdictions, a clouded future for parole, parole boards, and parole supervision. The public may finally find that prisoners who return to society with no guidance or supervision after a long incarceration are even more in need of parole than were those graduates of past practices. The results will be difficult to determine, as it will be many years until the determinate prisoners begin to return in numbers.

Parole Remains a Major Segment of Corrections

Despite growing pressures for the determinate sentence and the elimination of supervision upon release, parole remains second only to probation as the largest segment of community corrections (see Table 12.3). Although many prisoners now are released unconditionally to the community, approximately 74 percent are still released to parole supervision. In some states the title of *parole officer* has been changed to *community corrections officer* to reflect a custodial leaning, but the inmates remain under essentially the same controls as before.

In those states known as "determinate-sentencing" states, the parole board has been stripped of its discretionary power to release. It should be noted, however, that only two of these states (Maine in 1976 and Connecticut in 1981) have eliminated parole supervision as well. The rest of the determinate sentencing states release offenders to parole supervision upon completion of a fixed term. As noted in a report by the Federal Bureau of Justice Statistics:

> Prisoners enter parole either by parole board decision (discretionary release) or by fulfilling the conditions for a mandatory release. In all but nine States the parole board has discretionary power to parole prisoners. Mandatory parolees are those who are not released from prison by a parole board; they enter parole supervision automatically at the expiration of their maximum term minus time off for good behavior or program participation. Mandatory parolees include those released from prison under determinate sentencing statutes (which provide for release to parole at a prescribed or "determined" date). Whether a prisoner is paroled by discretionary release or by mandatory release has little effect on his parole supervision.[32]

Both parole and probation have a similar history, and even though they occur at opposite ends of the correctional process their clients are supervised in much the same way. Thirty states have combined the administration of probation and parole into a single agency. Even probation, which

TABLE 12.3 Correctional Populations, Percent of Adult Population under Sanction, and Percent Change, 1983–86

	1983		1984		1985		1986		Percent Increase in Correctional Populations 1983–86
	Number	Percent of Adult Population	Number	Percent of Adult Population	Number	Percent of Adult Population	Number	Percent of Adult Population	
Correctional populations total	2,488,450	1.45%	2,705,525	1.56%	3,027,227	1.72%	3,240,552	1.82%	30.2%
Probation	1,582,947	.92	1,740,948	1.00	1,968,767	1.12	2,094,405	1.18	32.3
Jail*	221,815	.13	233,018	.13	254,986	.15	272,736	.15	23.0
Prison	437,248	.26	464,567	.27	503,271	.29	546,659	.31	25.0
Parole	246,440	.14	266,992	.15	300,203	.17	326,752	.18	32.6

Source: Thomas Hester, *Probation and Parole 1986* (Washington, D.C.: U.S. Department of Justice, 1987), p. 4.

had traditionally been a preincarceration option, now takes place in many cases after a brief period of jail or prison time. The main difference remains the method by which the offender is placed under either option. Probation remains a direct sentence by the court, whereas parole is a function of the executive branch, with discretionary parole being granted by the parole board and mandatory parole by corrections agencies under the governor.

The latest comprehensive data on parole come from the Bureau of Justice Statistics for 1985. Most of those released to parole were released by the discretionary decisions of parole boards, but sixteen states reported some growth in mandatory paroles in 1985. As a percentage of all paroles, mandatory entry ranged from 3 percent in Nebraska to 91 percent in California. More than half of all mandatory releases took place in just five states. California accounted for a large percentage of mandatory releases because it is the only state that has made its determinate sentencing structure applicable retroactively to all of its prison populaton. In the other states, parole boards retain the power to deal with those cases that occurred prior to passage of the determinate sentencing act.

Parole entry rates are effected by a number of factors. The obvious factor is the size of the prison population. The higher the rate of incarceration, the higher the parole entry rate. This factor can be confounded, however,

---

TIME SERVED IN PRISON AND ON PAROLE 1984

According to data from the National Corrections Reporting Program, the median time served in confinement (including jail time) for individuals released from prisons in 33 states in 1984 was 17 months or 45.4 percent of their original court-ordered sentences. Those released for violent offenses served a median time in confinement of 28 months, about twice as long as either property or drug offenders.

Other findings include these:

- Those released from prison for murder and nonnegligent manslaughter served a median of 78 months in confinement; rapists served 44 months; robbers, 30 months; burglars, 17 months; and drug traffickers, 16 months.
- Violent offenders with a history of prior felony incarcerations served about 6 months longer in prison than those with no such history; property offenders served about three months longer; and drug offenders, one month longer.
- The average amount of time spent in jail that was credited toward an offender's prison sentence was about four months.
- For persons discharged from parole in 1984, the total amount of time served in prison and jail and on parole was an average of 60 months for a violent offense, 42 months for a drug offense, and 37 months for a property offense.
- Males on parole were more likely than females to be returned to custody for a parole violation (22 percent versus 14 percent).

Source: S. Minor-Harper and C. Innes, *Time Served In Prison and on Parole 1984* (Washington, D.C.: U.S. Department of Justice, 1987): 1.

by the number of prisoners that are released unconditionally (the inmates "jam their time"). The parole entry rate for the United States in 1982 was 8 per 10,000 adults, whereas the median rate for states was 6 per 10,000 adults. These rates ranged from high of 23 in North Carolina to 1 in Maine. See Table 12.4 for the 1986 data on parole.

TABLE 12.4 Adults on Parole, 1986

Regions and Jurisdictions	Parole Population 1/1/86	1986 Entries	1986 Exits	Parole Population 12/31/86	Percent Change in Parole Population 1985–86	1986 Parolees per 100,000 Adult Residents
U.S. Total	300,203	223,182	196,633	326,752	8.9%	184
Federal	17,064	8,749	8,501	17,312	1.5	
State	283,139	214,433	188,132	309,440	9.3	174
Northeast	82,849	45,139	39,656	88,332	6.6	233
Connecticut	695	166	258	603	− 13.2	25
Massachusetts	4,496	3,382	3,880	3,998	− 11.1	89
New Hampshire	453	207	121	539	19.0	70
New Jersey	13,385	7,565	6,886	14,064	5.1	243
New York	28,289	13,444	12,408	29,325	3.7	219
Pennsylvania	34,785	19,762	15,539	39,008	12.1	432
Rhode Island	402	414	358	458	13.9	61
Vermont	344	199	206	337	− 2.0	84
Midwest	41,722	33,222	31,871	43,073	3.2	99
Illinois	11,421	8,358	7,468	12,311	7.8	145
Indiana	2,797	4,836	4,360	3,273	17.0	81
Iowa	1,971	1,592	1,634	1,929	−2.1	92
Kansas	2,282	1,255	1,177	2,360	3.4	130
Michigan	6,639	4,238	4,975	5,902	− 11.1	88
Minnesota	1,364	1,390	1,317	1,437	5.4	46
Missouri	4,485	3,166	2,455	5,196	15.9	138
Nebraska	246	440	390	296	20.3	25
North Dakota	166	158	165	159	−4.2	33
Ohio	6,509	4,932	5,294	6,147	−5.5	78
South Dakota	415	407	414	408	− 1.7	80
Wisconsin	3,427	2,450	2,222	3,655	6.7	104
South	110,894	77,236	63,482	124,648	12.4	205
Alabama	2,425	1,723	1,157	2,991	23.3	102
Arkansas	3,891	1,743	1,793	3,841	− 1.3	222
Delaware	864	522	408	978	13.2	207
District of Columbia	3,504	1,651	1,435	3,720	6.2	762
Florida	4,214	3,011	3,747	3,478	− 17.5	39
Georgia	8,538	9,480	7,597	10,421	22.1	237
Kentucky	3,694	2,637	2,779	3,552	−3.8	131
Louisiana	3,346	2,795	1,975	4,166	24.5	132

TABLE 12.4 *Continued*

Maryland	7,308	4,924	4,738	7,494	2.5	224
Mississippi	3,392	1,644	1,582	3,454	1.8	189
North Carolina	3,184	5,522	5,384	3,322	4.3	71
Oklahoma	1,625	611	494	1,742	7.2	72
South Carolina	3,261	879	1,236	2,904	− 10.9	119
Tennessee	7,899	6,828	6,127	8,600	8.9	242
Texas	47,471	27,255	17,217	57,509	21.1	489
Virginia	5,640	5,506	5,376	5,770	2.3	133
West Virginia	638	505	437	706	10.7	50
West	47,674	58,836	53,123	53,387	12.0	150
Alaska	155	114	150	119	− 23.2	33
Arizona	1,717	2,613	2,296	2,034	18.5	85
California	30,127	45,553	42,518	33,162	10.1	167
Colorado	2,003	2,013	2,025	1,991	− .6	83
Hawaii	716	292	123	885	23.6	114
Idaho	483	274	226	531	9.9	77
Montana	634	312	278	668	5.4	114
Nevada*	1,313	1,446	1,230	1,529	16.5	211
New Mexico	1,092	1,162	1,107	1,147	5.0	114
Oregon	1,894	2,084	1,839	2,139	12.9	106
Utah	1,169	678	659	1,188	1.6	114
Washington*	6,039	2,105	478	7,666	26.9	232
Wyoming	332	190	194	328	− 1.2	93

Source: Thomas Hester, *Probation and Parole 1986* (Washington, D.C.: U.S. Department of Justice, p.3

Summary

We have seen that nearly every offender who enters prison is eventually released in some fashion. The question to ask is not "When?" but "How?" And the answer today is most often through parole. Two functions are involved in parole: the surveillance function, ensuring adequate supervision and control (in the form of a parole officer) to prevent future criminal activity, and the helping function, marshaling community resources to support the parolee in establishing noncriminal behavior patterns.

The parole process is a series of steps that frequently includes an appearance before a parole authority, establishment of a set of conditions to be met by the parolee, the assignment to a parole officer followed by regular meetings with the officer, appearance at a revocation hearing if parole is violated, and the eventual release from conditional supervision. This process has sometimes been changed or modified by the heat of public opinion and court decisions.

Although the parole process is a valuable aid to the corrections system, it is far from perfect.[33] The quality of personnel, at both the parole authority and parole officer levels, must be greatly improved. Salary levels, tenure regulations, and professional standards have been described and recommended. If these standards are met, the parole officer will become a true professional in a short period of time.

All offenders should be placed on parole as soon as they are first eligible, unless one of the following conditions exists:

1. There is a substantial indication that they will not conform to conditions of parole.
2. Their release at that time would depreciate the seriousness of the crime or promote disrespect for the law.
3. Their release would have substantially adverse effects on institutional discipline.
4. Their continued correctional treatment, medical care, or vocational or other training in the institution will substantially enhance their capacity to lead a law-abiding life when released at a later date.[34]

What is needed most is a method to determine the moment when inmates are most likely to benefit from parole, so that quick action can be taken to release them from the institutional setting at that time. After this point, we need effective supervision and delivery of service to help control criminal behaviors.

Review Questions

1. Differentiate between determinate and indefinite sentences.
2. What are the three main models of parole boards?
3. What are the main differences between parole and probation?
4. Why should parole boards be independent of institutions?
5. How long do offenders spend time in prison? For how long are they under correctional control? How do you feel about this?
6. What are four promising new strategies for parole?
7. Should parole supervision be abolished?
8. How many inmates exit prison through death, and of what do they die?

Key Terms

1. **good-time** (p. 244)
2. **executive clemency** (p. 250)
3. **amnesty** (p. 250)
4. **reprieve** (p. 250)
5. **consolidated board** (p. 252)
6. **flopped** (p. 253)
7. **discretionary release** (p. 254)
8. **mandatory release** (p. 254)
9. **convict bogey** (p. 256)
10. **revocation** (p. 259)
11. **furlough** (p. 260)
12. **shock parole** (p. 261)

Notes _____

1. Cesare Beccaria, *An Essay on Crimes and Punishments,* trans. Henry Paolucci (Indianapolis: Bobbs-Merrill, 1963), p. 99.
2. Harry Elmer Barnes and Negley K. Teeters, *New Horizons in Criminology,* 3d ed. (Englewood Cliffs, N.J.: Prentice-Hall, 1959), p. 568.
3. The new "good-time" reduction for the federal system is for "superior achievement" and constructive use of prison time. Program areas in which permissible reductions in presumed sentence length before parole are to be awarded include educational, vocational, industrial, and counseling programs. See Richard Allinson, "Achieving Inmates May Win Earlier Release," *Criminal Justice Newsletter* 10, (June 18, 1979): 4–5.
4. Brockway pressed for the use of parole and the indeterminate sentence mainly because of the prostitutes who were being shuttled in and out of the Detroit House of Corrections.
5. National Advisory Commission on Criminal Justice Standards and Goals, *Corrections* (Washington, D.C.: U.S. Department of Justice, 1973), p. 389. See also Lawrence Greenfield, *Probation and Parole 1985* (Washington, D.C.: U.S. Department of Justice, 1987): 4.
6. New Hampshire and Washington.
7. Bureau of Justice Statistics, *Probation and Parole 1985* (Washington, D.C.: U.S. Department of Justice, 1987), p. 10.
8. Wayne Morse, *The Attorney General's Survey of Release Procedures* (Washington, D.C.: U.S. Government Printing Office, 1939), p. 23.
9. Dr. Samuel G. Howe, husband of famed suffragist and reformer Julia Ward Howe, is credited with the first use of the word *parole* in its present sense. It originally meant "word" (of honor) not to commit further crimes.
10. National Advisory Commission, *Corrections,* p. 396. In 1979, thirty-nine of the fifty-three paroling authorities in the United States were autonomous agencies. See Eric Carlson, *Contemporary United States Parole Board Practices* (San Jose, Calif.: San Jose State University Foundation, 1979), p. 11.
11. National Advisory Commission, *Corrections,* p. 396.
12. Ibid., p. 397.
13. Joseph E. Scott, "An Examination of the Factors Utilized by Parole Boards in Determining the Severity of Punishment," (Ph.D. diss., Indiana University, 1972), pp. 57–59.
14. Eric Carlson, p. 105.
15. Everette M. Porter, "Criteria for Parole Selection," in *Proceedings of the American Correctional Association* (New York: ACA, 1958), p. 227.
16. President's Commission on Law Enforcement and Administration of Justice, *Task Force Report: Corrections* (Washington, D.C.: U.S. Government Printing Office, 1967), p. 184.
17. Ibid., p. 185.
18. Reintegration centers are located in Columbus, Cleveland, and Cincinnati. They are designed to house technical parole violators for sixty to ninety days and to treat their immediate problems through programmed learning techniques and concerned supervision.

19. Larry Meachum, "House Arrest: The Oklahoma Experience," *Corrections Today* 48 (1986): 102–110.
20. Leonard Flynn, "House Arrest: Florida's Alternative Eases Crowding and Tight Budgets," *Corrections Today* 48 (1986): 64–68.
21. J. Robert Lilly, R. Ball, and W. Lotz, "Electronic Jail Revisited," *Justice Quarterly* 3 (1986): 353–361. See also J. Robert Lilly, R. Ball, and J. Wright, "Home Incarceration with Electronic Monitoring in Kenton County, Kentucky: An Evaluation," in B. McCarthy (ed.), *Intermediate Punishments* (Monsey, N.Y.: Criminal Justice Press, 1987), pp. 189–203.
22. Diane Vaughan, "Shock Probation and Shock Parole: The Impact of Changing Correctional Ideology," in D. Petersen and C. Thomas (eds.), *Corrections: Problems and Prospects* (Englewood-Cliffs, N.J.: Prentice Hall, 1980), pp. 216–237.
23. Diane Vaughan et al.: "Shock Parole: A Preliminary Evaluation," *International Journal of Criminology and Penology* 4 (1976): 271–284.
24. Bureau of Justice Statistics, *Probation and Parole 1986* (Washington, D.C.: U.S. Department of Justice, 1987), p. 4.
25. Robert K. Merton is credited with elucidating the concept of the self-fulfilling prophecy: If those around a prison *expect* an inmate to behave in a certain way—to be stupid or brilliant, successful or a failure—their expectations will tend to shape his or her behavior. Robert K. Merton, *Social Theory and Social Structure* (Glencoe: Free Press, 1949), pp. 136–140.
26. National Commission on Law Observance and Enforcement, *Report on Penal Institutions, Probation and Parole* (Washington, D.C.: U.S. Government Printing Office, 1931), p. 325.
27. George Camp and Camille Camp, *The Corrections Yearbook 1987* (South Salem, N.Y.: Criminal Justice Institute, 1987), pp. 40–41.
28. See P. McAnany and E. Tromanhauser, "Organizing the Convicted: Self-help for Prisoners and Ex-cons," *Crime and Delinquency* 23 (January 1977): 68–74.
29. National Advisory Commission, *Corrections,* p. 414.
30. Frederick A. Hussey and Stephen P. Lagoy, "The Determinate Sentence and Its Impact on Parole," *Criminal Law Bulletin* 19 (March–April 1983): 101–130.
31. Andrew Von Hirsh and Kathleen J. Hanrahan, *Abolish Parole?* (Washington, D.C.: National Institute of Law Enforcement and Criminal Justice, September 1978), p. iii.
32. Bureau of Justice Statistics, *Probation and Parole 1982* (Washington, D.C.: U.S. Department of Justice, 1983).
33. For a critique, see John R. Manson, Determinate Sentencing," *Crime and Delinquency* 23 (April 1977): 204–207. See also the *Comments* that follow, pp. 207–214.
34. Daniel Glaser, *The Effectiveness of a Prison and Parole System,* Indianapolis, Ind.: Bobbs-Merrill, 1969, Chapter 9.

Recommended Readings

Allen, Harry, Chris Eskridge, Edward Latessa, and Gennaro Vito. *Probation and Parole in America.* New York: Free Press, 1985.
American Bar Association. *Criminal Appeals.* Washington, D.C.: ABA, 1969.

American Bar Association. *Post-conviction Remedies*. Washington, D.C.: ABA, 1968.

Carlson, Eric. *Contemporary United States Parole Board Practices*. San Jose, Calif.: San Jose State University Foundation, 1979.

Carter, Robert M., Daniel Glaser, and Leslie T. Wilkins. *Probation, Parole and Community Corrections*. New York: John Wiley, 1984.

Elion, Victor, and Edwin Megargee. "Racial Identity, Length of Incarceration, and Parole Decision Making." *Journal of Research in Crime and Delinquency* 16 (July 1979): 232–245.

Goodstein, Lynne. "Inmate Adjustment to Prison and the Transition to Community Life." *Journal of Research in Crime and Delinquency* 16 (July 1979): 246–272.

Gottfredson, Michael. "Parole Guidelines and the Reduction in Sentencing Disparity." *Journal of Research in Crime and Delinquency* 16 (July 1979): 218–231.

Gough, A. R. "The Expungement of Adjudication Records of Juvenile and Adult Offenders." *Washington University Law Quarterly* (1966): 147–190.

Greenfield, Lawrence. *Probation and Parole* 1987. Washington, D.C.: U.S. Department of Justice, 1987.

Hoffmann, Peter. "Screening for Risk: A Revised Salient Factor Score (SFS 81)." *Journal of Criminal Justice* 11 (1983): 539–548

Irsin, John and James Austin, *It's About Time*. (San Francisco, Calif.: National Council on Crime and Delinquency, 1987.

McCarthy, Belinda (ed.), *Intermediate Punishments*. Monsey, New York: Criminal Justice Press, 1987.

Minor, William, and Michael Courlander. "The Post-Release Trauma Thesis: A Reconsideration of the Risk of Early Parole Failure." *Journal of Research in Crime and Delinquency* 16 (July 1979): 273–293.

Stephanie Minor-Harper and Christopher Innes, *Time Served in Prison and on Parole* 1984. Washington, D.C.: U.S. Department of Justice, 1987.

Morris, Norval, and Gordon Hawkins. *The Honest Politician's Guide to Crime Control*. Chicago: University of Chicago Press, 1970.

National Advisory Commission on Criminal Justice Standards and Goals. *Courts*. Washington, D.C.: U.S. Department of Justice, 1973.

National Sheriffs' Association. *Inmates' Legal Rights*. Alexandria, Va.: NSA, 1987.

Packer, Herbert L. *The Limits of the Criminal Sanction*. Stanford, Calif.: Stanford University Press, 1968.

The Rights of the Convicted Criminal

Prisoners' Rights in Confinement

Years of litigation have resurrected the convict from his civil death. The principle is pretty well accepted that he or she must be allowed all the rights that any citizen has except those which must be denied on account of the curtailment of liberty entailed by punishment.
—JOHN P. CONRAD

What Is the Convicted Offender's Status?

When defendants have gone through the whole criminal justice process, including all appeals, and their sentences have been upheld, they officially acquire the status of *convicted offender*. They may already have spent a long time in prison as their appeals made their tedious way through the courts. But with the final guilty verdict in, the offenders' relationship to the correctional system undergoes a significant change. In this section, we shall examine the offenders' new status and their rights during and after incarceration. Over the years, a body of folklore has grown up about the rights of prisoners and ex-prisoners. This chapter will disprove some of these myths and clarify recent developments.

There was a time when a prison conviction often meant *civil death*, a cruel form of punishment expressly acknowledging a prisoner's permanent removal from the free society. In a perverse sense, the civil death sentence benefited the prisoner's family: the "widows" of male prisoners were able to remarry and rebuild a shattered life. In the United States until 1974, the inmate was a "slave of the state."[1] Today, except in rare cases, convicted offenders eventually return to the community from which they came. Their families may try to stay together until they are released, when the ex-prisoners must begin to cope again with the free world.

Imprisonment by its very nature deprives the offender of some constitutional rights. It is not clear, however, which rights must be completely sacrificed and which may be retained, perhaps in modified form. Prison officials have always been able to wield enormous power over the lives of

---

A SLAVE NO MORE

In 1871, the U.S. Supreme Court decided the status of the inmate in *Ruffin* v. *Commonwealth*: "A convicted felon is one whom the law in its humanity punishes by confinement in the penitentiary instead of death. . . . For the time being, during his term of service in the penitentiary, he is a slave of penal survitude to the State . . . for the time being, the slave of the State." In 1974, when the Court decided *Wolff* v. *McDonnell,* the legal status had shifted:

"Though his rights may be diminished by the needs and exigencies of the institutional environment, a prisoner is not wholly stripped of constitutional protections. . . . There is no iron curtain drawn between the Constitution and the prisons of this country. . . . He may not be deprived of life, liberty or property without due process of law." In a century, a slave had become an inconvenienced citizen.

---

incarcerated offenders. In the days when the sole purpose of imprisonment was punishment, the rights of offenders seemed unimportant. Because offenders seldom returned to the community, neither they nor their families were likely to complain that the offenders' rights had been infringed. As the philosophy of corrections moved toward reintegration, however, the complete deprivation of rights became intolerable.

With more than three million people[2] subject to the control of some kind of correctional authority in America each day, the status of those convicted offenders poses a significant problem. Correctional officials have been slow to draw up internal policies and procedures to guide their administrators in protecting the offenders' rights. Under the "hands-off" policy mentioned earlier, the courts were reluctant to criticize decisions and procedures developed by correctional administrators. That policy was abandoned in the mid-1960s, opening the door to case after case regarding prisoners' rights, with no end in sight. Prison practices have ranged from the total loss of offenders' rights upon conviction to various degrees of loss, but the new movement is toward the standards recommended by the National Advisory Commission on Criminal Justice Standards and Goals (see Figure 13-1):

Each state should immediately enact legislation that defines and implements the substantive rights of offenders. Such legislation should be governed by the following principles:

1. Offenders should be entitled to the same rights as free citizens, except where the nature of confinement necessarily requires modification.
2. Where modification of the rights of offenders is required by the nature of custody, such modification should be as limited as possible.
3. The duty of showing that custody requires modification of such rights should be upon the correctional agency.
4. Such legislation should provide adequate means for enforcement of the rights so defined. It should authorize the remedies for violations of the rights of offenders, where they do not already exist.[3]

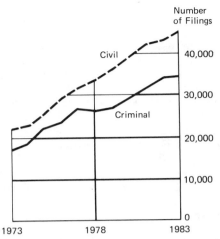

Figure 13-1 Civil and Criminal Appeals Filed, 1973–1983 (38 States) (Thomas Marvell and Sue Lindgren, *The Growth of Appeals* [Washington, D.C.: U.S. Department of Justice, 1985], p. 2)

Community Ties: A Basic Need

Visitation

The vestiges of civil death are probably most visible in correctional practices that pertain to the privilege of having visitors. There is continuous debate as to whether the visitor privilege is in fact a right. The practice of having visitors is not new; occasional visitors were allowed even as early as the Walnut Street Jail. If a prisoner were diligent and good, he was allowed a visit from a close family member—but only once every three months, for fifteen minutes, through two grills, and under the scrutiny of a keeper.[4] This procedure may seem absurdly strict, but it closely resembles the current practice in many correctional institutions. The security psychosis at most prisons dictates that visits be limited and subject to highly regimented conditions, likely to discourage close physical or emotional contact. The dehumanizing rules and procedures for visiting do not accord with modern goals of rehabilitation and correction. Although security is important in maximum security prisons, it could be tempered with humanity in such a personal thing as a visit from a friend or family member.

Limitations on visiting hours, restricted visitor lists,[5] overcrowded visiting rooms, and the constant presence of guards all contribute to the inmate's difficulty in maintaining ties with the outside world. Most institutions are located far from large urban centers (where most inmates' families live), requiring long hours of travel and expense for visitors.[6] Not only family

THE BILL OF RIGHTS
AND THE FOURTEENTH AMENDMENT

Amendment 1

Congress shall make no law respecting an establishment of religion, or prohibiting the free exercise thereof; or abridging the freedom of speech, or of the press; or the right of the people peaceably to asssemble, and to petition the Government for a redress of grievances.

Amendment 2

A well-regulated Militia, being necessary to the security of a free state, the right of the people to keep and bear Arms, shall not be infringed.

Amendment 3

No soldier shall, in time of peace be quartered in any house, without the consent of the Owner, nor in time of war, but in a manner to be prescribed by law.

Amendment 4

The right of the people to be secure in their persons, houses, papers, and effects, against unreasonable searches and seizures, shall not be violated, and no Warrants shall issue, but upon probable cause, supported by Oath of affirmation, and particularly describing the place to be searched, and the persons or things to be seized.

Amendment 5

No person shall be held to answer for a capital, or otherwise infamous crime, unless on a presentment or indictment of a Grand Jury, except in cases arising in the land or naval forces, or in the Militia, when in actual service in time of War or public danger; nor shall any person be subject for the same offense to be twice put in jeopardy of life or limb; nor shall be compelled in any criminal case to be a witness against himself, nor be deprived of life, liberty, or property, without due process of law, nor shall private property be taken for public use, without just compensation.

Amendment 6

In all criminal prosecutions, the accused shall enjoy the right to a speedy and public trial, by an impartial jury of the State and district wherein the crime shall have been committed, which district shall have been previously ascertained by law, and to be informed of the nature and cause of the accusation; to be confronted with the witnesses in his favor, and to have the Assistance of Counsel for his defense.

Amendment 7

In Suits at common law, where the value of the controversy shall exceed twenty dollars, the right of trial by jury shall be preserved, and no fact tried by a jury, shall be otherwise re-examined in any court in the United States, than according to the rule of common law.

Amendment 8

Excessive bail shall not be required, nor excessive fines imposed, nor cruel and unusual punishments inflicted.

Amendment 9

The enumeration in the Constitution, of certain rights, shall not be construed to deny or disparage others retained by the people.

> **Amendment 10**
> The powers not delegated to the United States by the Constitution, nor prohibited to it by the states, are reserved for the States, or to the people.
> **Amendment 14**
> Section 1. All persons born or naturalized in the United States, and subject to the jurisdiction thereof, are citizens of the United States and of the State wherein they reside. No State shall make or enforce any law which shall abridge the privileges or immunities of citizens of the United States; nor shall any State deprive any person of life, liberty, or property, without due process of law; or deny to any person within its jurisdiction the equal protection of the laws.

ties but friendships as well must wither under these conditions. This alienation creates serious problems for both the inmate and the institution. Typically, an inmate receives a visitor once a month, usually a member of his or her immediate family. This is hardly representative of social life in contemporary America.

For the married inmate, family ties are inevitably weakened by long separation. With divorce almost inevitable, the social consequences to the family, community, and institution are incalculable; imprisonment itself is grounds for divorce in some twenty-eight jurisdictions.[7] Institution officials often face severe problems caused by the deterioration of an inmate's family situation. When, for example, a wife does not write, or the inmate hears through the grapevine that she has a lover, violence can and often does result—expressed in attacks against prison personnel or another prisoner or even in escape.

Deprived of even a semblance of normal relations with the outside, the inmate turns to the other inmates and the inmate subculture for solace. It seems ironic that inmates are cut off from both friends and relatives and drawn entirely into the company of criminals; yet some parole rules forbid the parolee to associate with known ex-offenders. Such paradoxical situations seem to counter the basic premises of American corrections. There is no better way to combat the inmate social system and prepare an inmate for freedom than by strengthening his or her ties with the outside world.

Another form of visitation, employed in many foreign countries and at least six states, is the so-called conjugal visit. In Sweden, this is generally referred to as an unsupervised visit. The strong feelings generated over this issue pertain to the common belief that part of the inmate's punishment should be the loss of his or her sexual outlet. But in the Swedish system the sexual aspect of the visit is not questioned. As Torsten Eriksson, former director of prisons in Sweden, stated,

> The question whether an inmate shall be permitted to have sexual intercourse with his wife or a female inmate with her husband within the institution is the subject of considerable discussion in many countries. In the Latin American

countries this is regarded as obvious and even necessary to the inmate's mental health; the Anglo-Saxons, on the other hand, usually regard it as an impossibility. In Sweden we generally allow unsupervised visits in the open institutions. An inmate may take a visitor to his private room, whether it is his father, mother, brother, sister, wife, fiancee, or someone else close to him. Since the inmate has a key to his room, nobody pays any attention if he locks himself in with his visitor. Moreover, unsupervised visits in special rooms may be permitted in closed institutions also. I do not know whether sexual intercourse occurs during such visits, although I can always hazard a guess. In our opinion, sexuality is strictly a personal matter. We do not ask questions, we make no special provisions. We merely ask whether the individual inmate can be trusted to receive a visitor without supervision.[8]

Research on the relative effectiveness of conjugal visiting or unsupervised visits in the United States has not been extensive, but conjugal visiting is believed to strengthen family ties, reduce homosexuality among inmates, lessen tensions between officers and inmates, make inmates easier to manage, and lessen isolation from the outside community. Opponents argue that it puts too much emphasis on the physical aspects of marriage, is unfair to the unmarried resident, raises welfare costs through increased family size, and decreases the intensity of punishment to offenders.

It seems probable that our Anglo-Saxon heritage will prevent conjugal visitation reforms in this country on a par with those in Sweden. The logical solution here, used increasingly, is the home furlough. This permits the deserving prisoner to visit his or her family under unsupervised circumstances in a natural situation. The U.S. Army permits its major offenders incarcerated under maximum custody a seven-day leave each year to visit family. So far, when it has been used, the home furlough has not resulted in mass escapes or crime waves. This is but another step in the march toward community corrections. Ties with family and friends are critical to the rehabilitation of offenders, and correctional administrators must give them maximum opportunities to maintain these ties.

Use of the Mails

The mail system is closely tied to visitation as another essential contact with the outside world. As in the case of visits, stated reasons for the limitation and censorship of mail are tied either to security or to the prison's orderly administration. Although the use of the mail system is a right, case law has established that correctional administrators can place reasonable restrictions on prisoners in the exercise of this right if there is a "clear and present danger" or "compelling state need."[9] As with most situations behind the walls, over the years mail rules were systematically stiffened to facilitate the institutions' smooth operation. If it became too much of an administrative burden to read all the incoming and outgoing mail, the number of letters or the list of correspondents was reduced.

Eventually, a small maximum of allowed letters and very restrictive lists of correspondents became the standard. As long as the prisoners could not turn to the courts, this practice did not create a stir. When the attorneys appointed to help prisoners began to see the unjustness of restrictions concerning mail and other "privileges," they began to question the rules and reestablish these "privileges" as rights.

How much mail should a prisoner receive? Administrators have usually restricted it to an amount that can readily be censored. During personnel shortages (in wars, for example), the amount of mail was often limited to one letter a month. Outgoing mail was similarly restricted. Communications with an attorney could be opened and read, but not censored unless the correspondence referred to plans for illegal activity or contained contraband. More recently, court decisions have found that most censorship of communications between inmates and their lawyers is unconstitutional; this direction also appears in decisions regarding communications with the news media.

When an inmate wishes to communicate with a second inmate, either a friend or "jailhouse lawyer" at another institution, the courts have stuck to a hands-off policy, leaving this problem to the discretion of the administrators. The general policy has been to prohibit the passage of any correspondence between inmates. This policy is under attack, however, and has been rejected by some states.[10] In most court cases, the test for permissibility of mail and literature has been the "clear and present danger" standard:

> We accept the premise that a certain literature may pose such a clear and present danger to the security of a prison, or to the rehabilitation of prisoners, that it should be censored. To take an extreme example, if there were mailed to a prisoner a brochure demonstrating in detail how to saw prison bars with utensils used in the mess hall, or how to provoke a prison riot, it would properly be screened. A magazine detailing for incarcerated drug addicts how they might obtain a euphoric "high," comparable to that experienced from heroin, by sniffing aerosol or glue available for other purposes within the prison walls, would likewise be censorable as restraining effective rehabilitation. Furthermore, it is undoubtedly true that in the volatile atmosphere of a prison, where a large number of men, many with criminal tendencies, live in close proximity to each other, violence can be fomented by the printed

---

CONTRABAND

Contraband is any material that might be used for an escape or used to take advantage of other prisoners. Such items as matches, money, pornographic pictures, guns, knives, lubricants, drugs, and tools are generally considered as contraband. Any item can be placed on the contraband list if it is seen as a threat to the prison's orderly operation.

> **DEATH ROW INMATE MAIL**
> Death row inmates frequently receive photocopies of correspondence sent to them from persons other than attorneys. There is a "clear and present danger" of poisoning from chemicals sprayed on stationery at the inmate's request. Stamps can also be affixed to envelopes, using a liquid poison to moisten the stamp. Finally, lethal poison can also be suspended in ink. Death row inmates cannot be allowed to kill themselves before their execution, although three did commit suicide in 1986.

word much more easily than in the outside world. Some censorship or prior restraint on inflammatory literature sent into prisons is, therefore, necessary to prevent such literature from being used to cause disruption or violence within the prison. It may well be that in some prisons where the prisoners' flash-point is low, articles regarding bombing, prison riots, or the like, which would be harmless when sold on the corner newsstand, would be too dangerous for release to the prison population.[11]

The courts have also upheld restrictions on incoming newspapers and magazines that would permit "only the publisher" to be the sender.[12] Ohio took the lead in the reform of mail censorship, eliminating all of it in Ohio's prisons on August 3, 1973.[13] Under the Ohio system, both incoming and outgoing mail is merely inspected for contraband and delivered unread. Each inmate may write and receive an unlimited number of items of mail. The adoption of these standards has caused few if any problems. Most states, however, still inspect, electronically, incoming packages and open letters in order to look for contraband.

Religion in Prison

The idea underlying the penitentiary was drawn from religious precepts. It thus seems ironic that there would be any conflict in providing freedom of religion in prisons, but this has indeed been the case. The early efforts to restore the criminal through penitence and prayer were conducted in small homogeneous communities. As immigration to America expanded, it became the most heterogeneous nation in the world. Because the United States was founded on a belief that freedom of worship could not be infringed by the government, the First Amendment addressed these issues: "Congress shall make no law respecting an establishment of religion, or prohibiting the free exercise thereof. . . ." It is the conflict between what constitutes an established religion and the individual's right to exercise it that has caused grief in the nation's prisons.

A clear example of this problem is the Black Muslim decision, which has dominated case law for over a decade. After a long string of cases,[14] the courts finally held that the Black Muslim faith did constitute an

A Typical Prison Chapel for Religious Services (Courtesy of the Washington State Department of Corrections)

established religion and that the Muslims were therefore entitled to follow the practices that the religion prescribed.[15] The resolution of the Black Muslim issue means that the standards applied there can be applied to any duly recognized religion. This puts a strain on the prison administrator, who must allow equal protection for all inmates. The question of whether the state really grants each inmate "free exercise" simply by ensuring access to a minister of his or her particular faith is still being settled. It is clear that totally free exercise of all religions would result in chaos in a closed environment such as a prison. In earlier cases, the test used to restrict a religious practice was the "clear and present danger" to the institution or its personnel, including inmates. In more recent years, the courts have relaxed the standards and now may require "reasonable and substantial justification".[16] Such tests have arisen over such related religious practices as inmates' wearing hats, eating special diets, having special feeding times, wearing religious emblems, beards, and so on. Generally, the courts have upheld restrictions of religious practice when there are reasonable and substantial justifications.[17] However, administrators have been alerted that religious freedoms are of special interest to the courts and will receive strong review, with the burden resting on the correctional administration to prove why the restrictions were imposed.

Access to Court and Counsel _____

Access to the federal courts was not established as a constitutional right for inmates until 1940, in a case called *Ex Parte Hull*.[18] In this decision, the U.S. Supreme Court established that "the state and its officers may not abridge or impair a petitioner's right to apply to a federal court for a writ of habeas corpus." Despite this clear ruling, the courts still maintained a strict hands-off policy in this regard until the 1969 case of *Johnson* v. *Avery*.[19] This case established the right of prisoners who could not afford adequate legal assistance to use "jailhouse lawyers" in the preparation of habeas corpus proceedings. The need for the smooth operation of the prison was subordinated to the right to habeas corpus.

Once the prisoners' right to use jailhouse lawyers was established, inmates needed to be assured of an adequate supply of legal research materials. And in 1971, the case of *Younger* v. *Gilmore*[20] guaranteed the inmate writ writers such assistance. But the extent of materials provided has varied considerably, from complete law libraries in the state prisons to the bare essentials elsewhere. Meanwhile, other states allow law students to run legal clinics inside institutions, under the supervision of a law school faculty member qualified to practice in that jurisdiction. It seems that the courts must continue to require that administrations offer adequate legal counsel to inmates, or they will have to live with the continued use of jailhouse lawyers and the problems that result.

The right to consult with counsel has been clearly established. The problem, before *Gideon* and the cases it generated, was that most inmates could not afford a lawyer to defend them or prepare later appeals. And early prison rules restricted the use of jailhouse lawyers, so few prisoners were able to file writs in the federal courts. After the courts established the right to counsel, those administrative agencies that could not or would not comply were covered by *Johnson* v. *Avery*. Though not all jurisdictions have been able to provide counsel for all inmates, the remedies incorporated in the court decisions have helped fill the void—incidentally creating a flood of writs.

The Right to Medical Treatment and Services _____

The issue of adequate medical care in our prisons has finally prompted a decision from the Supreme Court. Only when a constitutionally guaran-

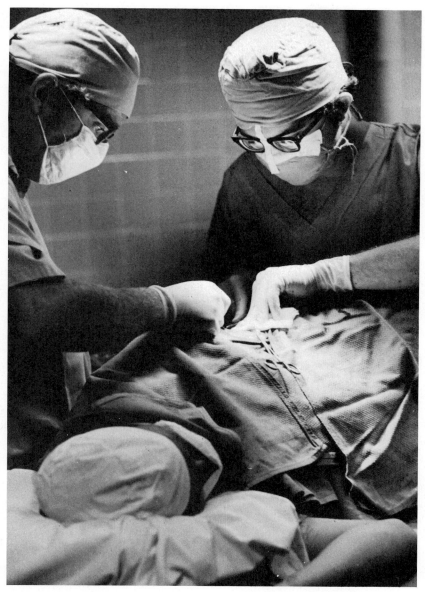

Surgical Treatment in a Federal Prison (Courtesy Federal Bureau of Prisons)

teed right has been violated has the Court become involved in the provision of medical care. Because both medical programs and the backgrounds of prison medical personnel are extremely diversified, the quality of medical aid varies among institutions.

The U.S. Supreme Court has taken the position that inmates in state prisons should seek remedy in the state courts. In the 1976 case of *Estelle* v. *Gamble*,[21] this position was made even clearer. Although suits in the past have shown that prisoners' rights to proper diagnosis and medical treatment of illness have been violated on a grand scale, the courts have moved slowly in this area. In *Estelle* v. *Gamble*, however, the Court stated, "We therefore conclude that deliberate indifference to serious medical needs of prisoners constitutes the unnecessary and wanton infliction of pain . . . proscribed by the Eighth Amendment. This is true whether the indifference is manifested by prison doctors in their response to the prisoner's needs or by prison guards in intentionally denying or delaying access to medical care or intentionally interfering with the treatment once prescribed."[22] This is a giant step forward in the provision of medical treatment, but it still falls short of the individual remedies provided by decisions in other areas.

Gamble states a position of sympathy for complaints about the system-wide failure to provide adequate and humane medical care. The test of deliberate indifference, however, a requirement for evoking the Eighth Amendment, seems to be a major hurdle for most who choose to use *Gamble* as a basis for action. Mere negligence òr malpractice leaves the prisoner with remedy only in a state civil case. Total deprivation of medical service seems to be the current standard for application of constitutional prohibitions.

Because of the relative ineffectiveness of using state and tort courts to remedy inadequate medical services and treatment in institutions, inmates have more recently begun to sue correctional administrators through Section 1983 of the U.S. Code. This section, passed in 1871 to protect the civil rights of recently freed slaves, allows petitioners to sue in a federal court without having first exhausted all existing state courts' remedies. The federal district and circuit courts are currently deciding a number of important cases, and some of those will eventually come before the U.S. Supreme Court.

TORT SUITS

A *tort* is a civil wrong and in corrections typically means that the plaintiff alleges the defendant failed to perform a duty required by the defendant's position or owed to the plaintiff. The objective of the suit is usually compensation for damages. A tort case alleges the defendant was negligent, or grossly negligent, or deliberately negligent. These same objectives are seen in medical malpractice suits brought by inmates against the facility and, in cases where the inmate has been attacked by others, for negligence in not protecting the inmate from attack.

Not only are tort cases handled in state courts, but they are also time-consuming. If lost, damages and attorneys' fees may be awarded by the court. Inmates are successful in lawsuits in less than 2 percent of the cases that go to trial.

> **CIVIL RIGHTS ACTS**
>
> Title 42, Section 1983 of the U.S. Code, commonly known as the Civil Rights Act, reads as follows:
>
> Any person who, under color of any statute, ordinance, regulation, custom, or usage, or any state, or territory, subjects or causes to be subjected, any citizen of the United States or other person within the jurisdiction thereof to the deprivation of any rights, privileges, or immunities secured by the Constitution and laws, shall be liable to the party injured in an action at law, suit in equity, or other proper proceedings for redress.

One example of the use of Section 1983 to redress medical malpractice and mistreatment can be seen in *Tucker* v. *Hutto*,[23] a Virginia case in which Tucker's arms and legs became permanently paralyzed as a result of improper use of antipsychotic drugs while he was a patient at the Virginia State Penitentiary Hospital. The suit was initiated by the National Prison Project[24] and, settled out of court for $518,000. Section 1983 suits can be an effective, although unwelcome, avenue for defining and improving prisoner rights while under confinement.

Many times the federal courts have been forced to overlook the issue of constitutional rights in order to correct situations involving a flagrant disregard of the need for adequate medical service. This disregard has often produced prison riots in the past, and it will continue to be a factor in right-to-treatment cases over the next decade. Right to treatment is covered in detail in Chapter 22.

Remedies for Violations of Rights

The first steps to remedy the almost standard practice of depriving convicted offenders of all rights have been taken, starting with the recognition that the Constitution does entitle these individuals to retain a substantial portion of their rights, even while incarcerated. The push for this recognition has come from the offenders themselves, often with the assistance of jailhouse lawyers, and has resulted in active and sympathetic judicial intervention. The writ of habeas corpus, designed as a tool for prisoners to test the legality of their confinement, has been the main weapon in the battle for prisoner rights. This battle continues today, especially with regard to increased maintenance of community ties and the abolition of the death penalty.

The strengthening of offenders' rights was a major area of study for the National Advisory Commission. This issue is highly charged, and correctional authorities are understandably concerned that the press for rights may disrupt the programs at their institutions. The standards suggested by the commission attempt to address the central problems:

COURT MASTERS IN CORRECTIONS

Both a federal or state court in which litigation over correctional issues has been filed may appoint a servant of the court, a functional adjunct whose task is to assist the court in whatever manner the court directs. Typically, the Master oversees the day-to-day compliance of the institution to the decree of the court or the consent decree. A decree of the court implies that the defendant (correctional unit) lost the case and the court has issued orders that are to be implemented. A consent decree occurs where the complainants (inmates) or defendants agree to a set of actions that both would find acceptable.

Generally, Masters monitor the lawsuit, report to the court, investigate complaints by inmates, have access to prisoners and their files, hold hearings, and write reports that inform the appointing judge on progress in the settlement of the orders. They also advise the court (through their special expertise in corrections, in particular), and help arrange compromises between the extremes of the demands of the inmates and the realities of prison administration.

When a Master is appointed, correctional administrators tend to resist the intrusion of the Master into the routine affairs of the institution. Some Masters have their own reform agenda, or fail to represent the correctional unit in securing compromise. Finally, the defendant (correctional system) must pay for the Master and any staff, and there usually is little disincentive to the Master's office running up long hours of work at high rates of compensation. Currently, Masters are seen as providing correctional expertise to a court that has no competence in correctional administration. Future correctional administrators will need to develop positive working relationships with the court, and negotiate with all parties to define clearly the powers, role and scope of the Master, to minimize any negative fall-out from the appointment of an intervention agent.

Each correctional agency immediately should adopt policies and procedures, and where applicable should seek legislation, to insure proper redress where an offender's rights are abridged.

1. Administrative remedies, not requiring the intervention of a court, should include at least the following:
   a. Procedures allowing an offender to seek redress where he believes his rights have been or are about to be violated.
   b. Policies of inspection and supervision to assure periodic evaluation of institutional conditions and staff practices that may affect offenders' rights.
   c. Policies which:
      (1) Assure wide distribution and understanding of the rights of offenders among both offenders and correctional staff.
      (2) Provide that the intentional or persistent violation of an offender's rights is justification for removal from office or employment of any correctional worker.
      (3) Authorize the payment of claims to offenders as compensation for injury caused by a violation of any right.

2. Judicial remedies for violation of rights should include at least the following:
   a. Authority for an injunction either prohibiting a practice violative of an offender's rights or requiring affirmative action on the part of governmental officials to assure compliance with offenders' rights.
   b. Authority for an award of damages against either the correctional agency or, in appropriate circumstances, the staff member involved to compensate the offender for injury caused by a violation of his rights.
   c. Authority for the court to exercise continuous supervision of a correctional facility or program including the power to appoint a special master responsible to the court to oversee implementation of offenders' rights.

ALTERNATIVES TO LITIGATION

Civil litigation abounds over correctional issues such as prison overcrowding, compensation for lost personal property, need for a special diet, and restoration of good time credits, increasing every year at great expense and time consumed by institutional mangers. Further, court litigation is not a speedy technique for resolving inmate needs. Finally, correctional administrators have become increasingly concerned with the impact of lawsuits on the institution, including the reluctance of correctional staff to take actions, decline in staff morale, officer stress, and general reluctance to comply with discretionary duties. In the search for alternatives to litigation, four basic approaches have been proposed: grievance boards, inmate grievance procedures, ombudsman, and mediation.

The *grievance board* is usually staffed by institutional employees or an occasional concerned citizen, to accept and investigate inmate complaints and then propose solutions, as relevant, to correctional administrators.

The *inmate grievance procedure* is similar to the grievance board, except that inmates are selected to serve as part of the grievance committee, a procedure many correctional managers find unacceptable, as it might strengthen the influence inmate grievance committee members would have over staff and other inmates.

The third alternative is the *ombudsman*, a public official who investigates complaints against correctional personnel, practices, policies, and customs, and who is empowered to recommend corrective solutions and measures. Empowered to investigate, the ombudsman has access to files, inmates, records, and staff. The ombudsman (and office staff) tend to be impartial, have special expertise, and are independent of the correctional administrator. Reports are filed not only with the institutional manager, but also with the correctional department director and funding agent for the office of the ombudsman. There are at least seventeen correctional systems in the nation that operate with the ombudsman to protect inmates.

Mediators are relatively new on the correctional scene, and represent a third party skilled in correctional work who agree to hear differences and to render a decision to remedy the condition that would be binding on both parties. Maryland, Rhode Island, Arkansas, and more recently, South Carolina, have experiments with this approach.

An inmate might file a lawsuit in conjunction with any of these alternatives. The methods are seen as promising ways to avoid litigation over correctional issues.

    d. Authority for the court to prohibit further commitments to an institution or program.

    e. Authority for the court to shut down an instutition or program and require either the transfer or release of confined or supervised offenders.

    f. Criminal penalties for intentional violations of an offender's rights.[25]

A Shift in Direction

During the court terms when Warren Burger was Chief Justice, and in conjunction with the appointment of more conservative Justices to the U.S. Supreme Court, the shift toward judicial recognition of prisoner rights slowed down.[26] Under the current Rehnquist court, it is expected that additional conservative decisions will be made. However, it is too soon to detect major changes in the Court's philosophy.

Yet some things appear certain. First, the role of the federal courts in responding to inmate complaints is significant, and even more conservative decisions by the Supreme Court are not likely to abate this trend. The number of complaints filed in state and federal court over jail and prison conditions, violations of inmate civil rights, due process violations, mistreatment and lack of treatment of inmates, has increased every year for the last two decades (see Tables 13.1 and 13.2).

TABLE 13.1 Civil and Criminal Cases Filed in U.S. District Court During 12-Month Periods Ending June 30, 1970–1986

Year	Number of Cases Filed	
	Civil	Criminal
1970	87,321	39,959
1971	93,396	43,157
1972	96,173	49,054
1973	98,560	42,434
1974	103,530	39,754
1975	117,320	43,282
1976	130,597	41,020
1977	130,567	41,464
1978	138,770	35,983
1979	154,666	32,688
1980	168,789	28,921
1981	180,576	31,287
1982	206,193	32,682
1983	241,842	35,872
1984	261,485	36,845
1985	273,670	39,500
1986	254,828	41,490

Source: Administrative Office of the U.S. Courts, *Annual Report of the Director*, 1970–86, Table C-1, D-1.

TABLE 13.2 Types of Civil Cases Filed in U.S. District Court in 12-Month Period Ending June 30, 1980, 1985, and 1986

	Number of Cases Filed		
	1980	1985	1986
Total civil cases	168,789	273,670	254,828
Cases where U.S. is plaintiff or defendant	63,628	117,488	91,830
Contract	24,063	65,647	48,257
Land condemnation	4,621	608	423
Other real property	3,660	5,679	6,278
Tort	4,438	3,116	3,351
Antitrust	39	30	39
Civil rights	1,459	2,081	2,256
Prisoner petitions	3,713	6,262	4,432
Forfeitures/penalties	3,019	4,908	3,480
Labor	2,241	1,202	1,239
Social security	9,043	19,771	14,407
Tax	3,254	2,990	2,779
Other	4,078	5,194	4,889
Private party litigation	105,161	156,182	162,998
Contract	24,989	36,995	40,095
Real property	2,786	3,831	3,973
FELA	1,990	2,186	2,534
Personal injury			
Marine	4,875	4,320	4,052
Motor vehicle	5,752	6,871	7,016
Other	10,878	21,448	21,676
Other torts	4,606	3,652	3,697
Antitrust	1,457	1,052	838
Civil rights	11,485	17,472	17,872
Commerce	1,031	794	823
Prisoner petitions	19,574	27,206	29,333
Copyright/patent/trademark	3,774	5,398	5,643
Labor	6,399	10,547	11,600
Other	5,565	14,410	13,846

Source: Administrative Office of the U.S. Courts, *Annual Report of the Director*, 1980, 1985, 1986, Table C-3.

Second, liability exposure of correctional administrators and managers has increased with several legal decisions. The sheriff, for example, has absolute liability for jail operations, whether or not he or she knew of the conditions.[27] The shield of the principle of sovereign immunity is gone; the State can do wrong. Third, many correctional systems have agreed to submit complaints to a mediator in an effort to avoid the time, cost, expenses, and damages of litigation. Whether this becomes a major trend will depend on the success of initial efforts in this direction. Finally, the trends of the 1960s–1980s must be monitored to be certain that the gains in rights by inmates are not reversed by court decisions, or actions by correctional administrators to limit access to the courts or to secure limitations on the number of suits an inmate may file. In the light of massive prison over-crowding, corrections must do everything possible to keep prisons from sliding back into the morass from which they have emerged over the last three decades.

Summary

As civil cases are increasingly filed in state and federal courts by inmates seeking to improve their lot in prisons and jails throughout the country, we sense an insurgent reactionary move in the political realm. Court appointees are more conservative; and the test used to determine if corrections can restrict conditions has partially slid from "clear and present danger" to "reasonable and substantial justification." Further, the proportion of offenders being committed to prisons is increasing, and legislatures have taken steps to see that the incarcerated remain in prison for longer periods. It is against this background that we point with enthusiasm to the comments of a former practitioner and expert witness, John P. Conrad:

> Prisoners' rights don't excite the public as a righteous cause. I want to propose that in the interest of both the prisoners, the employees of the prison and the general public, every prisoner has a right to conditions that won't make him a worse man. We know how hard it is to help prisoners to become better men, and many penal authorities have given up too easily on that task. But whatever prisons do, they must not make men needlessly worse. As to that requirement, there can be no competition of rights. Those who believe in justice as the essential virtue of social institutions in a democracy face only the difficulty of prodding prison bureaucracies into recognition of their plain duty. Every bureaucracy cares more about its survival than the performance of plain duties and of few can this be said more surely than those charged with the administration of prisons. Only the continuous vigilance of an informed public can assure that survival requires that performance of duty is manifest in the observance of rights.[28]

Review Questions

1. Why is it important for offenders to retain their ties with the community?
2. What is the difference between conjugal visits and unsupervised visits?
3. What is the name of the writ that tests the legality of confinement?
4. How have offender rights been developed by the courts?
5. What are four alternatives to litigation by which inmates might secure their rights?
6. What impacts have the more conservative courts had on the definition of inmate rights?
7. What are the advantages and disadvantages of having the court Master?

Key Terms _____

1. civil death (p. 279)
2. hands-off policy (p. 280)
3. conjugal visit (p. 283)
4. contraband (p. 285)
5. jailhouse lawyer (p. 285)
6. censorship (p. 285)
7. Black Muslims (p. 286)
8. free exercise of religion (p. 286)
9. habeas corpus (p. 287)
10. tort suits (p. 290)
11. Section 1983 suit (p. 291)
12. court master (p. 292)
13. mediation (p. 293)
14. ombudsman (p. 293)

Notes _____

1. In *Ruffin* v. *Commonwealth*, 62 Va. (21 Grat.) 790, 796 (1871). See also *Wolff* v. *McDonnell*, 418 U.S. 539, 94S. Ct. 2963 (1974).
2. Lawrence Greenfield, *Probation and Parole 1986* (Washington, D.C.: U.S. Department of Justice, 1987), p. 4.
3. National Advisory Commission on Criminal Justice Standards and Goals, *Corrections* (Washington, D.C.: U.S. Department of Justice, 1973), p. 439.
4. Harry Elmer Barnes and Negley K. Teeters, *New Horizons in Criminology*, 3d ed. (Englewood Cliffs, N.J.: Prentice-Hall, 1959), p. 505.
5. Visiting lists may be restricted, and persons who have violated visiting regulations may be removed from the list. *Patterson* v. *Walters*, 363 F. Supp. 486 (W.D. Pa. 1973). In addition, any person who previously attempted to help an inmate escape may be required to visit via noncontact means. *In re Bell*, 168 Cal. Rptr. 100 (App. 1980).
6. Ohio Citizens' Task Force on Corrections, *Final Report* (Columbus: Ohio Department of Urban Affairs, 1972), p. C-66.
7. Velmer Burton, Francis Cullen, and Lawrence Travis, "The Collateral Consequences of a Felony Conviction: A National Study of State Statutes," *Federal Probation* 51 (1987): 52–60.
8. Torsten Eriksson, from an unpublished speech to a group in Sydney, Australia.
9. *Brown* v. *Wainwright*, 419 F.2d 1308 (5th Cir. 1969); *Ortega* v. *Ragen*, 216 F.2d 561 (7th Cir. 1954); *Medlock* v. *Burke*, 285 F.Supp. 67 (E.D. Wisc. 1968). These three decisions found insufficient jurisdiction for federal court interference on behalf of inmates against prison authorities. The *Brown* decision refused a prisoner's request that a three-judge court be convened to enjoin prison censors from removing postage stamps from his outgoing mail. In *Ortega* v. *Ragen*, civil rights action was denied to a prisoner alleging the warden's failure to deliver letters of appeal. The *Medlock* decision refused the prisoner's appeal for court intervention to prevent alleged deprivation of medical care. In 1980, the U.S. Bureau of Prisons reduced the number of letters per week that inmates could mail at the expense of the bureau but left intact its unrestricted mail-out policy for inmates paying their own postage.
10. Some courts have upheld the restriction of communications between inmates at different institutions for security reasons. *Schlobohm* v. *U.S. Attorney General*, 479 F. Supp. 401 (M.D. Pa. 1979).
11. *Sostre* v. *Otis*, 330 F.Supp. 941, 944–954 (S.D.N.Y. 1971). The district court

upheld the prisoner's petition against prison officials for interfering with his receipt of literature.

12. *Guajardo* v. *Estelle*, 580 F. 2d 748 (5th Cir. 1978).
13. Executive Order Number 814 for incoming mail, 814A for outgoing mail. Office of the Governor, State of Ohio, August 3, 1973.
14. *Sewell* v. *Pegelow*, 304 F.2d 670 (4th Cir. 1962); *Banks* v. *Havener*, 234 F.Supp. 27 (E.D. Va. 1964); *Knuckles* v. *Prasse*, 435 F. 2d 1255 (3rd Cir. 1970). These three cases dealt with the right of Black Muslim inmates to freedom of religion. In *Knuckles* v. *Prasse*, the court of appeals held that prison officials were not required to make available to prisoners Black Muslim publications that urged defiance of prison authorities and thus threatened prison security, unless properly interpreted by a trained Muslim minister. In the *Sewell* decision, a clear instance of discrimination against a Black Muslim prisoner was brought before the court of appeals, which dismissed the case on the grounds that it properly came under the jurisdiction of the district court. In *Banks* v. *Havener*, responding to a petition under the Civil Rights Act by Black Muslim prisoners, the district court held that the antipathy of inmates and staff occasioned by the Black Muslims' belief in black supremacy was alone not sufficient to justify suppression of the practice of the Black Muslim religion. See also *Hasan Jamal Abdul Majid* v. *Henderson*, 533 F. Supp. 1257 (N.D. N.Y., March 11, 1982).
15. Although correctional personnel originally feared them, the Black Muslims are paradoxically now viewed as a source of stability among inmates. See Keith Butler, "The Muslims Are No Longer an Unknown Quality," *Corrections Magazine* 4 (June 1978):55–65.
16. See National Sheriffs' Association, *Inmates Legal Rights* (Alexandria, Va.: NSA, 1987): 64–66.
17. *Brown* v. *Johnson*, 743 F. 2d. 408 (6th Cir. 1985).
18. *Ex Parte Hull*, 312, U.S. 546 (1940). This case upheld the right to petition for a writ of habeas corpus for a parolee whose parole was revoked for committing a second offense.
19. *Johnson* v. *Avery*, 393 U.S. 483, 484 (1969). Through a writ of certiorari, a court of appeals decision was reversed in favor of an inmate who had been disciplined for violating a prison regulation that prohibited inmates from assisting other prisoners in preparing writs. The court of appeals had reversed a district court decision that voided the regulation because it had the effect of barring illiterate prisoners from access to general habeas corpus.
20. *Younger* v. *Gilmore*, 92 S. Ct. 250 (1971).
21. *Estelle* v. *Gamble*, 97 S. Ct. 285 (1976). The standard for judging the adequacy of medical treatment is the level of care offered to free people in the same locality. The prison must furnish comparable services, and inmates may collect damages for inadequate medical treatment. See *Newman* v. *Alabama*, 559 F. 2nd. 283 (1977). Medical treatment in jails is generally less adequate than that in prisons.
22. Ibid.
23. In *Tucker* v. *Hutto*, entered as a civil case under 78-0161-R, Eastern District of Virginia, the trial judge approved the out-of-court settlement on January 5, 1979, just five days before the trial was to open. See also R. Allinson, "Inmate Receives $518,000 Damage Award," *Criminal Justice Newsletter* 10 (January 15, 1979): 7.

24. The National Prison Project, American Civil Liberties Union Foundation, 1346 Connecticut Avenue, N.W., Washington, D.C. 20036.
25. National Advisory Commission, *Corrections*, p. 70.
26. "Supreme Court Decisions May Signal Halt to Expansion of Prisoner's Rights," *Criminal Justice Newsletter* 5 (August 12, 1974): 1.
27. *Tatum* v. *Houser*, 642 F. 2d 253 (8th Cir. 1981).
28. John P. Conrad, "The Rights of Wrongdoers," *Criminal Justice Research Bulletin* 3 (1987): 6.

The Death Penalty

> The useless profusion of punishments, which have
> never made men better, induces me to inquire
> whether the punishment of *death* be really useful
> in a well-governed state? What *right*, I ask, have
> men to cut the throats of their fellow creatures?
> —CESARE BECCARIA

The Death Penalty as a Public Spectacle

On March 14, 1984, shortly before his death by lethal injection at Huntsville Prison, James David "Cowboy" Autry petitioned the Texas Board of Corrections to allow his execution to be televised. Twenty-six of forty-four television stations in Texas refused to show it; twelve said they would; and six were undecided. To see a death by execution in the family living room posed a number of philosophical and moral issues for the ambivalent American public in regard to the death penalty. The viewer would have seen the young, somewhat attractive Autry strapped down and injected with a lethal substance.

What they would not have seen would be the 43-year-old mother of five, gunned down for a $2.70 six-pack of beer, or the 43-year-old former priest who picked up the phone to call for help and was also gunned down when Autry and his partner turned back. As it turned out, Autry died the way most offenders who have been executed in the United States have died—in the relative obscurity of a prison death house—at 12:40 A.M., the fourteenth of almost 100 persons to die since the moratorium on executions was lifted in 1976. The decades-long legal and moral debates had intensified, focusing on the questions of how, where, and why the death penalty should be used. After all, it was argued, why shouldn't executions in all their finality and horror be seen by the largest possible audiences? Isn't the purpose of capital punishment to *deter* other potential murderers (see Figure 14–1)?

CAPITAL PUNISHMENT
Execution of an offender by the state, usually for the crime of murder.

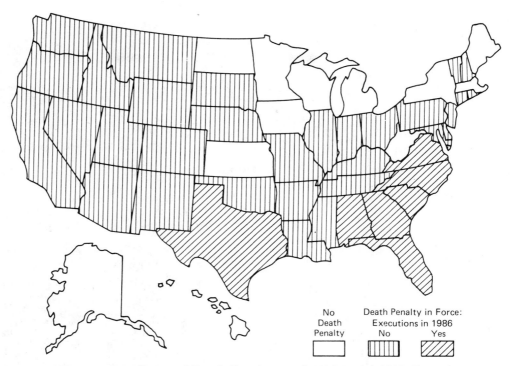

Figure 14-1 Status of Death Penalty as of 1/1/87 and 1986 Executions (Steven Schlesinger, *Capital Punishment 1986* [Washington, D.C.: U.S. Department of Justice, 1987], p. 1)

As discussed in Part 1, the death penalty was perhaps the earliest form of punishment—and, until recent times, the most common. At one time in England there were over two hundred crimes for which the death penalty was imposed. The argument supporting the death penalty—its theoretical deterrent power—led to many public executions. This practice was finally stopped in England, legend has it, partly to curb the flourishing pickpocket business at the executions (picking pockets, ironically, was a capital offense). Early public executions in America were well attended, to say the least:

> The day of the execution was dark and cloudy. A slight, drizzling rain fell during the greater part of the morning, and the streets presented an unbroken surface of slop and mud. A large crowd had gathered from the country at an early hour—arriving by the first trains from the east, west, north and south. Many came into town on horseback and in carriages and wagons," and the streets were thronged with a moving mass of human beings, eager to gratify curiosity. A rope had been stretched across the enclosure in which the gallows stood, at a distance of forty or fifty feet from it, and guards, armed with muskets, were stationed inside of the rope to keep the crowd

The Public Hanging of President Garfield's Assassin (Courtesy United Press International)

from pressing upon the place of execution. Outside of the stretched rope the streets were filled. . . . The only incident that diverted the intense interest of this vast multitude was the appearance of a traveling auctioneer, who had selected that time to cry his goods and dispose of his wares.[1]

The last public execution in the United States took place in Owensboro, Kentucky, on August 14, 1936.[2] It is estimated that over twenty thousand people crowded into the small Kentucky town to witness the spectacle. Various reform groups, disturbed that such a solemn event should take place in a holiday atmosphere, moved to have executions transferred behind the high stone walls of our prisons. As the executions began to take place in private, methods were improved to make them more efficient. Without the emotional power of an execution before an audience, the grisly task became a sort of ritualistic slaughter. Over twenty-five hundred prisoners have died on the gallows, in the gas chamber, the electric chair, by lethal injection, and by gunshot since Ramsey Bethea was hanged in Kentucky in 1936. For capital offenses by state, see Table 14.1

TABLE 14.1 Capital Offenses by State, 1986

Alabama. Murder during kidnaping, robbery, rape, sodomy, burglary, sexual assault, or arson; murder of peace officer, correctional officer, or public official; murder while under a life sentence; murder for pecuniary gain or contract murder; multiple murders; aircraft piracy; murder by a defendant with a previous murder conviction; murder of a witness to a crime.
Arizona. First-degree murder.
Arkansas. Capital murder as defined by Arkansas statute (41-1501).
California. Treason; aggravated assault by a prisoner serving a life term; first-degree murder with special circumstances; train wrecking.
Colorado. First-degree murder; first-degree kidnaping.
Connecticut. Murder of a public safety or correctional officer; murder for pecuniary gain; murder in the course of a felony; murder by a defendant with a previous conviction for intentional murder; murder while under a life sentence; murder during a kidnaping; illegal sale of cocaine, methadone, or heroin to a person who dies from using these drugs; murder during first-degree sexual assault; multiple murders.
Delaware. First-degree murder with aggravating circumstances.
Florida. First-degree murder.
Georgia. Murder; kidnaping with bodily injury when the victim dies; aircraft hijacking; treason.
Idaho. First-degree murder; aggravated kidnaping.
Illinois. Murder.
Indiana. Murder.
Kentucky. Aggravated murder; kidnaping when victim is killed.
Louisiana. First-degree murder.
Maryland. First-degree murder, either premeditated or during the commission of a felony.
Mississippi. Capital murder includes murder of a peace officer or correctional officer, murder while under a life sentence, murder by bomb or explosive, contract murder, murder committed during specific felonies (rape, burglary, kidnaping, arson, robbery, sexual battery, unnatural intercourse) and murder of an elected official; capital rape is the forcible rape of a child under 14 years by a person 18 years or older.
Missouri. First-degree murder.
Montana. Deliberate homicide; aggravated kidnaping when victim dies; attempted deliberate homicide, aggravated assault, or aggravated kidnaping by a State prison inmate with a prior conviction for deliberate homicide or who has been previously declared a persistent felony offender.
Nebraska. First-degree murder.
Nevada. First-degree murder.
New Hampshire. Contract murder; murder of a law enforcement officer; murder of a kidnap victim.
New Jersey. Purposeful or knowing murder; contract murder; murder during a kidnaping.
New Mexico. First-degree murder.
North Carolina. First-degree murder.
Ohio. Assassination; contract murder; murder during escape; murder while in a correctional facility; murder after conviction of a prior purposeful killing or prior attempted murder; murder of a peace

TABLE 14.1. *Continued*

officer; murder arising from specified felonies (rape, kidnaping, arson, robbery, burglary); murder of a witness to prevent testimony in a criminal proceeding.

Oklahoma. Murder with malice aforethought; murder arising from specified felonies (forcible rape, robbery with a dangerous weapon, kidnaping, escape from lawful custody, first-degree burglary, arson); murder when the victim is a child.

Oregon. Aggravated murder.

Pennsylvania. First-degree murder.

South Carolina. Murder with statutory aggravating circumstances.

South Dakota. First-degree murder; kidnaping with gross permanent physical injury inflicted on the victim.

Tennessee. First-degree murder.

Texas. Murder of a public safety officer, fireman, or correctional employee; murder during the commission of specified felonies (kidnaping, burglary, robbery, aggravated rape, arson); murder for remuneration; multiple murder.

Utah. First-degree murder.

Vermont. Murder of a police officer or correctional officer; kidnaping for ransom.

Virginia. Murder during the commission of specified felonies (abduction, armed robbery, rape); contract murder; murder by a prisoner while in custody; murder of a law enforcement officer; multiple murders; murder of a child under 12 years old during an abduction.

Washington. First-degree premeditated murder.

Wyoming. First-degree murder including felony murder.

Federal statutes include 14 crimes for which the death penalty may be imposed.

Source: Steven Schlesinger, *Criminal Punishment 1986* (Washington, D.C.: Department of Justice, 1986), p. 3.

In 1978, even before Autry's attempt, a convicted murderer in Texas tried to have his execution broadcast on live television. There has been speculation as to whether such a spectacle would turn the public against the execution of criminals (as it is postulated that the televising of the Vietnam War did in regard to wars in general) or whether the execution would attract the public to a new thrill in an era of increasing television violence and jaded sensibilities of viewers.

America's most innovative solution to execution was probably the electric chair. Although this invention was extolled as a more humanitarian way to kill the offender, many considered it merely a promotional scheme of the New York electrical company that developed it. The first electrocution was conducted at the Auburn Penitentiary in New York in 1890. Opponents of the chair, claiming that it must be excessively painful (a claim vehemently denied by prison administrators who used it), advocated lethal gas as the most humane execution method. It is interesting to note that seventeen states have passed legislation to use a lethal injection of chemicals as the latest, "most humane," form of execution. Physicians' associations are expressing concern that their members, whose profession it is to save lives, may be asked by the state of take lives. It seems that we are still seeking a way to make more humane the process, if not the practice, of execution. See Table 14.2 for the current methods of execution used in those states that have the death penalty.

The physical pain of the execution is probably the smallest concern of the offenders during their prolonged wait in the death house, a wait that often takes eight to ten years.[3] The mental anguish they must endure, which that long wait can only intensify, has been a primary focus of the recent widespread controversy surrounding the death penalty, as the more industrialized societies have moved to abolish it.[4]

The use of the death penalty in the United States peaked in the crime-laden 1930s, when a total of 1,513 prisoners were excuted,[5] an average of about twelve per month. The increased number of appeals and rising opposition to the death penalty peaked in the turbulent 1960s, and in 1972 the U.S. Supreme Court placed a moratorium on the death penalty, while states considered legislation that could meet strict Constitutional guidelines. That moratorium was dissolved in 1976, and executions began anew in 1977 with Gary Gilmore's cry, "Let's do it!".

Origins of the Death Penalty ————————————————————————————

In earlier chapters, brief references were made to some of the issues regarding capital punishment, or the death penalty. The frequency with

TABLE 14.2 Method of Execution, by State, 1986

Lethal injection	Electrocution	Lethal gas	Hanging	Firing squad
Arkansas[a]	Alabama	Arizona	Delaware[a]	Idaho[a]
Delaware[a]	Arkansas[a]	California	Montana[a]	Utah[a]
Idaho[a]	Connecticut	Colorado	New Hampshire[c]	
Illinois	Florida	Maryland	Washington[a]	
Mississippi[b]	Georgia	Mississippi[b]		
Montana[a]	Indiana	Missouri		
Nevada	Kentucky	North Carolina[a]		
New Jersey	Louisiana	Wyoming[a]		
New Mexico	Nebraska			
North Carolina[a]	Ohio			
Oklahoma	Pennsylvania			
Oregon	South Carolina			
South Dakota	Tennessee			
Texas	Vermont			
Utah[a]	Virginia			
Washington[a]				
Wyoming[a]				

[a]Authorizes two methods of execution.
[b]Mississippi authorizes lethal injection for those convicted after 7/1/84; executions of those convicted prior to that date are to be carried out with lethal gas.
[c]Lethal injection authorized effective 1/1/87.

Source: Steven Schlesinger, *Capital Punishment 1986* (Washington, D.C.: U.S. Department of Justice, 1987), p. 4.

which this topic occurs demonstrates how intertwined it is with all the other aspects of criminal justice. The term *capital punishment* generally refers to the execution, in the name of the state, of a person who has been convicted of some serious crime. The crimes for which this punishment has been imposed have varied over the centuries, but murder and rape have been the most common. The means by which the punishment has been carried out have varied even more.

In preindustrial society, the death penalty was relatively simple to carry out. Offenders were usually forced out into the wilderness (banished), where their demise was relatively certain. When human skills and culture advanced, the chances for survival in the wilderness increased, and the effectiveness of banishment diminished. These persons often became outlaws and continued to prey on the social group. When society began to execute (rather than banish) individuals for serious transgressions (usually murder) based on *talion,* the procedure returned to simply effectiveness.

Society has always been able to devise countless imaginative and cruel methods for the destruction of a condemned offender. The condemned have been hanged, burned, flayed alive, boiled in oil, thrown to wild beasts, crucified, drowned, crushed, impaled, stoned, shot, strangled, torn apart, beheaded, disemboweled, electrocuted, buried alive, smothered, gassed, and now, injected with lethal drugs. This list only partially exhausts the creative methods that executioners have employed throughout history. In search of vengeance against the condemned, society has also resorted to all sorts of ritual punishment, with mutilation and degradation preceding the final coup de grâce.

As noted earlier, executions were almost always administered as a public spectacle, in the hope that they would serve as a warning and a deterrent to others. It could be argued that the human desire to obtain retribution for crimes was transferred from the individual to the state in a way that finally became repugnant to many enlightened societies. Still, long after the elimination of the more bloody forms of capital vengeance, controversy still centers on its possible deterrent value.

The arguments for and against the death penalty concern the issues of deterrence, excessive cruelty (Eighth Amendment arguments), equability (Sixth and Fourteenth Amendment considerations), and attitudes toward capital punishment.[6]

Cruel and Infrequent Punishment

Arbitrary Use of the Death Penalty

To understand better the magnitude of the death penalty issue, one must examine the somewhat incomplete records on the subject. The total numbers of executions in this country between 1930 and 1986 are shown in

Table 14.3. As mentioned earler, the death penalty has most often been prescribed for murder and rape. One thus would reasonably expect a fairly high correlation between the number of such offenses and the number of executions. In the 1930s, the earliest period for which relatively reliable statistics are available, the average number of executions was about 165 per year. And the number of murders and rapes reported per year during the 1930s averaged about 3,500 and 3,800, respectively, a ratio of about 1:44.[7]

Also significant is the number of executions in different states and regions. As Figure 14-3 indicates, most executions have taken place in the South (over 50 percent of the total in the ten states of Texas, Arkansas, Louisiana, Mississippi, Tennessee, Alabama, Georgia, Florida, South Carolina, and North Carolina). The six industrial states that extend from Illinois to New York account for another 22 percent of the executions. When California is added into the equation, these seventeen states accounted for over 80 percent of the executions in America between 1930 and 1967. From 1977 to 1987, however, the first ten states listed accounted for 92.5 percent of the executions. Only Indiana (with 2 executions) of the other states listed had any executions at all. The eight remaining executions were in Virginia (5), Nevada (2), and Utah (1).[8]

TABLE 14.3 Number of Executions, 1930–1986

	Number Executed	
State	Since 1930	Since 1977
U.S. total	*3,927*	*68*
Georgia	373	7
New York	329	
Texas	317	20
California	292	
North Carolina	266	3
Florida	186	16
Ohio	172	
South Carolina	164	2
Mississippi	155	1
Pennsylvania	152	
Louisiana	140	7
Alabama	137	2
Arkansas	118	
Kentucky	103	
Virginia	97	5
Tennessee	93	
Illinois	90	
New Jersey	74	
Maryland	68	
Missouri	62	
Oklahoma	60	
Washington	47	
Colorado	47	

TABLE 14.3 *Continued*

State	Number Executed	
	Since 1930	Since 1977
Indiana	43	2
West Virginia	40	
District of Columbia	40	
Arizona	38	
Federal system	33	
Nevada	31	2
Massachusetts	27	
Connecticut	21	
Oregon	19	
Iowa	18	
Kansas	15	
Utah	14	1
Delaware	12	
New Mexico	8	
Wyoming	7	
Montana	6	
Vermont	4	
Nebraska	4	
Idaho	3	
South Dakota	1	
New Hampshire	1	
Wisconsin	0	
Rhode Island	0	
North Dakota	0	
Minnesota	0	
Michigan	0	
Maine	0	
Hawaii	0	
Alaska	0	

Source: Steven Schlesinger, *Capital Punishment 1986* (Washington, D.C.: U.S. Department of Justice, 1987), p. 8.

This leaves an average of only twenty executions per state for the remaining thirty-three between 1930 and 1987. Seven states had no executions during that period (North Dakota, Minnesota, Wisconsin, Michigan, Maine, Alaska, and Hawaii). It is worth noting that 80 percent of those executed for rape between 1930 and 1986 were black. All 405 of these executions took place in the Deep South, with the exception of seven in Missouri, a border state. This indicates that, in the case of rape, the death penalty was most readily imposed on blacks in the South, where the idea of interracial sex relations stirred deep emotions (see Figure 14–2).

The broad gap between the number of capital crimes and the number of executions is even more evident when one examines the data for the 1960s. From 1960 to 1967, the year that the moratorium on the death penalty apparently took effect, there were only 135 executions in America, an average of only a little over 17 a year.

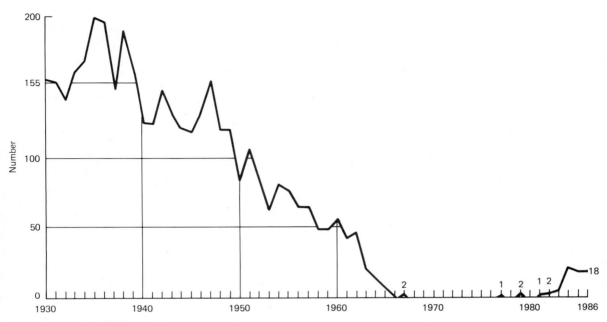

Figure 14-2 Persons Executed, 1930–1986 (Steven Schlesinger, *Capital Punishment 1986* [Washington, D.C.: U.S. Department of Justice, 1987], p. 8)

Actually, as the 1960s progressed, the number per year dropped to only 7 in 1965, 1 in 1966, and 2 in 1967. There was 1 in 1977, another in 1979, and none in 1980. The pace since then has picked up, with 1 in 1981, 2 in 1982, 5 in 1983 and, most recently, 18 in 1986. When one considers that the number of murders and rapes reported during that period averaged about 10,000 and 25,000 per year, respectively,[9] one tends to agree with Justice William Brennan:

> When a country of over 200 million people inflicts an unusually severe punishment no more than fifty times a year, the inference is strong that the punishment is not being regularly and fairly applied. To dispel it would indeed require a clear showing of nonarbitrary infliction.[10]

Even if one agrees that the number of murders and rapes[11] committed does not necessarily reflect the number for which the death penalty might have been imposed, the difference is still staggering. As Justice Potter Stewart explained, the death penalty is "freakishly" or "spectacularly" rare in its occurrence. In a telling argument in *Furman* v. *Georgia*, Justice Brennan in 1976 summed up the arbitrary nature of the death penalty:

> *When the punishment of death is inflicted in a trivial number of cases in which it is legally available, the conclusion is virtually inescapable that it is being inflicted arbitrarily.* Indeed, it smacks of little more than a lottery

system. The states claim, however, that this rarity is evidence not of arbitrariness, but of informed selectivity: Death is inflicted, they say, only in "extreme" cases.

Informed selectivity, of course, is a value not to be denigrated. Yet presumably the states could make precisely the same claim if there were ten executions per year, or five, or even if there were but one. That there may be as many as fifty per year does not strengthen the claim. When the rate of infliction is at this low level, it is highly implausible that only the worst criminals or the criminals who commit the worst crimes are selected for this punishment. No one has yet suggested a rational basis that could differentiate in those terms the few who die from the many who go to prison. Crimes and criminals simply do not admit of a distinction that can be drawn so finely as to explain, on that ground, the execution of such a tiny sample of those eligible. Certainly the laws that provide for this punishment do not attempt to draw that distinction; all cases to which the laws apply are necessarily "extreme." Nor is the distinction credible in fact. If, for example, petitioner Furman or his crime illustrates the "extreme," then nearly all murderers and their murders are also "extreme." Furthermore, our procedures in death cases, rather than punishment, actually sanction an arbitrary selection. For this Court held juries may, as they do, make the decision whether to impose a death sentence wholly unguided by standards governing that decision, _McGautha_ v. _California_ 402 U.S. 183, 196–208 (1971). In other words, our procedures are not constructed to guard against the totally capricious selection of criminals for the punishment of death.[12]

This argument is further reinforced by the fact that the two crimes of murder and rape have accounted for nearly 99 percent of the executions in the United States since 1930, with 87 percent of the total for murder alone. All the 18 executions in 1986 were for murder (see Figure 14–3).

It appears that the original practice of mandating the death penalty for murder has become repugnant to American society as a whole. This is demonstrated by the reluctance of juries to convict in these cases, despite the earlier efforts of state legislators to pass laws that call for mandatory executions for certain types of murder. (Even mass murders result in often strangely diverse punishments. In the "Chinatown massacres," which resulted in thirteen deaths in the 1983 holdup of a gambling club in Seattle, one of the three defendants received the death penalty, a second thirteen life sentences, and the third only received sentences for thirteen counts of robbery.)

The concept of _malice aforethought_,[13] usually an essential element of proof in the capital murder statutes, provided a rationale for juries to opt for a lesser penalty. The legislature finally recognized that the juries were using this concept to avoid the death penalty and passed statutes that attempted to differentiate between the degrees of various capital crimes (for example, first- and second-degree murder, and first- and second-degree rape), thus trying to restrict mandatory execution to the first offenses. In response, juries simply refused to convict in cases in which they felt — arbitrarily — that the death penalty was inappropriate. The further refine-

Figure 14-3 The Roster of Executions

At the time of this writing, Following the Supreme Court decision in *Gregg* v. *Georgia* (1976), there have been 98 executions in the United States. The majority of the executions took place in the southern states (94%), and all but one of those executed were male. Whites constituted 53% of the executions, blacks made up 41%, and Hispanics accounted for 6% of all executions. Texas leads the nation with a total of just over a quarter of all executions. The roster, since 1976, is as follows:

Executions #	State	Name	Race–Sex	Date of Execution
1.	Utah	Gary Gilmore	(wm)	1/17/1977
2.	Florida	John Spenkelink	(wm)	5/25/1979
3.	Nevada	Jessie Bishop	(wm)	10/22/1979
4.	Indiana	Steven Judy	(wm)	3/9/1981
5.	Virginia	Frank Coppola	(wm)	8/10/1982
6.	Texas	Charlie Brooks	(bm)	12/7/1982
7.	Alabama	John Evans	(wm)	4/22/1983
8.	Mississippi	Jimmy Gray	(wm)	9/2/1983
9.	Florida	Robert Sullivan	(wm)	11/30/1983
10.	Louisiana	Robert Williams	(bm)	12/14/1983
11.	Georgia	John Smith	(wm)	12/15/1983
12.	Florida	Anthony Anton	(wm)	1/26/1984
13.	Louisiana	Johnnie Taylor	(bm)	2/29/1984
14.	Texas	James Autry	(wm)	3/14/1984
15.	North Carolina	James Hutchins	(wm)	3/16/1984
16.	Texas	Ronald O'Bryan	(wm)	3/31/1984
17.	Louisiana	Elmo Sonnier	(wm)	4/5/1984
18.	Florida	Arthur Goode	(wm)	4/5/1984
19.	Florida	James Adams	(bm)	5/10/1984
20.	Florida	Carl Shriner	(wm)	6/20/1984
21.	Georgia	Ivon Stanley	(bm)	7/12/1984
22.	Florida	David Washington	(bm)	7/13/1984
23.	Florida	Ernest Dobbert	(wm)	9/7/1984
24.	Lousiana	Timothy Baldwin	(wm)	9/11/1984
25.	Florida	James Henry	(bm)	9/20/1984
26.	Virginia	Linwood Briley	(bm)	10/12/1984
27.	Louisiana	Earnest Knighton	(bm)	10/30/1984
28.	Texas	Thomas Barefoot	(wm)	10/30/1984
29.	North Carolina	Velma Barfield	(wf)	11/2/1984
30.	Florida	Timothy Palmes	(wm)	11/8/1984
31.	Georgia	Alpha Stephens	(bm)	12/12/1984
32.	Louisiana	Robert Willie	(wm)	12/27/1984
33.	Louisiana	David Martin	(wm)	1/4/1985
34.	Georgia	Roosevelt Green	(bm)	1/9/1985
35.	South Carolina	Joseph Shaw	(wm)	1/11/1985
36.	Texas	Doyle Skillern	(wm)	1/16/1985
37.	Florida	James Raulerson	(wm)	1/30/1985
38.	Georgia	Van Solomon	(bm)	2/20/1985
39.	Florida	John Witt	(wm)	3/6/1985
40.	Texas	Stephen Morin	(wm)	3/13/1985

Figure 14-3 *Continued*

Executions #	State	Name	Race–Sex	Date of Execution
41.	Georgia	John Young	(bm)	3/20/1985
42.	Virginia	James Briley	(bm)	4/18/1985
43.	Texas	Jesse DeLaRosa	(hm)	5/15/1985
44.	Florida	Marvin Francois	(bm)	5/29/1985
45.	Texas	Charles Milton	(bm)	6/15/1985
46.	Virginia	Morris Mason	(bm)	6/25/1985
47.	Texas	Henry Porter	(hm)	7/9/1985
48.	Texas	Charles Rumbaugh	(wm)	9/12/1985
49.	Indiana	William Vandiver	(wm)	10/16/1985
50.	Nevada	Carroll Cole	(wm)	12/6/1985
51.	South Carolina	James Roach	(wm)	1/10/1986
52.	Texas	Charles Bass	(wm)	3/12/1986
53.	Alabama	Arthur Jones	(bm)	3/21/1986
54.	Texas	Jeffrey Barney	(wm)	4/15/1986
55.	Florida	Daniel Thomas	(bm)	4/15/1986
56.	Florida	David Funches	(bm)	4/22/1986
57.	Texas	Jay Pinkerton	(bm)	5/15/1986
58.	Florida	Ronald Straight	(wm)	5/20/1986
59.	Texas	Rudy Esquivel	(hm)	6/9/1986
60.	Texas	Kenneth Brock	(wm)	6/19/1986
61.	Georgia	Jerome Bowen	(bm)	6/24/1986
62.	Virginia	Michael Smith	(bm)	7/31/1986
63.	Texas	Randy Woolis	(wm)	8/30/1986
64.	Texas	Larry Smith	(bm)	8/22/1986
65.	Texas	Chester Wicker	(wm)	8/26/1986
66.	North Carolina	John Rook	(wm)	9/19/1986
67.	Texas	Michael Evans	(bm)	12/5/1986
68.	Texas	Richard Andrade	(hm)	12/18/1986
69.	Texas	Raymond Hernandez	(hm)	1/3/1987
70.	Texas	Elisiao Moreno	(hm)	3/4/1987
71.	Georgia	Joseph Mulligan	(wm)	5/15/1987
72.	Georgia	Richard Tucker	(bm)	5/19/1987
73.	Mississippi	Edward Earl Johnson	(bm)	5/20/1987
74.	Georgia	William Boyd Tucker	(wm)	5/28/1987
75.	Texas	Anthony Williams	(bm)	5/28/1987
76.	Louisiana	Benjamin Berry	(wm)	6/7/1987
77.	Louisiana	Alvin Moore	(bm)	6/9/1987
78.	Louisiana	Jimmy Glass	(wm)	6/12/1987
79.	Louisiana	Jimmy Wingo	(wm)	6/16/1987
80.	Texas	Elliott Johnson	(bm)	6/24/1987
81.	Virginia	Richard Whitley	(wm)	7/6/1987
82.	Texas	John R. Thompson	(wm)	7/8/1987
83.	Mississippi	Tommy Ray Evans	(bm)	7/8/1987
84.	Louisiana	Willy Celesting	(bm)	7/20/1987
85.	Louisiana	Willy Watson	(bm)	7/24/1987
86.	Louisiana	John Bogdon	(wm)	7/30/1987
87.	Louisiana	Sterling Rault	(wm)	8/24/1987
88.	Florida	Beauford White	(bm)	8/28/1987
89.	Alabama	Wayne Ritter	(wm)	8/28/1987
90.	Utah	Dale Pierre Selby	(bm)	8/28/1987
91.	Georgia	Billy Mitchell	(bm)	9/1/1987

Figure 14-3 *Continued*

Executions #	State	Name	Race–Sex	Date of Execution
92.	Texas	Joseph Starvaggi	(wm)	9/10/1987
93.	Georgia	Timothy McCorquodale	(wm)	9/21/1987
94.	Texas	Robert Streetman	(wm)	1/7/1988
95.	Florida	Willy Darden	(bm)	3/15/1988
96.	Louisiana	Wayne Felde	(wm)	3/15/1988
97.	Louisiana	Leslie Lowenfield	(bm)	4/13/1988
98.	Virginia	Earl Clanton	(bm)	4/14/1988

Source: Telephone conversation with National Criminal Justice Reference Service, Department of Justice, Washington, D.C., May 24, 1988.

ment of the distinction between capital and noncapital cases was abandoned by legislation in many jurisdictions, and juries were given legal discretion to continue the practice they had already established in fact. The sentence of death is now discretionary in every jurisdiction in which it is still used. Many states have done away with the death penalty entirely, and others prescribe it only in very rare cases.[14]

As the power of imposing death moved from the impersonal and mandatory statutory approach to the hands of the jurors, the use of this final punishment declined to the point of insignificance. Of course, this decline was not so insignificant to the few who were still being executed by the state. Thus, in the 1960s appeared another series of cases attacking the death penalty on the grounds of cruel and unusual punishment.

The Eighth Amendment Versus the Death Penalty

American jurisprudence has borrowed much from the English law. The ban against cruel and unusual punishment embodied in the Eighth Amendment was lifted from the English Bill of Rights of 1689. As Justice Thurgood Marshall indicated in *Furman* v. *Georgia:*

> Perhaps the most important principle in analyzing "cruel and unusual" punishment questions is one that is reiterated again and again in the prior opinions of the Court: i.e., the cruel and unusual language *"must draw its meaning from the evolving standards of decency that mark the progress of a maturing society."* Thus, a penalty which was permissible at one time in our nation's history is not necessarily permissible today.
>
> The fact, therefore, that the Court, or individual justices, may have in the past expressed an opinion that the death penalty is constitutional is not now binding on us.[15]

This reference to unusual punishment helps clarify the relationship between this particular amendment and the customs and practices of any given period. The death penalty was surely not an unusual punishment in the early nineteenth century.

Cruelty was examined by the Supreme Court in 1878 in *Wilkerson* v. *Utah.*[16] It was Utah's practice to punish premeditated murderers by shoot-

> **EIGHTH AMENDMENT**
> Excessive bail shall not be required, nor excessive fines imposed, nor cruel and unusual punishments inflicted.

ing them at a public execution. In this case, the concept of the developing frontier and the execution practices in vogue in other areas around the world were examined. The Court did not stick to the doctrine of traditional practice but examined contemporary thought on the matter of cruel punishment. It found that the case against Utah was not cruel in the context of the times but that it left open the door for future Court examinations of the cruelty issue:

> Difficulty would attend the effort to define with exactness the extent of the constitutional provision which provides that cruel and unusual punishments shall not be inflicted: but it is safe to affirm that punishments of torture . . . and all others in the same line of unnecessary cruelty, are forbidden by that amendment to the Constitution.[17]

Only with the introduction of the electric chair in New York was the issue of cruel and unusual punishment raised again. The 1890 case of *In re Kemmler* challenged the use of this new form of execution as cruel and unusual punishment, but the Court was unanimous in its decision that electrocution was not unconstitutional just because it was unusual. It also came very close to employing the due process clause of the Fourteenth Amendment in this case, giving early warning that it might do so at a later, more substantial hearing. In the 1892 case of *O'Neil* v. *Vermont,* the court again affirmed that the Eighth Amendment did not apply to the states, but this time there were three strong dissenting opinions. One of the dissenting justices wrote:

> That designation [cruel and unusual], it is true, is usually applied to punishments which inflict torture, such as the rack, the thumbscrew, the iron boot, the stretching of limbs and the like, which are attended with acute pain and suffering. . . . The inhibition is directed not only against punishments of the character mentioned, but against all punishments which by their excessive

> **FOURTEENTH AMENDMENT**
> All persons born or naturalized in the United States, and subject to the jurisdiction thereof, are citizens of the United States and of the State wherein they reside. No State shall make or enforce any law which shall abridge the privileges or immunities of citizens of the United States; nor shall any State deprive any person of life, liberty, or property, without due process of law; nor deny to any person within its jurisdiction the equal protection of the laws.

length or severity are greatly disproportioned to the offenses charged. The whole inhibition is against that which is excessive. . . .[18]

This logic, though a minority attitude at the time, prevailed to dominate the 1910 "landmark" case of *Weems* v. *United States*[19] — the first time the court invalidated a penalty because they found it excessive. Clearly, excessive punishment had become as objectionable to the Court as that which was inherently cruel.

Not until 1947 did the Court decide another significant case on the issue of whether the Eighth Amendment applied to the states. In the case of *Louisiana ex rel. Francis* v. *Resweber*[20] the Court was virtually unanimous in its agreement that the infliction of unnecessary pain is forbidden by traditional Anglo-American legal practice. This unusual case involved a convicted murderer (Francis) who was sentenced to die in the electric chair. The electrical system malfunctioned at the execution, so Francis was not killed the first time the current passed through his body. Pleading that a second attempt at electrocution would be cruel and unusual punishment, Francis took his case to the Supreme Court. Although this case brought out many of the crucial Eighth Amendment issues, the Court stopped short of enforcing that amendment on the states, and Francis lost his appeal on a five to four split. He thus was finally executed, but his case paved the way for several that came in the 1960s.

The 1968 *Powell* case was the last to be heard on the issue of cruel and unusual punishment until the landmark 1972 case on capital punishment, *Furman* v. *Georgia*. The Court's decision was five to four in favor of a ban on using capital punishment as it was currently being practiced. Indeed, the justices were so widely divided on the issue that each wrote a separate opinion.[21] Only two of the justices (Brennan and Marshall) held that the death penalty was cruel and unusual punishment under all circumstances. The due process clause of the Fourteenth Amendment was evoked, leaving the states with the problem of passing legislation that met the Court's requirements, as described in the opinion of Chief Justice Warren Burger:

The legislatures are free to eliminate capital punishment for specific crimes or to carve out limited exceptions to a general abolition of the penalty, without adherence to the conceptual strictures of the Eighth Amendment. The legislatures can and should make an assessment of the deterrent influence of capital punishment, both generally and as affecting the commission of specific types of crimes. If legislatures come to doubt the efficacy of capital punishment, they can abolish it either completely or on a selective basis. If new evidence persuades them that they acted unwisely, they can reverse their field and reinstate the penalty to the extent it is thought warranted. An Eighth Amendment ruling by judges cannot be made with such flexibility or discriminating precision.[22]

The Electric Chair (left), Modern Science's Answer to the Gallows, and a Gas Chamber (right) in the 1930s (Photos courtesy of United Press International)

Although the minority opinion seemed to feel that the Court had overstepped its jurisdiction, the tenor of the dissenting remarks made it clear that they were willing to hear a new appeal when the findings in *Furman* were challenged. The high level of legislative activity in the states, seeking to reinstate the death penalty under the Court's new guidelines, suggested that there would be a challenge in the near future.

Though *Furman* gave a new lease on life to the over six hundred men who had been sitting on death row,[23] new death sentences continue to be handed down, awaiting final resolution of the issue.

The 1976 Decision

On January 17, 1977, the firing squad of the Utah State Prison ended the moratorium on the death penalty that the *Furman* decision had imposed for a decade. Amid a great amount of controversy and in a circus-like atmosphere, Gary Mark Gilmore made his way into the history books as the first American to be executed in the nation's third century. The Supreme Court, in a series of cases, had clarified the conditions in which the death penalty could and could not be imposed.

On July 2, 1976, five cases were decided as to whether certain state provisions were acceptable under the *Furman* decision. The statutes of three states (Texas, Florida, and Georgia) were affirmed, and the statutes of two others (North Carolina and Louisiana) were struck down. The case of *Gregg* v. *Georgia* is the model for those that were upheld. As noted in that decision:

> We think that the Georgia court wisely has chosen not to impose unnecessary restrictions on the evidence that can be offered at such a hearing and to approve open and far-ranging argument. So long as the evidence introduced and the arguments made at the presentence hearing do not prejudice a defendant, it is preferable not to impose restrictions. We think it desirable for the jury to have as much information before it as possible when it makes the sentencing decision.
>
> Finally, the Georgia statute has an additional provision designed to assure that the death penalty will not be imposed on a capriciously selected group of convicted defendants. The new sentencing procedures require that the state supreme court review every death sentence to determine whether it was imposed under the influence of passion, prejudice, or any other arbitrary factor, whether the evidence supports the findings of a statutory aggravating circumstance, and "whether the sentence of death is excessive or disproportionate to the penalty imposed in similar cases, considering both the crime and the defendant." In performing its sentence review function, the Georgia court has held that "if the death penalty is only rarely imposed for an act or it is substantially out of line with sentences imposed for other acts it will be set aside as excessive." The court on another occasion stated that "we view it to be our duty under the similarity standard to assure that no death sentence is affirmed unless in similar cases throughout the state the death penalty has been imposed generally. . . ."
>
> It is apparent that the Supreme Court of Georgia has taken its review responsibilities seriously. In *Coley,* it held that the prior cases indicate that the past practice among juries faced with similar factual situations and like aggravating circumstances has been to impose only the sentence of life imprisonment for the offense of rape, rather than death." It thereupon reduced Coley's sentence from death to life imprisonment. Similarly, although armed robbery is a capital offense under Georgia law, the Georgia court concluded that the death sentences imposed in this case for that crime were "unusual in that they are rarely imposed for [armed robbery]. Thus, under the test provided by statute, . . . they must be considered to be excessive or disproportionate to the penalties imposed in similar cases." The court therefore vacated Gregg's death sentence for armed robbery and has followed a similar course in every other armed robbery death penalty case to come before it.
>
> The provision for appellate review in the Georgia capital-sentencing system serves as a check against the random or arbitrary imposition of the death penalty. In particular, the proportionality review substantially eliminates the possibility that a person will be sentenced to die by the action of an aberrant jury. If a time comes when juries generally do not impose the death sentence in a certain kind of murder case, the appellate review procedures assure that no defendant convicted under such circumstances will suffer a sentence of death.

The basic concern of *Furman* centered on those defendants who were being condemned to death capriciously and arbitrarily. Under the procedures before the Court in that case, sentencing authorities were not directed to give attention to the nature or circumstances of the crime committed or to the character or record of the defendant. Left unguided, juries imposed the death sentence in a way that could only be called freakish. The new Georgia sentencing procedures, by contrast, focus the jury's attention on the particularized nature of the crime and the particularized characteristics of the individual defendant. While the jury is permitted to consider any aggravating or mitigating circumstances, it must find and identify at least one statutory aggravating factor before it may impose a penalty of death. In this way the jury's discretion is channeled. No longer can a jury wantonly and freakishly impose the death sentence; it is always circumscribed by the legislative guidelines. In addition, the review function of the Supreme Court of Georgia affords additional assurance the concerns that prompted our decision in *Furman* are not present to any significant degree in the Georgia procedure applied here.

For the reasons expressed in this opinion, we hold that the statutory system under which Gregg was sentenced to death does not violate the Constitution. Accordingly, the judgment of the Georgia Supreme Court is affirmed.[24]

The decision in *Gregg* set off a chain of legislative actions in state houses across the nation, aimed at providing death penalty statutes that would meet the Supreme Court's challenge. Again, they sought to activate the most cherished beliefs about the death penalty (see Figure 14–4):

No other punishment *deters men so effectually* from committing crimes as the punishment of death. This is one of those propositions which it is difficult to prove, simply because they are in themselves more obvious than any proof can make them. It is possible to display ingenuity in arguing against it, but that is all. The whole experience of mankind is in the other direction. The threat of instant death is the one to which resort has always been made when there was an absolute necessity for producing some result.... No one goes to certain inevitable death except by compulsion. Put the matter the other way. Was there ever yet a criminal who, when sentenced to death and brought out to die, would refuse the offer of a commutation of his sentence for the severest secondary punishment? Surely not. Why is this? It can only be because "All that a man has will he give for his life." In any secondary punishment, however terrible, there is hope; but death is death; its terrors cannot be described more forcibly.[25]

The abolitionists try to amass vast statistical bases to show the lack of correlation between statutes in various jurisdictions. Although such evidence is not without flaws, the abolitionists have a clear and convincing case that the death penalty is not useful as a deterrent to crime in America. What is the alternative to a death penalty in punishing offenders who have committed crimes such as murder and rape? Life imprisonment, without hope for parole, is considered the most logical substitute, though prison administrators claim that offenders who know they are in prison for life

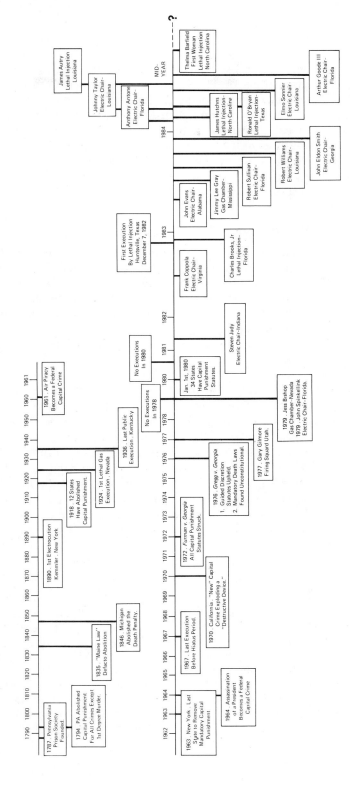

Figure 14-4 Capital Punishment Time Line (Sandra Nicolai et al., *The Question of Capital Punishment* [Contact Inc.])

will feel they have nothing to lose if they commit further crimes behind the walls. In fact, there is an overwhelming body of evidence that the presence or absence of the death penalty has no effect on the homicide rate inside prisons. Murderers (who account for almost 90 percent of capital cases) are usually model prisoners. It has even been postulated that the death penalty itself creates an atmosphere that fosters violence in prison. The day of an execution is charged with extreme tension. The prisoners are often placed under more security than usual, and acts of violence in defiance of the authorities seem to be more prevalent.

Public Opinion

There have been wide fluctuations in the American public's attitude toward the death penalty, as reflected in public opinion polls. Although most polls show strong support for the death penalty—with a low of around 60 percent showing support compared to the current rates of over 86 percent—this fact seems to have as little impact on death penalty legislation as public opinion has on gun control. Those who advocate the death penalty claim that there is no viable alternative that provides equal protection for society.

Many who oppose the life sentence as a replacement for the death penalty observe that the parole laws in many states make it possible for a "lifer" to get out in a relatively brief time. Usually, those who receive life sentences become eligible for parole in thirteen years, but the national average served under a life sentence is currently less than seven years. The proposed answer to this argument is to remove the hope of parole from a prisoner given life sentence *(life certain),* but this action would constitute an admission that certain prisoners could not be rehabilitated and would destroy the offenders' possible incentive to change their behavior patterns. The chance that an innocent person might be convicted also detracts from the acceptability of the irreversible death penalty.

DETERRENCE OF DEATH PENALTY

While there are substantial claims that the death penalty may or may not act as a deterrent to others in an act of general deterrence, depending on the ideological position of the debater, one should realize that if the death penalty were a deterrent, no crime would occur. Retentionists point out that a lighthouse sits beside a dangerous, rock-strewn coastline to warn ships away. The fact that a few ill-fated ships run afoul of the dangers the lighthouse proclaims is no reason to tear the lighthouse down—or to abolish capital punishment. For those ships the lighthouse warns away, there is no evidence of deterrence. Only the ones that ignore to their peril the lighthouse's warning will show up as "failures" of the deterrent effect.   Anonymous

---

The Controversy Continues _____

In 1983, a symposium was held on the issues surrounding the death penalty. An overview of this symposium was prepared by the distinguished scholars Michael Meltsner and Marvin Wolfgang:

In 1976, a divided United States Supreme Court upheld state capital sentencing laws on the assumption that explicit sentencing guidelines, separate sentencing hearings and automatic appellate review of all death sentences would remove the substantial risk of arbitrariness of previous capital punishment sentencing schemes. Eight years later, the premises supporting the constitutionality of the new laws appear to have little practical currency. That a set of scholarly contributions from lawyers, criminologists, and other investigators would uncover flaws in the operation of the death-case legal system is not surprising; earlier research into the operation of the discretionary death penalty systems raised significant doubts about the reliability, fairness, and necessity of capital punishment and contributed to the Court's landmark 1972 decision in *Furman* v. *Georgia*. But both the depth and bite of recent investigations are startling. Discretionary death sentencing was rejected in *Furman* for a complex of factors amounting to legal arbitrariness — lack of even-handedness, caprice, discrimination, excessiveness. The statutory schemes approved in 1976 and those adopted thereafter were formulated to avoid unconstitutional arbitrariness in capital sentencing systems.

Though there may have been a shift in the stage of the system at which arbitrariness occurs, the new laws have not eliminated the disparate treatment of minority group members. Sentencing standards, evidentiary hearings, and appellate review of lower court death sentences have neither screened out racial or economic factors in death sentencing nor reduced to satisfactory levels the system's capacity to produce inconsistent and "freakish" results. Decisions of prosecutors to seek the death penalty are related to the race of the victim and defendant. Wide geographical variations in the imposition of the death penalty mean that the likelihood of receiving the death sentence may depend solely upon the locus of the trial. Appellate courts have not proven themselves capable of rectifying inconsistency in trial court death sentencing and indeed the principles and processes employed by reviewing courts are not designed to produce consistent and evenhanded capital sentencing.

The results of recent research offer little comfort to those who seek to justify the death penalty because it allegedly deters more effectively than prison sentences; there is much evidence which validates previous studies which found the death penalty ineffective as a marginal deterrent.

Additionally, recent studies have added to the weight of earlier investigations that found that capital punishment was in fact a spur to murder, the so-called brutalization effect. The legal system has not fared well in attempting to implement a more defensible and even-handed selection of those to be executed. The new laws have raised vexing legal problems; the operation of these laws to date suggests that these problems can be resolved only at the cost of abandoning fundamental due process values.

Though Supreme Court decisions are often characterized as watersheds, the process of constitutional lawmaking is actually marked by gradualism. *Furman* overturned the laws of most death penalty states by a slim margin but the constitutional ruling emerged from years of moratorium, scholarly doubt, public debate, and misuse of the death sentencing apparatus. *Furman* gave the states the choice of whether to continue a regime of capital sentencing, and the states responded by sending a clear message that such a system was desired — at least on the law books. The 1976 decisions may be seen as permitting the states to make the case that a rationally selective, nondiscriminatory, and nonexcessive capital sentencing system might be constitutional. With more than a thousand persons waiting on death row, their numbers growing daily, and a handful of extraordinarily bizarre and troubling executions, researchers have come to grips with the statutory generalizations approved by the Court. On the basis of the scholarship presented here, the judgment must be that the arbitrariness that gave rise to *Furman* v. *Georgia* remains, and the states have failed to show that a death penalty system can reduce arbitrariness to constitutionally permissible levels. [footnotes deleted][26]

After a long and tortuous process, the Court has finally made clear what it feels are the boundaries for imposition of the death penalty. Despite this effort, many states still believe that the death penalty is too harsh a punishment to impose. The arguments in the Supreme Court may be settled, at least for the time being, but the arguments continue.

Death Row Populations Mount: What to Do? _____

With almost two thousand prisoners on death rows across this nation, what will the reaction by the public be to an unprecedented number of executions in the late 1980s and early 1990s? Administrators, politicians, legislators, and the public wrestle with what to do about this backlog of incarcerated evil. No one seems to be ready to deal with it, and so the appeals wend their ways through the courts. The median time since the death sentence was imposed for the 1,781 prisoners was forty months.[27] As Benjamin Renshaw noted in 1982:

> The United States will witness a spate of executions beginning in 1983–84 without parallel in this Nation since the depression era. Whatever views one may hold on the use of capital punishment, that is the reality behind the numbers — both those dealing with prisoners on death row and the number of State capital punishment statutes that have passed Federal or State constitutional muster.
>
> The number of persons on death row has been rising steadily for 5 years; only four persons were executed during this period, three of whom chose not to exhaust their avenues of appeal. A similar buildup on death row occurred during the sixties, but these persons were all removed from the threat of capital punishment as a result of the Supreme Court decision in *Furman* v. *Georgia*.

TABLE 14.4 Prisoners under Sentence of Death, by Region and State, Yearend 1985 and 1986

Region and State	Prisoners Under Sentence 1985	Changes during 1986			Prisoners Under Sentence 1986
		Received Under Sentence	Removed from Death Row (Excluding Executions)	Executed	
U.S. Total	1,575	297	73	18	1,781
Federal	0	0	0	0	0
State	1,575	297	73	18	1,781
Northeast	75	25	3	0	97
Connecticut	0	0	0	0	0
New Hampshire	0	0	0	0	0
New Jersey	17	6	0	0	23
Pennsylvania	58	19	3	0	74
Vermont	0	0	0	0	0
Midwest	216	58	7	0	267
Illinois	78	25	2	0	101
Indiana	34	6	0	0	40
Missouri	36	10	3	0	43
Nebraska	12	2	0	0	14
Ohio	56	15	2	0	69
South Dakota	0	0	0	0	0
South	999	174	47	18	1,108
Alabama	79	8	3	1	83
Arkansas	26	4	4	0	26
Delaware	4	0	0	0	4
Florida	227	39	9	3	254
Georgia	107	11	6	1	111
Kentucky	23	8	0	0	31
Louisiana	40	3	4	0	39
Maryland	17	2	1	0	18
Mississippi	40	2	4	0	38
North Carolina	56	11	3	1	63
Oklahoma	58	16	2	0	72
South Carolina	40	13	5	1	47
Tennessee	47	7	1	0	53
Texas	208	41	3	10	236
Virginia	27	9	2	1	33
West	285	40	16	0	309
Arizona	55	6	2	0	59
California	159	24	7	0	176
Colorado	1	0	0	0	1
Idaho	14	1	1	0	14
Montana	5	0	0	0	5
Nevada	31	5	1	0	35
New Mexico	5	0	5	0	0
Oregon	0	2	0	0	2
Utah	7	0	0	0	7
Washington	5	2	0	0	7
Wyoming	3	0	0	0	3

Source: Steven Schlesinger, *Capital Punishment 1986* (Washington, D.C.: U.S. Department of Justice, 1987) p. 5.

Now again time is running out for a large proportion of individuals awaiting capital punishment. States have drafted and redrafted capital punishment measures and the Supreme Court is overturning fewer and fewer on Eighth Amendment or other constitutional grounds. Further, many death-row residents are exhausting their appeal process under these statutes. Thus the situation is ripe for the Nation to witness executions at a rate approaching the more than three per week that prevailed during the 1930's. We will then have a grim arena in which to conduct our national debate on the efficacy of the death penalty.[28]

As seen in Table 14.4, the number of executions has already begun to meet the dire predictions of 1982. The Supreme Court seems to be aware of the need to get on with the grisly business of deciding what to do with the nearly eighteen hundred inmates on death row. A ruling in mid-1983 gave the death penalty states a "green light" for speeding up executions by as much as six months or more, through more efficient procedures adopted by the Court. Though the majority of death row inmates have not exhausted their appeals to the final stage of the Supreme Court, over ten percent have. The new rules accomplish the following:

Under the Supreme Court ruling, issued July 6 in the case of Texas death row inmate Thomas Barefoot, the onslaught of executions could begin a little sooner than expected.

From now on, when an execution date is set and imminent, the 12 U.S. Circuit Courts of Appeals may step up the speed with which they handle a final-hour appeal from a death row inmate.

Instead of automatically postponing the execution and taking the usual six months or longer to consider an inmate's last-chance appeal, a Federal appeals court may use new streamlined procedures to avoid delays in executions.

If they choose, the courts may compress the time they usually take to consider a legal claim, hurriedly schedule arguments, issue a rejection and let the execution take place on schedule.

Although the ruling affects death penalty claims only when they reach the Federal appeals court, the results are crucial. The U.S. appeals courts are generally the next-to-last hope for inmates trying to avoid execution.[29]

This decision has not been good news for those who have traditionally taken over a decade to exhaust the appeals mechanisms. Executions will soon become more numerous, with less time between them. Whether this will dull the nation's senses to the death penalty or focus action against it has yet to be seen (see Chart 14.3).

Time May Also Be Running Out for Women on Death Row _____

Since 1977, forty-four women were sentenced to death, from seventeen states (see Table 14.5). Of these, twenty-five had their death sentences vacated or commuted, or they died in confinement. Prior to 1967, the last woman to have been executed legally in the United States was Elizabeth Ann Duncan, who died in the California gas chamber on August 8, 1962 (see Table 14.6). Duncan was so infatuated with her son that she hired two killers to murder her daughter-in-law. In 1986, there were eighteen women on the death rows across the nation, as shown in Table 14.7.

In 1984, Thelma Barfield was executed by lethal injection in North Carolina—the first woman to be executed in twenty-two years. Despite the reluctance to execute women, the Supreme Court's desires for equity in imposing the death penalty seem to require that sex also be removed as a barrier. Of the over seventeen hundred inmates on death row, only eighteen are women, even though about one out of seven arrests for murder (1986) were of women. This unequal ratio of sentences to death for women who commit murder seems to foretell a more equitable push for the death penalty for women in the future.

Since the first woman was executed in 1638, only 286 out of the 12,264 legal executions in the United States (including during the colonial period) have been women. But it looks as though this situation will soon change.

TABLE 14.5 Movement of Women Under Sentence of Death, by State, 1977–1986

State	Prisoners Under Sentence on 1/1/77	Changes from 1977–1986			Prisoners Under Sentence on 12/31/86
		Received Under Sentence	Death Sentence Removed	Executed	
U.S. Total	7	37	25	1	18
Alabama	0	3	1	0	2
Arkansas	0	1	1	0	0
Californa	2	0	2	0	0
Florida	1	2	1	0	2
Georgia	1	4	4	0	1
Idaho	0	1	1	0	0
Indiana	0	3	0	0	3
Kentucky	0	1	1	0	0
Maryland	0	3	2	0	1
Mississippi	0	3	1	0	2
Nevada	0	2	1	0	1
New Jersey	0	1	0	0	1
North Carolina	0	2	1	1	0
Ohio	3	3	5	0	1
Oklahoma	0	2	1	0	1
Tennessee	0	1	0	0	1
Texas	0	5	3	0	2

Source: Steven Schlesinger, *Capital Punishment 1986* (Washington, D.C.: U.S. Department of Justice, 1987) p. 9

TABLE 14.6 Women Executed under Civil Authority, 1930–1986

Year	Number Executed	States with Executions
Total	33	
1984	1	North Carolina
1962	1	California
1957	1	Alabama
1955	1	California
1954	2	Ohio
1953	3	Alabama, Federal (Missouri, New York)
1951	1	New York
1947	2	California, South Carolina
1946	1	Pennsylvania
1945	1	Georgia
1944	3	Mississippi, New York, North Carolina
1943	3	Mississippi, North Carolina, South Carolina
1942	1	Louisiana
1941	1	California
1938	2	Illinois, Ohio
1937	1	Mississippi
1936	1	New York
1935	3	Delaware, Louisiana, New York
1934	1	New York
1931	1	Pennsylvania
1930	2	Alabama, Arizona

Source: Steven Schlesinger, *Capital Punishment 1986* (Washington, D.C.: U.S. Department of Justice, 1987), p. 9.

TABLE 14.7 Number of Women on Death Row, by State, Yearend 1972–1986

State	1972	1973	1974	1975	1976	1977	1978	1979	1980	1981	1982	1983	1984	1985	1986
U.S. total	4	3	3	8	7	6	5	7	9	11	14	13	17	17	18
California	3			1	2										
Georgia	1	2	1	1	1	1	1	2	3	4	4	3	2	2	1
North Carolina		1	2	3			2	1	1	1	1	1			
Ohio				2	3	4						2	2	2	1
Oklahoma				1				1	1	1	2	2	1	1	1
Florida						1	1	1	1	1			1	2	2
Alabama							1	1		1	1	2	2	2	2
Texas								1	2	2	2		1	2	2
Kentucky									1	1					
Maryland										1	2	1	2	1	1
Mississippi											1	1	1	1	2
Nevada											1	1	2	2	1
New Jersey													1	1	1
Arkansas													1		
Idaho													1		
Indiana														1	3
Tennessee															1

Source: Steven Schlesinger, *Capital Punishment 1986* (Washington, D.C.: U.S. Department of Justice, 1987), p. 6.

EQUITY

Freedom from bias or prejudice in the application of the law. Regarding the death penalty, the principle of equity would mean that capital punishment would be applied without favoritism to men and women, and to blacks and whites alike.

Juveniles on Death Row: Should They Be Executed? _____

In 1986, thirty-six states had capital punishment statutes that provided for the execution of persons who committed their crimes while they were still juveniles, (under the age of eighteen). In February 1987, the Supreme Court agreed to decide whether "cruel and unusual punishment" is an aspect of the execution of juveniles. If so, such executions would be in violation of the Constitution. This case may decide this issue once and for all. The United States has executed 281 juveniles over the past 211 years, the latest in May 1986. That person was the third juvenile criminal to be executed in that year. This spate of executions is undoubtedly what prompted the Court to consider reviewing this issue. Although opponents of the death penalty are clearly trying to stop this practice, they do not advocate that society not punish these offenders. To first be selected to be tried as an adult, then to be convicted of a capital crime, and then to be sentenced to execution indicates that the juvenile committed a serious and heinous crime.

The details of the case that is of such concern to the thirty-seven sentenced to die for crimes committed before they were eighteen are noted in *Parade Magazine*:

> Wayne Thompson was 15 when he was arrested along with his half-brother, then 27, and two other men, also in their 20s, for the shooting and stabbing death of Charles Keene, Thompson's former brother-in-law, who lived in rural Amber, Oklahoma.
>
> After Keene's body was found in the Washita River, Thompson and the others were convicted of first-degree murder. They were all given the death penalty and sent to McAlester, Oklahoma's turn-of-the-century maximum-security prison. There are 64 convicts currently awaiting execution on McAlester's death row. According to Warden Gary Maynard, Wayne Thompson is the first juvenile locked within its all-brick cells.[30]

All of the juveniles on death row are in there for murder, usually in conjunction with several other crimes. Many of the murders were extremely vicious or gratuitous, often involving sadism or torture. As shown in Table 14.8, the states that have the death penalty for juvenile offenders are divided into those with specific minimum ages (27) and those with no minimum age (6). Oklahoma, South Dakota, and Delaware have neither a minimum age nor consider age to be a mitigating factor (see Table 14.8).

TABLE 14.8 Minimum Age Authorized for Capital Punishment, Yearend 1986

10 years	Indiana
13 years	Mississippi
14 years	Maryland
	Missouri
	North Carolina
15 years	Arkansas
	Louisiana
	Virginia
16 years	Nevada
	Oregon[a]
17 years	Georgia
	New Hampshire
	Texas
18 years	California
	Connecticut
	Colorado
	Idaho
	Illinois
	Nebraska
	New Jersey
	New Mexico
	Ohio
No minimum age specified	Federal
	Alabama
	Arizona
	Delaware
	Florida
	Kentucky[b]
	Montana
	Oklahoma
	Pennsylvania
	South Carolina
	South Dakota[c]
	Tennesse
	Utah
	Vermont
	Washington
	Wyoming

[a]After removal to adult court.
[b]Effective 7/1/87, the minimum age in Kentucky will be 16 (KRS 640.040).
[c]Must be tried as an adult.

Source: Steven Schlesinger, _Capital Punishment 1986_ (Washington, D.C.: U.S. Department of Justice, 1987), p. 4.

Who are these juvenile criminals on death row? Fifteen are white, eighteen are black. Two are females, making them a double problem for the prison administration and another factor in this knotty problem. Twenty-five of them are from southern states. Texas leads the states with five juveniles on death row, Georgia has four, Florida has three, and several other states have two (see Table 14.9). The average age of those convicted

TABLE 14.9 **Juvenile Criminals on Death Row**

Name	State	Age When Crime Was Committed	Time on Death Row
Joseph Anlisio	Pennsylvania	15	2½ years
Paula Cooper	Indiana	15	2 months
Wayne Thompson	Oklahoma	15	2¾ years
Ronald Ward	Arkansas	15	1 year
Leon Brown	North Carolina	15	2 years
Kevin Hughes	Pennsylvania	16	3 years
Carnel Jackson	Alabama	16	5 years
James Morgan	Florida	16	8¾ years
Frederick Lynn	Alabama	16	3 years
Heath Wilkins	Missouri	16	3 months
José High	Georgia	16	7¾ years
Joseph John Cannon	Texas	17	4½ years
Robert A. Carter	Texas	17	4½ years
Timothy Davis	Alabama	17	6 years
Johnny Frank Garrett	Texas	17	4 years
Gary Graham	Texas	17	5 years
Curtis Paul Harris	Texas	17	7 years
Lawrence Johnson	Maryland	17	4 years
Larry Jones	Mississippi	17	11½ years
Frederick Lashley	Missouri	17	4 years
Andrew Legare	Georgia	17	8¾ years
Jesse James Livingston	Florida	17	1 year
Daleone Prejean	Louisiana	17	8 years
David Rushing	Louisiana	17	3 years
Kevin Stanford	Kentucky	17	4 years
Freddie Lee Stokes	North Carolina	17	4 years
Jay Thompson	Indiana	17	4½ years
George Tokman	Mississippi	17	5 years
Christopher Burger	Georgia	17	8 years
Janice Buttrum	Georgia	17	5 years
James Trimble	Maryland	17	4½ years
Paul Magill	Florida	17	9 years
Marko Bey	New Jersey	17	3 years

Source: Parade Magazine, October 18, 1986, p. 5.

offenders was sixteen and one-half at the time of their offense. They have been on death row for up to nine years. Whether the states, as many have, take the lead and set minimum ages for the death penalty (probably eighteen) or wait for the Supreme Court to present clear constitutional guidelines, it appears clear that this issue may be resolved soon.

Summary ——

As of January 1, 1987, 68 men and women have died by state execution since the day that Gary Gilmore was shot through the heart in 1977. The Supreme Court of the United States has streamlined and expedited its procedures for appellate review and seems to have tackled the issue of capital punishment head-on. However, the death rows in thirty-three states are packed, with a total of 1,781 persons sentenced to die by hanging, electrocution, lethal injection, gas, and the firing squad. Five states—Connecticut, New Hampshire, Oregon, South Dakota, and Vermont—have the death penalty on the books, but have no inmates on death row.

After it showed clearly what provisions it was willing to accept in regard to the death penalty in *Gregg*, the Court has been relatively supportive of the states implementing them. It is clear, however, that the limited circumstances acceptable for the ultimate punishment must be administered on a scrupulously equitable basis or the Court will surely hold that even such limited application of the sanction of death is unconstitutional. The matter of equity is the one that must be watched over the next few years, as the number of convictions continues to grow.

All but five of those executed since the lifting of the ban on capital punishment in 1976 have been executed in states in the deep South. The southern tradition of retribution seems to be ready now to spread to the rest of America. Perhaps this attitude will spread to states like Washington, Pennsylvania, or California. As we complete the last years of the 1980s, the Supreme Court of *all* the United States is keeping a sharp eye on the patterns of executions that seems reserved to one geographical region. The Court will need to rethink this matter of equity and, perhaps, take action to correct this pattern.

Women and juveniles who have been sentenced to death present issues that seem to fly in the face of an equity doctrine. These issues must be resolved. The public still supports the death penalty for adults on a fairly consistent rate of about 70 percent. However, statistics are not so clear for women and juveniles on death row. There seems to be no really valid polling figures in regard to women, who are generally lumped in with "adults." Some polls show a 50 percent level of support for the execution of juveniles on death row, so the Court has its work cut out for it.

It can be hoped that, someday, we will choose to work toward improved and innovative correctional programs that leave the death penalty ritual for future anthropologists and historians to ponder. The legacy may well stand as an example of the callous disregard for the value of human life in the twentieth century. One way to modify such a legacy lies in the efforts to improve the entire criminal justice system, and to make sure that all offenders are treated equitably.

Review Questions _____

1. Explain the guidelines that came out of *Furman* v. *Georgia*.
2. Prepare an argument *for* the retention of the death penalty, and then prepare an argument *against* it.
3. What are the major issues related to the question of the execution of juveniles?

Key Terms ——

1. **capital punishment (p. 302)**
2. **capital crimes (p. 303)**
3. **equability (p. 306)**
4. **arbitrarily (p. 309)**
5. **malice aforethought (p. 310)**
6. **cruel and unusual punishment (p. 314)**
7. **deterrence (p. 320)**
8. **life certain (p. 320)**
9. **equity (p. 327)**

Notes ——

1. "Public Executions," *Journal of Prison Discipline and Philanthropy* (July 1859): 117–123; quotation from p. 120.
2. Harry Elmer Barnes and Negley K. Teeter, *New Horizons in Criminology,* 3d ed. (Englewood Cliffs, N.J.: Prentice-Hall, 1959), p. 308.
3. Ibid., p. 309.
4. For a good reference to this controversy, see Ernest van den Haag and John Conrad *The Death Penalty: A Debate* (New York: Plenum Press, 1983).
5. Federal Bureau of Prisons, *National Prisoner Statistics* 18 (February 1958), p. 5.
6. The most readable discussion of these issues can be found in P. Lewis et al., "A Post-*Furman* Profile of Florida's Condemned — A Question of Discrimination in Terms of the Race of the Victim and a Comment on *Spinkellink* v. *Wainwright,*" *Stetson Law Review* 9 (Fall 1979): 1–45.
7. J. Edgar Hoover, *Uniform Crime Reports* (Washington, D.C.: U.S. Government Printing Office, 1931–1939). A rough average of these crimes known to the police is presented here.
8. *Capital Punishment, 1986,* U.S. Department of Justice, Bureau of Justice Statistics, Washington, D.C.: US Government Printing Office, (September 1987), p 8.
9. Hoover, *Uniform Crime Reports,* 1960–1967. Again, an average of the number of these crimes known to the police is presented. A note of caution: the reported crimes in the early era of the *Uniform Crime Reports* should not be compared with those of the later reports as crime definitions have varied across decades. They are cited only to call attention to the difference between crimes that could result in the death penalty and those that did result in an execution.
10. Justice William J. Brennan, *Furman* v. *Georgia,* 408 U.S. 238 (1976).
11. The U.S. Supreme Court recently rendered three decisions that further restricted the applications of the death penalty. In 1977, the case of *Coker* v. *Georgia* (433 U.S. 584) decided that the death penalty was "grossly disproportionate punishment" for the crime of rape of an adult woman, even though the offender had been previously convicted of rape and was, at the time of the crime, an escapee from prison. The second case (*Roberts* v. *Louisiana,* 431 U.S. 633) was decided in 1977 and prohibited the mandatory death penalty following conviction for the killing of a firefighter or police officer in performance of his or her duties. The last cases (*Lockett* v. *Ohio,* 434 U.S. 889, and *Bell* v. *Ohio,* 434 U.S. 887) were 1978 decisions, striking down Ohio's death penalty statute for "impermissibly restricting the mitigating factors that may be considered on behalf of an offender at sentencing."
12. Brennan, *Furman* v. *Georgia.*

13. Malice aforethought means malice in fact or implied malice in the intent of one who has had time to premeditate an act that is unlawful or harmful.

14. The states without the death penalty (prior to *Furman* v. *Georgia*) were: Mandatory implementation of the death penalty, mandatory death penalty for murder of a law enforcement officer or firefighter in the line of duty, and mandatory death penalty for rape of an adult person are no longer permissible. See note 11.

15. Justice Thurgood Marshall, *Furman* v. *Georgia*. Actually, the U.S. Supreme Court shifted from the earlier standard (concerned only with historical techniques for imposing punishment) to the "emerging standards" doctrine in 1910 (*Weems* v. *United States*, 217 U.S. 349).

16. *Wilkerson* v. *Utah*, 99 U.S. 130 (1878). The State Supreme Court of Utah upheld a lower-court decision sentencing a prisoner convicted of murder in the first degree to be shot publicly.

17. Justice Nathan Clifford, *Wilkerson* v. *Utah*, 99 U.S. 130 (1878).

18. Justice Stephen Field, *O'Neil* v. *Vermont*, 1944 U.S. 323 (1892).

19. *Weems* v. *United States*, 217 U.S. 349 (1910). This decision represented a broad interpretation of the Eighth Amendment, asserting that cruel and unusual punishment could apply to prison sentences of a length disproportionate to the offense.

20. *Louisiana ex rel. Francis* v. *Resweber,* 329 U.S. 459 (1947). The State Supreme Court of Louisiana denied a writ of habeas corpus against a second attempt to execute a prisoner convicted of murder, the first attempt at electrocution having failed because of mechanical difficulty.

21. For briefer analysis of the varied opinions, see F. C. Rieber, "Supreme Court Bars Death Penalty As It Is Now Imposed by the States," *American Journal of Corrections* 35 (1973): 10–14.

22. Chief Justice Warren Burger, *Furman* v. *Georgia*.

23. These included such notable figures as Sirhan Sirhan, the convicted killer of Senator Robert Kennedy, and Charles Manson, leader of the group of mass killers in California known as the "Family."

24. *Gregg* v. *Georgia,* 428 U.S. 153 (1976).

25. Sir James Stephen (as quoted in *Furman* v. *Georgia* by Justice Marshall).

26. Marvin Wolfgang and Michael Meltsner, "Introduction to Symposium on Current Death Penalty Issues," *Journal of Criminal Law and Criminology* 74 (Fall 1983): 659–670.

27. *Capital Punishment, 1986,* p. 1.

28. Benjamin H. Renshaw III, "Death Row Prisoners: 1981," *Bureau of Justice Statistics Bulletin* (Washington, D.C.: U.S. Department of Justice, July 1982), p. 1.

29. Editors, "Supreme Court Speeds Up Death Penalty Appeal Process: Issues Streamlined Procedures," *Corrections Digest* (Washington, D.C.: Washington Crime News Services, July 13, 1983), p. 2.

30. *Oklahoma's Violent Young: Kids as Killers, Oklahoma Observer* (Oklahoma City: September 10, 1987), p. 68.

Rights of Ex-Offenders

Young, unskilled, poorly educated, the typical
offender has few marketable capabilities to offer
potential employers. Unable to find or keep a job
upon his release from prison, the offender often
returns to crime—the only "business" he knows.
  Breaking the cycle of recidivism is a difficult
task, involving many complex contributing factors.
One of these is employment potential. Effective
programs for building relevant job skills do ease
the offender's reentry into society.
—GERALD M. CAPLAN, Former Director,
National Institute of Law Enforcement
and Criminal Justice

The Legend of the Ex-Con

The highly stylized version of the "ex-con" presented in the movies and
on television usually depicts a tough, scar-faced thug, able to survive on
his wits and muscle, with a good-looking blonde always somewhere in the
background. He is depicted as a man to be feared and never trusted. With
a granite jaw and shifty eyes, he talks out of the corner of his mouth,
and he prefers a life of crime. The real-life ex-offender, of course, is something quite different from our legendary ex-con of movie and dime-novel
fame.

The newly released ex-offenders found in most cities are young, with
little experience outside prison walls; they are poor, with only the funds
they managed to acquire while in prison; uneducated, with less than a
high school degree; former illicit drug users,[1] and frightened, having spent
several years away from a rapidly changing world. After release from
prison, these individuals must start a new life and make it in the free
world while being watched by the correctional authorities, local police,
employers, friends, and family. They often return to the same social and
environmental conditions that gave rise to their trouble in the first place.
The wonder is not that so many ex-offenders recidivate but that more do
not. If one adds to this already heavy burden the legal and administrative

restrictions placed on ex-offenders, it becomes evident that the happy-go-lucky ex-con is indeed a legend invented for the reading and viewing public. This chapter will consider the restrictions on ex-offenders and the current status of efforts to give them additional rights.

Collateral Consequences of Conviction

Conviction for an offense carries with it the punishment imposed by statute. In addition, the convicted offender must carry several other disabilities and disqualifications that result from the conviction per se.

Even after offenders have served their sentences, these secondary handicaps continue to plague them in the form of social stigma, loss of civil rights, and administrative and legislative restrictions. Each of these areas interacts with the others, and their overall effect is to prevent the successful reintegration of ex-offenders into the free community. The problems first surface when ex-offenders attempt to find employment,[2] as this account by one such job seeker illustrates:

> Now if you're out there on the bricks and looking for work, Joe, don't bother applying for any of those jobs I told you about and you'll save yourself a bundle of heartaches. Whenever you apply for any job, my advice is not to mention your record. That's right, lie to 'em. If they have a place on the employment application where it asks you if you've ever been convicted of a crime, put down N-O, no! If you don't, you're screening yourself out of 75 percent of all jobs, and damned near 100 percent of the better jobs. You have to look ahead too, Joe. Big Willie, the trustyland barber, has a brother working for one of the big steel companies. A friend got him the job, white collar too. That was seven, eight years ago. He's still on the same job, but guys who have only been with the company two or three years are moving right up the line to higher job classifications and better pay. Why? His boss told him why. He's got a record, and the company knows it's on his original employment application. His boss told him he was terribly sorry, that wasn't

---

COLLATERAL CONSEQUENCES

Many state and federal statutes restrict some of the rights and privileges ordinarily available to law-abiding citizens in the nation. These include the rights to vote, to hold offices of private and public trust, to assist in parenting, to be on jury duty, to own firearms, to remain married, and to have privacy. These and other rights may be lost upon conviction. These are collectively called *collateral consequences* of criminal conviction.

Just how many citizens face collateral consequences is unknown, but a conservative estimate is that there are at least 50 million persons who have been arrested for some offense in the nation, and at least 14 million persons have been convicted of a felony.

his fault, but the higher-ups passed him up because fifteen years ago he served two years in prison. See, Joe, crime don't pay, because they ain't never going to let you up once they got you down. That's just the way it is.

Go ahead and tell 'em if you want to, Joe. You're taking a chance no matter what you do. If you tell 'em you don't get the job most of the time. If you don't tell 'em, and they find out, they fire you. You know Louie, the cellhouse clerk? He got a job and didn't tell 'em about his record. Louie's parole officer came around checking on him and blowed the job for Louie. How do you like them apples? And Gabby, the four block runner, went out and got a job that'll knock you out. He was hired as a credit investigator! Yeah, handling confidential financial reports all day long. While he was still on parole too. His parole officer was an OK guy and said more power to 'em. Well, it took about two months because the employment application investigation isn't handled by regional offices but is done by the main office in New York. One day his boss calls him in, red faced and all, and says to him, why didn't you tell us? Louie says, if I'd told you, would you have hired me? His boss says, of course not! Louie was canned.[3]

The great dilemma faced by the ex-offender in search of a job is obvious.

Stigma

The stigma of a prison record is to ex-offenders a millstone to be worn around their necks until death. Though we pride ourselves that we have advanced beyond the eye-for-an-eye mentality of the past, we do not show it in the treatment of our offenders who have allegedly paid their "debt" to society. Aaron Nussbaum pointed out some of the problems of stigma for the discharged prisoner:

> It is a grim fact that total punishment for crime never ends with the courts or jails. None can deny that a criminal record is a life-long handicap, and its subject a "marked man" in our society. No matter how genuine the refor-mation, nor how sincere and complete the inner resolution to revert to lawful behavior, the criminal offender is and remains a prisoner of his past record long after the crime is expiated by the punishment fixed under the criminal codes.
>
> This traditional prejudice and distrust stalks him at every turn no matter what crime he may have committed or the nature of the punishment meted out to him. It strikes at the first offender as ruthlessly, and with as deadly effect, as upon the inveterate repeater or the professional criminal. It pursues those alike who have served time in imprisonment, of long or short duration, and those who have been merely cloaked with a criminal record in the form of a suspended sentence, a discharge on probation, or even a fine.[4]

One needs self-esteem to survive in the competitive atmosphere of the free world. Thus the diminished self-esteem of the offender makes it difficult to bridge the gap between institutional life and the community. It is this search for self-esteem and status that leads many ex-offenders back to the circle of acquaintances that first led them afoul of the law. The personal disintegration encouraged by the fortress prisons of America makes the discharged offender both a social and economic cripple. We can only hope that the new techniques in corrections, designed to strengthen self-esteem and produce reasonable readjustment in the community, will help offset this effect, as will increased use of community corrections.

The Transition Period: A Time of Readjustment

Many ex-inmates, particularly those having served longer sentences, face a difficult transitional period when paroled. Not only do they have breaks in their employment histories that are difficult to explain to potential employers, but many are taken aback by the cost of food and services on the outside, especially as inflation has more than doubled the cost of basic commodities since 1973. Because of these problems, many ex-offenders need intensive assistance from reintegration services, such as halfway houses. In the Federal Bureau of Prisons, a large portion of prerelease inmates in fact spend their last six months in halfway houses, where they receive training in how to fill out employment applications, how to get and hold a job, how to deal with family problems and crises, where to secure services available in their communities, how to manage money, and so on. Such services will be even more important as tax revolts decrease parole services, more inmates are incarcerated, and sentences lengthen.[5] Charging fees for parole services may further aggravate the situation.[6]

Loss of Civil Rights

Though most people recognize that released prisoners do not automatically regain all their civil rights, there is widespread confusion as to which rights are permanently lost and which suspended, and what machinery is available to regain them. Sol Rubin, a lawyer and writer on penology, discussed the offender's loss of the rights to vote and engage in certain kinds of employment:

> [W]hen a convicted defendant is *not* sentenced to commitment, but is placed on probation, and receives a suspended sentence, he should lose no civil rights. This is a recommendation of the Standard Probation and Parole Act published as long ago as 1955.
>
> It is a contradiction of the purposes of probation and parole that this view does not prevail. A California case cites the following instruction to a new parolee: "Your civil rights have been suspended. Therefore, you may not enter into any contract, marry, engage in business, or execute a contract without the restoration of such civil rights by the Adult Authority." A look at the rights restored by the Adult Authority at the time of release on parole is just as sad, hardly more than that on release he may be at large. He may rent a habitation, he is told, buy food, clothing, and transportation, and tools for a job; and he is advised that he has the benefit of rights under Workman's Compensation, Unemployment Insurance, etc.

When the sentence is commitment, the principle of *Coffin* v. *Reichard* ought to apply, that a prisoner retains (or should retain) all rights of an ordinary citizen except those expressly or by necessary implication taken away by law.[7]

To determine the current status of collateral consequences, Burton, Cullen and Travis surveyed the fifty states and the District of Columbia statutes, case law, and attorneys general in a systematic review of the specific privileges, immunities, and rights that felons might lose after conviction. The basic results are found in Tables 15.1 and 15.2. The researchers found that states are generally becoming less restrictive in depriving felons of their civil rights.

Some eleven states permanently disenfranchise the felon unless he or she is pardoned or restored to citizenship through the vacating of the original sentence, expungement of record, or other judicial procedure unique to the jurisdiction. In the survey, over three-fourths of the jurisdictions restored the right to vote after specific periods of time had lapsed. Other major findings were as follows:

1. In some sixteen states (nearly one-third of the jurisdictions surveyed), courts may terminate parenting rights on the conviction or incarceration of a parent.
2. More than half (twenty-eight states) permit divorce for conviction or imprisonment of a felony.
3. Some 30 percent of the jurisdictions permanently bar convicted felons from public employment in their home states, unless pardoned or restored to full citizenship.
4. If one is a felon in nineteen states, one may not hold public office.
5. Almost every state forbids a felon from possession of a firearm.
6. Only eight states require felons to register as a former offender, and only four states continue the practice of civil death.[8]

Recognition of the inequities in these denials is expressed in the provisions of Section 306.1(1) of the American Law Institute's Model Penal Code:

No person shall suffer any legal disqualification or disability because of his conviction of a crime or his sentence on such conviction, unless the disqualification or disability involves the deprivation of a right or privilege which is:

a. necessarily incident to execution of the sentence of the court; or
b. provided by the Constitution or the Code; or
c. provided by a statute other than the Code, when the conviction is of a crime defined by such statute; or
d. provided by the judgment, order, or regulation of a court, agency, or official exercising a jurisdiction conferred by law, or by the statute defining such jurisdiction, when the commission of the crime or the conviction or the sentence is reasonably related to the competency of the individual to exercise the right or privilege of which he is deprived.[9]

TABLE 15.1 Restrictions of Felony Offenders' Civil Rights

	Restrictive vs. Less Restrictive, by Right & Jurisdiction								
Jurisdiction	Voting: Permanently Lost vs. Restorable	Parental: Yes vs. No	Divorce: Permanently Yes vs. No	Public Employment: Permanently Lost vs. Restorable	Juror: Permanently Lost vs. Restorable	Holding Office: Permanently Lost vs. Restorable	Firearm: "Violent" Felony vs. "Any" Felony	Criminal Registration: Yes vs. No	Civil Death: Yes vs. No
Alabama	X	X	X	X	X	X		X	
Alaska			X		X		X		
Arizona	X	X					X	X	
Arkansas	X		X		X	X	X	X	
California		X			X	X^1	X		
Colorado		X					X		
Connecticut			X				X		
Delaware				X	X	X^1	X		
D.C.			X		X	X	X	X	
Florida	X				X	X	X		
Georgia			X		X	X	X		
Hawaii					X		X		
Idaho			X		X				X
Illinois			X				X		
Indiana		X	X		X		X		
Iowa	X			X	X	X	X		
Kansas		X					X		
Kentucky	X	X			X	X	X		
Louisiana			X						
Maine						X^1	X		
Maryland		X	X		X				
Massachusetts		X				X^1	X		
Michigan		X					X		

State	1	2	3	4	5	6	7	8
Minnesota								
Mississippi	X	X	X	X				X
Missouri					X			
Montana			X		X			
Nebraska			X		X			
Nevada		X		X	X			X
New Hampshire							X	
New Jersey			X	X	X		X	
New Mexico			X	X	X		X	
New York	X				X	X	X	
North Carolina							X	
North Dakota							X	
Ohio				X	X		X	
Oklahoma			X		X		X	
Oregon								X
Pennsylvania					X		X	
Rhode Island	X			X	X	X	X	X
South Carolina				X	X	X	X	X
South Dakota							X	X
Tennessee			X	X	X		X	
Texas		X		X	X		X	
Utah					X		X	
Vermont		X					X	
Virginia				X	X		X	
Washington								
West Virginia			X	X			X	
Wisconsin			X				X	X
Wyoming					X		X	X

X = right is restricted or jeopardized

1 = right is restricted for specific offenses

Source: Velmer Burton, Francis Cullen and Lawrence Travis, "The Collateral Consequences of a Felony Conviction," *Federal Probation* 51 (1987): 55.

TABLE 15.2 **Restricted Rights by Jurisdiction**

Number of Rights That Are Restricted	Jurisdictions
9	None
8	Mississippi
7	Alabama and Rhode Island
6	Nevada and Tennessee
5	Arkansas, California, Florida, Iowa, and New York
4	Delaware, District of Columbia, Georgia, Indiana, Kentucky, New Mexico, Texas, and Virginia
3	Alaska, Arizona, Idaho, Massachusetts, New Jersey, Ohio, Oklahoma, Pennsylvania, South Carolina, Utah, and Wisconsin
2	Connecticut, Hawaii, Illinois, Kansas, Maine, Maryland, Michigan, Montana, Nebraska, New Hampshire, Oregon, South Dakota, and Wyoming
1	Colorado, Louisiana, Minnesota, Missouri, North Dakota, Vermont, and West Virginia
0	North Carolina and Washington

Rights considered were in the areas of voting, parenting, divorce, public employment, jury duty, holding public office, owning firearms, criminal registration, and civil death.

Source: Velmer Burton, Francis Cullen, and Lawrence Travis, "The Collateral Consequences of Felony Conviction," *Federal Probation* 51 (1987): 52–60.

Right to Work Versus Need to Work

Ex-offenders are often faced with the cruel paradox that they must have employment to remain free, even though the system denies them employment because they have a record.[10] Many studies have shown that employment is one of the most important factors in the successful reintegration of ex-offenders into the community. In the past, ex-offenders could move on to a new territory and establish a new identity, thus escaping the stigmatization that goes with a prison record. On the advancing frontiers of early America, the new settlers asked few questions, judging individuals on their present actions rather than past records. But today computers record every aspect of our lives, and privacy has become less a right than a very rare privilege. To many people, the informational expansion is a boon; to ex-offenders it often represents a catastrophe. Even citizens who find themselves involved in an arrest that does not result in conviction may suffer the worst consequences of a record, including the failure to obtain a job, or its loss.

There appear to be two levels where action is necessary to alleviate this crushing burden for the ex-offender. At the community level, barriers to employment that work against the poor and uneducated must be overcome; that is, more realistic educational requirements for jobs must be negotiated. (Degrees and diplomas are often used as screening devices for jobs that

A Job: The Ultimate Rehabilitation (Courtesy Pioneer Human Services)

do not require them.) A structural framework must be constructed in which the community has jobs to fill, training to give, and a willingness to offer these to offenders and ex-offenders. These conditions can be met only by basic changes in society, not by programs for the individual. The use of ex-offenders as parole officer agents by some states is an example of such a favorable development.

At the individual level, the offender must overcome his or her personal handicaps. Many recent programs are aimed at the employability of the offender and ex-offender, often the young, the unemployed, and the unskilled (frequently also members of minority groups), who comprise the bulk of official arrest statistics.

In community-based programs to help in the employment of offenders and ex-offenders, it must be assumed that the person has the capability for regular employment but is unfamiliar with and inexperienced in certain of the behavioral skills demanded. In other words, behavioral training, rather than therapy, is needed. It must also be assumed that if offenders learn to handle themselves in the community while under correctional control, they will be able to do so when these controls have been lifted. In planning employment assistance for offenders and ex-offenders who may need it, program planners are faced with many questions:

- How much support service is necessary?
- Should supportive services be provided in-house or be contracted?

- How good a job should be sought ("dead-end," having job mobility, on a career ladder, etc.)?
- Who should be trained, and what kind of training should be offered?
- When, what kind, and how much training should be provided in the institutions?

To answer these questions, a comprehensive service program should include the following:

- Assessment of the client's skills and abilities.
- Training in job-hunting and job-readiness skills and in acquiring acceptable work attitudes.
- Job training and basic education, if necessary.
- Job development and job placement.
- Follow-up with employee and employer after placement.
- Other supportive services, as required (medical or legal aid).

Restricted Trades: Barriers to Employment

Although there are still some barriers to employment in general for ex-offenders, today's standards are more likely to apply to the individual and his or her offense. Ex-offenders as an identified class (or minority) are appealing more and more to the courts. The nineties will see great strides in this area, especially in the removal of employment restrictions for ex-offenders, simply because they are ex-offenders.[11] We are happy to report that the trades outlined in the third edition of this book are now opening to all classes of persons. It is only the general unemployment picture that most severely affects the ex-offender. When work is scarce for all, the ex-offender finds it more and more difficult to find any kind of employment. This tends to highlight the overall problem, in all aspects of society, that results from a criminal record.

The National Alliance for Business and the Probation Division of the Administrative Office of the U.S. Courts undertook a partnership venture in June of 1980, designed to test a delivery system for ex-offender training services and employment. The model is designed to use existing resources, coordinated to attain the model's objectives. The Alliance provides technical assistance to localities attempting to implement the model, and it is proving to be a promising venture.[12]

The Problem with a Record _____

As we have seen, the person with a record of conviction is at a major disadvantage in regard to reintegration into the community. The depriva-

Learning a Trade Can Mean a Good Job (Courtesy of American Correctional Association, photo by UNICOR)

tion of rights and bars to employment are related to that record, and so it is vital to know what having a record means in the age of information. It seems that a record, even a record of mere contact with the criminal justice system, is extremely difficult to shed once it has been acquired. This record becomes the basis for special attention by the police and harassment from credit agencies. Once the record has been placed in the computers, it can be retrieved whenever requested by an authorized agency and, inevitably, by some unauthorized agencies.

One way to overcome the problem of a record is to construct a system that will annul the conviction after certain specifications are met. The National Council on Crime and Delinquency[13] makes this provision in its Model Act for Annulment of Conviction of Crime:

> The court in which a conviction of crime has been had may, at the time of discharge of a convicted person from its control, or upon his discharge from imprisonment or parole, or at any time thereafter, enter an order annulling, canceling, and rescinding the record of conviction and disposition, when in

---

ANNULMENT

An annulment is a judicial proceeding that nullifies, abolishes, cancels, and abrogates a judgment or former judicial proceeding. An annulment results in a legal statement that the arrest and conviction never existed, and deprives the former judgement of all force currently or in the future.

---

the opinion of the court the order would assist in rehabilitation and be consistent with the public welfare. Upon the entry of such order the person against whom the conviction had been entered shall be restored to all civil rights lost or suspended by virtue of the arrest, conviction, or sentence, unless otherwise provided in the order, and shall be treated in all respects as not having been convicted, except that upon conviction of any subsequent crime the prior conviction may be considered by the court in determining the sentence to be imposed.

In any application for employment, license, or other civil right or privilege, or any appearance as a witness, a person may be questioned about previous criminal record only in language such as the following: Have you ever been arrested for or convicted of a crime which has not been annulled by a court?" Upon entry of the order of annulment of conviction, the court shall issue to the person in whose favor the order has been entered a certificate stating that his behavior after conviction has warranted the issuance of the order, and that its effect is to annul, cancel, and rescind the record of conviction and disposition. Nothing in this act shall affect any right of the offender to appeal from his conviction or to rely on it in bar of any subsequent proceedings for the same offense.[14]

This kind of proposal has aroused interest but little action in state legislatures. Because annulment is, in fact, the only reasonable way to protect the ex-offender from questions about prior convictions, some courts are getting around the legislative inaction by failing to enter the record of conviction and keeping an informal "vest-pocket" record.[15]

The problem of a record in this country is especially critical when an arrest does not result in a conviction. In most foreign countries, an arrest with no conviction cannot be used against the person in later actions. In the United States, in most jurisdictions, employment applications can include questions about an arrest, regardless of whether or not there was a conviction. Even a pardon, exonerating the suspect from guilt, does not remove the incident from the record. Not surprisingly, the current attack on this perpetual record is based on the cruel and unusual punishment clause of the Eighth Amendment.[16] Another legal approach is reflected in recent suits claiming that prisoners and ex-offenders are being discriminated against as a class, instead of being treated on the basis of individual merit:

It is a truism that we find hard to accept that the protections of the Bill of Rights against police and other official abuse are for all of us, the criminals and the noncriminals. But when we consider the tens of millions who have a record of arrest, perhaps as many as 50 million, it is clear that the civil rights of those who are in conflict with the law are, indeed, in the most pragmatic way, the interest of all. We are in an era of struggle for civil rights, for blacks, for women, for the mentally ill, for the young, even the delinquent young. Perhaps we are in a period of civil rights for homosexuals and others whose sexual practices are unreasonably subject to legal condemnation.

It is timely, indeed, that we awake to the excesses in punishing those in conflict with the law. It is a field of great discrimination, and must be remedied, just as much as other discriminations must be remedied. Not all people with a criminal record are vicious or degraded to begin with, or if their crime was vicious, are they doomed to remain as they were; unless, of course, we strive by discrimination and rejection to make them so.[17]

Registration of Criminals

Registration of criminals has been a practice ever since society started imprisoning individuals. In ancient times, registration was used to identify prisoners in penal servitude; prisoners were branded or marked to decrease their already minimal chances of escape. Because penal slaves had no hope of ever being free, the markings were a sign of their permanent status. The "yellow card" was later used in European countries to identify former prisoners who were lucky enough to live through their sentences.[18] The registration of felons has also been a widespread practice in America, especially at the local level. A problem with local registration is that it tends to single out offenders for special attention from authorities to which they would not otherwise be subject. Most of these requirements are obsolete today. As information on offenders and arrested persons is placed into computer data banks, a public official can easily query the computer to check the status of almost anyone.

The most common form of local registration concerns sex-related offenses. The "pervert file" is used to check out former offenders in the event of similar crimes. This kind of file is no doubt an asset to law enforcement, but it becomes a real problem for the ex-offender who is seriously trying to conform. These inquiries are legitimate for law enforcement personnel;

EXPUNGEMENT

The process by which the record of crime conviction is destroyed or sealed after expiration of statutorily required time. This means the act of physically destroying information — including criminal records — in files, computers, or other depositories.

A related process is "erasure of record" of juveniles. This is a procedure by which a person's criminal record may be sealed or destroyed if certain conditions (as may be set forth in the jurisdiction) are met. This is commonly provided for by statute for juvenile records.

however, the discretion with which they are conducted can make a great difference to the ex-offender.

The practice of registering felons is on the decline, mainly because of the mobility of our present American society, but it remains in force in eight jurisdictions. Registration may be much more subtle than the practice of branding with a scarlet letter,[19] but it also has the potential to become a permanent stigma. There is considerable room to improve on these tactics in an age of modern informational techniques.

Expungement as a Response

It is clear that the debilitating effect of a criminal conviction is often heightened, rather than reduced, when the ex-offender returns to the free society. Some states have recognized this fact and attempted to develop *expungement* statutes, which erase the history of criminal conviction and completely restore the ex-offender's rights, thus removing the stigma of a criminal record. This idea was first developed in 1956, at the National Conference on Parole:

> The expunging of a criminal record should be authorized on a discretionary basis. The court of disposition should be empowered to expunge the record of conviction and disposition through an order by which the individual shall be deemed not to have been convicted. Such action may be taken at the point of discharge from suspended sentence, probation, or the institution upon expiration of a term of commitment. When such action is taken the civil and political rights of the offender are restored.[20]

The American Law Institute also saw the need for some way to vacate a conviction record in selected cases. A section of the Institute's Model Penal Code was compiled in 1961, recommending that the court use its authority to erase a record when an offender "has been discharged from probation or parole before the expiration of the maximum thereof" or "when the defendant has fully satisfied the sentence and has since led a law-abiding life for at least five years."[21]

These early recommendations of expungement did not specify procedures for the expungement order and did not go into great detail in identifying the real issues. The Model Act for Annulment proposed by the National Council on Crime and Delinquency, containing the comprehensive provisions for expungement quoted earlier, would give the ex-offender better protection than the Model Penal Code provides. But it remains too limited in its application and fails to recommend adequate procedures. Its effect on someone who is convicted is clear, as it only takes effect after conviction. But it does not help the individual who is arrested and not convicted. A viable annulment statute must also permit erasure of an arrest record.

Almost two decades ago, the American Bar Association Project on Standards for Criminal Justice made the following points regarding the need to remove the record stigma. These statements are still valid, but general adoption of these points has been agonizingly slow:

> Every jurisdiction should have a method by which the collateral effects of a criminal record can be avoided or mitigated following the successful completion of a term on probation and during its service.
>
> The Advisory Committee is not as concerned with the form which such statutes take as it is with the principle that flexibility should be built into the system and that effective ways should be devised to mitigate the scarlet letter effect of a conviction once the offender has satisfactorily adjusted.[22]

Clearly, there is growing support for the principle that ex-offenders (especially those who have demonstrated that they are in fact reformed) should be given a means of eliminating the brand of the felon. Though expungement is not the only answer to the problem of the burden and consequences of a criminal record, a sensible approach to the method is sorely needed.

Restoring Offenders' Rights _____

Some states restore civil rights when parole is granted; others when the offender is released from parole. In still others, it is necessary for a governor to restore all rights, usually through a pardon. California's procedures for pardon illustrate the latter. What is required for a pardon in California?

First, the offender must have led a crime-free existence for ten years following release from parole. The offender must initiate a petition for pardon in a superior court (also called a court of common pleas in other jurisdictions). A formal hearing is held, and the presiding judge solicits opinions from the local district attorney and chief law enforcement officer

---

PARDON

An act of executive clemency that absolves the party in part or in full from the legal consequences of the crime and conviction. For the accused, a pardon stops further criminal justice proceedings.

Pardons can be *full* or *conditional*, and the former generally applies to both the punishment and the guilt of the offender, and blots out the existence of guilt in the eyes of the law. It also removes an offender's disabilities and restores civil rights. The conditional pardon usually falls short of the remedies available in the full pardon, is an expression of guilt, and does not obliterate the conviction but may restore civil rights.

The U.S. Supreme Court decisions on pardons and their effects are directly contradictory, and thus state laws usually govern pardons. While pardons are not frequent in the nation at this time, it is reasonable to expect they will become more frequent as prison overcrowding becomes more critical.

---

in the jurisdiction. A computer search is made for any arrests and convictions. The local probation department prepares a prepardon hearing report. If the preponderance of evidence is favorable and no arrest or conviction record is found, the petition is approved by the superior court and is forwarded to the governor's office. The governor may then order the equivalent of a parole board (Board of Prison Terms) to prepare an investigation that would contain a recommendation for pardon. If the report is favorable, the governor may pardon the petitioner, thereby restoring to him or her all of the rights and immunities of an ordinary citizen. It is evident that most ex-offenders, though no doubt preferring a pardon, may even more favor having the crime and conviction put as far behind them as possible. They may also not have the perseverance to endure such an involved and expensive procedure. Finally, almost all ex-offenders are rearrested within the ten-year time period, even if there is no further action by criminal justice system officials. No wonder so few ex-offenders seek and receive pardons!

Laws that deprive ex-offenders from civil rights are vestiges from distant times and contradict both the principles of reintegration and the purposes of correction. We propose that all laws that deprive ex-offenders from civil rights should be abolished until and unless it is proved that the public's safety and protection require them. Doing so would advance the goals of corrections and reintegration and is more defensible than is the continuing disenfranchisement of currently law-abiding persons.

Summary

Many organizations contend that when convicted felons have paid their debt to society, they should have a chance to start over, with a clean record. This belief has been translated into statutes that provide for the annulment and expungement of criminal records in a number of states, but many of them lack adequate mechanisms to implement the provisions. Only when the general public has fully accepted the idea of a fresh start for the ex-offender will our legislators pass the revisions necessary to make the statutes fully effective.

Review Questions

1. What are the collateral consequences of a conviction? Discuss.
2. How could expungement improve the reintegration process for ex-offenders?
3. Why does registration of criminals have such a drastic effect on the ex-offender? What are the alternatives?

Key Terms _____

1. **collateral consequences** (p. 334)
2. **stigma** (p. 335)
3. **civil rights** (p. 336)
4. **restricted trades** (p. 342)
5. **annulment** (p. 344)
6. **criminal registration** (p. 345)
7. **yellow card** (p. 345)
8. **pervert file** (p. 345)
9. **expungement** (p. 345)
10. **pardon** (p. 347)

Notes _____

1. "Study Links Crime and Drug Use," San Francisco Chronicle (January 22, 1988): A-9.
2. R. H. Walkman, *Employment Services for Ex-Offenders Field Test: Summary Report* (Washington, D.C.: U.S. Department of Justice, 1985). His primary finding of interest was that employment decreased recidivism among ex-offenders.
3. Georgetown University Law Center, *The Closed Door: The Effect of a Criminal Record on Employment with State and Local Public Agencies* (Springfield, Va.: National Technical Information Service, 1972), p. v.
4. Harry Elmer Barnes and Negley K. Teeters, *New Horizons in Criminology,* 3d ed. (Englewood Cliffs, N.J.: Prentice-Hall, 1959), p. 544.
5. Joan Potter, "Growth Slows—At Least for Now," *Corrections Magazine* 6 (April 1980): 25–30. A study of United Kingdom prisoners who rejected help from prison aftercare workers over a twelve-year period indicated that only 29 percent of the rejection group was not reconvicted. See Keith Soothill, "The Outcome for Prisoners Who Rejected Offers of Help," British Journal of Criminology 25 (1985): 172–181.
6. For a parallel discussion of fees in probation, see Christopher Baird, Douglas Holien, and Audrey Bakke, Fees for Probation Services (Madison, Wis.: National Council on Crime and Delinquency, 1986).
7. Sol Rubin, "The Man with a Record: A Civil Rights Problem," *Federal Probation* (September 1971): 4.
8. Velmer Burton, Francis Cullen, and Lawrence Travis, "The Collateral Consequences of a Felony Conviction: A National Study of State Statutes," *Federal Probation* 51 (1987): 52–60.
9. American Law Institute, *Model Penal Code: Proposed Official Draft* (Philadelphia: American Law Institute, 1962), p. 43.
10. There is a potential liability in disclosing a parolee's background to a potential employer if this results in the client's not getting the job. See Rolando del Carmen and Eve Trook-White, Liability Issues in Community Sevice Sanctions (Washington, D.C.: U.S. Department of Justice, 1986): pp. 19–21.
11. See Reynoso's dissenting opinion in *Heatherington* v. *California*, 147 Cal. 300 (1978). Here, Judge Reynoso argued that ex-offenders should not be denied the right to work simply because of the prior felony conviction. (Judge Reynoso was recalled from the California Supreme Court in 1987 in part because of a conservative backlash against the Chief Justice of the time.)
12. National Alliance of Business. *Employment and Training of Ex-Offenders: A Community Approach* (Washington, D.C.: National Alliance of Business, 1983).

13. The National Council on Crime and Delinquency was founded in 1907. (77 Maiden Lane, Fourth Floor, San Francisco, Calif. 94108).
14. National Council on Crime and Delinquency, *Annulment of a Conviction of Crime, A Model Act* (Paramus, N.J.: National Council on Crime and Delinquency, 1962).
15. A vest-pocket record is an informal record that the court keeps unofficially and holds over the defendant for a set period of time.
16. "Excessive bail shall not be required, nor excessive fines imposed, nor cruel and unusual punishment inflicted."
17. Rubin, pp. 6–7.
18. Most European countries have required residents to carry identification cards for population-control purposes. A "yellow card" (identification card of yellow color) was, in many countries, a sign of an ex-offender.
19. The scarlet letter was a scarlet "A" that the Puritans required known female adulterers to wear around the neck as a punitive mark. The practice is fully described in Nathaniel Hawthorne's novel *The Scarlet Letter*.
20. Georgetown University Law Center, *The Closed Door*, p. 58.
21. American Law Institute, *Model Penal Code*.
22. Georgetown University Law Center, *The Closed Door*, p. 61.

Recommended Readings _____

Alpert, Geoffrey. *Legal Rights of Prisoners*. Lexington, Mass.: Heath, 1978.

Bureau of Justice Statistics. *Federal Drug Law Violators*. Washington, D.C.: U.S. Department of Justice, 1984.

Bureau of Justice Statistics. *Report to the Nation on Crime and Justice*. Washington, D.C.: U.S. Department of Justice, 1983.

Burton, Velmer, Francis Cullen, and Lawrence Travis. "The Collateral Consequences of a Felony Conviction: A National Study of State Statutes." *Federal Probation* 51 (1987): 52–60.

Dolinko, David. "How to Criticize the Death Penalty." Journal of Criminal Law and Criminology 77 (1985): 546–601.

Gest, Ted. "Bulging Prisons: Curbing Crime—Or Wasting Lives?" *U.S. News and World Report* (April 23, 1984): 42–44.

National Advisory Commission on Criminal Justice Standards and Goals. *Corrections*. Washington, D.C.: U.S. Department of Justice, 1973.

National Institute of Corrections. *The Handicapped Offender*. Washington, D.C.: U.S. Department of Justice, 1982.

National Institute of Corrections. *Prison and Jail Health Care*. Washington, D.C.: U.S. Department of Justice, 1981.

President's Commission on Law Enforcement and Administration of Justice. *Task Force Report: Challenge of Crime in a Free Society*. Washington, D.C.: U.S. Government Printing Office, 1967.

President's Commission on Law Enforcement and Administration of Justice. *Task Force Report: Corrections*. Washington, D.C.: U.S. Government Printing Office, 1967.

President's Commission on Law Enforcement and Administration of Justice. *Task Force Report: Courts*. Washington, D.C.: U.S. Government Printing Office, 1967.

The Correctional Client

16

Adult Offenders

> Conviction for a crime, still more a sentence of
> imprisonment, may itself undermine family
> cohesion and security, destroy the offender's
> prospects, result in loss of employment and assets,
> all quite apart from any legal measures . . . those
> who commit crimes as youths outgrow criminality
> in their twenties. But they may never be able to
> outgrow their criminal records.
> —LEON RADZINOWICZ and MARVIN WOLFGANG

As we saw in Part 1, until very recently, incarceration practices were not intended to "correct" the behavior of inmates. Consequently, the young and the old, the sick and the well, the women and the men, and the dangerous and the naive all were placed indiscriminately in one facility. As the concepts of penitence and corrections were developed, men and women were segregated in separate institutions. Later, institutions were further specialized, with different kinds of institutions for the younger inmates, who were separated from the more hardened felons (though these groups are still sometimes hard to tell apart).

If corrections and prisons can be considered businesses, it becomes convenient to consider inmate groups as *clients* with different needs, problems, and demands. As we shall see from the growth of corrections in all areas, the business analogy can be further described as a "boom." We now shall address three major subdivisions into which the modern-day correctional client may be categorized: *adults, juveniles,* and *special category offenders.* We begin this study with the adult offender, using further subcategories to investigate the treatment and incarceration of males and females. First, we examine all these categories in the context of the beginning point of the correctional system, the jail (see Figure 16–1).

Men and Women, Boys and Girls in Jail

Of all the institutions through which offenders pass in the correctional funnel, none has a more diverse population or a more sordid past than

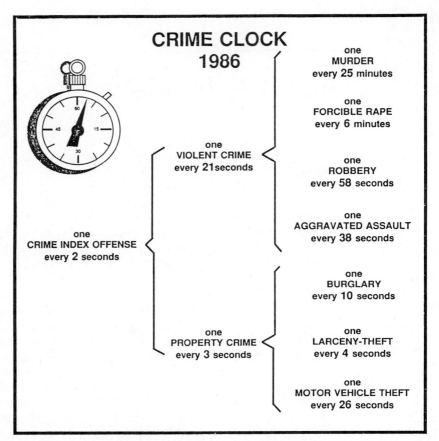

Figure 16-1 The Crime Clock. The crime clock should be viewed with care. Being the most aggregate representation of UCR data, it is designed to convey the annual reported crime experience by showing the relative frequency of occurence of the Index Offenses. This mode of display should not be taken to imply a regularity in the commission of the Part I Offenses; rather, it represents the annual ratio of crime to fixed time intervals.

do the jails. Jails are confinement facilities usually operated by a local law enforcement agency, holding persons detained pending adjudication and/or persons committed after adjudication for sentences generally lasting one year or less. The jail is the first facility within the criminal justice system with which adult males and females (and many juveniles) have contact.[1]

Characteristics of the Jail Population

Both the felon and the misdemeanant, the first-time and the repeat offender, the adult (male and female), and the juvenile, the accused and

> **JAIL**
> Confinement facility, usually operated by a local law enforcement agency, that holds persons detained pending adjudication and/or persons convicted after adjudication and serving sentences of generally one year or less.

the convicted, not to mention the guilty and the innocent, are housed in America's jails. Those held in jail include the accused who are awaiting arraignment, transfer to other authorities (mental hospitals, federal courts, the military), trial, or final sentencing. About 49 percent of the nation's jailed are actually serving sentences, though this number is rising, as local jurisdictions "crack down" on those who drive while intoxicated (DWI) and on domestic disturbance crimes.[2] Some 92 percent of the jail population is male. Statistics on jails are difficult to obtain and national surveys are infrequent and often suspect. However, based on the last national jail census, there are an estimated 274,444 men, women, and children in some 3,400 jails on any given day.[3] Men held in jails are in many ways the "losers" of society in terms of economic and social status, occupation, marital status, education, and almost any other factor.

The persons incarcerated in our jails are subjected to the most degrading forms of behavior as well as to personal danger, and they soon learn the meaning of *dead time*. The problems in jails are covered in detail in Chapter 23.

Adult Male Prisons: Warehouses for Men _____

As pointed out in Part 1, the prison was one of America's contributions to the Western world. Whereas accused offenders were once housed in detention facilities only until their trial and punishment (which was usually severe), the Walnut Street Jail of 1790 and its successors provided a facility for punishment, penitence, treatment, and reformation.

In the nineteenth and early twentieth centuries, America built dozens of massive bastion-like prisons, capable of warehousing literally thousands of inmates in their multitiered cellblocks. Offering few treatment services, these castles for the more impoverished of society were rapidly filled with offenders and remained full until the late 1960s and early 1970s, when prison populations began to drop. This drop, in part due to the increased use of community-based corrections, particularly probation, has come to a halt, and the prison population has achieved new heights. It appears that a variation of Parkinson's law is operating in corrections: as rapidly as prisons are built, court commitments expand to fill all available cells. As Simon Dinitz would say, "Nothing fails like success."[4] The proliferation of prisons and the almost instant overcrowding of the new institutions seem to doom the men within to no help at best and to too much help (punishment) at worst.

Who are the prison inmates? What are their needs, and what programs should be devised to address these needs? What should we know about their backgrounds? What happens to the men in the prisons of America?

Characteristics of the Prison Population

The number of male offenders in America's prisons is rising at an alarming rate, along with the total prison populations, despite a brief decline in the early 1970s. Between January 1, 1977, and January 1, 1987, the prison population increased by 198 percent, from 275,378 to 546,659 (not including 13,770 inmates sentenced to state prisons by the courts but who were, at the time, being held in county facilities because of prison overcrowding; see Figure 16-2). Of the total number, 44,408 (8 percent) were incarcerated in federal facilities under the Bureau of Prisons (see Chapter 25), and 502,251 (92 percent) were in state prisons. In total, there were 216 Americans in prison for every 100,000 citizens[5] (see Tables 16.1 and 16.2).

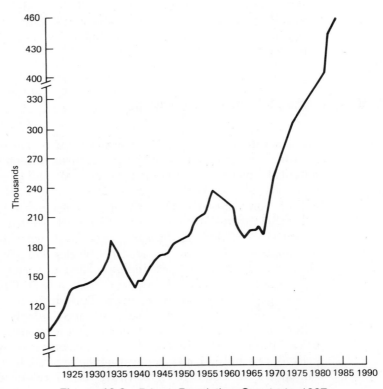

Figure 16-2 Prison Population Counts to 1987

TABLE 16.1 Prisoners under the Jurisdiction of State and Federal Correctional Authorities, by Region and State, Yearend 1985–1986

Region and State	Total			Sentenced to More Than 1 Year			Incar- ceration Rate 1986*
	Advance 1986	Final 1985	Percent Change 1985–1986	Advance 1986	Final 1985	Percent Change 1985–1986	
U.S., total	546,659	503,271	8.6%	523,922	481,393	8.8%	216
Federal	44,408	40,223	10.4	36,531	32,695	11.7	15
State	502,251	463,048	8.5	487,391	448,698	8.6	201
Northeast	82,388	75,706	8.8%	79,071	72,656	8.8%	158
Connecticut	6,905	6,149	12.3	4,043	4,326	7.0	135
Maine	1,316	1,226	7.3	1,165	967	20.5	99
Massachusetts	5,678	5,390	5.3	5,678	5,390	5.3	97
New Hampshire	782	683	14.5	782	683	14.5	76
New Jersey	12,020	11,335	6.0	12,020	11,335	6.0	157
New York	38,449	34,712	10.8	38,449	34,712	10.8	216
Pennsylvania	15,201	14,227	6.8	15,165	14,119	7.4	128
Rhode Island	1,361	1,307	4.1	1,010	964	4.8	103
Vermont	676	677	− 0.1	476	443	7.4	88
Midwest	103,101	95,704	7.7%	102,689	95,245	7.8%	173
Illinois	19,456	18,634	4.4	19,456	18,634	4.4	168
Indiana	10,175	9,904	2.7	9,963	9,615	3.6	181
Iowa	2,777	2,832	− 1.9	2,777	2,832	− 1.9	98
Kansas	5,425	4,732	14.6	5,425	4,732	14.6	220
Michigan	20,742	17,755	16.8	20,742	17,755	16.8	227
Minnesota	2,462	2,343	5.1	2,462	2,343	5.1	58
Missouri	10,485	9,915	5.7	10,485	9,915	5.7	206
Nebraska	1,953	1,814	7.7	1,863	1,733	7.5	116
North Dakota	421	422	− 0.2	361	375	− 3.7	53
Ohio	22,463	20,864	7.7	22,463	20,864	7.7	209
South Dakota	1,045	1,047	− 0.2	1,014	1,035	− 2.0	143
Wisconsin	5,697	5,442	4.7	5,678	5,412	4.9	119
South	215,713	202,926	6.3%	208,374	195.868	6.4%	249
Alabama	11,710	11,015	6.3	11,504	10,749	7.0	283
Arkansas	4,701	4,611	2.0	4,701	4,611	2.0	198
Delaware	2,828	2,553	10.8	2,026	1,759	15.2	324
Dist. of Columbia	6,746	6,404	5.3	4,786	4,604	4.0	753
Florida	32,228	28,600	12.7	32,219	28,482	13.1	272
Georgia	17,363	16,014	8.4	16,291	15,115	7.8	265
Kentucky	6,322	5,801	9.0	6,322	5,801	9.0	169
Louisiana	14,580	13,890	5.0	14,580	13,890	5.0	322
Maryland	13,326	13,005	2.5	12,559	12,303	2.1	280
Mississippi	6,747	6,392	5.6	6,565	6,208	5.8	249
North Carolina	17,762	17,344	2.4	16,460	16,007	2.8	258
Oklahoma	9,596	8,330	15.2	9,596	8,330	15.2	288
South Carolina	11,676	10,510	11.1	11,022	9,908	11.2	324
Tennessee	7,182	7,127	0.8	7,182	7,127	0.8	149
Texas	38,534	37,532	2.7	38,534	37,532	2.7	228
Virginia	12,930	12,073	7.1	12,545	11,717	7.1	215
West Virginia	1,482	1,725	− 14.1	1,482	1,725	− 14.1	77

TABLE 16.1 *Continued*

Region and State	Total			Sentenced to More Than 1 Year			Incar- ceration Rate 1986*
	Advance 1986	Final 1985	Percent Change 1985–1986	Advance 1986	Final 1985	Percent Change 1985–1986	
West	101,049	88,712	13.9%	97,257	84,929	14.5%	198
Alaska	2,460	2,329	5.6	1,666	1,530	8.9	306
Arizona	9,434	8,531	10.6	9,038	8,273	9.2	268
California	59,484	50,111	18.7	57,725	48,279	19.6	212
Colorado	3,673	3,369	9.0	3,673	3,369	9.0	111
Hawaii	2,180	2,111	3.3	1,521	1,428	6.5	142
Idaho	1,451	1,294	12.1	1,451	1,294	12.1	144
Montana	1,111	1,129	− 1.6	1,111	1,129	− 1.6	135
Nevada	4,505	3,771	19.5	4,505	3,771	19.5	462
New Mexico	2,701	2,313	16.8	2,545	2,112	20.5	170
Oregon	4,737	4,454	6.4	4,737	4,454	6.4	175
Utah	1,845	1,633	13.0	1,817	1,623	12.0	108
Washington	6,603	6,909	− 4.4	6,603	6,909	− 4.4	147
Wyoming	865	758	14.1	865	758	14.1	170

Note: Prisoner counts for 1985 may differ from those reported in previous publications and are subject to revision as updated figures become available.

*The number of prisoners sentenced to more than 1 year per 100,000 resident population. Population estimates are for July 1, 1986.

Source: Bureau of Justice, *Prisoners 1986* (Washington, D.C.), p. 2.

The most common offenses for which sentences are being served in state correctional facilities include robbery, homicide, burglary, major drug offenses (excluding possession), minor drug offenses (including possession), assault, sexual assault, forgery, fraud, and embezzlement. Fifty-seven percent of all state prisoners serve time for crimes against the person (including armed robbery), and 43 percent are imprisoned for crimes against property.[6]

Males have historically and overwhelmingly predominated in the prison population. Although the number of females sentenced to prison is increasing rapidly, (17.5 percent from January 1986 to January 1987 alone),[7] over 95 percent of the total number of inmates in prison are male. In corrections, as in the overall criminal justice system, women tend to receive more favorable disposition at each major decision point in the system.

One must remember that those in prison are at the bottom of the correctional funnel. As a group, men in prisons are undereducated and underemployed, primarily because of their social class and lack of opportunity (see Figure 16-2). These men are often beset with medical and psychological problems. Many, if not most, are poor and have been unable to cope with the complexities of city life (see Figure 16-3).[8] Often recent arrivals to urban areas, they have limited job skills and do not know how to use available social services in the community. Many come from broken homes with low annual incomes, and a large number are drug and alcohol abusers. These characteristics suggest the number of treatment challenges faced by

TABLE 16.2. Change in the State and Federal Prison Populations, 1980–1986

Year	Number of Inmates	Annual Percent Change	Total Percent Change Since 1980
1980	329,821		
1981	369,930	12.2%	12.2%
1982	413,806	11.9	25.5
1983	437,248	5.7	32.6
1984	464,567	6.2	40.9
1985	503,271	8.3	52.6
1986	546,659	8.6	65.7

Note: All counts are for December 31 of each year and may differ from previously reported numbers because of revision.

Source: Bureau of Justice Statistics: *Prisoners 1986* (Washington, D.C.), p. 4.

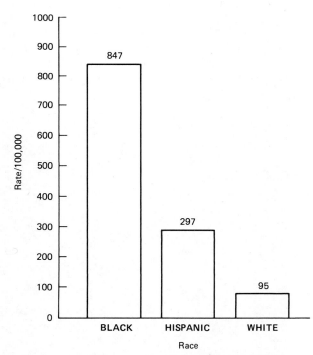

Figure 16-3 California Prison Commitment Rates by Race (John Irwin and James Austin, *It's About Time* [San Francisco, CA: National Council on Crime and Delinquency, 1987], p. 20)

correctional administrators whose mandate it is to provide reasonable and effective reintegration services while protecting society from the offenders. The problems in meeting this mission are exacerbated by a hardening of public attitudes toward and opinions about the male felon.

Jails, detention facilities, and prisons are overcrowded to the danger point,[9] and it is obvious that the present male prison system will be unable to meet the increasing demands. Not only must we reexamine all of our institutions that hold male offenders, but we must also seriously consider alternatives to incarceration. Some male offenders are extremely dangerous and must be isolated from others. In the 1970s it was estimated that only some 15 to 25 percent of the male population in prison fell into this category. This situation, however, has changed; overcrowding has tended to force correctional administrators to find ways to release those men considered least dangerous back into the community, and this has left an increasingly greater percentage of violent offenders smoldering in a potential tinderbox. In most states, the number of violent offenders committing crimes against the person is closer to 75 percent and growing, as property offenders are given alternatives to incarceration.[10]

As stated earlier, male offenders tend to be heavy users of alcohol and drugs. In 1987, well over one-half of the men in prison had been drinking at the time of the instant offense and another large percentage were under the influence of drugs. These statistics indicate that drug and alcohol abuse are serious problems that contribute negatively to the offenders' behavior, both in the community and in the institution. Drug and alcohol treatment programs both in and out of prison are no longer a luxury—they are a necessity.

A Typical Male Institution (Courtesy of the Ohio Department of Rehabilitation and Corrections)

TABLE 16.3   The Prison Situation among the States at Yearend, 1986

10 States with the Largest 1986 Prison Population	Number of Inmates	10 States with the Highest Incarceration Rates, 1986*	Prisoners per 100,000 Residents	1985–86	10 States with the Largest Percent Increases in Prison Population	
					Percent Increase	1980–86*	Percent Increase
California	59,484	Nevada	462	Nevada	19.5%	Alaska	191.9%
Texas	38,534	Delaware	324	California	18.7	California	148.1
New York	38,449	South Carolina	324	Michigan	16.8	Nevada	145.0
Florida	32,228	Louisiana	322	New Mexico	16.8	Hawaii	143.8
Ohio	22,463	Alaska	306	Oklahoma	15.2	New Hampshire	139.9
Michigan	20,742	Oklahoma	288	Kansas	14.6	Kansas	117.5
Illinois	19,456	Alabama	283	New Hampshire	14.5	New Jersey	116.0
North Carolina	17,762	Maryland	280	Wyoming	14.1	New Mexico	112.3
Georgia	17,363	Florida	272	Utah	13.0	Arizona	107.3
Pennsylvania	15,201	Arizona	268	Florida	12.7	Oklahoma	100.1

Note: The District of Columbia as a wholly urban jurisdiction is excluded.   *Prisoners with sentences of more than 1 year.

Source: Bureau of Justice Statistics: *Prisoners 1986* (Washington, D.C.), p. 3.

Education is an important factor in American society; it is viewed by many as an essential prerequisite for economic stability and success. In a "high-tech" society such as the United States, education is crucial for getting a job and earning an adequate income. Despite this need for education, the most recent national survey found that one in five Americans can be considered functionally illiterate.[11] This sad situation is becoming even worse as more and more youths pass through our public school systems without being properly prepared to function with developed problem-solving skills in an urban environment. It is not too surprising that crime is often chosen as one alternative for survival under these circumstances. It is not enough that many inmates are now given a chance to earn a high school education in prison; the nation as a whole must insist that the education provided by our public school systems supply the skills needed to keep these men out of prison (see Table 16.1).

Finally, almost one in four imprisoned men are eligible to be furloughed into an early-release procedure, but fewer than half of those eligible are given the opportunity to take such a furlough. Most inmates (74 percent) have some kind of institutional work assignment, but six out of ten are earning less than twenty cents per hour for their work. It is hard to motivate an incarcerated man to make a serious effort to learn a trade while he is working in prison for such low wages, when the same man has made up to $500 a day illegally in his community—and knows it can be done again.

Prisonization

Every venture intended to elevate humanity (or at least to encourage improvement) has as many unplanned and unwanted effects as it has desired effects. Efforts to give male offenders a setting in which to do penance and be "reformed" have resulted in a number of unwanted side effects, ranging from the mental and physical deterioration caused by extreme solitary confinement at Sing Sing to a more contemporary unwanted phenomenon called *prisonization*. The originator of the term, Donald Clemmer, described this process as "the taking on in greater or less degree of the folkways, mores, customs, and general culture of the penitentiary."[12] Clemmer observed that the acculturation into the prison community subjects the inmate to certain influences that either breed or deepen criminal behaviors, causing the prisoner to learn the criminal ideology of the prison—to become "prisonized." Prisonization is a process that includes accepting the subordinate role into which one is thrust as an inmate; developing new habits of sleeping, dressing, eating, and working; undergoing status degradation; adopting a new language; and learning that one is dependent on others (including one's fellow inmates) for the scarce pleasures found in incarceration, including food, work assignment, freedom from assault, and privileges. Students of prisonization believe that this process not only leads the inmate

---

PRISONIZATION

The process by which the inmate learns, through socializaiton, the rules and regulations of the penal institution, as well as the informal values, rules, and customs of the penitentiary culture. Once these values have been inculcated, the inmate becomes generally inoculated against conventional values. Thus prisonization can be seen as a criminalization process whereby a criminal novice is transformed from basically a prosocial errant to a committed predatory criminal.

It is important to remember that correctional staff can be prisonized as well, although the degree and extent of socialization is not as extensive, nor long-lasting. Prisonization for the officer generally reflects the necessity of managing and interacting with inmates; the officer has to know and manipulate the inmate system to attain individual and institutional goals.

---

to identify with criminal codes, goals, and behaviors but also serves to undercut reintegration programs and to lessen the offender's ability to adjust to society after release.[13]

The phenomenon of prisonization appears to exist in all prisons, not just the large Gothic bastions that testify to archaic prison philosophies. It can be brought into the prison by older inmates, but even in new prisons that receive first-time offenders, the inmates' pains of imprisonment can generate the prisonization process.

Because prisonization occurs in every institution, although to varying degrees, it is necessary to understand the benefits that accrue to the men who adhere to the inmate codes. The future correctional administrator must also understand the pains of imprisonment that encourage socialization into the inmate subculture. These pains are status deprivation, sexual deprivation, material deprivation, and enforced intimacy with other deviants.

The inmate subculture reduces the pains of imprisonment by encouraging the sharing of the few benefits and pleasures inside prisons, by helping prevent naked aggression by inmates against other inmates, and by providing a circle of friends who can and will come to an inmate's assistance if he is attacked. It also offers alternative sexual outlets, defines appropriate roles for getting along with other inmates, and supplies companions with whom an inmate can share confidences and interact comfortably. In addition, this process makes available contraband drugs (including glue, "pruno,"[14] and prescription drugs stolen from prison dispensaries) on which an inmate can get high. There are also many other, less tangible benefits.

Fortunately, recent research suggests that the extent, and thus the negative impact, of prisonization may be reduced through the staff's institutional administration and orientation.

We would expect to find more solidarity (of the inmate code) and more traditional inmate types in a correctional system with only one institution for adult felons and where that institution is characterized by more severe material and sociopsychological deprivations.[15]

Others have suggested that the nature and extent of endorsement of prisoner norms ("don't rat on another inmate," "mind your own business," "never exploit another inmate," "never cooperate with correctional officers," "do your own time," "be a man," "don't whine") can be significantly reduced.

In addition to the problems of prisonization, institutional populations are increasingly divided along ethnic and racial lines. The resulting groups frequently engage in power struggles for control of the institution, fighting among themselves and attacking prison officials and correctional officers. The fracturing of the inmate population into racial and ethnic groups (primarily a white/black/Mexican-American gang phenomenon in maximum security prisons) poses serious new problems for prison administrators, raises the level of anxiety among inmates, works against reintegration, and creates an atmosphere of perceived danger among the prison staff. Prison administrators will need to develop new techniques for coping with inmate trichotomization and prison gangs so as to bring order to the prison setting and make reintegration programs more effective.

If the institutional administrator and staff emphasize individual and group treatment rather than custody and discipline, if a pattern of cooperation can be developed between informal inmate leaders and institutional authorities, if a medium or minimum custody level can be achieved, and if violators of rules governing the use of force by the correctional staff are consistently reprimanded, then the prison culture and the prisonization process can be markedly reduced. Some researchers have suggested that shorter prison terms tend to undercut the power of the prison culture, as inmates can and do participate in "anticipatory socialization" as they near

---

BABY BOOM

After World War II, returning soldiers tended to marry young and begin families. The result was a large number of offspring born between 1945 and 1954, some 200 percent larger than would have been expected had the war not created delays in family formation and childbearing.

The large numbers of children worked their ways through the school system as time progressed and the children matured creating overcrowding first in grade-school and then in high-school populations. Many "baby-boomers" entered college, creating another service-delivery crisis.

The significance of the baby boom for corrections lay in the high-crime rate years of ages 19–29, when offenders were most likely to commit crime. Thus the baby boom struck the correctional system from about 1970–1985. Because there is a "commitment lag" (generally ten years) between early onset of criminal behavior and being sent to prison, correctional overcrowding in the late 1980s can be seen as caused in part by World War II!

"Baby boomers" have themselves begun families and there is an "echo-boom" in the offing that will affect the criminal justice system in the late 1990s; it will particularly cause crises in corrections in the first part of the twenty-first century.

the end of their prison sentences and begin to prepare for their participation in the activities of the free world. It thus is reasonable to assume that short, fixed periods of incarceration would help reduce the negative effects of prisonization.

The Prison Population Boom

In the six years between 1980 and 1986, prison populations sharply increased, much to the dismay of both prisoners and concerned correctional administrators. There is little agreement on the exact reasons for the population boom, although some correctional personnel are quick to note that the police and courts may have become more efficient more quickly than the correctional subsystem did. As one administrator observed, "The police tooled up, the prosecutor's office has expanded along with the use of plea bargaining, and the courts finally stepped into the twentieth century. We in corrections have received the benefits of efficiency through sharply increased commitments."

Others have identified the hardening of public opinion as a factor, pointing out that judges are perceiving considerable local pressure to commit offenders rather than use probation. It could be that the reaction to crime in America has exceeded the threshold of fear[16] and reached panic proportions, with widespread public clamor for commitments contributing to prison overpopulation.

It is more likely, however, that a principal cause is the increase in the population at risk,[17] those males in the age range of eighteen to thirty. Inasmuch as crime is a young person's occupation and considering the fact that the number of persons in the high crime rate ages doubled between 1965 and 1985, one would expect the factor of age to contribute heavily to the overpopulation of American prisons. The "age at risk" problem was made worse by a population shift over the last fifteen years, during which families with young sons moved to urban areas from rural environments. The rural settings had provided more control and more wholesome outlets for young men. Historically, such population shifts—regardless of the population group in motion—meant that the second generation engaged in more frequent criminal behavior. In this case, recent population shifts coincided with an increase in the population at risk, and we can therefore expect the committed population to rise for several more years.

Two economic factors that could curb this trend are reduced unemployment and an expansion of the economy. The population at risk is traditionally overrepresented in the ranks of the unemployed; with a national unemployment rate of over 5.7 percent, the unemployment rate for the population at risk is reported to be in the 14 to 32 percent range. If unemployment were reduced, the crime rate should also drop. However, a decrease in the rate of unemployment depends on an expansion of the economy at a sufficiently high annual growth rate (above 4 percent). With economic conditions uncertain at best as America enters the late-1980s, this problem bears watching. A plummeting stock market, huge budget and trade deficits, unemployment, and worsening energy problems would bode ill for the already severe problems of growing numbers of ex-offenders.[18] America seems determined to resolve its crime problems with a "lock 'em up and throw away the key" philosophy.[19] Although incapacitation may be an effective way temporarily to prevent crime, helping offenders expand their opportunities and enter the mainstream of American society might be a more permanent way of lowering crime rates and the collateral national costs of incarceration.

Rape in All-Male Prisons

In a detailed study of aggression among men behind prison walls, Anthony Scacco suggested that sex is a vehicle for exploitation rather than an expression of pathological personality or situational frustration.[20] The sexual assaults that occur within prisons and jails cannot be categorized solely as homosexual attacks; rather they often are assaults made by heterosexually oriented males for political reasons—that is, to show power and dominance over other human beings. It is a depressing fact that victimization, degradation, racism, and humiliation of victims are the foremost reasons that sexual assaults are perpetrated on men in this setting.

Scacco also addressed a topic seldom openly discussed by correctional administrators: the polarization of inmates in prison, a phenomenon that has accelerated in recent years. Younger and more aggressive inmates appear to be polarizing into racial and ethnic groups, and the conflict between these groups—and with the correctional staff—has led to greater tension behind the walls.[21] As prison populations continue to grow, this polarization will probably also increase.

To reduce the potential for further disturbances among men in prison, Scacco proposed several steps:

1. The staff of a correctional institution should openly admit that they must meet together as a body and discuss their views on sexuality if they are to render assistance to the inmates in their care.
2. Masturbation for relief of sexual tension should be allowed within an institution, not denied to men within prison walls.
3. Classification at reception and orientation centers should keep sexually different and sexually attractive men from mixing with the rest of the inmate population, to keep the weaker and often younger inmates apart from other inmates with sexual desires which they would fulfill through sexual assault.
4. Conjugal visits, which reduce recidivism and homosexuality, are a more socially acceptable solution than rape.
5. Furlough programs should be implemented to maintain normal sexual relations.

6. Coeducational correctional institutions should be expanded, rather than prisons, and populations reduced to the remaining 30 percent of the inmate population which requires confinement.[22]

In institutions for only male felons, homosexual behavior between consenting adults has been a recurrent phenomenon, as in other such unisexual settings as naval ships and religious monasteries. It is unreasonable to expect inmates to abandon sexual behavior in prison, particularly when they face increasingly long sentences. As Peter Buffum noted:

> [The present pattern of homosexuality in prisons] means that as long as the prison is an environment which is largely devoid of situations where legitimate affectional ties can be established, there will be a tendency for the formation of homosexual relationships, especially among those persons serving long sentences who have concomitantly lost contact with meaningful persons in the free community. If in addition the prison does not allow legitimate attempts of the inmates to control their own lives and does not give an opportunity for expressions of masculinity and self-assertion that are meaningful among men at this social level, there will be homosexual relationships created to fulfill this need.[23]

Especially among younger inmates and those who accept passive roles, homosexual behaviors and relationships could impair future commitments to heterosexuality as well as create exploitative situations. When such relationships create jealousy among inmates, the potential for serious violence and administrative problems increases. If a third inmate becomes involved in a dyadic relationship or there is a transfer of affection, extreme violence can occur. The once-frequent pattern of transferring the passive partner to another institution is no longer an adequate or constitutional response by prison management. Segregating passive partners may cause

---

CONJUGAL VISITATION

During a family visit, inmate and spouse are allowed to spend time together on the prison campus, unsupervised and alone in private quarters, trailers, houses, and rooms. During this time, they may engage in sexual intercourse.

European and Latin American countries have been the leaders in permitting conjugal visiting, but several states (California, Mississippi) have formal programs of conjugal visiting. Others (like Montana) permit the program without granting formal approval.

Advantages cited in some studies include lessening forced and voluntary homosexual acts within prison, maintaining a more normal prison environment, lowering tension levels, lessening attacks on correctional officers, reinforcing gender-appropriate roles, helping to preserve marriages, and (from the perspective of the prison administration) encouraging appropriate behavior by inmates hoping to earn a conjugal visitation pass.

the active inmates to coerce others into sexual behavior, as well as to raise legal issues of inmate rights and to create the potential for lawsuits arising from such isolation.

Prison administrators will need to consider and implement home visits at known intervals for those under long sentences, as well as provide activities and programs that will attack the real problems. At the beginning of 1987, however, only eight states reported permitting inmates to have family (conjugal) visits.[24] This allowed inmates to have some control over their own lives; the ability for some self-expression; and to exhibit some affectional relationships and stable interpersonal relationships are a result of efforts from the establishment of family visiting. What will emerge will include opportunities for inmates to participate in inmate organizations; effective vocational, educational, and recreational programs; and co-correctional institutions.[25] The Federal Bureau of Prisons has expanded the number of co-correctional institutions to nine co-correctional institutions in 1987. Encouraging correspondence with and visits from relatives and employment of female correctional officers will also help reduce homosexual behavior, as will more involvement by volunteers in corrections.

Alternatives for the Future

Male offenders who are not dangerous men can be diverted into such programs as deferred prosecution, house arrest, probation, weekend confinement, restitution and community work-release programs, and community reintegration centers. The last two of these programs are at least as effective as are prisons, and cost much less than the outrageous $100,000 per cell and up to $16,000 per year-average per-prisoner cost. These community programs, rather than the prisons, should be expanded. Prisons, however, seem to be almost impossible to get rid of, although they require enormous annual outlays for upkeep and corrupt both the keeper and the kept. These monuments to an age gone by do not and cannot achieve their stated mission unless correctional administrators are trained and dedicated, have sufficient resources, abide by the Constitution, and understand the effects of inaction and indecisiveness.

Expanding the alternatives for male offenders has another benefit: to the extent that male offenders are integrated into the community, their future criminal behavior will be sharply reduced, if not eliminated. Community-based corrections can reduce the crime problem in the United States to a far greater extent than can the current prison operations, by actually making offenders useful citizens.

Although a large number of prisons are under construction and there will be men in prisons for a long time to come, the more cost-effective and cost-beneficial community programs may eventually reduce the number of inmates under lock and key to only those who are too dangerous to be released. Corrections must and will divert its resources into those programs that offer humane treatment without sacrificing the protection of society.

Women, Crime, and Corrections

The 1970s and early 1980s were the years when women's equality and rights were asserted, if not established, on almost every front. Yet only recently has there been a movement to push for the rights of female offenders in corrections. In a way, women still receive differential, even preferential, treatment at almost every station of the criminal justice system, partly in deference to traditional female sex roles. This section examines the more common kinds of offenses committed by women, dispositional alternatives for women, and some correctional facilities, issues, and programs for women in a rapidly changing environment.

Crime Statistics for Women

Although the criminal statistics contained in the FBI's *Uniform Crime Reports* (UCR) are somewhat limited, especially for crimes involving women, they are the best available and can at least be accepted as an indicator of trends. During the four years from 1982 to 1986, the amount of female crime, as indicated by arrest figures, rose by 13.5 percent.[26] During the same period, male arrests grew by only 5.2 percent. This dramatic difference can be seen in certain kinds of crime in which women offenders have become more and more involved (and reported) in those four years. Arrest figures for females under eighteen years of age (+5.9 percent) have increased in contrast to those for males of the same age group (-2.6 percent). The greater increase was in aggravated assault (up 17.7 percent), whereas for male offenders under eighteen, this crime increased by only 10.4 percent, a 7.3 percent difference. Overall, violent crime arrests for all female offenders increased 12.8 percent, almost twice the increase reported for men. These figures clearly indicate the growing role of the female offender in the entire spectrum of crime and in the criminal justice system (see Table 16.4). Data on female offenders in California during 1985 are shown in Figures 16-4 and 16-5. Almost half of the 260,673 female arrestees were between 18 and 28 years of age, and minorities were vastly overrepresented among these women.

Prostitution

The general increase in female criminality can also be seen as reflecting the changing patterns of criminal opportunity for women. It is interesting that arrests for prostitution, the crime Freda Adler calls "the oldest and newest profession,"[27] decreased 10.2 percent between 1982 and 1986. But these figures contrast dramatically with the rate of decrease in prostitution among females under eighteen, which decreased 18.2 percent between 1982 and 1986. This seems to continue the pattern that occurred between 1978

TABLE 16.4 Total Arrest Trends, Sex, 1982–1986

Offense Charged	Males Total			Males Under 18			Females Total			Females Under 18		
	1982	1986	Percent Change	1982	1986	Percent Change	1982	1986	Percent Change	1982	1986	Percent Change
TOTAL	7,244,900	7,623,244	+5.2	1,222,846	1,190,876	−2.6	1,414,064	1,604,298	+13.5	322,087	341,080	+5.9
Murder and nonnegligent manslaughter	13,863	13,006	−6.2	1,222	1,207	−1.2	2,116	1,850	−12.6	106	88	−17.0
Forcible rape	24,488	27,489	+12.3	3,645	4,168	+14.3	245	265	+8.2	59	53	−10.2
Robbery	112,493	107,434	−4.5	29,201	24,410	−16.4	8,948	9,163	+2.4	2,152	1,835	−14.7
Aggravated Assault	202,105	232,528	+15.1	25,893	28,598	+10.4	30,245	35,613	+17.7	4,954	5,159	+4.1
Burglary	361,798	309,770	−14.4	143,767	110,151	−23.4	26,353	27,360	+3.8	10,449	9,209	−11.9
Larceny-theft	698,356	721,148	+3.3	237,590	241,228	+1.5	296,478	318,826	+7.5	86,785	87,620	+1.0
Motor vehicle theft	86,959	106,001	+21.9	30,547	40,209	+31.6	8,676	11,090	+27.8	3,834	4,888	+27.5
Arson	12,857	11,813	−8.1	4,896	4,974	+1.6	1,946	1,881	−3.3	691	544	−21.3
Violent crime[1]	352,949	380,457	+7.8	59,961	58,383	−2.6	41,554	46,891	+12.8	7,271	7,135	−1.9
Property crime[2]	1,159,970	1,148,732	−1.0	416,800	396,562	−4.9	333,453	359,157	+7.7	101,759	102,261	+.5
Crime Index total[3]	1,512,919	1,529,189	+1.1	476,761	454,945	−4.6	375,007	406,048	+8.3	109,030	109,396	+.3
Other assaults	322,197	444,413	+37.9	46,985	57,682	+22.8	54,939	79,899	+45.4	12,932	17,008	+31.5
Forgery and counterfeiting	47,916	45,953	−4.1	4,755	4,299	−9.6	23,213	23,347	+.6	2,264	2,090	−7.7
Fraud	139,288	146,151	+4.9	14,010	12,891	−8.0	93,381	110,519	+18.4	3,804	4,156	+9.3
Embezzlement	4,732	5,989	+26.6	392	385	−1.8	2,049	3,380	+65.0	141	244	+73.0
Stolen property; buying, receiving, possessing	88,421	90,802	+2.7	22,637	23,060	+1.9	11,421	11,542	+1.1	2,278	2,271	−.3
Vandalism	155,291	173,351	+11.6	70,183	74,507	+6.2	16,089	20,593	+28.0	6,331	7,531	+19.0
Weapons; carrying, possessing, etc.	128,863	133,472	+3.6	18,047	21,127	+17.1	10,543	10,675	+1.3	1,273	1,439	+13.0
Prostitution and commercialized vice	26,392	31,883	+20.8	724	673	−7.0	67,243	60,364	−10.2	1,623	1,328	−18.2
Sex offenses (except forcible rape and prostitution)	54,412	69,215	+27.2	8,912	11,364	+27.5	4,393	6,017	+37.0	589	866	+47.0
Drug abuse violations	424,253	546,293	+28.8	55,389	53,418	−3.6	67,243	92,664	+37.8	10,821	8,920	−17.6
Gambling	24,924	20,091	−19.4	754	522	−30.8	3,089	4,287	+38.8	42	33	−21.4
Offenses against family and children	32,745	34,681	+5.9	843	1,459	+73.1	3,984	6,286	+57.8	504	882	+75.0
Driving under the influence	1,117,782	1,102,041	−1.4	19,714	16,481	−16.4	136,612	141,594	+3.6	2,614	2,471	−5.5
Liquor laws	298,706	341,842	+14.4	77,162	81,881	+6.1	52,722	67,425	+27.9	23,480	27,894	+18.8
Drunkenness	859,734	658,417	−23.4	25,990	20,557	−20.9	79,149	64,616	−18.4	4,416	3,700	−16.2
Disorderly conduct	396,073	401,592	+1.4	58,236	58,707	+.8	73,032	91,410	+25.2	13,018	13,347	+2.5
Vagrancy	25,653	25,842	+.7	2,668	1,792	−32.8	3,525	3,239	−8.1	533	372	−30.2
All other offenses (except traffic)	1,489,525	1,723,787	+15.7	223,610	196,886	−12.0	265,204	314,733	+18.7	55,168	51,472	−6.7
Suspicion (not included in totals)	6,669	5,356	−19.7	1,859	1,744	−6.2	1,145	1,069	−6.6	445	453	+1.8
Curfew and loitering law violations	54,472	47,455	−12.9	54,472	47,455	−12.9	15,192	15,968	+5.1	15,192	15,968	+5.1
Runaways	40,602	50,785	+25.1	40,602	50,785	+25.1	56,034	69,692	+24.4	56,034	69,692	+24.4

[1] Violent crimes are offenses of murder, forcible rape, robbery, and aggravated assault.
[2] Property crimes are offenses of burglary, larceny-theft, motor vehicle theft, and arson.
[3] Includes arson.

Source: Federal Bureau of Investigation, *Crime in the United States 1987* (Washington, D.C.), p. 171.

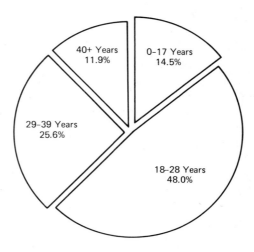

Figure 16-4 Female Arrestees, 1985 (Percent by Age) (John Van De Camp, *Women in Crime: The Female Arrestee* [Sacramento: California Department of Justice, 1987], p. 3)

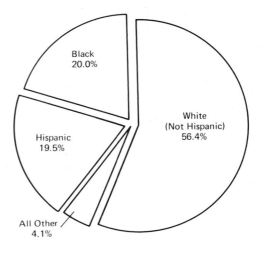

Figure 16-5 Female Arrestees, 1985 (Percent by Race/Ethnic Group) (John Van De Camp, *Women in Crime: The Female Arrestee* [Sacramento: California Department of Justice, 1987], p. 3)

and 1982, when arrests for prostitution decreased by 5 percent for those under eighteen. For the group over eighteen, arrests increased by 14 percent between 1978 and 1982.

The *arrest* figures for prostitution, however, represent only the tip of the iceberg. Because prostitution is one of the so-called victimless crimes, and clients seldom complain, as they would be implicating themselves, the number of arrests for prostitution usually reflects only cases of flagrant solicitation, rampant disease, or a "local cleanup" campaign. Considerable folklore surrounds prostitution, most of it with no basis in fact. Those who profit from prostitution (almost never the prostitutes themselves) are not about to compile statistics or seek publicity. It is a business that thrives on sexual appetite, with the ultimate motive being simple profit.

Careers in prostitution range from that of the corner hooker to the jet-set courtesan, the main difference being the age, beauty, and price of the merchandise. The business of organized vice is not a simple question of boy-meets-girl; many levels of profit-taking and payoff winnow down the prostitute's nightly earnings of, say, $350 to a weekly figure of less than $100. The pimp, the madam, the landlord, the crooked vice cop, and others all take their cut. The real victim of this "victimless crime" is often the prostitute herself.

It is conservatively estimated that there are between 200,000 and 250,000 prostitutes in America. If this estimate is only 50 percent correct, the business is still staggering in its financial potential. At the lowest market price of $25 for a "trick,"[28] with each prostitute averaging six tricks a day, the volume could range from $10 to $15 billion a year. This tax-free income for prostitution is approximately one-third of the 1986 expenditures for the entire criminal justice system: federal, state, county, and municipal. Small wonder that arrests for prostitution are so few, with such great monetary resources available.

Crime Classes for Women: A Changing Pattern? _____

As shown in Table 16.4, in 1982 the crimes for which women were arrested most often were the index crimes of larceny-theft (296,478), aggravated assault (30,245), and burglary (26,353). These three categories accounted for 94 percent of the female arrests for index crimes in 1982. In 1986, the same three categories still accounted for 94 percent of the arrests for index crimes, with percent increases in numbers of arrests for females of +17.7 percent, 3.8 percent, and 7.5 percent respectively.

Prostitution and fraud are included in the UCR under "other" offenses and accounted for 67,243 and 93,381 arrests respectively in 1982. There were 60,364 (a 10.2 percent decrease) and 110,519 (a 18.4 percent increase) in 1986. Aggravated assault, a traditionally "male" crime, showed a 17.5

percent increase in arrests for females in 1986 over 1982. But by far the largest increase in arrests for women came from motor vehicle theft (a 27.8 percent increase) in 1986 over 1982.[29] This is yet another generally accepted "male" offense and one not usually associated with female criminals. Whether these trends will continue into the 1990s is still unknown. But it seems that women are edging closer to the patterns of their male counterparts in their arrest patterns.

A Differential Justice System for Women? _____

The previous scarcity of research in the area of women's equality in general, and on their role in the criminal justice system in particular, makes this area the current "gold mine" for researchers and writers.[30] It is unfortunate that much of the earlier literature was a warmed-over repetition of the old myths and inaccuracies of the 1940s and 1950s. In the rapidly changing 1970s, there began a knowledge explosion regarding female crime.

The first point at which the female offender comes into contact with the criminal justice system is at the point of arrest. Although arrest is a traumatic experience for the male offender, it has special problems for the female. It is estimated that 80 percent of the female offenders in America have dependent children at home and that a great percentage of these children have no one else to care for them. Concern for the children and a tendency among officers to identify female offenders with their mothers or sisters cause arresting officers to be more discreet than they might be with a male in the same situation. A recognition of the need to provide more pretrial services for female offenders has prompted many communities to develop volunteer programs to assist with the women's problems at home. It is important to remember that the children of female offenders often become residents of juvenile institutions as a result of their mothers' actions. To the juveniles who are removed from the community and placed in what they perceive as a facility for other juveniles who have committed offenses, it becomes hard to accept the concept that protection, not punishment, is the state's motivation (see Chapter 17).

An officer's reluctance to arrest the female offender is also the result of age-old customs, mores, and laws that have created great distinctions between men and women who are under apprehension.[31] Although a policeman seldom hesitates to place a male offender "up against the wall" and to respond to force with equal force, he is often loath to do so with a female. Most police departments have strict rules and regulations in regard to the apprehension, search, and detention of women. In most cases, a female officer or matron is assigned to detain women and conduct searches of their persons. The female offender is sometimes treated like someone from a far-off planet rather than a person who has committed a criminal act.

The female offender seldom spends much time in detention before trial. Concern for the family and the lack of adequate female detention facilities or female personnel in the police department almost demand pretrial release for women.[32] Also, until quite recently, female offenders usually committed less serious offenses and could therefore be released on bail or on their own recognizance. In more recent years (1982–1986), women have been committing more serious crimes,[33] and, perhaps owing to the move to equalize punishments for codefendants, they have been receiving more severe sentences.[34]

This view of the female offender's possible preferential treatment in the criminal justice system is not shared by all, however, as is noted by Rita Simon:

> Others believe that judges are more punitive toward women. They are more likely to throw the book at the female defendant because they believe there is a greater discrepancy between her behavior and the behavior expected of women than there is between the behavior of the male defendant and the behavior expected of men. In other words, women defendants pay for the judges' belief that it is more in man's nature to commit crimes than it is in woman's. Thus, when a judge is convinced that the woman before him has committed a crime, he is more likely to overact and punish her, not only for the specific offense but also for transgressing against his expectations of womanly behavior.
>
> The existence of such statutes as the indeterminate sentence for women, or the sanctioning of a procedure whereby only convicted male defendants have their minimum sentences determined by a judge at an open hearing and in the presence of counsel, while the woman's minimum sentence is decided by a parole board in a closed session in which she is not represented by counsel, are cited as evidence of the unfair, punitive treatment that is accorded to women in the court.
>
> However, as women are arrested in greater numbers for crimes now committed mainly by men, they can expect the paternalistic attitude of judges—if such an attitude exists—to diminish rapidly.[35]

Though statistics show that about one out of five persons arrested in the United States is a woman, only one woman out of every twenty-five arrested is sent to prison. For example, New York State has a population of 14,632,000 and 1,126,704 index crimes, but the state incarcerated fewer than 1,400 women in 1986.[36]

The differential treatment accorded to women in many cases does not automatically mean better treatment or consideration. Moreover, as an alternative to differential treatment, the model of the male prison is sometimes copied, even to the point of ignoring the female inmates' obvious physical differences. At the other extreme, the best programs of differential treatment, filled with compassionate understanding for the female residents, could serve as models for institutions housing either sex—or both:

Built around multilevel and beautifully landscaped courtyards, the attractive buildings provide security without fences. Small housing units with pleasant living rooms provide space for normal interaction between presumably normal women. The expectation that the women will behave like human beings pervades the place. Education, recreation, and training areas are uncramped and well [designed]. Opportunity for interaction between staff and inmate is present everywhere.

About 200 yards away from the other buildings are attractive apartments, each containing a living room, dining space, kitchen, two bedrooms, and a bath. Women approaching release live in them while working or attending school in the city. These apartments normally are out of bounds to staff except on invitation.[37]

This kind of model reflects the relatively humane feeling toward the female offender that was in vogue when the Purdy Corrections Center was built in Washington state in 1976. The idea seems to continue to motivate the male-dominated criminal justice system to send very few women to prison. However, the situation is changing. The Purdy facility now has a

The Purdy Treatment Center for Women (Courtesy Washington State Department of Corrections)

fence, razor wire, and tighter security to reflect the reality of more violent inmates and hardening of public attitudes.

It is true that men are also being filtered out of the correctional funnel in greater numbers, but it appears that women can be returned to society with less chance of further criminal activity that might endanger society. Follow-up studies, reported since those in the 1975 *Uniform Crime Reports*, indicate that women seem to do better in regard to recidivism than men in every age category.[38]

For these and other reasons, the female offender has traditionally received discretionary treatment by police and prosecutors, with only those women who are considered particularly hard cases finally coming before a judge. It is also a fact that no politically minded prosecutor can enjoy bringing a mother with three small children to trial. Thus, such trials seldom occur unless the case is both serious and airtight. The result is that cases against women are often no-papered, and the correctional funnel for them narrows sharply. Those women brought to court are still apt to receive consideration for probation, fines, and suspended sentences more often than men who commit comparable crimes. However, the few who are sentenced to prison are less likely to receive early consideration for parole.

Despite the preferential treatment of female offenders, the number of incarcerated females in the United States jumped from 6,239 in 1971 to 26,610 in 1986, a whopping 426 percent increase. California alone held

TABLE 16.5   Women in State and Federal Institutions at Yearend, 1986

Jurisdiction	Number of Women Inmates	Percent of All Inmates	Percent Change in Women Inmate Population, 1985–86
U.S., total	26,610	4.9%	15.1%
Federal	2,833	6.4	17.8
State	23,777	4.7	14.8
States with at least 500 women inmates:			
California	3,564	6.0%	22.6%
Texas	1,758	4.6	10.3
Florida	1,630	5.1	25.0
New York	1,326	3.4	25.6
Ohio	1,213	5.4	5.2
Michigan	1,018	4.9	25.1
Georgia	947	5.5	13.7
North Carolina	827	4.7	10.7
Illinois	764	3.9	13.5
Oklahoma	679	7.1	33.9
Louisiana	637	4.4	4.4
Alabama	616	5.3	9.6
South Carolina	601	5.1	20.0
Pennsylvania	591	3.9	18.2

Source: Bureau of Justice Statistics: *Prisoners 1986* (Washington, D.C.), p. 3.

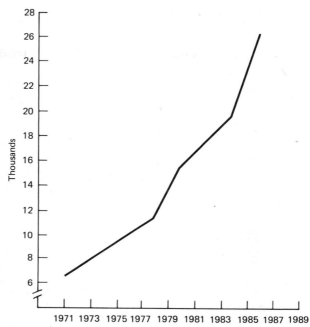

Figure 16-6 Female Felons in Prison, 1971 to 1987

over 6 percent of the incarcerated female offenders. If preferential treatment were not offered, the number of female prisoners in the nation would probably approach 100,000, rather than the mere 26,610! (See Figure 16-6 and Table 16.5.)

Why has the women's prison population increased so sharply? No one knows for certain, but some of the reasons given are that women are committing more crimes and being arrested more often, and that they are committing more serious crimes and are being sentenced more severely by judges. Other theories are that presentence investigators and the judiciary, influenced by the women's liberation movement, are less likely to give favorable sentencing considerations than they were in the past; that parole boards are using uniform sentencing guidelines that force female inmates to serve more time;[39] and that women are getting their "just desserts" under the conservative backlash to treat all offenders more severely. There are many theories, but not many data to support any one theory in particular.

Women Behind Bars _____

The plight of the woman behind bars is often a difficult one. In terms of institutions, the male-oriented criminal justice system may totally ignore

A Minimum Security Dormitory (Courtesy of American Correctional Association, photo by CRSS Constructors, Inc.)

the special requirements of the female offender. The nature of punishment for female offenders has come a long way from the time when they were thrown into the holds of hulks as diversions for the incarcerated male felons, but much more needs to be done before treatment of the female offender can be said to be an integrated part of corrections.

Detainment Facilities for Women

As noted earlier, the problems with female prisoners start with the requirement for a search in the police station. Many large urban police departments are able to maintain a matron on duty and provide separate facilities for female detainees. In most jurisdictions, however, there are no matrons and no separate facilities.

At the local level, places of confinement for women range from a few well-designed jail facilities for female offenders to whatever can be improvised, such as a separate floor or cell next to those for male offenders. The screening process at the point of arrest creates great problems for jail personnel. Because only the most serious female offenders are selected for arrest and detention, there is a more immediate need for effective security measures. This problem is made more acute because of the lack of qualified personnel[40] and adequate facilities to supply the extensive security required.

In addition, certain tangential problems relate to the detention of a woman. The first is what to do with her children, if she has any. If there is a husband at home, he is likely to be working during the day. The need to detain the female offender should not mean neglecting the innocent children she leaves behind. Provision of adequate services for them requires close coordination with the local child welfare service agencies. These services are often nonexistent in the smaller jurisdictions and, although it requires a special kind of sensitivity to deal with such children, often the job is left to men trained to react only to relatively simple situations, if these men are trained at all. Confinement itself is a problem in most jails, and it is often solved by temporarily using a portion of the facility designed for men. In some cases, law enforcement officials might arrange with the local hospital or mental institution to house the female prisoner for a short period of time. Others arrange to transfer the female prisoner to a larger urban facility until trial.

All of these temporary measures create problems for both the corrections administration and the offender. Security and logistics become a drain on resources that were not planned for such use. The defendant has problems concerning visitation, contact with counsel, and the welfare of her family. All these problems may be shared by the male defendant, but he is much less likely to have the woman's acute worry for her children. If he has any children, there is probably a wife to take care of them, whereas the woman often has no husband (or has one who works). In addition, some of the women are pregnant or require medical attention for problems unique to their sex. The average small-town police station is hardly prepared to handle this kind of situation. Because of the almost total lack of standards for female confinement, the situation at the local jail or correctional facility presents only a token of the problems that characterize prisons for women.

Women's Prisons

There were fifty-two institutions for women offenders only, and eighteen co-correctional listed in 1988.[41] The picture in regard to the administration of these women's prisons has changed greatly in recent years. In 1966, only ten of the nation's institutions for women were headed by a female correctional administrator. In 1984, twenty-nine of the correctional administrators of these institutions for women were females.

Because the conditions in the women's institutions vary greatly, it would be fruitless to attempt to describe them individually. They are not all horror stories; it is sufficient to state that the best and the worst aspects of the male institution are also in evidence in the women's prison, the only major differences being the variations based on the traits unique to each sex and the more numerous and varied training and education programs available to males.

Diversionary procedures seem to be especially applicable to the kinds of offenses for which women are corrected; yet almost no diversion is utilized for females once they have been convicted and sentenced. A large percentage of the women incarcerated have children who must be placed in foster homes or under the supervision of childcare agencies. The female offender is excluded from the decision making regarding the disposition of her children in most cases. Women also are faced with telling their children about the coming absences, a painful and sometimes traumatic process.[42] Another problem with the female institutions is the fact that, until very recently, most "vocational training" centers were providing "female-type" services for the rest of the correctional system (for example, laundry, tailoring, mending, making flags, and other traditionally "female" tasks). This kind of program does little to prepare the female offender for an occupation on the outside. As shown by Ryan's study, that situation has now improved considerably:

> There has been a marked increase in educational and vocational programs for adult female offenders. Adult Basic Education programs have increased by 22%, GED/high school diploma programs have increased by 21%, and college programs have increased by 19%.[43]

Although there was a wing of the Sing Sing Prison set aside for female offenders early in the nineteenth century, the first prison for women was the Indiana Reform Institute for Women (1873);[44] the first federal women's facility was the Federal Correctional Institution at Alderson, West Virginia (1927). One of the assumptions underlying the development of prisons for female offenders was that women were "naturally passive" and hence not as dangerous as their incarcerated male counterparts.[45] This perception allowed women's prison administrators a freer rein in programming. In fact, many of the innovations in corrections were first developed and implemented in women's prisons, including educational classes, libraries, art and music programs, work release, recreation, vocational programming, classification based on behavioral criteria, and progressive grading. Many important aspects of contemporary corrections were pioneered by female administrators in charge of institutions for female offenders!

The problems of the female correctional institution were addressed in the following recommendations:

1. Develop policy to facilitate communication and development of interagency agreements and cooperative actions between correctional agencies and among correctional agencies and other agencies, such as state departments of education, state departments of postsecondary/technical schools, state departments of higher education, vocational rehabilitation, and women's bureaus of the state departments of labor.
2. Expand the networking of managers and supervisors in correctional systems with adult female offenders.

3. Provide regional and national forums for the exchange of ideas and models, and identification of resources.

4. Provide special issue training programs for managers and supervisors of female offenders to address identified needs and problem areas; and to develop skills, techniques, and tools for addressing these needs and problem areas. There is a need for continued study of differing organizational structures and different combinations of program variables to determine the differential effects of organizational structures and program variables on the delivery of effective programs and services to meet the needs of adult female offenders. There is also a need to replicate this study with youthful female offenders.[46]

The problem of inadequate statistics and information on the female offender is a major one, although the number of studies on female offenders and institutions is increasing rapidly. The significance of this lack of data is highlighted by Ryan:

This state of the art analysis of adult female offenders and the programs and services provided for these offenders was conducted because: (1) relatively little empirical data have been reported to describe female offenders and the program opportunities available to these offenders; (2) it is important to have current information on female offenders for management decision-making; and (3) state of the art information will facilitate and contribute to networking and resource development.[47]

It is hoped that research now in progress will offer the student of corrections with an even more meaningful and useful data base on female correctional facilities.

The Co-Correctional Institution _____

The single-sex experience and long-term deprivation of heterosexual outlets create the same kinds of problems in female institutions that are found in male prisons. The recommendations for coeducational institutions may seem extreme to the uninitiated, but the leavening effect of a system that allows at least social contact in daily activity with members of the opposite sex is considerable. Excessive administrative concern about overt signs of friendship as indicative of possible homosexual activity conflicts with many standard practices for women outside the walls. If one observed two males holding hands as they walked down the street, they would be suspected of deviant behavior. This same behavior, though not considered strange for women (and particularly girls) on the outside, is viewed with great suspicion inside the walls, for girls and women alike. This situation is described by an inmate:

COED INSTITUTIONS

Coed or co-correctional institutions hold both male and female offenders who interact and share the facility except for sleeping areas. They study, eat, dance, work, and engage in leisure activities within one campus.

Coed institutions are believed to lower the volume of homosexual behavior — both voluntary behavior and homosexual rape — as well as encourage reintegration of offenders selected to participate in the program. Further, men tend to fight with each other less, take more care in their personal appearance, buttress self-esteem, and encourage learning of appropriate gender-relations. Most males entering coed prisons are carefully selected: they must be eligible for minimum custody assignment, be close to parole date, have few institutional infractions, no escapes in their records, and so on. The penalty for engaging in sexual behavior for men in coed institutions is usually transfer to an all-male, higher-security institution and, sometimes, parole date setback.

It's tough to be *natural*. The thing that most of us are trying to accomplish here, we're trying to get our minds at a point to where we can handle whatever comes our way, to get our emotions balanced, to maybe straighten up our way of thinking. You know, it just makes it hard when you're trying to be a natural person — to react to things normally — when the staff won't let you be normal — when you do a normal thing that being a woman makes it normal, and then have them say no, you can't do that because if you do, that's personal contact and that's homosexuality. So there's our mental hassle.

I know that when women are thrown together without men or without the companionship of men it makes it pretty rough on them — women being the emotional people that they are. They have to have a certain amount of affection and close companionship. You know, a woman, if she's with a man she'll put her hand on him or maybe she'll reach up and touch him. This is something that a woman does naturally without thinking, and so if a woman has a good friend, or an affair, she does the same thing because this is her nature. The thing of it is — like I have a friend at the cottage — neither one of us have ever played. We're never gonna play. And if somebody tried to force us into it, we couldn't, wouldn't, or what have you. But being a woman and after being here for quite a while, we put our arms around each other, we don't think there's anything the matter with it, because there's nothing there — it's a friendship. We're walking down the hall, our records are both spotless, she's a council girl, I'm Minimum A [minimum custody classification]. I've never had anything on my record that was bad and my god, the supervisor comes out and says, "Now, now girls, you know we don't allow that sort of thing here." And we look at her and say "What sort of thing?" "This personal contact." And yet this same supervisor, we saw her up at the corner putting her arm around another supervisor the same way we were doing. So this is where part of our mental hassle comes in.[48]

The redefinition of the natural acts described above into something considered evil and proscribed is another reason that institutionalization is so crippling to the long-term prisoner. As inmates, male or female, learn that simple signs of friendship are prohibited, they learn to repress their impulses toward interpersonal warmth when they get out. The kind of behavior that makes them acceptable on the inside makes them appear "hard-case" (unfeeling, unresponsive) on the outside. In the male this kind of coldness can be viewed as "tough" or "macho," but in the woman it is almost always considered unattractive.

Very few studies have been conducted on the homosexuality of female prisoners. A lot of conjecture is found in the literature, but true scientific research is rare. Even the monumental effort to compile statistics on female offenders in Sheldon and Eleanor Glueck's *500 Delinquent Women*[49] did not consider homosexuality, but sex role research is increasing.[50]

The freedom from intensive supervision makes it difficult to prevent homosexual activity. There are never enough personnel to watch all the inmates, and so lovers get together despite the staff's efforts. In many institutions the staff adopts the attitude of "looking the other way" in regard to the female inmates' sexual activity. (The same is true in many men's institutions). It is possible that homosexuality is an even more prevalent problem in the women's institutions than in men's, because a high percentage of the inmates have been so misused by men that they had already turned to other females to fulfill their emotional needs on the outside. It is also quite possible that the impact of imprisonment is significantly different for women, tending to encourage a homosexual response. Women appear more likely to view arrest, jailing, the court trial, and commitment to prison in highly personal terms. This personalized reaction could harden antisocial attitudes and lead to further illegal behavior.

One study has identified three psychological deprivations that might lead to homosexual behavior:

1. Affectional starvation and need for understanding
2. Isolation from previous symbiotic interpersonal relations
3. Need for continued intimate relationships with a person[51]

It would be hard to imagine an incarcerated felon, male or female, who does not suffer these deprivations to some degree.

The co-correctional prison, while a relatively new development in corrections, has had a rocky existence. Two were opened in 1971 in the Federal Bureau of Prisons system. Since that time, there have been a good number of attempts at coed adult state and federal facilities, but only a few still remained coed in 1986.[52] J. O. Smykla defined adult co-corrections as an adult institution, the major purpose of which is the institutional confinement of felons, managed by one institutional administration and having regular programs or areas in which female and male inmates have daily opportunities for human interaction.[53]

Juvenile co-correction programs have existed for at least a century in some states, and the concept of adult co-corrections is being rapidly accepted. When these programs were established, co-corrections had twelve objectives:

1. To reduce the dehumanizing and destructive aspects of confinement by allowing continuity or resumption of heterosexual relationships
2. To reduce the institutional control problems through the weakening of disruptive homosexual systems, reduction of predatory homosexual activity, lessening of assaultive behavior, and the diversion of inmate interests and activities
3. To protect inmates likely to be involved in "trouble" were they in a same-sex institution
4. To provide an additional tool for creating a more normal, less institutionalized atmosphere
5. To cushion the shock of adjustment for releasees, by reducing the number and intensity of adjustments to be made
6. To realize economies of scale in terms of more efficient utilization of available space, staff, and programs
7. To provide relief of immediate or anticipated overcrowding, sometimes of emergency proportions
8. To reduce the need for civilian labor, by provision of both light and heavy inmate work forces
9. To increase diversification and flexibility of program offerings, and equal access for males and females
10. To expand treatment potentials for working with inmates having "sexual problems," and development of positive heterosexual relationships, and coping skills
11. To provide relief of immediate or anticipated legal pressures to provide equal access to programs and services to both sexes
12. To expand career opportunities for women, previously often "boxed into" the single state women's institutions, as co-correctional staff[54]

The question of whether these objectives have been met cannot yet be answered, primarily because evaluations of their effectiveness have been weak at best. The recidivism research studies to date, however, indicate probable success.[55]

Women's Liberation and Women's Prisons _____

One of the rallying cries of the women's liberation movement is "equal pay for equal work." In the case of female prisoners, there is a need for equal treatment—for access to some of the new correctional programs, including alternatives to incarceration being offered to male offenders. More co-correctional prisons are another possibility, but not in the immediate future. A third way to equalize treatment is by adding more women as members of the criminal justice team. Female correctional workers are now firmly established as members of the corrections team in the field. This has in turn caused correctional administrators and personnel to address underlying problems inherent in the introduction of opposite-sex custodial and treatment personnel into single-sex prisons, including security of staff, privacy of inmates, and the suitability of females to work in male prisons. The courts have generally ruled that Title VII of the Civil Rights Act of 1965 forbade sexual discrimination at all levels of government, unless the gender were a *bona fide occupational qualification* (BFOQ) or if morality were crucial. There are now female correctional officers in every state, many working in all-male institutions.

Although equality is a noble goal for the female offender, it also has a negative side. Female arrest, conviction, and incarceration rates have risen sharply in the last five years, in comparison with those of male offenders. Even with the reduction in crime rates in the United States, female offenders are imprisoned at a higher rate than are male offenders. Such rates of incarceration may increase at an accelerated rate, as the attitudes toward and treatment of female offenders change. Available data indicate that sentencing is getting tougher for women and that they are becoming more involved in serious crimes. Repetitions of these kinds of findings will be common for the next few years, as the criminal justice system adjusts to the "liberated" female offender.[56]

The great wall of mystery as to the handling of the female offender must be broken down so that more women who need treatment will be placed in the right programs. Screening as drastic as that which takes place in the female offender system is perhaps counterproductive to the goals of rehabilitation. At this stage in the development of America's correctional system, these comments represent pure speculation; it is possible, of course, that the recidivism rate for those women informally screened is very low.

Summary _____

As men and women engage in illegal activities and are caught up in the criminal justice system, many are eventually concentrated in America's potpourri of jails, workhouses, and prisons. Although a few of these institutions are exceptionally well-administered facilities, with adequate programs and dedicated staffs, it seems that most male offenders await trial and serve time in units that are lacking in these factors so necessary to an effective correctional process. The by-products of the public's inattention to this tragic situation, aggravated by uninspired correction leadership, ruptured family ties, increased welfare rolls, dead time in jails, socialization into a dysfunctional "prisonized" culture, rape in prison, embitterment and hostility, and the decreased ability of former inmates to function in the free world. Men and women in prison sense—even if they cannot articulate—that the gulf is great between the treatment and expected reformation on the one hand and the realities of practice on the other.[57] The whole process is viewed as a cruel sham perpetuated in the name of an abstract ideal to which only lip service, if that, is given.

The increase in jail and prison populations in the last few years and the probable continued growth in the numbers of caged adult offenders do not bode well for the quality of life behind bars. Aggression in prisons, polarization of inmates, riots and disturbances, and inmate attacks on guards are likely to increase. Prison crowding in the absence of meaningful programs and concerned administrators is a time bomb that will eventually explode unless steps are taken to defuse the situation. Because the population at risk is not expected to decline in the immediate future, programming and diversion alternatives, including community-based corrections, are the avenues that must now be explored (see Chapter 26).

In examining the situation of the female offender as a special issue, we must bear in mind that incarceration intensifies a female offender's antisocial attitudes, thereby increasing the likelihood of her return to criminal behavior. Two alternatives are suggested:

1. Diversionary programs should be made available for handling suspected or convicted female offenders, including the increased use of the summons, probation, deferred prosecution, community treatment centers, and halfway houses.
2. Those women who are incarcerated in prisons should have maximum contact with the outside world, including more frequent visitation privileges, uncensored mail, home visitations, and home furloughs.

Further examination, too, is needed regarding the approximately twenty-four out of every twenty-five convicted female offenders who are not imprisoned. Perhaps, as we have suggested, the rate of recidivism for this group is very low.[58] The discretionary diversion presently employed with nonincarcerated female offenders may well be a model for the rest of the criminal justice system.

The problems faced by both male and female adult offenders seem to be coming more to a point of parity. All the problems, and some of the benefits and programs, that are seen in male institutions are now seen in the female institutions as well. As a reflection of equal rights on the outside, this blurring of the differences (to include co-correctional institutions) seems to be the wave of the future. It is important that these changes result in more correctional capabilities, not less, as they are implemented.

Review Questions

1. Why have prison populations increased recently? What short-term effects will result from this increase?
2. What is meant by the "population at risk"? How does it contribute to the population problem in male prisons?
3. Explain the dynamics of rape in prison.
4. What factors contribute to prisonization?
5. What can be done to reduce homosexuality in prisons?
6. What are some of the main reasons women are treated so differently in the correctional system?
7. What are the major crimes for which women are convicted? Explain.
8. How would a more "equal" system of criminal justice for women affect the correctional system?

Key Terms

1. crime clock (p. 356)
2. jail (p. 357)
3. dead time (p. 357)
4. prisonization (p. 364)
5. baby boom (p. 366)
6. echo boom (p. 366)
7. conjugal visitation (p. 369)
8. trick (p. 374)
9. co-correctional (p. 383)
10. hard-case (p. 385)
11. women's liberation (p. 386)
12. parity (p. 388)

Notes

1. U.S. Department of Justice, *Jail Inmates 1986* (Washington, D.C.: U.S. Government Printing Office, 1987), p. 3.
2. Ibid.
3. Ibid. This includes 33,027 Hispanics, or 14 percent of the males in jails.
4. Simon Dinitz, "Nothing Fails Like a Little Success," in Edward Sagarin, ed., *Criminology: New Concerns* (Beverly Hills, Calif.: Sage Publications, 1979), pp. 105–118.
5. Bureau of Justice Statistics, *Prisoners in 1986* (Washington, D.C.: U.S. Department of Justice, May 1987), p. 1. See also, George M. Camp and Camille Graham Camp, *The Corrections Yearbook* (South Salem, New York: Criminal Justice Institute, 1987), p. 7.
The ten states with the highest rates were

Nevada	462	Alabama	283
Louisiana	322	Florida	272
Maryland	280	North Carolina	258
South Carolina	324	Arizona	268
Georgia	265	District of Columbia	753

6. See Benjamin Ward, "Development of Jail Overcrowding in the New York Department of Corrections, June 1983." Paper presented at the annual meeting of the American Society of Criminology, Denver.

7. Between 1985 and 1986, the number of women in prison has increased by 15.1 percent. See Bureau of Justice Statistics, _Prisoners in 1986_, p. 1.

8. Bureau of Justice Statistics, _Prisoners and Drugs_ (Washington, D.C.: U.S. Department of Justice, March 1983). See also Bureau of Justice Statistics, _Prisoners and Alcohol_ (Washington, D.C.: U.S. Department of Justice, January 1983).

9. Bureau of Justice Statistics, _Prisoners, 1986_, p. 5. Only ten states are operating at less than 100 percent of capacity. On January 1, 1987, state and federal institutions were operating at 106 percent of their estimated capacity. In general, 1 of every 250 adult Americans was behind bars on January 1, 1987, one of the highest rates in the world.

10. See Bureau of Justice Statistics, _Prisoners and Drugs_.

11. Charles Bailey, "Prison Populations Surging, and Not Just Because of the Nation's Economic Slowdown," _Corrections Digest_ 7 (February 1976): 9.

12. Donald Clemmer, _The Prison Community_ (New York: Rinehart & Co., 1940), p. 8.

13. Lynne Goodstein, "Inmate Adjustment to Prison and the Transition to Community Life," _Journal of Research in Crime and Delinquency_ 16 (July 1979): 246–272. This article has an excellent bibliography for students.

14. _Pruno_ is alcohol made from fruit scraps, potato peelings, raisins, or any other biodegradable fruit and sugar.

15. Gene Kassebaum, David Ward, and Daniel Wilner, _Prison Treatment and Parole Survival: An Empirical Assessment_ (New York: John Wiley, 1971), p. 301.

16. Ron Akers et al., "Fear of Crime and Victimization Among the Elderly in Different Types of Communities," _Criminology_, 25 (1987): pp. 487–505.

17. Rob Wilson, "U.S. Prison Population Sets Another Record," _Corrections Magazine_ 4 (June 1980): 5.

18. Richard Allison, "Does Recession Bode Rise in Imprisonment?" _Criminal Justice Digest_ 10. (October 22, 1979): 5–6. See also Bruce Cory and Stephen Gettinger, _Time to Build?_ (New York: Edna McConnell Clark Foundation, 1984).

19. A term developed in the 1930s.

20. Anthony Scacco, _Rape in Prison_ (Springfield, Ill: Chas. C. Thomas, 1975).

21. John Ramirez, "Race and the Apprehension of Inmate Misconduct," _Journal of Criminal Justice_ 11 (1983): 413–427.

22. Scacco, _Rape in Prison_, pp. 99–116.

23. Peter Buffum, _Homosexuality in Prisons_ (Washington, D.C.: U.S. Government Printing Office, 1972), p. 28.

24. This is an increase over the past and the numbers continue to expand. The spread of AIDS through homosexual acts may cause even more jurisdictions to adopt family visiting as a more acceptable outlet for sexual pressures for married inmates.

25. John Smykla, _Probation and Parole_ (New York: Macmillan, 1984).

26. William Webster, _Crime in the United States, 1986_ (Washington, D.C.: U.S. Department of Justice, 1987), p. 171.

27. Freda Adler, _Sisters in Crime_ (New York: McGraw-Hill, 1975).

28. A trick is an act of intercourse, generally considered completed by the orgasm of the male participant.

29. Webster, *Crime in the United States*, p. 171.

30. See Nichole Hahn, "Matrons and Molls: The Study of Women's Prison History"; and Carol Fenster, "Females As Partners in Crime." Papers presented at the American Society of Criminology meeting, Philadelphia, November 1979.

31. Marvin Krohn, James Curry, and Shirley Nelson-Kilger, "Is Chivalry Dead? An Analysis of Changes in Police Dispositions of Males and Females," *Criminology* 21 (1983): 228–244. See also Cassia Spohn, John Gruhl, and Susan Welch, "The Impact of Ethnicity and Gender of Defendants on the Decision to Reject or Dismiss Felony Charges." *Criminology* 25 (1987): 175–191. For a view of discrimination against women attorneys, witnesses, and litigants, see William Eich, "Gender Bias in the Courtroom: Some Participants are More Equal Than Others," *Judicature* 69 (1986): 339–343.

32. There are ten separate jail facilities for females, located in such large cities as New York and Los Angeles. In 1978, there were also forty-six prisons in thirty-seven states, devoted entirely to female felons. Another thirteen states had no separate facility. See Clarice Feinman, "Prison for Women: The Multipurpose Institution." Paper presented at the American Society of Criminology meeting, Philadelphia, November 1979.

33. Joan Potter, "In Prison, Women Are Different," *Corrections Magazine* 4 (December 1978): 14–24. See also Webster, *Crime in the United States 1982*.

34. See Fenster, "Females As Partners in Crime."

35. Rita Simon, *The Contemporary Woman and Crime* (Washington, D.C.: U.S. Department of Health, Education and Welfare, 1976), p. 50.

36. Webster, *Crime in the United States 1986,* p. 173. Inmate data are from the American Correctional Association, *Directory: 1984* (College Park, Md.: ACA, 1984), pp. 228–244.

37. National Advisory Commission on Criminal Justice Standards and Goals, *Corrections* (Washington, D.C.: U.S. Department of Justice, 1976), p. 346. This is a description of the Women's Treatment Center, Purdy, Washington.

38. Clarence Kelley, U.S. Department of Justice, *Uniform Crime Reports: 1975* (Washington, D.C.: U.S. Government Printing Office, 1976), p. 47.

39. See Ellen Mowbray, "Parole Prediction and Gender." Paper presented at the American Society of Criminology meeting, Toronto, November 1982.

40. T. A. Ryan, *Adult Female Offenders and Institutional Programs: A State of the Art Analysis,* U.S. Government Printing Office, Washington, D.C., 1984, pp. 102–103.

41. American Correctional Association, *1988 Directory of Juvenile and Adult Correctional Departments, Institutions, Agencies and Paroling Authorities* (College Park, Maryland: ACA, 1988), p. xvii.

42. Phyllis Jo Baunach, *Mothers in Prison* (New Brunswick, N.J.: Transaction Books, 1985).

43. Ryan, *Adult Female Offenders*, p. 28.

44. Feinman, "Prison for Women," p. 2.

45. Clarice Feinman, "Sex Role Stereotypes and Justice for Women," *Crime and Delinquency* 25 (January 1979): 87–94.

46. Ryan, *Adult Female Offenders and Institutional Programs*, p. 29.

47. Ibid, p. ix.

48. David Ward and Gene Kassebaum, "Sexual Tension in a Women's Prison," in, Marvin Wolfgang and Leon Radzinowicz, eds., *The Criminal in Confinement*

(New York: Basic Books, 1971), pp. 149–150. See also Candace Kruttschnitt, "Race Relations and the Female Inmate," *Crime and Delinquency* 29 (1983): 577–592.

49. Sheldon and Eleanor Glueck, *500 Delinquent Women* (New York: Knopf, 1934). See also, J. O. Smykla, *Co-Corrections: A Case Study of a Co-ed Federal Prison* (Washington, D.C.: University Press of America, 1979).

50. J. O. Smykla, *Co-Corrections: A Case Study of a Co-Ed Federal Prison* (Washington, D.C.: University Press of America, 1979).

51. David Ward and Gene Kassebaum, *Women's Prison: Sex and Social Structure* (Chicago: Aldine, 1965), pp. 9–10.

52. J. O. Smykla, "The Impact of Co-corrections," p. 1. Paper presented at the annual meeting of the Academy of Criminal Justice Sciences, Cincinnati, March 1979. As of 1984, there were at least sixteen state prisons that housed both male and female felons, but few of these meet Smykla's definition of a coed prison.

53. Ibid., p. 2. See also J. Ross et al., *Assessment of Coeducational Corrections* (Washington, D.C.: U.S. Government Printing Office, 1978), pp. 3–4.

54. J. Ross et al, *Assessment of Coeducational Corrections,* pp. 1–2.

55. Smykla, "The Impact of Co-corrections," pp. 12–16.

56. Ineke Haen Marshall, "Women's Rights and Female Criminality in the Netherlands." Paper presented at the American Society of Criminology, Toronto, November, 1982. Marshall found little evidence that the women's movement has had any impact on the patterns of female crime in the Netherlands.

57. See Geoffrey Alpert and Donald Hicks, "Prisoners' Attitudes Toward Components of the Legal and Judicial Systems," *Criminology* 14 (February 1977): 461–482.

58. There is reason to suspect that the recidivism rate is, on the other hand, quite high. See Margarite Warren and Jill Rosenbaum. "Criminal Careers of Female Offenders." *Criminal Justice and Behavior* 13 (1986), pp. 393–418.

17

Juveniles: Punish or Protect?

The belief that the state has both the right and
responsibility to act on behalf of juveniles in
trouble was the key element in juvenile justice in
twelfth-century England and remains central to
the juvenile justice system in the United States
today. . . . The dispute between legalists and
therapists remains unresolved after a century or
more of debate and continues to be problematic
for practitioners.
—STEVEN M. COX and JOHN C. CONRAD

The Juvenile Crime Problem

It has been estimated that approximately one out of every six boys and
one out of every nine children in the United States will be referred to a
juvenile court before his or her eighteenth birthday. The rise in juvenile
crime has been considered the most serious aspect of the crime problem
in America. There have been some improvements, however. In 1982, 31
percent of the serious index crimes, and 18 percent of all crimes cleared
by arrest were committed by persons under eighteen years of age. In 1986,
these figures were 33 percent and 17 percent respectively. At these rates,
which we know reflect only reported crimes—a small part of the true
picture, as confirmed by victimization studies—498,823 index crimes
against property and 65,518 index crimes against persons cleared by arrest
in 1986 involved a juvenile offender.[1]

JUVENILE

A person subject to juvenile court proceedings because a statuatorily defined
event was alleged to have occurred while his or her age was below the statuatorily specified limit of original jurisdiction of a juvenile court. A juvenile
delinquent, then, has been adjudicated by an officer of a juvenile court for law
violations that would be crimes if they had been committed by an adult.

TABLE 17.1 Number of Persons Arrested Under 18

	Number of Persons Arrested					
	Total all Ages			Under 18 Years of Age		
Offense Charged	1982	1986	Percent Change	1982	1986	Percent Change
Total	8,658,964	9,227,542	+ 6.6	1,544,933	1,531,956	− .8
Murder and nonnegligent manslaughter	15,979	14,856	− 7.0	1,328	1,295	− 2.5
Forcible rape	24,733	27,754	+12.2	3,704	4,221	+14.0
Robbery	121,441	116,597	− 4.0	31,353	26,245	−16.3
Aggravated assault	232,350	268,141	+15.4	30,847	33,757	+ 9.4
Burglary	388,151	337,130	−13.1	154,216	119,360	−22.6
Larceny-theft	994,834	1,039,974	+ 4.5	324,375	328,848	+ 1.4
Motor vehicle theft	95,635	117,091	+22.4	34,381	45,097	+31.2
Arson	14,803	13,694	− 7.5	5,587	5,518	− 1.2
Violent crime	394,503	427,348	+ 8.3	67,232	65,518	− 2.5
Property Crime	1,493,423	1,507,889	+ 1.0	518,559	498,823	− 3.8
Crime Index total	1,887,926	1,935,237	+ 2.5	585,791	564,341	− 3.7

Source: Federal Bureau of Investigation, *Crime in the United States 1987* (Washington, D.C.), p. 173.

Although the percentages remained rather consistent between 1982 and 1986, they fell slightly in absolute numbers, even as the overall population grew. This could be another indication of the shrinking of the population at risk, or the fact that real progress is being made in the juvenile justice system. But juveniles contribute to a significant and alarming portion of the crime problem (see Table 17.1).

Juveniles today are handled differently and separately from adults in almost every phase of the criminal justice system. Differential treatment and discretion by individual officials at various stages of the criminal process cloud the juvenile crime picture. There have been some major adjustments in the juvenile justice system in the past few years, and many more changes will probably be initiated in the next decade.

Because a very large percentage of incarcerated felons spent time as juveniles in training institutions and schools for delinquents, we shall briefly look at the development and function of the juvenile courts and the juvenile system, starting with the philosophy that produced them.

Juvenile Justice

Parens Patriae

Like most of America's criminal justice system, our juvenile justice system derives from the common law of England. In regard to criminal responsibility, the English common law made three assumptions concerning age.

> ### *PARENS PATRIAE*
> A legal philosophy by which the state would assume the role of the parent of a juvenile.

First, children under the age of seven were presumed to be incapable of holding criminal intent. Second, from the ages of eight to fourteen, offenders were not held responsible unless the state could prove that they could clearly distinguish between right and wrong. Lastly, if offenders were over the age of fourteen, they were assumed to be responsible for their acts and therefore deserving of punishment. In this last case, the burden was on the defendants to prove that they were not responsible.

The king was considered the father of his country *(parens patriae),* who assumed responsibility for protecting all orphans and otherwise dependent children. In England this responsibility was fulfilled by the chancery courts,[2] in which the needful child became a ward of the state under the protection of *parens patriae.* The chancery court was designed to act more flexibly than the more rigid criminal courts. The main concern was for the welfare of the child; legal procedures that might hamper the court in its beneficial actions were either circumvented or ignored. Thus, there were two concepts under the common law: that children under certain ages were not responsible for their actions and that a certain category of children was in need of protection by the state. It was not until the ages of possible responsibility were raised to sixteen and eighteen that these two concepts merged into the concept of juvenile delinquency.

Despite concern for their children's welfare, most communities have a tolerance point for juveniles' disruptive behavior. When children go beyond this point, they can be taken into custody and recorded as delinquents. The mixing of juvenile offenders and adult felons was a practice that had existed for centuries but in America's early history was looked on as repugnant. It was not until 1899 that the delinquent juvenile began to receive differential attention in the courts. The first juvenile court was established in that year in Chicago, and the delinquent joined the dependent and neglected child as a ward of the state. When the juvenile delinquent was thus placed under the cloak of *parens patriae,* he or she was removed entirely from the formal criminal justice system. The general procedures for the handling of juvenile delinquents today are outlined by the National Juvenile Justice Clearinghouse:

> ARREST: The juvenile justice process often begins with an investigation by a police officer either because he or she observes a law violation or because a violation is reported to the police.
> *The police officer may decide to release the child to his or her parent with a warning or reprimand, or the officer may release to the parents on condition that the juvenile enroll in a community diversion program.*

Or the officer may take the juvenile into custody and refer the matter to the Juvenile Court's intake officer for further processing.

INTAKE: The intake officer is responsible for determining whether or not a case should move ahead for further court processing.

The intake officer may decide to release the juvenile to the parents with a warning or reprimand or may release the child on condition that the child enroll in a community diversion or submit to informal probation (supervision) by a Juvenile Court officer.

If not, the intake officer will recommend that a petition be filed, equivalent to filing a charge, and will refer the case to the Juvenile Court prosecutor. The intake officer also makes the initial decision as to whether the child shall be detained pending further court action or released to the parents pending hearing. If the juvenile is detained, the decision is reviewed by a judge or a court administrator at a Juvenile Court detention hearing.

ADJUDICATION: The Juvenile Court judge must review all the evidence presented at a hearing and determine whether to sustain or reject the allegations made on the petition.

The Juvenile Court judge may reject the allegations made in the petition; then the juvenile is released. In some cases the judge may believe that the allegations are true but withhold adjudication on condition the child agrees to enroll in a community program that the court feels will help resolve the problem. By withholding adjudication, many of the problems identified by labeling theorists are avoided or, at least, lessened.

DISPOSITION: At a hearing, the Juvenile Court judge reviews the recommendations of all concerned parties as to what should happen to the child.

Even now, the judge may decide that a severe form of treatment is not to the advantage of the youth or the community. In this case, the disposition may be probation, a warning or reprimand, some form of community service, a fine, or "home detention," in which the juvenile continues to live at home but receives rigorous daily counseling.

Other dispositions are more stringent. They may be such nonsecure custodial treatment as foster care or group home placement—but they may range up to incarceration in a secure juvenile correctional facility. The judge's disposition will depend on the seriousness of the offense and the child's previous court history.

AFTERCARE: *Whatever disposition is made of the case, the court may make the termination of that disposition contingent upon the juvenile's acceptance of aftercare—probation, counseling, enrollment in a community program, or any of a number of other forms of treatment designed to lessen the chance that the youth will get in trouble again.* [3]

A Whole New Vocabulary

Even after the juvenile delinquent was officially removed from the criminal justice system, administrators continued to practice many aspects of that system in dealing with juveniles. Various terms used in the criminal courts were changed to apply to juvenile justice, but the meanings remained the same. It is essential in understanding the juvenile justice process to recognize how the new terms relate to the old. For example, *petition* replaces "complaint," *summons* is used in place of "warrant," *finding of involvement* replaces "conviction," and *disposition* is the new term for "sentencing." Table 17.2 covers most of the significant terms used in the juvenile system. (A detailed glossary of terms used in the criminal justice system as a whole may be found at the end of this text.)

By 1945, juvenile courts had been established in every state, and it became apparent that different terms were being used for the same older concepts. A major problem developed from the practice of combining all the different categories of juveniles under the same rubric of *parens patriae*.

TABLE 17.2 Glossary of Terms Used in the Juvenile Justice System

Juvenile Term	Adult Term
1. **Adjudication:** a decision by the judge that the child has committed delinquent acts.	**Conviction of guilt**
2. **Adjudicatory hearing:** a hearing to determine whether the allegations of a petition are supported by the evidence beyond a reasonable doubt or by a preponderance of the evidence.	**Trial**
3. **Adjustment:** a reference to matters that are settled or brought to a satisfactory state so that the parties can agree without the official intervention of the court.	**Plea bargaining**
4. **Aftercare:** the supervision given to a child for a limited period of time after he is released from the training school but still under the control of the school or of the juvenile court.	**Parole**
5. **Commitment:** a decision by the judge that the child should be sent to a training school.	**Sentence to imprisonment**
6. **Court:** the court having jurisdiction over children who are alleged to be or found to be delinquent. Juvenile delinquency procedures should not be used for neglected children or those needing supervision.	**Court of record**
7. **Delinquent act:** an act that if committed by an adult would be called a crime. The term *delinquent acts* does not include such ambiguities and noncrimes as *being ungovernable, truancy, incorrigibility,* and *disobedience.*	**Crime**
8. **Delinquent child:** a child who is found to have committed an act that would be considered a crime if committed by an adult.	**Criminal**
9. **Detention:** the temporary care of a child alleged to be delinquent who requires secure custody in physically restricting facilities pending court disposition or execution of a court order.	**Holding in jail**
10. **Dispositional hearing:** a hearing held after the adjudicatory hearing in order to determine what order of disposition should be made concerning a child adjudicated as delinquent.	**Sentencing hearing**

TABLE 17.2 *Continued*

Juvenile Term	Adult Term
11. **Hearing:** the presentation of evidence to the juvenile court judge, his consideration of it, and his decision on disposition of the case.	**Trial**
12. **Petition:** an application for an order of court or for some other judicial action. Hence, a "delinquency petition" is an application for the court to act in the matter of a juvenile apprehended for a delinquent act.	**Accusation or indictment**
13. **Probation:** the supervision of a delinquent child after the court hearing but without commitment to a training school.	**Probation (with the same meaning)**
14. **Residential child-care facility:** A dwelling other than a detention or shelter-care facility, which provides living accommodations, care, treatment, and maintenance for children and youth and is licensed to provide such care. Such facilities include foster family homes, group homes, and halfway houses.	**Halfway house**
15. **Shelter:** the temporary care of a child in physically unrestricting facilities pending court disposition or execution of a court order for placement. Shelter care is used for dependent and neglected children and minors in need of supervision. Separate shelter-care facilities are also used for children apprehended for delinquency who need temporary shelter but not secure detention.	**Jail**
16. **Take into custody:** the act of the police in securing the physical custody of a child engaged in delinquency; avoids the stigma of the word *arrest*.	**Arrest**

The words *child*, *youth*, and *youngster* are used synonymously and denote a person of juvenile court age. Juvenile court laws define a *child* as any person under the specified age, no matter how mature or sophisticated he may seem. Juvenile jurisdiction in at least two-thirds of the states include children under eighteen; the others also include youngsters between the ages of eighteen and twenty-one.
Source: National Advisory Commission on Criminal Justice and Goals, *Corrections* (Washington, D.C.: U.S. Government Printing Office, 1973), p. 248; Ruth S. Cavan, *Juvenile Delinquency*, 2d ed. (New York: Lippincott, 1969), p. 367.

Categories of Juveniles _____

Essentially three kinds of children come into contact with the juvenile court system — a significant event in their lives. The children in two of these categories have committed no offense and are referred to today as *status offenders,* as their only problem is their *status.* They are either *dependent* (without family or support) or *neglected* (having a family situation that is harmful to them). The only category that involves an offense is the *delinquent juvenile.*

Dependent children are those who need the protection of the state to meet their basic life needs. Usually their parents have died, and they have no other adult relatives who can take care of them. In the early days of

America, these unfortunates were taken in by other families. Later, when their numbers increased, orphans and other dependent children gravitated to the growing cities, and various types of institutions were opened to handle them. Orphanages, common in the nineteenth century, are seldom found in America today. Some of the dependent children were kept in almshouses and other institutions, public and private, to give them food and shelter.

Dependent children now are wards of the state, subject to at least some control by the courts; whenever possible, these children are placed in foster homes. Neglected children have problems similar to those of dependent children. However, they need the protection of the state, not because their

Juveniles in Cages (Courtesy Justice Assistance Center)

parents are dead, but because their parents either mistreat or ignore them. Often these children are the victims of a tragic circumstance known as the *battered child syndrome*,[4] in which the parents' mental problems lead them to hurt their offspring. The child who is physically abused by a parent or guardian usually comes to the attention of the authorities through reports from neighbors, friends, or relatives. Even when badly abused, children are usually very loyal to their parents, and seldom report their neglect to the authorities. Sexual abuse by parents (incest) is also seldom reported by the young victims.

The care of neglected and dependent children is important, of course, but the juvenile courts were established primarily to handle delinquent juveniles. For judicial purposes, delinquents are divided into several categories. The first is composed of children who have allegedly committed an offense that would be a crime if it had been committed by an adult. This group makes up about 75 percent of the population of the state institutions for delinquent juveniles.

The second category of delinquents consists of those who have allegedly violated regulations that apply only to juveniles: curfew restrictions, required school attendance, and similar rules and ordinances. The third and last group is labeled the incorrigible juveniles (those who have been declared unmanageable by their parents and the court).[5] The second and third groups are often referred to as PINS (persons in need of supervision) or MINS (minors in need of supervision). Most concerned juvenile correctional officials would like to remove children in these PINS and MINS classifications (as well as status offenders) from the facilities designed primarily for the first category of delinquent juveniles.[6]

In addition to the three major categories of juveniles, the court may also have to deal with other children's problems such as adoption, termination of parents' rights, appointment of a guardian, custody in divorce, nonsupport, and related situations. It is this broad overreach of the juvenile court and the resultant conglomeration in juvenile dentention and correctional facilities that generates most of the attacks on the system. Juvenile facilities, though generally much more humane than the adult systems are, have had and still have many drawbacks.

Facilities for Juveniles

Schools built to house the homeless and dependent children who roamed the street of Europe in the nineteenth century became the model for many later establishments in the United States. In England, the Reformatory School Acts of 1854, 1857, and 1866 offered methods whereby courts could send offenders under the age of sixteen to reformatories and, later, to industrial schools. The New York City House of Refuge became the first real American response to the juvenile problem in 1825. These early efforts were prisonlike structures, and the courts were still allowed to send juvenile offenders to adult prisons instead if they so desired.[7] Juvenile institutions attempted to protect the children from the bad influence of the adult institutions, even though the system was crude and decentralized. Most of these schools were established by private organizations that recognized the need for special attention to both juvenile offenders and neglected or dependent children. The first cottage housing systems for juveniles, now the most popular systems, were founded in Massachusetts (1854) and Ohio (1858).[8] Not until 1899, however, in Chicago, was the juvenile court system coordinated within a political jurisdiction, as an integral part of the county's criminal justice system. Since that time, the juvenile court system has extended to cover every jurisdiction in the country, and a fairly standard pattern of juvenile confinement has ensued.

Detention Facilities

The main type of facility for juveniles is the detention "home" where juvenile victims of crime are often kept in the same facilities as are juvenile offenders, with the same treatment afforded to both, under *parens patriae*. There were over 400 short-term facilities in America, which admitted over 520,000 juveniles in 1985.[9] These figures, though only an estimate, suggest the enormity of the juvenile-detention problem. Even more tragic is the fact that most jurisdictions do not have enough youthful offenders to justify the construction of separate juvenile detention facilities, and so an estimated 1,708 juveniles are held in local jails and police lockups each year.[10] Many states have statutory provisions for the detention of juveniles in jails, as long as these prisoners are segregated from adult offenders. Some states have statutes or policies prohibiting the detention of juveniles in jails, but practical problems frequently require the violation of such statutes (see Table 17.3). Some 92,856 juveniles were admitted to jails in 1986.[11]

Facilities designated exclusively for juvenile detention are usually not the best examples of how an ideal juvenile correctional facility should be designed and operated. Most of these structures were originally built for some other purpose and converted to their present use with as little expenditure as possible. Most are overcrowded before they reach their rated capacities. In the adult institutions the emphasis is on custody, and the same preoccupation with security shapes the programs and the general environment in the juvenile detention facilities. Most of these programs are located in urban areas and are virtually sealed off from the community by their physical structure and other security measures. The youths are placed in dormitory-style housing, or single cells in some cases, often with the fixed furniture and dreary interiors that are typical of adult institutions. Most juvenile detention centers lack services and programs that

TABLE 17.3 Admissions and Discharges from Public Juvenile Facilities by Region and State

	Admissions	Discharges
United States, total	521,607	515,301
Northeast	41,638	40,730
Connecticut	1,704	1,678
Maine	784	777
Massachusetts	2,784	2,737
New Hampshire	847	847
New Jersey	13,649	13,024
New York	7,377	7,409
Pennsylvania	13,861	13,629
Rhode Island	632	629
Midwest	112,110	110.008
Illinois	16,111	15,562
Indiana	15,821	15,478
Iowa	2,725	2,677
Kansas	3,179	3,179
Michigan	13,318	12,966
Minnesota	8,640	8,462
Missouri	10,101	10,023
Nebraska	2,456	2,389
North Dakota	557	579
Ohio	32,737	32,372
South Dakota	1,598	1,575
Wisconsin	4,867	4,746
South	158,007	156,123
Alabama	7,512	7,197
Arkansas	1,919	1,906
Delaware	1,021	1,047
District of Columbia	6,012	5,819
Florida	32,462	32,154
Georgia	14,466	14,552
Kentucky	5,420	5,280
Louisiana	5,370	5,337
Maryland	8,653	8,491
Mississippi	4,642	4,660
North Carolina	4,392	4,368
Oklahoma	2,480	2,516
South Carolina	4,546	4,464
Tennessee	13,824	13,515
Texas	30,509	30,263
Virginia	13,405	13,164
West Virginia	1,374	1,390
West	209,852	208,440
Alaska	2,441	2,381
Arizona	10,636	10,470
California	133,462	132,619
Colorado	9,322	9,197
Hawaii	2,863	2,847
Idaho	1,176	1,173
Montana	478	421

TABLE 17.3 *Continued*

	Admissions	Discharges
Nevada	5,697	5,666
New Mexico	8,014	8,027
Oregon	7,965	8,067
Utah	5,414	5,374
Washington	22,107	21,931
Wyoming	277	267

Source: U.S. Department of Justice, Bureau of Justice Statistics, *Children in Custody*, Bulletin NCJ-102457 (Washington, DC: U.S. Department of Justice, October 1986), p. 3, Table 4.

might improve the residents' chances of staying away from crime. These juveniles are denied most of the good found in adult programs and are subject to the worst aspects of institutional programs. Twenty years ago, the National Advisory Commission on Criminal Justice Standards and Goals made specific recommendations with regard to juvenile detention facilities. These recommendations remain sound and deserve review:

1. The detention facility should be located in a residential area in the community and near court and community resources.
2. Population of detention centers should not exceed thirty residents. When population requirements significantly exceed this number, development of separate components under the network system should be pursued.
3. Living area capacities within the center should not exceed ten or twelve youngsters each. Only individual occupancy should be provided, with single rooms and programming regarded as essential. Individual rooms should be pleasant, adequately furnished, and homelike rather than punitive and hostile in atmosphere.
4. Security should not be viewed as in indispensable quality of the physical environment but should be based on a combination of staffing patterns, technological devices, and physical design.
5. Existing residential facilities within the community should be used in preference to new construction.
6. Facility programming should be based on investigation of community resources, with the contemplation of full use of these resources, prior to determination of the facility's in-house program requirements.
7. New construction and renovation of existing facilities should be based on consideration of the functional interrelationships between program activities and program participants.
8. Detention facilities should be coeducational and should have access to a full range of supportive programs, including education, library, recreation, arts and crafts, music, drama, writing, and entertainment. Outdoor recreational areas are essential.
9. Citizens advisory boards should be established to pursue development of in-house and community-based programs and alternatives to detention.
10. Planning should comply with pertinent state and federal regulations and the Environmental Policy Act of 1969.[12]

It would do well for administrators and legislators to dust off these documents and see where they stand two decades later in their implementation (see Table 17.4).

Training Schools

According to the 1985 *Census of Public Juvenile Facilities*, approximately 48,701 individual juveniles were housed within state and local government facilities on December 31, 1983, and 49,322 on December 31, 1985.[13] (See Table 17.5 for details.) The average cost for institutional confinement was $25,200 per resident per year, as shown by Table 17.6; cost comparisons are presented there state-by-state. When compared with approximately $8,000 for community residential facilities and less than $3,500 for foster home placement.[14], institutional confinement is expensive. The number of residents housed nationwide in publicly operated facilities for juveniles decreased by less than 700 individuals, or 1 percent, during the two-year

TABLE 17.4 Juveniles in Public Juvenile Facilities by Sex and Reason Held, United States, on February 1, 1985

	Total	Male	Female
Total	49,322	42,549	6,773
Juveniles detained or committed for			
Delinquent acts[a]	46,086	40,929	5,157
Violent	12,245	11,214	1,031
Murder, forcible rape, robbery and aggravated assault	8,656	8,096	560
Other	3,589	3,118	471
Property	22,020	19,978	2,042
Burglary, arson, larceny-theft, and motor vehicle theft	16,129	14,948	1,181
Other	5,891	5,030	861
Alcohol/drug offenses	2,660	2,319	341
Public order offenses	1,936	1,505	431
Probation violations	4,557	3,652	905
All other offenses[b]	2,668	2,261	407
Status offenses[c]	2,293	1,096	1,197
No·offenses[d]	644	364	280
Juveniles voluntarily admitted	299	160	139

[a] Acts that would be criminal if committed by adults.
[b] Includes unknown and unspecified offenses.
[c] Acts that would not be criminal for adults such as running away, truancy, and incorrigibility.
[d] Those held for dependency, neglect, abuse, emotional disturbance, or mental retardation.

Source: U.S. Department of Justice, Bureau of Justice Statistics, *Children in Custody*, Bulletin NCJ-102457 (Washington DC: U.S. Department of Justice, October 1986), p. 4, Table 6.

TABLE 17.5   Juveniles Held in Public Juvenile Facilities on February 1 by Demographic Characteristics and Adjudication Status, United States, 1983 and 1985.

	1983	1985
Total	48,701	49,322
Sex		
Male	42,182	42,549
Female	6,519	6,773
Race[a]		
White	27,805	29,969
Black	18,020	18,269
Other[b]	1,104	1,084
Ethnicity[a]		
Hispanic	5,727	6,551
Nonhispanic	41,202	42,771
Age on census data		
Total under 9 years	42	60
10 to 13 years	3,104	3,181
14 to 17 year	39,571	40,640
18 to 20 years	4,804	5,409
21 years and older	86	32
Not reported	1,094	0
Adjudication status		
Detained	13,156	14,474
Committed	35,178	34,549
Voluntarily admitted	367	299

[a] Excludes 1,772 cases for which race and ethnicity were not reported in 1983.
[b] American Indians, Alaskan natives, Asians, and Pacific Islanders.

Source: U.S. Department of Justice, Bureau of Justice Statistics, *Children in Custody*, Bulletin NCJ-102457 (Washington, DC: U.S. Department of Justice, October 1986), p. 3, Table 5.

TABLE 17.6   Number of Juvenile Public Facilities and Average Cost per Resident per Year

	Number of Facilities on February 1, 1985	Average Cost to House One Resident for One Year (1984)
United States, total	1,040	$25,200
Northeast	146	39,900
Connecticut	4	66,100
Maine	1	25,400
Massachusetts	9	39,500
New Hampshire	2	30,000
New Jersey	54	26,300
New York	39	52,600
Pennsylvania	35	44,000
Rhode Island	32	35,900

TABLE 17.6 *Continued*

	Number of Facilities on February 1, 1985	Average Cost to House One Resident for One Year (1984)
Midwest	278	26,100
Illinois	20	24,100
Indiana	33	17,800
Iowa	13	29,200
Kansas	12	28,800
Michigan	52	35,900
Minnesota	19	39,100
Missouri	43	22,900
Nebraska	4	21,900
North Dakota	3	27,000
Ohio	65	22,600
South Dakota	5	16,800
Wisconsin	9	29,000
South	381	22,700
Alabama	23	19,100
Arkansas	5	22,400
Delaware	4	21,800
District of Columbia	4	33,700
Florida	53	15,200
Georgia	26	24,100
Kentucky	39	25,200
Louisiana	13	21,900
Maryland	18	16,800
Mississippi	8	15,700
North Carolina	25	28,200
Oklahoma	12	54,000
South Carolina	12	35,200
Tennessee	21	20,800
Texas	54	22,100
Virginia	59	26,100
West Virginia	5	23,200
West	235	22,900
Alaska	4	46,700
Arizona	17	21,900
California	109	21,300
Colorado	12	28,100
Hawaii	3	29,900
Idaho	3	43,100
Montana	7	27,400
Nevada	8	28,500
New Mexico	11	19,200
Oregon	14	25,100
Utah	15	32,000
Washington	30	29,300
Wyoming	2	22,400

Source: U.S. Department of Justice, Bureau of Justice Statistics, *Children in Custody*, Bulletin NCJ-102457 (Washington, DC: U.S. Department of Justice, October 1986), p. 5, Table 10.

period ending December 31, 1985. There were 1,040 public juvenile facilities at the end of 1984, four out of ten of which could be classified as "open" as opposed to "institutionalized."

The issue of whether it is productive to place juveniles in institutions is being hotly debated in correctional circles. One state has closed all of its juvenile institutions,[15] and others are phasing them out as soon as is practical.[16] Various Supreme Court decisions in the 1960s and 1970s and subsequent court orders in the 1980s have influenced the programs of the state training schools to some extent, but many continue to do "business as usual."

Institutions provide the most expensive and least successful method of handling juvenile offenders (see Figure 17-1). But until the services needed for supervision and treatment in the community are forthcoming, judges often have no other choice but to commit offenders. The junior prisons are not all bad, but the custody philosophy is the prevailing model, and it creates the same problem at this level as at the adult level. The dangers that these institutions present to the civil rights of the juvenile offender were forcefully brought to public attention in a series of landmark court decisions, outlined in the next section.

Learning is Often a One-on-One Situation With Kids (Courtesy Justice Assistance Center)

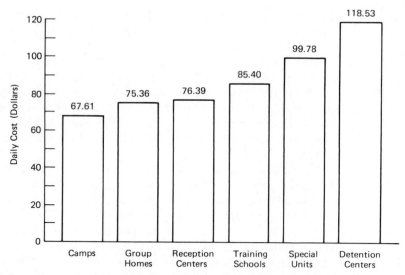

Figure 17-1   Average Daily Cost per Juvenile by Type of Facility (George and Camille Camp. *The Corrections Yearbook* [South Salem, NY: Criminal Justice Institute, 1987], p. 62)

The Legal Rights of Juveniles

The "new" court system, which was over one hundred years in coming, defined all procedures of the juvenile courts as civil rather than criminal. (*Civil* suits relate to and affect only individual wrongs, whereas *criminal* prosecutions involve public wrongs.) It is evident, therefore, that the greatest effort in the juvenile justice system has been aimed at creating a separate court system for youths and delinquents. This separate system and the perpetuation of the doctrine of *parens patriae* have resulted in a system that has largely ignored the legal rights of juveniles. Those rights accorded adults, such as the right to a speedy trial, the right to trial by jury, the right to bail, the right to confront one's accusers, and the right to protection from self-incrimination,[17] were seen as unnecessary for juveniles.

However, as the rights of adults were being pursued, as in *Miranda* v. *Arizona,* some court decisions did have a bearing on juvenile rights. The decision in *Gideon* v. *Wainwright,* 372 U.S. 335 (1963), set the stage for legislation regarding due process. Although concerned with the right to legal counsel in adult, noncapital felony cases, several states have required that indigent children who request counsel be so provided and at public expense. *Gault* established this as a right for juveniles.

Some Landmark Cases

In the landmark opinions in *Kent* v. *United States,* 383 U.S. 541 (1966), and *In re Gault,* 387 U.S. 1 (1967), the Supreme Court at long last evaluated juvenile court proceedings and children's constitutionally guaranteed rights. In *Kent* v. *United States,* the Court noted that the child involved in certain juvenile court proceedings was deprived of constitutional rights and at the same time not given the rehabilitation promised under earlier juvenile court philosophy and statutes. It pointed out that "there may be grounds for concern that the child receives the worst of both worlds."[18]

In the *Kent* case, the Court did not have occasion to pass directly on the right to counsel and the notice of this right because the juvenile involved had been given counsel within twenty-four hours of his arrest. The next year, however, the Supreme Court did have occasion to render a decision on these rights in *In re Gault.* On May 15, 1967, the Supreme Court rendered its first decision in the area of juvenile delinquency procedure. Gerald Gault allegedly made a telephone call to a woman living in his neighborhood, during which he used some obscene words and phrases. The use of a telephone for such purpose violated an Arizona statute, and hence Gerald, aged sixteen, was subject to adjudication as a juvenile delinquent. The adjudication was in fact made after a proceeding in which he was not offered the basic procedural protections to which he would have been entitled had he been charged in a criminal court. In this decision, Justice Abraham Fortas ruled that a child alleged to be a juvenile delinquent had at least the following rights:

1. Right to notice of the charges in time to prepare for trial.
2. Right to counsel.
3. Right to confrontation and cross-examination of his or her accusers.
4. Privilege against self-incrimination, at least in court.

The *Gault* decision ended the presumption that the juvenile courts were beyond the scope or purview of due process protection. The primary lesson learned here was that juvenile courts would have to become courts of law and follow standard procedures concerning the constitutional rights of those on whom they passed judgment. *In re Gault* did, however, fail to answer one question: whether a juvenile must be advised of his or her rights at some point in the pre-judicial stage. When serious offenses are involved and the juvenile might be transferred to an adult criminal court, some police forces are giving such warnings.

Some states like California apply, as a general rule, *Miranda*[19] restrictions to juvenile interrogation. In another case related to the *Gault* decision, *In re Winship,* 397 U.S. 358 (1970) the Supreme Court held that to justify a court finding of delinquency against a juvenile, the proof must be beyond a reasonable doubt that the juvenile committed the alleged delinquent act. Before this case, the requirement seemed to be that the judge be influenced only by a preponderance of evidence against the accused delinquent.

Finally, the Supreme Court agreed to hear arguments about whether juveniles had a constitutional right to a jury trial. In *McKeiver* v. *Pennsylvania,* 403 U.S. 528 (1971), implying that the due process standard of "fundamental fairness" applied, the Court rejected the concept of trial by jury for juveniles. The Court contended that the "juvenile proceeding has not yet been held to be a 'criminal prosecution' within the meaning and reach of the Sixth Amendment. . . ."[20] The Supreme Court stated that it was as yet unwilling to "remake the juvenile proceeding into a full adversary process" and put "an effective end to what has been the idealistic prospect of an intimate, informal protective proceeding."[21] The Court concluded by encouraging the states to "seek in new and different ways the elusive answers to the young."[22]

The Supreme Court has not been the only source of change in the area of juvenile rights. Federal acts and legislation have also played an important role. For example, until the Uniform Juvenile Court Act of 1968, a child could still be taken into custody by police or others in a situation in which the Fourth Amendment would have exempted an adult. The Uniform Juvenile Court Act therefore set some limits on nondiscriminatory home removals of children. It provides for the removal of a child from his or her home only if there are reasonable grounds to believe that the child is suffering from illness or injury or is in immediate danger from the environment and that removal from that environment, therefore, is necessary.

In 1974, the U.S. Congress passed the Juvenile Justice and Delinquency Prevention Act (Public Law 93-415). This act requires

> a comprehensive assessment regarding the effectiveness of the existing juvenile justice system. This legislation also provides the impetus for developing and implementing innovative alternatives to prevent juvenile delinquency and to divert status offenders from the criminal justice system. The intent of the Act is to clearly identify those youth who are victimized or otherwise troubled but have not committed criminal offenses and to divert such youth from institutionalization. Simultaneously this will promote the utilization of resources within the juvenile justice system to more effectively deal with youthful criminal offenders.[23]

It appears, then, that the courts and the legislative bodies (state and federal) are still reluctant to allow children to be treated as the legal equals of adults. As a doctrine, *parens patriae* is as firmly entrenched as was the earlier doctrine to treat delinquent children by having them whipped and put to bed without supper.

Juveniles do not have full protection under the law, and their constitutional rights are being violated. However, once equitable protection is recognized, then delinquents will have to be considered (in most cases) criminally responsible for their misbehavior. Equal protection under the law can work both ways. Present juvenile court procedures, though denying some rights to juveniles, do, nevertheless, extend to them certain privileges and immunities not afforded to adults. A new legal system for juveniles will of necessity imply trade-offs of these immunities in return for the granting of full constitutional rights.

Procedural Rights

As a result of the Supreme Court cases mentioned earlier, the juvenile court is now a court of law. Most procedural guarantees are therefore mandatory, as stated in the due process provisions of the Fourteenth Amendment of the Constitution, which protect the rights of the accused. Procedural rights are rights pertaining to statutory laws and are accorded to juveniles during the fact-finding process of a juvenile case. Such rights range from the right to a trial by jury (not yet a reality) to the right to legal counsel. The Supreme Court's decisions regarding juveniles have thus far dealt with only the procedural rights of children.

Procedural rights accorded juveniles in court are still lagging behind those of adults. The *McKeiver* decision, which declared that the concept of due process in juvenile court proceedings does not include the right to a jury trial, is the most significant of these. Thus far, the procedural rights guaranteed to juveniles in court proceedings are (1) the right to adequate notice of charges against him or her; (2) the right to counsel and to have counsel provided if the child is indigent; (3) the right to confrontation and cross-examination of witnesses; (4) the right to refuse to do anything that would be self-incriminatory; (5) the right to a judicial hearing, with counsel, prior to the transfer of a juvenile to an adult court;[24] and (6) the right to be considered innocent until proven guilty beyond a reasonable doubt.

Right of Notice of Charges. The *Gault* case established that a juvenile has a constitutional right to be given a timely notice of the charges against him or her. This is required in order to give the juvenile's defense counsel adequate time to prepare for the trial.[25] To provide this timely notice, most states use a summons. A *summons* is the legal instrument to give notice to the acccused of the proceedings against him or her.

Gault held that the due process requirements of notice in juvenile court proceedings were to be the same as in other criminal or civil proceedings.

Right to Counsel. In *Gault*, it was held that the accused juvenile has the right to counsel. Counsel may be of the person's own choosing or may be appointed by the court for financial or other reasons. By the time the *Gault* decision was made, several states had already taken steps to provide legal counsel for juveniles. Since *Gault*, the regular participation of defense counsel in juvenile court has become commonplace. However, whether the juvenile uses private or assigned counsel, such defense counsels are likely to be unfamiliar with the proceedings of a juvenile court, for many will have had only civil court experience. Notice of the juvenile's right to counsel must be clearly understood by both the child and the family and should be given both in writing and orally. This notice contains two important elements: (1) the child and/or parents may be represented by counsel (2) if they cannot afford and therefore cannot employ counsel, the child and parents are, in the absence of a competent waiver, entitled to be represented by counsel at public expense.

Procedures direct that notice of the right to counsel shall be given to the child and parents at the first intake interview, or when the child is admitted to a detention center or shelter-care facility. Counsel should be given to children whenever possible. No simple action holds more potential for achieving procedural justice for the juvenile in court than does legal representation.

Rights of Confrontation and Cross-examination. The juvenile's right to confront and to cross-examine hostile witnesses was upheld in *In re Gault*. Most states apply this ruling to only the first phase of the criminal court proceedings—that is, to that part dealing with the determination of one's guilt or innocence. However, many statutes and cases allow the juvenile the right of confrontation and cross-examination at dispositional hearings at which the second phase of criminal court proceedings is carried out, designed to determine appropriate sentencing. For example, in *Strode* v. *Brorby*,[26] a commitment order that would have sent a boy to an industrial school rather than place him on probation was reserved. The court ruled that the juvenile had been refused the opportunity to present witnesses in his favor who would have testified that he deserved probation rather than institutionalization.

Right of Privilege against Self-incrimination. The Fifth Amendment right to remain silent (that is, the privilege against self-incrimination) is the last entitlement conferred upon juveniles by the *Gault* decision. The Court concluded that the constitutional privilege against self-incrimination is as applicable in juvenile cases as it is in adult cases.

If the juvenile court judge in the *Gault* case had reached a decision as to Gerald Gault's guilt based on Gault's own admissions, it would have been based on admissions obtained without regard to his privilege against self-incrimination. In ruling on the *Gault* decision, Justice Abraham Fortas obviously felt that juvenile court judges should not be influenced by confessions, admissions, and like acts that may have been obtained under dubious circumstances and without regard to the provisions of the Fifth Amendment.

Right to a Judicial Hearing. In 1966, *Kent* v. *United States*[27] was argued in the U.S. Supreme Court, raising the issue of whether juveniles receive less legal protection than adults do.

The Supreme Court ruled that the lower court decision on the waiver of this right was unconstitutional. It found that: (1) in waiver of jurisdiction, a hearing must be granted; (2) assistance of counsel at such hearings must be granted; (3) the plaintiff's counsel must have access to social service records; and (4) a statement of the facts of the full investigation and a statement of the judge's reasons for waiver must accompany the waiver. In making this ruling, the Court emphasized that although juvenile court procedures were still civil in nature and that consequently juveniles were not entitled to all the protections given to adult criminals, waiver hearings must still provide all of the protections implied in the Fourteenth Amendment's due process clause.

Right of Proof beyond a Reasonable Doubt. In 1970, in the *Winship* case, the Supreme Court held that juveniles were entitled to have accusations and/or charges against them proven beyond a reasonable doubt. Twelve-year-old Samuel Winship was adjudicated delinquent as the result of a theft of $112 from a woman's purse. Consequently, he was committed to a training school for one and one-half years, subject to annual extensions of commitment, until his eighteenth birthday. The case was appealed to the New York Court of Appeals and was upheld by that court. The Supreme Court, however, later reversed that decision. The Supreme Court contended that the loss of liberty is no less significant for a juvenile than for an adult. Therefore, no juvenile may be deprived of his or her individual liberty of evidence less precise than that required to deprive an adult of his or her individual liberty. With this ruling the Court mandated that the criminal law burden—rather than the traditionally less stringent civil law burden of the mere preponderance of all evidence—is applicable in juvenile cases.

As in adult cases, the defense now has an advantage over the prosecution in regard to the burden of proof. The prosecution must prove every allegation with facts, whereas the defense merely has to raise a reasonable doubt.[28]

Right to Trial by Jury. As stated earlier, the Supreme Court held, in *McKeiver* v. *Pennsylvania* (1971), that due process of law does not require a jury in juvenile court trials. However, the Supreme Court was careful to note that there "is nothing to prevent a juvenile court judge in a particular case where he feels the need, or when the need is demonstrated, from using an advisory jury."[29]

Jury trials for juveniles in most cases, however, are the exception rather than the rule, unless a motion specifically requesting the statutory provision of a trial by jury is made in the court jurisdiction in which the case is to be heard.[30] Until the door is opened wide to jury trials for juveniles accused of crimes, young people will not receive fair treatment through procedural rights in the courts and will remain the second-class citizens that so many persons in the juvenile justice system feel they are.

In addition to procedural rights in court, juveniles do have certain other procedural rights within the various stages of the juvenile justice system, to include arrest, interrogation, detention, and bail.

The Supreme Court has not yet considered the question of whether the constitutional rights of individuals who come into contact with police (for questioning, temporary detainment, arrest, or other perceived intrusions upon their freedom) also apply to juveniles. However, many courts, police departments, and legislatures assume that they do. It has been reported that there is a trend to amend juvenile court acts to extend arrest laws to juveniles,[31] and the Uniform Juvenile Court Act does include a section regarding search and seizure.[32]

Arrest. Many states, though they do not consider the taking of a child into custody by police an arrest, do require that this act be legal under the state and federal constitutions.[36] Since the *Gault* decision, many courts have required that the police have probable cause before taking a child into custody as a suspect in a criminal act. "In the near future, courts will have to decide whether the taking of a juvenile into custody for noncriminal misbehavior, ungovernability, is subject to these or other standards. Certainly, there are some constitutional limitations on how the police handle problem children."[33]

Though laws applicable to the arrest of adults may be applicable to the arrest (or taking into custody) of juveniles, provisions found in juvenile acts relating to detention, custody, and interrogation may differ decidedly from those accorded adults.

Interrogation. The issue of whether warnings (*Miranda* decision) must be given at the interrogation of a juvenile suspect has yet to be decided by the Supreme Court. As noted earlier, the *Gault* decision gives the accused juvenile the right to refuse to give self-incriminating evidence; however, this privilege has generally been applied to court proceedings only. In fact, the Supreme Court in the *Gault* decision declined to discuss the questioning of juveniles by the police.

The Supreme Court concluded that the very fact of custodial interrogation exacts a heavy toll on individual liberty and trades on the weakness of individuals. If the Court felt this way about confessions abstracted from adults, they logically would be even more sensitive to those obtained from juveniles. If, according to *Miranda,* an individual does not knowingly waive his or her constitutional privilege against self-incrimination, then the police cannot submit that person to custodial interrogation.

To summarize, several courts have already taken the position that a confession or statement of guilt by a juvenile during pre-judicial investigation (interrogation by police or probation officers) is not admissible in court unless the juvenile has previously been notified of the right to remain silent and the right to counsel and knowingly waives those rights. This implies, therefore, that there are efforts to bind police officers to procedures similar to those used in adult arrests. Procedures that are just like those of the adult system may not be the answer in the juvenile system.

Anthony Travisono, long-time executive director of the American Correctional Association, echoes the opinion that organizations should stress prevention as the best course for juveniles:

> It makes more sense to intervene now, while there is still time, with a healthy dose of care and concern. We can teach them to read, educate them, give them jobs, and offer them counseling. But the best thing we can do for them now is show we care about them, prove that society has not given up on them, and demonstrate that they are capable of assuming the responsibilities of adulthood. If we do these things, some of them will change, and the tide could turn.
>
> Prevention—not corrections—is still society's best defense. Correctional professionals need to communicate this thought to politicians and community leaders as often as possible. Even though it often seems that our voice is not being heard, we should continue to speak out because, as we say among ourselves when we meet, "who knows better than we do?"[35]

By following this policy, police forces will be in tune with the current practices regarding the needs to help the juvenile offender, if possible, and still protect a juvenile's legal rights and will thereby be offering the juvenile fair treatment.

Detention and Bail. Since the decision to detain a juvenile before court proceedings affects the way the court will later see that child, it is important that this decision be arrived at fairly. Placing a juvenile in a detention facility simply because he or she has no place else to go, for example, appears to be a questionable practice, especially in light of the potential harm it may cause the juvenile. Also, statutory law and appellate courts in some states require that a juvenile be given a formal detention hearing with the right to confront and cross-examine the witnesses.[36]

There are many factors to be considered in regard to bail for juveniles. For example, where does a fourteen-year-old teen-ager get the money for bail, especially when his or her parents cannot pay it? Would the right to bail simply widen the gap between justice for the rich and justice for the poor? Bail is a constitutional guarantee in most adult cases, and the disparity between rich and poor exists there. The adult who posts bail usually suffers if he or she skips bail, especially if the bail money was his or her own or a friend's or a relative's. Would a juvenile feel any responsibility to the person who put up the money to ensure the child's temporary freedom? Would bail bondsmen be willing to provide bail money for indigent juveniles, especially those who receive no financial support from their parents?

These and other questions will have to be considered in devising a system of bail for juveniles accused of criminal acts, especially if the courts rule in favor of this provision as a constitutional right for juveniles. A ruling to this effect appears imminent in light of the current trend in the area of juvenile rights. Will the juvenile justice system be prepared to implement the provisions of a such a ruling? It will have to be if the juvenile is to move closer to full protection under the Constitution.

The Correctional Funnel for Juveniles _____

In Chapter 7, we saw the dramatic effects of the correctional funnel in the adult system. A similar process is at work in the juvenile system, along with a number of other factors. The problem is sometimes referred to as *hidden delinquency.* In an attempt to get to the bottom of this problem, the Law Enforcement Assistance Administration set aside $10 million for research projects on the diversion of juveniles from the system. Figure 17-2 illustrates the funnel effect. The rising number of juvenile offenders and offense rates are shown in Table 17.7, covering the years

TABLE 17.7 Number and Confinement Rate (per 100,000 Juveniles) of Juveniles in Public Juvenile Facilities

Region and State	Number of Juveniles			Number of Juveniles in Custody per 100,000 Juveniles in Population		
	1983	1985	Percent Change	1983	1985	Percent Change
United States, total	48,701	49,322	1%	176	185	5%
Northeast	5,335	5,015	− 6	99	99	0
Connecticut	163	202	24	56	74	32
Maine	208	242	16	137	167	22
Massachusetts	143	187	31	23	32	39
New Hampshire	138	152	10	111	127	14
New Jersey	1,775	1,508	−15	184	166	−10
New York	1,708	1,516	−11	104	98	− 6
Pennsylvania	1,082	1,060	− 2	73	76	4
Rhode Island	118	148	25	100	133	33
Midwest	11,456	11,382	− 1	159	166	4
Illinois	1,621	1,534	− 5	127	126	− 1
Indiana	1,157	1,334	15	160	193	21
Iowa	377	399	6	101	112	11
Kansas	636	651	2	222	233	5
Michigan	1,754	1,733	− 1	163	170	4
Minnesota	678	634	− 6	127	125	− 2
Missouri	878	815	− 7	166	158	− 5
Nebraska	250	269	8	126	140	11

TABLE 17.7 *Continued*

North Dakota	108	94	−13	126	111	−12
Ohio	3,160	3,058	− 3	225	230	2
South Dakota	174	193	11	195	222	14
Wisconsin	663	668	1	105	112	7
South	15,318	14,905	− 3	162	162	0
Alabama	716	680	− 5	135	133	− 1
Arkansas	288	274	− 5	95	93	− 2
Delaware	253	190	−25	329	264	15
District of Columbia	360	281	−22	554	461	−17
Florida	2,161	2,179	1	183	189	3
Georgia	1,261	1,053	−16	190	161	−15
Kentucky	650	609	− 6	132	130	− 2
Louisiana	1,469	1,188	−19	274	200	−27
Maryland	1,201	1,377	15	214	263	23
Mississippi	423	410	− 3	114	114	0
North Carolina	724	798	10	125	142	14
Oklahoma	468	314	−33	117	80	−32
South Carolina	696	647	− 7	184	175	− 5
Tennessee	1,047	1,128	8	174	195	12
Texas	1,936	2,209	14	110	125	14
Virginia	1,523	1,456	− 4	219	218	− 1
West Virginia	142	112	−21	55	45	−18
West	16,592	18,020	9	297	327	10
Alaska	159	201	26	265	314	18
Arizona	632	905	43	170	244	44
California	11,559	12,524	8	390	430	10
Colorado	561	581	4	148	156	5
Hawaii	144	149	3	117	123	5
Idaho	186	118	−37	140	87	−38
Montana	193	204	6	184	198	8
Nevada	419	451	8	395	425	8
New Mexico	453	511	13	237	275	16
Oregon	712	702	− 1	218	222	2
Utah	155	170	10	70	73	4
Washington	1,252	1,342	7	237	260	10
Wyoming	167	162	− 3	226	231	2

Source: U.S. Department of Justice, Bureau of Justice Statistics, *Children in Custody,* Bulletin NCJ-102457 (Washington, DC: U.S. Department of Justice, October 1986), p. 2, Table 2.

1983 to 1985, the most recent figures available as this text goes to press. These show a clear flattening trend. As more of the status offenders are removed from the juvenile process, these rates should decline, but the serious offenses can be expected to continue according to the trends now indicated.

The Direction of Juvenile Justice _____

Disenchantment with and criticisms of the *parens patriae* juvenile court and its procedures have been voiced by voluntary organizations, private

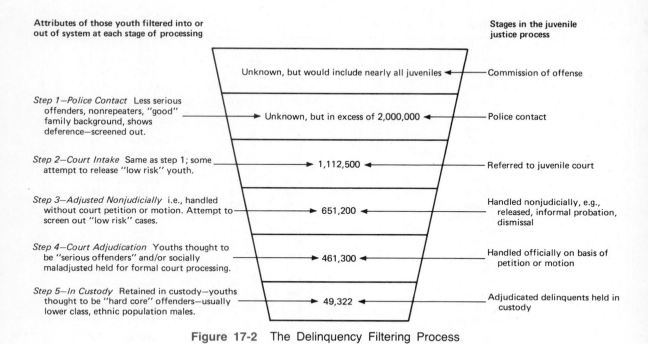

Attributes of those youth filtered into or out of system at each stage of processing

Stages in the juvenile justice process

Unknown, but would include nearly all juveniles ◄——— Commission of offense

Step 1—Police Contact Less serious offenders, nonrepeaters, "good" family background, shows deference—screened out. ——► Unknown, but in excess of 2,000,000 ◄——— Police contact

Step 2—Court Intake Same as step 1; some attempt to release "low risk" youth. ——► 1,112,500 ◄——— Referred to juvenile court

Step 3—Adjusted Nonjudicially i.e., handled without court petition or motion. Attempt to screen out "low risk" cases. ——► 651,200 ◄——— Handled nonjudicially, e.g., released, informal probation, dismissal

Step 4—Court Adjudication Youths thought to be "serious offenders" and/or socially maladjusted held for formal court processing. ——► 461,300 ◄——— Handled officially on basis of petition or motion

Step 5—In Custody Retained in custody—youths thought to be "hard core" offenders—usually lower class, ethnic population males. ——► 49,322 ◄——— Adjudicated delinquents held in custody

Figure 17-2   The Delinquency Filtering Process

nonprofit organizations, the judiciary, and the bar, practitioners, researchers, and the federal government, among others. Such efforts, coupled with the major decisions of the U.S. Supreme Court, have led to four major trends in the handling of juveniles; *diversion*, *decriminalization*, *removal of status offenders*, and *decarceration*.

Diversion

The due process model that we have noted is derived from the *Gault*, *Winship*, and *Kent* cases, by defining those constitutionally guaranteed rights that must be accorded to every citizen, whether adult or juvenile. The differences between costs at the various levels of custodial care are shown earlier in Figure 17-1.

DIVERSION

The official halting or suspension, at any legally prescribed processing point after a recorded justice system entry, of formal juvenile (or criminal) proceedings against an alleged offender, and referral of that person to a treatment or care program administered by a nonjustice agency or private agency. Sometimes no referral is given.

Recently, there has been a trend toward the diversion of juveniles. Diversion programs function to divert juveniles out of the juvenile justice system, encourage the use of existing private correctional agencies and facilities for such youths, and avoid formal contact with the juvenile court. These programs include remedial education programs, foster homes, group homes, and local counseling facilities and centers (see Figure 17-3). The effectiveness of such programs has not yet been demonstrated, but Rausch and Logan summarized the existing studies and concluded as follows:

> One common component to all rationales for diversion seem to be that *less* intervention is better than *more* intervention. Thus whatever else it involves, diversion necessarily implies an attempt to make the form of social control

Type	Facilities		Population	
	Number	Percent	Number	Percent
Detention Centers	74	11.6	1,394	4.3
Training Schools	126	19.6	21,929	67.3
Ranches	75	11.7	2,668	8.2
Group Homes	243	37.9	2,329	7.1
Special Security & Treatment Centers	94	14.7	2,423	7.4
Separate R&D Centers	29	4.5	1,834	5.6

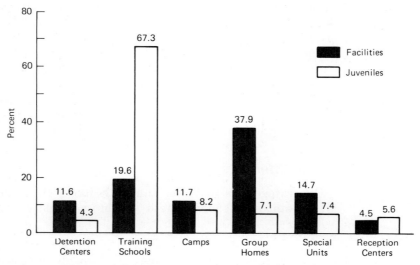

Figure 17-3 Types of Facilities and Juveniles Confined in Them on January 1, 1987 (George and Camille Camp, *The Corrections Yearbook* [South Salem, NY: Criminal Justice Institute, 1987], p. 61)

more limited in scope. Studies of diversion programs . . . indicate that instead of limiting the scope of the system, diversion programs often broaden it. They do this by either intensifying services or by taking in more cases. The latter is referred to as a "widening of the net" effect.[37]

Decriminalization

The principal aim in the juvenile and criminal justice systems is to remove from the scope of law and social control certain types of currently proscribed behaviors that pose little perceived danger to society. These behaviors are frequently seen as "deviant" rather than illegal and thus "not the law's business." Decriminalization is an "official act generally accomplished by legislation, in which an act or omission, formerly criminal, is made non-criminal without punitive sanctions."[38] The decriminalization movement, then, would delete deviant behavior from juvenile laws and proceedings and leave to social agencies the task of providing assistance if and when requested. Treatment under the decriminalization theory would be on a voluntary basis.

The types of acts to be decriminalized vary among the proponents of decriminalization. Adultery, homosexuality between consenting adults in private (as in the Netherlands and California), fornication (frequently termed *unruliness* in female juveniles), prostitution (as in France and Holland), drunkenness, and social gambling are frequently identified as deviant acts by adults that should be decriminalized.[39] In the juvenile area, these are largely status offenses. The crucial difference is that decriminalization calls for repeal of the legal rules defining status offenses and delinquencies,[40] rather than the diversion of status offenders to alternative service agencies. Social control would still exist; treatment would not be voluntary; and the juvenile court would retain some jurisdiction (forcing noncooperative juveniles to reappear before the juvenile court judge) for noncompliance if status offenses were not decriminalized. Although decriminalization may be a more logical response to the problem of the status offender, court administrators, probation officers, and even parents ("teach the brat a lesson") have vested interests in maintaining the juvenile court's scope of authority.[41] Decriminalization seems to be a policy whose time has come.

Status Offenders

One category of juveniles that falls under the aegis of the juvenile court is the status offender. These youths commit offenses that would not be

---

DECRIMINALIZATION
An act removing from statutes any formerly forbidden or required behavior. Generally accomplished by a legislature, such formal action removes criminal penalties from statutes.

STATUS OFFENSE

Behavior or conduct that is an offense only when committed by a juvenile. A status offender would be one so designated by adjudication by a judicial officer of a juvenile court.

crimes if committed by an adult, according to the statutes or ordinances of the jurisdiction in which the offense was committed, and that are specifically applicable to them because of their status as juveniles. Status offenses include ungovernability, running away, unruliness, school truancy, disregard for or abuse of lawful parental authority, repeated use of alcoholic beverages, and so on. Approximately one-third of the 600,000 children in 1971 being held in detention prior to a court hearing were status offenders.[42]

The Institute of Juvenile Administration of the American Bar Association, a national standards-setting organization, recommended the following:

1. A juvenile's acts of misbehavior, ungovernability, or unruliness which do not violate the criminal law should not constitute a ground for asserting juvenile court jurisdiction over the juvenile committing them.
2. Any law enforcement officer who reasonably determines that a juvenile is in circumstances which constitute a substantial and immediate danger to the juvenile's physical safety may, if the juvenile's physical safety requires such action, take the juvenile into limited custody (subject to the limitations of this part).[43]

These recommendations reflect the earlier intent of the Juvenile Justice and Delinquency Prevention Act (JJDPA) to divert status offenders to shelter facilities, rather than juvenile detention centers or jails, as well as not to detain or confine status offenders in any institution in which they would have regular contact with adult offenders.

The Juvenile Justice and Delinquency Prevention Act of 1974, as amended through 1980, directs the Office of Juvenile Justice and Delinquency Prevention (OJJDP) to encourage programs to divert minor juvenile offenders from formal police and court processing, to substitute nonsecure community-based facilities for secure confinement, and to assist in the development of local youth services that reabsorb delinquents into the normal community life. One of the Act's directives was to discontinue the use of juvenile detention of correctional facilities for youths charged with status offenses.[44]

Despite the massive research, funding, and efforts to keep juveniles out of adult jails, there were 1,629 juveniles locked up in adult jails at mid-year 1985.[45] Even though the effort to remove status offenders from the juvenile court system may be bearing fruit, the attempt to keep them out of adult jails has not yet been successful.

A Classroom in a Modern Juvenile Institution (Courtesy of American Correctional Association, photo by Jefferson Youth Center)

Decarceration

The concept of juvenile decarceration is recent, as 1969 is seen as the birth date of this movement. In that year, Jerome Miller was appointed youth commissioner for Massachusetts. His opinion was that training schools were receiving the failures of every social agency that had a responsibility for youths: families, schools, welfare and health care agencies, and mental health and social service agencies. He asserted that the era of involuntary confinement of juveniles in large correctional institutions was over and that an age of more humane, decent, and community-based care for delinquents had begun. In a few short years, he closed the major institutions in Massachusetts, placing one thousand of his charges in small group homes; and using existing community-based correctional services and private agencies ("vendors") to handle the delinquents in that state. (Currently only Vermont does not have *any* juvenile institutions.)

Critics of the deinstitutionalization movement became exasperated, and the policy entered the realm of partisan politics. Miller's peers, Massachusetts juvenile correctional personnel, unions, and the media first expressed concern and then dismay. Earlier program evaluators found higher recidivism rates for the decarcerated group than for earlier juveniles processed through the correctional units. Later, however, these evaluators were satisfied that community corrections did not require the sacrifice of public protection.[46]

In 1980, a new governor of Massachusetts, Michael Dukakis, pledged to crack down on the burgeoning juvenile crime and appointed a task force on juvenile crime.[47] The "dreadful swing of the penal pendulum" had occurred.[48] In reality, "an outbreak of lawfulness" had begun, and juvenile crime was dropping in most Massachusetts jurisdictions: there was scant evidence to support the contention of increasing juvenile crime.[49]

As anticipated, the Massachusetts governor's task force on juvenile crime recommended construction of additional secure beds, greatly increased judicial sentencing discretion, mandatory sentences for certain categories of delinquents, and easing of the criteria for transferring juveniles to stand trial in adult courts.[50] Later published outcome studies indicated that the violent recidivists actually increased the seriousness of their later crimes when subjected to a secure setting! Proponents of the Massachusetts decarceration movement noted that the initial placements in the early years had overwhelmed the ability of private vendors to care for their charges. They also found that the administrators of the Massachusetts Department of Youth Services had failed to assume effective control over and to manage the complicated system of private-sector treatment programs, a failure of imagination and leadership. The main source of the control problems, they argued, appeared to be the private-sector agencies under contract to the Department of Youth Services, as they had become increasingly selective about intake cases, being quick to reject those juveniles believed to be potentially disruptive or runaways or to cause other problems.[51] Benedict Alper observed, "The measures which governments are taking can only be described as child abuse on a massive, unprecedented scale."[52] The debate over decarceration continues.

The Washington State Experience: Accountability _____

In 1978, the state of Washington's new juvenile court legislation became effective, representing a radical shift in the United States from the *parens patriae* philosophy and objectives of the juvenile court system. The new law adopts the adversarial procedure and philosophy found in the adult criminal justice system of American law. Schram and Schneider described the new model:

> Among its many provisions, the new legislation requires juvenile courts to formalize their procedures, extends to juveniles the same due process available to adults in criminal proceedings (with the exception of trial by jury), institutes methods to prove accountability for diversion at various points in the juvenile justice system, and creates formal, accountability-based diversion systems. In addition, the code mandates that punishment for violations of crim-

inal statutes are to be guided by presumptive sentencing standards that are based on the seriousness of the crime committed and the culpability (age and prior offense history) of juvenile offenders.[53]

Included in this codification are provisions that mandate and formalize new responsibilities and functions for the juvenile justice system actors: police, prosecutors, judges, and juveniles. Though it is not possible to define here in great detail the many new proceedings and rights, the law stresses accountability: to make the juvenile offenders accountable for their criminal behavior and to provide a punishment commensurate with the crime, prior criminal history, and age. Preliminary evaluation research indicates that the diversion components of the legislation had a tremendous impact, and about one-half of the juvenile cases were diverted. Further, the probability of confinement as a sanction increased significantly. Courts were more likely to hold juveniles accountable for their behavior than previously. More importantly, status offenders were effectively removed from the juvenile court.

The shift in Washington may signal a new movement in the juvenile justice field. Time and further research will indicate the effectiveness of these innovations.[54] It is recognized that training institutions may decline in number and populations and that community alternatives may proliferate. The poor facilities in juvenile correctional institutions, the inmate social system, the reduction of services because of a heavy emphasis on custody, and a fossilized bureaucratic organization all contribute to the relative ineffectiveness of the juvenile system. But by realizing this problem and by developing alternatives, the burden that inadequate treatment of juvenile delinquents places on the adult correctional system can be reduced—creating a double benefit for our society. Although some states will continue with the *parens patriae* model, the Supreme Court will be watching to see that the rights of young citizens are not abused.

Summary

There is some hope for the future in the efforts by the Office of Juvenile Justice and Delinquency Prevention (OJJDP) and the American Correctional Association to establish national resource centers to serve as models for the rest of the country:

Located in Berrien Center, Michigan, Fort Meyers, Florida and Louisville, Kentucky, these facilities vary in size and organizational structure. After a comprehensive evaluation of program materials and on-site inspection, these three national resource centers were selected from among eight accredited juvenile detention centers.

The national resource centers are important because of their contribution to the practice of juvenile detention. Each center presents approximately four two-day workshops per year. . . . Not only do these workshops permit participants to experience an excellent physical plant, but there is also ample opportunity to ask direct questions about the realities of implementing model programs in a variety of institutional settings.[55]

Although these centers are truly a great accomplishment, many more of them must be implemented if they are to have a significant impact on the stumbling juvenile justice system, especially on institutions.

It is reasonable to consider that the relatively high proportion of adult felons processed through the juvenile treatment delivery systems and training institutions as youths may decrease sharply as alternatives to formal processing, institutionalization, and labeling are developed for juveniles. Unfortunately, those youths who are left to go through the ever-hardening juvenile institutions are being labeled more and more like their adult counterparts.

Although there are occasional examples of programs for our youth that seem to be breaking the patterns of delinquent and criminal behavior, the public seems to have little patience with wayward youth. The number of community-based beds for juvenile programs is shrinking. It is essential that the impacts of poor programming and systems that punish instead of treat our children become known to the general public. Only with informed public support can the patterns of "crime schools" and neglect be broken, so that juveniles will be able to escape the further impact of the adult system. The public seems to be responding to this kind of logic by *lowering* the age of responsibility for criminal remand to adult courts.

It seems that juvenile justice in America will continue at least to give lip service to the ideals of *parens patriae,* but with the Supreme Court watching closely to see that the rights of young citizens are not abused. If we abandon our young people and begin to assume that their behavior is adult because it is repugnant or violent, the jails and prisons of the 1990s will continue to be overcrowded to the extreme and we will have a million adults behind bars.

Review Questions

1. Explain the concept of *parens patriae.* How does this apply today?
2. Describe and differentiate between the three kinds of children who come into contact with the juvenile courts.
3. What were the major findings in the case of *In re Gault?*
4. What effect does differential treatment have on juvenile justice? Explain.
5. What are the major trends in the juvenile justice system?
6. Differentiate between diversion and decriminalization.

Key Terms _____

1. juvenile (p. 393)
2. *parens patriae* (p. 394)
3. adjudication (p. 396)
4. aftercare (p. 396)
5. status offender (p. 398)
6. neglected (p. 398)
7. dependent (p. 398)
8. delinquent (p. 398)
9. MINS (p. 399)
10. PINS (p. 399)
11. training school (p. 404)
12. diversion (p. 418)
13. decriminalization (p. 420)
14. decarceration (p. 422)
15. accountability (p. 423)

Notes _____

1. William Webster, *Uniform Crime Report: 1986* (Washington, D.C.: U.S. Department of Justice, 1987), p. 170.
2. Chancery courts date back to England's feudal era. They traditionally had broad power over the welfare of children but exercised this authority almost exclusively on behalf of minors whose property rights were in jeopardy. In America, this authority was extended to minors in danger of personal as well as property attacks.
3. Office of Juvenile Justice and Deliquency Prevention, *Facts About Youth and Delinquency: A Citizen's Guide to Juvenile Justice* (Washington, D.C.: U.S. Department of Justice, 1982), pp. 7–10.
4. Ann Kuhl, "An Expert Witness in Child Sexual Abuse Evaluations: The Dilemma." Paper presented at the Sixth International Symposium on Victimology, Jerusalem, August 29, 1988.
5. Peter Greenwood and Frank Zimring, *One More Chance: The Pursuit of Promising Strategies for Chronic Juvenile Offenders.* (Santa Monica, Calif.: Rand Corporation, 1985). See also Jeffrey Fagan, Elizabeth Piper, and Melinda Moore, "Violent Delinquents and Urban Youths," *Criminology* 24 (1986): 439–471.
6. Marc LeBlanc and Louise Biron, "Status Offenses: A Legal Term Without Meaning," *Journal of Research in Crime and Delinquency* 17 (January 1980): 114–125. See also Charles Logan and Sharla Rausch, "Why Deinstitutionalizating Status Offenders Is Pointless," *Crime and Delinquency* 31 (1985): 501–517.
7. Remanding juveniles to adult courts, sometimes called "bind-over," is a hotly debated topic in the juvenile delinquency area. See M. A. Bortner, "Traditional Rhetoric, Organizational Realities: Remand of Juveniles to Adult Court," *Crime and Delinquency* 32 (1986): 53–73. See also Jeffery Fagan, Martin Forst, and T. Scott Vivona, "Racial Determinants of the Judicial Transfer Decision: Prosecuting Violent Youth in Criminal Court," *Crime and Delinquency* 33 (1987): 259–286. On the difference in punishment, see C. Rudman, J. Fagan, and M. Moore, "Violent Youth in Adult Court: Process and Punishment," *Crime and Delinquency* 32 (1986): 75–96.
8. The cottage system is composed of a series of small houselike structures within a compound. These usually contain open living and sleeping areas or separate rooms for residents and separate living areas for cottage "parents." The Ohio Boys' Industrial School (Lancaster) was closed in 1981.

9. Bureau of Justice Statistics, *Sourcebook of Criminal Justice Statistics: 1986* (Washington, D.C.: U.S. Department of Justice, 1986), p. 390.

10. Susan Kline, *Jail Inmates 1986*, (Washington, D.C.: U.S. Department of Justice, 1987), p. 1.

11. Ibid, p. 2.

12. National Advisory Commission, *Corrections,* p. 269.

13. Bureau of Justice Statistics, *Survey,* p. 389.

14. Ibid., p. 392.

15. Massachusetts originally tried to close its juvenile institutions, but one remains open. Vermont closed its institutions by using extensive contracts for private correctional services and by reducing the age to ten that juveniles could be remanded to adult courts!

16. Vermont is the only state that has been successful. The most recent data indicate that twenty-three states have increased the number of their juvenile institutions; thirteen retain the same number; and fourteen have decreased the number.

17. Larry Holtz, "*Miranda* in a Juvenile Setting: A Child's Right to Silence," *Journal of Criminal Law and Criminology* 78 (1987): 534–536.

18. M. L. Midonick, *Children, Parents and the Courts: Juvenile Delinquency, Ungovernability and Neglect* (New York: Practicing Law Institute, 1972), p. 1.

19. *Miranda* v. *Arizona,* 384 U.S. 436, 448 (1966).

20. *McKeiver* v. *Pennsylvania,* 403 U.S. 541 (1971).

21. Ibid., p. 545.

22. Ibid., p. 547.

23. Juvenile Justice and Delinquency Act of 1975: P.L. 93–415. Signed into law on September 7, 1974.

24. Barry Field, "The Juvenile Court Meets the Principle of the Offense: Legislative Changes in Juvenile Waiver Statistics," *Journal of Criminal Law and Criminology,* 78 (1987): 471–533.

25. *In re Gault,* 387 U.S. 1, 33 (1967).

26. *Strode* v. *Brorby,* 478 F. 2d 608 (Wyoming, 1970).

27. *Kent* v. *United States,* 383 U.S. 541 (1966).

28. The doubt must be one that a reasonable man or woman would express when presented with all of the evidence.

29. *McKeiver* v. *Pennsylvania:* 408.

30. For example, see *M.* v. *Superior Court,* 4 Cal. App. 3d 370, 482 P. 2d 664, 93 Cal. Rptr. 752 (1971).

31. E. Z. Fester and T. F. Courtless, "The Beginning of Juvenile Justice: Police Practices and the Juvenile Offender," *Vanderbilt Law Review* 22 (1969): 567–608.

32. Commissioners on Uniform State Laws, Uniform Juvenile Court Act, Section 27 B, 1968.

33. Besharov, *Juvenile Justice Advocacy,* p. 97.

34. *Miranda* v. *Arizona,* 384 U.S. 436, 448 (1966). See also Peter Lewis and Harry Allen, "Participating Miranda: An Attempt to Subvert Constitutional Safeguards," *Crime and Delinquency* 23 (January 1977): 75–80.

35. Anthony Travisono, "Prevention, Not Corrections Is Best For Juveniles," *Corrections Today* 49 (October 1987), p. 4.

36. See, for example, California Welfare and Institutions Code §702.5.

37. Juveniles do not have a constitutionally guaranteed right to trial by jury, however. In more than a dozen states, jury trials are permitted under state laws.

38. Sharla Rausch and Charles Logan, "Diversion from Juvenile Court: Panacea or Pandora's Box?" Paper presented at the annual meeting of the American Society of Criminology, Toronto, November 6, 1982.

39. Henry Black, *Black's Law Dictionary* (St. Paul: West Publishing, 1979), p. 371.

40. Sue Titus Reid, *Crime and Criminology* (New York: Holt, Rinehart & Winston, 1982), pp. 40–42.

41. Lamar Empey, "The Social Construction of Childhood, Delinquency and Social Reform," in Malcolm Klein, ed., *The Juvenile Justice System* (Beverly Hills, Calif.: Sage Publications, 1976), pp. 27–54.

42. Rausch and Logan, "Diversion."

43. Edward Healey, "Status Offenders: Non-Criminal Offenders, Court As the Last Resort." Paper presented at the Second Asian-Pacific Conference on Juvenile Delinquency, Seoul, November 7, 1982.

44. Institute of Judicial Administration, *Standards.*

45. Anne Voight, "OJJDP Evaluation Finds Program for Status Offenders Reduced Detention by 43 Percent," *Justice Assistance News* 3 (October 1982): 6.

46. John Smykla, *Community-based Corrections* (New York: Macmillan, 1981) p. 23.

47. Michael Sherrill, "Massachusetts: A Harder Line Toward Juveniles," *Corrections Magazine* 7 (1981): 29–31.

48. Benedict Alper, "Massachusetts Ten Years Later," in John Sullivan, Joseph Victor, and Donal MacNamara, eds., *Criminal Justice 83/84* (Guilford, Conn.: Dushkin, 1983), pp. 183–185.

49. Harvey Lowell and Bruce Bullington, *Rediscovering Juvenile Justice: The Cost of Getting Tough* (Hackensack, N.J.: National Council on Crime and Delinquency, 1981).

50. Ibid.

51. Sherrill, p. 29.

52. Alper, p. 184.

53. Donna Schram and Anne Schneider, "The Effects of Juvenile Justice System Reforms on Case Processing and Sentences for Juveniles: The Experience of Washington State." Paper presented at the annual meeting of the American Society of Criminology, Toronto, November 4, 1982. See also Anne Schneider, *An Assessment of Juvenile Justice System Reform in Washington State* (Washington, D.C.: Office of Juvenile Justice and Delinquency Prevention, U.S. Department of Justice, 1984).

54. For a comparison of the juvenile system in the Netherlands, see Josine Junger-Tas, *Child Protection and Juvenile Justice in Holland* (The Hague: Ministry of Justice, 1982); and Josine Junger-Tas, *Juvenile Court Structures: Problems and Dilemmas* (The Hague: Ministry of Justice, 1979). A futuristic view can be found in Josine Junger-Tas and Leo Tigges, *Probation, After-Care, Child-Care and Protection Today and in the Future* (The Hague: Ministry of Justice, 1982).

55. David Roush, "Setting the Standard: National Juvenile Detention Resource Centers," *Corrections Today*, 49 (October 1987): p 33.

CHAPTER
18

Special Category Offenders

Social groups create deviance by making the rules
whose infraction constitutes deviance and by
applying those rules to particular people and
labeling them as outsiders.
—H. S. BECKER

Special Kinds of Deviants

This chapter deals with some of the "rejects" of society who are too
often found in America's jails and correctional facilities. Many of these
individuals are handicapped by their mental processes, and others are
labeled by their specific behavior or personal background.

Of the many categories that could be examined, we have chosen to
discuss the *mentally disordered offender,* the *mentally retarded offender,*
the *sex offender,* and the *elderly offender.* Although these categories do not
exhaust the possible types of special category offenders, they offer a spectrum of the problems faced by correctional administrators and individual
offenders in their custody and treatment.

The Mentally Disordered Offender

What kind of illness would civilized people find so repulsive that they
would reject the sufferers in the most barbaric fashion and brand them
with a stigma that would remain, even if a cure were achieved? These
unfortunates—the mentally disordered—used to be scorned and burned,
but, in more enlightened times, we have built backwoods fortresses for
them, presumably to protect ourselves from contagion. They have been
executed as witches, subjected to exorcisms, chained, or thrown into
gatehouses and prisons to furnish a horrible diversion for the other prisoners.[1] In some countries they were gathered together and placed on a
"ship of fools" (*das Shiff der Narren*) and shipped off to uninhabited lands
where they were left to wander on their own. The methods recommended
by Celus, a first-century Roman scholar, established the pattern of treat-

ment for the years to come: "When he [the mentally disordered person] has said or done anything wrong, he must be chastised by hunger, chains, and fetters."[2] In line with that approach, throughout human history the mentally disordered have been subjected to misguided, cruel, sadistic, and fear-based treatment, ranging from burning at the stake to banishment from society.

Before the Middle Ages, the mentally disturbed were generally tolerated. They were usually cared for locally by members of their own family, tribal system, or primitive society. However, the advent of widespread poverty, disease, and religious fanaticism seemed to trigger intolerance for any deviation. The mentally disturbed were thought to be possessed by devils and demons and were punished harshly because of it. At that time, the insane were driven out of society; later they were confined — another form of isolation from society.

The first insane asylum was constructed in Europe in 1408.[3] From that date until recently, the asylum has been a dumping ground for all the mentally disordered people we could neither understand nor cure. The states, one after another, responded to this compelling method of ridding society of misfits, and built numerous institutions during the mid-1800s. The inflated claims of cures for mental illness could not stand up against the process of institutionalization, however, and long-term commitments, not cures, became the rule of the day.

Asylums became another "invisible empire" in America, with the excesses and lack of care or caring ignored by society. With the discovery of tranquilizing drugs, they became places where patients were put into a controllable stupor, until the "magic cure" for mental illness could be found. Longer and longer periods of institutionalization, often ordered at the whim of family members, finally got the attention of the courts. In the 1960s the rights of all citizens, to include the mentally ill and the convict, were being reexamined at every level. The abuses of the asylums were brought to light and the counterreaction was extreme. In the early 1970s, state after state adopted policies under the Community Mental Health Act that swept the country. The essential goal was to release all inmates of the asylums who were not a "clear and present danger" to themselves and others.

While benign in their approach, these acts flooded the central cities of America with mentally impaired street people. The response by most jurisdictions has been to move the problem into the jails and correctional institutions of America. In Seattle, Washington, the King County Executive, Randy Revelle, was fond of saying that the King County Jail was the "third largest mental health facility in the state. The first being the Western State Hospital, the second the section of I-5 between the jail and the hospital."[4]

As the mentally ill became a larger segment of the population in jails and prisons, professionals in the mental health field became essential to

---

MENTAL ILLNESS AND CORRECTIONS

Most persons familiar with the justice system will understand that the courts are concerned with the three major types of pleas that could be entered in the preadjudication phases: "incompetent to stand trial," "not guilty by reason of insanity," and "guilty but mentally ill." The special issues in determining guilt are described in this chapter.

In addition, there are two categories of postadjudication offenders whose special psychological needs pose problems for institutional corrections: inmates whose mental health deteriorates to episodic crises, and those sentenced to death who become mentally disturbed.

For some inmates, the impacts of prison life overwhelm their usual coping patterns. Some factors that lead to "prison psychosis" include the routine of the prison, fear of other inmates, forced homosexual behavior, assault and fear of assault, deterioration in affairs and circumstances of family on the outside of prison, depression, and so on. When the psychological crisis comes, correctional administrators frequently transfer affected inmates to prison infirmaries or psychological treatment wards, or initiate inmate transfer to a mental health system. Long-term and intensive psychotherapy for "mentally ill" inmates, however, is believed to be rare. Treatment for episodic mental crisis tends to remain at the "first aid" level in many states.

Death rows do not usually contain a large proportion of a prison's population but subsume a disproportionate share of the per-inmate cost due to the demands of observing, caring, and maintaining death row. This includes a lower staff-inmate ratio, mail processing, death-watch officer workload, closer custody during recreational periods, and so on. Some inmates on death row become mentally ill and, as such, cannot be executed (*Ford* v. *Wainright*, 106 S. Ct. 2595, 1986). The state has an additional burden of determining if the death-row inmate is insane, establishing some procedure to restore the inmate to sanity, and then of certifying the sanity of the patient-inmate. Because this would be tantamount to a "death sentence" and thus not a favor for the inmate, it is unlikely that mental health physicians would undertake this process alone or with great enthusiasm. It remains for the states to develop procedures for identifying, diagnosing, treating, and certifying the sanity of death-row inmates who claim to be "insane."

---

the correctional administrators. Although the ratio of mental health practitioners remains much too low, there has been some progress. Because many institutions must deal with mental health issues on a priority basis, little to no services are provided for the majority who do not exhibit violent or bizarre behavior. It is a practical fact in corrections that "the squeaky wheel gets the oil."

For the extreme behavior cases, there are special units for more intensive treatment, such as the one in Washington state. That unit is a model of how to deal with extreme mentally and behaviorally disordered prisoners. Unfortunately, this fine facility can handle only 144 inmates. Though commendable, this is only about one-tenth of the commonly recognized population of inmates who could use more intensive mental health services. One quickly finds that only the really severe cases are able to be referred to the Special Offender Center.

Is the mentally disordered person more prone to criminal behavior? Or does the criminal justice system respond to these misfits in a *legal* manner, just because the mental health system has been rendered helpless to deal with most of them? Steadman and his group have studied that relationship and have made some rather interesting discoveries:

> The correlates of crime among the mentally disordered appear to be the same as the correlates of crime among any other group: age, gender, race, social class, and prior criminality.
>
> Likewise, the correlates of mental disorder among criminal offenders appear to be the same as those in other populations: age, social class, and previous disorder. Populations characterized by the correlates of both crime and mental disorder (e.g., low social class) can be expected to show high rates of both, and they do.[5]

It appears that the relationship between crime and mental disorder (at least in *groups*, as shown in this study) has no real causal effect. It is essential that we learn more about distinguishing between different kinds of mental illness and their impacts on correctional administration. It is important to remember that the real link to look for is one that indicates the potential harm to the mentally ill person and others. It may be a long time before such options are available to corrections.

Two Ways to Escape Criminal Responsibility

There are two justifications that defendants can invoke to relieve themselves of criminal responsibility for an act. The first is "not guilty by reason of insanity"; the second is "incompetent to stand trial." In the first instance, offenders do not deny the commission of the act but assert that they did not have the capacity to understand the nature of the act or that it was wrong. The second instance is based on the common-law criterion that defendants must be able to understand the charges against them and to cooperate with their counsel in the preparation of their own defense. The procedures for determining competency vary considerably from jurisdiction to jurisdiction, but most make it a court decision based on psychiatric testimony. If defendants are found incompetent to stand trial, they are usually committed to a mental institution until declared competent.

The Criminally Insane

With the advent of legal insanity and incompetency as defenses against criminal conviction came the development of special asylums for the criminally insane, in most cases just another form of prison without due process protections. These institutions are reserved for the following categories of offender:

a. Persons adjudicated incompetent to enter a plea or stand trial.
b. Defendants found not guilty by reason of insanity.
c. Persons adjudicated under special statutes, e.g., "sexually dangerous persons," "defective delinquents," "sexual psychopaths," etc.
d. Convicted and sentenced offenders who have become mentally disturbed while serving a prison sentence and have been transferred to a mental health facility.
e. Other potentially hazardous mentally ill persons requiring special security during the course of their evaluation and treatment.[6]

In more recent years, those claiming to be not guilty by reason of insanity (NGRI) have been the subject of considerable debate.[7] President Richard M. Nixon persistently sought to have the NGRI defense abolished. More informed criminologists point to the problems with the insanity defense as being excessive media coverage, suspicion of malingering by the defendant, and conflicting and suspicious testimony by professional colleagues testifying for either the defense or the prosecution.

Prosecutors often hope that those accused offenders acquitted through the plea of NGRI will be institutionalized for a period sufficient to reduce their dangerousness and will receive both public safety and retribution. The debate continues. Perhaps the best solution would be to determine guilt and then shift the issue of diminished capacity (insanity, in this case) to the sentencing or case disposition stage. This position was recognized by the American Psychiatric Association following the attack of John Hinckley on the life of President Ronald Reagan.

As a response, by 1986 twelve states abolished the insanity defense entirely, then created "guilty but mentally ill" (GBMI) statutes in their place.[8] Under these statutes, an offender's mental illness is acknowledged but not seen as sufficient reason to allow him or her to escape criminal responsibility. If convicted, offenders will be committed to prison. Some states will provide mental health treatment in the prison setting but others may transfer the offender to a mental health facility for treatment.

The position of the American Psychiatric Association is that significant changes in the legislation should be made to deal with the disposition of violent insanity acquittees:

1. Special legislation should be designed for those persons charged with violent offenses who have been found not guilty by reason of insanity.
2. Confinement and release decisions should be made by a board including both psychiatrists and other professionals representing the criminal justice system and akin to a parole board.
3. Release should be conditional on having a treatment supervision plan in place, with the necessary resources available to implement it.

4. The board having jurisdiction over the released insanity acquittees should also have the authority to reconfine them.
5. When psychiatric treatment in a hospital setting has obtained the maximal treatment benefit possible, but the board believes that for other reasons confinement is still necessary, the insanity acquittee should be transferred to the most appropriate nonhospital facility (prison).[9]

While the public remains upset by a seeming "loophole" in the net of justice, the courts continue to try to find equitable ways to deal with the offender who has diminished mental capacity.

The Problem of Prediction

It is unfortunate that the long indeterminate sentences often given to mentally disordered offenders reflect a fear that those committed might be a problem in the future. Lewis Carroll presented the problem effectively in *Through the Looking Glass:*

> "[T]here's the King's Messenger," said the Queen. "He's in prison now, being punished; and the trial doesn't even begin till next Wednesday; and of course the crime comes last of all."
>
> "Suppose he never commits the crime?" said Alice.
>
> "That would be all the better, wouldn't it?" the Queen said, as she turned the plaster round her finger with a bit of ribbon.
>
> Alice felt there· was no denying *that.* "Of course it would be all the better," she said, "but it wouldn't be all the better his being punished."
>
> "You're wrong *there,* at any rate," said the Queen. "Were you ever punished?"
>
> "Only for faults," said Alice.
>
> "And you were all the better for it, I know!" the Queen said triumphantly.
>
> "Yes, but then I *had* done the things·I was punished for," said Alice. "That makes all the difference."
>
> "But if you hadn't done them," the Queen said, "that would have been better still; better, and better, and better!"[10]

It is the requirement for prediction of criminal inclination that makes so questionable the programs for treating the mentally disordered. Who can predict potential dangerousness with any degree of accuracy? Bernard Rubin stated that "the belief in the psychiatrist's ability to predict the likely dangerousness of a patient's future behavior is almost universally held, yet it lacks empirical support." And he added, "Labeling of deviancy as mental illness or predicting dangerousness is just a convention to get someone to treatment. Once in treatment the concept of dangerousness is forgotten."[11]

So we see the paradox of requiring psychiatrists to predict behavior and to attach a label to offenders, when this might result in an indefinite, or even lifelong, commitment to a mental institution for someone who is not really dangerous (a "false positive" prediction). Further, this individual is then labeled for custody and treatment in a special area within that institution. When one considers the wealth of folklore surrounding mental institutions, it becomes clear that a dreadful stigma accompanies the label of "criminally insane."

The Developmentally Disabled Offender

Within the correctional system there are offenders who, though considered legally sane and competent to stand trial, are developmentally disabled. (An IQ score of 69 or below on a standardized test is the generally accepted measure for identifying the mentally retarded.) Their intellectual level and social adaptability measure well below average; yet they are adjudged legally responsible for their actions.

In their guidelines for incarcerated mentally retarded offenders, Santamour and West address the problems encountered:

1. In prison, the retarded offender is slower to adjust to routine, has more difficulty in learning regulations, and accumulates more rule infractions, which, in turn, affect housing, parole, and other related matters.

Dealing With the Hearing Impaired Offender (Courtesy Federal Bureau of Prisons)

2. Retarded inmates rarely take part in rehabilitation programs because of their desire to mask their deficiencies.
3. They often suffer the brunt of practical jokes and sexual harassment.
4. Such inmates are more often denied parole, serving on the average two or three years longer than other prisoners for the same offense.[12]

Administrators in both fields (corrections and retardation) have a tendency to regard the developmentally disabled offender as a misfit in their system of services. They look to one another to assume responsibility for programming and funding. Because of the few resources available to each system and even more pressing concerns, the result is often very limited programming.

The special needs of the devolpmentally disabled offender are unique, and the program models are few. Those models that do exist are limited primarily to special education programs geared more to the needs of the individual with learning disabilities other than those of the retarded person.

It should be emphasized that all offenders within the correctional system, whether or not they are retarded, demand our attention. Abuses are all too frequent, and few inmates are spared from the pervasively negatively impact of the correctional system itself. The consideration given here to the special needs of the retarded offender is not meant in any way to endorse the conditions under which prisoners in general are treated but, rather, to draw attention to this group's special needs.

A Historic Perspective

In reviewing historical and philosophical trends in the study of the retarded offender, it is noteworthy that before the late nineteenth century, there was little attempt to differentiate between the mentally retarded individual and one who commits a crime. Farber,[13] tracing the development of theories with respect to mental retardation and criminality, found that for the majority of theorists there was a general equation between criminality and subnormal intelligence. Brown and Courtless[14] outlined three phases that characterized the late nineteenth and early twentieth centuries in the development of theories concerning the mentally retarded person and criminal behavior. From 1890 to 1920, theorists felt that mental retardation predisposed a person to commit criminal acts—linking mental retardation and criminality with poverty, insanity, and moral and physical degradation. Close to the onset of World War I, intelligence testing was begun, with the earliest attempt to discriminate between the effects of mental retardation and criminal behavior. Studies based on testing reported the numbers of criminals falling in the retarded range as generally high.

The second period to which Brown and Courtless referred—1921 to 1960—has been called the time of "denial and neglect." Theorists questioned whether in fact mental retardation predisposed one to commit criminal acts.

They adopted the view that levels of intelligence must be considered within their environmental context. For the first time an attempt was made to link social factors with intelligence levels. There was thus a move away from the constitutional explanations offered by theorists such as Lombroso.

Currently there is less reluctance to associate retardation directly with delinquency. Much of the revived interest of the 1960s to date has been generated by the legal community and not by criminologists. Such a phenomenon stems from a growing awareness that the preponderance of mentally retarded individuals in the criminal justice system may be more an administrative and legal artifact than evidence for a causal relationship between mental retardation and criminality.

The landmark *Ruiz* decision has also set the tone for judicial consideration of the mentally retarded inmate.[15] This class action suit involved issues of overcrowding, medical care, inmate trustees as guards, and other conditions; the federal court declared the Texas prison system to be unconstitutional. Judge Justice found that between 10 and 15 percent of the Texas Department of Corrections inmates were retarded and that they were distributed throughout the system. The judge echoed Santamour and West concerning the retarded inmates' special problems and added that

1. They are abnormally prone to injury, many of which are job-related.
2. They are decidedly disadvantaged when appearing before a disciplinary committee. This raises basic problems of fairness and the special need for assistance.[16]

It seems obvious that the issue of the mentally retarded inmate is slowly coming to the forefront, led by the efforts of the courts.

Issues in Law Enforcement and Court Proceedings

Several abuses and problems were found by Brown and Courtless in research on the criminal justice system's procedures in handling the developmentally disabled offender. In about 8 percent of the cases studied there was evidence that the retarded person was not represented by an attorney. Where representation was found, in 69 percent of such cases the representation was court-appointed.

Fifty-nine percent entered pleas of guilty. In those cases where pleas of not guilty were entered, 40 percent of the retarded individuals waived jury trial.

In 80 percent of the cases, the original charge was the same as the convicting charge. Confessions or incriminating statements were obtained from the retarded in two-thirds of the cases studied.

In almost 78 percent of the cases, no pretrial psychological or psychiatric examinations were made. In only 20 percent of the cases, presentence examinations were made. The issue of competency to stand trial and criminal responsibility were not raised in 92 percent of the cases under study. In 88 percent of the cases, no appeals were made and post conviction relief was not requested in 84 percent of the cases.[17]

Much of the literature points out that developmentally disabled suspects confess more easily, react to friendly suggestions as well as intimidations, and plead guilty more often. The President's Commission on Law Enforcement and Administration of Justice reported that when a retarded person does go to trial, his or her ability to remember details, locate witnesses, and testify credibly is limited. Here is found a framework for serious abuse within the criminal justice system, supporting the conclusion that the disproportionate number of retarded offenders is a legal and administrative artifact and not necessarily the result of a direct causal relationship between mental retardation and criminal behavior.

Too often a client's defense may be hampered or even mishandled because attorneys, as a group, are not aware of the retarded person's problems. Allen emphasized this same point: the criminal justice system fails to recognize the retarded offender. The following quotations from interviews provided by Allen illustrate this lack of awareness:

> . . . we all thought he was dumb, but he was a mean - - - , and we were all a little afraid of him. (Taken from a discussion with a prosecuting attorney. The defendant was later retested at an I.Q. score of 57.)
>
> I don't recall that any of my clients were retarded. (Taken from discussion with a public defender, and later, several of his clients were found to be retarded.)[18]

This general confusion from the professionals' lack of comprehensive knowledge about mental retardation is further compounded by the many legal definitions of mental retardation, which vary from jurisdiction to jurisdiction. Very often laws make no distinction between mental illness and mental retardation, and very often the solution employed in handling the retarded individual is to place him or her in a mental hospital. Under certain defective delinquency laws, the mentally retarded are categorized with the sociopath and certain sexual offenders.

Labeling

The question of special facilities and special programs leads to a discussion of the pros and cons of labeling. Much of the recent literature in the fields of metal retardation and delinquency expresses concern with the labeling process. The concern here stems from the possible overclassification and stigmatization from the use of labels.

For the individual who is retarded and has come in contact with the criminal justice system, the liability of labeling is often the assumption that the retarded offender is incorrigible. The result may be that appropriate services are withheld.[19]

The problems of testing demand the careful application of labels. The cultural biases of the tests themselves and the problems of administering them should forewarn one about indiscriminate use of lables. Even though tests may indicate retardation, it is important that such individuals have the opportunity to demonstrate that they are not retarded.

Some professionals have begun to question the diagnostic benefits of labeling. They feel that such diagnosis seldom indicates specfic treatment procedures.[20] However, if adaptive behavior assessments are made on each individual retarded offender, along with IQ testing, then they can be used to develop a treatment plan, and this criticism of labeling would no longer be valid.

Labeling, or classification, is often important and, as one researcher suggested, "there may be circumstances in which using such labels is justifiable, and if we provide due process safeguards . . . then we can rightfully use that label.[21] Another researcher presented some convincing arguments in support of labeling, making two points. The first is that all problems associated with labeling cannot be the result of the labeling process itself but are also the outcome of public ignorance. The solution to the problem may not be to abandon the system entirely but, rather, to refine it and educate society, changing negative attitudes with regard to labels of retardation and delinquency. The second point is that to discontinue any system of classification because of the potential abuse would "punish those who need help the most."[22]

The retarded offender is often an individual who has never been accepted by society at large. Becoming a part of the "society of captives" is often their first experience of acceptance and thus has a pervasive impact. At Massachusetts' Bridgewater State Hospital and Prison, personnel commenting on the strengths of the association between the retarded inmate and the prison culture noted that it was only the retarded inmates who returned to prison for social visits.

Are mentally retarded offenders in need of special consideration in regard to criminal responsibility? As noted by Professor Richard C. Allen:

> Historically, society has pursued three alternative courses with the mentally retarded offender: we have ignored his limitations and special needs; or we have sought to tailor traditional criminal law processes to fit them; we have grouped him with psychopaths, sociopaths, and sex deviates in a kind of conventicle of the outcast and hopeless.[23]

One way to accomplish such consideration would be with a special court, similar to a juvenile court, where the mentally retarded offender is handled both for the crime and the condition of the offender. Findings and recommendations for the handling of the mentally retarded offender are shown for consideration in Figures 18-1 and 18-2.

Figure 18-1

Major Findings

- Few jails or prisons have sufficient facilities and programs to handle the special needs of developmentally disabled offenders, while hospitals and other health facilities are seldom capable of administering correctional programs with sufficient security to protect society's rights. Without alternatives, judges are left with no other choice than to sentence these individuals to prison.
- Some mentally retarded offenders require incarceration because of the seriousness of their crimes or their records as repeat offenders, but most other mentally retarded offenders could be diverted from prison to community treatment programs while still insuring the safety of the community.
- There is tremendous variation in estimates of the number of mentally retarded persons incarcerated in prison: earlier reseach indicates that the percentage of these offenders is higher than the percentage within the general population, while the most recent studies place the percentage at about the same level as within the general population.
- Mentally retarded offenders are often used by their peers, reflecting their great need for approval and acceptance. They have no long-term time perspective, and little ability to think in a causal way and understand the consequences of their actions.
- Retarded persons are often victimized or abused by other inmates.
- Identifying these offenders who have special needs is essential for planning individualized programs. Due process and functional diagnosis and evaluation performed by specially trained staff utilizing sophisticated assessment tools and procedures are essential.
- Since mental retardation is usually undetected, violation of the legal rights of these persons is frequent.
- Criminal justice and corrections personnel are not presently trained to handle the special problems and needs of these offenders.
- Matters of competency relating to diminished mental capacity should be considered at the first point of contact with the criminal justice system and at each decision point in the continuum.
- Developmentally disabled offenders should be assigned to programs that meet their individual needs: some may be mixed in with the regular prison population; some need a segregated environment; some would benefit most from a community setting; and others might be placed in a regular mental retardation group home or guardianship arrangement.
- The survey of local jurisdictions revealed the need for training about mental retardation for criminal justice personnel who normally do not distinguish between mental retardation and mental illness, the need for

early identification of mentally retarded persons once they come in contact with the criminal justice system, and the need for more community resources, particularly residential programs, to serve mentally retarded offenders.

Figure 18-2

Recommendations

It Is Recommended That . . .
1. All criminal justice personnel receive basic training in regard to mental retardation.
2. Every effort be made to identify offenders who are mentally retarded at each stage of the criminal justice process, especially in the earlier stages.
3. Funding be increased, both for adult probation and parole, for the purchase of community services for the mentally retarded probationer and parolee.
4. In all appropriate cases the mentally retarded offender be diverted to community programs.
5. For those mentally retarded offenders who are sentenced to prison, great care be taken to protect them from abuse and manipulation by other inmates; and special program activities be provided which take into consideration their handicap of mental retardation.
6. Experts in the field of mental retardation in Texas direct some of their efforts to development of prevention programs to keep mentally retarded persons from becoming offenders.
7. Mentally retarded offenders be accepted by all programs designed for mentally retarded persons.
8. The Texas Code of Criminal Procedures be amended to allow for the transfer of mentally retarded offenders form Texas Department of Corrections to an appropriate TDMHMR program where the prisoner may, in fact, serve out the full prison term.
9. The question of competency be considered at the first possible stage in the criminal justice system.
10. Mental retardation be considered in the law as a mitigating circumstance and therefore be taken into consideration at the time of sentencing if, in fact, the offender has been found competent but mentally retarded.
11. The standards of Texas Commission on Jail Standards include specific references to mentally retarded inmates and their needs.
12. Ultimately, the Texas Department of Mental Health and Mental Retardation provide services to all mentally retarded adult offenders.
13. In Texas IQ tests be developed which are less culturally biased against blacks and minorities.

The Sex Offender

Are sex offenders being let off too easily in American courts, or are they being punished too harshly?[24] Are there some sex offenders in correctional institutions who might better be treated on probation? Are some who should be incarcerated being released on probation? Are sentences too long or too short? Are incarcerated sex offenders being paroled too soon, or is parole too-long delayed? Should unconventional approaches—castration, for example—be tried?

Currently, nothing in particular is being done about the large majority of sentenced sex offenders. Those serving time in correctional institutions are lodged in the same cell blocks as are those incarcerated for nonsex offenses and are subjected to the same correctional routines. Those out on probation and parole are, with few exceptions, treated like other probationers and parolees. Little or no attention is paid to the particular factors

TABLE 18.1

States with Highest Number of Sex Offenders

California	5,984
Texas	3,836
Florida	3,569
Ohio	2,515
Michigan	2,416
New York	2,395
Illinois	2,048
Georgia	1,907
Washington	1,865
North Carolina	1,800

Increase in Number of Sex Offenders in Prison

37	Number of Prison systems reporting increase
1	Number of reporting decrease
13	Number reporting no change
3	No data

Reasons for Increase

- Greater public awareness and better reporting
- More prosecutions and convictions
- Changes in statutes on sex offenses
- Longer sentences
- Reluctance/delay in paroling sex offenders
- More sex offenders sent to prison, some on mandatory sentences
- Overall increase in prison population

Source: Contact Center; *Corrections Compendium* (1987), p 5.

that made these individuals *sex* offenders — and that may (or may not) lead them to commit future sex offenses.

The number of sex offenders as a part of the corrections systems of America is growing. A recent survey by Contact Center shows that there are about 55,000 inmates who are sex offenders in the fifty-four systems that were examined. Table 18.1 summarizes the findings of this extensive study. Table 18.2 breaks out the number of sex offenders by state, as reported to Contact Center in the study.[25]

"Sex Fiends" Versus Sex Offenders

Attitudes toward sex offenders widely held by the public as well as by legislators, judges,[26] and others in positions of power are largely influenced by traditional beliefs. Since the turn of the twentieth century, rape-murders and rape-mutilations have continued to occur. There is no evidence that such crimes are either more rare or more common than in earlier days, but they continue to exert a powerful hold on the public's attention and to perpetuate the false notion of the "sex fiend" as the typical sex offender.

A visit to a treatment program for American sex offenders in the 1980s shows a very different perspective. Those currently in treatment cannot, by the widest stretch of the term, be classified as "sex fiends." The fewer than 1 percent of these lust-murderers and rape-mutilators are not found in treatment programs but are usually incarcerated in maximum security institutions, often awaiting execution.

Not one of the programs makes any claim that it can rehabilitate or safely restore to society the exceedingly small group of sex offenders — perhaps a dozen per year in the entire country — whose murders, tortures, and mutilations make newspaper headlines. Treatment programs do not want these "sex fiends" and do not get them. Rather, treatment programs are concerned with the bulk of sex offenders, the more than 99 percent whose offenses fall far short when compared with the sordid cases described in nineteenth-century literature.

It is possible, of course, that tomorrow an alumnus of one of these treatment programs may commit a lust-murder of the more heinous type. The same is true of an alumnus of a local high school or a member of a church choir. Treatment programs are specifically designed to minimize the likelihood that an offender will commit any sex offense following release — either a crime of the grossly offensive type or a lesser offense like the ones committed in the past.

The Common Sex Offenses

Any analysis of sex offenses is complicated by the fact that state legislatures are often too inhibited to describe specifically the acts they are seeking to punish. Thus punishment may be decreed for "lewd and lascivi-

TABLE 18.2 Sex Offender Survey

State	No. of Sex Offenders Incarcerated	Trend		
		Increased	Decreased	No Change
Alabama	1,050	x		
Alaska	530	x		
Arizona	987	x		
Arkansas	667			x
California	5,984			x
Colorado	450	x		
Connecticut	360		x	
Delaware	144			x
District of Columbia	385	x (slight)		
Florida	3,569	x		
Georgia	1,907	x		
Hawaii	254	x		
Idaho	230	x		
Illinois	2,048	x		
Indiana	1,692	No previous data for comparison		
Iowa	430	x		
Kansas	811	x		
Kentucky	668	Not available		
Louisiana	1,097	x		
Maine	325 to 390	x		
Maryland	1,100			x
Massachusetts	766			x
Michigan	2,416			x
Minnesota	426	x		
Mississippi	144			x
Missouri	1,300	x		
Montana	210	x		
Nebraska	193	x		
Nevada	535			
New Hampshire	130	x		
New Jersey	362	x		
New Mexico	280	x		
New York	2,395			x
North Carolina	1,800			x
North Dakota	85	x		
Ohio	2,515	x		
Oklahoma	780			x
Oregon	1,717	x		
Pennsylvania	509	x		
Rhode Island	137			x
South Carolina	1,214	x		
South Dekota	157	x		
Tennessee	1,315			x
Texas	3,836	x		
Utah	400	x		
Vermont	134	x		
Virginia	1,200	x		
Washington	1,865	x		
West Virginia	148	x		
Wisconsin	991	x		
Wyoming	200	x		
Federal Bureau of Prisons	385	x		
Canada	1,316	x		
Puerto Rico	128			x

Source: Contact Center, *Corrections Compendium* (1987), p 6.

ous conduct," "acts against nature," "carnal knowledge," "imperiling the morals of a minor," and so on. Almost any sexual activity may be prosecuted under one or another of these vague and broad rubrics. The same term, moreover, means different things in different states. Thus *sodomy,* which in many states refers primarily to male homosexual acts, may or may not also be applied to heterosexual oral or anal intercourse or to sexual contacts with animals.

Highly misleading terms may be used, such as *statutory rape* for an offense that is not rape at all but sexual intercourse with a fully consenting female who has not yet reached the age of legal consent (eighteen in some states).[27]

Discussions of sex offenses are further complicated by the fact that a man charged with a serious offense such as rape may be permitted, in the course of plea bargaining, to plead guilty to a lesser offense; hence, men who are in fact rapists may be lodged in correctional institutions for such apparently nonsexual offenses as breaking and entering or assault. In the following discussion we shall consider the actual offenses committed, rather than the vague legal terminology often used or the lesser offenses to which an offender may plead.

Until the past few years, the term *sex offense* commonly called to mind a lust-murder of the most irrational type. More recently, the intense and proper concern of the women's movement with rape and related crimes, such as assault with intent to commit rape, has tended to make rape the predominant sex offense in the minds of many people. Certainly, rape is among the most important of the sex offenses, and it is an offense with which the public will be continually concerned. Many experts feel that rape, in its more violent forms, is not a sex crime at all but a crime of power and dominance over women.[28]

By far the most common sex offenses, however, are three that are rarely prosecuted: fornication, adultery, and male homosexual contact.

Fornication, which is sexual intercourse between persons not married to each other, remains a crime in most states but is generally ignored by the law enforcement and criminal justice systems.

Adultery is sexual intercourse between two persons, at least one of whom is married to someone else. This also remains a crime in most states, rarely punished and almost never leading to participation in a treatment program.

Male homosexual conduct and other acts classed as *sodomy* are the most common of all sex offenses; the Kinsey reports and more recent data indicate that millions of sodomy offenses are committed each week.

These offenses were not lightly punished during past eras of American history. In the 1640s in Massachusetts, for example, "buggery"—anal intercourse with man, woman, or beast—was punishable by death for both parties. In 1648, rape also became punishable by death. Rapists whose lives were spared might be sentenced to have their nostrils slit and to wear halters around their necks. Adultery with a married or engaged woman was punishable by death for both parties, but adultery between a married man and a single, unbetrothed woman was considered mere fornication, punishable by a public whipping. Also punishable by public whipping was sexual intercourse between unmarried persons and pregnancy of unmarried women.

Times have changed, however. Many states have repealed their laws against sodomy—including both male homosexual acts and heterosexual oral and anal acts. Most states that have repealed their sodomy laws have similarly decriminalized fornication, adultery, and other sexual activities engaged in by consenting adults in private. Similar repeals are under consideration in other states. Even in states in which such laws remain on the books, they are rarely enforced, and even more rarely do they lead to the person's participation in a treatment program for sex offenders.

Laws governing public indecency and solicitation—solicitation for both prostitution and male homosexual contact—are still enforced in many jurisdictions. But they commonly lead to fines, probation, or short sentences in local correctional institutions. Rarely if ever do they lead to participation in a sex offender treatment program.

With these enormous categories of offenses eliminated or almost eliminated and with the very small number of rape-murders, sex-torture cases, and sex-dismemberments similarly eliminated as grounds for providing treatment, there remain five categories of sex offenses that account for the overwhelming majority of treatment program participants:

1. Rape, attempted rape, assault with intent to rape, and the like.[29]
2. Child molestation.[30]
3. Incest.[31]
4. Exhibitionism and voyeurism.
5. Miscellaneous offenses (breaking and entering, arson, and the like) in cases in which there is a sexual motivation.

The great majority of sex offenders currently participating in treatment programs are predominantly heterosexual and are there for heterosexual offenses—though some of them, like some heterosexual nonoffenders, have had occasional or incidental homosexual contacts. Most homosexual participants in treatment programs are there for sexual contacts, rarely violent, with male children or adolescents. Some are homosexual incest offenders. A few have committed homosexual rape or rape-related offenses.

Almost all sex offenses prosecuted in the United States today (except for prostitution-related offenses and offenses involving indecent stage performances) are committed by men. The only significant exceptions are the rare cases of child molestation in which a woman is prosecuted along with a man, often her husband. As a rough estimate, two or three hundred males are prosecuted for sex offenses for every female prosecuted. It is possible, of course, that the ratio of offenses committed by females is higher than is the ratio of prosecutions.

Most sex offenders in treatment programs are aged eighteen to thirty-five. A significant minority (mostly child molesters) are past fifty. How do the sex offenders enrolled in treatment programs differ from the remainder of sex offenders? At least five "sorting processes" distinguish the two groups. Some sex offenses are reported to the police; others are not. Most rapes and a wide range of lesser offenses go unreported. No man ends up in a treatment program as a result of an unreported offense. After an offense is reported, the perpetrator may or may not be apprehended and prosecuted. Those who escape arrest and prosecution no doubt differ in significant respects from those who reach the courts.

Of those prosecuted, a small number are found not guilty and a very large number (mostly minor offenders) receive suspended sentences or are placed on probation without assignment to a treatment program. Of the offenders remaining after these three sorting processes, some are sent to ordinary correctional institutions and others to treatment programs. Who will be sent to treatment programs depends in part on state law, in part on the judge, and in part on the availability of a treatment program.

Finally, most treatment programs can (and do) reject or transfer to other institutions those offenders whom they deem unsuitable for treatment. The net effect of these five sorting processes is a population of program participants from which most of the very serious offenders and most of the very minor offenders have been screened out.

Impact of New Public Attitudes toward Sexual Behavior

Since the 1950s, there has been a profound change in sexual tolerance in America. Current policies in many jurisdictions come closer and closer to providing that all forms of sex are legally tolerated, with three exceptions:

- Acts such as rape, involving force or duress (threats).[32]
- Sexual contacts with children.
- Acts in public that are deemed a public nuisance.

Legislatures, as we have noted, have recognized the new attitudes by repealing a wide variety of laws providing criminal penalties for acts between consenting adults in private. Law enforcement agencies are devoting less and less effort to enforcing laws of this kind that remain on the statute books. The courts, too, are increasingly accepting the change from "all sex is prohibited except . . ." to "all sex is permissible except. . . ." And as might be expected, this change in policy has had a profound impact on treatment programs for sex offenders.

One effect has been to alter the definition of successful treatment and to make success much easier to achieve. To cite the most conspicuous example, a significant minority of offenders in the early programs were male adults incarcerated for homosexual acts with other consenting adults. Successful treatment in those days meant that these men, following treatment, would no longer engage in homosexual activities.

As judged by that standard, treatment almost always failed. Under today's policies, success with homosexual offenders is judged by the same standards as is success with heterosexuals. Treatment of a homosexual offender (usually a child molester) is deemed successful if, following treatment, he meets the same three criteria:

- No use of force or duress.
- No sexual contacts with children.
- No acts in public that might be deemed a public nuisance.

One outstanding example of a sensible, but apparently successful, program for the treatment of the sex offender is the 180 Degrees, Inc. program at a halfway house in Minneapolis. This program involves all prospective members in a *men's sexuality group*. There seems to be some hope in this program:

> After several years of operation, the program's long-term impact on its participants is not clear. Short-term statistics, however, are encouraging. Of the men who have participated in the sexuality group and who are no longer residents of 180 Degrees, almost 75 percent successfully completed their stay at the halfway house, 7 percent absconded from the program, and 18 percent were terminated administratively.[33]

Although the history of success with the sexual offender is poor, there is no hope for the future if new approaches to this age-old problem are not tried.

The Elderly Offender

In the United States, those over sixty-five and older constitute one-ninth of the total population, approximately 26 million in all. Current statistics indicate that this figure is greater than the entire population of Canada. The fastest-growing group in the so-called "senior citizen" category is those who are seventy-five and older. Because of medical advances the *average* life expectancy in the year 2000 could be well into the low *nineties*! This trend will affect society in terms of retirement, education, healthcare . . . and corrections.[34]

As in the general population, the average age of offenders is rising (up from twenty-six in 1982 to over twenty-eight in 1986). This points up another category of special offender that needs to be discussed: the elderly offender, those inmates over fifty-nine years old. There are three forces at work that will increase the proportional representation of the aged in American prisons. The first is a statistical suggestion that crimes committed by the elderly may be on the increase. The second is the relatively longer sentences that courts are imposing on all offenders, and the third is the incremental effects of "enhancement" statutes that define prior convictions or incarcerations as factors that sentencing judges must consider in determining sentence length.

For example, if an offender has met or exceeded the legislatively established minimum of prior convictions, the judge in some jurisdictions must impose the prison-sentence length specified by the state legislature and also must enhance the prison term by a specified number of years (such as three or five) because the offender has been convicted or incarcerated before. In California, previous incarceration in a state prison requires that the sentencing judge impose the maximum sentence for the "aggravating" circumstance of the previous incarceration.

This creates three categories of elderly offenders and inmates: those who were sentenced to prison as young persons and who reach old age while incarcerated; another group has been in and out of incarceration most of their lives and now find themselves incarcerated again and over fifty-nine years old; the third group is from that new breed of criminal who is an active and aggressive person who committed a crime after reaching the age of fifty-nine. Each category has a different set of problems and requires different handling in the institution.

The possible results are numerous. If the prison population contains many aged inmates, who will care for the infirm? What special medical and geriatric programs will be created? How can prison administrators staff a maximum security nursing home? Will the public pay for so costly a nursing home? These and other questions will have to be addressed. Some were covered by Kelsey:

> Elderly offenders have unique problems in most facets of incarcerated life, including abusive treatment from other inmates, physical handicaps, and needs for special diets. Because of these special needs, correctional administrators need solid input from medical/health care staff concerning housing, program development, and security arrangements for geriatric offenders.
>
> Correctional administrators are faced with providing safe and humane care without taxing budgets or manpower. But most elderly offenders fall into rather long-term (and therefore expensive) sentencing groups. Because aged inmates frequently require medical attention, cost projections for these inmates are difficult because of various medical conditions that arise as after-effects of original illnesses.[35]

This rapidly growing segment of the offender population is one that requires forethought and understanding of the problems ahead. Those inmates with very long sentences, to include life without parole, are the geriatric inmates of the future. The intelligent administrator will prepare for them, as there is no way to stop the march of time.

Summary _____

The process of labeling is strong and pervasive in our society. Once labeled as *mentally disordered, mentally retarded, sex fiend,* or just *old*[36] a person's lot is rough indeed. Add to these heavy labels the added term *offender* and the problems multiply. Although mental illness is the nation's largest health problem, affecting one out of ten citizens, it is still frequently regarded with the "snakepit" philosophy of the Middle Ages, especially if some criminal act has been linked to the condition.

The developmentally disabled citizen is in a real dilemma if placed in a treatment program that requires measurable improvement as a condition of release. This concept led to laws in the 1930s that essentially gave retarded persons life sentences if he or she were placed in an institution until they "improved."

The sex offender is involved in a situation in which society's sexual mores are in transition. Some behaviors that put many in prison just a few years ago are no longer considered criminal. This change has not removed the stigma of the label *sex offender,* however, and the tolerance of the outside world is low for those so labeled.

These problems, along with the "right to treatment" issues discussed in Chapter 21, seem at constant odds with one another. When treatment programs fail, blame is often placed on the attendant, the overworked and undertrained staff, the legislators, and the courts. In the final analysis, however, it is up to society to decide whether or not it wants to spend the time and money to provide care and treatment for its bottom-line "losers" and then to attempt to remove the labels and reintegrate these individuals into the mainstream. Without a firm commitment for change, the castoffs of society will continue to return to institutions and then be released to the public, either with no change or with a decided change for the worse.

Review Questions

1. What spurred the growth of asylums in America?
2. How can one avoid criminal responsibility?
3. What are the most common sex offenses?
4. What would the American Psychiatric Association do with insanity acquittees?
5. What problems do developmentally disabled offenders pose for correctional administrators?
6. Why does the aged inmate create problems in corrections?
7. What types of former sex offenses have been decriminalized?
8. What recommendations have been offered for correctional processing of developmentally disabled offenders?

Key Terms

1. **mentally disordered offender** (p. 429)
2. **criminally insane** (p. 432)
3. **NGRI** (p. 433)
4. **developmentally disabled offender** (p. 435)
5. **mentally retarded** (p. 435)
6. **labeling** (p. 438)
7. **"sex fiends"** (p. 443)
8. **fornication** (p. 446)
9. **sexual tolerance** (p. 447)
10. **elderly offender** (p. 448)

Notes _____

1. G. Ives, *A History of Penal Methods* (London: S. Paul, 1914). Exploitation of the incarcerated mentally retarded offenders by more aggressive and stronger inmates remains a problem in all facilities: mental institutions, juvenile centers, nursing homes, jails, and prisons. In 1980, Congress passed the Civil Rights of Institutionalized Persons Act, authorizing the attorney general to intervene in correctional settings if violations of inmates' civil rights are suspected. For an example of juvenile victimization, see C. Bartollas, S. Miller, and S. Dinitz, *Juvenile Victimization: The Institutional Paradox* (New York: Holsted Press, 1976), pp. 53–76.
2. J. Wilpers, "Animal, Vegetable or Human Being?" *Government Executive,* May 1973, p. 32.
3. Ibid, p. 33.
4. Randy Revelle, former King County Executive, while accepting the National Association of Counties award for the "6 East" project for mentally ill inmates at the King County Jail, 1982.
5. Henry J. Steadman and John Monahan, *Crime and Mental Disorder* (Washington, D.C.: U.S. Department of Justice, 1984), p. 5.
6. National Institute of Mental Health, *Directory of Institutions for the Mentally Disordered Offenders* (Washington, D.C.: U.S. Government Printing Office, 1972).
7. Valerie Hans, "An Analysis of Public Attitudes Toward the Insanity Defense," *Criminology* 24 (1986) pp. 393–413. Among her more interesting findings were that the public wants insane lawbreakers punished, believes that insanity defense procedures fail to protect the general public, and wildly overestimates the use and effectiveness of the insanity defense.
8. John Klofas and Ralph Weisheit, "Guilty But Mentally Ill: Reform of the Insanity Defense in Illinois," *Justice Quarterly* 4 (1987): 40–50.
9. American Psychiatric Association, *Standards for Psychiatric Facilities* (Washington, D.C.: American Psychiatric Association, 1981), pp. 17–18.
10. Lewis Carroll, *Alice's Adventures in Wonderland and Through the Looking Glass and What Alice Found There* (London: Oxford University Press, 1971), p. 123.
11. B. Rubin, "Prediction of Dangerousness in Mentally Ill Criminals," *Archives of General Psychiatry* 27 (September 1972): 397–407.
12. Miles Santamour and Bernadette West, *Sourcebook on the Mentally Disordered Prisoner* (Washington, D.C.: U. S. Department of Justice, 1985), p. 70.
13. B. Farber, *Mental Retardation: Its Social Context and Social Consequences* (Boston: Houghton Mifflin, 1968).
14. Brown and Courtless, *The Mentally Retarded Offender.*
15. *Ruiz* v. *Estelle,* 503 F. Supp. 1265 (S.D. Tex. 1980), aff'd in part. 679 F. 2d 1115 (5th Cir. 1982), cert denied 103 S. Ct. 1438 (1983) at 1344.
16. Ibid., at 1344.
17. Brown and Courtless, pp. 9–10.
18. R. Allen, "The Retarded Offender: Unrecognized in Court and Untreated in Prison," *Federal Probation* 32 (September 1968): 3. See also Alex Moschella, "In Search of the Mentally Retarded Offender: The Massachusetts Bar Association's Specialized Training and Advocacy Program (1974-1978)," *Prison Journal* 116 (1986): 67–76.

19. Norm Kramer, "Treatment Program for the Developmentally Disabled/Mentally Retarded Offender," *The Prison Journal* 116 (1986): 85–92.
20. S. Shah, "The Mentally Retarded Offender: A Consideration of Some Aspects of the Criminal Justice Process," in *Readings in Law and Psychiatry* (Baltimore: Johns Hopkins University Press, 1968).
21. R. Burgdorf, Jr., "The Legal Rights of the Mentally Retarded Offender: Some Underlying Issues," in M. B. Santamour, ed., *The Mentally Retarded Citizen and the Criminal Justice System: Problems and Programs* (Newport, R.I.: James A. Maher Center, 1976), p. 43.
22. M. Kapp, "Legal Disposition of the Mildly Retarded Offender: A Vote for Segregation and Special Treatment." Unpublished Paper, Spring 1973. For more information on the developmentally disabled, see the special volume, "The Developmentally Disabled Offender." *The Prison Journal* 116 (1986).
23. Richard C. Allen, "Reaction to S. Fox: The Criminal Reform Movement," in M. Kindred, ed. *The Mentally Retarded Citizen and The Law* (Washington, D.C.: U. S. Government Printing Office, 1976), p. 645.
24. E. Brecher, *Treatment Programs for Sex Offenders,* National Institute of Law Enforcement and Criminal Justice (Washington, D.C.: U.S. Government Printing Office, 1978), pp. 1–12. The material for this section has been extracted from this document and reflects the current literature on this subject.
25. Survey, "The Number of Sex Offenders in Prison Growing," *Corrections Compendium* (May 1987): 5.
26. Anthony Walsh, "Placebo Justice: Victim Recommendations and Offender Sentences in Sexual Assault Cases," *Journal of Criminal Law and Criminology* 77 (1986): 1126–1141.
27. This area of legal procedure is rampant with charges of false accusation and victim's psychological trauma. See Andrew Soshnick, "The Rape Shield Law Paradox: Complaint Protection Amidst Oscillating Trends of State Judicial Interpretation," *Journal of Criminal Law and Criminology* 78 (1987): 644–698.
28. The relationship between offender and victim is under intense study, particularly for stranger and serial rapists. See James LeBeau, "Patterns of Stranger and Serial Rape Offending: Factors Distinguishing Apprehended and At-Large Offenders," *Journal of Criminal Law and Criminology* 78 (1987): 309–326.
29. See Patricia Cluss et al., "The Rape Victim: Psychological Correlates of Participation in the Legal Process," *Criminal Justice and Behavior* 10 (1983): 342–357.
30. David Finkelor, "Removing the Child—Prosecuting the Offender in Cases of Sexual Abuse: Evidence from the National Reporting System for Child Abuse and Neglect," *Child Abuse and Neglect* 7 (1983): 195–205.
31. Jean Goodwin et al., *Sexual Abuse: Incest Victims and Their Families* (Boston: John Wright, 1982).
32. Lynda Lytle Holmstrom and Ann Wolbert Burgess, *The Victim of Rape* (New Brunswick, N.J.: Transaction Books, 1983).
33. John Driggs and Thomas H. Zoet, "Breaking the Cycle—Sex Offenders on Parole," *Corrections Today* 49 (1987), p. 124.
34. Gennaro Vito and Deborah Wilson, "Forgotten People: Elderly Inmates," *Federal Probation* 49 (1985): 18–24.
35. O. W. Kelsey, "Elderly Inmates Need Special Care," *Corrections Today* 48 (1986), p. 56.
36. Ann Goetting, "Racism, Sexism and Ageism in the Prison Community," *Federal Probation* 54 (1985): 10–22.

Recommended Readings _____

Adams, Kenneth. "Former Mental Patients in a Prison and Parole System: A Study of Socially Disruptive Behavior," *Criminal Justice and Behavior* 10 (1983): 358–384.

American Friends Service Committee, *Struggle for Justice*. New York: Hill and Wang, 1971.

Busher, Walter. *Jail Overcrowding: Identifying Causes and Planning For Solutions. A Handbook for Administrators*. Washington, D.C.: American Justice Institute, 1983.

Cory, Bruce and Stephen Gettinger. *Time to Build? The Realites of Prison Construction*. New York: Edna McConnell Clark Foundation, 1984.

Greenfield, Lawrence. *Prisoners in 1986*. Washington, D.C.: U. S. Department of Justice, 1987.

Grossman, Jody, and Donald McDonald. *Survey of Inmates 65 Years of Age and Over, February 1981*. Albany, New York: Department of Correctional Services, 1981.

Handler, Joel, and Julie Katz, eds. *Neither Angels Nor Thieves: Studies in the Deinstitutionalization of Status Offenders*. Washington, D.C.: National Academy Press, 1982.

Harrington, Maxine, and Ann O'Regan Keary. "The Insanity Defense in Juvenile Proceedings," *Prosecutor* 17 (1983): 31–35.

Harry, Joseph. *Gay Children Grow Up*. New York: Prager, 1982.

Innes, Christopher. "The Effect of Prison Density on Prisoners," *The Criminal Justice Archive and Information Network*. Ann Arbor, Michigan: CJAIN, 1987. *Profile of State Prison Inmates, 1986*. Washington D.C.: U. S. Department of Justice, 1988.

Kline, Susan. *Jail Inmates 1986*. Washington, D.C.: U. S. Department of Justice, 1987.

Nacci, Peter, and Thomas Kane. "Sex and Sexual Aggression in Federal Prisons: Inmate Involvement and Employee Impact," *Federal Probation* 48 (March 1984): 46–53.

National Sheriffs' Association. *Inmates' Legal Rights*. Alexandria, Virginia: National Sheriffs' Association, 1987.
  Manual of Jail Administration. Washington, D.C.: National Sheriffs' Association, 1976.

Sickman, Melissa, and Phillis Jo Baunach. *Children in Custody*. Washington, D.C.: U. S. Department of Justice, 1986.

Simonsen, Clifford and Marshall Gordon. *Juvenile Justice in America*. New York, NY: Macmillan, 1982.

Stephan, James and Phillis Jo Baunach. *1984 Census of State Adult Correctional Facilities*. Washington, D.C.: U. S. Department of Justice, 1987.

Stinchcombe, Arthur, et al. *Crime and Punishment: Changing Attitudes in America*. San Fancisco: Jossey-Bass, 1980.

U. S. Bureau of the Prisons. *Female Offenders in the Federal Prison System*. Washington, D.C.: U. S. Bureau of the Prisons, 1977.

Wilson, Rob. "Who Will Care for the 'Mad and the Bad'?" *Corrections Magazine* 6 (February 1980): 5–17.

Correctional
Administration

CHAPTER

19

Management and Organization

As a formal analytical point of reference, primacy
of orientation to the attainment of a specific goal
is used as the defining characteristic of an
organization which distinguishes it from other
types of social systems.
—TALCOTT PARSONS

According to the U.S. Department of Justice, $13,034,221,000 was expended by federal, state, county, and municipal governments for corrections at yearend 1985, an increase of $2,000,000,000 in just one year.[1] This reflects a 197 percent increase for corrections in the decade between 1976 and 1985.[2] California alone plans to spend $1.2 billion to build state prisons over the next five years in order to accommodate the doubling of its inmate populations. Before prison construction bonds are retired (paid off) over a thirty-year period, the real cost to California will come closer to $12 billion.[3]

Corrections is a truly *big* business, in terms of costs, resources, personnel and payroll. The average annual cost per inmate in prisons alone was over $17,000 in 1986. The quality of people who manage this huge sum of money, the kinds of efficient and effective organizational techniques they employ, and the ways in which they try to improve the corrections "nonsystem" will probably in large part determine whether corrections moves ahead or reverts to already proven guidelines for failure.

This chapter is devoted to an update and examination of organizational and management theory as it is, or is not, applied to corrections. It is perhaps in this arena that the professional can show the public that corrections can be made cost effective and, if it cannot always improve an offender, at least it will not make him or her worse. We are especially grateful for the use of materials from the Research Report of the Joint Commission on Correctional Manpower and Training, *Developing Correctional Administrators,* to illustrate that not only is correctional administration developing, but it is occasionally at the cutting edge of development—although in too few instances.

Evolution of the Management Function in Corrections[4] _____

Daniel Glaser summarized the history of corrections by suggesting that we have passed through three stages, each characterized by a particular emphasis in the handling of offenders: first, *revenge;* second, *restraint;* and finally, *reformation.*[5] Correction management has mirrored these changing emphases and presently reflects increasing commitment of the system to a fourth goal, that of *reintegrating* the offender into the community.[6]

We must recognize, however, that each new emphasis was superimposed upon the earlier ones. Thus the present network of services is a bewildering combination of all of the functions mentioned. The nation's jails, for example, although primarily serving the function of revenge and restraint, occasionally develop programs for reforming and rehabilitating individual offenders. On the other hand, even the most advanced probation and parole agencies seek to restrain as well as to reform and reintegrate offenders, as evidenced by concern with varied sanctions designed to induce conforming behavior by those under correctional supervision.[7]

The nature of the "mix" between reformation and restraint as correctional management modalities has varied greatly by type of organization. Table 19.1 indicates some of the major tendencies. There are, however, interesting contradictions and reversals of these tendencies. Some forms of intensive individual treatment are not available to offenders until they establish criminal career patterns or commit violent crimes and are institutionalized. Some of the most advanced forms of treatment (for example, "milieu therapy," in which both staff and inmates are given responsibility for implementing the treatment goal) are found more often in institutions than under probation or parole auspices.[8]

Influence of the Prison

The traditional prison (the archetype of all correctional organizations) was an autocracy. Its single purpose was to maintain custody over the

TABLE 19.1 **Reformation and Restraint in Corrections**

Tendency Toward Restraint	Tendency Toward Reformation
Programs for adult offenders	Programs for juvenile offenders
Programs for male offenders	Programs for female offenders
Programs for recidivistic offenders	Programs for infrequent offenders
Programs for "dangerous" offenders	Programs for "nondangerous" offenders
Institution-based programs	Community-based programs (probation and parole)

inmates. To accomplish this, it developed a rigid and highly stratified hierarchy along the lines of a military organization. Authority and status were related to rank, from the warden to the guard. Each separate institution became its own small kingdom and the warden became the king.

Staff tended to be highly protective of this structure, holding to the closely defined prerequisites and prerogatives attached by custom to the various positions and levels. The reorganization of many correctional institutions within the last few decades has added another kind of hierarchy, the noncustodial personnel, to the framework of organization. A deputy warden in charge of treatment, heading a battery of professional and specialized services, was given formal authority and position equal to those of the deputy warden in charge of custody.

Business managers, heads of prison industries, and directors of honor camp programs were added, according to local needs. The special authority connected with worker function and specialization was fitted into the structure alongside the traditional authority of rank and seniority held by custodial personnel. These trends led to major redistributions of power and authority in the formal organization and resulted in a variety of stresses and adjustments in the informal organization of most institutions.[9]

In addition, these developments have tended to confuse and affect the expanded number of environments in which to make decisions and restrict choices that would be made by other administrators in the prison. This environment has changed drastically for correctional organizations as they have evolved from the traditional form. In the authoritarian prison, all significant decisions were made at or very near the top of the hierarchy. Moreover, these decisions were made according to simple and well-understood criteria. Such values as good control and safe custody have a concrete quality when compared with such vague prescriptions as "helping each individual to the extent that he is able to help himself" or "individualizing treatment according to the needs and problems of each inmate."[10]

One effect of adding more complex and nebulous criteria to the administrator's decision-making matrix has been to force the actual making of decisions downward toward the level of functional operations. The more difficulty that administrators have encountered in harmonizing treatment and custodial values in statements of policy and procedure, the more they have left to their subordinates the responsibility for making significant decisions. Even while the prison was establishing itself as the dominant organizational form for adjudicated offenders, other approaches developed. Institutions for juveniles, although influenced by their adult counterparts, tended to be smaller, less monolithic, and more committed to the goal of individual treatment. Probation and parole organizations, operating in the free community, produced less encapsulated, formal, and hierarchical management structures. Nevertheless, certain characteristics of penitentiaries and reformatories have conditioned the process of management and the style of managers in all correctional settings.

Characteristics of Correctional Management

Three pervasive themes have run through correctional management. First, the goals of restraint and reformation have helped reenforce correctional administrators' perceptions of offenders as morally, psychologically, physically, and educationally inferior human beings who must be upgraded and, in the meantime, controlled. As a result of this perception, correctional administrators focus the resources at their command primarily on the individual offender.

Because the offender is the principal target of organizational activity, little effort is made to mobilize and co-opt community resources, a function that is the very essence of the reintegration model of correctional intervention. This management posture has many consequences, such as the division of offenders into "caseloads" for purposes of treatment and supervision, recruitment of varied specialists (therapists) whose efforts are seldom coordinated and, as mentioned above, the scarcity of well-conceived efforts to work cooperatively with such community institutions as the schools, employment services, and neighborhood centers. As Richard Cloward pointed out:

> In order to ease the process of reintegration in the community, we shall have to give much greater attention than we do now to our aftercare [parole] programs. Since the real struggle between conformity and deviance takes place back in the community, the aftercare program is strategic. Yet aftercare tends to be the weakest program in most correctional systems. Somehow correctional administrators are reluctant to allocate funds for aftercare if that means reducing the scope of prestigeful clinical activities within the institution itself. Professional personnel, in turn, often tend to shun aftercare work. Somehow the thought of spending one's time working with families, teachers, and employers in the interests of mobilizing social opportunities for [an offender] seems distasteful; such activities do not carry the same prestige as therapeutic activities. But whatever the reasons, aftercare programs seem to get short shrift in the allocation of personnel and money.[11]

A second persistent attribute of correctional management has been a gradualist approach to program development and change. This approach has been characterized by a somewhat frivolous subscription to "new" ideas and generally nonrigorous, nonscientific rules of thumb for determining what to delete from the old system and what to add to it. The predominant conservatism of system managers has militated against deviations from familiar ways and has led to tokenism in the launching of new measures.

Correctional administrators are not so much responsible for this condition as they are victims of two realities: society's uncertainty about the causes and solutions of the crime problem, and the present inability of social science and research to provide a solid frame of reference for considering alternative courses of action and estimating their consequences.[12] Nevertheless, in any effort to understand how correctional executives might be effective innovators, it is necessary to confront the difficulties and frustration that currently surround the process of change.

It is important to note that there are numerous small-scale examples of change in correctional organization and programming that run counter to the general pattern we have described.[13] Some experimental programs have been firmly supported by theoretical premises and have been evaluated objectively. Some correctional administrators and consultants have made an effort to make change additive rather than fragmentary. Some executives in the system have attempted to move toward change along relatively rational lines while still coping skillfully with a plethora of "irrational" forces in their environments. It is this growing edge of innovation, of improved dissemination of knowledge, and of close connection between discovery and implementation of technique that offers hope for gains in the near future.

The third and final theme, which has its roots in the "prison culture" of the past and still runs through correctional management today, is the syndrome of isolationism and withdrawal. This condition has helped conceal from the public the realities of life in institutions and probation and parole agencies and has thus acted to perpetuate stereotypes and myths. Prisons, after all, were designed and located to keep criminals out of the sight and mind of the larger populace. Prison administrators found it expedient to honor that mandate. When community-based correctional programs gingerly sought to gain a foothold, their managers seems intuitively to avoid exposure to public scrutiny and judgment. Whereas the police tend to publicize aggressively their views of crime and punishment, the leaders of corrections tend to avoid public debate, particularly debate centering on controversial issues.[14]

This tendency has had serious consequences. The correctional field has had little success in developing public understanding and support for needed changes. Simplistic or erroneous conceptions of the nature of crime and its treatment have flourished, partly because there have not been effective spokespeople for more sophisticated interpretations, especially at times of "opportunity" when conflict or crisis have awakened the interest of an otherwise apathetic public.[15]

Pressures Toward Integration of Services

One of the most important developments in American corrections over the past three decades has been a movement toward the centralization and integration of services in some of the more progressive systems. The concept of a coordinated correctional system possessing a variety of rehabilitative services and custodial facilities was in direct contradiction to the historic pattern in which the head of each penal institution reigned almost as a monarch, typically under the large umbrella of a multipurpose "administrative" board. As one researcher pointed out as early as 1951:

> The trend is marked and distinct. Increasing centralization of authority and responsibility is evident in correctional organizations. The movement is in the direction away from decentralization.... The single state department with a professional administrator is doubtless the most satisfactory administrative form developed to date. More extensive authority and direction over corollary functions—probation, parole, local jails—reflect the growing unity of correctional administration.[16]

Generally, most of the significant innovations in correctional practice have occurred within professional, centralized administrative systems whose parts were related through a coherent framework of policy and whose programs were implemented through planning, research, and varied staff services. The field of corrections needs more unification.[17]

Yet, although centralization of correctional services within jurisdictions has been a major trend, the correctional services of the nation as a whole remain balkanized. Different levels of government operate the same services. There are schisms between services for juveniles and services for adults, between institutional facilities and community-based programs. The jails are more attached to the world of law enforcement than to the corrections establishment. The correctional field is still undecided as to whether a board or a single administrator can provide more effective management for correctional systems and programs. It is still divided, for example, as

Training Mid-Level Managers (Courtesy Federal Bureau of Prisons)

to whether the administration of field parole services should be controlled by the boards that make release decisions or by the departmental structures that administer institutional services.

Corrections and the Development of a Science of Management _____

As corrections has evolved and changed, producing new styles of management and proliferating new environments for administrators, so also have there been pervasive changes in theories of formal organization and in concepts related to administration leadership and behavior. The evolution of correctional management has moved along pathways that run generally parallel to this larger movement.

Conceptions of formal organizations and the roles of their managers have changed radically in the past half-century. Frederick Taylor's "scientific management" movement portrayed the administrator as a highly skilled technician who ensured the smooth operation of such organizational processes as planning, organizing, staffing, directing, coordinating, reporting, and budgeting.[18] Seen from this vantage point, the ideal executive is a rational individual who manipulates the levers of a human machine, correcting deficiencies by rearranging the span of control, the line of command, or the interrelationships of the structural components. Taylor's emphasis was on the anatomy of the system as symbolized by the organizational chart. The basic human tendency not to conform to official specification was ignored, a fact that contributed greatly to the early demise of the scientific management movement.

The so-called human relations movement that followed proclaimed somewhat pompously (as it now seems) that the needs and predilections of the human participants within formal organizations exert a powerful influence, and management would do well to recognize and accommodate them.[19] It was argued that the workers' need to find rewarding social satisfactions in their relationships with one another operates as a strong determinant of morale, and therefore of production. Research findings soon reinforced this position.[20]

One contribution of this school of thought was an elaboration of the idea of "informal organization," which takes into account how the actual dynamics of status and influence differ from the static lines and boxes on a organization chart. The boss's secretary, it was pointed out, may exercise great influence, though he or she has little formal status, because he or she can control the access of people and information to his or her superior. In the correctional institution, the warden would often relate better to shift lieutenants or line staff than to treatment or other noncustodial staff, even though the latter may be higher ranked in the formal organizational structure.

In recent years, more sophisticated theories and research methodologies have been brought to bear on the informal side of organization life. Just as prisons came to be conceived of as social systems, generic theories of organization began to define all of the systems within which workers join together to accomplish work goals as "complex" and "open."[21]

Concern for the psychological and social ingredients of organization life emphasized the responsibility of management to create conditions under which participants could use their capacities fully and creatively.[22] Attention was given to the dilemma of satisfying concurrently the legitimate requirements of the individual and the organization.[23] In contrast with the former preoccupation with hierarchy and the downward flow of authority, modern theorists argue that organizations should be seen as composites of problem-solving groups in which the leaders are primarily concerned with generating wide participation among the members and in which the decision-making power is shared with the members.[24]

Some recent formulations concerning management techniques seem especially applicable to developments in the field of corrections and therefore help provide a context for much research. Schein pointed out that the work styles of managers reflect the assumptions that they make about people.[25] He set forth four views or assumptions about the nature of humankind that seem to have been operative in correctional management.

The first view sees people as rational and economic in nature, primarily motivated by materialistic rewards, requiring from management a firm structure of incentives and controls in order to carry out predetermined tasks.

The second view sees the worker as social, primarily motivated by a need for meaningful relationships with others, requiring from management a concern for personal feelings and a structuring of work to bring about satisfying human interactions and group experiences.

The third view sees humankind as potentially self-actualizing. After satisfying lower-level needs, such as survival, self-esteem, and autonomy,[26] people respond to internal forces in seeking a sense of achievement and meaning in their work. The function of management, under this view, is to facilitate the efforts of correctional staff members to use their energies in creative and productive ways.

The fourth view sees the worker as complex and, though capable of self-actualization, highly varied in responding to different situations. This view challenges management to develop diagnostic skills and wide flexibility in meeting the needs, and thereby maximizing the contribution, of different organization members under constantly changing circumstances.

Some aspects of all these views can be found in both historic and contemporary correctional administration. The staffs of large, routinized institutions have generally been treated by management as rational-economic. Smaller institutions (especially those for juvenile offenders) and community-based correctional programs have moved toward the view that employees are motivated by social as well as economic satisfactions. Some of the most interesting experimental programs (for example, institutional efforts to develop "therapeutic communities," and demonstrations of intensive treatment on probation or parole)[27] have given the staff many opportunities for self-actualization. And some managers do view their staff as complex and seek to use varied skills and methods in working with them, along the lines suggested by Schein.

We must remember, of course, that correctional administrators have managerial relationships not only with staff but also with offenders. Indeed, it is the balancing and harmonizing of these two sets of relationships that create some of the most difficult problems, perhaps because administrators (consciously or unconsciously) adopt one view of people when dealing with staff and another when dealing with offenders. Consider, for example, the dynamics that might occur in an institution in which the management treats staff as motivated by social and economic needs, while viewing inmates as capable of responding only to coercion.[28]

The historic and contemporary picture of correctional management's view of offenders seems even more varied than its view of staff. Many offenders have been, and still are, viewed as responding only to force or threat of force. Both the time-honored penal work programs,[29] which offer opportunities for small earnings on a sliding scale, and the practice of reducing the time of incarceration (giving "good time") for conforming behavior stem from a rational-economic view of inmates.

One of the most significant developments in correctional rehabilitation — the use of small-group process to bring about changes of attitude and behavior — seems to rest on the concept that offenders are social humans. Other innovations, such as work or educational furloughs, have overtones of both the self-actualization and the complex views of offenders. Our position is that correctional management will be most effective if it is generally consistent in its view of all participants, whether staff or offenders, and if it seeks to develop approaches to them based on the assumption that, though complex, they are capable of self-actualization.

Another formulation from management theory that seems useful in assessing trends in correctional administration is the typology of organization and management styles suggested by Likert.[30] Distinguishing basically between authoritative and participative organizations, Likert posited four approaches to management, each with specified consequences for the motivation of participants, their job satisfaction, communication, decisionmaking, production, and other variables. The four types, which Likert viewed as stages of development, from ineffective and pathological to effective and healthy management are (1) exploitive-authoritative, (2) benevolent-authoritative, (3) participative-consultative, and (4) participative-group.

It appears that aspects of all four approaches are found in contemporary correctional organizations. The general trend, however, has been away from type 1, which is illustrated by the traditional prison with its dependence on coercive uses of authority, and into types 3 and 4 through a mixture of benevolently applied authority and limited democratization of the management process. The use of inmate advisory counsels, the delegation of case management authority to probation and parole officers, and the involvement of junior staff in long-range planning are examples of the participative-consultative practices adopted in many correctional agencies, particularly those based in or closely tied to the community. The general pattern in corrections, however, seems closer to Likert's benevolent-authoritative type than to any of the other three.

Some progressive correctional programs operate along lines similar to Likert's fourth type, participative-group. Examples of such an approach can be found in the New Jersey Highfields experiment, the Pinehills project in Utah, and the California Community Treatment project. Though differing from one another in many ways, these and similar experimental ventures distribute influence and decisional power widely among the staff and the offenders involved and use extensively the group process in guiding program operation.

Correctional administrators should seek to develop participation at all levels within their organizations. It should be recognized, however, that much empirical research is needed (both in correctional administration and in generic management processes) to refine understanding of how participative techniques may be employed successfully and how they may be adapted to the realities of particular programs.[31] As has already been noted, precipitous efforts to democratize correctional organizations not only tend to be dangerous but also are usually destined to fail. The introduction of participative methods into programs that are oriented toward the goals of revenge and restraint requires great sensitivity to the forces at work in the organization and in its environment.

Fragmentation of Corrections ————————————————————————————————

The preceding chapters have examined the various components of the correctional system, their development, and the clients they serve. It should now be apparent that the segment of the criminal justice system we call *corrections* is actually a poorly connected network of many other subsystems, most of them directed to a specific kind of clientele. Probation and parole are often not in tune with institutional programs; juvenile courts, adult institutions, and community programs often vie with one another for resources and personnel. Women's institutions and special-category offender programs are pushed into the background, whereas the larger correctional units get top priority.

These various programs all compete for the same limited dollars in state and local correctional budgets, often resulting in an attempt by administrators to distribute shortages equitably, rather than making a coordinated

TABLE 19.2 Sentencing Options Available to Courts

Sentencing Option

Death Penalty—In some States for certain crimes such as murder, the courts may sentence an offender to death by electrocution, exposure to lethal gas, hanging, lethal injection, or other method specified by State law.

Incarceration—The confinement of a convicted criminal in a Federal or State prison or a local jail to serve a court-imposed sentence. Custody is usually within a jail, administered locally, or a prison, operated by the State or the Federal government. In many States, offenders sentenced to less than 1 year are held in a jail; those sentenced to longer terms are committed to the State prison.

Probation—The sentencing of an offender to community supervision by a probation agency, often as a reult of suspending a sentence to confinement. Such supervision normally entails the provision of specific rules of conduct while in the community. If violated, a sentencing judge may impose a sentence of confinement. It is the most widely used correctional disposition in the United States.

Split sentences and shock probation—A penalty that explicity requires the convicted person to serve a period of confinement in a local, State, or Federal facility (the "shock") followed by a period of probation. This penalty attempts to combine the use of community supervision with a short incarceration experience.

Restitution—The requirement that the offender provide financial remuneration for the losses incurred by the victim.

Community Service—The requirement that the offender provide a specified number of hours of public service work, such as collecting trash in parks and other public facilities.

Fines—An economic penalty that requires the offender to pay a specific sum of money within the limit set by law. Fines are often imposed in addition to probation or as an alternative to incarceration.

Source: Bureau of Justice Statistics, *Report to the Nation on Crime and Justice* (Washington, D.C.: U.S. Department of Justice, 1983), p. 73.

and effective use of whatever funds are available. The fragmentation of the criminal justice system as a whole is one of the major barriers to developing effective rehabilitative programs; disorganization at the correctional level only aggravates an already critical situation.

The correctional system is divided into six administrative areas: (1) jails and detention facilities, (2) probation and parole, (3) adult institutions, (4) special category institutions, (5) community corrections, and (6) juvenile corrections. (The military offender belongs in a separate and distinct category with an organizational structure of its own, not generally integrated into state and local correctional programs.) We shall now examine these separate and semiautonomous organizational subcategories, their characteristics and administrative problems (see Table 19.2).

There are over 5,000 correctional facilities of various types in the United States and almost 2,500 probation and parole agencies. It is estimated that only some 16 percent of the adult and juvenile correctional facilities are operated at the federal and state level. The remaining 84 percent, consisting mostly of jails and detention facilities, are operated by the counties and cities of the nation. The major organizational issues are addressed in a 1971 report by the Advisory Commission of Intergovernmental Relations:

All but four states have highly fragmented correctional systems, vesting various correctional responsibilities in either independent boards or noncorrectional agencies. In forty-one states, an assortment of health, welfare, and youth agencies exercise certain correctional responsibilities, though their primary function is not corrections.

In over forty states, neither state nor local governments have full-scale responsibility for comprehensive correctional services. Some corrections services, particularly parole and adult and juvenile institutions, are administered by state agencies, while others, such as probation, local institutions and jails, and juvenile detention, are county or city responsibilities.

More than half of the states provide no standard-setting or inspection services to local jails and local correctional institutions.[32]

The details of these organizational problems, with regard to each of the basic areas in the correctional system, are discussed below.

Jails and Detention Facilities

It should be recalled that the local jail or detention facility is essentially used to hold accused persons prior to trial and sentencing. Most jurisdictions also use such facilities to hold a mixture of other categories as well, including those awaiting transfer to a prison, those on appeal, those serving short misdemeanor sentences, some who are serving longer sentences, mentally disordered persons, juveniles, and federal and military offenders awaiting transfer. Thus, the jails are used for a variety of short-term detention purposes, becoming a convenient warehouse for the storage of assorted suspects, offenders, and social outcasts.

The jails have basically remained under local control. Two of the main problems with the administration of these facilities are the demand that they accept and handle almost any kind of offender presented to them and the expectation that they can deal with such cases. When such offenders are thrust upon officials who often lack facilities and personnel to cope with them, there is little hope for organizational development beyond whatever stop-gap operations can be devised to maintain minimal functions.

The organizational structure of the jails and detention facilities across America is quite varied, as might be imagined. There are some common characteristics, however. Because most are operated by a law enforcement officer, either a county sheriff or a municipal police chief, the major emphasis is generally on security rather than on rehabilitation. These law enforcement officers impose their own background and personal orientation on the care and treatment of prisoners; more often than not, their approach is at odds with advanced corrections philosophy and movements. The jail and detention facility units constitute by far the most neglected area of the criminal justice system.[33]

The National Advisory Commission addressed the problem of fragmented, localized jail services and the need to merge them into a state-controlled system: "All local detention and correctional functions, both pre- and post-conviction, should be incorporated within the appropriate state system by 1982."[34] While this concept still holds a great deal of merit, such a plan has met considerable resistance at the local level, but the transitions could be encouraged by increased state funding, having periodic state inspection, and allowing state-established operational standards to be phased in over a period of time. Personnel training, facility improvement, and program development should be taken over by the states as soon as possible. Only when the detention stage—the stage at which most offenders enter the corrections process—begins to stress service over custody can the process as a whole work effectively. Improvement in jails and other detention institutions (the largest segment of the process in terms of volume of prisoners and number of facilities) is essential if the goals of the entire criminal justice system are to be realized.[35]

Probation and Parole

The question of which government agency should be responsible for probation—the correctional authority in the executive branch or the courts in the judicial branch—has been the focus of recent controversy. This argument is further aggravated by proponents of a statewide system who wish to avoid the problems of local control and local politics. At present, most states include probation with the correctional components in the executive branch, and others have optional or mixed arrangements.

Dividing parole into the decision-making and supervision processes helps to demonstrate the organizational problems in this subsystem. The decision-making body, in particular, faces a broad range of problems. As mentioned in Chapter 12, the current trend favors a consolidated model. More than 60 percent of state parole boards now integrate their activities with other agencies for offenders, through common administrative structures. This positive move helps relieve the problems of the second area: supervisory services. In recent years, state corrections departments have begun to absorb the supervisory function in adult parole. Consolidation of services is a first step toward providing a real spectrum of programs for adult, juvenile, and misdemeanant parolees. These benefits will also accrue to probationers as they are transferred into correctional systems supervised or administered by the state.

The probation and parole systems, similar in function and goals, have been combined in many jurisdictions, usually at the state and federal levels. Those who argue for maintaining separate probation services at the local level and under the judicial branch are frequently opposed to a similar arrangement for the parole system. There are valid arguments for both sides of this issue of state versus local control of probation, but most of the large urban states have opted for local control, usually at the county level. Several advantages are seen in this approach: probation is more closely tied to the community; there is less bureaucratic red tape in processing; and there is more support from local citizens.

If one examines some of the largest local probation agencies, however, it is difficult to see how a coordinated statewide program could be any less responsive. In the final analysis, it may well be the individual jurisdiction that must weigh the advantages and disadvantages and decide which way to organize for effective probation services.

No matter which type of organization is finally employed, the state must become more involved in the planning, funding, and maintenance of standards for probation services, ensuring that they are uniform and effective across both large and small jurisdictions.

Adult Institutions

Adult institutions include state and federal prisons for both men and women. There are enough similarities among these facilities to consider them as a group in discussing organizational components. Exceptions are special rules or laws that apply only at a particular level of government or to a particular gender; these will be discussed later.

It is difficult to describe a "typical" organizational structure for adult correctional institutions. There are so many different kinds of adult institutions that one can analyze this organization only in terms of the major functions that most of them are supposed to fulfill. Two of these functions — custody and treatment — are so complicated that a separate chapter is devoted to each of them; thus, we shall touch on them only briefly in this discussion of adult institutions.

At the top of the prison staff is the superintendent; the title of *warden* is less common today because of the negative associations it has for so many people. As the staff member whose job most often involves contact with the outside world, the superintendent is responsible for the effective operation of the institution and the quality of the personnel who run it. Thus, the superintendent is considered the "outside" administrator for the correctional institution. The "inside" administrator is one of the superintendent's deputies, usually the deputy in charge of custody rather than treatment.

The original purpose of prisons and, therefore, of the prison staff was to keep offenders confined. The concepts of rehabilitation and correction are relatively new, and the idea of a professional treatment staff is even newer. Modern prisons are the scene of a continuing power struggle between treatment and custody staffs regarding whose function is more important and who deserves the greater share of power and resources inside the walls. The remaining functions are more straightforward; there is no argument as to the necessity and importance of the basic services involved, and so personnel have less of a stake in any internal power struggle. As it exists today, the organization of most correctional institutions is primarily designed to ensure calm and secure operations.

"Don't feel too bad, you might have the solution to prison overcrowding."

Courtesy of the American Correctional Association, *Corrections Today*.

In the past few years, the long-term offender has become a special problem for the correctional administrator. Since about 1979, the attitude of America has become more punitive and has called for longer sentences. In the past, long-term inmates composed a relatively small portion of the residents of the nation's adult institutions. That ratio has grown steadily over the past few years and begins to be a major issue in prison administration and in planning for construction. As prisoners remain in bed space longer and longer periods of time, overcrowding becomes impossible to manage through movement of inmates to less restrictive environments. At the beginning of 1985, the long-term male population averaged 24.8 percent of the total institutional populations, with a range by prison of from 9 percent to 55 percent. Long-term female populations were 18.9 percent of total female institutional population, with these ranging from .3 percent to an incredible 68 percent.[36]

A survey of agencies dealing with the long-term inmate problem gave some guidelines for these difficult management problems. A summary of the findings in the area of correctional administration issues will be of interest to the student of corrections:

Eighty of the responding agencies reported that they were subject to laws influencing the number of long-term inmates they managed (e.g., sentence enhancement, determinate sentencing, and parole eligibility requirements). All but four of the respondents said that they used good time credits to reduce sentences or time served. Approximately 70% also stated they were subject to laws affecting the management of long-termers (e.g., statutes related to work release and furloughs). Over half of the respondents reported that they had been involved in litigation—usually regarding conditions of confinement, classification, or parole eligibility—that impacted upon management of their long-term populations.

Such legislative and legal factors have influenced correctional administration in a variety of ways. As the proportion of long-termers in both the male and female prison populations has risen in most reporting jurisdictions, agencies noted that bed space, particularly in maximum security, was tied up for longer periods, thwarting appropriate housing assignments for all inmates. Respondents also indicated that stress and disruptive behavior tended to increase.

In what seems to be an effort to better manage their growing long-term populations, 76.9% of the male survey respondents and 55.2% of the female survey respondents reported that they considered long-termers in current agency planning. Areas of consideration included physical plant construction or renovation, bed space projections, staffing, and budgeting.[37]

The stress on custody in most prisons has led to a movement to include the private sector in running prisons or portions of traditional prison programs. Private enterprise runs some juvenile institutions, such as the Weaversville Intensive Treatment Unit in Pennsylvania.[38] Private medical organizations have contracted to supply comprehensive medical services to state prison systems, and more and more, private enterprise is entering the prison industry area.[39] The effectiveness and profitability of these efforts remains to be proved, but the movement represents a realistic appraisal of the potential for the private sector's involvement in prison activities.

Special Category Institutions: In Transition

The special category institutions have traditionally been the domain of mental health administrators. In some states, the administration of these institutions lies in a gray area overlapping corrections and mental health. The issues of right to treatment and indeterminate commitment have created considerable confusion as to the appropriate administrative procedures, especially in jurisdictions in which inmates in ordinary correctional institutions have no recourse to due process.

The organizational structure of most special category institutions parallels that of most prisons. Although treatment is usually the stated purpose of these institutions, the main emphasis is on custody and control, often for very long periods of time. Both correctional and mental health authorities want to keep special category offenders out of prison, and stays in specialized institutions are lengthened accordingly.

The recent emphasis on forensic psychiatry, which focuses on the special legal problems of the mentally disturbed offender, has encouraged the creation of new organizational divisions, sometimes under corrections and sometimes under mental health. When these forensic psychiatric divisions are able to offer the same range of services to their special clients that other correctional subsystems offer, especially when they are constitutionally required, then the threat of continued legal action by these clients to obtain these services will diminish. The community-based correctional system will probably serve as a model for forensic psychiatric programs over the next few decades.

A total continuum of services, from outpatient care to maximum security, will be administered by trained professionals who are attuned to the needs of the special category offender. This movement is only just beginning, and it has yet to encounter many of the obstacles that have plagued the development and humanization of other treatment delivery systems.

Community Corrections

Corrections has undergone great change in the years since the emphasis shifted from custody to rehabilitation. Public safety demands that the convicted offender emerge from our correctional system a better person, certainly no worse, than when he or she entered it. These high expectations have stimulated the search for more effective ways to handle offenders. One reason for the pressure to create community-based corrections has been the recognition that prisonization can actually aggravate an offender's criminality.

It is clear that the future of corrections lies in these community-based programs. A major obstacle, however, is the prominence of the institutional model, with its physical plants and other programs already in operation, whereas no organized community program has yet gained widespread acceptance. So far, most community programs have emerged as demonstration projects or individual experiments, rather than as the products of systematic interaction among police, courts, and conventional correctional services.[40]

Community-based correctional systems vary in scope from state-controlled networks of halfway houses and reintegration centers to volunteer programs operating a single residential unit for as few as six inmates or for a single court. The goals of such programs are seen as humanitarian, restorative, and economic. These goals will be discussed in detail in Chapter 25, but it is important to understand why they offer a greater potential for rehabilitation than past institutional goals did. Incarceration clearly is a series of destructive situations: for the offender, the custody model intensifies the likelihood of physical danger, deprivation of human values, and loss of self-esteem. It is a basic humanitarian concept that only offenders who pose a threat to society should be subjected to the trauma of incarceration. This last issue demands, of course, a valid system of diagnosis, classification, and evaluation.

One weakness apparent in analyzing the administrative or management functions in a community corrections agency is that the director, supervisors, and counselors are promoted from within the ranks because of their abilities as professionals or practitioners, with little regard for their training or qualifications as administrators. Or, if they have received training, it is too specialized in nature, too related to a specific field. Although those who find themselves in such positions do the best they can to perform adequately as administrators, they are nevertheless handicapped by their training or background.

Juvenile Justice: Courts or Corrections?

The juvenile justice system, like most other correctional subsystems, is weakened by fragmentation and lack of agreement on the needs of the juvenile offender, as opposed to the protection needs of society. The model most used in the past centers on a benevolent judge, acting as a guardian of the youth's rights in the name of the state *(parens patriae)*. The common approach to the juvenile as a delinquent rather than a criminal has resulted in overly casual juvenile justice procedures.[41] One might expect such informality to benefit the young offender, but a more common result is that the juvenile's rights are ignored and violated instead of protected.

The basic organizational structure of the juvenile court was designed to keep the judge in control at all stages of the procedure, from adjudication to release back into the community. When the concept of corrections and rehabilitation emerged in the adult criminal justice system, the gap between the goals of the two systems narrowed. The provision of due process and many other rights to the adult system highlighted the absence of these basic considerations in most juvenile courts, and this problem was remedied with the U.S. Supreme Court's decision *In re Gault* (see Chapter 17). It has become obvious that with decreased emphasis on *parens patriae* and the affirmation of due process in the juvenile system, new organizational structures are now necessary.

Summary ——

Correctional administrators will face a series of challenging tasks in the last half of the 1980s. It is clear that the inmate population for which they must provide custody and treatment has changed drastically, both in the level of violent behavior and in the time to be incarcerated. The correctional administrator has also been alerted to certain rights and has had to provide inmates with counsel to ensure them. Citizen groups, official and unofficial, have begun to take an interest in corrections. Union activity among the correctional staff and the correctional population has begun to spread. As treatment techniques are developed to correct some categories of offenders, the issue is raised as to the administration's right to use them—and the offender's right to receive them. It sometimes appears that every step forward is counteracted by two steps back.

Modern management techniques have had a hard time gaining acceptance in a system that was an autocracy for over 150 years. It is not hard to understand that wardens of the 1950s would want to become the superintendents of the 1980s, if they have to give up the absolute control they had held in the past. Systems in transition have made it difficult for these leaders, many of whom came up through the ranks of custody staff, to change easily. The complexities of the modern correctional institution, with a broad range of staff that is often better educated and more attuned to the needs of a complex organization, are a major difficulty for the "new" *superintendent* role. Budgets, accountability, planning, personnel issues, legal issues, and many other knotty problems make the job hard to deal with.

In an era of shrinking governmental treasuries and rapidly growing inmate populations, the major problem for the correctional administrator seems to be able to do more with less. The educational needs for the upper-level management in corrections continue to grow. It will not be long before the correctional administrator will find himself or herself having to complete an MBA or an MPA degree in order to deal with the issues. When a relatively small institution puts a $12–13 million budget in the hands of the superintendent, it seems essential that the profession rethink the needs of staff at all levels, but especially those of the superintendent (CEO) of the facility.

Despite these problems facing the correctional administrator, there are hopeful signs of progress. Public disenchantment with the prison as a solution to the rehabilitation and reintegration of offenders has caused a general movement toward community-based corrections.[42] This in turn has stimulated a general upgrading of corrections personnel, accompanied by a movement toward professionalism and collective action by both custody and treatment staffs.

Corrections is becoming a more attractive career for the new graduate of criminal justice programs at the community colleges and universities across the country. The infusion of young professionals will be of significant help to hard-pressed correctional administrators as they face the even more complex emerging issues of the 1990s.

Review Questions _____

1. Why do prisons receive the largest share of the correctional budget?
2. What is meant by "unification of corrections"?
3. Historically, what are the three main stages in handling offenders?
4. Why are prisoners isolated from the outside?
5. Superintendents can be thought of as the "outside administrators" of prisons. What does this mean?
6. What are the four sets of assumptions about the nature of humankind that have operated in correctional management?

Key Terms _____

1. revenge (p. 456)
2. restraint (p. 456)
3. reformation (p.456)
4. autocracy (p.456)
5. caseloads (p. 458)
6. scientific management (p. 461)
7. informal organization (p. 461)
8. fragmentation (p. 464)
9. superintendent (p. 473)
10. public disenchantment (p. 473)

Notes _____

1. *Sourcebook of Criminal Justice Statistics—1986*, (Washington, D.C.: U.S. Department of Justice, 1987), p. 2.
2. Based on Ted Gest, "Bulging Prisons: Curbing Crime or Wasting Lives?" *U.S. News and World Report* (April 23, 1984): 42–45.
3. Bruce Cory and Stephen Gettinger, *Time to Build? The Realities of Prison Construction* (New York: Edna McConnell Clark Foundation, 1984). See also Jim Galvin, "What Does Incarceration Really Cost?" *Criminal Justice Newsletter* 14 (August 29, 1983): 5.
4. Elmer K. Nelson and C. Lovell, *Developing Correctional Administrators* (Washington, D.C.: Joint Commission in Correctional Manpower and Training, 1969), pp. 4–6, 8–11. We are grateful to the authors for allowing us to use their materials, on which much of the first half of this chapter is based.
5. Daniel Glaser, "The Prospects for Corrections," p. 203. Paper prepared for the Arden House Conference on Manpower Needs in Corrections, mimeographed, 1964. See also Clarence Schrag, "Contemporary Corrections: An Analytical Model." Paper prepared for the President's Commission on Law Enforcement and Administration of Justice, mimeographed, 1966.
6. Richard Allison, "Massachusetts Recidivism Drop Cited As Proof of Success of 'Reintegration' Model," *Criminal Justice Newsletter* 11 (March 3, 1980): 1–2.
7. Stanford Kadish, "The Advocate and the Expert-Counsel in the Peno-Correctional Process," *Minnesota Law Review* 45 (1961): 803. See also Fred Cohen, *The Legal Challenge to Corrections* (Washington, D.C.: Joint Commission on Correctional Manpower and Training, 1969).
8. See *Offenders As a Correctional Manpower Resource* (Washington, D.C.: Joint Commission on Correctional Manpower and Training, 1968).
9. For the understanding of the bases of power in prison, see John Hepburn: "The Exercise of Power in Coercive Organizations: A Study of Prison Guards," *Criminology* 23 (1985): 145–164.

10. Elmer K. Nelson, "The Gulf Between Theory and Practice in Corrections," *Federal Probation* 18 (1954): 48.

11. Richard Cloward, "Social Problems, Social Definitions, and Social Opportunities." Paper prepared for the National Council on Crime and Delinquency, New York, mimeographed, 1963, pp. 9–10. This earlier position is being reexamined in light of recent legal developments, influx of funds, and spread of services available for offenders. See: Harry Steadman et al., "Reevaluating the Custody-Therapy Conflict Paradigm in Correctional Mental Health Settings," *Criminology* 23 (1985): 165–179.

12. But see the excellent evaluation of Joan Petersilia, *The Influence of Criminal Justice Research* (Santa Monica: Rand, 1987).

13. See David Busby, "A Combination That Worked for Us," *Federal Probation* 48 (March 1984): 53–57; and Freddie Smith, Alabama Prison Option: Supervised Intensive Restitution Program," *Federal Probation* 48 (March 1984): 32–35.

14. Francis Cullen and Karen Gilbert, *Reaffirming Rehabilitation* (Cincinnati: Anderson, 1982).

15. See Clifford Simonsen, "Juvenile Justice in the '80s: Myth and Reality," *Liaison* 6 (November 1980): 18–20. An essay on the impacts of "low profilism" in corrections can be found in John Irwin and James Austin, *It's About Time*, (San Francisco: National Council on Crime and Delinquency, 1987).

16. Richard McGee, "State Organization for Correctional Administration," in Paul Tappan, ed., *Contemporary Corrections* (New York: McGraw-Hill, 1951), p. 89. For a more recent affirmation of the same view, see American Correctional Association, *Manual of Correctional Standards,* 3d. ed. (Washington, D.C.: ACA, 1966). The National Academy of Corrections in the National Institute of Corrections conducts many advanced correctional management seminars to teach leadership in corrections. The current mailing address for the National Academy of Corrections is 1790 30th Street, Suite 140, Boulder, Colo., 80301.

17. For an excellent blueprint for further unification, see E. Kim Nelson, R. Cushman, and N. Harlow, "Unification of Community Corrections," (Washington, D.C., U.S. Department of Justice, 1980).

18. Frederick W. Taylor, *The Principles of Scientific Management* (New York: Harper, 1911).

19. For a series of papers illustrating and testifying to this point of view, see Robert Dubin, *Human Relations in Administration* (Englewood Cliffs, N.J.: Prentice-Hall, 1951).

20. Fritz J. Roethliesberger and William J. Dickson, *Management and the Worker* (Cambridge, Mass.: Harvard University Press, 1939).

21. Daniel Katz and Robert L. Kahn, *The Social Psychology of Organizations* (New York: John Wiley, 1966).

22. Douglas McGregor, *The Human Side of Enterprise* (New York: McGraw-Hill, 1960).

23. Chris Argyris, *Integrating the Individual and the Organization* (New York: John Wiley, 1964).

24. Rensis Likert, *New Patterns of Management* (New York: McGraw-Hill, 1961).

25. Edgar H. Schein, *Organizational Psychology* (Englewood Cliffs, N.J.: Prentice-Hall, 1965).

26. Abraham H. Maslow, *Motivation and Personality* (New York: Harper & Row, 1954).

27. Edward Latessa, *Fifth Evaluation of the Lucas County Adult Probation Department's Incarceration Diversion Unit* (Cincinnati: University of Cincinnati, 1984). See also Frank Pearson, "New Jersey's Intensive Supervision Program: A Progress Report," *Crime and Delinquency* 31 (1985): 393–410 and L. Meachum, "House Arrest: The Oklahoma Experience," *Corrections Today* 49 (1986): 102–110.

28. A report of just this situation can be found in James Marquart, "Prison Guards and the Use of Physical Coercion as a Mechanism of Prisoner Control," *Criminology* 24, (1986): 347–391.

29. Barbara Auerbach, "New Prison Industries Legislation: The Private Sector Re-Enters the Field," *Prison Journal* 42 (1982): 25–36.

30. Likert, pp. 223–234.

31. Office of Development, Testing and Dissemination, *Putting Research to Work: Tolls for the Criminal Justice Professional* (Washington, D.C.: U.S. Department of Justice, 1984).

32. Advisory Commission on Intergovernmental Relations, *State-Local Relations in the Criminal Justice System* (Washington, D.C.: U.S. Government Printing Office, 1971), p. 15.

33. See Larry Mays and Joel Thompson, "Mayberry Revisited: The Characteristics and Operations of America's Small Jails." Paper presented at the Annual Meetings of the Academy of Criminal Justice Sciences, St. Louis, March 17, 1987.

34. National Advisory Commission on Criminal Justice Standards and Goals, *Corrections* (Washington, D.C.: U.S. Government Printing Office, 1971), p. 292.

35. Nicholas Demos, "The Future Jail: A Professionally Managed Corrections Center That Controls Its Population," *Federal Probation* 48 (March 1984): 35–40. See also Teri Martin, "Jails and Houses of Correction in Massachusetts: Statewide Planning for the 21st Century," *American Jails* 1 (1987): 25–27.

36. Cindie Unger and Robert Buchanan, *Managing Long-Term Inmates: A Guide For The Correctional Administrator*, (Washington, D.C.: U.S. Government Printing Office, 1985), p. 1.

37. Ibid., p. 3.

38. Kevin Krajick, "Punishment for Profit," *Across the Board* 9 (March 1984): 20–27. See also William Collins, "Privatization: Some Legal Considerations from a Neutral Perspective," *American Jails* 1 (1987): 28–34 and Bruce Rich, "Missouri Joins Private Business to Meet Inmate-Housing Needs," *Corrections Today* 49 (1987): 60–62.

39. CONTACT, Inc., "Prison Industry," *Corrections Compendium* 7 (1982): 5–11; Gail Funk et al., "The Future of Correctional Industries," *Prison Journal* 42 (1982): 37–51.

40. Perhaps the best exception to this generalization is Colorado, a state with an extensive community corrections thrust and organization. Extensive networking and local provision of community service marks Colorado's efforts. See also Tom Powell, "Corrections in Colorado," *Corrections Today* 49 (1987): 124–128.

41. Anne Voight, "Juveniles Commit 23% of Violent Crimes Against Persons," *Justice Assistance News* 2 (September 1981): 1. See also Larry Holtz, "*Miranda* in a Juvenile Setting: A Child's Right to Silence," *Journal of Criminal Law and Criminology* 78 (1987): 534–556.

42. An excellent report on community service orders can be found in Josine Junger-Tas, *The Dutch Experiments with Community Service* (The Hague: Ministry of Justice, 1984).

20

Custody

Prisons are no longer places where just "well-adjusted" offenders are placed. The courts are confining a new breed of "offender"—the retarded, the mentally ill, the young delinquent now branded an adult by court fiat, the AIDS patient, the geriatric prisoner, and now (in serious numbers) the DWI offender. Combine this new population with tougher sentencing practices and parole boards reluctant to release, and there is no doubt the characteristics of prison populations are changing rapidly.
—ANTHONY P. TRAVISONO

Institutions: Bureaucratic Control

As noted in the previous chapter, the prevailing management climate for corrections institutions is bureaucratic control, especially in state institutions. In most major correctional facilities, the inmate population is usually controlled by a combination of coercive rules that prohibit certain kinds of behavior and punishments that are meted out when the rules are broken. Bureaucratic organization is insulated by rules, and violations are punished in the name of equity.

In institutions that hold thousands of prisoners, each with personal problems,[1] the bureaucratic style seems to be the only functional way to cope with control: the process takes precedence over the individual, and prisoners become faceless commodities to be housed, worked, fed, secured, and released. This nineteenth-century model stresses warehousing and processing offenders. Any rehabilitation is incidental, a welcome but low-priority by-product. This bureaucratic style clearly conflicts with any emphasis on rehabilitation. The separate functions of the rigid and formalized organizations create an impoverished climate for behavioral change.[2]

CUSTODY

Refers to the level of immediate control exercised over offenders within correctional institutions. The levels can range from maximum to close, to medium and minimum.

Maximum or close custody usually means that the inmate cannot be trusted to move from one area to another, in the general prison or in the cellblocks, without being escorted by a correctional officer. It also implies that inmates will not be allowed "contact visits," or be allowed to associate with other prisoners freely. They are also limited in their contacts with other persons in general. The ratio of correctional officers to inmates in most maximum to close areas is usually quite high, as many as one per each four inmates (1:4).

Medium and minimum custody levels generally accommodate less risky or dangerous offenders, or those closer to the end of their sentences. Generally speaking, the difference between medium and minimum is the presence of a high fence and armed guard towers surrounding the former, with reasonably free movement within the facility for both. Staff-to-inmate ratios generally decrease, with 1:8 or 1:12 not too uncommon. Generally speaking, administrators will err on the "side of the angels" and assign a higher level of custody level when there is any doubt.

Custody and control have traditionally been the warden's dominant concerns. Until very recently, the warden's principal adviser was almost always the chief of the guard force. And the prison guard was the main instrument of control, the stereotyped "screw" with little compassion and a ready fist. Even though *correctional officers* have now replaced the old-time *guards* in almost all prisons, many still follow the same oppressive custodial procedures, especially in times of unrest. Until the cause-and-effect relationship between bureaucratic organization and institutional disturbance is openly acknowledged, the advocates of strong custodial control will retain their influential role.

Administrative Problem: Punish, Control, or Treat? _____

The divisions of power outlined in the previous chapters suggest some of the reasons why correctional administrators are often confused and hampered in their efforts to correct inmates. Although the public is willing to espouse reformatory goals for corrections, it is not willing to provide the support and funding that would make such reform a legislative priority. This inconsistency places dedicated correctional administrators in an awkward position: they can implement only the most meager of programs, and even then they must maintain an overall emphasis on control and punishment. Regardless of the approach to this problem, some aspect of operations will suffer.[3] If required to increase the number of security guards, the

---

CORRECTIONAL OFFICERS

Whether they have been called "prison guards," "turnkeys," "screws," "hacks," "detention officers," "correctional officers," or "security staff," the general reference is to the persons charged with control, movement management, and observation of the inmates in the jails and prisons of America. There are over 125,000 "line-level" custody staff in our correctional institutions, about 13 percent of whom are women.

Relatively little research has been conducted about American correctional officers who are not supervisory staff. Few criminological studies have been conducted. This is further compounded by the relatively high turnover rates among correctional officers, as high as 25 to 40 percent in many jurisdictions. Much remains to be learned about why some people are attracted to institutional custody work, how long they remain employed, their salaries, and why they choose to leave. These questions are important because correctional officers form the backbone of institutional efforts to control and rehabilitate those offenders committed to the correctional institutions of America.

---

administrator must obtain the necessary funds by decreasing the support for some treatment program. And if the administrator tries to amplify the treatment programs, this must usually be done at the expense of the custody staff.

As if these problems were not enough, a new element has been added in recent years: the unionization of the correctional officers in many jurisdictions. Administrators must deal with unions if their institutions are to function effectively, and collective action by the officers has swung the institutional balance of power in the direction of custody (as opposed to treatment). Preventing a return to outmoded procedures in the face of union strength will be a major task for correctional administrators in the next decade.

Unionization: The Correctional Officers _____

Unionization, found in almost every sector of business and industry, has in recent decades spread to the ranks of state and federal employees. In the past twenty years, the union movement has extended to the "sworn" officers charged with police, fire, and the correctional protection of the public. Police officers and firefighters have established collective bargaining agencies in most urban departments, with improved working conditions and wages as a result. Prohibited in many states by law from going on strike to back up their demands, law enforcement and fire protection officers developed the strategy of massive outbreaks of "blue flu" to emphasize their plight. In the correctional field, the union movement has taken root more slowly.

> **"BLUE FLU"**
> Because many jurisdictions forbid government employees from striking, other tactics are employed to create power negotiation in collective bargaining. One of these is called the "blue flu," the practice of uniformed personnel of taking sick leave *en masse* to back up their demands for improved working conditions, salary increments, and other items on their agenda. This method permits negotiating leverage without forcing the employees to strike, an illegal act.

As agents of public protection became more successful in their demands, their counterparts in the correctional institutions took notice. The great move in the late sixties toward more professionalism, the sharp increases in prisoner populations, community corrections, and other programs pointed up some of the needs of the long-neglected correctional officer. Initial efforts to organize met with disapproval from administrators, often because of limited budgets and already overtaxed security forces in the crowded prisons. Most administrators wanted the few available funds to be used for new personnel, not pay raises for the officers they already had. In some cases the correctional officers did go on strike, and their duties were assumed by the administrative and office personnel.[4]

Because correctional institutions tend to be widely scattered, the growth of the union movement has been slow and fragmented. In addition, as we have suggested, the goals of these collective bargaining agencies sometimes do not correspond to the administration's rehabilitation goals. Organization and collective action have brought many benefits to correctional officers so far, but they will get little sympathy from the administrators and the public until they show concern for the overall mission of the institution as well as their personal needs.

Inmate Organization: The Social System

Prisons are total institutions[5] in which the resident's every activity, moment, movement, and option are carefully regulated by the correctional staff. Inmates are given little individual responsibility and autonomy, important characteristics of everyday life in a modern achievement-oriented society. This tight regime compounds their personal inadequacies rather than correcting them. Cut off from ordinary social intercourse and their families and friends and isolated in bastionlike prisons, inmates are quickly taught by the other residents how to exist in this environment. The process of learning how to exist in prison—learning appropriate attitudes and behaviors, the norms of prison life—is called *prisonization*. This process leads to the adoption of the folkways, mores, customs, and general culture of the prison.[6] Evidently prisonization occurs spontaneously even in newly opened institutions; the process is handed down from prisoner to prisoner, remaining a strong force that is transmitted between prisons, working against the rehabilitation goals of even the most enlightened administrator. It impedes rather than facilitates treatment efforts, preventing inmates from acquiring the skills, talents, attitudes, and behavior necessary for successful adjustment in free society.

Indeed, the opposite tends to occur; inmates are infantalized[7] rather than matured. This situation led the President's Commission on Law Enforcement and Administration of Justice to note that "the conditions in which [inmates] live are the poorest possible preparation for their reentry into society, and often merely reinforce in them a pattern of manipulation and destructiveness."[8]

As part of the process of prisonization, inmates learn codes and roles, and they are subjected to a reward and punishment system that encourages them to act appropriately. Prison codes emphasize a number of specific behaviors: loyalty to other inmates ("never rat on a con," "don't be too nosy or talk too much," "never report a grievance against another inmate to the guards"); maintenance of calm ("keep cool," "don't start feuds"); avoidance of trickery or fraud ("always share with your cellmates," "sell hoarded goods at the going rate"); manliness ("don't complain"); quick-wittedness in prison dealings ("don't be a sucker," "guards are screws, never to be confided in or trusted").

Inmates who conform to these expectations become "real men" who can be trusted and are looked up to by other inmates. They share in the privileges available in prisons, and they can count on support if another inmate attacks them physically. Those who violate the normative structure become outcasts and are referred to by various descriptive and unpleasant names (e.g., "rat," "snitch," "fag," "merchant," "fink," etc.).

Two recent developments in America's prisons have exacerbated these problems. The first is the rise of gangs in prisons. There are four major gangs in California prisons: two Chicano gangs (ghetto Chicanos and the Mexican mafia or "Eme"), the Black Brotherhood, and the Aryan (Caucasian) Brotherhood. Conflicts between the gangs have led to stabbings, murder outside prison, rape, blackmail, and exploitation of nonaligned prisoners. Many wardens have ordered "lockdowns" that confine prisoners to their cells in order to avoid bloodshed and violence, leading to criticism from legislators and prison staff.[9] Prison overcrowding has made matters worse, and many a warden has resigned because of a sense of hopelessness.

The other development resulted from the abolition of parole as a mechanism for the early release of rehabilitated prisoners and those who have benefited from their terms of imprisonment. In this case, motivating inmates to participate in institutional programs has suffered; rehabilitation programs have been less effective; and considerable tension has been created between inmates and correctional staff.[10] Only now are we beginning to learn more about the consequences of abolishing parole, an issue that will be explored in more detail in Chapter 26.

It should be stressed again that the importance of prisonization lies in its negative impact on attempts to provide rehabilitative programs that encourage inmates to engage in legitimate, noncriminal activities.

Institutions: Custody Is a Way of Life _____

The "assistant superintendent for custody" or "security," also known as the deputy warden, is one of the most important figures in the correctional institution. The main responsibility of such deputies is to know where all prisoners are at all times. Techniques employed to ensure that all prisoners are accounted for have become more humane and permissive in recent years, but in most institutions the *count* is still the principal method of determining the prisoners' whereabouts, and counts are sometimes conducted as often as every two hours. Preoccupation with counting and recounting prisoners makes it difficult to conduct meaningful programs or permit individualized operations. To some extent, however, outside work details and opportunities for educational and vocational training and furloughs have been included in more streamlined counting methods. Today, counts are often called in to a central office in the prison's control room and tabulated against the daily tally of inmates, in some cases using

Contraband Can Move in an Institution (Courtesy of American Correctional Association, photo by Michael C. Dersin)

computers.[11] Although the count is more sensibly administered, it remains one of the most important tasks for which the custody staff is responsible.

Another function of the custody staff is to establish and maintain security procedures. Security procedures, at a minimum, include the inspection of persons and vehicles passing in and out of the institution, usually at a sally port at entry and exit points. The sally port is an area enclosed by a double gate. A vehicle or individual enters through the first gate, which is then closed. Before the second gate is opened, the search for forbidden articles (contraband) is made. After the search is completed, the second gate is opened and the individual or vehicle passes through that gate. At no time may both gates be open, and many gate systems are mechanically adjusted so that it is impossible to open them both at the same time. Sometimes a visitor feels that it is as hard to get into the institution as it is to get out. The fear that inmates and visitors will try to smuggle in contraband or other items to assist escape pervades the maximum security prison. Searches of vehicles and the requiring of visitors to pass through electronic metal detectors have become standard practices and procedures at major institutions.

Unfortunately, under the assumption that all inmates are alike, similar security practices have also been adopted by medium and minimum security prisons. It took over a century before America was prepared to build a prison without massive walls; it may take even longer to convince "old-guard" custody personnel that less stringent security measures may serve as well to ensure control.[12]

Prison Rules

Inmate Traffic and Its Control

Rules and regulations for inmates are usually detailed and aimed at strict traffic control. Prisoners' movements are carefully planned and controlled in every detail. In the past, all prisoners were awakened, moved to work, and fed at the same time, always under the eye of custody personnel. This degree of planning has slackened in many institutions; the trend is toward more reasonable controls over inmate traffic within the walls. President Johnson's commission described how some of the highly restrictive rules came into existence:

> [U]nder conditions of mass treatment and great concern for custody there is a tendency to accumulate numerous restrictions on inmate behavior. Each disturbance inspires an attempt to prevent its recurrence by establishing a new rule. Once established, rules have great success at survival. Rarely is there any systematic review that looks to the elimination of unnecessary restrictions.

When a disturbance occurs, for example, as men are going from one place to another, it is decreed that if any group of five or more men is moving from one building or area to another, they must walk in a line and be accompanied by an officer. Later an argument between two men in such a line escalates into a fist fight, and henceforth no talking is allowed in line. Someone is attacked with a "shiv" made from a table knife smuggled into a cell and sharpened to a point, and henceforth no forks or knives may be used by inmates in the dining hall.

By such accumulations of permanent rules passed in reaction to episodic disturbances, many prisons have evolved into places of extreme regimentation. They go through periods of tense competition, with staff oriented primarily to enforcing rules and inmates to evading them. What is most striking on investigation is that these efforts do not clearly decrease the amount of disorderly or even dangerous behavior.

When the staff treat inmates as if they were dangerous, they become dangerous, although not so much to staff as to each other. For, if alienated from staff, they fall more than ever under threat of domination by other inmates whose claims to authority they resist by counter-hostility.[13]

The commission's suggestion that inmates treated as if dangerous will become so is generally considered a valid point. One way to avoid this problem is for staff and inmates to maintain meaningful communications. If the custody staff loses contact with inmates, the latter can respond only to the inmate subculture. All too often, such limited interaction results in violence among the inmates. The most effective controls over inmate traffic and movement may well be those that guide our behavior in the free community.

Discipline

Traffic control is but one aspect of the rules designed to regulate inmate behavior. The same factors that apply to discipline in any situation apply to discipline in jails and prisons:

> Despite the most sincere, intelligent, and painstaking efforts by capable officers to maintain good discipline, disciplinary problems will arise in any jail (corrections institution). If there are group problems such as racial conflicts, strikes, disturbances, or riots they must be dealt with firmly and without hesitation.
>
> The capable and experienced jail [corrections] officer can stop most outbreaks before they get started by *constantly analyzing and correcting conditions* that cause bitterness and unrest, and by spotting and segregating inmate ringleaders and agitators who are fomenting trouble.
>
> The word *discipline* is not intended here to suggest negative or punitive action. Rather, it means close supervision of inmates with an understanding of their problems and frustrations, backed up by thorough knowledge of inmates' personalities, potentialities, and characters.[14]

Some of the archaic rules employed at many correctional institutions and jails may have been necessitated by the widespread use of untrained rural personnel as correctional officers. Many of these individuals were already instilled with the idea of the "convict bogey" before undertaking correctional work, a situation that precluded meaningful interaction with inmates, even those with rehabilitation potential. The gap between the cultural backgrounds of basically urban prisoners and rural guards was often filled by unnecessarily severe discipline. Correctional administrators must acknowledge the importance of such cultural and philosophical differences in order to utilize the personnel they are able to attract. While many jurisdictions are now able to offer reasonable salaries, corrections is still perceived by many as a low-prestige occupation (see Table 20.1). Unfortunately, most administrators have been unable to convince their untrained officers that more progressive discipline methods could be effective. The administrators, therefore, are left with a staff clearly in a warehousing role.

TABLE 20.1 Correctional Officer Salary Levels at Entry and End of Probation Period: 1987

	Entry Level	After Probation
Alabama	$14,274	$16,955
Arizona	16,172	16,577
Arkansas	10,712	13,832
California	19,524	26,952
Colorado	21,576	21,576
Connecticut	20,393	20,393
Delaware	14,442	16,053
Dist. of Col.	16,869	18,738
Florida	13,561	14,917
Georgia	14,976	15,534
Hawaii	15,966	15,966
Idaho	11,731	15,766
Illinois	17,064	18,648
Indiana	13,910	13,910
Iowa	16,994	17,805
Kansas	15,480	16,248
Kentucky	12,408	13,032
Louisiana	11,664	13,620
Maine	13,458	13,458
Maryland	17,950	19,077
Massachusetts	20,017	26,215
Michigan	17,789	21,227
Minnesota	19,210	19,752
Mississippi	12,228	12,852
Missouri	15,120	15,684
Montana	13,427	14,542
Nebraska	14,556	15,284
Nevada	16,719	18,443

TABLE 20.1 *Continued*

	Entry Level	After Probation
New Hampshire	16,484	18,711
New Jersey	20,152	22,167
New York	17,304	21,136
North Carolina	15,486	16,104
North Dakota	13,932	14,628
Ohio	15,746	16,245
Oklahoma	14,148	15,600
Oregon	19,320	20,292
Pennsylvania	16,065	18,298
Rhode Island	17,701	18,134
South Carolina	12,765	13,276
South Dakota	12,480	12,480
Tennessee	12,384	12,384
Texas	14,544	17,028
Utah	15,496	18,325
Vermont	13,520	14,602
Virginia	14,016	15,326
Washington	18,144	19,032
West Virginia	11,604	13,204
Wisconsin	16,137	16,121
Federal System	16,521	18,358

Source: George and Camille Camp, *The Corrections Yearbook, 1987*, (South Salem, N.Y.: Criminal Justice Institute, 1987): pp. 47–48.

TABLE 20.2 Hours of Agency Training for Correctional Officers (1987)

	Pre	In
Alabama	320	40
Arizona[1]	280	20
Arkansas	160	40
California	316	40
Colorado	120	40
Connecticut	160	40
Delaware	280	0
Dist. of Col.	280	48
Florida	360	40
Georgia	160	20
Hawaii	160	40
Idaho[2]	300	40
Illinois	240	40
Indiana	152	40
Iowa	160	40
Kansas	200	80
Kentucky	40	40
Louisiana	88	

TABLE 20.2 *Continued*

	Pre	In
Maine	80	20
Maryland	178	24
Massachusetts	300	40
Michigan	640	40
Minnesota	80	40
Mississippi	160	40
Missouri	200	40
Montana	120	40
Nebraska	120	40
Nevada	360	0
New Hampshire[3]	160	40
New Jersey	320	40
New Mexico	120	
New York	262	32
North Carolina	160	0
North Dakota	80	48
Ohio	120	32
Oklahoma	300	40
Oregon	80	40
Pennsylvania	280	40
Rhode Island	320	0
South Carolina	240	40
South Dakota	160	40
Tennessee	120	40
Texas	140	80
Utah	360	40
Vermont	40	40
Virginia	352	12
Washington	160	20
West Virginia	120	40
Wisconsin	280	20
Federal System	160	40

[1] After the first year, 40 hours required annually
[2] 100 hours of preservice is OJT
[3] Includes preservice classroom hours only

Source: George and Camille Camp, *The Corrections Yearbook, 1987* (South Salem, N.Y.: Criminal Justice Institute, 1987): pp. 47–48.

It should be noted, however, that most correctional officers are dedicated and humane persons, and marshaling their potential is an important challenge to concerned administrators. The situation with regard to educating these officers is improving. As shown in Table 20.2, most states now offer extensive preservice training to ensure a minimal level of competence in the officers before they are placed on the job. The vast majority also provide in-service training on a regular basis after employment. As this trend continues, salaries, the quality of personnel, and working conditions will improve. The tendency to use outdated and counterproductive forms of discipline should decrease accordingly, and the correctional officer, long recognized as the single most important agent for change in institutions, will be able to realize his or her[15] potential contribution to the new rehabilitation approach.

Contraband and Shakedowns

In early years of corrections in America's jails and prisons, *contraband* was officially defined as any item that could be used to break an institution's rule or to assist in escape. In practice, the term usually ended up referring to anything the custody staff designated as undesirable for possession by the inmates. Such banning power is unrestricted. It can start with a particular object, such as a knife, and extend to anything that might conceivably be made into a knife—a policy that has placed some relatively innocuous items on contraband lists. The following definition illustrates the extensive power held by correctional officers:

> Any item that is not issued or not authorized in the jail is contraband. Control of contraband is necessary for several reasons:
> 1. To control the introduction of articles that can be used for trading and gambling.
> 2. To control the collecting of junk and the accumulation of items that make housekeeping difficult.
> 3. To identify medications and drugs and items that can be used as weapons and escape implements.
>
> Controlling contraband requires a clear understanding of what contraband is, of regulations that are designed to limit its entry into the jail, and of effective search procedures. The definition of contraband given above is simple and clear. However, this definition can become useless if the jail attempts to supplement it with a long list of approved items. If the jail permits prisoners to have packages, the problem of contraband control will be made difficult, since the list of authorized items may grow long.[16]

What appears to be a relatively simple definition is often then complicated by long lists of approved and forbidden items. Overdefinition can only result in a bureaucratic nightmare for correctional officers who must continuously search for contraband. A broad and clear definition, followed by the use of common sense by trained correctional officers, will usually result in better control and less conflict over what is or is not contraband. An excessively long contraband list is often seen as a challenge to the inmate and an indication of suppression by prison administrators.

Such items as guns, however, are clearly dangerous contraband, and prison administrators must continually check packages, visitors, and correc-

Contraband Is a Big Problem in Corrections: Sometimes a Fatal Problem
(Courtesy American Correctional Association)

tional officers to detect such material. This is usually accomplished by means of modern metal-detecting equipment.

The generally accepted way of defining contraband in the late-1980s is to use the affirmative approach. That is, "contraband is any item, or quantity of an item, that is not specifically authorized by the institution rules."

This leaves the decision as to what *is* contraband to the inmate. Contraband is more often defined as acquisition of excess items that are authorized, rather than as those items that are dangerous *per se*, (e.g., extra blankets, extra books, hoarded food). Contraband in this sense is seen as power to the inmate, plus a way to beat the system and show fellow inmates that the forbidden can be done. This power is used to trade favors or show favoritism to more powerful inmates. Contraband is often used as currency, just as we use barter on the outside.

Because the loss of contraband is the loss of power, searches and shakedowns are another source of potential conflict with inmates in security institutions. The most common type of search to prevent contraband entry into and movement within institutions is the *frisk* search. This type of search is used whenever prisoners enter or leave the institution and when institutional personnel suspect that a prisoner may be hiding contraband on his or her person. Figure 20-1 shows the proper procedures for a frisk.

When it is suspected that the prisoner has had access to drugs, weapons, or other items that can be secreted on the body or in a body cavity, and a frisk reveals nothing, a strip search may be conducted. The strip search is ordinarily made in a location where the prisoner will not be observed by other inmates, subjected to ridicule. The basic strip search requires only the visual observation of the entire body and orifices. If a more extensive, body cavity search, is merited it must be conducted with the knowledge and permission of the chief administrator of the facility (superintendent, sheriff, etc.). A body cavity search must be conducted by qualified medical personnel. Failure to follow these procedures can result in serious lawsuits against the institution.

Suppositories are one way to hide "keester" drugs and other small items of contraband, and so body cavities, with probable cause, may need to be examined. The strip search frequently follows visits, usually for every inmate or on a random sample basis. In the past, frequent strips were used to debase and abuse prisoners, a practice that greatly increased prison tension, and that resulted in many legal actions against offending staff. Frisks are a necessary part of institutional security, but if strip searches are made an everyday routine, the procedure soon degrades not only the searched but the searcher as well.

As rules prohibiting contraband grow more detailed, inmates seek ways to secrete these items in the living area and throughout the institution. There is virtually no limitation to the ingenuity employed in hiding contraband in prisons. Ironically, the older—and presumably more "secure"—institutions and plants lend themselves best to secret hiding places. The process could almost be seen as a game, with correctional officers periodically searching the same old spots. The need for shakedowns (searching of an entire cell or cellblock) is lessened when contraband rules are made realistic and humane; prohibiting such items as family pictures and tooth-

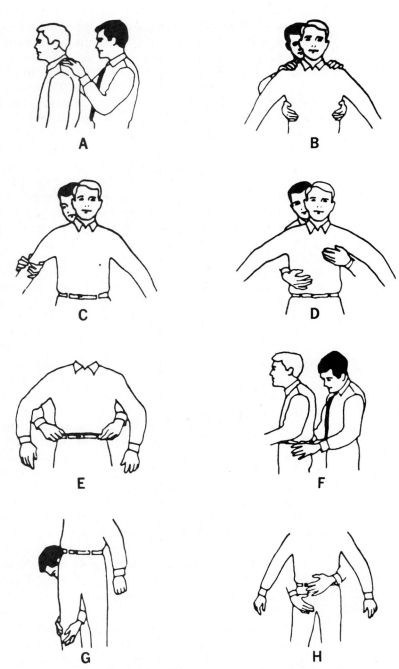

Figure 20-1 The Frisk Search (Nick Pappas, *The Jail: Its Operation and Management* [Lompoc, Calif.: Federal Prison Industries, 1971], p. 23)

picks creates a needless irritant. The shakedown also has greater effect if used only to locate items that represent a clear and present danger to the institution, not just for the sake of what inmates call "Mickey Mouse" harassment.

Prevention of Escape _____

Maximum security adult prisons were built as though they had to contain the most dangerous creature imaginable. "A prison is designed to be as strong as the strongest inmate" is an old correctional chestnut. The high walls, corner towers, and armed guards are external signs of preoccupation with escape. The nature of the prison population, while changing, does not really justify this model.

> [I]t's a mistake to think U.S. jails and prisons are seething with oppressed and vicious criminals just waiting their chance to get out and ravage the innocent.
>
> The broad facts are quite different. About [89] percent of felony arrests in the country are for taking money or other property. The percentage is higher for felonies committed by repeaters. Of the approximately [547,000] prisoners in federal and state prisons, between one-half and two-thirds are there for nonviolent crimes, like forgery, embezzling, larceny, auto-theft, and house-breaking. A little over [11] percent are in prison for homicide, rape, robbery, and assault.
>
> The typical prisoner is more likely to be the tax accountant from Montana who received a sentence of 31 years and 31 days on tax-fraud charges. He was well past middle age, had raised his family, and nowhere in his previous years was there a suggestion of misconduct. A momentary break in a lifetime of rectitude put him behind bars.[17]

The picture with twice as many inmates increases the concern over the possibility of escape.[18] The issue is complex but revolves around two problems. The first is the philosophy of mass treatment, firmly established since the time when lockstep and silence were required for all prisoner movements. The second reason is political. Seasoned superintendents know that frequent escapes will be extremely damaging to their records, and so they take extreme measures to prevent them—directed toward all prisoners, rather than toward the few who might actually try to escape. In a few prisons, however, administrators have begun to realize that a tax evader and an ax murderer do not have the same potential for escape attempts.

The Federal Correctional Institution at Seagoville, Texas, is perhaps one of the best models of a truly "open" prison. There is no wall around Seagoville, and entry to the main facilities is through an open gate. The

The Ubiquitous Tower (Courtesy National Clearinghouse for Criminal Justice Planning and Architecture)

only barrier around the installation is a low chain-link fence similar to those used in residential backyards. The clean, campuslike appearance of the installation demonstrates that it is possible to confine and rehabilitate men without subjecting them to the dreary, claustrophobic atmosphere of the walled prisons. There are few escapes in this atmosphere of trust. The administration believes in encouraging inmate responsibility, self-discipline, and judgment.

Seagoville serves as a model in the development of prisons that offer both humanity and hope for the inmate. Work-release programs and other progressive transitional steps make the adaptation from institution to community-based correctional programs smooth and effective. Security is a normal part of the daily activity at Seagoville, but not the only activity. The Federal Correctional Institution at Pleasanton, California, presents another model of an open institution that is co-correctional. These and other innovations in the federal system will be covered in detail in Chapter 24.

Correctional Officers _____

The Military Model

The need for an organized and effective control force in prisons has instilled a paramilitary flavor in most security staffs. The adoption of militaristic organizational structures and procedures has made it easier to train a force with limited background to do a specific job. The paramilitary approach is seen in the uniforms, titles, and procedures of custody personnel. Training is directed to the mission of security, and there is little if any emphasis on interaction with inmates. The model of the aloof but efficient guard has emerged, and the hiring of custody personnel is more often based on height and weight than on the applicant's ability to work with people. To a great extent, correctional hiring practices bar those people who can best fulfill the newer mission of rehabilitation. The seniority system and the growing power of correctional officer unions may further discourage the infusion of custody personnel with behavioral science backgrounds.

In order to provide the best entry-level personnel, and to maintain a level of quality and growth in their staff, many jurisdictions have established rigid training standards along the lines recommended in Table 20.3, by the American Correctional Association. These types of requirements will ensure that all staff are eventually exposed to methods that are not simply "more of the same."

To reflect the population in institutions, personnel should actively recruit from minority groups, women, young persons, and prospective indigenous workers, and see that employment announcements reach these groups and the general public.

It is useful to conduct, from time to time, a task analysis of each correctional position (to be updated periodically) to determine those tasks, skills, and qualities needed. Testing based solely on these relevant features in a "hands-on" manner to assure that proper qualifications are considered for each position helps the administrator know what is needed in training. These procedures will lead to an "open" system of selection in which any testing device used is related to a specific job and is a practical test of a person's ability to perform, at an acceptable standard, the tasks identified for that job.

These are a few of the steps that might help span the presently large communication gap between keepers and kept. Correctional officers and custody staff spend more time with the inmate population than does anyone else in the institution. They should relate well to others, as they can be the most positive agents of change in that corrections subsystem.[19] They can also destroy any efforts toward change that are attempted by a treatment staff that tries to bypass them. A move away from the military/police image to the correctional image is critical to effective change in the institutional setting.

TABLE 20.3 **Summary of Orientation and Minimum Training Hours**

The following description of general job categories should be used in determining minimum training requirements as outlined in standards 2-4088 thru 2-4094. Contract or part-time employees should receive training similar to that of full-time employees in their particular category and pertinent to their role in working with inmates.

Title	Position	Prior to Job	First Year On the Job	Each Year Thereafter
Clerical/Support (Minimum contact):	Secretaries, Clerks, Typists, PBX Operators, Computer and Warehouse Personnel, Accountants, Personnel Staff	40	16	16
Support (regular or daily contact):	Food Service, Industry Work Supervisors, Farm Work Supervisors, Maintenance Work Supervisors	40	40	40
Professional Specialist:	Case Managers, Counselors, Social Workers, Psychologists, Teachers, Librarians, Medical Personnel, Chaplains, Recreational Leaders	40	40	40
All Correctional Officers	All staff assigned to full-time custodial and/or security posts	40	120	40
Administrative Management Personnel: (Additional Training)	Wardens/Superintendents, Deputy or Assistant Wardens/Superintendents, Business Managers, Personnel Directors, Case Manager Supervisors, Unit Managers, Shift Supervisors	—	40	40
Emergency Unit Staff:	Members of emergency or confrontation units	*40	—	**16

* May be part of 120 hours of on-the-job training required in first year as correctional officer
** May be part of 40 hours annual training required of all correctional officers

Source: American Correctional Association, *Standards for Adult Correctional Institutions* (College Park, Md.: 1986), p. 2.

Upgrading Correctional Personnel

The most important rehabilitative tool is the impact of one person on another. Thus, a primary goal for the correctional system is the recruitment, training, and retention of employees who are able—physically, emotionally, educationally, and motivationally—to work as a team.

In the correctional system it is hard to hire or keep qualified personnel. Including the nation's prisons and jails, there are an estimated 125,000 women and men working in custody jobs alone. About 13 percent of these custody workers are now represented by women. There is no real reason for the correctional officer and jailer to cry "poormouth" about salaries in this field. The national average entry-level starting pay of about $15,500 (around $17,000 after probation) is not a bad salary when one considers the current minimum qualifications for the applicants.

But even during the mid-1970s, when national unemployment rates reached new post-Depression highs, some prison custody jobs went begging. Current correctional officer turnover rates in some states are so high that some administrators openly confess that it is almost impossible to operate

Whether They Are Called "Jailers," "Guards," or "Corrections Officers," They Keep Order in Our Jails and Prisons (Courtesy of American Correctional Association, photo by BOP)

their facilities with consistent policies. Over the past seven years this situation has stabilized with the lowered unemployment rates and low-priced "high-tech" jobs competing with corrections and losing.

Turnover rates do remain high, however, with burnout[20] and low wages in some maximum security institutions. Some institutions report that it is not unusual for them to lose at least half of their new officers in the first year.

One major exception is the Illinois' Vienna Correctional Center—a minimum security institution—that has file cabinets full of job applications. In October 1987, it had a backlog of 1,400 applications for the custody staff alone.

For most security managers and personnel directors, however, the human resource dilemma is shortage, not a surplus: Because of the persistent problem of unfilled slots on most shifts, supervisors ask officers on duty to work another shift ("work doubles"). This situation leads to tired staff and high overtime budgets, but legislators are seldom willing to increase expenditures for staff, fearing that correctional officers are just padding the roles. The concept of audits for "minimum critical staffing" has been tried many times, but budget needs still seem to override attempts at rationalizing staffing patterns.[21]

While many consider salaries in corrections to be too low, they are improving. Ranging from $21,000 in Colorado to $10,700 in Arkansas per year, the national average of around $15,500 compares with many other professions. Attempts to raise salary levels have included some unorthodox ideas. In Ohio, for example, hazardous duty and overtime pay for correctional officers were initiated, skewing the salary schedules so that correctional officers could earn more than a deputy warden or professional-technical staff with special skills and higher education.

Perhaps more important than salary is the employees' sense of public rejection, reinforced in some institutions by the belief that the administrators do not consult them, treat them fairly, or care what they think.[22] New channels of communication must be opened between administrators and employees, as well as between employees and inmates.

Administrators should meet with staff to discuss employee problems; custodial and treatment staff should also meet together.[23] These meetings should be regularly scheduled and formally integrated into the institutional procedures.

After two or three weeks of basic orientation, new staff learn the ways of the institution by working with one or more officers in a modified apprenticeship program, which can institutionalize the bad habits of the past. Correctional officers spend twenty-four hours a day with inmates. The officers' actions, words, training, and skills make the difference between a hostile and destructive environment for prisoners and one that is constructive and humane. Correctional personnel are too often punitive, contemptuous and degrading, reflecting a suspicion of inmates that may lead to a self-defeating game of "cops and robbers." It is in this adversarial relationship that rehabilitation breaks down.

The following recommendations would counteract some of these problems and reduce the conflict between custody and treatment staffs:

1. A position of program director should be created to integrate all services in the institutions. All present deputy wardens would report to this individual.
2. The model of the collaborative institution should be adopted. In this model, lines of communication are continuously open between prisoners and staff, and between treatment and security personnel. Inmates, custodial officers, and professional staff meet regularly to discuss mutual problems and their

possible solutions. Under the Program Director, this collaborative effort should engender better treatment as well as better custody.

3. The academy approach to employee training should be adopted. It should be noted that federal funds now support academy programs and in-service training. To achieve the goal of up-grading training, it is absolutely necessary for states to commit themselves to on-going appropriations for the extension and improvement of these training programs.

4. A Corrections Academy should be established in a centrally located area, close to a major university.

5. All person hired for the management of prisoners should be thoroughly screened through the use of written tests and psychological interviews. This screening process should be followed by at least six months, and perhaps a year, of probationary status on the job.

6. Courses should be designed for all supervisory personnel by the Academy with special emphasis on the behavioral sciences and rehabilitative penology.

7. New officers should be trained in basic penology before assuming their posts.

8. Continued in-service training should be made mandatory at the Academy and at the institutions.

9. Promotions and salary increases should be contingent on the successful participation in and completion of these in-service training programs, as well as monitoring on the job. This recommendation is contingent upon alterations to existing civil service regulations.[24]

Like the recommendations of numerous commissions over the past sixty years, these recommendations retain the ring of logic and truth, along with common sense. Many of these recommendations have been adopted in progressive jurisdictions. These are essentially the basis recommendations for the *Standards* adopted by the American Correctional Association in regard to hiring and training of corrections officers. Their adoption should be considered by any correctional system, even though they were made almost two decades ago in Ohio.

Summary

According to the *Standards for Adult Correctional Institutions:*

The humane administration and direction of institutional care are paramount in preserving individual rights and responsibilities and, in turn, the ultimate protection of society.[25]

Historically, correctional institutions probably have done a more effective job in security than in any other aspect of the institutional program. The pitfalls in exercising this responsibility include opportunities for the excessive use of force by some personnel, the debilitating effects of excessive routinization on inmates, and the frustration of treatment programs when security needs are seen as paramount. These negative possibilities become probabilities because the custodial portion of the institutional program is carried out by the persons least trained in treatment techniques.

Even though the official policy of the institution may be humane, the people who are in direct contact with the inmates may have an entirely different view of their role, leading to degrading and sometimes brutal treatment of inmates. Recruitment and hiring standards, practices, and procedures have not established sufficiently high educational or personality standards for the position of corrections officer. Salaries authorized by most legislatures for custodial personnel are not yet high enough to attract and retain treatment-minded persons with high levels of education. It speaks well for today's correctional personnel that relatively few have been identified as brutal persons. The nature of the situation, however, lends itself to individual expressions of punitiveness.[26]

One of the most vexing problems of prison management concerns the relationship between security and treatment. Too often, this relationship pits custody and treatment personnel against each other. Both under the law and in fact, the primary emphasis in corrections is on security. Thus, the deputy warden or associate superintendent for custody becomes the institution's key operating officer.

Disciplinary infractions and other security considerations can prevent, hamper, or terminate inmate involvement in academic, vocational, educational, and other recommended activities (recreation, Alcoholics Anonymous, visiting, drug therapy, and so on). Furthermore, many important services are usually not available at night; thus, inmates who work during the day are excluded. Adequate staffing could permit the expansion of treatment services to the evening hours and weekends.

Treatment-oriented personnel at all levels express concern about the conflict between security and program needs. Although institutional rules and regulations are vital to the correctional process, unnecessary rules that regiment minor aspects of daily life can impede the development of individual responsibility. For example, lockdowns, shakedowns, and skin searches are inherently humiliating and engender bitterness and resentment. In a cell shakedown, the inmates' possessions are often knocked to the floor and trampled. It is true that occasional thorough searches of person and premises are necessary to protect the institutional community. Nevertheless, the basic principles of human dignity need to be observed.

In regard to security, a few final recommendations. First, policies should be developed to define the relationships between essential security functions and rehabilitative program needs for the institutions. The obvious dichotomy of custody and treatment must be erased and greater recognition given to the fact that each is supportive of the other. Clarification must be made of the essential roles of all aspects of the institutional program so that none can be unduly hampered by the needs of others.

Second, policies and guidelines for institutional rules and regulations should be developed and all present rules and procedures revised to insure that the demands of security do not negate the objectives of treatment. In policy formation and in specific rules, the principle of clear and present danger should apply; if the regulation is required for the safety of the institutional community, it should be kept. If not, it should be abolished. These policies should provide for periodic review of institutional compliance. At each institution, a permanent standing committee, representing all major services, should be made responsible for implementing these guidelines and policies.

Third, in cases where force has been used upon an inmate, in addition to an investigation by the institution and/or an outside agency, a report should routinely be submitted to the corrections authority by the prison physician and by the inmate himself or herself.

Finally, the correctional authority should respond to requests from families that they be permitted to visit and see an inmate if they believe excessive force has been used against him or her. If they desire an outside physician to examine the prisoner, this request should be granted without delay, in accordance with rules to be promulgated by the correctional authority. Copies of all "Use of Force" reports should be filed with the correctional authority and be made available for inspection by the inmate's family, attorney, and, with the inmate's written permission, other appropriate people.

It is recognized by all involved in corrections that custody and security are necessary but are not the only correctional goals. The next chapter deals with treatment as another essential goal for corrections.

Review Questions _____

1. What is the primary focus of the bureaucratic style of prison management?
2. Where have prison guards been obtained in the past? How does this situation create problems?
3. Why has the military model been so popular in the prisons?
4. Why do disciplinary and security considerations so greatly affect treatment programs? How can this issue be resolved?
5. What are the effects of imprisonment on inmates? Staff?
6. In what ways have the roles and positions of correctional officers improved over the last two decades?

Key Terms _____

1. **bureaucratic control** (p. 478)
2. **custody** (p. 479)
3. **"screw"** (p. 479)
4. **correctional officers** (p. 480)
5. **unionization** (p. 480)
6. **"blue flu"** (p. 481)
7. **lockdowns** (p. 482)
8. **prison rules** (p. 484)
9. **"convict bogey"** (p. 486)
10. **"keester" drugs** (p. 491)
11. **frisk search** (p. 492)
12. **military model** (p. 495)

Notes _____

1. See Bureau of Justice Statistics, *Prisoners and Drugs* (Washington, D.C.: U.S. Department of Justice, 1983); Bureau of Justice Statistics, *Prisons and Prisoners* (Washington, D.C.: U.S. Department of Justice, 1982); Bernard Gropper, *Probing the Links between Drugs and Crime* (Washington, D.C.: U.S. Department of Justice, 1985); and Richard McGee, George Warner, and Nora Harlow, *The Special Management Inmate* (Washington, D.C.: U.S. Department of Justice, 1985).

2. Clifford English, "The Impact of the Indeterminate Sentence on an Institutional Social System," *Journal of Offender Counseling, Services and Rehabilitation* 8 (Fall–Winter 1983): 69–82.

3. John Hepburn and C. Albonetti, "Role Conflict in Correctional Institutions: An Empirical Examination of the Treatment-Custody Dilemma Among Correctional Staff," *Criminology* 17 (February 1980): 445–460. See also Rob Wilson, "Who Will Care for the 'Mad and the Bad'?" *Corrections Magazine* 6 (February 1980): 5–17; Eric Poole and Robert Regoli, "Professionalism, Role Conflict, Work Alienation and Anomia," *Social Science Journal* 20 (1983): 63–70; and Nancy Jurik and M. Mushenko, "The Internal Crisis of Corrections: Professionalism and the Work Environment," Justice Quarterly 3 (1986): 457–480.

4. Correctional officers have gone on strike in Washington State and in institutions in the Ohio State system. When this happens, administrative personnel or state police are required temporarily to fill the correctional officers' posts. Although police strikes have been found to have a limited impact on the rates of reported crime, little is known about institutional disturbances and rule violations in prison when correctional officers strike. Erdwin Phufl, "Police Strikes and Conventional Crime," *Criminology* 21 (November 1983): 489–503.

5. See David Shichor and Harry Allen, "Correctional Efforts in the Educated Society: The Case of Study Release," *Lambda Alpha Epsilon* 39 (June 1976): 18–24. See also James Marquart, "Prison Guards and the Use of Physical Coercion as a Mechanism of Inmate Control," Criminology 24 (1986): 347–366.

6. Donald Clemmer, *The Prison Community* (New York: Rinehart, 1940); Anthony Scacco, *Rape in Prison* (Springfield, Ill.: Chas. C. Thomas, 1975).

7. Shichor and Allen, p. 21.

8. President's Commission on Law Enforcement and Administration of Justice, *The Challenge of Crime in a Free Society* (Washington, D.C.: U.S. Government Printing Office, 1967), p. 159.

9. Ann Bancroft, "San Quentin to Get New Warden, Reform," *San Francisco Chronicle,* November 2, 1983, p. 6. See also Bruce Porter, "California's Prison Gangs: The Price of Control," *Corrections Magazine* 8 (1982): 6–19. George Camp and Camille Camp, *Prison Gangs: Their Extent, Nature and Impacts on Prison* (Washington, D.C.: U.S. Department of Justice, 1985); Steve Daniels, "Prison Gangs: Confronting the Threat," *Corrections Today* 49 (1987): 66, 126, 162.

10. English, "The Impact of the Indeterminate Sentence." See also Peter Nacci and Thomas Kane, "Sex and Sexual Aggression in Federal Prisons: Inmate Involvement and Employee Impact," *Federal Probation* 48 (1985): 46–52.

11. David Hagar, "Computers Aid Rehabilitation in New Zealand," *Corrections Today* 49 (1987): 118.

12. Ernest van den Haag, "Prisons Cost Too Much Because They Are Too Secure," *Corrections Magazine* 6 (April 1980): 39–43. See also Don Gibbons, *The Limits of Punishment as Social Policy* (San Francisco: National Council on Crime and Delinquency, 1988).

13. President's Commission on Law Enforcement and Administration of Justice, *Task Force Report: Corrections* (Washington, D.C.: U.S. Government Printing Office, 1967), p. 67.

14. *Jail Officer's Training Manual*, (Alexandria, Virginia: National Sheriff's Association, 1984), p. 95.

15. Lynn Zimmer, "Female Guards in Men's Prisons: Creating a Role for Themselves" (Ann Arbor, Mich.: University Microfilms International, 1982), as cited in R. Allison, ed., *Criminal Justice Abstracts* 15 (June 1983): 199. Lois Shawyer, "On the Question of Having Women Guards in Male Prisons," *Corrective and Social Psychiatry and Journal of Behavior Technology Methods and Therapy* 33 (1987): 154–159.

16. Nick Pappas, *The Jail: Its Operation and Management* (Lompoc, Calif.: Federal Prison Industries, 1971), p 23.

17. Robert Osterman, *Crime in America* (Silver Springs, Ohio: Newsbook, 1966), pp. 149–150, data are current (1987).

18. For a discussion of prison security, see *Corrections Today* 49 (July 1987). Here the reader will find a number of articles dealing with inmate anger control, training, special glass, perimeter security, electronic security, etc.

19. Carol Fewell, "Successful Strategies: Integrating Health Care and Security Functions," *Corrections Today* 50 (1988): 20–22.

20. John Whitehead and Charles Lindquist, "Correctional Officer Job Burnout: A Path Model," *Journal of Research in Crime and Delinquency* 23 (1986): 23–42. See also Nigel Long, et al., "Stress in Prison Staff: An Occupational Study," *Criminology* 24 (1986): 331–345.

21. John Shuiteman, "Playing the Numbers Game: Analysis Can Help Determine Manpower Requirements," *Corrections Today* 49 (1987): 40–42.

22. Frances Cheek and Marie Di Stefano Miller, "Reducing Staff and Inmate Stress," *Corrections Today* 44 (1982): 72–76, 78. For a discussion of frustrations within the workforce, see Jurik and Mushenko, "The Internal Crisis . . ." *supra* note 3.

23. Michael Sherrill and Peter Katel, "New Mexico: An Anatomy of a Riot," *Corrections Magazine* 6 (April 1980): 6–24. See also Steven Dillingham and Montgomery Reid, "Can Riots be Prevented?" *Corrections Today* 44 (1982): 54–56. See also American Correctional Association, "After Atlanta and Oakdale: ACA Pays Tribute to Federal Officials, Staff," *Corrections Today* 50 (1988): 26, 64.

24. Ohio Citizens' Task Force on Corrections, *Final Report* (Columbus: State of Ohio, 1971), pp. C-25, C-26.

25. American Correctional Association, *Manual of Corrections Standards for Adult Correctional Institutions,* 2d ed. (Washington, D.C.: ACA, 1981), p. xviii.

26. For a candid look at correctional officer use of excessive force in coercive prison situations, see James Marquart, *supra* note 5.

21

Treatment

There is no behavior or person that a modern
psychiatrist cannot plausibly diagnose as
abnormal or ill.
—THOMAS S. SZASZ

The Treatment Model

Treatment services, which generally include vocational training, education, counseling, teaching, casework, religious activities, and clinical activity, are believed to play a significant role in offender rehabilitation. In the past, especially in the larger institutions, the allocation of resources and personnel for treatment bore little, if any, relation to this assumed significance. As a national average, the resources allocated for treatment services amounted to only about 10 percent of the expenditures of the institutional staffs. This disproportionate distribution of resources in the 1960s was well addressed by that era's *Manual of Correctional Standards:*

> Over the past thirty years, there has been increasing recognition that a major function of a correctional agency is to influence change in the attitude and behavior of the offender. The disciplines of psychiatry, psychology, and social casework have provided corrections with tools which are useful in stimulating change.[1]

Part of the disproportionate allocation of resources is a basic difference in nature between treatment and custody operations. Staff in the custody side must work 24 hours per day, 7 days a week, 365 days a year. Treatment staff, on the other hand, usually work 8 hours a day, 5 days a week and have holidays, vacations, and weekends off. When a custody officer is sick or takes vacation, he or she must be replaced (the common term is "back-filled") by another corrections officer, often on overtime, because *minimal critical staffing* must be maintained in order to protect the public. This protection is still the primary mission of corrections. When treatment staff are sick or take vacation, their position usually goes unfilled until they return to work. Because each 24-hour post requires 5.4 to 5.6 staff, the ratio will always seem heavily weighted toward custody staff (see Table 21.1).

TABLE 21.1 Ratio of Correctional Inmates to Officers as of January 1987

	Male	Female	Total	Ratio
Alabama	1,444	216	1,660	6.1
Arizona	1,650	361	2,011	4.6
Arkansas	667	103	770	5.9
California	7,293	1,515	8,808	6.7
Colorado	338	42	380	9.7
Connecticut	1,276	132	1,408	4.5
Delaware	564	88	652	3.9
Dist. of Col.			1,778	3.5
Florida	5,352	1,174	6,526	4.8
Georgia	2,476	421	2,877	6.0
Hawaii	478	81	559	3.5
Idaho	208	27	235	6.0
Illinois	4,216	521	4,737	4.1
Indiana	1,432	336	1,768	5.8
Iowa	865	115	980	3.0
Kansas	602	139	741	7.1
Louisiana	1,956	427	2,383	4.5
Maine	290	28	318	3.8
Maryland	2,456	476	2,932	4.4
Michigan	3,987	1,038	5,025	3.7
Minnesota	654	109	763	3.3
Mississippi	751	226	977	7.0
Missouri	1,082	155	1,237	8.2
Montana	173	15	188	5.2
Nebraska	348	69	417	4.5
Nevada	575	73	648	6.9
New Hampshire	63	13	76	10.5
New Jersey	3,013	298	3,311	3.7
New York	12,086	1,129	13,215	2.9
North Carolina	3,383	221	3,604	5.0
North Dakota	43	9	52	8.5
Ohio	2,298	353	2,651	8.4
Oklahoma	902	314	1,216	6.2
Oregon	439	82	521	7.7
Pennsylvania	1,788	182	1,970	7.5
Rhode Island	479	21	500	2.7
South Carolina	1,823	505	2,328	4.4
South Dakota	159	39	198	5.3
Tennessee	1,825	385	2,210	3.2
Texas	6,355	1,179	7,534	5.1
Virginia	2,861	499	3,360	3.3
Washington	1,439	299	1,738	3.4
West Virginia	303	47	350	3.4
Wisconsin	1,414	214	1,628	3.3
Wyoming			150	5.8
Federal System	3,747	417	4,164	9.8

Source: George and Camille Camp, *The Corrections Yearbook*, (South Salem, N.Y.: Criminal Justice Institute, 1987): pp. 45–46. These are line-level, nonsupervisory correctional officers.

In the entire corrections system, a very small percentage of institutional personnel are employed in social work or psychological services, and the number of psychiatrists in corrections is infinitesimal. Diagnostic workups and testing processes tend to consume the workday of those involved in these services. Also, treatment personnel must often spend long hours sitting on disciplinary courts, classification and reclassification committees, and honor placement committees. Thus, a minute staff has almost no time to spend on ongoing treatment with inmates. In addition, correctional administrators and the treatment staff frequently have to contend with the deeply ingrained antagonism of the staff members who are oriented toward custody, security, and maintenance of calm.[2]

Only in recent times has the "associate superintendent for treatment" (or deputy warden for treatment) been selected from candidates with training in the social sciences, rather than through the promotion of a faithful custody supervisor. This is important, as the typical rank-and-file custody person was usually not someone who had earned the job through training and education, but through experience and staying out of trouble. This often placed a person with a high school education (or less) over psychiatrists, psychologists, medical doctors and nurses, social workers, and educators who possessed far more academic credentials. Understandably, these roles created many problems as treatment became more important.

The treatment model for corrections arose from the three basic services first offered to prisoners: *religious*, *medical*, and *educational*. The development of these services will be traced in this chapter, along with an analysis

---

INMATE PROGRAM INVOLVEMENT

One of the fears of correctional experts when states began to shift to determinate sentences was that, since the best motivator for inmate program participation appeared to be the need to convince releasing authorities of prisoners' reform through completion of prison treatment programs, determinate sentences would render treatment programs underenrolled if not superfluous. After all, if inmates were "playing the reform game" to convince a parole board of their readiness for release, and the parole board's discretion to release were abolished, inmates might very well stop participating in any treatment programs.

This fear has been proven unfounded. The rates of program participation in Illinois, Minnesota, and Connecticut, for example, remained about the same or increased somewhat. How much of the noted participation was voluntary, however, remains in question. Prison administrators need concrete criteria for making decisions about transfers to less secure institutions, institutional job and housing assignments, furlough eligibility, and awarding of meritorious good time credits based on program participation. The incentives for inmate involvement may have changed, but participation rates and levels appear to be unaffected by the determinate sentence.

Source: John Hepburn and L. Goodstein, "Organizational Imperatives and Sentencing Reforms," *Crime and Delinquency* 32, (1986): 339–365.

of some recent treatment innovations. Much of the public still view treatment as a form of "coddling," and many administrators have responded to this view by rejecting new and promising rehabilitation techniques created by behavioral scientists. In fact, the protection of society, not the pampering of offenders, is the basic reason for treatment. If the sources of an individual's criminality can be treated before he or she is referred back to the community, they should be. As noted in Chapter 20, inmates are most strongly influenced by those persons who spend the most time with them. At present, it is the correctional officers and work supervisors, rather than treatment specialists, who are most likely to exert that influence.

The sharp split between the treatment and custody staffs is being bridged in many jurisdictions. In these programs, the treatment staff is directly involved with the custody staff, both to accomplish control and to be involved in rehabilitation, a process that actually begins with the initial classification.[3] The treatment model in corrections is under attack, however (see Chapter 25). The model of *unit team management*, pioneered by the federal system combines the skills of all the staff and works to provide a climate that helps in rehabilitation (see Chapter 24).

Classification: Security or Treatment? _____

In Chapter 13, we noted that classification is a relatively recent innovation in corrections. The classification process can frequently intensify the conflict between treatment and custody staffs if it is not carefully handled.[4] In most correctional classification processes (either at the individual institution or at a central classification facility), there is more concern with the danger that the new inmates might present to the institution than with the possibility that they might respond to treatment. As a result, new inmates are often assigned to higher custody grades than their backgrounds warrant, until they can "prove" themselves. This security-oriented concept of classification often excludes inmates from participation in the programs that could lead to their rehabilitation. Their early treatment, in fact, may be restricted to health care — an essential program, as most offenders are in poor physical condition when they enter the institution.

The Three Basic Services _____

Health and Medical Services

Even in the earliest days of American prisons, certain times were set aside for sick call. Of course, the treatment provided was less than one would expect to receive at a clinic in the community. In many cases, prisoners use sick call merely to obtain a brief respite from prison labor or from the dull routine. Time wasted on "goldbrickers" is time the medical staff cannot give those who really need care. Because the correctional funnel selects out all but the most serious offenders, the cream of society does not often end up in prisons. As described so well by the Ohio Task Force on Corrections in the early 1970s, the prison doctor must deal with a unique brand of patient:

> The prison physician faces one of the most difficult problems in medical service. To him are sent the very essence of society's misfits, for his patients are not only the abnormal, the subnormal, and the maladjusted—the handicapped, the sick, the surgically unfit, the degenerate, the dissipated, the diseased, the psychotic, the psychopathic, the neurotic, and the feebleminded—but they are also the socially undesirable—men and women whom society has cast out, who cannot or will not cooperate according to the rules of the game. To this beginning must be added all the complicating forces which are peculiar to a prison and which so materially affect the prison physician's patients.
>
> They begin with the mental worry and disgrace of imprisonment and they by no means end with the drab, dull existence which characterizes prison life. Not only does lack of stimulating work weaken the mental keenness of active minds, but lack of any work in most prisons today saps the moral fiber out of the most stalwart spirits. Crowded together in the narrow confines of a walled institution, housed in cages like animals where insufficiency of light and air and no privacy wilt the hardiest, fed on a monotonous diet, allowed only a restricted amount of exercise—the problem of keeping people well under such condition is itself a problem.[5]

As noted in Chapter 13, medical services are often a source of inmates' complaints and frequently become a real headache for administrators.[6] In many areas throughout the country, qualified medical personnel are generally in short supply, and this shortage is felt even more acutely in correctional institutions. To supply the total medical care for which an institution is responsible, it is often necessary to combine the services of full-time medical employees, contractual consultants, and available community resources.[7] Even with all these efforts, inmates and the public often tend to look down on any medically trained person who is willing to become involved with a correctional institution. Any doctor who accepts the prison physician's relatively low income and standard of living, it is thought, must have been a failure in the community.

Proper medical care is important to the overall rehabilitation effort. In many cases, the offender's health condition is one of the main reasons that authorities decided to opt for the prisoner's placement in a correctional institution instead of a road camp unit. Poor diet, drug abuse, a history of inadequate medical attention, and other debilitating conditions are not uncommon among inmates. Once they have been restored to reasonable health, however, it is often easier to work on the causes behind their problems.[8]

In the most progressive prisons, cosmetic medicine—plastic surgery—is available on request of the treatment staff, to reshape the offender's self-image and thus increase his or her self-confidence. As a matter of fact, in a survey of over one hundred types of treatment, it was noted that plastic surgery appeared to be one of the most effective rehabilitation treatments.

Another major service to the offender is found in the dental clinic, as most prisoners have very bad teeth. Even in an institution fortunate enough to have good dental care facilities, this service can take many months for a prisoner who needs a lot of work, as their teeth have suffered from long neglect. The effects of this kind of treatment are similar to those of plastic surgery: improved appearance enhances the offender's feelings of confidence and well-being, and he or she may be relieved of chronic pain and irritation, as well.

Chaplaincy Services

One service that has always been available to the incarcerated felon is religious assistance and guidance. Solitary meditation in the Walnut Street Jail was intended to make offenders realize the error of their sinful ways and make them penitent. Penitence was often encouraged by visits from the local ministers and priests. Later, the large institutions of the early 1800s created the need for a full-time chaplain on the premises.

The correctional chaplaincy has been and is currently the least sought-after position among ministers, who evidently prefer to serve more conventional congregations. Part of the problem, too, is the remote location of most prisons and a widespread public belief (shared by many administrators) that religion in prisons should be confined to the chaplain's traditional duties. A movement has sprung up to establish a core of clinically oriented clerics, but the correctional field is less attractive to them than are other kinds of institutions. There is a definite need to upgrade the role of the correctional chaplain in order to attract the best into the institutions. The role of the chief chaplain can be enhanced if it becomes accredited by the Association for Clinical Pastoral Education. With this background, the chaplain can develop programs, recruit and train chaplaincy candidates, and even use seminary students to augment his or her resources.

The new and growing special-interest groups inside prisons—those whose religious orientation is toward a particular ethnic group, culture, or subculture—do not accord with the traditional religious outlets. As discussed in Chapter 13, their right to pursue their faiths while confined has been firmly established. The traditional institution has provided Protestant, Roman Catholic, and (sometimes) Jewish chaplains as representatives of the three major religious groups in this country, because it was not feasible to have a cleric for each and every religion observed by different inmates. These chaplains attempt to offer ecumenical services and have tried to provide worship for all prisoners. However, the more vocal members of the smaller sects have protested this arrangement.

It is possible, if the chaplain's salary and image are sufficiently upgraded, that ministers trained in the behavioral sciences will become part of the contemporary prison scene—a far cry from the Walnut Street missionaries whose sole function was to provide Bible reading and prayer. These new chaplains might well play an integrated part of the treatment team in future rehabilitation programs.

Education for Inmates

In most state correctional systems, education of incarcerated inmates is a legislative mandate. The largest group of treatment personnel are the teachers, who usually far outnumber those in counseling services. Although most institutions have some kind of educational program, there are marked differences in kind and extent. Early efforts were aimed simply at teaching prisoners to read. With 12 million people in the United States considered to be functionally illiterate, it is not too suprising that those at the "bottom of the barrel" have literacy problems in even greater measure.

Education Can Be the Way Back to A Productive Life (Courtesy Justice Assistance Center)

Today, most inmates are able to achieve at least a high school education (or GED) through institutional programs, and the more progressive institutions are offering courses at the two-year and four-year college level.[9] It is acknowledged that lack of education is a serious handicap when these people return to the free world: former offenders who cannot get jobs because of insufficient education are likely to return to crime. For this reason, education has long been regarded as a primary rehabilitative tool in the correctional field. The gap between the need for educational services and the provision of adequate educational and vocational training is wide, however.

One of the first barriers to effective educational programs is, once again, the problem of administrative considerations: operational requirements, security needs, shortage of teachers, shortage of educational materials, tight budgets, and a lack of inmate motivation.[10] Inmates and staff are often handicapped by unsuitable or out-of-date textbooks, often below the level of the "street" sophistication of the average adult prisoner. Inmates who are prevented from attending classes for disciplinary reasons[11] may miss enough to be required to miss the rest of the term. Denying education as part of disciplinary action devalues its effectiveness as a treatment component and doubles the punishment factor.

The classes held in most institutions are conventional and relatively old-fashioned, in contrast with those that use the new learning technology and innovations available to students at all levels on the outside. Most prisoners have had little formal education and probably resisted whatever teaching they were exposed to. Material that bored them as children or truant teenagers is not likely to hold them enthralled as adults. What these mature felons do not need are "Dick and Jane" readers or other textbooks designed for children. But because of the low priority and minimal funds assigned to education in most institutions, it is these useless texts that prisoners are offered, often by public schools that no longer use them. Small wonder that most prison programs are neither accredited nor enthusiastically supported by inmates.

The surprising fact is that some educational services not only survive but even contribute to the inmates' rehabilitation.[12] In Ohio, the Department of Rehabilitation and Correction was finally able to establish a complete school district composed entirely of the educational programs within the state prison system. In the states of New York and Washington, education programs are contracted with local community colleges and they provide excellent programs, from adult basic education to degree programs in the institutions. Project Newgate, a program bringing the first years of college into the prisons, along with instructors and a complete curriculum, was the model for such programs in the 1970s.

Two other education-related programs that have been attempted, with varying results, are work/training release or furlough, and educational release. In educational release, inmates are allowed to leave the institution to attend college, high school, or vocational-technical schools during the

Working with Learning Disabled Inmates (Courtesy of American Correctional Association, photo by Stephen Steurer)

day, though they must return to the institution or an approved site when not at school, or at night. The use of educational release became quite widespread in the United States, but these programs were usually curtailed by highly visible failures or by budget cuts. In the work/training-release program, an inmate may be allowed to leave the limits of confinement to secure education and a job; this enables the offender to develop a work history, learn a trade, support dependents, or even make restitution to the victim of his or her crime.

Education, medical care, and religious practice have served as the "basic treatment" programs in America's prisons since the days of the Walnut Street Jail. In recent years, this limited three-sided approach to treatment has expanded to include a wide variety of programs aimed at the rehabilitation of incarcerated offenders.

The Vocational-Rehabilitation Model _____

Vocational and technical training in prisons have been available to prisoners ever since the industrial prison was established in the early 1800s. This early training, however, was aimed not at prisoner rehabilitation but at institutional profit. Later, at the Elmira Reformatory, the concept of

---

PRISON RELEASE PROGRAMS

To obtain work, occupational training, and education are three major objectives for which inmates are allowed to leave the prison. In most states, the legal mechanism for allowing an inmate to leave prison is the furlough program: the legislature extends the limits of confinement to include placement in the community while the prisoner pursues some common and identifiable correctional goal.

Furloughees are usually screened carefully and supervised by an agency. Although the extent of recidivism amongst furloughees is unknown, it is generally believed to be low. One reason for the low recidivism probably is that furloughees in most jurisdictions remain inmates and can be returned to prison easily if they show overt signs of being unable to conform their behavior to community expectations.

Oklahoma has used home furlough (house arrest of inmates) as a mechanism to reduce prison overcrowding, and the recidivism rate is markably low. More states are exploring the opportunities of increasing furlough programs to extend the limits of confinement for low-risk inmates, and plan to couple house arrest with electronic monitoring, unscheduled drug and alcohol testing, and supervision fees. This may become a major prison-release mechanism in the next decade.

---

training for the purpose of teaching a trade to ex-offenders was introduced, and it has slowly taken root over the years.

A major setback to adequate vocational training came with the passage of restrictive federal laws on the interstate transport of prison industry goods. These laws, passed in the mid-1930s, sounded the deathknell for many work programs in state prisons. Only in the past twenty years have institutions begun to reemphasize vocational training programs.

The waste of prisoners' time in idleness is staggering. Neil Singer conducted an analysis of potential inmate economic benefits and found that 208,000 felons in prison could earn an average of $8,038 each year, or $1.67 billion in total.[13] With today's prison population of approximately 594,000, that amount could be estimated at closer to $9 billion! Such economic realities cause legislators, managers, and citizens to wince when they appraise current forms of "treatment."

The goals of vocational training, when oriented too much toward institution-oriented goals can have some problem. As noted by Guynes and Grieser:

> Vocational training consumes both raw materials and staff instructional time. When these costs are imposed on industries, the institutional cost reduction goals are endangered.
>
> The development of good work habits in a real-world environment requires production with a minimum of "featherbedding." In a correctional environment, this is contrary to the need to maximize the number of inmates on the work force (i.e., reduce idleness).
>
> In order to maximize inmates' capacity to learn to manage their pay,

adequate salaries must be provided. While this goal is compatible with the institutional goal of cost reduction (to the degree that the offender is then responsible for room and board and commissary needs), the associated managerial expense may well increase product costs rather than reduce them. Certainly, the increased salary required to provide gate money runs counter to reducing the state's incarceration expenses.[14]

A common problem with prison industries is their multiple goals, for they sometimes shift and are always ambiguous. The prison administrator may believe the goal of prison industries to be generation of profits; shop managers are convinced it is to train inmates; and inmates believe it is "make work" and that they will receive some wage unrelated to productivity.[15] Leadership in resolving these conflicting goals was exerted by Congress in 1979, when it passed the Prison-Industries Enhancement Act, selectively repealing portions of the federal laws limiting prison industries. Since then, at least twenty states (such as Arizona, Minnesota, and Kansas)[16] have authorized some form of private-sector involvement with state penal industries,[17] such as in the areas of data processing, hotel-chain reservations, and manufacturing. Many of these private industry efforts must deal with insurance, initial plant investment costs, and quality control problems. It remains to be seen how effective private industry will

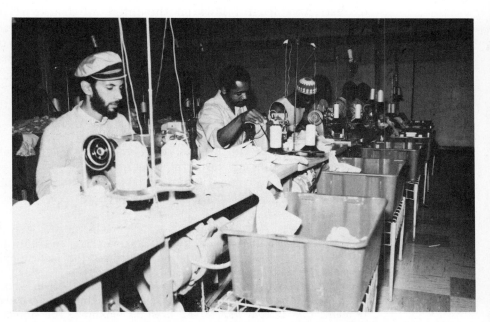

Part of Treatment is Learning the Discipline of Working (Courtesy of American Correctional Association, photo by UNICOR)

be in collaborating with prisons,[18] but such efforts are welcome signs in times of prison overcrowding!

These procedures, taken together, offer a realistic solution to one of the most serious problems impeding the successful return of offenders to an employment-oriented society.

Professionals in the Field of Corrections _____

Psychologists

Psychology is concerned with measuring and evaluating an individual's intellectual capability and his or her ability to cope and adjust in society. The use of mass testing, popularized in World War I, clearly had possibilities for prisons. With the advent of the first classification program in New Jersey in 1918, the psychologist became a dominant force in the classification process. Today, IQ tests and other measurements developed by psychologists have become standard in classification and treatment decisions. Psychologists have continued to outnumber other professionals who seek to determine the cause of and cure for criminal behavior; with their measurements and questionnaires, psychologists are generally more acceptable to the correctional staff than psychiatrists are.

Psychiatrists

Although psychiatrists became involved in prison activity early in the development of treatment programs, the correctional team has not readily accepted their presence. It is often difficult for the mission-oriented custody staff to accept the abstract, seemingly indecisive approach that is the hallmark of psychiatric treatment. The correctional officer would prefer to have all offenders with psychiatric problems relegated to mental institutions.[19] This distrust of prison psychiatrists also stems from an awareness that competent psychiatrists in private practice can make several times the salaries offered by prisons.

Another stumbling block to really effective psychiatric service in prison is the institutional environment itself: many psychiatrists would argue that little can be done in the way of treatment inside the monolithic institutions. Their efforts in prisons, as a result, stress diagnosis rather than treatment. This combination of circumstances means that some state systems have very few full-time psychiatric staff members and others have none. To gain maximum help from the psychiatrist, the whole function of most prisons would have to be changed.[20] The new pattern envisioned by the psychiatrist would be along the lines of the hospital model, in which treatment diagnoses can be seen through to completion. An alternative might be a small, urban-based, short-term treatment facility for handling moderately disturbed offenders.

Sociologists

Sociologists have been latecomers into correctional treatment programs. They are especially helpful in identifying and developing the roles and structures of the prison subcultures and the administrative personnel. Many of the current research projects in prisons and other areas of correctional treatment are being directed by sociologists. This group of professionals has also been helpful in determining the social factors that cause offenders to commit or repeat crimes. The findings and recommendations from many sociological studies are helping to push corrections back into the community.[21]

Sociologists have also worked their way into administrative positions in corrections, where they can exert more influence on the complex organization and its programs. Many of the higher-education programs in corrections are housed in university sociology departments, where criminology is handled as an integral part of the discipline of sociology.

Social Workers

Social work became particularly important in the spectrum of corrections when it began to emphasize rehabilitation. The caseworker is essential in the presentence investigation phase, and many probation officers and parole officers received their training in social work. It seems reasonable that the social worker became more involved in institutional programs as these programs develped a stress toward treatment. Social workers had already taken their places in school programs, hospitals, and mental health institutions, among others. The basic concepts of social casework can be successfully applied in the authoritarian atmosphere of the prison.[22] The social worker has the training to help the offender adapt to the prison situation inside the walls.

Barnes and Teeters, in their classic text on criminology, list four prerequisites for effective casework in prison:

> First, it must be accepted by the administration that there are constructive elements in a prison experience; second, that these elements can be translated into a sound correctional program; third, that the staff dedicate itself to the task of helping the inmate find maturity as a mark of social responsibility; fourth, that the administration provide the structure or climate in which the case worker can operate effectively.[23]

Clearly, the role of the social caseworker is especially suited to working out inmate problems.

Treatment and the Reintegration Model _____

The movement toward treatment and corrections in the community has highlighted the need to make programs inside the walls relate to circumstances in the outside world. Crime cannot be controlled by the reformation of prisoners alone. There must be continued reformation and reintegration efforts in the community.

Toward this end, many of the barriers shutting off the prison from the community have come down in the last decade. The treatment concept has been expanded to encompass the efforts of community-oriented professionals, and community volunteers have begun to give offenders the support and guidance needed to ensure successful reintegration.[24] The main objective of the reintegration model is to return the offender to the community as a responsible and productive citizen, rather than a feared and shunned "ex-con" with little hope for success. Institutions dedicated to this objective have learned to overcome deficits in funding and personnel by using the ingenuity of prison staff and the resources available in the community. Teachers and graduate students are encouraged to offer courses on topics that will help reintegrate the inmate, including such subjects as social problems, mental health, and the use of community resources.

Other assistance and support by outsiders help reduce the feeling of isolation and stigma that inevitably overtakes the incarcerated offender. No discussion of treatment would be complete without at least a mention of some of the various treatment modalities used in both prison and community corrections.

Some treatment program can be found in every institution, although the treatment personnel might be given titles that would not reflect the particular training or discipline of a "counselor." These treatment modalities cannot be covered in depth in an introductory course but include transactional analysis, psychodrama, behavior modification, individual and group psychotherapy, therapeutic communities, emotional maturity instruction, and guides to "better living."[25] Students interested in these treatment techniques should consult their instructors for more information.[26]

In many institutions, the barriers are coming down for traffic in both directions ("the door swings both ways"). Outside activity by inmates and prison personnel ranges from touring lecture programs to work and educational furloughs. These latter programs serve as a method of graduated release back to the community. The rationale for graduated release has its roots in the problems faced by the newly released inmate. Release is a very stressful time for an inmate, especially when he or she emerges directly from an institution. Inmates know they have failed in the past and fear that they will fail again. Without a chance to ease back into society in stages, as happens in graduated release, the inmate is a babe in the woods if he or she has been inside the walls for a long period of time. The released prisoner needs new social skills and a chance to catch up with a rapidly moving society.

The reintegration model allows the inmate to take on increasing responsibilities until he or she is ready for complete acceptance by the community. It is the wave of the future, and treatment programs built around such a comprehensive and integrated plan will have much higher potential for success than the old custody/control methods. The true reintegration model recognizes the need to give the ex-offender a reasonable means of support. Hence, good vocational training is important.

Unionization: The Inmates

A movement that has caused problems with treatment programs, primarily because of the custody-oriented fear of inmate organization, is the rise of prison unions. The prisoner union movement began at California's Folsom Prison in 1970, when the climate was ripe for what then seemed to be revolutionary demands by the Folsom inmates. They had just suffered several internal disturbances and had been through a nineteen-day strike. The strike had focused on the prisoners' demands for eliminating indeterminate sentences and was punctuated by the fatal shooting of three black inmates at Soledad Prison. The "Soledad Brothers" became a rallying point for prisoners who sought to form a union. The three main goals of the California union started at that time were the following:

1. The abolishment of the indeterminate sentence system and all its ramifications.
2. The establishment of workers' rights for the prisoner, including the right to organize collectively and bargain.
3. The restoration of civil and human rights for the prisoners.[27]

The movement spread rapidly, and today, locals have been established in almost all the California state prisons. The basic structure of the California model keeps the control on the outside, in the hands of ex-offenders in the community. These ex-offenders are also active in helping prisoners in other states set up union operations.

A prisoner union was established in New York, at Greenhaven Prison, and was affiliated with the Distributive Workers of America. Other unions were established in Massachusetts, North Carolina, Kansas, Georgia, Minnesota, and Washington. The New England Prison Coalition covered Maine, Vermont, Rhode Island, Massachusetts, and New Hampshire.[28] However, with the great advances in populations and the attendant overcrowding, prisoners unions have lost their effectiveness. Some institutions still allow inmate groups, based on ethnic or racial lines, to exist but not to form protest groups and foment trouble.

Most correctional administrators in this country strongly oppose inmate unionization, as this comment by a state director of corrections suggests: "These men are convicted felons — convicted of breaking the laws of society. Under no circumstances will I recognize their so-called union."[29] Inmate union organizers are often dispersed to other institutions around the state (through "bus therapy") when they begin to become a nuisance. These are only stopgap resistance measures, however; the prisoner union is here to stay, and some procedure for collective bargaining has been established. Correctional administrators, however, will not cooperate unless inmates can convince them that unions will not threaten security and control within the institution. The concerned administrator's main fear is that the union power will soon gravitate to a few particularly magnetic or authoritative inmates, who will use that power to advance only their own philosophies and interests. Based on the development of such subculture powers in the past, this concern appears to be a valid one.

The right to form a prisoner union is in one of the gray areas of correctional law. The general expansion of prisoner rights, which can be interpreted as including the right to form a union, derives from the 1944 decision in *Coffin* v. *Reichard*.[30] This landmark case held that "a prisoner retains all the rights of an ordinary citizen, except those expressly, or by necessary implication, taken from him by law." The issue was approached more directly in the 1972 decision on *Goodwin* v. *Oswald,* however:

> There is nothing in federal or state constitutional or statutory law of which I am aware that forbids prison inmates from seeking to form, or correctional officials from electing to deal with, an organization or agency or representative group of inmates concerned with prison conditions and inmates' grievances. Indeed, the tragic experience at Attica . . . would make correctional officials, an observer might think, seek more peaceful ways of resolving prison problems than the old, ironclad, solitary-confinement, mail-censoring, dehumanizing methods that have worked so poorly in the past. Promoting or at least permitting the formation of a representative agency might well be, in the light of past experience, the wisest course for correctional officials to follow.[31]

This statement may constitute judicial approval of inmate unions, but it offers no solution to the administrative problem of juggling security against inmate rights. Prisoners have always found some way to bargain with their keepers. A formal procedure to accomplish this purpose could have beneficial as well as negative effects in terms of institutional order.

Unionization, for the staff or the inmates, creates many dilemmas for the correctional administrator. How these problems are resolved in the next decade may either encourage or negate the development of a flexible corrections approach aimed at rehabilitation and reintegration of offenders.

For example, the need for flexibility would not coincide with the rigid requirements that tend to develop out of labor union negotiations. It is important to meet these challenges so that solutions can be achieved that are both flexible and fair to all sides.

Summary

Within the serious problems of the correctional institution, the correctional treatment process has many elements. From the more formalized approach of the social scientists, the medical professionals, and the educators to the efforts of community volunteers and release programs, the key to treatment is an organized program designed to prepare the inmate for successful reintegration within the free society. It is obvious how important the cooperation and understanding of the security and custody staff can be in the success of any of the efforts described as "treatment." As the single most influential agent of change, the correctional officer is the keystone to the success or failure of any kind of treatment program. A cooperative effort by custody and treatment staffs is the essence of an effective institutional program.[32] But treatment cannot end at the prison gate. To ensure maximum success, the treatment must be continued and reinforced in the community. These community programs will be discussed in Chapter 25.

Review Questions

1. What are the general categories of treatment services?
2. Is classification more properly a security or a treatment function? Why?
3. Explain the various roles of psychologists, psychiatrists, and sociologists in correctional institutions.
4. Explain the rationale of the reintegration model and how it applies to graduated release.
5. Why does the custody staff seem to feel that most innovative treatment amounts to being "soft"?

Key Terms

1. "back-filled" (p. 504)
2. unit team management (p. 507)
3. "gold brickers" (p. 508)
4. Project Newgate (p. 511)
5. vocational-rehabilitation model (p. 512)
6. prison release programs (p. 513)
7. reintegration model (p. 517)
8. "Soledad Brothers" (p. 518)
9. bus therapy (p. 519)
10. prisoner union (p. 519)

Notes _____

1. American Correctional Association, *Manual of Correctional Standards,* 3d ed. (Washington, D.C.: ACA, 1966), p. 17.

2. See Rob Wilson, "Who Will Care for the 'Mad' and the 'Bad'?" *Corrections Magazine* 6 (February 1980): 5–17.

3. Ray Nelson, "Isolation of Staff from Inmates," *Corrections Today* 46 (April 1984): 106–108, 110. See also Carol Fewell, "Successful Strategies: Integrating Health Care and Security Functions," *Corrections Today* 50 (1988): pp. 20–22

4. Gary Bingham, "Inmate Assignments," *Corrections Today* 46 (June 1984): 58–59.

5. Ohio Citizens' Task Force on Corrections, *Final Report* (Columbus: State of Ohio, 1972): pp. C-55–C-56.

6. Stanley Grosshandler and Parker Eales, "Dilemmas of Correctional Medicine," *Corrections Today* 46 (June 1984): 114–116. For a recent survey of existing healthcare services and court-defined inmate rights to healthcare, see Carlton Hornung, "The Courts and an Inmate's Rights to Health Care," *Journal of Offender Counseling, Services and Rehabilitation* 6 (1982): 5–19.
   For a description of legal liabilities of the sheriff in the medical areas, see National Sheriffs' Association, *Inmates' Legal Rights* (Alexandria, Va: NSA, 1987): pp. 17–23.

7. Several states contract with health maintenance services for comprehensive healthcare skills. Not only do such private organizations recruit and pay physicians, nurses, dentists, and psychiatrists, but most also assist in defending against lawsuits and carry malpractice insurance. One example is the Prison Health Services, Inc., of Wilmington, Delaware.

8. The relationship between chemical ingestion of drugs and crime appears quite strong. See in particular the National Institute of Justice reports, *Prisoners and Drugs (1983)* and *Prisoners and Alcohol (1983)* (U.S. Department of Justice, 1985). See also Bernard Gropper, *Probing the Links Between Drugs and Crime,* (Washington, D.C.: U.S. Department of Justice, 1985), and Toni Atmore and Edward Bauchiero, "Substance Abuse: Identification and Treatment," *Corrections Today* 49 (1987): 22, 24, 26, 110.

9. See the special feature issue on education found in *Corrections Today* 49 (June 1987); and Hans Tock, "Reintegrating Inmates Through Education," *Federal Probation* 51 (September 1987): pp. 61–66.

10. William Reed, "Motivation of Inmates for College Enrollment and the Effect of Higher Education and Vocational Training upon Inmate Discipline" (Ann Arbor, Mich.: University Microfilms International, 1982). See also James Austin, "Assessing the New Generation of Prison Classification Models," *Crime and Delinquency* 29 (1983): 561–576; Ted Palmer, "Treatment and the Role of Classification: A Review of the Basics," *Crime and Delinquency* 30 (1984): 245–268.

11. Carolyn Buser, Peter Leone, and Mary Bannon, "Segregation: Does Education Stop Here?" *Corrections Today* 49 (1987): 16-18.

12. See Rick Linden and Linda Perry, "The Effectiveness of Prison Educational Programs," *Journal of Offender Counseling, Services and Rehabilitation* 6 (1982): 43–57.

13. Neil Singer, *The Value of Inmate Manpower* (Washington, D.C.: American Bar Association Commission on Correctional Facilities and Manpower, 1973).

14. Randall Guynes and Robert C. Grieser, "Contemporary Prison Industry Goals," *A Study of Prison Industry: History, Components, and Goals*, (U.S. Department of Justice, Washington, D.C.: January 1986), p. 25.

15. Joint Subcommittee on the Economic Productivity of the Prison Population and on Work Release Programs, *Report to the Governor and General Assembly of Virginia* (Richmond: Senate Document 22, 1982).

16. CONTACT, Inc., "Prison Industry," *Correctional Compendium* 7 (1982): 5–11.

17. Barbara Auerbach, "New Prison Industries Legislation: The Private Sector Re-enters the Field," *Prison Journal* 42 (1982): 5–11.

18. Gail Funke et al., "The Future of Correctional Industries," *Prison Journal* 42 (1981): 37–51. See also Joan Mullen, Kent Chabotar, and Deborah Carrow, *The Privitization of Corrections*, (Washington, D.C.: U.S. Department of Justice, 1985); Charles Logan, "The Propriety of Proprietary Prisons," *Federal Probation* 51 (September 1987): 35–40.

19. See Stephen Hardy, "Dealing with the Mentally Disturbed and Emotionally Disturbed," *Corrections Today* 46 (June 1984): 16–18, 126; Sol Chanales, "Medical and Psychiatric Responses to Prisoners," *Journal of Counseling, Services and Rehabilitation* 8 (1983): v–viii.

20. Steven Schreiber, "The Physician's Assistant," *Corrections Today* 46 (June 1984): 70, 135.

21. Daniel Kennedy, "Clinical Sociology and Correctional Counseling," *Crime and Delinquency* 30 (1984): 245–268.

22. Daniel Juda, "On the Special Problems of Creating Group Cohesion Within a Prison Setting," *Journal of Offender Counseling, Services and Rehabilitation* 8 (1983): 47–60.

23. Harry Elmer Barnes and Negley K. Teeters, *New Horizons in Criminology*, 3d ed. (Englewood Cliffs, N.J.: Prentice-Hall, 1959), pp. 472–473.

24. Edward Latessa, Larry Travis, and Harry E. Allen, "Volunteers and Paraprofessionals in Parole: Current Practices," *Journal of Offender Counseling, Services and Rehabilitation* 8 (1983): 91–107.

25. John Dierna, "Consulting in Federal Probation: The Introduction of a Flowchart in the Counseling Process," *Federal Probation* 51 (September 1987): 4–16.

26. For the student with an interest in correctional counseling, see Peter Kratcoski, *Correctional Counseling and Treatment* (Monterey, Calif.: Duxbury, 1982).

27. John Irwin and Willie Holder, "History of the Prisoners' Union," *The Outlaw: Journal of the Prisoners' Union* 2 (January–February 1973): 1–3.

28. C. Ronald Huff, "Unionization Behind Walls," *Criminology* 12 (August 1974): 175–194.

29. Ibid., p. 186.

30. *Coffin* v. *Reichard,* 143 F. 2nd 443 (1944).

31. *Goodwin* v. *Oswald,* 462 F. 2nd 1237 (1972).

32. A review of research (from 1973) on family intervention, counseling, diversion, and biomedical techniques with offenders suggests that such approaches are successful with offender populations. See P. Gendreau and Bob Ross, "Effective Correctional Treatment: Bibliotherapy for Cynics," *Crime and Delinquency* 25 (October 1979): 463–489. Currently, most "cutting edge" programs focusing on reintegration are house arrest, community service orders, intensive supervised probation, furlough from prison, and halfway house services (see Chapter 25).

Recommended Readings _____

Breda, Renato, and Franco Ferracuti. "Alternatives to Incarceration in Italy." *Crime and Delinquency* 26 (January 1980): 63–69.

Chaiken, Jan et al. *The Impact of Fiscal Limitation on California's Criminal Justice System.* Santa Monica, Calif.: Rand Corporation, 1981.

Cohen, Jacqueline. "Incapacitating Criminals: Recent Research Findings." *Research in Brief.* Washington, D.C.: U.S. Department of Justice, 1983, pp. 1–5.

Cullen, Hoan, Kent Chabotar, and Deborah Carrow. *The Privatization of Corrections.* Washington, D.C.: U.S. Department of Justice, 1985.

Currie, Elliott. *What Kind of Future? Violence and Public Safety in the Year 2000.* San Francisco, Calif.: National Council on Crime and Delinquency, 1987.

Greenwood, Peter, and Frank Zimring. *One More Chance: The Pursuit of Promising Intervention Strategies for Chronic Juvenile Offenders.* Santa Monica, Calif.: Rand Corporation, 1985.

McCulloh, Robert. *A Comparative Analysis of Juvenile Justice Standards and the JJDP Act.* Washington, D.C.: U.S. Department of Justice, 1981.

National Advisory Commission on Criminal Justice Standards and Goals. *Corrections.* Washington, D.C.: U.S. Government Printing Office, 1973.

National Association of Attorneys General. *Religion in Correctional and Mental Institutions.* Raleigh, N.C.: Committee on the Office of Attorney General, 1976.

Pointer, Donald, and Marjorie Kravitz. *The Handicapped Offender.* Washington, D.C.: U.S. Government Printing Office, 1981.

Pointer, Donald, and Marjorie Kravitz. *Prison and Jail Health Care.* Washington, D.C.: U.S. Government Printing Office, 1981.

Shannon, Lyle. *Assessing the Relationship of Adult Criminal Careers to Juvenile Careers.* Washington, D.C.: U.S. Government Printing Office, 1982.

U.S. Department of Justice. *Report to the Nation on Crime and Justice.* Washington, D.C.: U.S. Department of Justice, 1983.

Petersilia, Joan. *Expanding Options for Criminal Sentencing.* Santa Monica, Calif.: Rand Corporation, 1987.

Correctional Systems

22

Jails and Detention Facilities

Crowded jails have also brought attention to yet
another situation the public was not aware of: the
difficult position correctional officers in local jails
are put in and the demands that are placed on
them. . . . Truly they are jacks of all trade and
masters of none.
—JAMES GONDLES JR.

Jails: A Grim History

The housing of offenders and suspected criminals in local detention
facilities is a practice as old as the definition of crime. The local gaol,
lockup, workhouse, stockade, or jail has changed little over the centuries.
Only recently has there been any serious attempt to treat jail inmates,
and even these efforts must be continuously monitored or officials are
likely to abandon them. Originally devised as a place to lock up and
restrain all classes of misfits, the jail has a long and sordid history. As
discussed in Chapter 2, John Howard was made keenly aware of the appalling jail conditions in eighteenth-century England when he found himself the proprietor of one of the worst. His effort to reform the practices
and improve the conditions in the gaols and prisons of England and the
rest of Europe parallels the periodic attempts by American reformers to
clean up our jails.

The early jails in America were similar to those in Europe. Most were
composed of small rooms in which as many as twenty to thirty prisoners
were jammed together. The purpose of jails, as originally conceived by Henry
II of England when he ordered the construction of the first official English
jail at the Assize of Clarendon in 1166, was to detain suspected or accused
offenders until they could be brought before a court. Seldom were the jails
adequately heated or ventilated, and food was either sold by the jailer or
brought in by family or friends. Conditions within these early jails defy
description, and the problems of overcrowding and poor sanitation continue to
plague many jails today. At best, most are warehouses for the misdemeanant,
vagrant, petty offender, and common drunk. At worst, they are "festering

---

JAILS

A jail is a confinement facility, usually administered by a local law enforcement agency, intended for adults but sometimes also containing juveniles, that holds persons detained pending adjudication and/or persons committed after adjudication for sentences of a year or less. Jails are usually supported by local tax revenues and, as such, are particularly vulnerable to resource reductions.

Additional categories of jail inmates include mentally ill persons for whom there are no other facilities, parolees and probationers awaiting hearings, federal prisoners awaiting pick up by marshals, and offenders sentenced to departments of corrections for whom there is not yet space but who cannot be released.

---

sores" as described by Richard Velde, former director of the Law Enforcement Assistance Administration. The jail, perhaps more than any other segment of the correctional system, is resistant to change and tends to deteriorate more quickly than it can be improved. Jails are the "cloacal region of corrections."[1]

The jail has been at the end of the line for receiving public and governmental support since the days when John Howard inherited the abomination at Bedfordshire in 1773. Though public attention may turn to jails from time to time—when politicians or the media expose a particularly appalling situation—the jails quickly revert to their original deplorable state. In the last few years, a number of new facilities have been constructed to provide better conditions and programs for the misdemeanant prisoner and felony detainee, but these are all too few. Community programs and facilities are sometimes used to provide work and educational programs for short-term sentenced prisoners—again, not very often.[2]

Of all the problems that plague the criminal justice system, none is more confused and irrational than the question of what should be done with the felon in the period preceding trial. In the United States, the concept of "innocent until proven guilty" creates many problems for the local jail (see Table 22.1). Pretrial detention and procedures for pretrial liberty have been the subject of hot debate among personnel in the criminal justice system for many decades. The presumption of innocence is difficult to maintain once the defendant has been arrested and detained in jail. The police find this presumption difficult to accept if they have acted on probable cause (high probability of guilt) in first making the arrest. Several projects studying the effects of pretrial decisions on sentencing offer evidence that this period is critical to later correctional efforts.[3]

This is especially true when one considers that the Sixth Amendment to the Constitution guarantees a "speedy and public trial." Felony case-processing time was examined in twelve major jurisdictions, and it was found that the average time for a felony case to be filed in court was 3½ months, and the average time for being indicted and bound over for trial was 4¾ months. Those electing for a trial showed the longest time frames, a little over seven months for filing in court to 7½ months for indictment and being

TABLE 22.1 Number of State Prisoners Held in Local Jails because of Prison Crowding, by State, Yearend 1985 and 1986

States Housing Prisoners in Local Jails	Prisoners Held in Local Jails			
	Number		As Percent of All Prisoners	
	1985	1986	1985	1986
Total	10,143	13,770	2.2%	2.7%
Alabama	398	514	3.6	4.4
Arkansas[a]	115	458	2.5	8.9
California	1,122	1,566	2.2	2.6
Colorado[a]	245	343	6.8	8.5
Idaho	9	0	.6	0
Illinois	43	48	.2	.2
Kentucky	791	886	13.7	14.0
Louisiana	2,923	3,449	21.0	23.7
Maine	51	36	4.2	2.7
Massachusetts	2	1	—	—
Mississippi	933	1,169	14.6	17.3
New Jersey[a]	1,486	2,244	11.6	13.2
South Carolina	429	451	4.1	3.9
Tennessee[a]	628	1,201	8.3	14.3
Utah	33	77	2.1	4.2
Vermont[b]	11	8	1.7	1.2
Virginia	786	1,257	6.5	9.7
Washington	49	62	.7	.9
Wisconsin	89	0	1.6	0

— Less than 0.05%
[a] For States not including jail backups in their jusrisdiction counts, the percentage of jurisdiction population was calculated on the combined total of jail and prison.
[b] Vermont reported 8 inmates in local lockups.

Source: Lawrence Greenfield, *Prisoners in 1986* (Washington, D.C.: U.S. Department of Justice, 1987), p. 4.

bound over for trial.[4] This presents a problem for the "innocent" person being held, for he or she looks more guilty with each passing day in confinement.

Jails Today _____

Urban dwellers in America have responded to the need for local lockups and correctional facilities in a number of ways. The most common confinement facility is the lockup, but the size and quality of these facilities varies greatly. There is quite a difference between the one-cell lockup[5] of a small southern town and those of the gigantic facilities of New York City and Los Angeles. (The counterpart of the city lockup is the county jail, but jails, lockups, detention facilities, workhouses, and a number of other units all are commonly referred to as *jails*. We shall refer to all of these facilities as *city or county jails* except when it is more relevant to refer to them by another designation.) Policies and programs vary greatly among cities and counties, but some general descriptions and suggestions can be made for small, medium, and large systems. As many as 80 percent of the jails in this country hold between less than 50 up to 249 inmates. (See Table 22.2).

TABLE 22.2 Twenty-Five Largest Jails: Average Daily Population and 1-Day Count, June 30, 1986

City and Jail	Average Daily Population, 1986*	One-Day Count, June 30, 1986
Los Angeles, Calif.—Men's Central Jail	8,002	7,703
Chicago, Ill.—Department of Corrections County Jails	5,052	5,113
Houston, Tex.—County Downtown Central Jail	3,765	3,765
Washington, D.C.—D.C. Detention Facility**	2,365	2,635
Queens, N.Y.—NYC Correctional Institute for Men**	2,112	2,017
Queens, N.Y.—Anna M. Kross Center**	2,100	2,100
Los Angeles, Calif.—Sybil Brand Institute	1,877	2,204
Pleasanton, Calif.—County Jail Santa Rita	1,873	1,877
Baltimore, Md.—Baltimore City Jail	1,833	1,899
Los Angeles, Calif.—Hall of Justice Jail	1,717	1,696
Saugus, Calif.—Pitchess Honor Rancho—maximum security	1,683	1,609
Santa Ana, Calif.—Orange County Jail	1,580	1,636
Queens, N.Y.—NYC Adolescent Detention Center	1,575	1,567
Saugus, Calif.—Pitchess Honor Rancho—minimum security	1,506	1,599
Miami, Fla.—County Pre-Trial Detention Center	1,459	1,495
Fort Worth, Tex.—Tarrant County Jail	1,425	1,502
Los Angeles, Calif.—Biscailuz Center	1,301	1,524
Philadelphia, Pa.—House of Correction	1,286	1,279
Seattle, Wash.—King County Jail Facilities	1,282	1,443
Philadelphia, Pa.—Holmesburg Prison	1,195	1,104
Philadelphia, Pa.—Detention Center	1,160	1,115
Memphis, Tenn.—County Justice Center	1,143	1,263
Indianapolis, Ind.—Marion County Jail	1,130	1,141
Elk Grove, Calif.—Rio Cosumnes Corrections Center	1,116	1,219
East Elmhurst, N.Y.—NYC Correctional Institute for Women	1,110	1,197

*For the year ending June 30, 1986.
**Data for these facilities were only available for earlier years.

Source: Susan Kline, *Jail Inmates 1986* (Washington, D.C.: U.S. Department of Justice, 1987), p. 3.

Jails Can Provide Productive Work For Offenders (Courtesy of American Correctional Association, photo by Michael C. Dersin)

Characteristics of the Jail Population

Although it is always difficult to obtain accurate data regarding jails and jail populations, the 1986 study *Jail Inmates*, from the Bureau of Justice Statistics, provides current and reliable information.[6]

More than 274,444 persons were held in locally operated jails on June 30, 1986, an increase of 17 percent over the 1985 total, and 23 percent greater than that of 1984. The latest profile of jail inmates reflected the traditional, twofold function of a jail: a place for the temporary detention of the unconvicted and a confinement facility where many convicted persons—predominantly misdemeanants—serve out their sentences.[7] More than five out of every ten jail inmates had not been convicted of a crime. Compared with state and federal prisons, jails held a much smaller percentage of inmates for violent crimes, but larger proportions for property and public order offenses (see Table 16.1).

In 1986, some 53 percent of the jail inmates stood accused but not convicted of a crime. Most of those who had counsel were being represented by court-appointed lawyers, public defenders, or legal aid attorneys. A large percentage of all unconvicted inmates remained in jail, even though bail had been set for them by the authorities.

Whites outnumbered blacks in the nation's jails (59 percent and 40 percent respectively), but the proportion of blacks in jail far exceeded their 12 percent share of the United States population. Inmates belonging to

TABLE 22.3 Demographic characteristics of jail inmates, 1985 and 1986

Characteristic	Percent of Jail Inmates	
	1985	1986
Sex		
Total	100%	100%
Male	92	92
Female	8	8
Race		
White	59%	58%
Male	55	54
Female	4	4
Black	40%	41%
Male	37	37
Female	3	3
Other*	1%	1%
Male	1	1
Female	—	—
Ethnicity		
Hispanic	14%	14%
Male	13	13
Female	1	1
Non-Hispanic	86%	86%
Male	80	80
Female	7	7

Source: Susan Kline, *Jail Inmates 1986* (Washington, D.C.: U.S. Department of Justice, 1987), p. 2.

other minority races accounted for only 1 percent of all jail inmates (see Table 22.3).

The 1986 jail population consisted predominantly of males (92 percent). Most inmates were young men in their twenties. There was an amazing number of admissions and releases in 1986 (16.6 million), a total of about 7 percent of the national population, if each case represented one individual! (Of course, these numbers represent multiple arrests in most cases). Three-fourths of all the jail population were housed in the 361 jurisdictions with an average daily population of over 100, representing 612 jails.

The Problem of Overcrowding

Pressure from state correctional systems to reduce institutional populations is rapidly changing the makeup of our jails (and probationers), with serious offenders being housed with local drunks and misdemeanants. Already overcrowded and difficult to control, many jails have become dumping grounds where little is done but locking up and feeding the population. The following description appeared in a 1979 article in *Corrections Magazine:*

"The best I have is worse than the worst conditions at the state pen," said one exasperated Mississippi county attorney. "And I have a feeling it may be like this all over the country."

"Asking which jails are the worst is like asking, like kids do, whether you'd rather die by burning or freezing," says Ronald Goldfarb, an attorney and author of the book *Jails*. "They are all pretty awful. And whatever the problems on the state level, they are worse in the jails."

No one denies that the prisoners suffer from crowded multiple cells, a lack of fresh air and exercise, rampant illness, vermin, and idleness. "It's a madhouse back there," said one young Alabama jailer. "They're sodomizing each other and beating each other up all the time."

Some of the stories are grotesque. In August of last year, two Mississippi prisoners were found hanged in their cell after their request for transfer to the state prison was denied; a protest note was found nearby. In Tennessee, in 1975, a juvenile status offender, unable to get medication he needed, acted out his frustration by setting fire to a mattress. Toxic fumes from the polyurethane material spread through the jail, killing forty-two people, including staff, visitors, and inmates. In 1977, in Meridian, Mississippi, two state prisoners started a fire in their cell and pushed a third inmate, a local inebriate, into the blaze.[8]

Although there have been many improvements, this dismal picture is relatively accurate. The improvements in many physical facilities have been set back by overcrowding and by the more violent populations.

The 1986 jail census found that jails held about one inmate for every two inmates in state and federal prisons and that prison overcrowding led to a backup in jails of thousands of persons sentenced to prison. Furthermore, 1 percent of all juvenile admissions and releases were at jails in 1986. Of particular interest is the rated capacity of the nation's estimated 3,500 local jails. As shown by Table 22.4, the rated capacity was up from 1983 to 1986 by over 24,000 beds, but the occupancy rate (the capacity occupied) grew to 96 percent! Most jail administrators acknowledge that all flexibility in a jail, in regard to classification and housing, is lost when the jail is at 90 percent of capacity (see Table 22.4).

TABLE 22.4 Jail capacity and occupancy, 1983, 1985, 1986

	National Jail Census	Annual Survey of Jails	
	1983	1985	1986
Number of inmates	223,551	256,615	274,444
Rate capacity of jails	261,556	272,830	285,726
Percent of rated capacity occupied	85%	94%	96%

Note: Data are for June 30 of each year.

Source: Susan Kline, *Jail Inmates 1986* (Washington, D.C.: U.S. Department of Justice, 1987), p. 2.

The twenty-five largest jails in the United States held 19 percent of the nation's total jail inmates, most exceeding their capacity. It is obvious that those jails with unused capacity will be the smaller jails. A major cause of overcrowding in facilities is the pressure to close other facilities that do not meet acceptable standards.[9] Between 1972 and 1978, the number of jails available to house adult prisoners dropped from 3,921 to 3,443. These figures have continued to decline in the 1980s. Although most of these buildings probably deserved to be closed, the expanding populations and related problems have been left to a system with a shrinking capacity to handle them, regardless of how poorly. Overcrowding and idleness have thus become the rule in jails.

Jail Structure and Design

Most jails are fairly uniform in their basic structural arrangements. Usually they are designed to operate with a minimum staff and still provide secure confinement for the inmates. In the older jails, a large central cagelike structure called the "bullpen" is used for most of the nonviolent prisoners and the drunks (for the latter group, the structure is called the "tank"). Larger jails may contain several bullpens and a separate drunk

A "New Era" Jail: Without Bars and Up to Standards (Courtesy American Correctional Association)

tank. The central area is usually surrounded by rows of cells, facing inward toward the bullpens. Like keepers of caged animals, officials often limit contact with inmates by passing food into the bullpens and cells through slots in the doors. Thus, the already minimal contact between inmates and staff is reduced still further. Although this lack of contact is usually justified in the name of security, it compounds the already highly impersonal atmosphere at most jails.

Sanitary facilities are another major problem, especially in the older jails. And even where there is adequate plumbing, the inmates' frustration is too often vented on these objects. The lack of privacy and the personal degradation associated with the open use of sanitary facilities heightens the resentment and dehumanization, leading inmates to vandalize the already limited sanitary equipment. Many jails visited by the 1970 National Jail Census did not have any functioning flush toilets; buckets and similarly medieval expedients still prevailed in several American jails. Although toilets are a problem, the need for showers and washroom facilities is even more critical.

The large percentage of drunks and others placed in the tank, some filthy with their own vomit and excrement, are often left in an unsanitary condition because of a lack of adequate cleanup facilities. As stated in the National Advisory Commission, "If cleanliness is next to godliness, most jails are securely in the province of hell."[10]

In the new generation of jails, built with the last vestiges of the funds from the Law Enforcement Assistance Administration, there is much more adherence to standards and the involvement of staff in every aspect of inmate activity. But the most expensive portion of every corrections budget (see Chapter 19) is people, so the new jails are often built to isolate staff in control centers that operate electronic equipment to move people around the facilities. The amount of space and the requirement for access to natural light make the new jails much more humane and less oppressive.[11] Overcrowding pressures, however, have caused many of these facilities to disregard the mandated standards, just so that they can keep up with population growth. These conditions result in the same frustrations and resulting vandalism to equipment and deterioration of morale in inmates (see Figure 22.1).

Problems with Personnel

The structures used to house our jails reflect the multitude of problems connected with these facilities.[12] Certainly, the lack of adequate personnel is a crucial factor.[13] Most jails are operated by the law enforcement agency that has jurisdiction in the particular area. Because most of the full-time jail personnel are county police officers, dedicated to putting offenders into jail, the primary emphasis is on custodial convenience rather than correc-

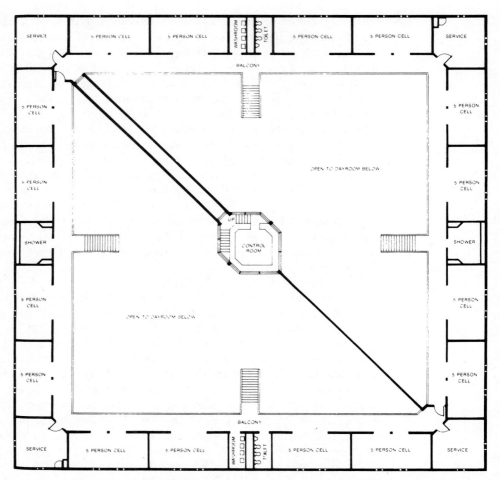

Figure 22-1 A Modern Jail Design (Charles DeWitt, *California Tests New Construction Concepts* [Washington, D.C.: U.S. Department of Justice, 1986], p. 8)

tional services. The philosophy behind this includes an almost fanatical concern with security, leaving the responsibility for the jails' internal operation to the inmates themselves. It is this situation that has produced the most reprehensible conditions in many of the large municipal jails. When jail personnel are not sworn officers but low-paid custodial individuals, the conditions become still worse. The need for preservice and in-service training of jailers[14] and other jail personnel has been clearly perceived by jail inspectors. The immediate requirement is not an influx of professional staff, but simple training aimed at breaking the habitual work patterns of uninterested, politically appointed, and unqualified jail personnel.

The national seven-day average ratio of jail workers to inmates is 1⅔ to 40. This ratio is only an average; the discrepancy becomes more noticeable during the night shift. The answer, however, is not so much more people as better people for the jobs already available.[15]

One problem with upgrading personnel and facilities has its roots in the long history of the jail "fee system," which stems from a practice in early England. The office of sheriff in those days was a position of pomp and prestige but little work. The distasteful duty of caring for the jail and its inmates was usually sold as a concession to a keeper, or gaoler. Fees for maintaining the inmates were extracted from their family, friends, or estate. Under this system, the greater the number of inmates was and the longer they were kept, the more income would accrue to the jailer. To increase his profit, the jailer cut his expenses to a minimum and operated the jail as cheaply as possible. This system remained unquestioned until 1773, when John Howard became the sheriff of Bedfordshire.

The fee system was used in America for many years, until it was largely replaced by a variation of itself. The inmates themselves are no longer required to pay for the jailer from the county treasury. In some states, this per-diem fee is paid by the state or by federal agencies with which the jail has a contract. Not surprisingly, a system that pays the sheriff to arrest and jail as many persons as possible is often exploited by the sheriffs who inherit it. Not until a professional police-officer position of sheriff and a civil service program is devised to replace fee systems in every jurisdiction will the corruption they encourage be eliminated.

The standards for jailers and related personnel have been a matter of concern for many years.

The key to success on your job and in pursuing a course of independent study . . . is self-discipline. You have to work at it on a regular basis when at times you would prefer to relax.

Make no mistake about it. The position of jail officer has assumed an importance that was not recognized even ten years ago. In the next decade you will see the training requirements and courses for study for those who would aspire to a career in corrections equal in length to the training and study required for other people in law enforcement.

The way of the world is change. For the professional jailer this fact means a continued life-long career of study and continuous training. This course is but a necessary first step.[16]

It is clear that the upgrading of personnel and their reorientation to this new and challenging mission is as critical in the jail system as it is anywhere else in the criminal justice system.

Alternatives to Jail

There are various alternatives to jail available to the pretrial defendant as well as to the convicted misdemeanant. We shall cover a few of these alternatives now.

Innocent until Proven Guilty?

Extended confinement of innocent persons—as with pretrial detention of the unadjudicated felon later found not guilty—is a serious problem. The defendant who is innocent and is exposed through pretrial confinement to the conditions of most jails will probably build up considerable animosity toward the criminal justice system and corrections in particular. The convicted offender eventually sent to a correctional institution also will have negative feelings about the inequities of a system that appears to confine arbitrarily some defendants before trial while releasing others.

Other Dispositions for the Misdemeanant

The confusion in defining and enforcing misdemeanor statutes is reflected in the absence of uniform techniques and systems for dealing with misdemeanants. Although different states vary greatly in their approaches, and jurisdictions within states may also be inconsistent, some patterns are fairly constant.[17] As mentioned earlier, the bulk of the misdemeanor cases are disposed of through confinement or probation. There are other alternatives for disposition as well, the most prevalent being the use of *fines*.

Fines are often called "price tag justice." In the case of misdemeanor offenses, the fine is in many cases offered as an alternative to a period of confinement, meaning that the offender who cannot pay is confined—in effect, for being poor rather than for being guilty. The sheer number of misdemeanor cases the lower courts must hear presents a major obstacle to all but the most cursory justice. Some lower courts may hear as many as one hundred or more misdemeanor cases in a single morning. It is difficult, under such circumstances, to conduct any kind of in-depth diagnosis of the offender, the offense, or the offender's ability to pay a fine. The amount of fine for a particular crime is virtually standardized, and paying it is like paying forfeited bail. For the individual unable to pay,

---

FINES

A fine is a penalty imposed on a convicted person by a court that requires him or her to pay a specified amount of money. The fine is a cash payment of a dollar amount assessed by the judge in an individual case or determined by a published schedule of penalties. Fines may be paid in installments in many jurisdictions, or by use of the offender's credit card.

WEEKEND CONFINEMENT

To lessen the negative impacts of short-term incarceration and allow offenders to retain current employment, some jurisdictions permit sentences to be served during nonworking weekends. Such weekend confinement generally requires a guilty misdemeanant to check into the jail on Friday after work and leave Sunday morning, sometimes early enough to permit church attendance. A "weekender" serving his or her sentence over a number of months would generally be credited with three days of confinement per weekend.

COMMUNITY WORK ORDERS

Sentencing judges sometimes order misdemeanants to perform a period of service to the community as a substitute for, or in partial satisfaction of, a fine. This disposition is generally a condition of a suspended (or partially suspended) sentence or of probation. It can be used in a variety of ways: a sentence in itself, work in lieu of cash fine, as a condition of suspended sentence, or as a condition of probation.

The offender "volunteers" his or her services to a community agency for a certain number of hours per week over a specified period of time. The total number of hours, often assessed as the legal minimum wage, is determined often by the amount of the fine that would have been imposed or by that portion of the fine that is suspended.

---

a term in the lockup is the only alternative. In some cases, however, fines can be paid on the installment plan. This procedure gives offenders a chance to keep their jobs or seek work to pay the fine. This system, combined with weekend confinement and community work orders, has greatly improved misdemeanor justice.

Other alternatives for the misdemeanant are *probation without adjudication* and the *suspended sentence*. These are both variations on the same theme: holding formal disposition over the head of offenders for a period of time, often under specified conditions, and then nullifying the conviction. In probation without adjudication (also known as deferred prosecution), offenders can forego prosecution as long as they meet certain established conditions, usually for a specific period of time. The suspended sentence is used when offenders obviously do not require supervision to ensure their good behavior. This alternative is usually used for first offenders considered to be so impressed with their arrest and conviction that further sanctions against them would be of little positive value.

The extent to which these alternatives are employed is not really known, as there has been little research in this area. It is apparent that the misdemeanants, like adult felons, often "fall out" of the correctional funnel before it narrows down. If they did not, the jails of the country simply could not hold them.

Misdemeanor Probation: Promise Unfulfilled

Another alternative to confinement for the misdemeanant is *misdemeanor probation*. John Augustus (1841) was the first misdemeanant probation officer in America. Then, as today, the jails were populated mostly with drunks and vagrants. Probation, though finding its origins in the adult misdemeanor system, had its greatest growth in the juvenile and adult felon systems. Even though misdemeanor crime occurs in both urban and rural jurisdictions, the majority of adult misdemeanor probation services are simply not available in rural areas. In a large portion of the United States there is literally no probation service for the misdemeanant. In some jurisdictions, probation services for felons and misdemeanants have been combined, but this situation has created even heavier caseloads for the already overworked probation officers.

A few states have at least nominal statewide systems for the supervision of adult misdemeanants on probation. In many of these systems, supervision is provided only if requested, making the service itself something of a farce—more of a check-in formality than a counseling process. Often the offender is seen only once a month for a few minutes, usually in the office of the probation officer. The hope and promise of the program started by Boston cobbler John Augustus have not been fulfilled in the modern version of misdemeanant probation. Some of the reasons are found in the general overload of the criminal justice system; others are found in the short-term nature of misdemeanor sentences. Some more progressive jurisdictions,

---

ELECTRONIC SURVEILLANCE

Electronic surveillance makes use of telemetry technology to monitor an offender's presence at a specified site, usually at the home, where residence is required. The offender wears an electronic receiver or transmitter, which must be used according to instructions.

There are two major types of electronic monitoring: random calling and radio frequency. With random calling, the most popular and perhaps most efficient approach, a computer randomly dials the telephone number of the residence in which the offender is required to stay. When the computer program so directs, the offender must insert a special transmitter (bracelet or anklet) into a special piece of equipment that receives and then transmits the signal back to the computer, verifying the presence of the offender. The computer thán dials the next telephone number randomly. When computers misfunction, some offenders have been known to have been called fifteen times in a single night, creating within the offender a (false) sense of capacity of the system to monitor the offender's presence.

The radio-frequency method sends a continuous signal to an attachment on a telephone. When the offender leaves the range of the equipment ("breaks the signal"), the signaling device dials the monitoring agency to report noncompliance.

Both systems will continue to be refined and it is reasonable to expect increased use of telemetry technology in the future of corrections.

however, are using electronic surveillance[18] of misdemeanor probationers to ensure that they are meeting the provisions of that probation. With this technique, a single operator can monitor up to more than 200 persons.

Other Alternatives

A serious problem with misdemeanant corrections lies in the hodgepodge of offenders and offenses thrown together in the short-term facilities built primarily for detention. In some misdemeanant facilities, the felons confined for various reasons—with no separation from misdemeanants—number as high as 50 percent. Thrown in with this group of convicted offenders, both misdemeanants and felons, is another large group of unconvicted persons who are awaiting trial or other action. The unrestricted mingling of these categories of convicted and unconvicted felons and misdemeanants is the target of several pilot projects across the country, and their implementation is important.

A number of high-impact treatment programs have been designed to be carried out in the brief periods covered by misdemeanant sentences. The development and expansion of these programs, with maximum involvement in the community, will greatly assist local misdemeanant correctional workers in their efforts.

In Des Moines, Iowa, several innovative programs have been created, with significantly reduced jail population, costs, and reductions in the collateral consequences of misdemeanant conviction, such as the offender's job loss, families having to go on welfare, repossession of items being purchased on time, and family dissolution. In implementing one such program, the state saved $4.00 average per-diem cost[19] per person for the literally thousands of misdemeanant cases diverted (some for over 110 days) from the jail on *release on personal recognizance* (ROR). This is a promise by persons who could not raise bail bond to show up in court on the day of trial. Other persons not otherwise eligible for ROR (those who had committed serious crimes against the person), who were likewise unable to raise bail bond, were diverted to the pretrial supervision program (probation without adjudication). Still other misdemeanants (and a few felons) were diverted into the Fort Des Moines Residential Facility for Men. In the latter facility, the offender contracts to perform certain tasks to resolve the problems that led him to commit the crime. These tasks may include getting a job, learning a trade, or participating in personal or marital counseling. He is told not only that someone cares about him but also that (1) only he can solve his own problems; (2) if he chooses not to do so, he will be choosing to be jailed; and (3) if he tries to solve his problems through the available opportunities, he will be freed.

All three of these programs have had remarkably high success rates; only 1.8 percent of the ROR and pretrial supervision cases have failed to appear for trial compared with 2.2 percent for the bail-bond procedure.

The rearrest rate of the residential facility offenders was a mere 36 percent, compared with 50 to 70 percent for releases from penal institutions.[20]

These favorable results did not require heavy technical, vocational, professional, or academic expenditures; only those resources available in the community were used. Because of the effective use of such local resources and programs, as well as the remarkable outcomes, the National Institute of Law Enforcement and Criminal Justice declared the Des Moines project to be an "exemplary project," suitable for replication in other jurisdictions. The correctional client who enters the criminal justice system as a misdemeanant may well be the future felon to be treated at the state prison. Effective correctional programs designed to reform the misdemeanant at the earliest possible stage are crucial. The volume of misdemeanor offenders is so great that more resources must be provided for upgrading the facilities, programs, and quality of personnel they encounter.

Alternatives to Jail at the Pretrial Stage

Incarceration is one of the most severe punishments meted out by the American criminal justice system. Yet over one-half of all persons in local jails are awaiting trial. In effect, we are using our most severe sanction against many individuals who have been convicted of no crime. If detention were necessary—if there were no reasonable alternative to the jailing of suspects—this situation would be understandable. But experience with alternatives to jail has indicated that many people now incarcerated could be released safely and economically pending disposition of the charges against them. Most of them will appear in court as required without being held in jail.

Some tentative conclusions can be drawn from the experience of existing programs:

- Pretrial alternatives generally cost much less than jail incarceration does.
- Persons released before trial seem to fare better in court than do those who are incarcerated.
- Pretrial release alternatives appear to be as effective as jail is in preventing recidivism and can reduce the size of criminal justice agency workloads.
- Alternative programs can reduce jail populations and eliminate the need for expansion or new construction.[21]

Pretrial alternatives to detention run along a continuum of increasing controls or sanctions (Figure 22-2). Any community wishing to maximize the use of alternatives will provide a series of options that offer varying levels of supervision and services. This will permit the release of more persons with less waste of expensive resources. The least interventionary

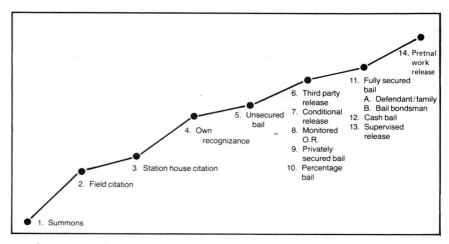

Figure 22-2 Pretrial Alternatives to Detention (*Instead of Jail: Pre- and Post-Trial Alternatives to Jail Incarceration: Volume I* [Washington, D.C.: U.S. Government Printing Office, 1977] p. 8)

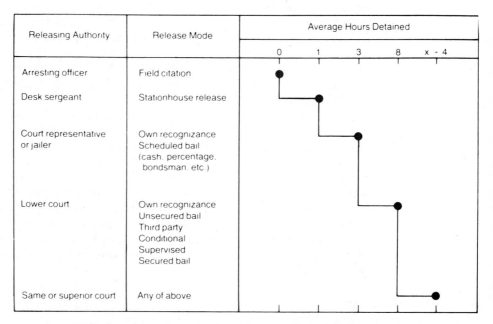

Figure 22-3 Locus of Authority to Release and Detention Time (*Instead of Jail: Pre- and Post-Trial Alternatives to Jail Incarceration: Volume I* [Washington, D.C.: U.S. Government Printing Office, 1977], p. 9)

and least costly options are used for low-risk cases. More expensive options and those involving greater interference in the life of the individual are reserved for cases in which these are the only alternatives to the even more costly option of jail incarceration.

Pretrial alternatives can be offered at various points in the criminal justice system. How long an arrested person will remain in custody largely depends on when and by whom the decision is made to opt for an alternative (Figure 22-3). Options made available early in the justice process (at the point of police contact, for example) are cheaper and have a greater impact on jail populations than do those offered at later stages. There are trade-offs, of course. Although early decisions to release or divert may save time and money, they may be less protective of either the rights of the suspects or the safety of the community.

Summary

Although improving jail facilities and upgrading jail personnel take a great deal of time and money, many other helpful procedures can be initiated more simply. Some were recommended back in 1937 by the National Jail Committee of the American Correctional Association. The fact that so many of these suggestions would still benefit jails today, almost fifty years later, reflects most of our jail systems' general resistance to change.

Jail administrators have an obligation to society to seek methods that can work in their own communities. Administrators are the practitioners who, with community involvement, must break the tradition of neglect and indifference that is the jail's legacy.[22] Unless vigorous and imaginative leadership is exhibited, even revitalized jails will soon regress to their squalid past.

The most effective way to reform inmates is either to keep them out of jail or to release them as soon as possible. Pretrial diversion, electronic monitoring, weekend confinement, community work orders, increased use of bail and personal recognizance, more extensive use of fines (including time payments), and various forms of work and study release all are viable alternatives to the destructive and expensive enforced idleness of most jails. Jails have proved highly resistant to change in the past and can be expected to remain so in the future. Until jails as we know them become mere relics, replaced by integrated community correctional centers, the best policy is to search for ways to keep people out of them and still protect the citizenry.

Review Questions

1. Why has the fee system been such a detriment to jail progress?
2. What effect does the changing role in corrections have on jail operations?

3. The community correctional center is a new concept. Does it differ much from the jails today? How?
4. What is the area of greatest weakness in the jails? Would more personnel be the answer? Why or why not?
5. What are the major alternatives to pretrial confinement? To the use of jail for post-conviction sentencing?

Key Terms

1. jails (p. 528)
2. "bullpen" (p. 534)
3. "tank" (p. 534)
4. fee system (p. 537)
5. per-diem fee (p. 537)
6. "price-tag justice" (p. 538)
7. weekend confinement (p. 539)
8. community work orders (p. 539)
9. electronic surveillance (p. 540)
10. pretrial alternatives (p. 542)

Notes

1. Hans Mattick and Alexander Aikman, "The Cloacal Region of Corrections," *The Annals* 381 (January 1969): 109–118.
2. Richard Frey and Kim Allen, "Community-Based Correctional Alternatives: Jefferson County's Response to Jail Crowding," *American Jails* 1 (Summer 1987): 37–38.
3. Charles Ares et al., "The Manhattan Bail Project: An Interim Report on the Use of Pretrial Parole," *New York University Law Review* 38 (1963): 67–83; Ann Rankin, "The Effect of Pretrial Detention," *New York University Law Review* 39 (1964): 651–659.
4. Bureau of Justice Statistics, "Felony Case-Processing Time: Special Report" (Washington, D.C., U.S. Department of Justice: August 1986), p 2.
5. James Pea, "Lewis County, Washington: A Well-Run Small Jail," *American Jails* 1 (Summer 1987): 35–36. See also Larry Mayes and Joel Thompson, "Mayberry Revisited: The Characteristics and Operations of America's Small Jails." Paper presented at the annual meeting of the Academy of Criminal Justice Sciences, St. Louis, March 17, 1987.
6. Bureau of Justice Statistics, *Jail Inmates 1986* (Washington, D.C.: U.S. Government Printing Office, October 1987). Most of the data in this section were drawn from this report.
7. In this report, a jail consists of a confinement facility administered by a local law enforcement agency, intended for adults but sometimes also holding juveniles, and confining persons detained pending adjudication and/or persons committed after adjudication for sentences of usually a year or less. Temporary holding facilities, or lockups, that do not hold persons after being formally charged in court (usually within forty-eight hours of arraignment) are excluded.
8. P. Taft, "Backed Up in Jail," *Corrections Magazine* 5 (June 1979): 28.
9. National Advisory Commission on Criminal Justice Standards and Goals, *Corrections* (Washington, D.C.: U.S. Government Printing Office, 1973), p. 276. See also Walter Busher, *Jail Overcrowding: Identifying Causes and Planning for Solutions* (Washington, D.C.: U.S. Department of Justice, 1983).

10. On jail standards, see Bruce Olsen, "New York Jail Standards," *American Jails* 1 (Fall 1987): 19–21; and Tom Reid, "Minnesota In-Servicing Training Methods: How to Exceed All Training Standards at a Low Cost," *American Jails*, 1 (Summer 1987): 10–12.

11. Jail designs and construction are undergoing rapid upgrading. See the excellent initial works by Charles DeWitt, all published in 1986: *Florida sets Example With Use of Concrete Modules*, *New Construction Methods For Correctional Facilities*, and *California Tests New Construction Concepts* (Washington, D.C.,: U.S. Department of Justice, 1986). See also the small-jail design in Rod Miller and Bill Clark, *Maine Jails: Progress Through Partnerships*, (Washington, D.C.,: U.S. Department of Justice, 1987), p. 4.

12. Jails are particularly vulnerable to fatal fires. See N. E. Schafer, "Fire Safety in Jails: Planning for Emergencies," *Federal Probation* 46 (1982): 41–45. See also Phillip Goldberg, "Avoiding Fatal Fires," *American Jails* 1 (Fall 1987): 46, 50, 53; and William and Betty Archambeault, *Correctional Supervisory Management* (Englewood Cliffs, N.J.: Prentice-Hall, 1982), pp. 382–386.

13. Kenneth Kerle and Francis Ford, *The State of Our Nation's Jails 1982* (Washington, D.C.: National Sheriffs Association, 1982).

14. QRC Research Corporation, *Study of Local Jails in West Virginia* (Lexington, Ky.: QRC, 1982).

15. Nicholas Demos, "The Future Jail: A Professionally Managed Corrections Center that Controls Its Population," *Federal Probation* 48 (March 1984): 35–39. The average starting salary for jail officers in 1982 was $10,780. See Kerle and Ford, *The State of Our Nation's Jails 1982*.

16. L. Cary Bittick, *Jail Officer's Training Manual*, National Sheriffs' Association, (Alexandria, Va.: NSA, 1984), p. iv.

17. Chris Eskridge, *Pretrial Release Programming: Issues and Trends* (New York: Clark Boardman, 1983).

18. Annesley Schmidt, "Electronic Monitoring: Who Uses It? How Much Does It Cost? Does It Work?" *Corrections Today*, 49 (1987), pp. 28, 30, 32, 34; Robert Hatrack, "Electronic Monitoring Throughout the U.S.," *American Jails* 1 (Fall 1987): 39–40.

19. Kerle and Fors, *The State of Our Nation's Jails 1982,* found the average cost per day of housing a jail prisoner to be $20.69.
    Data on 1987 costs reveal that the largest 50 jails cost no less than $27/per day and as high as $125/per day per inmate.

20. Law Enforcement Assistance Administration, *A Handbook on Community Correction in Des Moines* (Washington, D.C.: U.S. Government Printing Office, 1977), p. 66.

21. J. Galvin et al., *Instead of Jail: Pre- and Post-Trial Alternatives to Jail Incarceration: Volume I* (Washington, D.C.: U.S. Government Printing Office, 1977), pp. 7–9.

22. Proposed improvements can be found in Katherine Hooper Briar, "Jails: Neglected Asylums," *Social Casework* 64 (1983): 387–393; Statistical Analysis Center, *Jails in Arizona* (Phoenix: Department of Public Safety, 1982); and Dennis McCarthy, Henry Steadman, and Joseph Morrissey, "Issues in Planning Jail Mental Health Services," *Federal Probation* 46 (1982): 56–63; and Paul Paquette, "The Nuts and Bolts of Implementing the Regional Jail Concept," *American Jails* 1 (Fall 1987): 42, 44–45.

CHAPTER

23

State Prison Systems

The endurance of these monolithic structures is surpassed only by the tenacity of the assumptions and attitudes on which they were founded: the cause of crime is located in the individual offender; he should be punished for his acts; behavior is modifiable; and isolated institutions are appropriate settings in which to modify an individual's behavior. America had created a theory, reformation by confinement, and the system has been unwilling to abandon it although it has proved unworkable.
—WILLIAM G. NAGEL

Correctional Institutions: The Core of the System

This chapter will explore the systems that contain the correctional institutions in state-operated programs for offenders in the approximately 694 adult state prisons in America[1] (see Table 23.1). Juvenile institutions, detention centers, jails, workhouses, and other facilities for misdemeanants and minor offenders are not included. The major correctional institutions contained in the state systems are maximum, medium, and minimum security prisons, most of which are modeled after the nineteenth-century concepts in the Auburn penitentiary.

These institutions form the core of most state correctional programs, charged with the simultaneous functions of punishment and reform. Most are short on money and personnel, but they are still expected to prevent their graduates from returning to crime. Security and custody are the primary emphases in these prisons, and the environments are isolated both physically and philosophically from the mainstream of life. A former director of the Federal Bureau of Prisons described the ironic situation thirty years ago:

Even our modern prison system is proceeding on a rather uncertain course because its administration is necessarily a series of compromises. On the one hand, prisons are expected to punish; on the other, they are supposed to reform. They are expected to discipline rigorously at the same time that they teach self-reliance. They are built to be operated like vast impersonal machines, yet they are expected to fit men to live normal community lives. They operate in accordance with a fixed autocratic routine, yet they are expected to develop individual initiative. All too frequently restrictive laws force prisoners into idleness despite the fact that one of their primary objectives is to teach men how to earn an honest living. They refuse a prisoner a voice in self-government, but they expect him to become a thinking citizen in a democratic society. To some, prisons are nothing but "country clubs" catering to the whims and fancies of the inmates. To others the prison atmosphere seems charged only with bitterness, rancor, and an all-pervading sense of defeat. And so the whole paradoxical scheme continues, because our ideas and views regarding the function of correctional institutions in our society are confused, fuzzy, and nebulous.[2]

Correctional institutions are both a blessing and a curse. Reflecting a positive and humane movement away from the cruel punishments of the eighteenth century, they provided an alternative to death and flogging. But in terms of reforming inmates so that they can lead a noncriminal life in the free world, prisons have obviously failed. Still, the public's perceived need for security and the prison's effectiveness in isolating offenders from society have unfortunately made this system the primary answer to criminal behavior. The 502,251 inmates confined in state correctional institutions for adults at the start of 1987 were distributed in maximum, medium, and minimum institutions.[3] Maximum (or close) custody prisons are typically surrounded by a high wall or double fence, with armed guards in observation towers to prevent escape and prison disturbances in the institution's open areas. These facilities typically have large interior cell blocks to house the some 20 percent of state inmates (see Table 23.1).

TABLE 23.1 Prisoners under the Jurisdiction of State Correctional Authorities, by Region and State, Yearend 1985 and 1986

	Total		
Region and State	Advance 1986	Final 1985	Percent change 1985–86
U.S., total	546,659	503,271	8.6%
State	502,251	463,048	8.5
Northeast	82,388	75,706	8.8%
Connecticut	6,905	6,149	12.3
Maine	1,316	1,226	7.3
Massachusetts	5,678	5,390	5.3
New Hampshire	782	683	14.5
New Jersey	12,020	11,335	6.0
New York	38,449	34,712	10.8
Pennsylvania	15,201	14,227	6.8

TABLE 23.1. *Continued*

Rhode Island	1,361	1,307	4.1
Vermont	676	677	−0.1
Midwest	103,101	95,704	7.7%
Illinois	19,456	18,634	4.4
Indiana	10,175	9,904	2.7
Iowa	2,777	2,832	−1.9
Kansas	5,425	4,732	14.6
Michigan	20,742	17,755	16.8
Minnesota	2,462	2,343	5.1
Missouri	10,485	9,915	5.7
Nebraska	1,953	1,814	7.7
North Dakota	421	422	−0.2
Ohio	22,463	20,864	7.7
South Dakota	1,045	1,047	−0.2
Wisconsin	5,697	5,442	4.7
South	215,713	202,926	6.3%
Alabama	11,710	11,015	6.3
Arkansas	4,701	4,611	2.0
Delaware	2,828	2,553	10.8
District of Columbia	6,746	6,404	5.3
Florida	32,228	28,600	12.7
Georgia	17,363	16,014	8.4
Kentucky	6,322	5,801	9.0
Louisiana	14,580	13,890	5.0
Maryland	13,326	13,005	2.5
Mississippi	6,747	6,392	5.6
North Carolina	17,762	17,344	2.4
Oklahoma	9,596	8,330	15.2
South Carolina	11,676	10,510	11.1
Tennessee	7,182	7,127	0.8
Texas	38,534	37,532	2.7
Virginia	12,930	12,073	7.1
West Virginia	1,482	1,725	−14.1
West	101,049	88,712	13.9%
Alaska	2,460	2,329	5.6
Arizona	9,434	8,531	10.6
California	59,484	50,111	18.7
Colorado	3,673	3,369	9.0
Hawaii	2,180	2,111	3.3
Idaho	1,451	1,294	12.1
Montana	1,111	1,129	−1.6
Nevada	4,505	3,771	19.5
New Mexico	2,701	2,313	16.8
Oregon	4,737	4,454	6.4
Utah	1,845	1,633	13.0
Washington	6,603	6,909	−4.4
Wyoming	865	758	14.1

Source: Lawrence Greenfield, *Prisoners in 1986* (Washington, D.C.: U.S. Department of Justice, 1987), p. 2.

Medium custody prisons usually have double fences topped with barbed wire or razor wire to enclose the institution. Such prisons can have outside cell blocks in wings (or more recently "pods") of 150 or fewer cells, cubicles, or even dormitories. Some 42 percent of the inmates are under medium security; more than 87 percent of medium security institutions were constructed after 1925.

Minimum security prisons typically have neither the barbed wire nor the double fence, and armed posts are very rare. (As the type of prisoners incarcerated have become more violent and dangerous, many minimum security institutions have had to put fences and razor wire around them to make the public feel safer.[4] This "cosmetic" security makes little operational sense, as the inmates are typically outside the institution on work details all day.) Much more of the available housing is open-dormitory style. About 37 percent of the prison population resides in minimum custody prisons. More than 60 percent of minimum security institutions were constructed after 1950. (Table 23.2 details the distribution of populations in state institutions by custody category.)

The general trend today is toward medium rather than maximum security. Most medium security prisons were built in the twentieth century, in accordance with the new concepts of behavioral science. In fact, most of the medium security correctional institutions were built in the last twenty-five years. Although many of the ideals of early prison reformers could be realized in some medium security institutions, the primary emphasis still remains on security. The medium security correctional institution may well become the last resort in most state systems, as it offers much the same security as the maximum security prison does, but without the latter's oppressive and dehumanizing atmosphere and cost. The minimum security prison is intended to provide a model of reality for those inmates near the end of their sentence. Unfortunately, these facilities all too frequently tend to sacrifice individual programs for the needs of the major institutions, farms, forest-fire fighting, or work projects.

TABLE 23.2 Security Levels of American Prisons

Security Level	Percent of Prisons
Maximum	13%
High/Close	11
Medium	33
Minimum	22
Community	20
Total	99

Source: George Camp and Camille Camp, *The Corrections Yearbook* (South Salem, N.Y.: Criminal Justice Institute, 1987), p. 21.

Organization of State Systems _____

Of all the various types of correctional facilities in America, only 16 percent of them are under the control of state agencies. It is not surprising that the "correctional system" in most states is not really systematized at all. Organizational rigidity has handicapped meaningful revision and modernization of corrections. Rehabilitation and reintegration require that organizational structures be concerned with more than just institutional programs. In at least six states, this organizational need has been met by exercising control over all correctional activities at the state level.

Corrections at the state level generally is organized into a separate department of corrections (with a cabinet-level director appointed by the governor) or a division within a larger state department. Most correctional administrators consider the separate department to be more effective, and having the director at the cabinet level adds great flexibility and prestige to the correctional operation. Without an intermediate level of organization, the director of a separate department has the ability to move more freely at the policymaking level. An autonomous department is more able to control the allocation of personnel and fiscal resources, using economy of scale purchasing and operating with minimum competition from other divisions within the same department. Centralized control also has the advantage of providing more effective administrative functions that are unique to correctional problems.

Corrections is a human resource organization. As such, it is not amenable to analysis by the use of charts or the development of expenditure measures and empirical criteria. Human resources management presents special problems. One of the better descriptions of human resource management was written in 1966:

> Managing a human resource organization is probably even more difficult than managing other public agencies because many traditional management tools are not directly applicable. Data describing effects of the correctional process relate to behavior or attitudes and are subject to subjective, frequently conflicting interpretations. The feedback loops necessary for judging the consequences of policies are difficult to create and suffer from incomplete and inaccurate information. There has not been in corrections an organized and consistent relation between evaluative research and management action.
>
> The management of corrections as a human resource organization must be viewed broadly in terms of how offenders, employees, and various organization processes (communications, decision making, and others) are combined into what is called "the corrections process."[5]

The corrections process must include a system of multilevel programs and facilities to provide the spectrum of services required to make a statewide program work. Most state correctional systems are concerned only with the principal institutions and parole services, leaving the majority of correctional problems in the state to units of local government.

Development of State Systems _____

Each type of state correctional system has developed as a matter of historical accident as much as in response to a state's particular needs. As might be expected, the large industrial prisons are more in evidence in the major industrial states, generally in the area between Illinois and New York. Most of these institutions were built early in the prison movement and were designed to take advantage of the cheap labor force inmates represented. They were the hardest hit by the restrictions the government later placed on prison industries in the 1930s.

At present, the industry allowed in these giant institutions does not

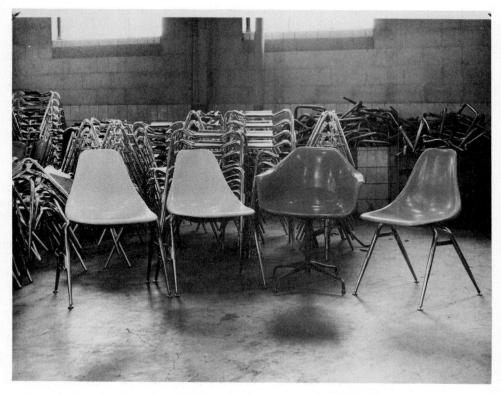

Products Typical of State Prison Shops (Courtesy Federal Bureau of Prisons)

Building a Greenhouse as Vocational Preparation (Courtesy of American Correctional Association, photo by Charles Gatje)

provide full employment for large inmate populations.[6] In an effort to spread the few jobs among the many inmates, supervisors try to slow down production and make the work last as long as possible. These procedures are not likely to provide the inmate with a model for job success on the outside. The general picture of activity in the one-time industrial prisons is one of idleness and boredom. Despite even the most dedicated attempts by the staff, inside and outside the institutions, there are just not enough meaningful jobs or other programs to help the huge populations housed in the Jacksons, Atticas, and San Quentins of the country.

The agricultural prison was begun in the southern states. These farms became very profitable ventures for the states and thus have been slow to change. Prisoners who served on public works and state farms replaced the pre-Civil War slave labor in many states, not only in the South. Here again, authorities may have rationalized that the training received from farm work helped prepare offenders for return to a basically agrarian southern economy, but the intent was to use free labor to produce farm products. Cheap prison labor was often leased out to farm owners at a great profit to both the farmer and the state that collected the fee. The use of prison farms has become less profitable, however, with the advent of highly mechanized farming methods in most agricultural states.

Other regions in the country have designated certain institutions as farm oriented. The food produced in these institutions has been used to feed the rest of the institutions in the state. Many states have now begun to abandon this practice, as it has been realized that farming experience is of little value to the primarily urban inmate found in most contemporary prisons. Another problem with prison farms has been the pressure from farm organizations, whose members argue that competition from the state is unfair—much as union workers did with regard to prison manufacturing industries in the early part of this century.

Other states have chosen to set up work camps and other forms of prisoner activity appropriate to their particular needs. Lumber camps have been used, as have road prisons or camps to construct and maintain roads. Recent versions of the work camp have been geared to provide a combination of hard work in the outdoors and programmed treatment aimed at preparing the offender for release. It is considered more beneficial for offenders to do time in the relatively healthful atmosphere of a small work camp than to languish in the idleness and boredom of the prison.

Inmates in State Prisons _____

In 1983, the U.S. Department of Justice conducted a national survey of inmates in state correctional facilities in the United States and found an estimated 381,955 offenders under the jurisdiction of state government.[7] (Since that study was conducted, the population of state prisons has skyrocketed to over 570,519)[8]. Almost all of these inmates (96 percent) had been sentenced, but 4 percent had been committed for a year or less or were not sentenced (see Figure 23.1).

An overwhelming majority of the inmates (95 of every 100) were males. The number of white inmates was slightly higher (50 percent to 46 percent) than the number of blacks, but equal to all minorities. All but a scant 1 percent were at least eighteen years of age, and 63 percent of all inmates were between the ages of eighteen and twenty-nine, the "high crime rate" years. The median age of inmates was twenty-eight.

As a group, state prison inmates were less educated than their counterparts in the civilian population. Sixty percent of the inmates had not received a high school diploma, in contrast with 36 percent of the general population eighteen years of age or older.

In terms of their criminal offenses, almost 60 percent had committed one of the big "three" crimes: robbery, burglary, or homicide. The average sentence length imposed was ten years,[9] although 10 percent of the prisoners were incarcerated under life sentences. Seventy percent had incurred at least one other sentence, in addition to the instant offense, and roughly one in three had served time as a juvenile offender.

There were many repeat offenders: 64 percent had been sentenced at least twice. These data suggest the difficulties faced in the state systems and indicate the inefficiency and general failure of current uncoordinated

---

TIME SERVED IN PRISON, 1984

In 1987, the Department of Justice reported that the median length of time served in confinement for a variety of offenses in state prisons was 17 months, about 45 percent of the original sentence imposed. In general, those prisoners committed for violent offenses served a median of 28 months, about twice as long as property or drug offenders. Other significant findings include these:

1. Those released from confinement from prison for murder and nonnegligent manslaughter served a median of 78 months in confinement. Rapists served 44 months, and robbers served 30 months. Burglars came in at the median (17 months), and drug traffickers served 16 months.

2. Original sentence length was reduced by a credit for time spent in jail, totaling about 4 months.

3. Violent offenders with a prior history of felony incarcerations served about 6 months longer than those with no such history. Similarly, property offenders with such a history served about 3 months longer.

4. For those going into parole following release from confinement, the total amount of correctional control time increased to an average of 60 months for violent offenses, 42 months for drug offenses, and 37 months for a property offense.

5. Males on parole were more likely than females to be returned to custody for parole violation (22 percent versus 14 percent). The average length of time on parole before revocation was about 18 months.

Source: Stephanie Minor-Harper and Christopher Innes, *Time Served in Prison and on Parole, 1984* (Washington, D.C.: U.S. Department of Justice, 1987), pp. 1–3.

correctional systems. The number of inmates in state institutions is shown in Table 23.1, along with the percentages of change between 1985 and 1986. As we approach 1990 with almost 600,000 persons in state prisons, it is clear that the problems for harried correctional administrators are only beginning. Fortunately, some of these problems are being addressed in actions in the Supreme Court.

Are Prisons "Cruel and Unusual Punishment"? _____

The problems of institutionalization are ever present in our state prisons. Understaffing, underbudgeting, and lack of citizen interest often become excuses for allowing conditions to deteriorate to the lowest levels. The following description relates the latest method used by inmates to strike back at such systems:

An air conditioner. Television, stereo, "Mr. Coffee" machine, tennis racket. And two Siamese cats. During his eight years in prison, Nick Palmigiano learned how to wheel and deal within the pliant rules of Rhode Island's maximum security institution. He accumulated, in his words, "a little bit of comfort." He had plenty of time to enjoy it, too—no work and no school.

Cruel? It sounds more like the "country club" in prison, that favorite whipping boy of campaigning district attorneys. Unusual? Not in Rhode Island. Other resourceful inmates there, using their own funds, had installed wood paneling in their cells, carpeting, even private telephones.

But to Palmigiano, those little comforts didn't compensate for what went on outside his cell: rats scurrying down trash-filled corridors, toilets overflowing with waste, mouse droppings in the food, 75 percent of the inmates on drugs, daily rapes and stabbings, nothing to do. As far as Palmigiano was concerned, making someone live like that was cruel and unusual punishment, prohibited by the Eighth Amendment to the U.S. Constitution.

So—motivated perhaps by a sincere desire to help less fortunate inmates, perhaps by a thirst to harass beleaguered prison administrators—he went to court. Federal court. That was hardly unusual. In 1975, 7,430 such petitions were filed by prisoners in the federal courts. Palmigiano himself had submitted well over 50 lawsuits against prison officials. *"Pro se"* Palmigiano, they called him, in honor of the phrase that describes suits accepted without fee because the plaintiff has no money. One of Palmigiano's suits, over disciplinary procedures, went all the way to the U.S. Supreme Court in 1975, but he lost there.

This time he won. Last August, several months after a probing trial, U.S. District Court Judge Raymond Pettine declared the maximum security unit of the Rhode Island prison system "irremediably obnoxious to constitutional standards" and ordered it closed within a year. He went on to declare the entire Adult Correctional Institution (ACI)—Rhode Island's only prison facility—un-constitutional. To see that the state met the standards he laid down, Judge Pettine appointed a "special master" with power to fire or transfer correctional personnel who didn't cooperate. "This case is not an exercise in making prison life more pleasant for prisoners, nor is the ACI about to be transformed into a Holiday Inn," the judge wrote. The conditions under which inmates in Rhode Island exist shocked the court, and the court is convinced that they would shock the conscience of any reasonable citizen who had a first-hand opportunity to view them."[10]

Beginning in the 1970s, both state and federal courts were asked to examine the operations and policies of correctional facilities and personnel to ensure compliance with the Eighth Amendment's prohibition against cruel and unusual punishment. By February 1983, the courts had declared unconstitutional the entire prison systems of Alabama, Florida, Mississippi, Oklahoma, Rhode Island, Tennessee, Texas, and all the male penal institutions of Michigan. In addition, at least one (or more) facilities in another twenty-one states were operating under either a court order or consent decree as a result of inmate crowding and/or the conditions of confinement. Yet another seven states were involved in ongoing litigation relating to overcrowding and/or the conditions of release from prison. Finally, in eight states, the courts had appointed receivers or masters to operate the state prison system or facility, had ordered the emergency release of inmates because of crowding, or had designated specific prisons to be closed[11] (see Table 23.3 for information on jail conditions).

TABLE 23.3   Jails in Jurisdictions with Large Jail Populations: Number of Jails under Court Order to Reduce Population or to Improve Conditions of Confinement, 1985

	Number of Jails in Jurisdictions with Large Jail Populations		
	Total	Ordered to Limit Population	Not Ordered to Limit Population
Total	614	137	477
Jails under court orders citing specific conditions of confinement	153	120	33
Subject of court order:			
Crowded living units	132	114	18
Recreational Facilities	88	68	20
Medical facilities or services	83	65	18
Visitation practices or policies	51	51	0
Disciplinary procedures or policies	62	48	14
Food service (quantity or quality)	49	38	11
Administrative segregation procedures or policies	57	45	12
Staffing patterns	59	45	14
Grievance procedures or policies	60	46	14
Education or training programs	48	33	15
Fire hazards	51	41	10
Counseling programs	38	29	9
Other	29	18	11

Source: Bureau of Justice Statistics, *Jail Inmates 1985* (Washington, D.C.: U.S. Department of Justice, 1987), p. 8.

The courts took these actions only as a last resort and when it was clear that the affected states had relinquished their responsibility to protect the constitutional rights of the inmates under their custody and care.

Facility construction began in earnest as a response to prison overcrowding. Between 1981 and 1982 alone, 42,000 beds were added to correctional systems.[12] At the start of 1983, more than 28,000 beds were under construction and another 74,000 were planned. During these two years alone, state

TABLE 23.4 **Prison Population Projections for 1990**

State	Population Predicted for 1990	State	Population Predicted for 1990
Alabama	11,845 inhouse	New Mexico	3,169
Alaska	12,179	New York	1986 pop.—36,078
Arkansas	5,662	North Carolina	19,926 (projected to
California	88,140		current legislative/
Colorado	7,125		policy use)
Connecticut	9,500	North Dakota	570
Delaware	1986 pop.—2,419	Ohio	26,000
District of		Oklahoma	1986 pop.—9,163
Columbia	9,606	Oregon	4,587
Florida	39,090	Pennsylvania	Not prepared that far
Georgia	1986 pop.—17,088		ahead. 1986 pop.—
Hawaii	2,103 (jail inmates		15,055
	and felons combined)	Rhode Island	1,900
Idaho	2,000	South Carolina	12,934
Illinois	21,855	South Dakota	1986 pop.—2,242
Indiana	11,750	Tennessee	12,000
Iowa	3,464 (if cap is lifted)	Texas	By law, TDC inmate
Kansas	5,642		population cannot ex-
Kentucky	8,482		ceed 95% of bed
Louisiana	15,091		capacity. 1986 pop.—
Maine	1,593		37,214
Maryland	14,200	Utah	2,850
Massachusetts	5,587	Vermont	Depends on implemen-
Michigan	22,000		tation of alternatives.
Minnesota	2,452		1986 pop.—665
Mississippi	8,505 (June 30,1989)	Virginia	13,372 (includes state
Missouri	13,880 (1991)		responsibility, backlog
Montana	1,153 to 1,220		in local jails)
Nebraska	1986 pop.—1,893	Washington	8,045
Nevada	5,953	West Virginia	1986 pop.—1,291
New Hampshire	998	Wisconsin	5,416
New Jersey	Expect growth of 2640	Wyoming	1,000
	to 2880 over next two	Federal Bureau	
	years. Current popula-	of Prisons	50,109
	tion is 14,928, including	Canada	14,175
	those backed up to		
	county jails.		

Source: Adapted from materials collected by Contact, Inc., Lincoln, Neb.

correctional systems spent more than $900 million for capital outlays (construction and renovations), and another $2.25 billion in bonds and other funds were allocated to support capital improvements.[13] For prison population projections, see Table 23.4.

The states, understandably, have reacted with great indignation over the Supreme Court's intruding into the domain of the executive branch at the state level. Where does the Court get the right to intervene in such matters? The Civil Rights Law of 1871 provides for the principal method of allowing such inmate complaints into the federal courts.[14] This statute provides that citizens denied constitutional rights by the state may sue in the federal court. Originally designed to protect the newly freed slaves in the post-Civil War era, the statute was generally forgotten until a landmark case in 1961 revived interest in this act. It was not until 1964, however, that the Court finally ruled in favor of a prisoner's seeking relief in federal court by way of the 1871 act (see Figure 23-1).

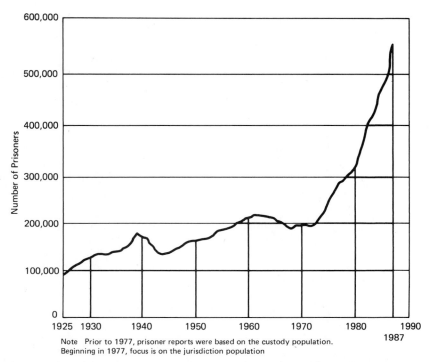

Note Prior to 1977, prisoner reports were based on the custody population.
Beginning in 1977, focus is on the jurisdiction population

Figure 23-1 Number of Sentenced State and Federal Prisoners, Yearend 1925 to Midyear 1987 (Extrapolated from Stephanie Minor-Harper, *State and Federal Prisoners, 1925–85* [Washington, D.C.: U.S. Department of Justice, 1986], p. 1)

The procedure has been tentative and careful, each step breaking new ground for prisoners' rights:

> These decisions provided almost all of the legal groundwork necessary for "conditions suits." They all came while Earl Warren was chief justice. But under Warren Burger, the Supreme Court has shown even more interest in prison cases. In some areas, it has extended prisoners' rights; in others it has held the line. But it has held fast to one principle: no one must interfere with the right of inmates to take their complaints to federal courts.
>
> With these sketchy guidelines, federal district judges have been feeling their way. In the first cases dealing with specific prison practices, the judges would balance the constitutional rights of the prisoners against the prison officials' legitimate interests in security, rehabilitation, and order. If the officials' defense was not sufficient, then the practice would be ordered changed. If such a ruling was upheld on appeal by one of the eleven U.S. Circuit Courts of Appeal, then it became a binding precedent within that circuit and was available to guide judges in other circuits. Only if the U.S. Supreme Court issues a ruling on a case is the precedent binding across the nation — although approval can be implied when the Court declines to hear an appeal. The Supreme Court has declined appeals on all the broad conditions suits that have been brought before it. District court judges have generally built upon each other's decisions in these areas.
>
> This judicial activism has not taken place in a vacuum, of course. In most areas of constitutional law inmates have ridden on the coattails of more popular causes such as school desegregation and voting rights for minorities. The extension of the class action suit has made broad-based challenges to prison conditions possible. Increased activism among lawyers and the growth of legal aid programs was an important factor.[15]

The states are not giving up easily, however, and have appealed these decisions. Each case is different, of course, but they have all been slowed in their immediate impact by the issuance of a decision of the Fifth Circuit Court of Appeals, written in regard to the Alabama order:

> This seemingly inexorable march toward greater judicial activism was slowed when the Fifth Circuit Court of Appeals issued its ruling on the state's appeal of the Alabama order. In an opinion by a three-judge panel, written by Judge J. P. Coleman, a former governor of Mississippi, the appeals court affirmed the basic finding of unconstitutionality, but it reduced the scope of Johnson's original order. The court ordered a new hearing on the judge's requirement of 60 square feet of space per inmate in new construction. It dissolved the Human Rights Committee and dismissed the hired consultant, although it said the judge could appoint a single monitor for each prison "*to observe,* and to report his *observations* to the court, with no authority to intervene in daily prison operations" [emphasis in original]. The court also overturned Judge Johnson's order forbidding the state to require women visitors to prisons to stand over a mirror and drop their underwear as part of a routine search for contraband.

The most significant part of Judge Johnson's order, that dealing with idleness, was also cut back. Rehabilitation programs, the court said, could not be required. Because the order that each inmate be assigned to a job "should not impose any real burden" on prison officials, it let that part stand. But it ruled that it could not be used as a precedent in future cases. "If the state furnishes its prisoners with reasonably adequate food, clothing, shelter, sanitation, medical care, and personal safety, so as to avoid the imposition of cruel and unusual punishment, that ends its obligations under Amendment Eight," the decision stated.[16]

Realistically, we must acknowledge that the prison has little control over who will be committed. Nor does it exercise much control over sentence length, parole eligibility, minimal sentence proportion to be served,[17] or legislative allocations. The current prison situation is a result in part of the high-risk age category (sixteen to twenty-nine) that the "baby boom" has brought about, the more conservative response to crime, the public fear of crime and criminals, the increased sentence length, and the higher failure rates of parolees who must then be returned to prison (see Figure 23-2). Yet the cruel and unusual punishment conditions continue.

One other response by corrections was to add more correctional personnel. Slightly more than 97,000 persons were employed in state correctional facilities in 1979, an increase of 60 percent over the number in 1974. As a result, the staff-inmate ratio dropped from 3.2 to 2.9 overall, but traditional institutions have lagged behind, with over 113,000 employees being responsible for an average of 4.1 inmates each at the beginning of 1985.[18] On January 1, 1987, there were more than 111,170 custiodial staff employ-

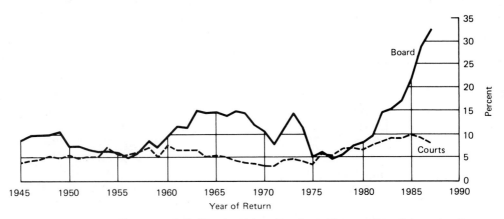

Figure 23-2 Percent of California Felon Parolees Returned to Prison by the Board and by the Court, 1945–1987 (Sheldon Messinger et al, *Parolees Returned to Prison and the California Prison Population* [Sacramento: California Attorney General's Office, 1988], p. 5)

ees, and the agency average of inmates to line-level staff was up to 5.4:1, a 32 percent increase since 1985.[19]

Correctional opportunities will continue to increase, and students will be sought who have the skills and willingness to work in the prisons of tomorrow. There is clearly a need for active citizen support for corrections, especially at the state level, and for active monitoring of our prison conditions.

Classification and Assignment In a State System

Most state codes provide for the separation or classification of prisoners, their division into different grades with promotion or degradation according to merit or demerit, their employment and instruction in industrial pursuits, and their education. Most also stipulate that reformation of prisoners is a primary goal, though there are some exceptions. California, for example, now advocates punishment.

The effective operation of a classification system rests on several elements: facilities and personnel to supply diagnostic information, a philosophy of treatment directed at inmate needs rather than institution convenience, diversification of treatment programs, and genuine opportunity for the inmate to participate in planning his or her own program.

Diagnostic information is assembled through several channels. One of the most important documents is the presentence investigation supplied by the courts. Information can also be gathered from the inmates, their families, community agencies, and official records. Other information is found through diagnostic examination, such as psychological aptitude and educational tests. Observations by staff members who have contact with inmates are also valuable. From these sources a picture of the needs and aspirations of the individual inmates emerges.

In most systems, the initial classification determines the institution to which an inmate will be assigned. The receiving institution then determines whether the individual shall remain in maximum security or be transferred to a medium or minimum security penitentiary. (Each state has at least one maximum security institution.) Most states base their transfer decisions on a perception of the individual's ability to handle the lowest level of security. Also important is an evaluation of the individual's ability to adjust to a program geared primarily to work, to academic or vocational training, or to the needs of older offenders.[20] A classification committee usually participates in making these decisions.

The classification process continues at the institutional level. Although each receiving institution emphasizes different programs, each has some version of education, counseling, and the other ingredients of a total program. Theoretically, individuals are assigned according to their needs but, realistically, assignments are too often made to conform to institutional needs. For example, an inmate may genuinely want to learn welding. If the welding class is filled—as it often may be—but there is a vacancy in the furniture shop, the inmate may be assigned to the furniture shop; no effort would be made to offer additional welding instruction. Also, inmates will often be assigned to a maintenance operation, such as food service or janitorial work, that is unlikely to conform to their own vocational ambitions. An essential element of effective classification is a periodic review of the inmate's progress through the recommended program. All institutions allow for this reevaluation, usually called reclassification. The purpose is to adjust the program in accordance with the inmate's progress and needs. Realistically, again, decisions are all too frequently made on the basis of the available vacancies and institutional needs.

Institution personnel may genuinely wish to provide the recommended program for an inmate; however, the need to keep the institution going inevitably shapes decisions. Personnel may rationalize maintenance assignments on the basis that many inmates need the experience of accepting supervision, developing regular work habits, learning to relate to coworkers, and the like. This may be true, but the treatment staff members are no less frustrated than the inmates are when prescribed programs are ignored. The classification and assignment process just described is only a composite of what the more effective programs provide.

Training in State Systems _____

One other way to improve the ability of state systems to react to a rapidly changing environment is to improve the requirements for entry-level staff, and then to improve the training of staff who are already in the system. The federal system has always had the advantage of high entry standards (now a bachelor's degree is required) and excellent training programs for staff (see Chapter 24). Most state systems require only the following requirements:

- High School diploma or GED
- No record of prior felony convictions
- That the person be 21 years of age (some states accept 18)
- Valid driver's license (of that state)

These seem to be quite minimal requirements for a job that commands so much influence over the lives and rights of inmates. Some of the more progressive states are beginning to raise those standards. California and Florida require extensive background investigations. California estimates it will need about 3,000 new corrections officers a year for the next 4–5 years to keep up with massive construction programs. Florida has a training program that amounts to over 500 hours, that must be completed before the employee can pass their probation period.

The general rule is for the employee to have at least 80 hours of training within their probationary period, usually 6 months. Some jurisdictions get around this requirement by making most of the training on-the-job activity. Most states try to provide at least some training. Before the efforts of the 1970s and subsequent lawsuits, most training amounted to the employee being handed a set of keys and told to go to work. Some states now work closely with their community colleges to provide preservice and postservice training, especially in the social sciences. Others have state training academies that provide basic and ongoing training.

The need to have better trained staff has caused the growth of many private and nonprofit agencies to start training academies for preemployment programs for corrections officers. Some of these programs have concentrated on finding interested minorities and females, and have done quite well. Others have tried the same approach, but lacking rigid standards, careful screening, and close association with the correctional agencies, they have failed.

Many administrators of correctional programs at the state level would like to raise entry-level standards to require a two-year degree, and promotional qualifications in line with that basepoint (e.g. a bachelor's degree for captains, master's degree for superintendents). They have a long battle ahead. Those in the system are usually afraid of these requirements and oppose the raising of such standards. These attitudes are enhanced by union activity that is primarily based on seniority, not training. It seems that some progress could be made if the incumbents were given a liberal opportunity to be "grandfathered" into the new programs. Training in the future "high-tech" prisons is essential; it is an area to watch carefully in the future.

Summary

The state correctional systems in America are as diverse as the states themselves. It has been our intent to give an overview of some of the problems that face most correctional administrators when they are trying to model a unified and coordinated system of corrections within the framework of fragmented and antiquated institutions and procedures. The prison remains the core of most state correctional systems, despite its patent failure as a means of rehabilitation and reintegration of offenders (the current goals of corrections). Classification of inmates and subsequent assignment and reassignment are still based more on the institution's needs and security than on individual needs. A few states have seen the advantage of a correctional system that is controlled by the state, but most are

TABLE 23.5 **The Prison Situation among the States at Yearend, 1986**

10 States with the Largest 1986 Prison Population	Number of Inmates	10 States with the Highest Incarceration Rates, 1986	Prisoners per 100,000 Residents
California	59,484	Nevada	462
Texas	38,534	Delaware	324
New York	38,449	South Carolina	324
Florida	32,228	Louisiana	322
Ohio	22,463	Alaska	306
Michigan	20,742	Oklahoma	288
Illinois	19,456	Alabama	283
North Carolina	17,762	Maryland	280
Georgia	17,363	Florida	272
Pennsylvania	15,201	Arizona	268

Source: Lawrence Greenfield, *Prisoners in 1986* (Washington, D.C.: U.S. Department of Justice, 1987), p. 3.

still moving toward an autonomous department of corrections for the 12 to 18 percent of offenders who now fall under state control.

Movements to absorb all correctional programs under the state's supervision and control encounter almost insurmountable political and practical obstacles at every step. New concepts are also hampered by the massive overcrowding in state institutions, causing funding to go for "bricks and mortar" rather than for managerial or administrative improvements. Proposed prison population projections are shown in Table 23-5, state by state. This mid-1987 study predicted a population of 547,497 in state facilities by 1990. With almost that many prisoners in the system by yearend 1987, these predictive models seem hard pressed to keep up with the growth of the corrections system. The population in terms of raw numbers and incarceration rate per 100,000 residents is shown at Table 23.5. It is interesting to note that these ten states represent 56 percent of the inmates held in state institutions at yearend 1986!

Women are not immune, as noted in Chapter 16, from the growth in incarceration in the United States. As shown by the data in Table 23.6, the population of state institutions for women with at least 500 inmates increased by an average of 14.8 percent in the single year between 1985 and 1986. And a recent one-day poll showed that 1 out of every 60 persons in the United States is under some kind of correctional supervision (that includes parole, probation and institutions). It seems difficult to imagine how budgets will be found to keep up with the state prisoners' plight with this massive growth (see Table 23.7).

Capacities of institutions also reflect the continuing problems created by overcrowding and growth. Table 23-7 lists populations over capacities that range from 183 percent (Connecticut) to 89 percent (North Dakota) of

TABLE 23.6   **Women in State Institutions at Yearend, 1986**

Jurisdiction	Number of Women Inmates	Percent of All Inmates	Percent Change in Women Inmate Population, 1985–86
State, Total	23,777	4.7	14.8
States with at least 500 women inmates:			
California	3,564	6.0%	22.6%
Texas	1,758	4.6	10.3
Florida	1,630	5.1	25.0
New York	1,326	3.4	25.6
Ohio	1,213	5.4	5.2
Michigan	1,018	4.9	25.1
Georgia	947	5.5	13.7
North Carolina	827	4.7	10.7
Illinois	764	3.9	13.5
Oklahoma	679	7.1	33.9
Louisiana	637	4.4	4.4
Alabama	616	5.3	9.6
South Carolina	601	5.1	20.0
Pennsylvania	591	3.9	18.2

Source: Lawrence Greenfield, *Prisoners in 1986* (Washington, D.C.: U.S. Department of Justice, 1987), p. 3.

TABLE 23.7   **Reported State Prison Capacities at Yearend 1986**

Jurisdiction	Rated Capacity	Operational Capacity	Design Capacity	Population as a Percent of:[a]	
				Highest Capacity	Lowest Capacity
Northeast					
Connecticut	6,072	4,968	3,781	1148%	183%
Maine	1,033	1,033	1,033	124	124
Massachusetts	3,265	—	—	174	174
New Hampshire[b]	689	689	539	110	141
New Jersey	10,401	11,394	9,777	105	123
New York	37,743	39,502	35,891	97	107
Pennsylvania	—	—	11,048	138	138
Rhode Island	1,456	1,440	1,359	113	124
Vermont	597	597	547	113	124
Midwest					
Illinois	19,705	19,705	15,943	98%	122%
Indiana	8,710	—	2,918	95	103
Iowa	—	2,702	2,918	95	103
Kansas	3,502	5,015	—	108	155
Michigan	—	16,784	—	124	124
Minnesota	2,495	2,495	2,633	94	99
Missouri	—	11,588	—	91	91
Nebraska	1,562	1,513	1,542	125	129
North Dakota	—	471	471	89	89

TABLE 23.7 *Continued*

Ohio	—	—	13,282	169	169
South Dakota	1,189	1,090	1,189	88	96
Wisconsin	—	4,591	—	124	124
South					
Alabama	10,374	10,374	10,374	108%	108%
Arkansas	—	4,620	—	102	102
Delaware	—	2,563	2,404	110	118
District of Columbia	6,769	6,577	—	100	103
Florida	35,982	32,290	25,561	90	126
Georgia	—	16,323	—	106	106
Kentucky	4,921	5,327	—	101	107
Louisiana	11,080	11,080	11,080	100	100
Maryland	—	13,646	9,544	98	140
Mississippi	5,878	—	—	95	95
North Carolina	—	—	16,575	107	107
Oklahoma	7,642	7,260	—	126	132
South Carolina	9,212	9,212	8,163	122	138
Tennessee	7,801	—	—	92	92
Texas	40,392	38,373	40,392	95	100
Virginia	10,159	10,159	9,753	115	120
West Virginia[b]	1,547	1,640	1,547	86	91
West					
Alaska	2,336	—	—	105%	105%
Arizona	—	9,911	—	95	95
California	32,853	53,887	32,853	107	176
Colorado	3,760	3,760	—	98	98
Hawaii	1,252	—	1,252	174	174
Idaho	1,149	1,470	1,149	99	126
Montana	936	1,190	936	93	119
Nevada	—	—	3,911	115	115
New Mexico	2,363	2,593	2,363	104	114
Oregon	—	4,057	2,815	117	168
Utah	1,805	1,805	1,537	98	115
Washington	5,324	6,040	5,324	108	123
Wyoming	—	950	—	91	91

—Data not available.

[a]Excludes State-sentenced inmates held in local jails due to overcrowding where they have been included in the total prisoner count.

[b]Capacity figures for males only.

Source: Lawrence Greenfield, *Prisoners in 1986* (Washington, D.C.: U.S. Department of Justice, 1987), p. 5.

various ratings. This amounts to an average of 136 percent of capacity, and it can be seen that all the major systems are extremely and critically overcrowded.

Longer sentences and stiffer enforcement measures have filled existing beds faster than they can be built. Alternatives to confinement have been used for all but the very few, and those few are not those we want out on the streets. Although the new institutions are being constructed, in the majority of cases, to constitutional standards in regard to square footage and other considerations, there seems to be little doubt that the single cells will soon become double-bunked. The taxpayers will not tolerate the allocation of funds to build more and more prisons, often at a total cost of over $80,000 per bed.

State correctional systems have inherited the legacy of a sometimes well-intentioned but often inhumane past. The purposes for which many of the crumbling old institutions were built and the procedures for operating these facilities are no longer in tune with society or behavioral science. The cry to tear down these monuments is a valid one, but practicalities dictate that the flood of inmates must be kept somewhere, and public safety must be ensured before ways can always be found constitutionally. Although many new programs outside the prisons are being attempted, they must be proved effective before they will be widely accepted. And the types of inmates now being placed in prisons do not lend themselves to lower security levels.

Much progress is being made, sometimes at the prodding of citizens' groups like the 1970s Ohio Citizens' Task Force on Corrections,[21] whose investigations uncovered the conditions in a typical state system of that era. But the death in 1981 of the Law Enforcement Assistance Administration, shrinking state budgets, and "get tough" attitudes from a public tired of being victimized make change much more difficult. In the next chapter we shall examine a truly centralized and integrated correctional system, the federal system.

Review Questions _____

1. Characterize the current inmate population in the nation.
2. How much time do inmates generally spend in prison?
3. What makes a prison "cruel and unusual" punishment?
4. Why are alternatives to incarceration beginning to be so necessary for correctional administrators?
5. What impact does overcrowding have on the reform of institutional progams in state systems?
6. How are inmates classified?
7. Has the institutional inmate-staff ratio gone up or down? Why?
8. What are three likely trends in state correctional facilities over the next ten years?

Key Terms _____

1. **cosmetic security (p. 550)**
2. **organizational rigidity (p. 551)**
3. **autonomous department (p. 551)**
4. **agricultural prison (p. 554)**
5. **institutionalization (p. 556)**
6. **Civil Rights Act of 1871 (p. 559)**
7. **conditions suits (p. 560)**
8. **grandfathered in (p. 564)**
9. **high-tech prisons (p. 564)**
10. **"get tough" (p. 568)**

Notes _____

1. Christoper Innes, *Population Density in State Prisons,* (Washington, D.C.: U.S. Department of Justice, 1986), p. 1.
2. Quoted in Harry Elmer Barnes and Negley K. Teeters, *New Horizons in Criminology,* 3d ed. (Englewood Cliffs, N.J.: Prentice-Hall, 1959), pp. 461–462.
3. Lawrence Greenfield, *Prisoners 1986* (Washington, D.C.: U.S. Department of Justice, 1987), p. 2.
4. For an analysis of the impacts of locating a low-security federal institution, see George Rogers and Marshall Haimes, "Local Impact of a Low-Security Federal Correctional Institution," *Federal Probation,* 51 (September 1987): 28–34.
5. National Advisory Commission on Criminal Justice Standards and Goals, *Corrections* (Washington, D.C.: U.S. Government Printing Office, 1973), p. 440.
6. But see the October 1986 issue of *Corrections Today* 48 (1986), particularly pp. 12–66. See also Gerald Farkas and Margaret Hambrick, "New Partnership: Industries and Education/Training Benefit Institutions and Inmates," *Corrections Today* 49 (1987): 52–54.
7. Bureau of Justice Statistics, *Prisoners in 1983*, U.S. Department of Justice (Washington D.C.: U.S. Government Printing Office, May 1984).
8. The nation's state and federal prison population soared to 570,519 inmates during the first half of the calendar year 1987. The estimated total as we go to press is 594,000 (January 1, 1988). See American Correctional Association, *On The Line* (College Park, Md: ACA, November 1987), p. 7.
9. Stephanie Minor-Harper and Christopher Innes, *Time Served In Prison and On Parole 1984* (Washington, D.C.: U.S. Department of Justice, 1987), p. 1.
10. S. Gettinger, "Cruel and Unusual Prisons," *Corrections Magazine* 3 (December 1977): 3.
11. Bureau of Justice Statistics, *Report to the Nation on Crime and Justice* (Washington, D.C.: U.S. Department of Justice, 1983), p. 80.
12. Bureau of Justice Statistics, *Prisoners 1983*, p. 5.
13. Ibid., p. 9.
14. This is Chapter 42 of the U.S. Code, Section 1983: Every person who under color of any statute, ordinance, regulation, custom, or usage of any State or Territory, subjects or causes to be subjected, any citizen of the United States or other person within the jurisdiction thereof to the deprivation of any rights,

privileges, or immunities secured by the Constitution and laws, shall be liable to the party injured in an action at law, suit in equity, or other proper proceeding for redress.

15. Gettinger, p. 6.
16. Ibid., p. 10.
17. To understand some of the ways that prison staff can shorten the length of incarceration time, even in states with determinate sentencing, see John Hepburn and Lynne Goodstein, "Organizational Imperatives and Sentencing Reform Implementation: The Impact of Prison Practices and Priorities on the Attainmant of the Objective of Determinate Sentencing," *Crime and Delinquency* 32 (1986): 339–365.
18. Bureau of Justice Statistics, *Population Density*, p. 1.
19. George Camp and Camille Camp, *The Corrections Yearbook 1987* (South Salem, N.Y.: Criminal Justice Institute, Inc., 1987), pp. 44–45.
20. Gennaro Vito and Deborah Wilson, "Forgotten People: Elderly Inmates," *Federal Probation*, 49 (1985): 18–24.
21. Harry Allen, *Final Report by the Ohio Citizens' Task Force on Corrections* (Columbus: State of Ohio, 1971).

24

The Federal System[1]

That there is hereby established in the
Department of Justice a Bureau of Prisons . . .
responsible for the safekeeping, care, protection,
instruction and discipline of all persons charged
with or convicted of offenses against the United
States.
—Acts Approved by President Herbert Hoover,
May 14 and May 27, 1930

With this proclamation, the federal government went into the business
of corrections in a big way. The history of incarcerating offenders for
violations of federal law is long and interesting. With the power of the
federal government (and the federal purse) behind it, the federal Bureau
of Prisons became an innovator and leader in correctional management
and operations.

Before 1895: The Use of State Facilities

During this period, federal prisoners were assigned to state and local
institutions to serve their sentences. One of the first acts of Congress was
to pass a bill (An Act to Establish the Judicial Courts of the United States)
that encouraged the states to pass laws providing for the incarceration of
federal offenders in state institutions. Most of the states did pass such
laws, and all federal offenders sentenced to one year or more served their
sentences in state facilities. Offenders who were sentenced to terms of less
than one year or those being held in detention awaiting trial were usually
confined in local jails, a practice that continues today on a limited scale.

In 1870, Congress established the Justice Department. A general agent
in the Department of Justice was placed in charge of all federal prisoners
in state and local institutions. Later, the general agent became the superintendent of prisons, responsible to an assistant attorney general for the
care and custody of all federal prisoners.

The state prisons became seriously overcrowded after the Civil War.
With increased numbers of both state and federal prisoners, many states

became reluctant to take federal prisoners when they could not even care properly for their own. Consequently, in some states only federal prisoners from that state were accepted. In states where neither suitable nor adequate facilities were available, lengthy travel and high costs were required to transport federal inmates to appropriate facilities. In 1885, there were 1,027 federal prisoners in state prisons and approximately 10,000 in county jails. By 1895, these numbers had risen to 2,516 federal prisoners in state prisons and approximately 15,000 in county jails.

On March 3, 1891, the U.S. Congress passed a bill (An Act for the Erection of United States Prisons and for the Imprisonment of United States Prisoners, and for other purposes) authorizing the construction of three penitentiaries, although their funding was not approved until later. The establishment of federal prison facilities was considered necessary because of the states' reluctance to house federal prisoners, the exclusion of federal prisoners from contract labor, and the increasing number of federal and state offenders.

The First Federal Prison Facilities: 1895–1929 _____

Until 1895, all military prisoners were confined at Fort Leavenworth. The War Department then decided to house its prisoners in several military installations. Consequently, the Department of Justice acquired the surplus military prison at Fort Leavenworth in eastern Kansas. For the first time, federal prisoners—those transferred from state institutions as well as new commitments—were confined in a federal facility. In short order the Department of Justice realized that the prison, adapted from former quartermaster warehouses, was inadequate. Therefore, on July 10, 1896, Congress appropriated funds for the construction of the previously authorized penitentiary capable of holding twelve hundred inmates, three miles from the prison at Fort Leavenworth. The site for the new penitentiary was on the Fort Leavenworth military reservation. Because the penitentiary was built by convict labor, construction took many years and was not completed until 1928.

The United States Penitentiary at Atlanta, Georgia, was authorized under the 1891 legislation, and the funding authority was secured from Congress in 1899. The third penitentiary, located on McNeil Island, Washington, was originally a territorial jail, constructed between 1872 and 1875. After repeated efforts to divest itself of the McNeil Island facility, the federal government designated it as a United States penitentiary in 1907.[2] The Auburn style of architecture, characterized by multitiered cellblocks and a fortresslike appearance, was adopted in all three penitentiaries.

Between 1900 and 1935, American prisons, including federal institutions, were primarily custodial, punitive, and industrial. Overcrowding at the

Metropolitan Correction Center, San Diego (Courtesy Federal Bureau of Prisons)

federal prisons during this period left few resources for anything but custodial care. Nevertheless, there were significant developments during the early 1900s that have affected the operation of federal institutions to the present day, including passage of the White Slave Act in 1910, the Harrison Narcotic Act in 1914, the Volsted Act in 1918, and the Dyer Act of 1919. All brought a larger number of people under federal criminal jurisdiction. The number of offenders incarcerated under these statutes swelled the federal prison population beyond the available physical capacity. Largely because of the population increase in federal prisons, Congress authorized in 1925 a reformatory for "male persons between the ages of seventeen and thirty," which was constructed in Chillicothe, Ohio.[3]

Female prisoners continued to be boarded in institutions operated by the states. By the 1920s, however, the number of female prisoners warranted the building of special federal facilities. In 1924 Congress acted, and in 1927 a new five-hundred-inmate institution opened at Alderson, West Virginia.

In 1929, when overcrowding reached a critical stage in the New York City area, the state and local authorities ordered all federal prisoners removed from the Tombs and the Raymond Street Jail. Responding to this crisis, a federal detention center in New York City was authorized by the attorney general under the authority given him through the U.S. Marshals Service. The facility acquired by the Department of Justice was a newly constructed three-story garage, which was remodeled into a jail and called the Federal Detention Headquarters.

The Establishment of the Bureau of Prisons _____

The federal prison system soon began to experience problems of severe overcrowding, inconsistent administration, the political spoils system, and a decentralized organizational structure. In 1929, the response of the seventieth Congress was to create the House Special Committee on Federal Penal and Reformatory Institutions to examine all facets of the treatment of federal prisoners, including inmate labor. It offered the following recommendations:

- Establishment of a centralized administration of federal prisons at the bureau level.
- Increased expenditure for federal probation officers, to be appointed by federal judges and exempt from civil service regulations.
- Establishment of a full-time parole board.
- Provision of facilities by the District of Columbia for its prisoners.
- Transfer of all military prisoners held in civil prisons to Fort Leavenworth Military Barracks.
- Removal of the minimum age of prisoners at the U.S. Industrial Reformatory at Chillicothe, Ohio.
- Expeditious establishment of the two narcotic treatment farms previously authorized.

- Passage of H.R. 11285 authorizing road camps for federal offenders.
- Provision of additional employment opportunities for federal offenders.
- Employment of an adequate number of nonfederal jail inspectors and linking payments for these facilities to conditions and programs found in them.
- Construction of institutions to include two additional penitentiaries, a hospital for the care of the criminally insane, and a system of federal jails and workhouses in the more congested parts of the country.

Legislation was drafted, passed, and signed into law by President Herbert Hoover on May 14, 1930, creating the Federal Bureau of Prisons within the Department of Justice. Other legislation generally enacted the recommendations of the committee during the summer of 1930.

Sanford Bates was appointed by President Hoover to be the first director of the Bureau of Prisons. The selection of Bates signified that the attitude toward penal administration in the federal government had shifted from one that depended on political patronage.

The Early Growth of the Federal Bureau of Prisons: 1930–1955 _____

It was obvious that three penitentiaries, a reformatory for young men and one for women, a jail, and eight camps did not meet the growing needs of the federal prison system. During the period before 1930, thousands of federal prisoners were receiving sentences of less than a year, particularly for violating liquor and immigration laws.

Federal prisoners with sentences of a year and less could not be legally confined in the penitentiaries, and many were unsuitable physically or custodially for open camps. Therefore, many were housed in county and city jails, which were already overcrowded. To meet this problem, it was decided to build new structures or remodel existing structures to serve as regional jails. In 1930 the old New Orleans Mint was transferred to the Department of Justice for use as a jail. In 1932, a new regional jail was opened at La Tuna, Texas, primarily to house the influx of immigration violators. In 1933 a similar institution was opened near Detroit at Milan, Michigan. To reduce overcrowding in the penitentiaries, another was added in 1932 at Lewisburg, Pennsylvania.

The need for a men's reformatory west of the Mississippi River resulted in the establishment of an institution at El Reno, Oklahoma, in 1933. In the same year, a hospital for mentally ill prisoners (and for those with chronic medical ailments) was opened at Springfield, Missouri.

During the early 1930s, new anticrime legislation was enacted that brought more serious types of offenders into federal prisons. The "crime wave" of this period, combined with the expanding role of the federal

A Federal Facility for Medium Custody Prisoners (Courtesy Federal Bureau of Prisons)

government in crime control, brought in 1934 the old military prison on Alcatraz Island in California under the control of the Department of Justice.

Congress gave support to the new agency. Subsequent legislation approved minimum security camps, the construction of new institutions, and a program of diversified industrial employment within the institutions under Federal Prison Industries, Inc. Today this program is more commonly known by its trade name, UNICOR.

Classification: A New Hope

Developed and implemented in 1934, the Federal Bureau of Prisons' classification system was the single most dramatic departure from the state systems. The federal institutions were sufficient in number and diversity by 1934 to make a classification program possible. Federal facilities were divided into penitentiaries, reformatories, prison camps, a hospital, and treatment facilities for drug addicts operated by the U.S. Public Health Service. Within each type of facility, offenders were further classified by age, offense, sex, and the like. The classification of offenders involved every institutional resource in evaluating each offender and planning his or her rehabilitation.

CLASSIFICATION

Classification in corrections usually means differentiating the prisoner population into custodial or security groups, thus permitting a degree of planning, custodial felixibility, and programming not previously possible. As such, classification breaks the inmate population up into groups with similar needs and security risks, and allows for more specific handling of offender needs.

In addition, classification also means that institutions within a correctional system will begin to specialize in custody and treatments for the risk level and needs of the incoming inmates. Some institutions can be set aside for inmates who have medical problem. Facilities would provide for surgery, dental reconstruction, or special diet and treatment for chronic ailments (high blood pressure, diabetes, cancer, and so on.) Other institutions can become educational and vocational centers, designed to improve the level of formal education and functioning of the inmates sent to that facility. Others would house recalcitrant, aggressive, and hostile offenders who need maximum custody.

As the Bureau of Prisons grew, its treatment staff were increasingly part of the prison complement, and institutions became more capable of handling and treating specific categories of inmates. This was Sanford Bates' most significant contribution to corrections.

World War II to 1955

During World War II, the Bureau manufactured a variety of wartime goods for the military. To meet the demand, several factories operated more than one shift per day, with some staying open seven days a week. Factory production increased significantly, and both staff and inmates believed their work to be an important contribution to the war effort.

Bureau administrators played a key role in convincing government officials to permit released offenders to enlist in the armed forces. Because ex-offenders had always been prohibited from serving in the military, the Bureau enthusiastically endorsed this change.

With an increase in population of over 3,400 between June 30, 1950, and June 30, 1955, practically all institutions became overcrowded. All close-custody institutions and the institutions on the West Coast were particularly crowded. In 1954, the Bureau of Prisons requested that the Navy return the Terminal Island, California, institution. This institution was reopened as a federal correctional institution in May 1955. A federal jail in Anchorage, Alaska, was opened in 1953 to meet the needs of that area for short-term detention.

The Intervening Years: 1955–1980 _____

The predominant goal of the Bureau of Prisons during the 1950s and 1960s was the rehabilitation of the individual offender. In agreement with this philosophy, Congress passed the Youth Corrections Act in 1950, offer-

A Federal Corrections Officer at Work (Courtesy of American Correctional Association, photo by BOP)

ing a broad range of correctional alternatives that had not been previously available. The Youth Corrections Act was the first of several legislative initiatives that advanced the Bureau's philosophy of rehabilitation.

The Youth Corrections Act was a milestone in federal sentencing. It envisioned intensive programs of diagnosis and treatment and imposed new responsibilities on the Bureau of Prisons. The law was implemented in 1954, and a Youth Division in the U.S. Board of Parole was established.

In 1958, diagnostic services and indeterminate sentences were made available for adults through legislation. The dream of the early reformers and original Bureau personnel was realized: a treatment program geared to the individual offender was now clearly established in the law. The medical model of correction had reached fruition.

The medical model reached its peak during the 1960s, fulfilling the charter given the Bureau by Congress to treat individually each person sentenced to serve time in a federal institution. The inmate population remained fairly constant throughout this period. The year 1955 ended with 21,606 prisoners in federal institutions, and by 1970 this number had decreased to 20,686. Thus, in the facilities area, the Bureau of Prisons was upgrading rather than expanding.

Recent Developments: 1970–1988 _____

Public attitudes toward criminals and the appropriate societal response to them were influenced by many factors during the 1980s. Chief among these have been increasing crime rates and the growing problems in administering prisons. Inmate disruptions at Attica and other institutions provided opportunities for the public to reexamine the prison's goals.[4] The neoclassical call for law and order prompted a public debate about crime and criminals similar to that which had occurred in the 1930s. In response to this public concern, the Bureau of Prisons devised a comprehensive master plan.

Four objectives for the Bureau of Prisons were established in the Bureau's master plan:

1. Increasing program alternatives for offenders who do not require traditional institutional confinement, thereby minimizing the negative effects of imprisonment, lessening alienation from society, and reducing economic costs to the taxpayer.
2. Enhancing the quality of the correctional staff by providing increased training opportunities, better working conditions, and heightened professional challenges to inspire continuous personnel growth and satisfaction.
3. Improving present physical plants and incorporating new facilities into the system to increase the effectiveness of correctional programs.
4. Expanding community involvement in correctional programs and goals because, in the final analysis, only through successful reintegration into the community can the ex-offender avoid reverting to crime.

A significant development during the 1970s and 1980s was the assignment of responsibility for the planning and management of inmate programs to treatment teams. Though the staff makeup of the teams varied among institutions, they usually consisted of a caseworker, a correctional counselor, and an educational representative. Also introduced was the functional unit approach, or unit management, in place of traditional casework programming. The unit management system provides for semiautonomous unit teams.

In the 1970s, institutional educational programs both academic and vocational, continued to be supplemented by outside educational agencies. Local colleges and universities came into some institutions to teach courses leading to degrees. In other cases, prisoners are allowed to attend colleges and universities located close to the institutions. Flexibility became the key word concerning education in the 1970s.

The Bureau's rehabilitation programs and their increasing sophistication were challenged in the mid-1970s by academicians, researchers, and practitioners who pointed out the bankruptcy of results obtained from traditional rehabilitation programming.[5] Accordingly, in 1975 the medical model of corrections in the Federal Bureau of Prisons was deemphasized, and in its place was substituted a philosophy of rehabilitation, retribution, deterrence, and incapacitation.

The 1970s gave the Bureau of Prisons more new facilities than at any time since the 1930s. A steady increase in inmate population during the first five years of the decade, from 20,208 in 1970 to 23,566 in 1975, and a dramatic increase to over 30,000 inmates at the end of fiscal year 1977 dictated the acquisition of additional facilities. The purpose of these additions was to reduce overcrowding, to create more humane and safe living conditions, and to close the three old penitentiaries at McNeil Island, Washington,[6] Atlanta, Georgia, and Leavenworth, Kansas.

Introduced in 1973, the administrative remedy procedure allows inmates to file formal grievances concerning treatment, custody, or regulations. The administrative remedy process is a mechanism for inmates to learn in writing why institutional actions, such as furloughs being denied, are taken. Many within the Bureau of Prisons feel the administrative remedy procedure has reduced perceived tensions between staff and inmates, thus creating a safer, more humane atmosphere in which they interact.[7]

One of the key developments in corrections was accreditation. Sponsored by the American Correctional Association and funded by the Law Enforcement Assistance Adminstration, the Commission on Accreditation for Corrections was created. This commission developed and issued ten sets of standards covering every aspect of corrections, including community and juvenile programs. Accreditation creates a widely accepted set of standards for corrections that will help agencies obtain the resources necessary to upgrade corrections and meet the courts' mandates. To maintain and improve conditions for inmates and staff, the federal prison system has begun the process of accreditation for its institutions.

The Federal Bureau of Prisons experienced as much change in the 1970s as in any other time in its history; yet many of the activities of the Bureau for the most part remain unchanged. This apparent contradiction could be explained as the result of contradictory input from the Congress, public, professional corrections personnel, and others who on the one hand wish prisons to be secure and protective of the public and, on the other, wish in some way to reform or change the individual.

Organization and Administration

The Federal Bureau of Prisons in the last quarter of the 1980s provides a career service, with the majority of new employees entering on duty as correctional officers. Administration is carried out by the Central Office in Washington, D.C., and by five regional offices. The Central Office is comprised of the Director's Office and four divisions: Correctional Programs; Administration; Medical and Services; and Industries, Education and Vocational Training. Each division is headed by an assistant director. There is also an Office of General Counsel and an Office of Inspections, both of which report to the director (see Figure 24-1).

The five regions are headed by regional directors and are located in Atlanta, Dallas, Philadelphia, Belmont (San Francisco), and Kansas City, Missouri.

WESTERN REGION
Burlingame, California

NORTH CENTRAL REGION
Kansas City, Missouri

SOUTH CENTRAL REGION
Dallas, Texas

SOUTHEAST REGION
Atlantic, Georgia

NORTHEAST REGION
Philadelphia, Pennsylvania

● FEDERAL PRISON SYSTEM FACILITIES
○ COMMUNITY PROGRAMS OFFICES
▲ FACILITIES UNDER CONSTRUCTION
▲ STAFF TRAINING CENTERS

Figure 24-1 Federal Correctional System (Federal Bureau of Prisons)

Inmate Population

The inmate population of the Federal Bureau of Prisons was 44,408 at the end of 1986. This number is 59 percent above the combined rated capacities of the 47 institutions and represents an increase of 2,901 over the population at the end of 1985 (see Figure 24-2).

There was a 22 percent increase in the number of unsentenced inmates in the Federal Prison System in 1986, due to the opening of the Federal Detention Center in Oakdale, Louisiana, and a detention unit at the Federal Correctional Institution, in Phoenix, Arizona. The sentenced inmate population increased by 14 percent over the 1985 population. The Bureau continues to house over 2,600 Cubans, most of whom are unsentenced.

From August 26, 1985, through January 14, 1986, the Federal Bureau of Prisons received over 1,700 inmates from the District of Columbia Superior and District Courts. This resulted in a 48 percent increase in the number of District of Columbia-code violators in the Federal Prison System during 1986.

Federal court sentencing of offenders to longer terms of confinement for serious crimes and the effort to combat organized crime and drug trafficking continued to contribute to the inmate population increase in 1986.

The percentage of inmates serving sentences for drug law violations increased from 26 percent in 1981 to 37 percent at the end of 1986. The number of offenders convicted of auto theft is now only 1 percent, compared to 22 percent in 1970. This decline is due to the shift in the policy of the Department of Justice in the 1970s to reduce prosecution of auto theft offenses at the federal level and a shift in the Bureau of Prisons' policy no longer to house juvenile offenders, who made up a large portion of those convicted of auto theft.

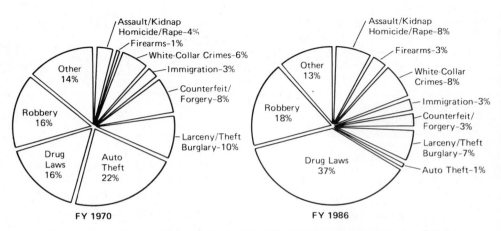

Figure 24-2 Percentage of Population Confined to Institutions by Offense

Bureau Construction and Renovation _____

In response to the increasing inmate population, the Bureau of Prisons continues to expand its capacity through the construction of additional housing units, facility renovation, and construction of new facilities. New housing units were open during 1986 at the Federal Correctional Institutions in Butner, North Carolina; Tallahassee, Florida; La Tuna, Texas; and Lexington, Kentucky. These units added 521 beds to the capacity of the Bureau of Prisons. In addition, a 24-bed special housing unit for inmates with mental health problems opened at the Federal Correctional Institution, in Butner, North Carolina, and 78 beds were added to the Federal Prison Camp in Marion, Illinois.

Renovations were completed at the Federal Prison Camp in Duluth, Minnesota, bringing its capacity to 711. Additionally, the Bureau activated a 1,000-bed Federal Detention Center in Oakdale, Louisiana, to house aliens held for administrative review by the Immigration and Naturalization Service.

New institutions currently under construction are medium security federal correctional institutions in Marianna, Florida (750 beds); and a Metropolitan Detention Center in Los Angeles, California (500 beds). An 800-bed federal correctional institution in Sheridan, Oregon, is under construction. The earliest opening date for any of these facilities will be 1988.

Housing units are now under design or construction at nine institutions. These units are located at the federal correctional institutions in Milan, Michigan; Seagoville, Texas; Texarkana, Texas; El Reno, Oklahoma; and Oxford, Wisconsin; the federal prison camps at Maxwell Air Force Base, Montgomery, Alabama and Eglin Air Force Base, Florida; the metropolitan correctional center in Miami, Florida; and the federal detention center in Oakdale, Louisiana. With the abandoning of the idea to scrap the two major prisons, massive housing unit renovations are underway at the U.S. Penitentiaries in Atlanta, Georgia, and Leavenworth, Kansas.

Community Programs _____

Prison space is a scarce and costly resource, to be used in situations where the interests of society must be protected. Because of the continued record-high prison population in 1986, the use of alternatives to incarceration for nonviolent offenders was expanded.

At the end of 1986, there were nearly 5,000 offenders confined in Bureau of Prisons contract facilities. Approximately 80 percent of eligible offenders released to the community were released through community treatment centers. These centers are used for offenders near release as a transition back to the home, job, and community. Time is used to find a job, locate a place to live, and reestablish family ties.

The centers are also used for offenders serving short sentences, for unsentenced offenders participating in the pretrial service program, and for offenders under community supervision who need guidance and supportive services beyond what can be provided through regular postrelease supervision. At the end of 1986, there were 3,100 federal inmates housed in over 330 contract centers operated by state, local, and private agencies (see Figure 24-3).

The Community Correctional Center project was implemented in Washington, D.C. in 1983. The project uses imprisonment alternatives such as community service, work, and victim restitution when recommended by the U.S. District Court. The center is available to federal courts in the District of Columbia, Maryland, and Virginia for sentenced offenders who are not a risk to the community and who may be in custody up to one year.

A second Community Correctional Center was opened in Detroit, Michigan, in September 1985. During the first half of 1986, 109 offenders were placed in the center, and almost $57,000 toward the cost of incarceration was collected from offenders. This represents approximately 18 percent of the total cost of incarceration.

All persons adjudicated under the Juvenile Justice and Delinquency Prevention Act are placed under contract in local and state facilities as well

Figure 24-3 Metropolitan Detention Center, Los Angeles, California. Scheduled to open in late 1988 (U.S. Department of Justice, *Federal Bureau of Prisons: 1986 Annual Report* [Washington, D.C.: U.S. Government Printing Office, 1987], p. 4)

as in such facilities as boys' ranches, group homes, or foster homes. Most adult inmates sentenced to serve less than six months are confined in local jails. There were 1,700 such inmates at the end of 1986.

Approximately 100 federal inmates were housed in state prisons at the end of that year. These inmates are housed in state facilities primarily for protection purposes, as most have cooperated with the federal government in providing court testimony. Use of more state beds is anticipated as federal inmate populations grow and a few spaces come available.

Inmate Classification System _____

The Bureau of Prisons' inmate classification system has been in effect since April 1979. Variables such as severity of offense, history of escapes or violence, expected length of incarceration, and type of prior commitments are used to determine an inmate's security level. This system groups the 47 institutions into six security levels; institutions labeled *Security Level 1* provide the least restrictive environment whereas the *Security Level 6* institution in Marion, Illinois, is the most secure.

An institution's security level is determined by the type of perimeter security, number of towers, external patrols, detection devices, security of housing areas, type of living quarters, and the level of staffing.[8]

The Federal Bureau of Prisons is now responsible for carrying out the judgments of federal courts whenever a period of confinement is ordered. There are 47 institutions, ranging from minimum to maximum security, and over 12,000 employees. Over 45,000 inmates are currently confined in federal institutions. All sentenced offenders who are medically able are required to complete regular daily work assignments. In addition, all offenders have opportunities to participate in education, vocational training, work, religion, and counseling programs.

The classification system, designed to place offenders in the least restrictive institution possible that is closest to their homes, has proven effective. Security Level 1 inmates account for approximately 37 percent of the inmate population. This means that more inmates can be moved into "open" institutions such as prison camps. The effect is that higher security level institutions become more humane through reduced crowding.

Federal Prison Industries, Inc. _____

Federal Prison Industries, Inc., with the corporate trade name UNICOR, is a wholly-owned government corporation that sells its products and services to other federal agencies. UNICOR's mission is to support the Federal

Bureau of Prisons through the gainful employment of inmates in diversified work programs.

At the end of 1986, 41.5 percent of all eligible inmates and 30 percent of all inmates confined in the Federal Prison System were employed by UNICOR. The 75 industrial operations located in 40 institutions constructively employ inmates and assist in preparing them for employment opportunities upon release. Inmate employment in UNICOR rose from 9,995 at the end of 1985 to 12,885 at the end of 1986.

Occupational training is also offered through UNICOR and includes on-the-job training, vocational education, and apprenticeship programs. There are 225 formal training programs in various trades offered by federal institutions. Apprenticeship programs, registered with the U.S. Department of Labor's Bureau of Apprenticeship and Training, exist at 34 institutions.

An active program of plant modernization and expansion of industries began in 1983 and continues. The program includes 66 projects at 41 institutions. UNICOR will have invested more than $67 million in this program, which will provide for the potential employment of over 3,600 additional inmates in prison industries and will ensure modern production capacity far into the future.

Education and Training

The Federal Bureau of Prisons provides academic and occupational training programs to prepare inmates for employment upon release. Although enrollment is voluntary, program options are extensive, ranging from Adult Basic Education (ABE) through college courses. Occupational training programs include accredited vocational training, apprenticeship programs, and preindustrial training.

A mandatory literacy program was implemented for inmates in 1983. This policy required all federal inmates who functioned below a sixth-grade educational level to enroll in the ABE program for a minimum of 90 days. In 1986, this standard was raised to an eighth-grade literacy level, the nationally accepted functional literacy level. All promotions in Federal Prison Industries and in institution work assignments are contingent upon the inmate's achieving an eighth-grade literacy level.

The Adult Basic Education program has been successful. Enrollments exceeded 8,000 in 1986, and there were over 5,000 completions. Certificates for completion of the General Education Development program were awarded to over 3,000 inmates. The transition to the eighth-grade literacy level has been smooth and is anticipated to increase substantially the number of enrollments in the ABE program.

Projects were funded by UNICOR to provide job training in such fields as computer sciences, business, diesel mechanics, water treatment, petroleum technology, graphic arts, and food service. Approximately 7,000 students completed occupational training courses in 1986 and another 7,000 completions were projected for 1987.

Inmate Financial Responsibility Program _____

The Bureau of Prisons implemented a pilot Inmate Financial Responsibility Program in the South Central Region in 1986 to assist inmates in paying fines, restitution, and debts. The program included identifying inmates with financial obligations, establishing a financial plan for him or her to meet these obligations, and holding the inmate accountable for these finances during and after incarceration.

The program has been successful and has assisted other criminal justice agencies such as the U.S. Parole Commission, the U.S. Probation Office, and the U.S. Attorney's Office in tracking inmate debts and fines. The Inmate Financial Responsibility Program was implemented throughout the Bureau of Prisons in 1987.

Staff Training _____

Staff training provides every bureau employee with the knowledge, skills, and abilities required to assure high standards of employee performance and conduct.

The staff training network is composed of the Staff Training Operations Office, Washington, D.C.; a Staff Training Academy at the Federal Law Enforcement Training Center in Glynco, Georgia; a Management and Specialty Training Center in Denver, Colorado; and a Food Service and Commissary Training Center at the Federal Correctional Institution in Fort Worth, Texas.

Each institution has a staff training officer who is responsible for all institution-based training. In addition, each region has a regional training administrator who is responsible for conducting training audits and coordinating the assignment of basic training at Glynco. All new employees are required to undergo four weeks of formal training during their first forty-five days with the Bureau of Prisons.

Automated Information Systems _____

The Bureau of Prisons has continued expansion of Sentry, its on-line inmate information system. The Sentry system monitors inmates in federal institutions and contract facilities, and plays an integral part in inmate designation, classification, and sentence computation.

The Sentry system is used by all Bureau installations, the U.S. Parole Commission, U.S. Marshals Service, Office of Enforcement Operations, Department of Justice Command Center, and selected offices of the U.S. Attorney, and the U.S. Probation and Pardon Attorney. Sentry's electronic mail component provides an important communication link between these offices.

Female Offenders _____

The Bureau of Prisons continues to focus on improving programs and services for female offenders. It operates four co-correctional facilities and one all-female institution located in Alderson, West Virginia.

The Federal Correctional Institution in Lexington, Kentucky, serves as the medical and psychiatric referral center for women who have acute physical or emotional problems. The Children's Center and Pregnant Women's Shelter Home programs are also available when children are born to incarcerated women at the Federal Correctional Institution in Pleasanton, California.

Eleven apprenticeship-training programs have been accredited by the Women's Bureau of the U.S. Department of Labor, Bureau of Apprenticeship and Training. These programs assist in preparing women in such nontraditional fields as auto mechanics, electricians, plumbing, painting, and brick laying. Sixty-two apprenticeship programs are offered for women in thirty-nine different trades.

Prisoner Transfers _____

The United States entered into the first prisoner transfer treaty with Mexico in 1977. Since that time, Canada, Panama, Peru, Bolivia, Turkey, and the Council of Europe, which includes the United Kingdom, France, Spain, West Germany, and Sweden, have signed similar treaties that allow eligible inmates to serve the remainder of their sentences in their native countries. Prisoners are transferred on a voluntary basis, and, during 1986, the Bureau of Prisons staff traveled to Great Britain, Peru, Mexico, and

Canada to escort returning Americans. The Attorney General has signed a transfer treaty with Thailand that, when ratified by both governments, will allow for transfers with a twelfth nation.

Chaplaincy Services

All inmates are afforded opportunities for pursuing their individual religious beliefs and practices. The Bureau's 76 full-time chaplains are assisted by religious advisers from the community working under contract and by more than 2,500 community volunteers. Religious activities are among the most well-attended programs in the institutions.

Psychological Services

The Bureau of Prisons' psychology staff provides a wide range of mental health services to inmates and provides psychological evaluations of offenders when requested by federal courts. Bureau psychologists coordinate suicide prevention, drug abuse, and employee assistance programs; screen new institution commitments; and classify offenders using empirically-derived topologies. Additionally, psychologists provide training to staff and serve on interviewing panels for new employees.

Medical Care

The Bureau of Prisons provides a wide range of medical and dental services to meet the needs of its inmate population. In the majority of cases, medical care is provided within the prison setting. Community facilities are used to supplement this care as necessary. The primary medical referral centers are located in Rochester, Minnesota; Springfield, Missouri; and Lexington, Kentucky. More limited medical services are available at the Federal Correctional Institution in Terminal Island, California, and psychiatric services are available at the Federal Correctional Institutions in Butner, North Carolina; Lexington (female only); and Terminal Island; and at the Medical Centers in Springfield and Rochester.

The Federal Medical Center in Rochester, Minnesota, was activated in 1985. Upon its full activation in the spring of 1987, the facility added 110 medical and surgical beds and 128 psychiatric beds to the capacity of the Bureau of Prisons. There will also be 128 outpatient beds for medical, surgical, and psychiatric cases. A Chemical Dependency Unit, with a capacity of 30 beds, will provide evaluation and treatment services for chemically-dependent patients when completed. The center will provide medical services to both male and female inmates and will obtain medical assistance from the Mayo Clinic, also located in Rochester.

Legal Activities

The Office of General Counsel also oversees and administers the inmate-grievance program, initiated in November 1974. The administrative remedy procedure provides a mechanism for formal resolution of inmates' complaints relating to any aspect of imprisonment if local attempts at informal resolution have failed. The process not only provides for the resolution of grievances but also reduces or eliminates many suits that would otherwise be filed. At the institution level, approximately 13,000 grievances were filed in 1985. Relief was granted in approximately 15 percent of these filings.
tort claims, personal liability actions against individual staff members, injunctive actions, and habeas corpus.

The Office of General Counsel also has responsibility for many nonlitigation matters, including legislation review and development, training of staff in the legal implications and requirements of corrections work, processing of employee discrimination complaints, and publication of rules in the federal register.

The Office of General Counsel also oversees and administers the inmate-grievance program, initiated in November 1974. The administrative remedy procedure provides a mechanism for formal resolution of inmates' complaints relating to any aspect of imprisonment if local attempts at informal resolution have failed. The process not only provides for the resolution of grievances but also reduces or eliminates many suits that would otherwise be filed. At the institution level, approximately 13,000 grievances were filed in 1985. Relief was granted in approximately 15 percent of these filings.

Staffing Patterns

The Bureau of Prisons is making significant progress in increasing the professionalism of its staff. Today, a third of the over 12,000 employees of the Federal Bureau of Prisons have college backgrounds.

Over 31 percent of all newly hired Bureau of Prisons employees in 1986 were members of minority groups, and 31 percent were women. Minorities now constitute nearly 26 percent of all employees, compared to 8 percent in 1971, when the Bureau first implemented a minority recruitment program.

Women are making significant advancements in traditionally male-dominated positions. Today, women comprise 21.6 percent of the workforce, compared to 11 percent in 1971. College and specialty recruitment continue to be the major sources for ensuring representative applicant pools.

Professional Standards _____

The Bureau of Prisons strives to acquire and maintain correctional accreditation for all its facilities, ensuring that correctional programs and operations are carried out in a humane and professional manner. In 1986, the Commission on Accreditation for Corrections awarded one initial accreditation and nine reaccreditations. This brings to 38 the total number of facilities accredited for three-year terms.

National Institute of Corrections _____

The National Institute of Corrections[9] was established by Congress in 1974 to assist state and local corrections agencies. The Institute is governed by a sixteen-member Advisory Board and is administered by a director who is appointed by the Attorney General.

Nearly $11,000,000 was awarded in 145 grants and contracts to state and local corrections agencies, organizations, and individuals during 1986. The awards were for training, technical assistance projects, research and evaluation, policy and program formulation, and clearinghouse activities.

The institute responded to 702 requests for technical assistance from state and local agencies in 50 states and the District of Columbia. These efforts led to improved record keeping and information management, and advancements in many other areas of correctional management programming.

Institutional overcrowding continued to prevail as the most critical problem in the field of corrections in 1986. The institute addressed crowding by assisting state and local corrections agencies in planning and designing new institutions, strengthening community corrections programs, and providing technical assistance to jurisdictions facing severe crowding.

The institute's information center provided information in response to nearly 8,300 inquiries from federal, state, and local practitioners during the year and continued to serve as a central source of practical, readily retrievable information on corrections.

The National Academy of Corrections,[10] the training arm of the Institute, provided training for approximately 3,000 managers, administrators, and staff trainers during the year. The academy also sponsored the participation of 144 state and local personnel at Federal Bureau of Prisons' training programs. Off-site, agency-based training was provided for 665 staff trainers who subsequently provided the same training for nearly 22,500 correctional staff in their respective agencies. Training needs were also met through grants and technical assistance to state and local agencies.

Summary

One objective of the Federal Bureau of Prisons is to be a model for state and local corrections. The bureau has attacked some of the major issues head-on and has made notable progress. But there are no simple solutions to the long-festering problems of corrections. Much hard work lies ahead — for the bureau and for all other correctional agencies in this country.

One of the bright spots on the horizon is the increasing use by the courts and corrections of community-based treatment as a humane, less costly alternative to incarceration for selected offenders. A substantial percentage of offenders, however, are not suitable for treatment in the relative freedom of community-based programs. In this category fall many multiple offenders who have long histories of serious, often violent, crimes.

To achieve maximum correctional benefits for all offenders, the Bureau of Prisons has sought to develop a balanced approach, recognizing that no single, all-purpose treatment method can be expected to produce effective results. One of the main challenges of the future undoubtedly will be to sustain the present level of public and legislative interest, which demands a concerted effort by the correctional community and by concerned citizens.

Although the Federal Bureau of Prisons is often described as a model that state systems might copy, it too has its problems and critics. In a 1987 uprising by 1,000 Cuban inmates held at the Oakdale facility in Louisiana and 1,400 held at the Federal Penitentiary in Atlanta, public outcry was raised. The Cubans, part of the Mariel group of 100,000 refugees admitted into the country in 1980, had taken hostages and overrun both facilities after hearing on their radios that 2,500 "undesirable" Cubans were about to be deported to Cuba. A siege of both facilities went on for eleven days, ending with the 89 hostages being released unharmed. The decision by the Department of Justice, that no one would be held responsible for the millions of dollars in damage to the institutions, was widely criticized. Attorney General Meese responded as follows:

> . . . the Cubans did not come out ahead of the government in the agreement ending the 11-day crisis.
> . . . when details of the agreement that freed the 89 hostages are fully understood, it will become clear it was fair and proper.

> You will learn as we proceed in this matter ... in no institution will people be able to gain by an uprising.[11]

The Bureau of Prisons no longer deals with just the "cream of criminals," but has some real problem inmates with which to deal. They are now experiencing some of the serious problems with overcrowding that has been the fate of the state facilities.

In 1984, Congress created the U.S. Sentencing Commission as an independent body, located in the judicial branch of the government. The Commission began its work in 1985 and submitted new guidelines on April 13, 1987. The guidelines will dramatically alter sentencing practices in the federal criminal justice system. A summary of these impacts is as follows:

- "Straight" probationary sentences (i.e., sentences that require no form of confinement) will be reduced significantly.
- For especially serious crimes, such as drug offenses and crimes against persons, probationary services will decline dramatically.
- For other crimes, like property offenses, the proportion of sentences involving some form of probation will not change appreciably, although probation with a condition of confinement may be substituted for straight probation.
- Average time served for violent offenses will increase substantially. For most property crimes, average time served will remain largely unchanged. Exceptions: burglary and income tax fraud, where average time served will go up.
- Federal prison populations will grow markedly by the end of this century, more as a result of the Anti-Drug Abuse Act of 1986 and the career offender provision of the Comprehensive Crime Control Act of 1984 than as a result of the guidelines.[12]

Wherever the blame is finally placed, the changes will have an impact on the correctional administrators in the Bureau of Prisons in the form of a massive increase in the numbers of inmates confined in federal institutions, institutions that are already overcrowded.

The National Institute of Justice conducted a study on more than 10,000 cases, using a very sophisticated computer model, to determine the possible impact on the system. Table 24.1 shows the dramatic increase in those who will receive "split sentences" (probation with confinement) for all offenses.

Even more dramatically, Table 24.2 shows the massive impact upon the populations projected for the Federal Bureau of Prisons. The "low-growth scenario" is bad enough, but the "high-growth scenario" *triples* the system's population in just ten years. This impact will be something to watch closely over the next few years. It may have more impact on the *model* correctional system in America than any other influence.

TABLE 24.1 Percentage of Defendants Receiving Probation and Split Sentences under Current Practice and as Projected under the Guidelines

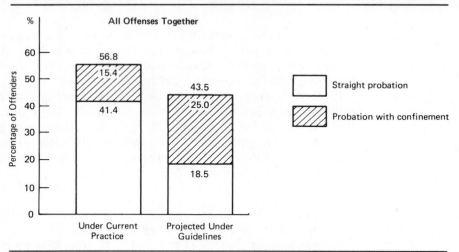

Source: National Institute of Justice, "The Impact of the Federal Sentencing Guidelines," *NIJ Reports: Research in Action* (Washington, D.C.: U.S. Department of Justice, September 1987), p. 3.

Review Questions

1. Explain the various categories of the institutions in the federal prison system.
2. What forces led to the shift in philosophy of the Bureau of Prisons in the 1970s?
3. Outline some of the community programs in which the bureau is involved.
4. Why does the bureau have such an advantage over state systems in evaluating programs?
5. Why has the prison population of the Federal Bureau of Prisons increased over the last few years?

Key Terms

1. White Slave Act (p. 574)
2. Volsted Act (p. 574)
3. UNICOR (p. 576)
4. classification (p. 577)
5. regional offices (p. 581)
6. Federal Prison Industries, Inc. (p. 585)
7. National Institute of Corrections (p. 591)
8. National Academy of Corrections (p. 591)
9. Mariel Cubans (p. 592)
10. U.S. Sentencing Commission (p. 593)

TABLE 24.2 Prison Population Projections

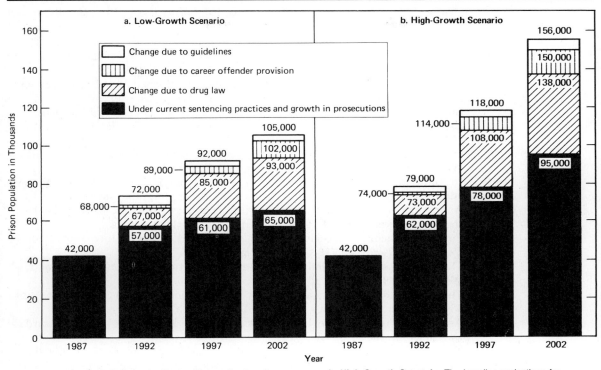

a. **Low-Growth Scenario**. The baseline projections for 1987–1989 are based on the average annual growth for the years 1982–1986. Thereafter, criminal cases were assumed to grow at a rate of 1 percent per year.

b. **High-Growth Scenario**. The baseline projections for 1987–1991 are based on the average annual growth for 1982–1986. Projections for 1992–2002 are based on the average annual growth that reproduces the same 15-year percentage growth for 1987–2002 that was observed for 1971–1986.

Source: National Institute of Justice, "The Impact of the Federal Sentencing Guidelines," *NIJ Reports: Research in Action* (Washington, D.C.: U.S. Department of Justice, September 1987), p. 6.

Notes _____

1. This chapter has drawn heavily from U.S. Department of Justice, *The Development of the Federal Prison System* (Washington, D.C.: U.S. Government Printing Office, 1979), and the U.S. Department of Justice, *Federal Bureau of Prisons: 1986 Annual Report* (Washington, D.C.: US Government Printing Office, 1987). See also the Federal Bureau of Prisons, *Federal Prison System 1982* (Lompoc, Calif.: U.S. Department of Justice, 1984).
2. The facility is now part of the prison system of the state of Washington.
3. This facility is currently an Ohio correctional institution.

4. Between November 21 and 23, 1987, eighty-seven federal prison staff were seized as hostages at the Atlanta Penitentiary and at the Alien Detention Center at Oakdale, Louisiana. These have been described as the most disruptive episodes in the history of the Bureau of Prisons. Hostages were eventually released after the Attorney General agreed to review each case of the Marielitos, Cubans who arrived in the nation during the Mariel boatlift. See "After Atlanta and Oakdale," *Corrections Today* 50 (1988): 26, 64–65.

5. See Harry Allen and Nick Gatz, "Abandoning the Medical Model in Corrections: Some Implications and Alternatives," *Prison Journal* 54 (Autumn 1974): 4–14; Simon Dinitz, "Nothing Fails Like Little Success," in Edward Sagarin, ed., *Criminology: New Concerns* (Beverly Hills, Calif.: Sage Publications, 1979), pp. 105–118.

6. Only McNeil Island has been closed, and has since been sold to the state of Washington to help solve some of its overcrowding.

7. In addition, the Office of General Counsel in the Federal Bureau of Prisons administers and oversees the inmate grievance program, initiated in 1974. Approximately fourteen thousand grievances were filled in fiscal year 1982; the inmate was granted relief in 20 percent of these filings.

8. For a discussion of security in jails and prisons, see the July 1987 issue of *Corrections Today* 49 (1987), in particular pages 16–102.

9. The address of the National Institute of Corrections is 320 First Street NW, Washington, D.C. 20534

10. The address of the National Academy of Corrections is 1790 30th Street (Suite 430), Boulder, Colo. 80301

11. Associated Press, "Meese Defends Prison Deal," *The Seattle Times* (Saturday, December 5, 1987), p. A2.

12. National Institute of Justice, "The Impact of the Federal Sentencing Guidelines," *NIJ Reports: Research In Action* (Washington D.C.: U.S. Department of Justice, September 1987), p. 2.

Community Corrections

The manifold implications of the concept of
community corrections pivot around a profound
idea: official reactions to the convicted offender
should be related to the community forces which
contribute to criminality, which are involved in
the definition of crime as a social problem, and
which largely determine whether or not
"rehabilitation" programs will produce his
integration within the control system regulating
the behavior of noncriminals.
—ELMER H. JOHNSON

Prisons: At a Turning Point

For almost two centuries, jails, prisons, reformatories, and training schools have embodied the primary societal response to criminal behavior in America. Increasingly, the public is becoming aware—especially in these short budget times—that these institutions are inefficient, ineffective, and expensive.[1] Unrelieved confinement may be necessary for a reasonable percentage of the inmate population, but to house all of the rest in bleak and cheerless places is a waste not only of human potential but also of costly security measures. More recently, as noted in Part 3, the correctional system has expanded to include four components: probation, intermediate punishments, institutional incarceration, and parole.

The four have grown separately, often in competition for the same limited fiscal, physical, and personnel resources. In recent years, authorities have recognized that an effective utilization of these scarce resources demands their coordination and consolidation. Still badly fragmented and divided in many ways, the correctional services in the United States are slowly, and often reluctantly, beginning to move toward the creation of an organized system. Foremost in this movement is the shift away from the total institution, toward alternatives to incarceration.

Although it might seem that the current trends in prison construction and overpopulation reflect a more punitive, conservative, and hard-line approach to crime and criminals, the crimes known to police in the United States have actually been decreasing, as is shown in Table 25-1. Furthermore, the "baby boomers" have moved through the high-risk ages of sixteen to twenty-nine. Also, the selective incapacitation of the highest-risk offenders for longer periods of incarceration may achieve the suppressive effects[2] sought by its advocates.[3]

Selective incapacitation is characterized as a sound concept in theory, but a nightmare in practice. David R. Struckoff quotes Walker's five questions (1985) about selective incapacitation:

- Can we correctly estimate the amount of crime reduction?
- Can we accurately identify chronic offenders and predict their future behavior?
- Can we afford the monetary costs of implementing selective incapacitation should it involve massive new detention center construction?
- Can we implement a policy of consistent selective incapacitation without violating constitutional rights?
- What will the side effects be?[4]

Clearly the jury is still out on this controversal attempt to link incarceration to crime reduction. As Struckoff says: "A vigorously joined debate continues on this topic, because it will affect police, prosecutors, judges, legislators, the public, and the correctional community."[5]

The correctional pendulum swings slowly, and probably will swing for many decades. But if the movement is toward the "hard line of increased incarceration" today, it also can swing in the opposite direction in the future. In today's correctional environment, the main aim remains to achieve the greatest possible use of supportive treatment back in the community. The custodial institutions have failed because most of them have virtually no access to community treatment programs, professional services, or public support.

Perhaps it would be better to raze all the prisons and start over again, but this cannot be done until workable alternatives have been firmly established. The number of alternatives is growing, however, and attempts to evaluate the effectiveness of these programs are under way.

Reentry into the Community from the Institution _____

Partial Incarceration: A Beginning

One of the earliest programs for releasing prisoners before their full sentences expired was the result of the first *work-release* legislation. The use of offenders for community work programs had its origins in ancient Rome, where prisoners aided in the construction of massive public works. Those workers, however, had no hope for release; their work was just another form of slave labor. The work-release philosophy, which permits inmates to work on their own in the free community, dates back to a 1913 Wisconsin statute that allowed misdemeanants to continue to work at their jobs while serving short sentences in jail. North Carolina applied the principles of the Wisconsin statute to felony offenders in 1957, under limited conditions; Michigan and Maryland soon followed suit with similar acts.

In 1965, Congress passed the Federal Prisoner Rehabilitation Act, which provided for work release, furloughs, and community treatment centers for federal prisoners. This act, an excerpt of which follows, served as a model for many states:

> The Attorney General may extend the limits of the place of confinement of a prisoner as to whom there is reasonable cause to believe he will honor this trust, by authorizing him, under prescribed conditions, to . . .
>
> 1. visit a specifically designated place or places for a period not to exceed thirty days and return to the same or another institution or facility. An extension of limits may be granted only to permit a visit to a dying relative, attendance at the funeral of a relative, the obtaining of medical services not otherwise available, the contacting of prospective employers, or for any other compelling reason consistent with the public interest; or
> 2. work at paid employment or participate in a training program in the community on a voluntary basis while continuing as a prisoner of the institution or facility to which he is committed. . . .
>
> The willful failure of a prisoner to remain within the extended limits of his confinement, or to return within the time prescribed, to an institution or facility, designated by the Attorney General, shall be deemed an escape from the custody of the Attorney General.[6]

Institutional work release is not intended to be a substitute for parole, but it can be a valuable tool for the correctional administrator and the parole officer who must eventually supervise an individual who has participated in work release. The work-release program is not really an alternative to incarceration. Rather, it is a chance for offenders to test their work skills and personal control over their behavior in the community. And it allows them to spend the major part of the day away from the institution. Because offenders must still return to the institution, the work-release program may be considered only a partial alternative.

Work release has other benefits besides allowing inmates to be outside the walls for a period of time each day. The income derived from the work can be used in a number of ways: if the inmates have families, the earnings can be used to keep them off welfare rolls or to augment the assistance they might be receiving; inmates can reimburse victims for their loss, if the judge has required it,[7] or they may be able to build a nest egg for the time when they will be released. One of the main fringe benefits is that their community becomes aware of their ability to maintain a job without creating problems for themselves or others. Also, their association with stable co-workers in the free world may give them support and guidance[8] that they could not find inside the walls. In the American tradition, the ability to "do a good day's work" both heightens the offenders' self-esteem and commands respect from others. Many Scandinavian prisons have factories attached to them, allowing inmates to work at real-world jobs for pay equal to that earned by the outside worker.

Another form of partial incarceration is the furlough. Both work release and furlough extend the limits of confinement to include unsupervised absences from the institution. Furloughs and home visits have been allowed for many years on an informal basis. The death of a family member or some other crisis situation was the most common reason for the furlough. As states have passed legislation making furloughs a legal correctional tool, furloughs have been used for a number of purposes, including a home visit during holidays or just before release, so that the return to the free world is a graduated process. Education has been another reason for extensive use of the furlough; it often allows the inmate to be in residence at the school during the week; he or she returns to the correctional institution on the weekend. One benefit of home furloughs, obviously, is decreased sexual tension in institutions. More uses for the furlough will be explored as correctional administrators gain experience with it. A major roadblock to progress in such programs in the late 1980s has been a few highly publicized and sensational failures. These failures, combined with the general increase in violent and dangerous inmates coming out of the prisons, cause it to be difficult to promote any kind of furlough program.

Halfway Houses as Alternatives to Incarceration

The search for alternatives to incarceration led to the development of the halfway house, a place where offenders can benefit from work or education in the free world while residing in the community.[9] The interest in the halfway house as an alternative to imprisonment has grown in recent years. Although the original halfway houses served as residences for homeless men released from prison, they have since been used for a variety of purposes. Small residences offering shelter have been managed by prison aid societies for over a century. In recent years, more attention has been given to halfway houses as the possible nuclei for community-based networks of residential treatment centers, drug-free and alcohol-free living space,[10] or as prerelease guidance centers.

In 1961 the U.S. Bureau of Prisons established prerelease guidance centers in major metropolitan areas. The offender is sent to these centers from a correctional institution several months before he or she is eligible for parole. Staff personnel are selected on the basis of their treatment orientation and aptitude for counseling. The offender is allowed to work and attend school in the community without supervision, and he or she participates in a number of programs in the halfway house itself. This approach has been copied by many states and appears to be a viable program when properly staffed and supervised. As possible uses for the halfway house are explored and outcomes are verified,[11] these units will offer not only short-term residency before the prisoner's placement on parole but also noninstitutional residence facilities[12] for a number of different classes of offenders.[13] At that point, halfway houses will constitute the first real alternative to institutional incarceration in the community.

Graduated Release: Toward a Community-Based Alternative _____

It has been generally recognized that offenders who serve long sentences in institutions suffer culture shock when they are suddenly returned to the community from which they originally came. Just as astronauts must reenter the atmosphere in a series of shallow passes, so should offenders reenter society in a gradual series of steps. Referred to as *graduated release,* some programs are intended to ease the pressures of culture shock experienced by institutionalized offenders. Some of the concepts for reducing the effects of reentry are presently being practiced; others must wait until there is a true correctional continuum available. Any preparation for release is better than none, but preparation that includes periods of nonincarcerated time is most effective.

The periods immediately before and after release are especially crucial to the ex-offender's adjustment to society. Despite an outward attitude of bravado, most ex-offenders know they will have a serious problem trying to reestablish a life outside the institution. Their apprehension builds as they approach release. Some inmates become "jackrabbits," escaping shortly before they are due for release.[14] Others commit some petty offense within a short period after their release.

These actions can be seen as deliberate efforts to ensure their quick return to the "safety" of the institution, where all their needs are met and no demands (except obedience to the rules) are made on them. Awareness of this phenomenon has led many thoughtful correctional administrators to establish prerelease and postrelease programs aimed at assisting the ex-offender through those critical periods. Topics covered in such programs include how to get a driver's license, how to spend money, how to find an apartment, how to find a job, and how to handle sex, family adjustment, credit buying, and so on.

The whole experience of incarceration is a prelude to the inmate's even-

tual release. Unfortunately, the institutional environment bears little relation to the free life. The inmate is seldom allowed to earn a meaningful
wage,[15] is deprived of heterosexual relations, and lives in an authoritarian
world dominated by the instutution's needs. To expect an individual to
switch overnight from that situation to a free community is asking a great
deal of even the most stable personality.

Many programs have problems because the prerelease preparation is
begun too late in the inmate's sentence. If possible, prerelease preparation
should begin far in advance.[16] The inmate must be a part of the planning
and be clearly aware of the purpose and intent of graduated release. These
goals must be realistic and part of the entire treatment process for the
inmate while he or she is incarcerated (e.g., if the inmate is to be released
to a job in a print shop as part of the plan, it is not relevant for him or
her to be assigned to a farm operation.) Choices should be made based on
the individual's needs, not on the needs of the institution. Wherever possible, work release should be part of the plan, allowing the inmate to
reintegrate to the free world and develop work habits with a support sytem
and minimal controls still in place. Again, graduated-release and prerelease
programs are not either/or alternatives to incarceration, but can help to
offset the destructive and dependency-producing effects of imprisonment.

New Ways to Do Old Things?

In recent years, more and more people—in the correctional field and
among the general public—have come to favor community-based corrections. The concept is often promoted as a new and revolutionary idea, but in
reality the concept of treating (or punishing) the offender in the community is
one of the oldest forms of social control. By comparison, the concept of imprisonment is new, and many of the problems in the ex-offender's readjustment to the community stem from long isolation in the artificial prison
environment. Even the harsh punishments common in our early history
were performed in the community (including subjecting the prisoner to
stocks, pillories, and even executions). When correctional efforts eventually
moved inside the prisons, the shift was really in emphasis rather than
procedures. The treatment and rehabilitation movements for convicted felons
and adjudicated deliquents alerted communities to the fact that the offenders
they sent away to prison almost always return to the community.

Thus the public has begun to question the effectiveness of institutional
corrections and to support the idea of community treatment. Community
involvement in correcting offenders reflects a reversal of the prison
philosophy that isolation is the only answer. The combination of rising
recidivism rates and skyrocketing costs for institutional programs has en-

couraged community programs, but many of them have not fulfilled their supporters' inflated claims. Even if the results are only equal in terms of rehabilitation or recidivism, the cost of community corrections is so much lower than that of institutionalization that its emphasis can be justified on economics alone. And if the costs were the same, the community programs would still be worth considering on humanitarian grounds, for they represent a more reasonable approach to social control than the fortress prisons.

Before we demolish all the prisons, however, it is essential to recognize that the correctional utopia promised by community-based correctional programs cannot be created overnight. Crime and violence will continue to generate public fear, concern, and overreaction. Overselling community-based programs as a panacea for all offenders misleads the public. Newspapers seldom note when an ex-offender who returns to crime *did not* have the benefit of community-based treatment, and the public assumes that community programs are worthless and that more offenders should be incarcerated. Conversely, the media will always note with glee when the resident of work release, or on furlough or parole, is involved with a crime while in that status.

A proper balance between small, humane, program-oriented maximum security institutions and community-based programs must be maintained for the foreseeable future. Until we develop effective programs for offenders who are so drug-dependent, violent, or disadvantaged that we cannot help them and they cannot help themselves, we must have some way to keep society safe from these people. The remaining offenders, however, should be given more and more opportunities for participation in community-based programs, which are generally divided into two categories: diversion programs and programs designed to augment the existing correctional system.

One of the principles underlying community-based corrections is to minimize the offender's contact with institutional incarceration. The emphasis away from the dehumanizing and alienating effects of institutionalization mandates avoidance of jails, workhouses, and prisons to an extent consistent with the need to protect society.

To be effective, community-based programs must take advantage of every aspect of the services available to the offender in the outside world. This goal requires a whole new set of roles for all involved in the correctional process. Citizens, correctional workers, and offenders themselves must adjust to new expectations and functions.

The role of "social change agent" includes more responsibility than the correctional worker held in his or her earlier control function. Even the traditional community roles of probation and parole officers must be changed in emphasis to give offenders the total services of the community-based system. This process will require extensive recruiting and retraining within the present system to provide the quality personnel with the orientation needed to make the system work.

The Private Sector's Role in Community Corrections _____

The role of the private, and private nonprofit, sector in institutional jails and prisons was discussed in some detail in the last chapter. The idea of having these sectors comes as some kind of shock to many people, but this should not be the case. The concept of having government services provided by contracting in the private sector was the primary method of obtaining those services for the first hundred or so years of the United States. Transportation, fire protection, police, and even armies were often provided on contract. The second century saw a change toward providing services through bureaucratic agencies. In recent years, however, the cost of government-provided services has risen so high that many services are now moving back to the private sector.

There have been a number of precedents in the correctional field: health-care, food service, education, mental health, transportation, and training have been provided by contractors to many systems. From the time of John Augustus, most juvenile and adult halfway houses and other services have been provided by private or charitable organizations. As the need for more community corrections has grown, many entrepreneurs have become involved in the "boom" industry of corrections. Many of these entrepreneurs are now expanding across state borders and operating organizations like a franchise.

The main advantage that is held by these operations is the ability to expand and contract their operations as needs change. When a government invests in the building of a major correctional facility in the community, it is obliged to staff it and operate it even if it is not cost-effective to do so. The entrepreneurs of community corrections can modify an existing facility, provide staff on a contract basis, use community resources for professional services, and then close it down when no longer needed. The federal community corrections programs house over 3,000 inmates in 330 contracted community correctional centers. Most states contract for their community corrections, so the business is burgeoning.

One of the major issues for the contractor concerns liability for potential public safety issues. Most government agencies are "self-insured."[17] This insurance protects them with the resources of the entire government entity. The private-sector operator, however, must have some type of liability insurance to cover these problems. With the incredible growth of litigation in the United States, government agencies have become targets for attorneys looking for new markets. This has caused insurance rates to skyrocket and affect operations by the private sector.[18] The small operator has been put in a squeeze, and the large ones are hurting as well. It will be seen how this phase of private corrections influences some of the efforts by private operations to move into jails and prisons (see Chapter 27).

Diversion: Keeping the Offender Out Of the System _____

Diversion from the criminal justice system has taken place in one form or another since social controls were first established. In most cases, informal diversions merely mean an official's exercise of discretion at some point in the criminal process.

More formal diversions include suspension of the criminal process in favor of some noncriminal disposition. Only about 30 percent of the reported offenses in America result in an arrest, and only about one-third of these arrests result in a criminal conviction,[19] an indication that preconviction diversion is not uncommon.

Diversion may occur at a number of points in the criminal justice system. The primary points are prior to police contact, prior to official police processing, and prior to official court processing. Three basic models emerge to determine what agency might be responsible for diversion. First we find *community-based* diversion programs. Second, we find *police-based* diversion programs. The other commonly used method is *court-based* diversion programs. While each of these models usually involves more than one agency or group, programs will generally be grouped according to who initiates the action and is primarily responsible for their implementation.

Most diversion programs now in effect constitute informal responses to the ambiguities of existing legislation. The value of such programs is difficult, if not impossible, to estimate. Their goals and procedures must be clearly articulated and integrated into the rest of the criminal justice system.

Community-Based Diversion Programs

Diversion projects are most effective when integrated into a community-based correctional system with alternative levels of supervision and custody. The currently informal options on an accountable basis must be formalized without rigidifying the process. If community-based programs are too restricted, they will merely become "institutions without walls." Diversion is seen as the first threshold of the community corrections system, designed to remove as many offenders as possible from the process before their conviction and criminalization.

Although programs that aim toward a total or partial alternative to incarceration are improvements, they do not eliminate the stigma of a conviction record. Diversion programs tied to treatment and services in the community, however, both avoid the problems of incarceration and remove the criminal label. These programs are seen not as a substitute for probation services but as a method of filling the gap between offenders eligible for probation and cases in which the charges can be dropped. Diversion should be accompanied by a formalized agreement with offenders

The "New Pioneer Fellowship House," Built Specifically as a Work-Release facility (Courtesy Pioneer Human Services)

as to what they are to do in return for the elimination of their arrest records. A set of alternative treatment services and residential reinforcements may be needed to help diverted individuals handle their problems. The diverted individuals should have the advantages available to all other categories of offenders and ex-inmates being treated in the local network.

Police-Based Diversion Programs

Police agencies have practiced diversion, informally, by using their power of discretion at the time of an offender's arrest. Several programs have been established to encourage more of these diversions on a formal basis. Police have been reluctant in the past to formalize their practice of discretion because of public reaction that the practice means that they are "being soft." Most formalized programs are aimed at the youthful offenders in an effort to keep them from beginning a career of crime.

Another example of diversionary tactics at the police level is the family crisis intervention approach. This approach, which has been used in several large cities, is especially important as the number of domestic violence laws across the country are toughened. Laws often now result in the arrest of both parties.

There are indications that the police, by identifying conflict situations at an early stage of development, can prevent the escalation of violence.

A general model involves the use of specially-trained family crisis intervention officers to respond to family disturbances; these officers attempt to resolve the conflict on the scene. If they cannot, the antagonists are referred to a community agency instead of jail.

Court-Based Diversion Programs

The courts are involved with diversion in several ways. One method is to use civil commitment for individuals who presumably can be treated more efficiently in a hospital situation. However, the constitutionality of these civil commitment procedures has been questioned, and their continued use is doubtful. A more common and reasonable use of diversion by the courts is found in pretrial intervention programs, which have been funded extensively by the U.S. Department of Labor. The general pattern of such actions is, at the end of the prescribed period of the continuance, to allow; (1) dismissal of pending charges based on satisfactory project participation and demonstrated self-improvement, (2) extension of the continuance to allow the program staff more time to work with the person (usually for an additional thirty to ninety days), (3) return of the defendant to normal court processing, without prejudice, because of unsatisfactory performance in the program.

Diversion is especially appropriate for the public drunk and the first-time drug abuser. The current alternative to incarceration for the public drunk is to send him or her to a *detoxification center*. Voluntary attendance at detoxification centers demonstrates the willingness of many problem drinkers to accept treatment, if only for free room and board.

The severity of criminal sanctions and public reaction to most drug offenses makes the diversion of drug abuse cases a sensitive area. With the country awash with illegal drugs, and drug use by the general population quite high, the wave of enforcement activity has made it difficult to divert all but the least violent of users, leaving the hard cases to sweat it out in institutions that seldom provide meaningful programs. Most diversion programs for drug users are concentrated on juveniles and are aimed at the first-time arrestees.

The spectrum of diversionary programs is geared toward the same goal: provision of a reasonable alternative[20] to incarceration in large, punitive prisons. Again, as in the development of many other aspects of correctional services, such programs often begin as independent actions by concerned professionals and community groups. These multifaceted efforts all are competing for the scarce dollars and personnel allotted to corrections as a whole; consequently, many of them are poorly staffed and underfunded. It is a real danger that these programs, without careful coordination at all levels of the criminal justice system, will produce poor results from good ideas — and will cause the inevitable return to an emphasis on incarceration. Signs of such a backlash are already in evidence.[21]

Probation and Parole: A Changing Role _____

Probation and parole have been the traditional modes of releasing offenders into the community. Probation gives nondangerous convicted offenders a chance to remain in their community and work toward an eventual release from supervision. Parole has been developed for institutionalized offenders who are ready to return to the community under supervision before their sentences have expired. Both programs were discussed in detail in Part 3. Essential to successful community-based corrections is the coordination of activities and services available for all offenders, whether on diversion, probation, or parole. These programs presently function as separate entities, under the control of different local units of government. As a comprehensive, community-based correctional system is developed, the traditional role of probation and parole officers will give way to that of "change agents." Such agents will have an array of correctional treatment and service alternatives at their disposal, with the ability to move offenders as needed from one type of program to another[22] (as opposed to the narrow options of returning offenders to court or prison, or ignoring their problems entirely).

Adjuncts to Institutionalization—An Intermediate Step _____

The sharp distinction between treatment methods in the institution and community-based treatment has become blurred as more and more offenders are released under supervision. The most effective response to their differential needs is to develop a spectrum of custody and supervision modalities. The problems of bridging the gap between the institution and the community have been recognized since the earliest prisons began to release offenders on "tickets of leave" in the mid-nineteenth century. The efforts of Ireland's Sir Walter Crofton gave prisoners a chance to work in the community for a period of time before their release. The concept of work release has since become an important adjunct to institutional programs. Under these programs, offenders are allowed to work at jobs in the community and still receive the benefit of certain programs available at an institution. Work release may often be the first step toward some form of residential and custodial facility in the community for offenders who are able to function at their job but are still in need of supervised treatment. Such community-based facilities are usually referred to as *halfway houses* (discussed earlier) because residents are considered to be halfway out of the institution.

Halfway houses are often operated by private organizations under state supervision. As funds have been made available from various sources, halfway houses have acquired different organizational and ideological orientations.

A Typical Room Inside the "New Pioneer Fellowship House" (Courtesy Pioneer Human Services)

Some states have begun to take a much closer look at their funding of halfway-house programs and require a better accounting of results. Halfway houses are often located in depressed neighborhoods in older buildings that were originally designed for some other purpose.[23]

The increasing use of diversionary and probationary alternatives to imprisonment resulted in the development of halfway-*in* houses for offenders who need supportive residential treatment but who are not so dangerous as to be sent to prison. An integrated system of the future might place halfway-out and halfway-in offenders in the same residence, with the emphasis on the kinds of treatment provided rather than the type of offender. These two categories may well be joined by a third as the new reintegration centers become part of the correctional system. In the future, residential care and custody will most likely emphasize referral to available community services and programs, rather than just personal contact with the offender.

The Community Correctional Center _____

The community correctional center is the most appealing step toward a community-based institution in recent years. Developed in a number of models, these centers are usually fairly open and are located in the com-

The Cleveland Reintegration Center, a Former Home For Unwed Mothers
(Courtesy of Ohio Department of Rehabilitation and Corrections)

munity, utilizing community resources for its services. Centers serve a variety of purposes, including detention, treatment, holding, and prerelease, and are based in a variety of facilities ranging from existing jails to hotels and motels. With growing support, the centers will offer a specific and integrated set of services.

Is Cheaper Better?

As mentioned earlier, proponents of community-based corrections have often made exaggerated claims for their results. Upon examination, however, it appears that community programs are no more and no less effective than institutional corrections are. But from a financial standpoint, community-based corrections are proving to be more practical.[24] In the community-based exemplary project conducted in Des Moines, Iowa, it was found that residential corrections were approximately four times cheaper than were the ongoing state institutional programs.[25] In community-based programs that do not require a residential facility, the cost differential is even more pronounced. The cost of maintaining an inmate in a correctional institution is estimated to be approximately $17,500 a year, as opposed to $600–$1000 for probation and parole.

Economics is not the only measure of a correctional program, however; the principal objective of such programs is to protect the public. Only when it is definitely established that shifts from institutional to community corrections can be accomplished with no increased danger to the public should they be made. It is clear that treatment in the community is more humane, and that it protects the offender from institutionalization. It has been proved that subjecting offenders to custodial coercion in the fortress prisons places them in physical danger, destroys their community ties, and reduces their self-esteem. A system is hard to fault that avoids these problems, costs less, is more (or equally) effective, and still protects the community. It is basically for these reasons that the movement toward community corrections has gained such great support in the past decade. Improvements and increased success for the programs that are now in an experimental stage will make the community-based programs the keystone of corrections in the decades to come.

High-Tech Enters Corrections: Electronic Monitoring _____

The public fear of having criminals in our midst has caused a wave of high-tech methods to be developed for tracking and monitoring persons in community corrections programs. These have ranged from simple call-back methods to ascertain that the individual is where he or she is supposed to be to computerized devices that are interactive and pervasive. In a recent review of such programs, Ralph Kirkland Gable sums up the main issues:

> The first electronic monitoring system in corrections was developed in 1964. It was used as an alternative to the incarceration of parolees and mental patients. More recently, with rapid advances in communications technology and data management, personal telemonitoring systems are being developed at several locations in the United States and other countries. Current case law suggests that at least some types of electronic monitoring may be legally permissible when they are used to verify compliance with other acceptable conditions of probation or parole and have demonstrated therapeutic effectiveness. Three major correctional objectives may be achieved through the use of telemonitoring systems: (1) reduced correctional costs, (2) extended protection of the public, and (3) improved rehabilitation of offenders. Consideration should now be given to the important legal and social issues involved in the large scale use of telemonitoring.[26]

No matter how effective telemonitoring can become, some offender is going to commit a heinous crime while being monitored. This will no doubt cause a major discussion to occur as to whether or not some classes of offenders should be allowed that option of control. If the users of such systems are careful to have clear and well-drawn policies and procedures, and if staff is trained in responses, the system will probably survive. No system designed by humans cannot be circumvented by humans who have devious minds to start with.

The Integrated Contract Model: A Possible Compromise? _____

We need not review the general procedures of processing offenders from arrest through parole; nor need we elaborate on the existence of varied alternatives to formal processing. These are briefly sketched in Figure 25-1 and are assumed to exist to divert offenders for reintegration purposes. Our focus is on the offender after pleading or being adjudicated guilty of a felony.[27]

With the integrated contract model, once guilt has been determined, and before disposition of the instant case, the judge would formally preside over and participate in the offender's choice of either punishment or reintegration. In this initial decision, the defense attorney would continue to provide legal advise and protect the offender's rights. The prosecution attorney should remain a viable entity and would also participate in the final contract.

Upon conviction of these offenders not opting for punishment, the state's department of corrections would institute a comprehensive reintegration plan predicated on maximum delivery of services, victim restitution, the least restrictive environment, and a detailed program for dealing with the offender. Various options would include behavior modification, intrusive therapy, halfway houses, house arrest, probation hostels for chemical-dependent offenders, restitution, community treatment centers, electronic monitoring, community reintegration centers, and education/vocation furlough programs. The individualized plan would be presented to the court in the form of a proposed contract. Both the defense and prosecuting attorneys could consent to or dissent from the plan; the court would retain authority in development of the final contract.

Once the contracts were approved and signed by all parties, the court would formally dispose of the offender by his or her commitment as a probationer to the state's department of corrections, whose responsibility would include implementation of the contract, provision of services, and supervision, the levels of which could be varied in accordance with the offender's progress toward defined goals within the contractual time period. Serious deviation from the contract, absconding, and technical violations

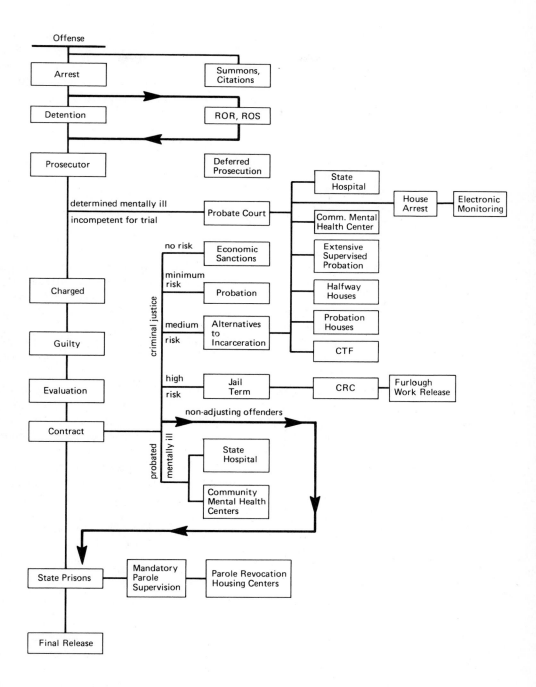

Figure 25-1 A Reintegration Model. (The authors are indebted to Dr. Richard Seiter for the original model of this concept.)

would be governed by at least the *Morrissey* conditions outlined in the landmark case. The court would retain the right to revoke formally the reintegration contract and to impose prison as the alternative.

There would be five categories of offenders for whom this would not be necessary, and mandatory prison terms would be required for those offenders who do the following:

1. Perpetrate murder in the first degree.
2. Commit any crime in which a firearm is used.
3. Are third-time felony conviction offenders.
4. Are rapists.
5. Are convicted as large-scale drug dealers.

The philosophy of prison would be incapacitation; sentence lengths would be determinate, with minor reductions for good-time behavior. Recidivists would receive multiples of the determinate sentence. Inasmuch as parole would not exist as a mandatory requirement and sentences would be determinate, a paroling agency would not be necessary. However, ex-prisoners desiring assistance would be eligible for all of the services, on a voluntary basis, available to probationers (see Figure 25-1).

At present, this system is much more dream than reality. Yet the various elements that are its foundation exist in most jurisdictions today. The major difference between the social justice model and the standard criminal justice model is the establishment of graduated and integrated levels of correctional treatment, related less to the offense than to the offender's individual problems and needs. Most social agencies now are taking this approach on a piecemeal basis, but the added element of coordination and control would ensure that all programs could contribute to the offender's rehabilitation. The social justice model seems to represent a logical conclusion for the present evolutionary trend in corrections. Like it or not, the correctional system today is under heavy fire; the emphasis is on accountability. Explanations must be given for the billions spent on corrections, rehabilitation, and processing of offenders. Excuses and glib platitudes are no longer the currency of the times. Results are.

Summary

The answer to all correctional problems may appear to lie in the closing down of America's prisons, but the total problem is not so simple to solve. When we speak of alternatives to incarceration, we speak of a carefully selected group of accused or convicted offenders. The primary mission of the correctional system is the protection of the public. All programs must be designed or proposed with that mission in mind, or they will be doomed to early failure and public rejection. All the systems described in this chapter have been programmed to meet the needs of certain categories of offenders. We do not propose that all offenders be given the chance for diversion or community treatment or any of the other programs described. What seems to be needed, however, is a system that offers as many alternatives to incarceration as are possible for the individuals who appear to have some hope of benefiting from them and who will present little, if any, danger to the community. The residual population may be required to remain in maximum security institutions until new treatments are found for them. Institutions for these residual inmates can be made more humane, more treatment-oriented, and more closely tied to the community. The community should be encouraged to come into the institution, providing models of behavior and friendship ties for the offenders who must remain incarcerated. The prison, in a modified form, still has a valuable place in the correctional system for the estimated 15 to 20 percent of the convicted offenders who require this level of control. For most convicted and diverted offenders, however, the use of either partial or total alternatives is a more reasonable response than is incarceration.

Review Questions

1. What are the traditional components of a correctional system? What are some recent additions?
2. Why is graduated release so beneficial to both the community and the offender?
3. Should all offenders be given the chance for diversion from the criminal justice system? Why or why not?
4. What is the primary mission of any correctional system?
5. Describe the contract model of corrections.
6. What are likely to be the major trends in corrections in the next decade? In prisons?
7. What are the major issues in the use of electronic monitoring?

Key Terms

1. selective incapacitation (p. 598)
2. partial incarceration (p. 598)
3. institutional work release (p. 599)
4. halfway house (p. 600)
5. graduated release (p. 601)
6. social change agent (p. 603)
7. self-insured (p. 604)
8. community-based diversion (p. 605)
9. police-based diversion (p. 606)
10. court-based diversion (p. 607)
11. community correctional center (p. 609)
12. integrated contract model (p. 612)

Notes

1. James Galvin, "What Does Incarceration Really Cost?" *Criminal Justice Newsletter* 14 (August 29, 1983): 5. Estimates of the annual cost of incarcerating an inmate in Minnesota range from $25,550 to $45,990, depending on the institution. The average cost is $36,500!

2. Daniel Glaser, "Supervising Offenders Outside of Prison," in James Q. Wilson, ed., *Crime and Public Policy* (San Francisco: Institute for Contemporary Studies, 1983), pp. 207–227.

3. Alfred Blumstein, "Prisons, Population, Capacity and Alternatives," in James Q. Wilson, ed., *Crime and Public Policy* (San Francisco: Institute for Contemporary Studies, 1983), pp. 229–250.

4. David R. Struckoff, "Selective Incapacitation," *Corrections Today* 49 (February 1987): 30.

5. Ibid.: 32.

6. American Academy of Political and Social Science, "The Continuum of Corrections," *The Future of Corrections (The Annals)* 38 (January 1969): 85.

7. James Bridges et al., "The Case for Creative Restitution in Corrections," *Federal Probation* 43 (September 1979): 28–35. See also Burt Galaway, "Probation as a Reparative Sentence," *Federal Probation* 46 (September 1983): 9–18. See also Jean Warner and Vincent Burke (eds.), *National Directory of Juvenile Restitution Programs: 1987* (Washington, D.C.: U.S. Department of Justice, 1987).

8. The longer a work-release participant remains employed in the same work-release job after earning parole status, the greater is the potential for parole success. Kyu Man Lee, "The Wichita Work Release Center: An Evaluative Study" (Ann Arbor, Mich.: University Microfilms International, 1983).

9. Roy Fisher and Charles Wilson, *Authority or Freedom? Probation Hostels for Adults* (Hants, England: Gover, 1982). See also James Bonta and Laurence Motiuk, "The Diversion of Incarcerated Offenders to Correctional Halfway Houses," *Journal of Research in Crime and Delinquency* 24 (1987): 302–323.

10. In Seattle, Pioneer Human Services has purchased a low-income hotel and several residences for the provision of alcohol and drug-free environments for recovering abusers. Participants must abstain from *any* alcohol or drug use during residency. They are also either in outpatient treatment, or following an aftercare plan in order to be admitted. Normal expectations for sobriety after six months for this type of group has been about 4 percent, but early results in this relatively new program have shown success rates of up to *87 percent*!

11. Marc Levinson, "In South Carolina, Community Corrections Means the Alston Wilkes Society," *Corrections Magazine* 9 (1983): 41–46. In Florida, presentence investigation reports are prepared by the Salvation Army.

12. Glaser, "Supervising Offenders Outside of Prison."

13. James Beck, "An Evaluation of Federal Community Treatment Centers," *Federal Probation* 43 (September 1979): 36–41.

14. *Jackrabbit* is a slang term for a prisoner who has nervous jitters just before release. Many of these inmates will deliberately attempt to escape so that they will be kept in prison. For this reason, "short-timers" are often kept in tight security immediately preceding their release date.

15. Those states participating in Prison-Industries Enhancement Act programs at the Federal Bureau of Prisons generally pay more substantial wages to inmates for penal industry participation.

16. See Jerry McGlone and James Mayer, "Industries and Education, the Vital TIE," *Corrections Today* 49 (1987): 32–34.

17. Self-insurance is achieved when the cash reserves of a governmental entity, or a private company, are large enough to cover the amount of anticipated

liabilities. If it is determined that the incidence of such losses is low enough that they would probably not exceed the cost of insurance, then risk is justified.

18. For example, the Pioneer Human Services agency in Seattle experienced a *tripling* of their liability rates in a one-year period.

19. National Advisory Commission on Criminal Justice Standards and Goals, *Corrections* (Washington, D.C.: U.S. Government Printing Office, 1973), p. 74.

20. Jim Galvin, "Midwest Group Provides Community Options," *Criminal Justice Newsletter* 14 (August 15, 1983): 1–2. See also his "Missouri Community Corrections Bill," *Criminal Justice Newsletter* 14 (August 15, 1983): 3.

21. Peter Finn, "Prison Crowding: The Responses of Probation and Parole," *Crime and Delinquency* 30 (January 1984): 141–153.

22. Gennaro Vito and Franklin Marshall, "The Administrative Caseload Project," *Federal Probation* 46 (1983): 33–41.

23. Harry E. Allen et al., *Halfway House: Program Model* (Washington, D.C.: U.S. Department of Justice, 1979).

24. Department of Court Services, *A Handbook of Community Corrections in Des Moines* (Washington, D.C.: U.S. Department of Justice, 1973), p. 145. For cost statements for probation, intensive supervised probation, and imprisonment, see Billie Erwin and Lawrence Bennett, *New Dimensions In Probation: Georgia's Experience With Intensive Probation Supervision* (Washington, D.C.: U.S. Department of Justice, 1986). The per-day costs are $.76, $4.37, and $30.43, respectively.

25. Estimating the costs of any correctional program is fraught with problems. It is very difficult to estimate human costs, recidivism costs, land costs, and lower taxes because the land does not yield tax revenue. Welfare payments to offenders' families, loss of property to victims, suffering and loss of income of victims, the cost of a life or a truncated life expectancy because of victim injury, and so on are difficult to estimate. One should consider such cost statements only as estimates.

26. Ralph Kirkland Gable, "Application of Personal Telemonitoring to Current Problems in Corrections," *Journal of Criminal Justice*, 14 (1986): 173. See also J. Robert Lilly, Richard Ball, and Jennifer Wright, "Home Incarceration with Electronic Monitoring in Kenton County, Kentucky: An Evaluation," in Belinda McCarthy, ed. *Intermediate Punishments* (Monsey, N.Y.: Justice Press, 1987), p. 203.

27. Much of this section was drawn from Nick Gatz and Harry Allen, "Abandoning the Medical Model in Corrections: Some Implications and Alternatives," *Prison Journal* 54 (Autumn 1974): 4–24.

Recommended Readings _____

American Correctional Association. *Manual of Correctional Standards*. Washington, D.C.: ACA, 1969.

Blumstein, A., J. Cohen, and D. Nagle. *Deterrence and Incapacitation: Estimating the Effects of Criminal Sanctions on Crime Rates*. Washington, D.C.: National Academy of Sciences, 1978.

Boorkman, David et al. *Community-based Corrections in Des Moines*. Washington, D.C.: U.S. Government Printing Office, 1976.

Chapman, Jane Robert et al. *Women Employed in Corrections*. Washington, D.C.: U.S. Government Printing Office, 1983.

Cohen, Jacqueline. *Incapacitating Criminals: Recent Research Findings*. Washington, D.C.: U.S. Department of Justice, 1983.

Cory, Bruce, and Stephen Gettinger. *Time to Build? The Realities of Prison Construction*. New York: Edna McConnell Clark Foundation, 1984.

Gibbons, Don. *The Limits of Punishment as Social Policy*. San Francisco, Calif.: National Council on Crime and Delinquency, 1988.

Glick, Ruth, and Virginia Neto. *National Study of Women's Correctional Programs*. Washington, D.C.: U.S. Department of Justice, 1977.

Greenwood, Peter, and Frank Zimring. *One More Chance: The Pursuit of Promising Intervention Strategies for Chronic Juvenile Offenders*. Santa Monica, Calif.: Rand, 1985.

Hershberger, Gregory. "The Development of the Federal Prison System." *Federal Probation* 43 (December 1979): 13–23.

Joint Commission on Correctional Manpower and Training. *Perspectives on Correctional Manpower and Training*. Washington, D.C.: JCCMT, 1969.

Latessa, Edward. *The Fifth-Year Evaluation of the Lucas County Probation Department's Incarceration Diversion Unit*. Cincinnati: University of Cincinnati, 1984.

Lieberman, Joel B. et al. *The Bronx Sentencing Project of the Vera Institute of Justice*. Washington, D.C.: U.S. Government Printing Office, 1972.

McCarthy, Belinda. *Intermediate Punishments*. Monsey, N.Y.: Criminal Justice Press, 1987.

Morris, Norval, and Gordon Hawkins. *The Honest Politician's Guide to Crime Control*. Chicago: University of Chicago Press, 1970.

National Institute of Law Enforcement and Criminal Justice. *How Well Does It Work? A Review of Criminal Justice Evaluation 1978*. Washington, D.C.: U.S. Government Printing Office, 1979.

Nelson, E. K., Howard Ohmart, and Nora Harlow. *Promising Strategies for Probation and Parole*. Washington, D.C.: U.S. Government Printing Office, 1978.

Newman, Oscar. *Architectural Design for Crime Prevention*. Washington, D.C.: U.S. Government Printing Office, 1973.

Pappas, Nick. *The Jail: Its Operation and Management*. Lompoc, Calif.: U.S. Bureau of Prisons, 1970.

Petersilia, Joan, *Expanding Options for Criminal Sentencing* Santa Monica, Calif.: Rand, 1987.

Ross, J. G. et al. *Assessment of Coeducational Corrections*. Washington, D.C.: U.S. Department of Justice, 1978.

Seiter, Richard P. et al. *Halfway Houses*. Washington, D.C.: U.S. Government Printing Office, 1977.

U.S. Department of Justice. *Prevention of Violence in Correctional Institutions*. Washington, D.C.: U.S. Government Printing Office, 1972.

U.S. Department of Justice. *The St. Louis Detoxification and Diagnostic Evaluation Center*. Washington, D.C.: U.S. Government Printing Office, 1973.

Summary and Overview

26

Corrections in the 1980s: Hope or Despair?

Correctional policy, particularly during times of rapidly increasing prisoner populations and prison overcrowding, can no longer remain confined to one level of government or one segment of society. State, local and federal authorities must focus on these problems and in concert — within the framework of federalism — develop a national correctional policy to deal with them.
— WARREN E. BURGER,
Former Chief Justice of the United States

The 1980s Are a Mixed Bag

The 1980s began with mixed signals. The executioner was back from forced retirement; the treatment model was declared dead; and the flat sentence was on its way back in more and more states. Parole was under attack and already abandoned in many states, and the public seemed to have acquired a "get tough" attitude. The prison population grew from 196,000 in 1970 to over 315,000 as the decade of the 1980s began.

The bloody uprising at Attica was almost ten years in the past, and the public was not aware of the growing cancer of overcrowding and violence in the nation's prisons. This "fool's paradise" was rudely interrupted during the thirty-six hours of rage and horror that riveted the populace to their television screens on the first weekend of February 1980. The New Mexico prison riot took its place in history, along with the many other incidents that have brought to the public's attention the conditions in the fortress prisons of America.

Even though no shots were fired, no guards were killed, and great restraint was shown by the prison authorities, the thirty-six hours of bloody rampage and wanton killing resulted in one of the most brutal riots in American penal history. When the rubble of the relatively modern facility (built in 1954) was sifted, it was found that thirty-three residents had died, most at the hands of their fellow prisoners. The extent of the brutality was the worst that most observers had ever seen. The episode was described in an article in *Newsweek* magazine.[1]

It is somewhat ironic that much of the progress in corrections is over-shadowed by such incidents as Attica and New Mexico. In contrast, the United States Penitentiary at Leavenworth announced that one of its inmates, a thirty-eight-year-old bank robber, became the first prisoner ever to be inducted into the elite Phi Beta Kappa scholarship society. The inmate earned a bachelor of science degree in psychology after five years of study in courses offered by the University of Kansas at Leavenworth, finishing with a grade-point average of 3.97 out of a possible 4.0.

As corrections in America approaches the 1990s and heads for the year 2000, the pattern seems to be "one step ahead and two steps backward." The changes underway are dynamic, but they offer a confused and often contradictory picture. We shall look at the basic problems here, but the future of corrections belongs to those who have mastered the knowledge and skills needed to effect real change in a system that resists it at almost every level. Without intelligent and informed leaders, the next edition of this chapter will no doubt begin with a story about yet another prison riot, caused by the apathy and ignorance of both the public and the correctional administrators who tolerate the conditions that make history repeat itself again and again.

Corrections in a Climate of Change _____

The last few decades have been a time of great social change. The industrialization of America eventually led to urbanization and the resulting problems connected with densely populated, poverty-ridden slums. Rising crime in the poorly designed urban centers contributed to an exodus to the suburbs by those who could afford the move. The inner city was left to the poor, the uneducated, and the minority groups. Cities became places of fear, and so-called street crime became a political issue. Presidential hopeful Senator Barry Goldwater alerted the nation to "law and order" as a campaign issue in the 1964 general elections. Lyndon Johnson was elected, but he too got the message that something had to be done about crime in the streets; hence, he appointed a commission to look into the problems of "crime in a free society."

The task force reports of that commission, especially the report on corrections, detailed what was already common knowledge to practitioners in the field: failure at all levels of the system, high recidivism rates from institutions, prisons depicted as schools of crime, and a lack of alternatives to incarceration. All of these points were variations on the themes contained in the Wickersham Commission Report of 1931 and several other reports in between. As in the past, most correctional administrators expected the 1967 commission reports to end up on dusty shelves, stimulating little or no action. Fortunately, the federal government was to provide the means to do something about the recommendations of this commission.

The Law Enforcement Assistance Act of 1965 (Public Law 89-197) was enacted to provide funds for the development of programs that would reduce the crime in the streets. The initial success of this legislation led to the development of the Omnibus Crime Control and Safe Streets Act of 1968 (P.L. 90-351). This legislation, implemented with generous funding by the Congress, pumped billions of dollars into the nation's fight against crime. Important to the field of corrections was the specific requirement that at least 20 percent of the money given to the Law Enforcement Assistance Administration (LEAA) be spent on action programs in corrections. These funds encouraged innovation, education, and evaluation across the spectrum of correctional services. This federal funding has been matched by significant permanent funds from the states as well, ensuring the continuation of the most promising of the pilot programs and procedures. The successor to the LEAA continues these efforts into the 1990s.[2]

Prisons continue to be at least microcosms of the outside society. It is not surprising that the issues that swept the cities in the 1960s spread to the prisons of America. The 1960s saw great advances in civil rights, but radical groups to the left and right perceived the changes as occurring either too slowly or too fast. The results increased polarization between the races and caused especially serious problems in the institutional setting. Divisions along racial, political, and ideological lines are strongly accentuated by the total institution. Many of the riots and disturbances in the prisons have been aimed at achieving political ends rather than at improving conditions in the institution.

The pressure-cooker environment of a total institution means that the slightest friction can explode the surface calm almost immediately. Thus, the highly volatile issues of the 1960s and 1970s have produced serious crises in the prisons in the 1980s. As correctional administrators turn more and more to incarceration alternatives, the prisons will be left with the residual, often hard-core and radicalized problem offenders as their cadre, further increasing the risk of prison violence. The serious overcrowding of the prisons, which now contain almost 600,000 inmates, exacerbates the problems of the administrator with a living "time-bomb" on his or her hands. Figures 26-1 and 26-2 depict the problems of the exploding prison population.

Public Correctional Policy: Direction at Last _____

Corrections has sometimes been described as "a concept in search of a discipline." Most state and local systems developed and expanded on an

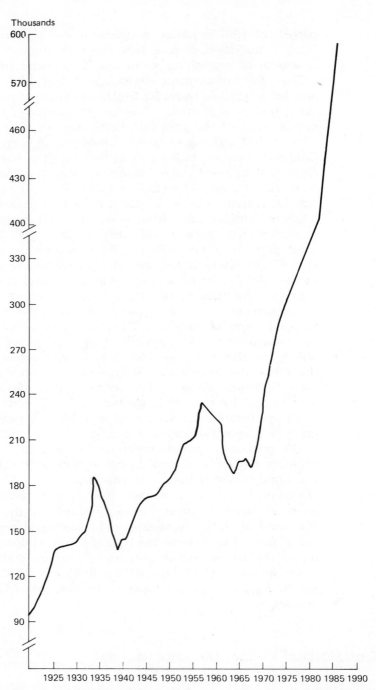

Figure 26-1 Number of Sentenced Prisoners in State and Federal Institutions, Yearend 1925–1987

Legend

Per 100,000 civilian population

☐ 0 – 99   ▨ 150 – 199

▨ 100 – 149   ☐ 200 or more

Figure 26-2 Sentenced Prisoners in State Institutions: Number per 100,000 Population (Bureau of Justice Statistics, *Prisoners in 1986* [Washington, D.C.: U.S. Department of Justice, 1987], p. 2)

ad hoc basis and resulted in neither true consensus nor planned coordination as to policy in regard to the major issues that face administrators, legislators,[3] courts, and the confused citizen. The American Correctional Association has been the leader in the effort to come up with cohesive and comprehensive policies for corrections. As shown in the box illustrating the ACA's Declaration of Principles, the basic ideals of the national organization have changed only slightly since 1870, when they were first presented.

These principles, established at a time of even more turmoil than that is experienced today, provided a clear blueprint for the corrections in America—a blueprint that appears to have withstood the test of time and that only requires the establishment of national policies to make them a reality. Although little was said or done about these principles outside the professional network of corrections itself, they waited for a vehicle to make America aware of the need for implementation strategies. In the early

ACA DECLARATION OF PRINCIPLES

Preamble:

More than a century ago, in 1870, leaders in American corrections first developed principles stating the ideas and objectives underlying the practice of their profession.

As members of the American Correctional Association, we continue in the spirit of our founders by renewing and revising these principles in 1982, so they may continue to guide sound correctional practices, make clear our philosophy and aims, and facilitate our seeking out and involving the leaders and citizens of the communities we serve.

The role of corrections is to assist in the prevention and control of delinquency and crime. We believe that the principles stated herein provide the conceptual foundation for correctional policy that will increase that contribution. Ultimately, however, preventing criminal and delinquent behavior depends in large measure on the will of the individual and the constructive qualities of society and its basic institutions—family, school, religion, and government.

Social order in a democratic society depends on full recognition of individual human worth and dignity. Thus, in all its aspects, corrections must be measured against standards of fairness and humanity. We share with the rest of the juvenile and criminal justice systems the obligation to balance the protection of individuals against excessive restrictions.

Finally, we are committed to conducting corrections in a manner reflecting rational planning and effective administration as measured by recognized professional standards.

Principles: Article I—Basic Precepts

1. Laws and administrative policies and systems stemming from them shall be based on respect for human dignity and worth with recognition that hope is essential to humane and just programs.

2. Victims, witnesses, and all other citizens who come in contact with the criminal justice system shall receive fair, concerned consideration and assistance including restitution and/or compensation when appropriate.

3. The accused or convicted offender shall be accorded the protection of recognized standards of safety, humaneness, and due process. Individuals who are neither accused nor charged with criminal offenses should be served by other systems.

4. Sanctions imposed by the court shall be commensurate with the seriousness of the offense and take into account the past criminal history and extent of the offender's participation in the crime. Unwarranted disparity, undue length of sentences, and rigid sentencing structures are an injustice to society and the offender and create circumstances that are not in the best interest of mercy, justice, or public protection.

5. The least restrictive means of control and supervision consistent with public safety shall be used. Use of institutions for control and supervision of pretrial detention and post-conviction disposition shall be based on judicious and restricted use of a limited resource. Incarceration shall only be used with juveniles or adults charged with or convicted of criminal offenses and for whom no other alternative disposition is safe or acceptable to society.

6. Juvenile and adult correctional agencies, whether federal, state, or local, or public, private, or voluntary, must regard themselves as part of a highly integrated larger system that must work together toward common goals.

7. Correctional agencies, in order to be accountable to and receive strong support from all branches of government and the public at large, must take an active role in setting future direction and must provide information on which public policy decisions can be made.

Article II — Programs and Services

8. Correctional programs at all levels of government require a careful balance of community and institutional services that provide a range of effective, just, humane, and safe options for handling adult and juvenile offenders. These services shall meet accepted professional standards and be accredited where appropriate.

9. Correctional agencies shall provide classification systems for determining placement, degree of supervision, and programming that afford differential controls and services for adult and juvenile offenders. These systems shall be based on sound theory and empirical knowledge of human behavior, giving consideration to such factors as age, sex, physical and mental conditions, and the nature of the offense.

10. All offenders, whether in the community or in institutions, shall be afforded the opportunity to engage in productive work and participate in programs including educational, vocational training, religious, counseling, constructive use of leisure time, and other activities that will enhance self-worth, community integration, and economic status.

Article III — Personnel

11. Adequately trained and well-supervised volunteers are essential adjuncts to effective delivery of services to adult and juvenile offenders at all stages of the correctional process.

12. Leadership selection for correctional agencies at all levels, public and private, shall be on the basis of merit without regard for political affiliation, race, sex, or religion, with tenure assured as long as there is demonstrated competent performance and compliance with professional and ethical standards.

13. The staff of correctional systems must be professionally competent and well-trained. They shall be selected and retained on the basis of merit without regard to political affiliation, race, sex, or religion and afforded training, career development experiences, and remuneration commensurate with job requirements and performance.

Article IV — Advancement of Knowledge

14. Correctional agencies have a continuing responsibility to promote, sponsor, and participate in research and program evaluation efforts. Doing so will contribute to both an understanding of the prevention and control of delinquent and criminal behavior and to assessment of the effectiveness and efficiency of programs and services.

1970s, the time was right for looking closer at the need for national policy on corrections. The questions about the rights of all citizens were being brought into the prisons and jails of America, backed by the force of the courts. No longer could the need for a national consensus about the course of corrections in the country be ignored. The vehicle for discussion was the Williamsburg Conference of 1971. This conference brought leaders of

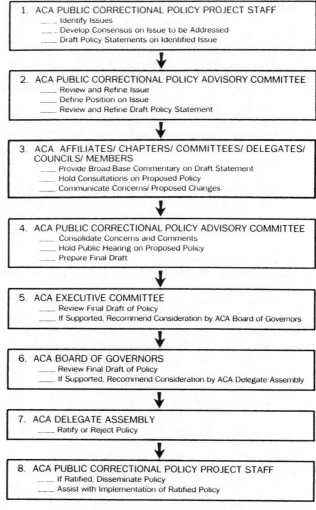

Figure 26-3 Public Correctional Policy Development Process, *Public Policy for Corrections*, American Correctional Association, College Park, MD, 1986, p. 5

corrections and representation from the courts, Congress, government, private citizens, and advocates from every spectrum of society to discuss the need for new directions for corrections. President Richard Nixon set the theme for this momentous conference by ensuring presence and support from the highest levels of government. This conference began the process that resulted in national policies on corrections.[4]

Finally, after years of discussion, the American Correctional Association's Policy/Resolutions Committee was charged with developing a proposal for funding a project to develop national correctional policies. The National Institute of Corrections funded this activity, with the following goals:

- To consolidate the significant correctional issues already identified by other groups and research efforts;
- To survey the ACA membership to determine their priorities on these issues;
- To outline a plan for an ongoing process of issue identification, and;
- To outline a plan of action to develop statements of rational policy addressing the identified issues.

That process was developed and is shown in graphic form in Figure 26-3.

In June of 1986, a second "Williamsburg" was held in Washington, D.C., with over three hundred representatives from every sector of American society. Presented to this group were the first twenty-one ratified and completed policies, for review and planning for the dissemination and acceptance by every system in the country. These twenty-one, along with five more that have since been addressed and ratified, are shown in Appendix B. Finally, America has a roadmap for finding its way into the twenty-first century! The persons who attended this great conference have since been spreading the word in jurisdictions all over the country. The effort now is for the new professionals in corrections to see that the process continues and that the policies are adopted in every sector of the field of corrections.

Personnel Improvements: A Major Goal _____

At the Staff Level

Perhaps no issue in corrections is as important as the training, educating, and recruiting of qualified staffs for the various systems.[5] In the past, institutional guards have been stigmatized by the general public almost as much as the inmates were whom they were expected to guard. In the nineteenth-century institution, the model of a strong, brutal guard was appropriate for the mission expected of him: he was in charge of custody and control. In today's correctional climate, however, that mission also includes rehabilitation and reintegration. The correctional officer, or change agent, is expected to possess a number of skills and abilities that were never envisioned by the original architects of the penitentiary. The comments of the Joint Commission on Correctional Manpower and Training still hold solid value today:

> In virtually every occupation and profession today, central themes of concern are the educational preparation, in-service training, and development of the manpower involved. In industry, the rapid advance of technology and automation has created a demand for higher levels of education and skills among workers. At the same time, the need for professionals and technicians in education, health, counseling, and the broad spectrum of other community services is growing faster than the education system can produce them. At the national level, a great deal of effort is going into a continuous and long-range study of the manpower resources of the country. Along with this is being developed a national policy dealing with the upgrading of educational levels and skills as well as with the distribution and most effective utilization of national manpower resources. In effect, the manpower problem is becoming defined more in terms of an educational and training crisis than in terms of manpower shortages. Corrections has not only been caught up in this complex of social and economic change but it is also feeling, more directly than in the past, the combined impact of new concepts and techniques in management, the technologies underlying the application of systems analysis to social problems, and the results of research on differential effectiveness of programs. Even the traditional boundaries which kept corrections confined within conventional limitations of institutions, probation, and parole are undergoing considerable reexamination. Implied in all of this change are some very critical issues relating to utilization of professional and nonprofessional personnel, the validity of existing formulas for staffing correctional agencies, and the kinds of in-service training that will contribute most effectively to the programmatic changes which seem imminent.[6]

Several approaches to the critical shortage of qualified personnel are either in operation or are proposed. In-service training is the first line of attack toward reshaping the ideological boundaries of corrections. Again, as noted in the 1968 Commission report:

> There are five kinds of in-service training: attitudinal, organizational, managerial, training for professional staff, and vocational training. I list attitudinal training first because persons come on our staffs through the indoctrination or orientation road. But it is my opinion that, in orientation or indoctrination training, in essence you are *not* orienting the employee to the company; you are *not* telling him about its benefits; you are *not* really answering his questions. What you are actually trying to do is to develop a productive attitude by means of what we call orientation. The truth of the matter is that trainees will remember only 10 percent of what they are told and will ask about these things again and again. The orientation-indoctrination for the new employee is really to set a productive attitude.[7]

In-service training is one of the easiest and least expensive ways for the correctional administrator to upgrade the quality and change the orientation of his or her current staff. Efforts to bring in new personnel with a different level of training and orientation may generate resentment in the present staff and may strengthen their resistance to change. Including all staff members in the program of in-service training will ensure the establishment of uniform policies and approaches to treatment.

A major leadership role in training programs is exercised by the Federal Bureau of Prisons and the National Institute of Corrections (attached administratively to the bureau). Every year the NIC trains thousands of state and local personnel through its National Academy of Corrections.[8] Courses include advanced correctional supervision, investigative supervisors' training, correctional management, and introduction to correctional techniques. Every institution in the Bureau has opened its courses to local correctional and law enforcement agencies. Basic training, management, food service, and locksmith training courses are also available at the Bureau's own training centers. These are separate from the mandated forty hours of postemployment annual training required of every Bureau employee. Much technological and administrative information is also being rapidly disseminated through this approach.[9]

Other resources for raising the level of the correctional personnel are the local universities and other educational institutions. Many educational programs for staff members were financed through the Law Enforcement Assistance Administration's Law Enforcement Educational Program (LEEP). The emphasis was on the social sciences and other courses designed to increase the staff's understanding of and sensitivity to the inmates' needs and problems. Many educational institutions have drawn up "package programs" for correctional administrators so that staff classes may be conducted inside the prisons. Using colleges and universities to upgrade personnel means that advanced-level courses will be available to some staff members whose previous education was extremely limited.

Ex-offenders have been used effectively in a number of programs throughout the nation. Recently the Adult Parole Authority of the state of Ohio has been using ex-offenders as case aides to parole officers. This was recognized as an "exemplary project" by the LEAA selection board, an accolade reserved for very few projects. The preliminary conclusions from that experiment are encouraging:

> Responses to interviews or questionnaires by parole supervisors, prison inmates, and parolees indicate general agreement that the Parole Officer Aide Program is worthwhile. Supervisors ranked parole officer aides higher than parole officers only on effort and ability to get jobs, yet saw them as a valuable source of information for parole officers and as able to teach parole officers how to relate to parolees. Inmates consistently indicated a preference for parole officer aides, with over two-thirds of them expressing a desire to be employed as an aide. Parolees supervised by aides consistently ranked aides

Corrections Officers Are Often Also "Heroes" and Are Recognized as Such: These Four Are from Arizona (Courtesy of American Correctional Association, photo by Thomas McGrath)

higher on all questions or scales than did parolees supervised by parole officers.

The researchers suggest this could be due to the smaller caseloads of parole officer aides, which allows them to devote more time to each of their parolees.[10]

Achievement of correctional programs staffed with those who are highly motivated, well educated, and oriented toward the mission of reintegration is still far down the road. The correctional system has traditionally been last in line for financial support, but the skyrocketing social cost of crime demands immediate personnel improvement. In-service training, educational opportunities, and imaginative recruiting are just a few methods for the correctional administrator to consider in the move toward crime reduction. It is ironic that just as some movement is being made toward improvement, the population crunch is causing the hiring of personnel to be done on a crisis basis—no doubt setting back progress in this area.

At the Administrative Level

Perhaps no problem concerning personnel is as important as that of correctional leadership. Throughout the United States, a very large percentage of the state directors of corrections have two or less years of experience in their positions;[11] only a small percentage have been in their job from two to four years. These proportions have not varied significantly over the past twenty-five years. These are extremely disturbing statistics given the monumental task of corrections. As pointed out by the Executive Director of the American Correctional Association:

> The responsibility for public safety and humane treatment for convicted offenders necessitates stability and continuity of leadership to plan and carry out programs. Experienced leaders with the opportunity to set goals, which are by and large long term, are a prerequisite for meeting the needs of the community and the offenders.

Momentum for correctional reform from above is hindered if lower-level

Education is Still a Viable Aid to Reintegration (Courtesy of American Correctional Association, photo by UNICOR)

staff have reason to suspect a new director may be imminent. Reform from below is frustrated when long-term goals cannot be maintained due to leadership changes. Staff should not have reason to be continually speculating about whom the new director will be and what his or her policies will be.

To increase the opportunity for a stable department of corrections with the best leadership available, chief executives or boards and commissions should seriously consider offering a contract for employment for a specified period of time such as three to five years for directors, wardens, and other persons in critical policy positions. With such a plan, governors and boards would still have the option to change leadership if necessary and would have a better chance of attracting the best qualified personnel. If the director, warden, etc., proves to be inadequate for any reason, he or she could be replaced under specific terms of the contract.

Selection of the best person for a corrections leadership position, with the anticipation of relatively long-term tenure, would help to provide the stability we need to manage and improve our highly volatile correctional systems. There is only room in our field for the best qualified professionals who are not only willing to invest a number of years to their posts and responsibilities, but may anticipate the opportunity to retain their positions long enough to implement and oversee much needed programs.

We are aware of the need for the governors to appoint persons who will be loyal to the administration. However, progress is usually effected when the best person is on the job without constant fear for survival in his or her post. Stability, continuity, and the opportunity for positive change without continual concern for job security are essential to fulfilling our responsibility to serve both the convicted offender and the public at large.[12]

For a number of decades, prison administrators have claimed, "If only I had the right staff, I could run a good prison in an old red barn." It seems that attention to this important area (pointed out as chief problems at Attica and New Mexico), is the touchstone to progress in our corrections system.

Prison Gangs: Something Old and Something New

Prison gangs have become a reflection of the street gangs found in America. The first gangs to be reported in prisons were found in Washington State in 1950, the *Gypsy Jokers* motorcycle gang. The second report on large gangs was from California, in 1957. These gangs were formed primarily along racial and ethnic lines, as well as by "bikers." Twelve years later, in Illinois, gangs began to appear in correctional institutions. This trend has continued in the 1970s and 1980s; the Department of Justice reported 114 individual gangs, with a total membership of over 12,000 in prisons nationwide in 1985. This study reported that gang members made up about 3 percent of prison populations in 1985.[13] Figure 26-4 shows the number of states with prison gangs in 1984. The figure reflects the most current data available.

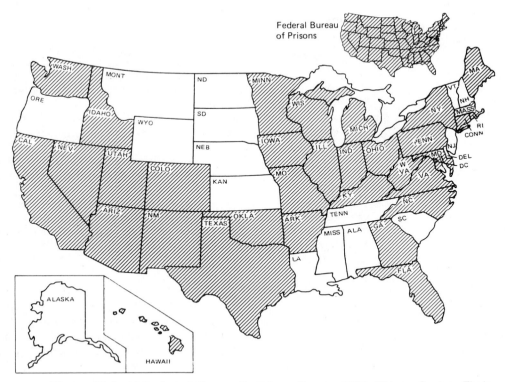

Figure 26-4 U.S. Jurisdictions with Prison Gangs, 1984 (*Prison Gangs: Their Extent, Nature and Impact on Prisons* [Washington, D.C.: U.S. Department of Justice, 1984])

Although the amount of illegal behavior by gangs varies considerably by jurisdiction, the problems gangs create are similar:

- Introduction and distribution of drugs;
- Intimidation of weaker inmates;
- Extortion and strong-arming;
- Violence associated with gang activities;
- Conflicts between gangs that create disturbances; and
- Contracted inmate murders.[14]

The study conducted by the Department of Justice made some specific recommendations about dealing with prison gangs:

1. Agencies should develop a general position (policy) and strategy concerning gangs.
2. Administrators should learn to detect early signs of gang activity and gang

members. Effective identification and tracking systems should be established or upgraded.

3. Models of gang control that have not worked under particular circumstances should be discarded and that information shared with other agencies to avoid replication of past failures. Models of gang control that have been successful under particular circumstances should also be shared so that they can be emulated as appropriate.

4. An overall screening system should be developed within an Interstate Compact clearinghouse to prevent difficulties such as spread of gangs, protective custody, jeopardy, etc.

5. Old, large, overcrowded prison facilities should be replaced with smaller facilities directly supervised by staff, thereby reducing the prisoners' perception that their "turf" is separate from staffs'.

6. Prison gang task forces have proven useful and should be extended to include other agencies and between agencies, regionally and nationally.

7. There should be a systematic debriefing procedure of former gang members to obtain pertinent and useful data, and a system for processing and using that data.[15]

It is clear from past efforts to control gangs that the most effective way to deal with them is try to establish good lines of communications between staff and gang members and to deal with the leadership of the gangs in a way that clearly indicates that the administration, not the gang, is in control. Problems with gangs will become more pressing as the prisons of America continue to become more and more overcrowded.

The Death of the Medical Model _____

Have we heard the death knell of the medical model in corrections?[16] Apparently so, if the research is to be believed. Bailey, Logan, and Martinson, among others, looked at hundreds of treatment programs evaluated over a broad scale of rigorousness and, given even biased evaluations the benefit of any doubt, concluded that none of these hundreds of rehabilitation programs was consistently effective.

The medical model in corrections was the outgrowth of the success of the biological and medical sciences, particularly in the last century. As the "ideology of evil" eroded in correctional practice, the medical model gradually became the dominant approach in correctional practices, especially over the last four decades. Wayson argued as follows:

> The social sciences, guided by an empiricist philosophy, led corrections to the individual in the search for the causes of crime, because he was "sick," "anti-social" or "deprived." One only had to describe the etiology of the disease and prescribe appropriate "cures." Philosophically, the approach denies free

will by positing that cultural, sociological, or psychological forces make the individual incapable of choosing. The objective of corrections, particularly incarceration, was to rehabilitate.[17]

Such significant correctional and criminal justice administrators and researchers as Raymond Procunier, Richard McGee, James Q. Wilson, David Fogel, and William Nagel are opposed to the medical model and/or its requisite, the indeterminate sentence.[18] Contemporary criticisms of the medical model do not follow political lines, and there are few distinctions between the right and left.

Increasingly, there are charges that institutions cannot rehabilitate, that prisoners are not sick, that incarceration does not cure, that treatment is a myth, and that nothing works. It might be better, conclude the disclaimers, if we faced reality and devoted our energies to more productive alternatives. Indeed, some states are seriously considering abandoning the existing models, including the parole board.[19] Sources of disaffection are numerous, and include *inter alia* researchers, inmates, courts, and economists.

The Fear of Crime: Where It Begins _____

Emphasis on violence in the media, instant visual coverage of criminal acts, and deterioration in the cities have intensified the public's fear of crime. It seems that these fears have been justified by the rising crime rates,[20] especially with regard to crimes of violence. The public has been told again and again that the majority of crimes are committed by individuals who have been arrested and processed through the correctional system before.[21] The inevitable result has been a loss of faith in the rehabilitative capability of our correctional systems and a cry for more punitive confinement. As noted in a brochure distributed by the United States Chamber of Commerce, "The conditions within many prisons achieve nothing but an increase in the number of recidivists (those released from institutions who commit additional crimes). Eighty percent of all felonies are committed by repeaters."[22] This kind of statement, though based on earlier facts, is damaging to the entire correctional system. It reflects, unfortunately, only the actions of those few offenders who passed through the entire correctional funnel and ended up in institutions.

We have already shown that those offenders who are selectively funneled into our prisons are the very ones most likely to return to criminal behavior. The increasing use of alternatives to incarceration is rapidly placing the largest portion of the correctional population outside the institution. Some diversionary and probation programs claim success rates as high as 60 to 90 percent. Because the offenders in these programs are not usually included in the calculations used to arrive at repeater rates, the public receives a distorted picture of the total system. Based on the figures above, an equally valid conclusion would be that offenders who participated in a noninstitutional program, or who were dealt with entirely outside the criminal justice system, were committing only 20 percent of the felonies. The point is that statistics can be interpreted in several ways, and the public's fear of the repeat offender is not often based on an accurate picture. Greater effort must be expended in the future to present the complete story to the public, so that they can understand the successes as well as the failures.

The reduction of public fear, when all the facts are presented, will help establish the value of alternatives to incarceration for most offenders. These facts will suggest that offenders who are not amenable to reintegration should be treated on the basis of their dangerousness, not simply as long as a specific sentence happens to last. Crime is a real danger, and some fear is certainly justified. But fear based on incomplete information can do more harm than good to the cause of safer streets.

Victims or Criminals? The Need for Change _____

Sexual and Physical Abuse of Children

When a child is abused by a parent, the traditional response has been to take action to remove the child from the family for placement in a juvenile care facility.[23] In rare cases these places are highly specialized centers in which the juvenile victim is given a chance to feel cared about. In most cases—far too many—the juvenile victim is processed in the same manner and by the same system as juvenile offenders are. It is small wonder that so many juvenile institutions are known as schools for crime.

Juvenile victims are hard pressed to understand that they are in an institution because of *parens patriae*—not to be punished, like others in the same environment. Embittered at being the only ones removed from the family and angry at being institutionalized, juveniles turn away from the authorities and toward the inmate subculture for support. Before the recognition of the need for "status offender" legislation, this was the familiar picture.

Society has begun to realize what has been done to juveniles who were victims of crime (abused children, incest victims, and children exploited for pornography, prostitution, and child labor). Today it is believed that family units should be maintained intact during treatment. The person to be punished for the crime clearly should not be the victim.

Victim advocates, along with many prosecutors across America, are looking at ways to provide for measures that will reduce stress for child victims of abuses. There have been many headline cases in the mid-1980s that have shown how treating child witnesses and victims in an insensitive manner can result in a weakening of the government's case. Great stress is put on the children. Figure 26-5 shows how legislation has handled testimony by child witnesses.

The National Institute of Justice holds that two areas need statutory reform:

- There should be an abolishment of special competency requirements for children, preferably through the establishment of a presumption that every witness is competent (as in the Federal Rules of Evidence). The determination of credibility should be left to the trier of fact.
- Legislatures should adopt special hearsay exceptions to admit certain out-of-court statements that do not fall within the existing exceptions to hearsay. These would not apply in every prosecution, but would be useful when a child freezes or recants on the witness stand, or when the defense asserts special exceptions for child victims of sexual abuse.[24]

As the problem with child sexual abuse becomes a growing major public issue, the field of corrections is faced with the problems of how to deal with the offenders in these emotionally charged crimes.

Victimless Crimes?

The handling of so-called *victimless* crimes has also come under close scrutiny and criticism. The users (victims) of drugs and alcohol are finding that the laws about possession and use of such substances are beginning to support decriminalization. Marijuana is the current target for decriminalization; or, in some cases there are statutory limits regarding how much marijuana may be possessed before the user becomes involved in a criminal act. Whether the use of "pot" is good or bad is not the question; those who use it are victims of the dealers of such substances, just as alcohol-users were victims of the bootleggers in the "roaring twenties." We do not advocate legalization or decriminalization of marijuana; we only posit this example as another case in which the victim of illegal activity becomes the one most often punished.

Prostitution is another "victimless" crime that does indeed have victims. The prostitute is victimized by the pimps who profit financially from her way of life. The customer may also be seen as a victim—of uncontrollable urges and a convincing sales pitch. Both of these "victims" of victimless crime can be, and are, punished as offenders. Prostitution has become an even more dangerous trade, as the prostitute is subject to the consequences of infection with the AIDS virus and the "John" faces the same problem. AIDS is thus a potential *death sentence* for this victimless crime.

FIGURE 26-5   Statutory Provisions Relevant to Child Witnesses in Sexual Abuse Cases*

	AL	AK	AZ	AR	CA	CO	CT	DE	DC	FL	GA	HI	ID	IL	IN	IA	KS	KY	LA	ME	MD	MA	MI	MN	MS	MO
LIVE TESTIMONY																										
Competency																										
• child < 14, court determines																										
• child < 10, court determines			S		S,2								S	S					S,3				S	S,4		S,2
• child competent if understands oath	S,R	R						C			S	S														
• competent if understands oath					R		C							C		S,R	S	S		R		S				
• every person competent			R	S	R		R			S												S	R		S	
Abused child hearsay exception																										
• child's age (in years)		<10			<15									<13	<10	M								<10		
• court finds reliable																	S							S		
• child testifies		S			S									S	S									S		
• child unavailable, statement corroborated		S			S										S			5							S	
• notice of introduction		S			S										S									S		
Exclusion of spectators from courtroom																										
• victim/witness age (in years)	any	≤16	any		any					<16	any			<13					≤15			<18	any	<18	any	
• during testimony only		S			6					S				S					S				9			
• public transcript provided	S	S			S																					
• media exception		S								S				S						8						
• family, guardian, moral support exceptions	S				S					S									S							
MECHANICAL TESTIMONY																										
Videotaped testimony admissible																										
• child's age (in years)	≤16	<15	<17	<15	<15					<16								≤12		<14						
• defendant's presence specified	S	S	S		S					S								9		S						
• opportunity for cross-examination specified	S		S		10															S						
• court findings required (footnote)			11	12	13					14										15						
• court findings include unavailability				S	S																					
• government may call child to testify			S															NO								
• other (footnote)		20			21															22						
Closed circuit testimony available																										
• child's age (in years)																		≤12		≤14						
• defendant present, but child cannot hear or see																		S		S						
• attorneys present																		S		S						
Abused child videotape/film hearsay exception																										
• child's age (in years)																		≤12		≤14						
• no attorneys present at taping																		S		S						
• interviewer/child available to testify																		S		S						

Source: Statutes were provided by State governments in the fall of 1984.

* Except for age limits, all numbers refer to footnotes.
See Figure §§-§ for statutory citations and a brief description of related laws *not* included on the chart.

1. State most likely uses "14-year-old" common law standard.
2. Exception: A child victim of a sexual offense is a competent witness and shall be allowed to testify without prior qualification in any judicial proceeding involving the alleged offense. Trier of fact is to determine the weight and credibility to be given to the testimony.
3. Child under 12 years may not testify under oath unless court is satisfied that child understands the nature of an oath.
4. Exception for sexual abuse cases repealed. New language reads: "A child describing any act of sexual contact or penetration performed on or with the child by another may use language appropriate for a child of that age."
5. Corroboration is *not* required.
6. This provision applies to the preliminary hearing.
7. This provision provides for in-camera testimony.
8. Exception for a reasonable but limited number of members of the public.

FIGURE 26-5 *Continued*

	MT	NE	NV	NH	NJ	NM	NY	NC	ND	OH	OK	OR	PA	RI	SC	SD	TN	TX	UT	VT	VA	WA	WV	WI	WY
LIVE TESTIMONY																									
Competency																									
• child < 14, court determines				C,1											C,1	C,1				C,1		C,1			
• child < 10, court determines						S,3				S,R								S,2				S			S
• child competent if understands oath																	R								
• competent if understands oath	R			R				R								S			R						
• every person competent		S	S		S	R			R		S	S	S			S					R			S	R
Abused child hearsay exception																									
• child's age (in years)																<10		M				<10			
• court finds reliable																S		S				S			
• child testifies																S		S				S			
• child unavailable, statement corroborated																S		S				S			
• notice of introduction																						S			
Exclusion of spectators from courtroom																									
• victim/witness age (in years)	any			<16				any	any	any						M				any		any			
• during testimony only				10					S							S								6	
• public transcript provided				S																					
• media exception																S									
• family, guardian, moral support exceptions																								S	
MECHANICAL TESTIMONY																									
Videotaped testimony admissible																									
• child's age (in years)						≤13	≤12			≤12						≤15		≤12						<18	
• defendant's presence specified	S					S				S								9						S	
• opportunity for cross-examination specified	10					S				S						S								S	
• court findings required (footnote)							16	17										18						19	
• court findings include unavailability																S									
• government may call child to testify						NO				NO								NO						S	
• other (footnote)	23					24	25											21							
Closed circuit testimony available																									
• child's age (in years)										≤12								≤12							
• defendant present, but child cannot hear or see										S								S							
• attorneys present										S								S							
Abused child videotape/film hearsay exception																									
• child's age (in years)																≤12									
• no attorneys present at taping																S									
• interviewer/child available to testify																S									

KEY **S** = Statute (includes codified rules)   **C** = Case law only
        R = Rule of evidence (not codified)   **M** = Minor; child

9. Defendant present, but the court to ensure child cannot hear or see defendant.
10. Testimony to be taken under the Rules of Evidence.
11. Court order "for good cause shown."
12. Court finding "that further testimony would cause the victim emotional trauma so that the victim is medically unavailable . . ."
13. Upon application, court to make preliminary finding whether "the victim is likely to be medically unavailable or otherwise unavailable . . ."; at trial, court to find whether, "further testimony would cause the victim emotional trauma so that the victim is medically unavailable or otherwise unavailable . . ."
14. Court finding that, "there is substantial likelihood that such victim or witness would suffer severe or emotional distress if required to testify in open court."
15. Court "expressly finds that the emotional or psychological well-being of the person would be substantially impaired if the person were to testify at trial."

(continued)

Figure 26-5 Statutory Provisions Relevant to Child Witnesses in Sexual Abuse Cases*
Cont.

16. Court Rule. Court order upon, "Showing that the child may be unable to testify without suffering unreasonable and unnecessary mental or emotional harm." (Statute. Court order "for good cause shown.")
17. For a child witness 12 years old or under, testimony may be videotaped *without* court findings. For a witness greater than 12 years old, court must find the witness "is likely to suffer severe emotional or mental distress if required to testify in person . . ."
18. Court finding that "further testimony would cause the victim emotional trauma, or that the victim is otherwise unavailable . . . or that such testimony would . . . be substantially detrimental to the well-being of the victim . . ."
19. Court order where "there is a substantial likelihood that the child will otherwise suffer emotional or mental strain."
20. The videotapes are listed as an exception to hearsay in R. Evid. R. 804.
21. Testimony to be videotaped at preliminary hearing.
22. Stenographical testimony or other court approved means also available. Videotapes are specified in the videotape law as an exception to hearsay.
23. Victim in prosecutions for sexual intercourse without consent if victim is less than 16 years; deviate sexual conduct, incest (no age specified).
24. Videotapes are specified in the videotape law as an exception to hearsay.
25. Videotape law applies to testimony presented to the Grand Jury.

Domestic Violence: Who Is the Victim?

Domestic violence has always been a part of American society. The changing roles of marriage partners; the changing attitudes toward the treatment of wives as other than property; and the attitude of regarding family disputes as private business have caused a crisis in local corrections. As shown in the box, there are serious consequences from the so-called "domestic" call to which the police respond. In most jurisdictions today, *both* parties are taken into custody and the judge is required to sort out who did what to whom. These formerly "victimless" events are now a major problem for the correctional administrator who already has to deal with an overflowing facility.

A more realistic approach to these "victimless" crimes is now being taken, but the tide of public opinion is hard to turn. From the standpoint of pragmatic correctional administration, removing these victims from the already overcrowded systems, both juvenile and adult, would help to relieve some of the deadly pressures that now plague corrections.

The Role of Research in Corrections _____

One of the handicaps to correctional reform is the lack of conclusive evidence as to which techniques work and which do not. Although many extensive research projects have attempted to explain, or justify, one or another of the hundreds of different approaches to correctional rehabilita-

---

FAMILY VIOLENCE

The family is the fundamental unit of American life. Thus, public policies that support the family are imperative for the survival of our society. To help families thrive within our communities, we must address the serious problem of family violence.

Family violence too often shatters families from all walks of life. Once considered a "hands off" issue, to be dealt with in the privacy of a family, these cases increasingly are brought to the criminal courts. No longer viewed simply as disagreements, arguments, or "family spats," they are recognized as violent crimes with victims suffering physical and psychological scars.

Research has found that such violence often continues and escalates over time, becoming both more frequent and more severe. Spouse abuse can mean a push down the stairs, a kick in the abdomen, a series of beatings, or even murder. One study found that in over 50 percent of domestic homicides, the police had previously been called to the residence five times or more.

Recent National Institute of Justice research has found that arresting the abuser can deter future violence in families. By making informed decisions based on careful evaluation of police methods, it appears that policies can either contribute to the decline or escalation of violent assault within the family.

Judges play a critical role in forming the criminal justice reaction to this kind of violence. Spouse abuse has traditionally been handled in family court. As police departments increasingly have developed arrest policies for both misdemeanor and felony domestic assault, more family violence cases are being heard before criminal court judges.

Within their own courtrooms, judges determine the kind of attention paid to family violence cases by probation agencies. They ensure that court orders and probation agreements are monitored closely. Special statutory provisions for protection orders are available in some jurisdictions. Judges can have an impact simply by talking to the parties involved in family violence cases.

Both the President's Task Force on Victims of Crime and the Attorney General's Task Force on Family Violence recognized that family violence is often much more complex in causes and solutions than crimes committed by unknown assailants.

James K. Stewart
Director
National Institute of Justice
Source: U.S. Department of Justice, *Confronting Domestic Violence: The Role of Criminal Court Judges* Washington, D.C. (November 1986), p. 1.

---

tion, most results are still inconclusive. In his massive examination of correctional research, Robert Martinson pointed out the crux of the evaluation problem in the field:

> In sum, even in the case of treatment programs administered outside penal institutions, we simply cannot say that this treatment in itself has an appreciable effect on offender behavior. On the other hand, there is one encouraging set of findings that emerges from these studies. For from many of them there flows the strong suggestion that even if we can't "treat" offenders so as to

make them do better, a great many of the programs designed to rehabilitate them at least did not make them do *worse*. And if these programs did not show the advantages of actually rehabilitating, some of them did have the advantage of being less onerous to the offender himself without seeming to pose increased danger to the community. And some of these programs—especially those involving less restrictive custody, minimal supervision, and early release—simply cost fewer dollars to administer. The information on the dollar costs of these programs is just beginning to be developed but the implication is clear: *that if we can't do more for (and to) offenders, at least we can safely do less.*

There is, however, one important caveat even to this note of optimism: In order to calculate the true costs of these programs, one must in each case include not only their administrative cost but also the cost of maintaining in the community an offender population increased in size. This population might well not be committing new offenses at any greater rate; but the offender population might, under some of these plans, be larger in absolute *numbers*. So the total number of offenses committed might rise, and our chances of victimization might therefore rise too. We need to be able to make a judgment about the size and probable duration of this effect; as of now, we simply do not know. . . .

[A] pattern has run through much of this discussion—of studies which "found" effects without making any truly rigorous attempt to exclude competing hypotheses, of extraneous factors permitted to intrude upon the measurements, of recidivism measures which are not all measuring the same thing, "of follow-up" periods which vary enormously and rarely extend beyond the period of legal supervision, of experiments never replicated, of "system effects" not taken into account, of categories drawn up without any theory to guide the enterprise. It is just possible that some of our treatment programs *are* working to some extent, but that our research is so bad that it is incapable of telling.[25]

There have been massive attacks on the problems of corrections since the end of WWII—which produced new methods of helping people as well as killing them. These efforts have ensured that change is here to stay and that the search for real solutions will continue. There is no doubt that correctional research has already altered many beliefs and practices with regard to the handling of inmates. Further research should be structured around specific objectives. As noted in 1973, still valid today, "two complementary sources of research are required to meet correction's continuing needs":

First, research must be incorporated as an integral instrument of correctional management. Modern administration depends on the collection and analysis of information as a basis for policy formulation and a guide for specific decisions. No information system can replace the decision maker, but availability of selected information, carefully interpreted, offers an invaluable aid to his reason and judgment. Every correctional manager should be afforded the tools of research methodology and the degree of objectivity an agency research program can provide.

Second, there is need for research done outside the agency. Not all sources of innovation can be found within the confines of any one agency or system. Continued improvement of corrections can be expected only from the application of new ideas and models derived from basic research and prototype projects. The support of such research by national funding agencies insures contribution of ideas from the private sector, the academic community, and other sources. Also required is a continuing hospitality to the conduct of research in the operating correctional agencies.

Research alone cannot create a new day in corrections. It offers the administrator opportunity to learn from the mistakes of others. The administrator's task in attempting to meet needs as they arise is to utilize tools with which innovations are forged.[26]

Research alone cannot solve the problems of correctional administrators. In some cases it may even dash cherished hopes and beliefs. But the knowledge gained can be used to progress in a sound, scientific manner.

Predictions of Future Trends _____

As American corrections edges toward the 1990s, prison populations are at an all-time high. In addition, a greater percentage of the population is incarcerated in the United States than in any other major Western nation. Per-bed construction costs are soaring to an average of as high as $100,000 per cell.[27] The per-capita costs of the nation's total criminal justice system average slightly over $126 in 1987. In California alone, often considered to be the national trend setter, the total male felon population has rocketed to over 67,514. It is projected that California will have a 16,500-bed deficit by 1992.[28] The $1.878 billion budget for the California Department of Corrections suggests an annual cost per inmate of over $17,338. In the early 1970s, one out of ten of its convicted felons was committed to California prisons; by the end of the 1980s, this number will grow to one out of three (see box).

GOING TO PRISON IN AMERICA

Criminals are increasingly likely to be imprisoned for their crimes later in the 1980s than before. Bureau of Justice Director Stephen Schlesinger noted that there is evidence that criminal justice policies have had this effect:

In 1980 there were 25 offenders committed to prison for every 1,000 murders, nonnegligent manslaughters, rapes, robberies, aggravated assaults and burglaries reported to police. By 1986 there were 43 prison commitments for every 1,000 such offenses.

Source: Bureau of Justice Statistics, *Prisoners in 1987* (Washington, D.C.: U.S. Department of Justice, 1988), p. 1.

Though these kinds of statistics are unnerving, extrapolations based on current trends for the year 2000 are even more ominous. The national prison population could reach 1.2 million! California prisons, even with a mere 6 percent growth rate, could exceed a population of 100,000 by the year 2000. Even with modest inflation rates, construction costs per bed could soar to over $110,000, not including debt service charges. The average annual cost per inmate could exceed $46,000, and the national per-capita cost for the criminal justice system could exceed $370. Although these are simple straight-line projections, they are useful indicators of some of the fiscal and space problems corrections may experience by the year 2000.

Policy Options and Implications

Departments of corrections have no choice but to accept court commitments.[29] The problems of scarcity of beds, prison overcrowding, lawsuits, and Eighth Amendment prohibitions (to say nothing of the problems of meeting minimum standards in the current accreditation movement) will dictate proactive administrative policies to protect institutions and inmates. Prisons can be constructed and renovated, but voters can defeat bond issues, resist taxes, and oppose prison construction in their local areas. It is becoming clear that resources are finite and that corrections will have to do more with less, as is true in every other segment of the government.

Corrections agencies will need to adopt a variety of defensive policies: probation subsidies to strengthen local corrections; split sentencing; use of paraprofessionals and volunteers; shock probation and shock parole; community-based residential facilities; and probation services for courts on an "as requested" basis.[30] These measures can only slow the crisis; they cannot eliminate the problem. The courts have used a somewhat remarkable process for diverting and deferring the costs from local government levels . . . and bucking the problem up to the state level, that simple process is commitment to *state* institutions.

As present trends continue, policies designed to purchase local correctional services from the private sector seem to be a viable option. Innovations include probation and diversion agencies and programs, halfway houses, community corrections centers, women's detention centers, jails, workhouses, and other community-based correctional programs. Adopting these programs can be accomplished piecemeal through subsidies, purchase of service plans, and cost-sharing programs. They can be done on a regional basis initially through planning commissions and consolidation.

Another spur for change would be providing minimum correctional standards for jails and legislation, giving authority for jail inspection to the state. Though some local autonomy in operations could be maintained, the basic policy would be to place local corrections under state control.

Community Corrections and the Private Sector Must Continue to Help
(Courtesy Pioneer Human Services)

Probationlike services could be concentrated in the state departments of corrections by implementing disposition contracts. This process would be initiated at the point of adjudication of guilt, but before sentencing. A state-operated probation department would, after a presentence report, assessment of offender risk and needs, and investigation of community resources, design a detailed reintegration plan and present it to the sentencing judge in the form of a contract. Both defense and prosecuting counsels would be active in the preparation of the proposed contract. The court would order the plan's implementation, retaining the authority to revoke the plan and to commit violators of the terms to a flat prison sentence. Offenders who reject the plan's terms would be sentenced to a flat term with no mandatory parole or parole services.

Other Innovations

Criminologists and correctional practitioners have, in general, concentrated on changing offenders but not on understanding human behavior.[31] In the next decade, surely before the year 2000, the focus will shift to human behavior, and interdisciplinary study of criminal behavior will be commonplace. Breakthroughs have already occurred in fields as diverse as physiology, dietetics, ecology, pharmacology, psychology, and physics.[32] Departments of criminology, criminal justice, and corrections in the colleges and universities of America are adjusting their curricula to the changing interdisciplinary thrusts. The focus on the biosocial, physiopharmacological, and biological dimensions of behavior raise formidable ethical,[33] moral, and legal questions in regard to application. The Bill of Rights may well be called into question if physical means for behavioral modification are applied.

On the other hand, surveys since 1948 have suggested that the Bill of Rights does not enjoy the widespread popular support it had in the nation's early years. Issues such as fear of crime, the Supreme Court's continuing pressure for individual rights in the face of the state's power, a conservative backlash in politics, increases in crime known to the police, an apparent failure to lower recidivism rates, along with the general disenchantment with the criminal justice process—all of these could coalesce into a public demand for a constitutional convention. It is possible that the rights and immunities enjoyed by Americans in general may be vastly altered by such a convention. It is necessary that the problem of crime be addressed more effectively, for personal rights and protections in America might become threatened if it is not.

We note that we have not been able to cover every possible change in corrections and the criminal justice system. We have not had space for likely developments in victim-compensation programs, crime insurance (somewhat like major medical insurance), the stepped-up use of capital punishment,[34] urban redesign and redevelopment, crime prevention through environmental design, the rapid expansion of probation, and the demise of mandatory parole services. These exclusions were intentional as they cover subjects currently in a stage of flux, more properly covered in other volumes.

Privatization of Corrections: A New Direction?

The current move toward privatization of corrections systems in America is controversial. There are strong advocates on both sides. Privatization refers to a process wherein the government relies on private corporations to construct and manage prisons and jails for an agreed-upon fee. There are sharply divided opinions in the field regarding the efficacy of using the private sector to implement public policy and public service.

As noted by the Director of the National Institute of Justice:

> Overcrowding and the escalating costs of American prisons and jails are among the factors prompting public officials and the private sector to experiment with new alliances in the field of corrections. Corrections departments have long relied on private vendors to furnish specific institutional services or to operate aftercare facilities and programs. But they now are turning to the private sector for help in financing new construction and in managing primary confinement facilities.
>
> Some of the controversial issues of such arrangements—quality, accountability, security, and cost—have been hotly debated and widely reported in the news

media, including *Newsweek, The Wall Street Journal,* and *Cable News Network.* Only fragments of experience, however, have been documented, and no comprehensive discussion of the issues has been available.

Administrative issues such as accountability and flexibility, legal issues such as authority, liability, security, and contract specificity, and financial issues such as efficiency, profitability, and visibility all remain to be settled before widespread privatization of the corrections field takes place.[35]

The report by the National Institute of Justice points out five circumstances under which careful experimentation with private sector facilities may work out:

1. *Rapid mobilization.* Given the widely acknowledged ability of the private sector to move more rapidly to bring additional facilities and man-power on-line, combined with the uncertainty that surrounds future population trends, contracting may be useful at the State level to avoid permanent facility expansion but still accommodate near-term population shifts.
2. *Experimentation.* An agency can test new models of institutional corrections practice without making a permanent commitment or laboring under the constraints to innovation typically present in traditional corrections bureaucracies.
3. *Decentralization.* Greater geographic and programmatic diversity may be possible by calling on local contractors rather than trying to provide the same community-oriented services under the direct control of a centralized agency.
4. *Specialization.* The flexibility of private contractors to satisfy unique demands suggests that contracting for the confinement of offenders with special needs may offer significant relief to general-purpose institutions as well as more opportunities for the successful treatment of the special "management" inmate.
5. *Regionalization.* Finally, the private sector is not typically bound by the jurisdictional politics that might otherwise impede efforts to develop shared facilities among States or counties within a State.[36]

Summary _____

The main response to crime in the corrections systems of America has been to place the offender in a penitentiary. This sort of response has been persistent, but in terms of reintegration of offenders into the free community, it has been an unsuccessful one. The industrial prisons that were built with such great expectations in the nineteenth century were not designed for reintegration, and efforts to make them serve that purpose have failed. In recent years, the advent of community-based treatment has created a correctional revolution in America, even during a period of skyrocketing populations in our fortress prisons.

The new correctional goals of rehabilitation and reintegration are difficult, if not impossible, to attain in the maximum security institution. The validity of these goals was reinforced with the infusion of many middle- and upper-class persons into the jails and prisons of America in the turbulent 1960s, primarily for drug offenses and civil disobedience. The problems of criminalization and prisonization are also addressed by the new correctional concepts. The maximum use of diversion from the criminal justice system allows many nondangerous offenders to receive treatment and support without incurring the stigma of a criminal record. The negative effects of a criminal record have been examined in detail, and the next great move in this area will be some form of mandatory expungement, after the ex-offender has lived in the community for a specified period of time without criminal involvement.

The correctional systems in America are slowly moving away from a philosophy that emphasized treatment aimed at the nonviolent offender's individual problems and toward punishment aimed at the offense. There is great pressure to punish the violent offender, with overcrowded prisons nearing the boiling point as a result. We look forward to writing about the outcome of this situation in a later edition.

It is hard to break down the boundaries between felonies and misdemeanors, federal and state crimes, and federal, state, and local correctional systems. All of these divisions encourage the development of separate policies, separate programs, separate systems, and separate drains on fiscal and personnel resources. It will probably be some time before individual offenders are treated in a network of separate programs and facilities geared toward classes of offenders, not offenses or jurisdictions. This movement is slowly getting underway, however, and it clearly heralds the direction of corrections in the next decades. It will be up to the professionals in the field to ensure that the new approaches do not jeopardize public safety and to provide alternatives for those who refuse to be reintegrated. It is a big job, but it represents the only effective solution to America's rising crime problem. The last chapter will address a few of the major problems that face the correctional administrator as we enter the 1990s and move toward the 21st century.

Review Questions

1. Why did the Attica and New Mexico prison riots have such impact upon corrections in the 1980's?
2. Why did the LEEA program have such a limited impact on the correctional systems in America?
3. What contribution did the American Correctional Association have in regard to national policy for the field of corrections?

Key Terms

NOTES

1. D. Williams, M. Kasindorf, and P. Katell, "The Killing Ground," *Newsweek* (February 8, 1980): 66–68. See also Ted Gest, "Bulging Prisons: Curbing Crime—Or Wasting Lives?" *U.S. News and World Report* (April 23, 1984): 42–45.
2. James Stewart, *Research Program Plan* (Washington, D.C.: National Institute of Justice, U.S. Department of Justice, 1987). The address of the National Institute of Justice is 633 Indiana Avenue NW, Washington, D.C. 20534. Additional technical assistance, research, and dissimenation efforts are to be found at the National Institute of Corrections, 320 First Street NW, Washington, D.C. 20534.
3. See in particular: Edmund McGarrell and Timothy Flanagan, "Measuring and Explaining Legislator Crime Control Ideology," *Journal of Research in Crime and Delinquency* 24 (1987): 102–118.
4. The complete text of each of the currently ratified National Policies on Corrections is contained in Appendix B.
5. Thomas McConnell, Charles Page, and John Kohls, "Entry-Level Selection and Training Standards Project," *American Jails* 3 (1987): 35–38.
6. Joint Commission on Correctional Manpower and Training, *Targets for In-Service Training* (Washington, D.C.: JCCMT, 1968), p. 1.
7. Ibid., p. 3.
8. The United States Attorney General mandated Department of Justice assistance in October 1981.
9. Federal Bureau of Prisons, *Federal Prison System 1982* (Lompoc, Calif.: U.S. Department of Justice, 1984), pp. 2, 6, 8–9.
10. Joseph Scott and Pamela Bennett, *Ex-Offenders As Parole Officers: An Evaluation of the Parole Officer Case Aide Program in Ohio* (Columbus: Ohio State University Research Foundation, 1973), p. 95.
11. The average length of service of heads of departments of corrections is 3.6 years. George Camp and Camille Camp, *The Corrections Yearbook 1987* (South Salem, N.Y.: Criminal Justice Institute, 1987), p. 42.
12. A. Travisono, "Building Correctional Leadership," *On the Line* 2 (May 1979): 1.
13. United States Department of Justice, *Prison Gangs: Their Nature, Extent and Impact on Prisons* (Washingtion, D.C.: U.S. Government Printing Office, 1985), p. vii.
14. Ibid., p. xi.
15. Ibid., p. xix.
16. Much of this section was drawn from Harry Allen and Nick Gatz, "Abandoning

the Medical Model in Corrections: Some Implications and Alternatives," *Prison Journal* 54 (Autumn 1974): 4–14.

17. William Wayson, "Correctional Myths and Economic Realities," *Proceedings, The Second National Workshop on Correctional and Parole Administration* (College Park, Md.: American Correctional Association, 1974), pp. 26–27. See also Bruce Cory and Stephen Gettinger, *Time to Build? The Realities of Prison Construction* (New York: Edna McConnell Clark Foundation, 1984).

18. Technically, this is incorrect, for the indeterminate sentence exists in many states that have abandoned the medical model. Jail-time credit, earned-time credit for good behavior, and credit for exemplary or participatory behavior can reduce even presumptive sentences by up to 50 percent—without the medical model! See John Hepburn and Lynne Goodstein, "Organizational Imperatives and Sentencing Reform Implementation: The Impact of Prison Practices and Priorities on the Attainment of the Objectives of Determinate Sentencing," *Crime and Delinquency* 32 (1986): 339–366.

19. Both Maine and Connecticut have abandoned parole boards as discretionary releasing authorities.

20. Crimes known to the police, as reported through the Federal Bureau of Investigation's *Uniform Crime Reports,* show that crime in the United States has declined over four of the last five years.

21. About one-half of all prison admissions do not return for subsequent reincarcerations. Patrick Lanagan and Lawrence Greenfield, *The Prevalence of Imprisonment* (Washington, D.C.: U.S. Department of Justice, 1985), p. 2. Also, the idea that career criminals perpetrate many and varied crimes, contributing disproportionately to the volume of crime in America, has been sharply called into question. Michael Gottfredson and Travis Hirschi, "The True Value of Lambda Would Appear to be Zero," *Criminology* 24 (1986): 213.

22. Chamber of Commerce of the United States, *Marshalling Citizen Power to Modernize Corrections* (Washington, D.C.: CCUS, 1973), p. 5.

23. James Spearly and Michael Lauderdale, "Community Characteristics and Ethnicity in the Prediction of Child Maltreatment Rates," *Child Abuse and Neglect* 7 (1983): 91–105.

24. The most recent bibliography for correctional treatment, management, community corrections, and so on is available in Office Development, Testing and Dissemination, *Putting Research to Work: Tools for the Criminal Justice Professional* (Washington, D.C.: U.S. Department of Justice, 1984), pp. 25–36.

25. Robert Martinson, "What Works?—Questions and Answers about Prison Reform," *Public Interest* (Spring 1974): p. 173.

26. National Advisory Commission on Criminal Justice Standards and Goals, *Corrections* (Washington, D.C.: U.S. Government Printing Office, 1973), p. 496.

27. If a bed in a correctional facility cost $30,000 and was financed by a state bond at, for example, 10 percent interest for thirty years, the true cost of building that bed would be $120,000.

28. This may be an underestimate, as the prison population is increasing by 400 inmates per month. To keep abreast of the current levels of commitment, California would have to open a 600-bed facility every six weeks! A rule of thumb in prison construction is that it takes six years for an institution to come on-line ("open"), beginning with the decision to build, through to a state's accepting the facility from the builder. See Harry Allen, "Intensive Supervised

Release from California Prisons: A Partial Solution to Prison Overcrowding."
Paper presented at the annual meeting of the Western Society of Criminology,
Monterey, Calif., February 27, 1988.

29. Milton Rector, "NCCD Urges America's Judges to Use Their Power to Move
Nation Away from Prison Use," *Corrections Digest* 10 (October 26, 1979): 1, 7–8.
30. Richard Allison, "Current Trends in Community Corrections: Favored Strategies
and Promising Projects," *Criminal Justice Newsletter* 10 (September 10, 1978): 1–3.
31. C. R. Jeffery, "Biology and Crime: The New Neo-Lombrosians," in C. R. Jeffery,
ed., *Biology and Crime* (Beverly Hills, Calif.: Sage Publications, 1979), pp. 7–18.
32. Alexander Schauss, *Nutrition and Behavior: A Biosociological Perspective: Implications for Criminology* (Tacoma: American Institute for Biosocial Research,
1982).
33. Dennis Longmire, "Ethical Dilemmas in the Research Setting," *Criminology* 23
(1983): 333–348.
34. Stephen Gettinger, "The Death Penalty Is Back—And So Is the Debate," *Corrections Magazine* 5 (June 1979): 70–78.
35. J. K. Stewart, National Institute of Justice: *Corrections and the Private Sector*
(Washington, D.C.: Department of Justice, 1984), p. 1.
36. Ibid., p. 7.

Recommended Readings _____

Baird, Christopher, Douglas Holien, and Audrey Bakke. *Fees for Probation Services.*
Washington, D.C.: U.S. Department of Justice, 1986.
Gibbons, Don. *The Limits of Punishment as Social Policy.* San Francisco, Calif.:
National Council on Crime and Delinquency, 1988.
Gottfredson, Stephen, and Sean McConville. *America's Correctional Crisis: Prison
Populations and Public Policy.* Westport, Conn.: Greenwood Press, 1987.
McCarthy, Belinda, (ed.) *Intermediate Punishments.* Monsey, N.Y.: Criminal Justice
Press, 1987.
Petersilia, Joan. *Expanding Options for Criminal Sentencing.* Santa Monica, Calif.:
Rand Corporation, 1987.
Petersilia, Joan, and Susan Turner. *Prison Versus Probation in California.* Santa
Monica, Calif.: Rand Corporation, 1986.

Big Questions: Hard Answers

While numerous factors have contributed to the increase in prison populations, criminal justice policy changes may be the most obvious and controllable factor. . . . When legislators expand the concept of criminality, set harsher penalties, institute determinate and mandatory sentencing, abolish or restrict parole release, and eliminate good-time credit, they must accept the consequences that longer sentences will be served and prison populations will grow.
—CONGRESSMAN ROBERT W. KASTENMEIR

Overcrowding Is the Major Problem: What to Do?

While the stock market plunged in October 1987, the population in state and federal adult institutions soared to new heights. By the time this book is printed, that population will surely exceed 600,000 and will continue to climb. In a system already bursting at the seams, we find correctional institutions, jails, camps, and detention facilities struggling to stay simply overcrowded and avoid the status of *crisis* crowding. This problem, more than any other, will influence the administrators of the 1990s. As a nation that already incarcerates more of its citizens than every other major westernized country, the United States needs to reevaluate where it is going in the field of corrections and then assess the social, fiscal, and human costs that this problem creates.

It has been estimated that a correctional facility (jail or prison) loses all flexibility in classification and assignment when the population reaches 90 percent of its rated capacity. What occurs then is simply "bed-availability assignment," resulting in persons who are not known for their ability to get along with others being assigned in a totally *random* fashion. When one considers that most correctional facilities in America are running at *over 110 percent* of capacity (some as high as 180 to 200 percent), it is clear that any planning for the handling of offenders is lost in the effort simply to *feed* these overpopulations. Perhaps treatment is not really dead; it just cannot survive in this kind of an environment.

Corrections Remains a Team Effort (Courtesy of American Correctional Association, photo by Michael C. Dersin)

The staff and management of jails and prisons are not the only ones affected by overcrowding. As noted by James Q. Wilson:

> Overcrowding is also of obvious concern to the large majority of prisoners who, in effect, become subject to harsher punishment as a result of the crowded conditions. Indeed, unreasonable crowding is one of the most frequently used bases for declaring a particular prison's conditions in violation of the Eighth Amendment's prohibition against "cruel and unusual punishment."[1]

This is a telling argument for the dangers that are associated with over-crowded and otherwise substandard conditions. The situation is further exacerbated by the rules of choice that must prevail if there is to be any logic in the assignment of offenders to incarceration as their punishment.

When there are more "customers" (offenders) than there are beds to serve them, the sanction of imprisonment must be reserved for those who are repeated offenders, or for those who commit the most serious crimes. With the great prison population growth in the 1970s and 1980s, this strategy has resulted in the prisons and jails being filled with a much different mixture of violent/nonviolent offenders than had been the case before. The ratio of those who have committed "crimes against property" and "crimes against the person" has more than been reversed in most jurisdictions, with many facilities holding, 75–80 percent of the latter. This does not bode well for the already understaffed, undertrained, and under-financed penal institutions in America. The answer, to date, has been to continue to build more and more institutions. Even with the opening of a new jail or prison in America almost every week for the past few years, the "correctional funnel" works in reverse to fill up every bed available!

Can Government Continue to Build Indefinitely?

The population problem in jails and prisons has gotten so bad that seldom are these words seen in the news unless they are preceded by the adjective overcrowded. The problem is not so easy to solve as it sounds. Not only are new facilities needed, but the old facilities are also frequently so decrepit that it would cost as much to make them constitutionally adequate as it would to build new ones. This is especially true in the case of jails, most of which were built before the 1950s and which are unable to be converted to meet contemporary standards. If this is the case, why do we not just abandon the old facilities and concentrate on building new ones?

It is a sad fact of life that most citizens wish to have more and more of their neighbors locked up, and for longer times than in the past. *But* (and this is critical to gaining an understanding of the problem), people do not want them locked up anywhere near their neighborhoods! Trying to get approval to build a new jail or prison in a community that is not desperate for the construction and correctional jobs is a long and difficult task. In Monroe, Washington, for example, there are now three major correctional institutions on "the hill," sharing an area with the state reformatory.[2] Such siting was due in part to the difficulty of finding a community close to a major population center (such as Seattle and Everett) that would allow them to be sited. This problem is often more acute when it is desirable to place a jail, work release center, or halfway house in a *community* setting.

If the states are not to continue to build an infinite number of jails and prisons, then policy issues must be addressed as to who is to be incarcer-

Modular Prisons May Be One Answer to Overcrowding (Courtesy of American Correctional Association, photo by David Skipper)

ated, for how long, and at what level of security. The major policy decision might be to avoid the tendency to use whatever space is available to the maximum, regardless of the outcome. If police are more efficient in *catching* criminals, prosecutors more efficient in *charging* criminals, and judges more efficient in *convicting* criminals, then the correctional system will be engulfed in a flood of inmates that it cannot possibly manage. Nevertheless, the system tries to keep up with the demand by inventing new construction strategies and methods of expansion.

New Construction Strategies

California presents a prime example of the pressing need for expansion in its state facilities. The largest state in the nation in population had not built a new prison since before 1965. In 1985 they set into motion plans to build 25,000 additional bed spaces in 14 new institutions (13 for men, 1 for women). The estimated cost of these projects shall exceed $1.8 *billion* between 1985 and 1990! The California Department of Corrections commissioned a major study to look into a number of different construction methods, deciding on a system of factory-produced concrete components.[3] These methods produce a campus-style atmosphere with single occupancy and dormitory versions of the same basic configuration (see Figures 27-1 and 27-2).

The first units of this plan were installed in the old (1955) California Medical facility at Vacaville, a high-security facility specializing in medical and psychiatric treatment. The Department was able to construct and open a new 300-bed addition in just 8 months, and then were able to add 900 more beds in less than a year. This experience shows that construction of

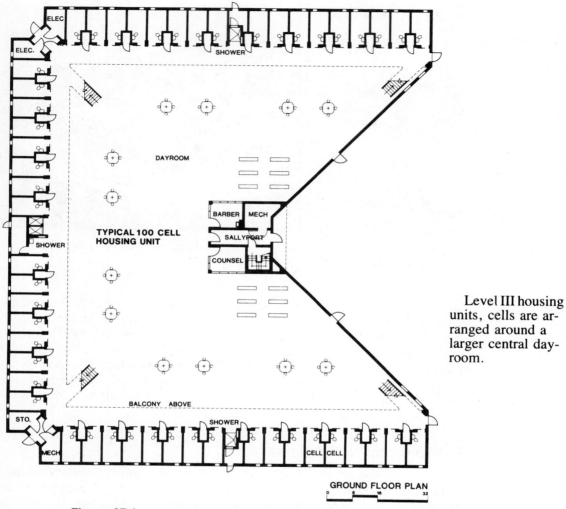

Level III housing units, cells are arranged around a larger central dayroom.

GROUND FLOOR PLAN

Figure 27-1 Single Occupancy Cells at the California Medical Facility at Vacaaville (Source: Charles Dewitt, *California Tests New Construction Concepts* [Washington, D. C.: U. S. Department of Justice, 1986], p. 4)

correctional facilities can be done quickly and effectively, using the following methods:

FAST TRACK—a procedure for acceleration of the building schedule by starting construction at the earliest possible moment, overlapping the design phase. Building phases are sequenced to complete construction of each stage in the order that buildings will be occupied.

Level II housing units, the facility is modified to create 5-, 8-, and 9-person dormitories.

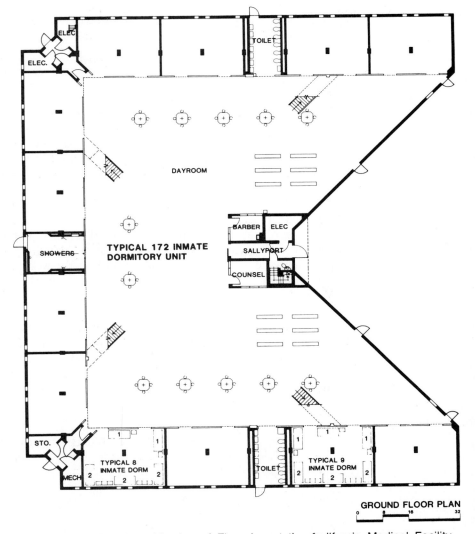

Figure 27-2 Dormitory Version of Floorplan at the California Medical Facility at Vacaville (Source: Charles DeWitt, *California Tests New Construction Concepts* [Washington, D. C.: U. S. Department of Justice, 1986], p. 4)

- *VALUE ENGINEERING*—the analysis of alternative systems, equipment, and materials to identify the relative benefits of each option. Initial costs and long-range operating costs are both analyzed to determine the best choice.[4]

Using the same concept of construction, California's Orange County Jail was expanded and ready for inmates in only seven months and at a cost of only $13,056 per bed.[5] The combination of concrete construction and tilt-up methods seems to hold a promising future for corrections facilities (see Figure 27.3).

Creative Ways to Finance Construction

The cost of building increasing numbers of prison and jail beds, often at a capital cost of up to $100,000 per bed, is met with resistance by the taxpayers. In New York, a bond issue was turned down for the construction of any new state prisons, despite critical overcrowding. Bond issues provide a complicated way to borrow money for capital expenses in a state or county (see box).

Although all borrowings by states, counties, or cities are subject to one of the conditions illustrated, the face value of the borrowing often represents only a fraction of the final cost. The cost of borrowing is explained in the box below. As can be seen, the total (real) cost of a $10 million, fixed-rate bond at 8 percent for twenty years will result in a total outlay of *$23 million* over the period of the borrowing.

With these problems in mind, the state of Ohio determined to find a better way to finance the prison construction they needed. Their method involved two major innovations of note: (1) prisons will be leased by the Department of Rehabilitation and Corrections, and, (2) the securities will carry a variable interest rate.[6] The method used in Ohio is one that employs lease bonds in order to stay under that state's constitutional debt limit. Just as creative financing has become necessary for the home buyer,

---

FACTS ABOUT MUNICIPAL BONDS

State and local governments may raise money for constructing correctional institutions by selling securities in the bond market. Most securities issued by public agencies are called municipal bonds. Compared to the stocks and bonds issued by private companies, municipal bonds offer investors an attractive combination of safety and tax-exempt income.

These securities usually offer stability and security that cannot be matched by the stocks and bonds issued by private companies. While a private company may lower or eliminate dividend payments at any time, interest payable by State and local governments represents a legal commitment. Similarly, municipal bonds offer a promise of return of the invested cash on their date of maturity; private-sector stocks provide no such assurances.

In addition to the safety of the investment, municipal bonds also offer tax-exempt income. As an obligation of State or local government, these securities are exempt from Federal taxes and generally exempt from State and local income taxes in the State of issuance. For investors who desire tax savings, this feature represents a significant benefit available only from municipal bonds.

Source: National Institute of Justice, *Ohio's New Approach to Prison and Jail Financing* (Washington, D.C.; U.S. Department of Justice, November 1986), p. 3.

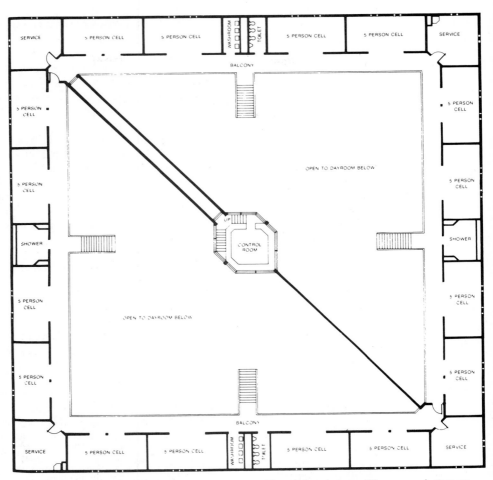

Figure 27-3 Orange County Floorplan. Floorplan shows differences between the jail unit and Vacaville. While the exterior wall design, building dimensions and roof are the same, a fourth wall of cells is shown and the building is divided into two distinct sections. (National Institute of Justice, *California Tests New Construction Concepts* [Washington, D.C.: U.S. Department of Justice, June 1986], p. 8)

so has it become necessary at the governmental level. The way the new approach works is shown in Figure 27-4.

Lease purchase is seen by the state of Ohio as a potential model for the use of many jurisdictions. The differences between this model and conventional financing is explained as follows:

COSTS OF BORROWING—ISSUANCE AND INTEREST

Like any consumer who buys with credit rather than cash, an agency that finances construction faces significant costs. As a general rule, financing a jail or prison will cost in total principal and interest payments more than 2 times the actual amount required for construction. For a 20-year fixed rate bond at 8 percent, the cost of a $10 million jail could actually represent a $23 million outlay over the duration of the financing period.

Issuance costs

Costs associated with the bonding process represent additional expenses for the State or local agency. Charges relating to the issuance of securities increases the issue by approximately 1.5 to 3 percent, and establishing a reserve fund equivalent to 1 year's payments of principal and interest, adds another 15 percent to the total. (The reserve fund may be invested at a rate which offsets the additional interest costs.) Altogether, an agency must plan on borrowing 15 to 20 percent more than the cost of the jail or prison. Costs include the following:

- Legal fees
- Printing and distribution of documents
- Credit ratings
- Bond discounts/underwriters fees
- Reserve fund

Interest costs

By far the most significant expense is the cost of interest on the debt. Twice each year, interest must be paid by the issuing unit of government to investors who purchased the bonds. The total amount of interest over the duration of financing depends ultimately upon several factors:

• **Interest rate:** Interest rates in effect at the time securities are issued represent a critical factor. During periods of high interest rates, borrowing is more costly for everyone—from the consumer to a government agency. From 1980 to 1985, interest rates as measured by The Bond Buyer Index of 20 Municipal Bonds varied from a high of 13.44 percent to a low of 7.11 percent. Interest rates in 1986 are the lowest since 1979.

• **Repayment schedule:** Although the term or repayment period is generally 20 to 30 years, some agencies have shortened the schedule to reduce interest costs. As with home mortgages, a shorter term may reduce both the interest rate and the cumulative interest cost. Unfortunately, an accelerated schedule requires much larger payments for principle, which many agencies cannot afford.

• **Type of securities:** The specific financial instrument or method of borrowing is the major determinant of interest cost. Unlike the preceding factors that are determined by the economy, selection of the specific security is a matter of choice.

Source: National Institute of Justice, *Ohio's New Approach to Prison and Jail Financing* (Washington, D.C.: U.S. Department of Justice, November 1986), p. 3.

Similarities

Tax-exempt income: As an obligation of a unit of state or local government, interest payments to investors are not subject to federal taxation and are also generally exempt from taxes in the jurisdiction of issue.

Ownership by public: After completion of all payments, the government

Figure 27-4 Profile of Ohio Finance Method

- Type of security: Lease-purchase demand bonds
- Size of issue: $79,000,000
- Rate on date of issue: 5.15 percent
- Operator/tenant: Ohio Department of Rehabilitation and Correction
- Issuing entity: Ohio Building Authority
- Interest provision: Variable rate, weekly interest adjustment
- Conversion features: Convert to fixed rate; also convert rate adjustments to weekly, monthly, or semiannual periods
- Liquidity: Demand provision permits bond holders to redeem or "put" securities with 1 week notice
- Security: Letter of credit from bank
- Current number of investors: Five institutional buyers
- Unit size: May be subdivided to $5,000 units, now set at $100,000
- Date of issue: 4/1/85
- Rating: S&P, P1+; Moody, Aaa/VMIG1
- Current rate: (July 7, 1986); 3.95 percent
- Due date: March 1, 2005

Source: National Institute of Justice, *Ohio's New Approach to Prison and Jail Financing*, (Washington, D.C.: U.S. Department of Justice, November 1986), p. 6.

entity ultimately acquires title to the facility. This is usually after 20 to 30 years, but may be accelerated by a shorter debt retirement schedule, requiring higher payments.

Differences

Legal agreement: This arrangement provides for legal ownership by another entity which leases the correctional facility to the unit of government. Many states permit creation of a public building authority for the purpose. The entity may be a public agency, nonprofit firm, or financial institution that legally owns the facility and sells the securities on the bond market. Although the corrections agency controls and operates the facility, the agency is technically a tenant. Since the leasing entity serves only as a nominal owner or "middleman," most rights and liabilities are assigned to a trustee bank.

Annual review: A legislative body must appropriate funds for lease payments, and the lease agreement may be terminated by action of the governmental agency. This provision is termed the "nonappropriation" clause and legally qualifies the arrangement as a lease.

Debt limit: Since the obligation is renewable each year, the amount borrowed is usually not categorized as an ongoing legal debt and does not count against debt capacity. Like equipment rental, the facility is not owned, a feature which distinguishes this method from general obligation bonds.

Taxing authority: Lease bonds are not guaranteed with the "full faith and credit" of the city, county, or state. Accordingly, they are not directly backed by the taxing power of the issuing jurisdiction, and general revenues are used to make lease payments.[7]

TABLE 27.1 Construction Finance Alternatives: Typical Examples

Traditional approach (General obligation bonds)

Fixed rate, 20- to 30-year maturity	Decline in use	• Provides tax-exempt interest to investors • Most secure investment — highest rating • Voter approval often required; new property taxes source of payments • Adds to public debt • Least costly fixed-rate security

New techniques (Tax-exempt lease-purchase bonds)

Fixed-rate securities	Most frequent alternative	• Bypasses many requirements and problems • Source of lease payments must be identified • Role of government agency unchanged • Raises capital quickly • More costly for issuer if rate is fixed
Variable-rate securities	Innovative technique	• Same benefits as fixed-rate lease-purchase • Risks of rising interest rates and remarketing • Usually convertible to fixed rate • Issued in Ohio, California, and Pennsylvania • Usually lowest interest rate at time of issue

Privatization (Taxable private financing)

Private ownership	Limited experience	• Owned by profitmaking company • Higher interest rate than public financing • Owners may receive special tax advantages • Tax-exempt income not available to owners • Financing and operation are separate issues

Source: National Institute of Justice, *Ohio's New Approach to Prison and Jail Financing* (Washington, D.C.: U.S. Department of Justice, November 1986), p. 9.

Although the financing of construction varies greatly from jurisdiction, there are some important considerations to examine in this area. As budgets shrink and taxpayers feel a greater crunch on their wallets, these alternatives, summarized in Table 27.1, are worth examination. These include the next topic: *privatization*.

Is Privatization an Answer?

Many jurisdictions are looking into the contracting out (privatizing) of their correctional facilities and the operation of these facilities as a way to save money and to get needed facilities on line as quickly as possible. The concept is not new, nor is it an answer for every problem. Many services, and some operations, have been contracted to private agencies

---

PRIVATIZATION

The lease examples explained in this *Construction Bulletin* do not change the role of governmental agencies. Another form of leasing—"privatization"—relies entirely upon the private sector and represents a major shift in policy.

With lease-purchase, government officials have created a nonprofit entity that acts on behalf of their agency. With "privatization," a profitmaking company actually owns the institution because private investors have put up money to build the facility.

Financing provided by a private company is almost always more costly because a unit of government can obtain a lower interest rate than a private company. A major reason for the higher cost is that lease payments on a privately owned institution must be treated as taxable income. In the recent past, the higher cost of private financing has been somewhat reduced because special tax benefits may be available to a company raising capital for construction. When tax benefits are available, private owners of a facility may pass their savings through to the governmental entity in the form of reduced lease payments.

Private owners of correctional facilities have been eligible to claim such tax benefits as depreciation and investment tax credits. However, Federal legislation pending in the summer of 1986 would disallow most of the tax advantages of private ownership. Accordingly, the cost of private financing will probably be even higher than in the past.

"Privatization" may also involve private-sector management and operation of a correctional facility, although this issue is not related to the type of financing. While private firms may offer contracts for both operations and financing, these issues should be examined separately. Although costs of operation may be discretionary, costs of private financing are necessarily higher when raising capital for construction.

Other features of private-sector participation may be of interest to State and local officials. Many firms now offer a comprehensive package of services called "turnkey" or "design-build" contracts in which a single company provides a variety of services ordinarily divided among several different firms. Depending upon the laws of each jurisdiction, consolidation into one contract may be an efficient approach that results in faster completion of the correctional facility.

Industrial development bonds, or "IDB" financing, represent a public-private partnership. This approach offers tax-exempt income to investors because securities are issued with the authorization of a governmental entity. However, total financing must be limited to $10 million, and the unit of government must pay full, fair market value for the facility upon termination of the lease. Use of industrial development bonds is tightly restricted by Federal law, and it is expected that Congress will impose further limitations on this approach in the future.

Source: National Institute of Justice, *Ohio's New Approach to Prison and Jail Financing* (Washington, D.C.: U.S. Department of Justice, November 1986), p. 9.

---

for years. These include medical services, food services, maintenance services, and many others. In the community corrections sector, work-release facilities have been operated on a *fee-for-services* basis for over a quarter

of a century. It has only been in the 1980s, however, that the pressure
has been put on governments at every level to examine the potential for
private contracts for every aspect of security institutions, to include jails
and prisons. The issues in this knotty problem are outlined in the following box.

The trends in private operation of correctional facilities, as of June 1987,
are as presented in the second box. As shown, only Tennessee has taken
the step to request bids for the private operation of a medium security
prison, a facility that is as yet not completed. The action by Tennessee,
however, was preceded by at least one private correctional corporation's
suggestion that they take over the entire state system.[8]

While many desperate correctional administrators are presently examining the privatization of even more operations and feel that there are opportunities for some expansion without extreme capital outlays, the jury
is still out on the role of total operation of security facilities by non-
governmental entities. The American Correctional Association provides a
National Correctional Policy on private-sector involvement in corrections
(see Appendix B). In their official document on the issue, they make the
following caveat:

TRENDS IN PRIVATE OPERATION OF CORRECTIONAL FACILITIES

Approximately 1,200 adults are held in secure correctional facilities privately
operated for State and local governments in the United States. Among the
institutions, by jurisdiction:

- State of Kentucky, Marion Adjustment Center, 200 males, minimum security,
  for-profit contractor.
- State of Florida, Beckham Hall Community Correctional Center, Miami, 171
  males, unsupervised work release, for-profit contractor.
- Bay County, Florida, Jail and Annex, 350 men and women, for-profit contractor.
- Hamilton County (Chattanooga), Tennessee, Silverdale Detention Center,
  workhouse, 340 men and women, for-profit contractor.
- Ramsey County (St. Paul), Minnesota, Roseville Detention Center, 42 females,
  not-for-profit operator.

The Tennessee Department of Corrections issued a request for proposals in
1986 for operation of a medium-security prison, but received no bids it considered responsive. The department is now considering revision and reissue of
the RFP.

Many States contract extensively for work release, prerelease, and other nonsecure detention space. For example, California contracts for 1,700 nonsecure
beds, Alaska has contracted out a correctional restitution center, and 5 of Illinois' 15 community correctional centers are privately operated.

Private companies or organizations operate juvenile facilities in 12 States;
secure juvenile facilities in Pennsylvania, Tennessee, Massachusetts, and Florida
were considered in the preparation of this report.

Source: National Institute of Justice, *Contracting for the Operation of Prisons and Jails* (Washington,
D.C.: U.S. Department of Justice, June 1987), p. 2.

The American Correctional Association believes strongly that leadership and guidance on this issue is needed. Therefore, the policy on private sector involvement emphasizes that *all* groups and individuals involved in correctional programs and services must operate according to the recognized professional standards of the field. Further, the policy affirms that the ultimate responsibility and authority for any correctional program, service, or facility rests with the governmental body, not the contractor. The role of contracted services and programs is to supplement agency operations where there is a demonstrated need, not to replace them. A clear understanding of this role is necessary by all parties to any contract, including legislators, executive officials, members of the judiciary, and contractors.[9]

One of the largest of the private corrections firms is the Corrections Corporation of America (CCA). In their bold plan of 1985 for the complete takeover of the Tennessee prison system, the leaders of CCA pointed out their view of the value in private contracting for correctional services:

> As governments continue to search for new and innovative ways to serve their constituencies, without burdening them with excessive taxes and adding more public employees, they are turning increasingly to private companies. They are seeking to do business with private firms with high levels of expertise, adequate financial resources and the desire to provide a quality service for a reasonable return on their investment.
>
> Of all government programs, corrections is unique. Because it has no constituency there are few pressures on the political system to do more than address the problems in the short term, and the correction department in Tennessee is a vivid illustration of this deficiency. Private contracting provides the one opportunity to provide for a system with stability and continuity of management, and a long range solution to the problem.[10]

There are strong positions on both sides of this issue, and the issue is exacerbated every day by growing populations and rising costs for prison construction. This situation will continue to be a major problem to watch into the twenty-first century.

AIDS: The Problem for Society Reaches Corrections ——————————————

Although most studies tend to show that Acquired Immune Deficiency Syndrome (AIDS) is spreading more slowly in correctional institutions than in the general public, it remains a serious issue for the correctional administrator who is already dealing with major problems. The need for more training and education on AIDS, to relieve the fear and apprehension of inmates and staff, is sorely needed. The following material is extracted from the National Institute of Justice study on the problem, published in 1987.[11]

Inmate Legal Issues

Before summarizing the inmate petitions and cases, it should be emphasized that most are still pending. Obviously anyone can file a suit for any reason. Many cases will undoubtedly be decided in favor of the correctional systems. The following discussion reflects the types of allegations that may be raised in inmates' AIDS-related lawsuits.

Equal Protection and Related Issues

This type of case involves inmates with AIDS, ARC, or HIV seropositivity who allege that the conditions of their confinement violate equal protection standards and/or constitute cruel and unusual punishment. The leading case is *Cordero* v. *Coughlin*,[12] in which the court upheld the New York State Department of Correctional Services' policy of medical segregation for inmates with AIDS. In an Oklahoma case, *Powell* v. *Department of Corrections*, the court took a very similar position regarding segregation of a seropositive inmate. Although it did not cite *Cordero*, the court declared that the segregation policy furthered legitimate correctional objectives, namely prevention of the spread of disease and protection of the seropositive inmate from other inmates. Further, the court stated that inmates have no constitutional right to be in general population and that the inmate had not been treated differently from other seropositive inmates — in fact, no other seropositive inmates had been identified in the Oklahoma prison system.[13]

In Colorado, by contrast, the Department of Corrections has eased its segregation policy for seropositive inmates, approximately .5 percent of Colorado prisoners. In motions filed under *Marioneaux* v. *Colorado State Penitentiary*, a broad correctional conditions case pending since the 1970s, seropositive inmates complained of being placed in a maximum security segregation unit next to death row, in violation of an objective classification system agreed to by the correctional department under *Marioneaux*. The state pleaded "special circumstances," but plaintiffs countered that the classification scheme contained no provision for special circumstances. Ultimately, the correctional department decided to move those seropositive inmates who ordinarily would have been classified as medium security or lower to a medium security unit. The department also held a national conference of experts to discuss comprehensive correctional AIDS policy.

Quality of Care and Related Issues

Typically, these are cases brought by inmates with AIDS alleging inadequate medical care or "deliberate indifference" to serious medical need. *Storms* v. *Coughlin*, another New York case, has been withdrawn. The plaintiffs' attorney reports that it became impossible to proceed in the absence of a measurable standard of adequate care for AIDS patients and without complete charting of their care while hospitalized.[13]

In Arizona, a case brought by the state prison system's only inmate with AIDS has been transformed by that inmate's death into a broader class action. The plaintiffs are seeking an injunction requiring a development of a comprehensive correctional policy on care of inmates with AIDS, ARC, and HIV seropositivity[14] (see Table 27.2).

Failure to Protect Others from AIDS or HIV Infection

Numerous cases have been filed by inmates alleging that correctional systems have not provided them adequate protection from HIV infection while in prison. The first case of this type was *La Rocca* v. *Dalsheim*,[15] in which New York State's policies were held to provide adequate protection. However, this case arose before the HIV antibody test became available and now a number of suits have been filed seeking antibody screening and other policies for the systematic identification and segregation of infected inmates. Many of these cases demonstrate that misinformation about AIDS still influences attitudes and actions in correctional institutions.

No cases have been filed as yet by inmates seeking damages for allegedly contracting HIV infection or AIDS while in a correctional facility. Correctional systems have been required by courts to adhere to a standard of

TABLE 27.2 AIDS Housing Policies in the State and Federal Prison Systems: 1986

Policy Combination	Housing Policy Combinations State/Federal Prison Systems				City/County Jail Systems			
	Original Survey: November 1985		Update Survey: October 1986		Original Survey: November 1985		Update Survey: October 1986	
	n	%	n	%	n	%	n	%
• Segregate AIDS Cases; ARC Cases and Seropositives Maintained in General Population	3	6%	8	16%	3	9%	3	9%
• Segregate AIDS and ARC Cases; Seropositives Maintained in General Population	10	20	8	16	3	9	4	12
• Segregate All Categories	8	16	8	16	13	41	9	27
• No Segregation of any Categories	2	4	6	12	0	0	1	3
• No Policy	8	16	5	10	1	3	0	0
• Combinations involving case-by-case determination	16	31	14	27	10	30	12	36
• Other Policy Combinations	4	8	2	4	3	9	2	6
• No Update	—	—	0	—	—	—	2	6
Total	51	101%	51	101%	33	101%	33	99%

Source: Theodore Hammett, *1986 Update: AIDS in Correctional Facilities* (Washington, D.C.: U.S. Department of Justice, 1987), p. 10.

reasonable care in protecting inmates. Breaches of this standard may constitute cruel and unusual punishment.[16] In several cases, correctional systems and their officials have been held liable for damages resulting from homosexual rapes and other inmate-on-inmate assaults on the ground that inadequate supervision had been provided to prevent such incidents.[17]

However, correctional systems have not been held responsible for insuring the *absolute* safety of persons in their custody. In several cases, for example, courts have held that a correctional system could be liable for damages from inmate-on-inmate assault only if its officials knew — or should have known — in advance of the risk to the particular inmate.[18]

Confidentiality and Other Issues

Several cases have been filed alleging improper disclosure, or seeking to halt disclosure, of AIDS-related information. In a pending New Jersey case, inmates allege that under certain policies AIDS-related medical records might be seen by guards. They also ask to be tested for HIV antibodies but to be freed from any disciplinary action for engaging in needlesharing activities that might have led to their infection.[19] A Florida case alleges improper disclosure of antibody test results by the correctional department.[20] The sharp increase in the number of AIDS-related inmate lawsuits underscores the continuing importance of education, training, carefully considered housing policies, and maintenance of the confidentially of medical information of all kinds.

NEEDLESHARING AND CONDOMS

Correctional administrators and investigators usually agree that major problems in prisons include the availability of illicit injectible drugs inside prison, and frequent voluntary and involuntary homosexual activity, including homosexual rape. Despite the clear evidence of the spread of AIDS through sharing dirty needles and anal intercourse, correctional presonnel and managers are unreasonably resistant to providing prophylactics and bleach to inmates.

Men in prison who wish to engage in anal intercourse are usually sufficiently capable of bringing that act to a successful completion. If the act is forcible intercourse with a passive male coerced into receiving an unwanted intrusion ("insertee"), and the HIV virus is spread, the matter of liability might mean considerable financial loss for the State, managing prison officer, and lowest-level correctional employee. Providing condoms to prisoners will soon be a constitutional right.

Dirty needles shared by prisoners can easily be effectively sterilized by double-rinsing of syringe and needle in common household bleach. Institutions with substantial availability of injectible illicit drugs should make distribution of household bleach a routine sanitary procedure. To do less is to invite liability and eventual punitive and exemplary damages.

There have been few cases of correctional staff-initiated lawsuits for contracting AIDS or HIV antibodies while on the job. Although no known cases of this type have yet been reported, administrators must be aware of the controversy regarding whether AIDS is a protected handicap under Section 504 of the Federal Rehabilitation Act of 1973.[21] If so, an employee could not be fired or otherwise discriminated against simply because he/she had AIDS. Several states and municipalities have passed laws and ordinances prohibiting discrimination against AIDS patients. By way of contrast, the U.S. Department of Justice issued an opinion in 1985 holding that measures taken to reduce the spread of AIDS could not be restricted under the Rehabilitation Act. This issue must be closely watched as it could result in a cost of billions of dollars to jurisdictions that do not handle the matter properly.

Drugs and Corrections

The problems with drugs on the streets of America are reflected in the drug use in the jails and prisons as well. The well-publicized "War on Drugs" seems to be lost in a flood of marijuana, cocaine, heroin, and a whole new family of "designer drugs," those that are made for specific reactions ... high or low. The drug industry is estimated to be a $60 *billion* industry and we are hard pressed to find the resources and will to fight this chemical plague. One method of fighting drug trafficking is shown in the following box, but the supply seems to always rise to meet demands. What does this issue have to do with corrections? A lot.

Contraband is *power* in a correctional institution, and drugs are the ultimate contraband, a way to escape the drudgery of prison life without having to risk towers and barbed wire. Drug profits, even inside the walls, can provide a way to "own" a guard or other staff member and make life easier for the trafficker. Few guards who work in facilities that pay poorly

---

FIGHTING DRUG TRAFFICKING WITH FORFEITURE SANCTIONS

Forfeiture is a legal procedure that enables a government to seize property used in the commission of a crime and, in some jurisdictions, assets traceable to criminal profits. Federal prosecutors are successfully wielding forfeiture sanctions as a powerful weapon against drug traffickers. In fiscal year 1986, total income to the Department of Justice Assets Forfeiture Fund was some $90 million. And, under the provisions of the 1984 Comprehensive Crime Control Act, approximately $25 million in cash and property forfeited in Federal cases in 1986 was shared with the State and local criminal justice agencies that participated in those cases.

Used effectively, forfeiture sanctions can cripple an ongoing criminal enterprise by seizing the tools of the drug trafficking trade—planes, vessels, cars, and trucks—as well as cash, bank accounts, and other goods used in criminal activity or obtained with illicit profits. The risk of losing such assets raises the stakes considerably for criminal enterprises such as drug trafficking. For example, Federal prosecutors in California seized land that had been used to grow marijuana. The prospect of losing prime real estate may well serve as a powerful deterrent to others contemplating an illegal harvest.

An additional advantage of forfeiture for jurisdictions is the financial windfall gained through successful forfeiture proceedings. In most States, proceeds from the sale of property seized go to the State of local treasury. Some States, however, allow law enforcement agencies to keep the funds or forfeited property for official use. Seized vehicles, for example, can be used in undercover operations, and cash can supplement the undercover drug "buy" fund.

Despite the potential of forfeiture as a drug enforcement strategy, its use remains relatively limited at the State and local levels. Two complementary efforts, sponsored by the National Institute of Justice and the Bureau of Justice Assistance, aim to change that picture.

With funds from the National Institute of Justice, the National Criminal Justice Association (NCJA), in conjunction with the Police Executive Research Forum (PERF), will develop an instruction manual on establishing and maintaining an asset seizure and forfeiture program at the State level. The project will also devise and pilot test a model training curriculum.

In a survey conducted by NCJA as part of a 1986 pilot program on asset seizure and forfeiture, every responding jurisdiction reported the need for training in this area. Existing forfeiture statutes were viewed as ambiguous and lacking procedural guidelines for implementation. Police and prosecutors were reluctant to use forfeiture sanctions in drug trafficking cases without firm knowledge and understanding of relevant statutes and procedures, and State officials were concerned about managing seized assets.

The manual is intended to guide development of a State asset seizure and forfeiture program. It will discuss recent developments in forfeiture laws and procedures—establishment of a seizure and forfeiture capability, management of an inventory of forfeited assets, cooperative enforcement and prosecution efforts, and the resource requirements of maintaining such a program. It will also cover investigative tools for forfeiture cases, with an emphasis on financial investigations.

The core document for the training curriculum, the manual is also designed to be an independent, "stand-alone" resource for officials who want to establish or review forfeiture programs. Publication of the guide is expected later this year, and its availability will be announced in *NIJ Reports*.

Concurrently, the Police Executive Research Forum and the National Criminal Justice Association will develop training for local criminal justice investigators on the tools and techniques for financial investigations in asset seizure and forfeiture cases. The training is funded by the Bureau of Justice Assistance. Four training sessions will be held later this year. For more information on these training sessions, write Richard Ward, Bureau of Justice Assistance, 633 Indiana Avenue NW., Washington, DC 20531 (202-724-5974).

Source: NIJ Reports, "Controlling Drug Abuse and Crime: A Research Update" (Washington, D.C.: U.S. Department of Justice, 1987), p. 3.

and train less can resist the temptation of a few hundred extra dollars a week to just "look the other way."

The introduction of the system of drug testing known by the acronym "EMIT," or *enzyme multiplied immune test* (see Box on page 1011) into most major institutions has given the staff a weapon to fight the problems associated with drugs in institutions. A major problem has been the unwillingness of *staff* to submit to random testing for the use of drugs. Arguments concerning such issues as rights against illegal search and seizure, privacy, and due process have been used by inmates and staff alike to

---

EMIT UNDER FIRE

Urinalysis Test

Although urine tests have long been used by the criminal justice system, only with the advent of more accurate and less expensive technology has urine testing become a viable option for screening large numbers of offenders. Primarily because of their low cost (under $5 for each drug tested) and ease of use, the EMIT™ (enzyme multiplied immune test) tests are the most commonly used urine tests today. These tests depend on a chemical reaction between the specimen and an antibody designed to react to a specific drug. The chemical reaction causes a change in the specimen's transmission of light, which is measured by a machine. If the reading is higher than a given standard, the specimen is positive for the drug. Because the determination of a positive is based on specific numbers, the level of subjectivity required by the EMIT test is less than that required by most other tests.

The growing popularity of the EMIT tests has made them the object of several legal challenges. The primary criticism is that the EMIT tests have too high a rate of false-positive errors. That is, the tests too often falsely indicate the presence of a drug. Much of the debate surrounds the possibility that some common *licit* drugs can cross-react with the test's reagents to produce a positive result. The ingestion of poppy seed bagels has been found to produce a positive test result for opiates, for instance. Furthermore, the EMIT test for opiates will detect prescribed drugs such as codeine as well as heroin (morphine). Sloppy recording procedures by laboratory staff and failure to maintain careful controls over the chain of custody of the specimen can also produce serious test errors.

The future of urine testing in the criminal justice system will probably depend on a satisfactory solution to the problem of false-positive errors. Preliminary Federal guidelines for testing specify that all positive test results from immunoassay tests, like EMIT, should be confirmed by gas chromatography/mass spectroscopy (GC/MS). GC/MS is the most accurate technique available for identifying drugs in the urine, but it costs $70 to $100 per specimen. It seems appropriate to require such a procedure when a single test result may end in loss of a person's job or liberty. However, when a test result is used to trigger further investigation to determine if a person is involved in drug use, confirmation by other methods (urine monitoring or diagnostic interview) may be equally acceptable. The courts have yet to decide this issue.

Source: Crime Files, *Drug Testing* (Washington, D.C.: U.S. Department of Justice, 1988), p. 2.

resist mandatory (even if random) testing. Even the EMIT system itself has drawn heavy fire.

Until there is a greater effort to remove drugs from the free society, there is little hope of removing this problem from within the walls of America's prisons. The fallacy behind a stepped-up testing program, when it is not followed by solid treatment, is that the public begins to believe that all the testing is part of a program to deal with the underlying dependencies. The generation of persons entering into leadership in corrections is now coming from the 1960s—the era of the flower children—and they need to understand the consequences to a correctional system that is as awash with drugs as are the streets (and suburban homes) of America. This issue is just as critical as the others we have mentioned.

Summary

It is extremely difficult to decide when to stop writing about this fascinating, complex, and dynamic field we call corrections. But reluctantly, we shall now close with a few observations. This text has been designed to give the student a broad view of the history, processes, systems, clientele, and problems shaping the functions and facilities that constitute corrections in America. In the beginning we asked the question, "What is corrections?" It should be apparent by now that corrections is a goal in search of a process, a process in search of a discipline, and a discipline that works. The history of corrections is long, but in America we are actually dealing with less than two centuries of experience.

The issues and challenges that corrections poses to the incoming correctional worker are complex. But they can be solved by dedicated, trained, and educated persons who are willing to propose constructive criticism and solutions. These new staff must learn to ask "Why?" and refuse to accept the answer, "It has always been done that way." As Walter C. Reckless was known to have said over many decades of working with corrections: "The fields are ripe for harvest and we need the hands to bring it in." It is with this spirit that we urge serious students to consider pitching in and providing the hands to help bring in the harvest of improved corrections in America.

Review Questions

1. What is the most pressing issue in corrections today? Why do you pick this topic?
2. What has the rising cost of corrections done to government planners in searching for solution?
3. Why is the problem of drugs even more acute in a correctional environment?

Corrections Can't Go Back to the "Old Days": Despite New Attitudes Toward Punishment (Courtesy American Correctional Association)

Key Terms

1. **bed-availability-assignment (p. 656)**
2. **creative financing (p. 662)**
3. **privatization contracting (p. 667)**
4. **CCA (p. 669)**
5. **seropositivity (p. 670)**
6. **needle sharing (p. 672)**
7. **condoms (p. 672)**
8. **war on drugs (p. 673)**
9. **emit (p. 675)**
10. **urinalysis (p. 675)**

Notes

1. James Q. Wilson, *Prison Overcrowding*, Crime File Study Guide (Washington D.C.: U.S. Government Printing Office, National Institute of Justice, 1987), p. 2.
2. The new facilities that were added are the Special Offender Center (144 beds), and the Twin Rivers Correctional Center (550 beds). In addition, $40 million

of renovation was done at the Washington State Reformatory, which was built in 1909.

3. Charles DeWitt, *California Tests New Construction Concepts* (Washington, D.C.: U.S. Department of Justice, June 1986), p. 3.
4. Ibid., p. 6.
5. Ibid., p. 10.
6. National Institute of Justice, *Ohio's New Approach to Prison and Jail Financing* (Washington, D.C.: U.S. Department of Justice, November 1986), p. 3.
7. Ibid., p. 4.
8. Corrections Corporation of America, *Adult Corrections Plan for the State of Tennessee*, (Nashville: CCA, November 1985).
9. American Correctional Association, *Public Policy for Corrections: A Handbook for Decision-Makers* (College Park, Md.: American Correctional Association, 1986), p. 51.
10. Corrections Corporation of America, *Adult Corrections Plan for the State of Tennessee*, (Nashville: CCA, 1985), p. 3.
11. Theodore M. Hammett, *AIDS in Correctional Facilities: Issues and Options* (Washington, D.C.: U.S. Department of Justice, May 1987), pp. xxiii–xxvi.
12. 607 F Supp 9 USDC (SDNY, 1984).
13. USDC, ND Oklahoma, Nos 85-C-820-C and 85-C-816-B, dismissed February 20, 1986. A similar Oklahoma case, *Morse* v. *Meachum*, was decided in favor of the correctional department in late December 1986. For a balanced and definitive statement of AIDS in prisons, see Rosemary Gido and William Guanay, "A Demographic Profile of New York State AIDS Inmate Mortalities: Research and Policy Implications." Paper presented at the annual meeting of the Academy of Criminal Justice Sciences, Las Vegas, April 1987. National data can be found in Theodore Hammett, *1986 Update: AIDS in Correctional Facilities* (Washington, D.C.: U.S. Department of Justice, 1987).
14. *Marioneaux* v. *Colorado State Penitentiary.* 465 Supp 1245 (1979); interview with David Miller, Colorado ACLU.
15. Interview with Anthony Carol Kahn, White Plains, N.Y.
16. 120 Misc 2d 697 (NY 1983).
17. See, e.g. *Doe* v. *Lally* 457 F Supp 1339 (USDC Maryland, 1979); *Campbell* v. *Bergeron* 486 F Supp 1246 (USDC Middle Dist, Louisiana, 1980), aff'd 654 F 2nd 719 (5th Cir, 1981); *Streeter* v. *Hopper* 618 F 2nd 1178 (5th Cir 1980); *Rhodes* v. *Chapman* 101 S Ct 2392 (1981).
18. See, e.g., *Raymond* v. *Baxely* 475 F Supp 1111 (USDC. E. Dist Mich, 1979); *Garrett* v. *United States* 501 F Supp 337 (USDC, N Dist, Georgia, 1980); *Saunders* v. *Chatham County* 728 F 2nd 1367 (11th Cir, 1982); *Kemp* v. *Waldron* 479 NYS 2d 440 (Sup Ct 1984); *Thomas* v. *Booker* 762 F 2d 654 (8th Cir 1985).
19. Notice of intent to sue, *Niosy* v. *Bowles.*
20. New Mexico Corrections Department, "Guidelines, Policies, and Procedures Relating to AIDS" (January 6, 1986): 21–22.
21. 29 USC 794. See also Theodore Hammett and Walter Bond, *Risk of Infection With the AIDS Virus through Exposure to Blood* (Washington, D.C.: U.S. Department of Justice, 1987).

Recommended Readings _____

Conrad, John P. "The Rights of Wrongdoers," *Criminal Justice Research Bulletin* 3 (1987).

Criminology. Volume 26, Number 1 (1988). Focus on criminal careers and career criminals.

Currie, Elliott. *What Kind of Future?* San Francisco: National Council on Crime and Delinquency, 1987.

Gibbons, Don. *The Limits of Punishment As Social Policy*. San Francisco: National Council on Crime and Delinquency, 1988.

Hackett, Judith et al.. *Contracting for the Operation of Prisons and Jails*. Washington, D.C.: U.S. Department of Justice, 1987.

Hammett, Theodore. *1986 Update: AIDS in Correctional Facilities*. Washington, D.C.: U.S. Department of Justice, 1987.

Hammett, Theodore et al. *Risk of Infection with the AIDS Virus through Exposure to Blood*. Washington, D.C.: U.S. Department of Justice, 1987.

Moriarity, Laura. "Ethical Issues of Selective Incapacitation." *Criminal Justice Research Bulletin* 3 (1987).

Petersilia, Joan. *Expanding Options for Criminal Sentencing*. Santa Monica, Calif.: Rand Corporation, 1987).

Appendix A
Glossary

The authors are grateful to the Law Enforcement Assistance Administration for the publication of the *Dictionary of Criminal Justice Data Terminology,* from which many of the following terms and definitions have been extracted. It is in the spirit of that effort to standardize criminal justice terminology that we have decided to include this section. We hope that students, especially those new to the field, will take the time to read and absorb the meanings of these tools of the trade. To obtain more detailed information about the terms in this glossary, the student should write to U.S. Department of Justice, National Criminal Reference Service, Washington, D.C. 20531.

Abscond (corrections). To depart from a geographical area or jurisdiction prescribed by the conditions of one's probation or parole, without authorization.

Abscond (court). To intentionally absent or conceal oneself unlawfully in order to avoid a legal process.

Acquittal. A judgment of a court, based either on the verdict of a jury or a judicial officer, that the defendant is not guilty of the offense(s) for which he or she has been tried.

Adjudicated. Having been the subject of completed criminal or juvenile proceedings, and convicted, or adjudicated a delinquent, status offender, or dependent.

Adjudication (criminal). The judicial decision terminating a criminal proceeding by a judgment of conviction or acquittal or by a dismissal of the case.

Adjudication (juvenile). The juvenile court decision, terminating an adjudicatory hearing, that the juvenile is a delinquent, status offender, or dependent or that the allegations in the petition are not sustained.

Adjudicatory hearing. In juvenile proceedings, the fact-finding process wherein the juvenile court determines whether or not there is sufficient evidence to sustain the allegations in a petition.

Adult. A person who is within the original jurisdiction of a criminal, rather than a juvenile, court because his or her age at the time of an alleged criminal act was above a statutorily specified limit.

Alias. Any name used for an official purpose that is different from a person's legal name.

Alternative Facility. An alternative place of limited confinement that may be an option for certain kinds of offenders. Such facilities may include treatment settings for drug-dependent offenders, minimum security facilities in the community that provide treatment and services as needed, work/study-release centers, and halfway houses or shelter-type facilities. All of these are less secure than the traditional jail but offer a more stimulating environment for the individual.

Appeal. A request by either the defense or the prosecution that a case be removed from a lower court to a higher court in order for a completed trial to be reviewed by the higher court.

Appearance. The act of coming into a court and submitting to the authority of that court.

Appearance, first (initial appearance). The first appearance of a juvenile or adult in the court that has jurisdiction over his or her case.

Appellant. A person who initiates an appeal.

Arraignment. The appearance of a person before a court in order that the court may inform the individual of the accusation(s) against him or her and enter his or her plea.

Arrest. Taking a person into custody by authority of law for the purpose of charging him or her with a criminal offense or initiating juvenile proceedings, terminating with the recording of a specific offense.

Arson. The intentional destruction or attempted destruction, by fire or explosive, of the property of another or of one's own property with the intent to defraud.

Assault. Unlawful intentional inflicting, or attempted or threatened inflicting, of injury upon another.

Assault, aggravated. Unlawful intentional causing of serious bodily injury with or without a deadly weapon or unlawful intentional attempting or threatening of serious bodily injury or death with a deadly weapon.

Assault, simple. Unlawful intentional threatening, attempted inflicting, or inflicting of less than serious bodily injury, in the absence of a deadly weapon.

Assault with a deadly weapon. Unlawful intentional inflicting, or attempted or threatened inflicting, or injury or death with the use of a deadly weapon.

Assault on a law enforcement officer. A simple or aggravated assault, in which the victim is a law enforcement officer engaged in the performance of his or her duties.

Assigned counsel. An attorney, not regularly employed by a government agency, assigned by the court to represent a particular person(s) in a particular criminal proceeding.

Attorney/lawyer/counsel. A person trained in the law, admitted to practice before the bar of a given jurisdiction, and authorized to advise, represent, and act for other persons in legal proceedings.

Backlog. The number of pending cases that exceeds the court's capacity, in that they cannot be acted upon because the court is occupied in acting upon other cases.

Bombing incident. The detonation or attempted detonation of an explosive or incendiary device with the willful disregard of risk to the person or property of another, or for a criminal purpose.

Bondsman-secured bail. Security service purchased by the defendant from a bail bondsman. The fee for this service ranges upward from 10 percent and is not refundable. The bail bondsman system, which permits a private entrepreneur to share with the court the decision on pretrial release, has been criticized for many years and is becoming obsolete in more progressive jurisdictions.

Booking. A police administrative action officially recording an arrest and identifying the person, the place, the time, the arresting authority, and the reason for the arrest.

Burglary. Unlawful entry of a structure, with or without force, with intent to commit a felony or larceny.

Camp/ranch/farm. Any of several types of similar confinement facilities, usually in a rural location, which contain adults or juveniles committed after adjudication.

Case. At the level of police or prosecutorial investigation, a set of circumstances under investigation involving one or more persons; at subsequent steps in criminal proceedings, a charging document alleging the commission of one or more crimes; a single defendant; in juvenile or correctional proceedings, a person who is the object of agency action.

Case (court). A single charging document under the jurisdiction of a court; a single defendant.

Caseload (corrections). The total number of clients registered with a correctional agency or agent during a specified time period, often divided into active and inactive or supervised and unsupervised, thus distinguishing between clients with whom the agency or agent maintains contact and those with whom it does not.

Caseload (court). The total number of cases filed in a given court or before a given judicial officer during a given period of time.

Caseload, pending. The number of cases at any given time that have been filed in a given court, or are before a given judicial officer, but have not reached disposition.

Cash bail. A cash payment for situations in which the charge is not serious and the scheduled bail is low. The defendant obtains release by paying in cash the full amount, which is recoverable after the required court appearances are made.

CCH. An abbreviation for computerized criminal history.

Charge. A formal allegation that a specific person(s) has committed a specific offense(s).

Charging document. A formal written accusation, filed in a court, alleging that a specified person(s) has committed a specific offense(s).

Check fraud. The issuance or passing of a check, draft, or money order that is legal as a formal document, signed by the legal account holder but with the foreknowledge that the bank or depository will refuse to honor it because of insufficient funds or closed account.

Chief of police. A local law enforcement officer who is the appointed or elected head of a police department.

Child abuse. Willful action or actions by a person causing physical harm to a child.

Child neglect. Willful failure by the person(s) responsible for a child's well-being to provide for adequate food, clothing, shelter, education, and supervison.

Citation (to appear). A written order issued by a law enforcement officer directing an alleged offender to appear in a specific court at a specified time in order to answer a criminal charge.

Citizen dispute settlement. The settlement of interpersonal disputes by a third party or the courts. Charges arising from interpersonal disputes are mediated by a third party in an attempt to avoid prosecution. If an agreement between the parties cannot be reached and the complainant wishes to proceed with criminal processing, the case may be referred to court for settlement.

Commitment. The action of a judicial officer ordering that an adjudicated and sentenced adult, or adjudicated delinquent or status offender who has been the subject of a juvenile court disposition hearing, be admitted into a correctional facility.

Community facility (nonconfinement facility, adult or juvenile). A correctional facility from which residents are regularly permitted to depart, unaccompanied by any official, for using daily community resources such as schools or treatment programs, or seeking or holding employment.

Community service. A period of service to the community as a substitute for, or in partial satisfaction of, a fine. This disposition is generally a condition of a suspended or partially suspended sentence or of probation. The offender volunteers his or her services to a community agency for a certain number of hours per week over a specified period of time. The total number of hours, often assessed at the legal minimum wage, is determined by the amount of the fine that would have been imposed or that portion of the fine that is suspended.

Complaint. A formal written accusation made by any person, often a prosecutor, and filed in a court, alleging that a specified person(s) has committed a specific offense(s).

Complaint denied. The decision by a prosecutor to decline a request that he or she seek an indictment or file an information or complaint against a specified person(s) for a specific offense(s).

Complaint granted. The decision by a prosecutor to grant a request that he or she seek an indictment or file an information or complaint against a specified person(s) for a specific offense(s).

Complaint requested (police). A request by a law enforcement agency that the prosecutor seek an indictment or file a complaint or information against a specified person(s) for a specific offense(s).

Conditional diversion. At the pretrial stage, suspension of prosecution while specific conditions are met. If conditions are not satisfied during a specified time period, the case is referred for continued prosecution.

Conditional release. The release of a defendant who agrees to meet specified conditions in addition to appearing in court. Such conditions may include remaining in a defined geographical area, maintaining steady employment, avoiding contact with the victim or with associates in the alleged crime, avoiding certain activities or places, participating in treatment, or accepting services. Conditional release is often used in conjunction with third-party or supervised release.

Confinement facility. A correctional facility from which the inmates are not regularly permitted to depart each day unaccompanied.

Convict. An adult who has been found guilty of a felony and who is confined in a federal or state confinement facility.

Conviction. A judgment of a court, based either on the verdict of a jury or a judicial officer or on the guilty plea of the defendant, that the defendant is guilty of the offense(s) for which he or she has been tried.

Correctional agency. A federal, state, or local criminal justice agency, under a single administrative authority, of which the principal functions are the investigation, intake screening, supervision, custody, confinement, or treatment of alleged or adjudicated adult offenders, delinquents, or status offenders.

Correctional day program. A publicly financed and operated nonresidential educational or treatment program for persons required, by a judicial officer, to participate.

Correctional facility. A building or part thereof, set of buildings, or area enclosing a set of buildings or structures operated by a government agency for the custody and/or treatment of adjudicated and committed persons, or persons subject to criminal or juvenile justice proceedings.

Correctional institution. A generic name proposed in this terminology for those long-term adult confinement facilities often called prisons, "federal or state correctional facilities," or "penitentiaries," and juvenile confinement facilities called "training schools," "reformatories," "boys ranches," and the like.

Correctional institution, adult. A confinement facility having custodial authority over adults sentenced to confinement for more than a year.

Correctional institution, juvenile. A confinement facility having custodial authority over delinquents and status offenders committed to confinement after a juvenile disposition hearing.

Corrections. A generic term that includes all government agencies, facilities, programs, procedures, personnel, and techniques concerned with the investigation, intake, custody, confinement, supervision, or treatment of alleged or adjudicated adult offenders, delinquents, or status offenders.

Count. Each separate offense, attributed to one or more persons, as listed in a complaint, information, or indictment.

Counterfeiting. The manufacture or attempted manufacture of a copy or imitation of a negotiable instrument with value set by law or convention, or the possession of such a copy without authorization, with the intent to defraud by claiming the copy's genuineness.

Court. An agency of the judicial branch of government, authorized or established by statute or constitution, and consisting of one or more judicial officers, which has the authority to decide on controversies in law and disputed matters of fact brought before it.

Court of appellate jurisdiction. A court that does not try criminal cases but that hears appeals.

Court of general jurisdiction. Of criminal courts, a court that has jurisdiction to try all criminal offenses, including all felonies, and that may or may not hear appeals.

Court of limited jurisdiction. Of criminal courts, a court of which the trial jurisdiction either includes no felonies or is limited to less than all felonies and which may or may not hear appeals.

Credit card fraud. The use or attempted use of a credit card in order to obtain goods or services with the intent to avoid payment.

Crime (criminal offense). An act committed or omitted in violation of a law forbidding or commanding it for which an adult can be punished, upon conviction, by incarceration and other penalties or a corporation penalized, or for which a juvenile can be brought under the jurisdiction of a juvenile court and adjudicated a delinquent or transferred to adult court.

Crime Index offenses, (index crimes). A UCR classification that includes all Part I offenses with the exception of involuntary (negligent) manslaughter.

Crimes against business (business crimes, commercial crimes). A summary term used by the National Crime Panel reports, including burglary and robbery (against businesses).

Crimes against households (household crimes). A summary term used by the National Crime Panel reports, including burglary (against households), household larceny, and motor vehicle theft.

Crimes against persons. A summary term used by UCR and the National Crime Panel reports, but with different meanings:
UCR
Murder
Nonnegligent (voluntary) manslaughter
National Crime Panel
Forcible rape
Robbery (against persons)
Aggravated assault
UCR
Negligent (involuntary) manslaughter
Forcible rape
Aggravated assault
National Crime Panel
Simple assault
Personal larceny

Crimes against property (property crime). A summary term used by UCR, both as a subclass of the Part I offenses and as a subclass of Crime Index offenses, but with different meanings:
As a subset of UCR Part I offenses
Robbery
Burglary
Larceny—theft
Motor vehicle theft
As a subset of UCR Crime Index offenses
Burglary
Larceny—theft
Motor vehicle theft

Crimes of violence (violent crime). A summary term used by UCR and the National Crime Panel, but with different meanings:
As a subset of UCR Index Crimes
Murder
Nonnegligent (voluntary) manslaughter
Forcible rape
Robbery

Aggravated assault
As a subset of National Crime Panel crimes against persons
Forcible rape
Robbery (against persons)
Aggravated assault
Simple assault

Criminal history record information. Information collected by criminal justice agencies on individuals, consisting of identifiable descriptions and notations of arrests, detentions, indictments, informations, or other formal criminal charges, and any disposition(s) arising therefrom, including sentencing, correctional supervision, and release.

Criminal justice agency. Any court with criminal jurisdiction and any other government agency or subunit that defends indigents, or of which the principal functions or activities consist of the prevention, detection, and investigation of crime; the apprehension, detention, and prosecution of alleged offenders; the confinement or official correctional supervision of accused or convicted persons; or the administrative or technical support of the above functions.

Criminal proceedings. Proceedings in a court of law undertaken to determine the guilt or innocence of an adult accused of a crime.

Culpability. The state of mind of one who has committed an act that makes him or her liable to prosecution for that act.

Defendant. A person against whom a criminal proceeding is pending.

Defense attorney. An attorney who represents the defendant in a legal proceeding.

Delinquency. Juvenile actions or conduct in violation of criminal law and, in some contexts, status offenses.

Delinquent. A juvenile who has been adjudicated by a judicial officer of a juvenile court as having committed a delinquent act, which is an act for which an adult could be prosecuted in a criminal court.

Delinquent act. An act committed by a juvenile for which an adult could be prosecuted in a criminal court but for which a juvenile can be adjudicated in a juvenile court or prosecuted in a criminal court if the juvenile court transfers jurisdiction.

De novo. Anew, afresh, as if there had been no earlier decision.

Dependency. The legal status of a juvenile over whom a juvenile court has assumed jurisdiction because the court has found his or her care by parent, guardian, or custodian to fall short of a legal standard of proper care.

Dependent. A juvenile over whom a juvenile court has assumed jurisdiction because the court has found his or her care by parent, guardian, or custodian to fall short of a legal standard of proper care.

Detention. The legally authorized holding in confinement of a person subject to criminal or juvenile court proceedings until the point of commitment to a correctional facility or release.

Detention center. A government facility that provides temporary care in a physically restricting environment for juveniles in custody pending court disposition.

Detention facility. A generic name proposed in this terminology as a cover term for those facilities that hold adults or juveniles in confinement pending adjudication, adults sentenced for a year or less of confinement, and in some instances postadjudicated juveniles, including facilities called "jails," "county farms," "honor farms," "work camps," "road camps," "detention centers," "shelters," "juvenile halls," and the like.

Detention facility, adult. A confinement facility of which the custodial authority is forty-eight hours or more and in which adults can be confined before adjudication or for sentences of a year or less.

Detention facility, juvenile. A confinement facility having custodial authority over juveniles confined pending and after adjudication.

Detention hearing. In juvenile proceedings, a hearing by a judicial officer of a juvenile court to determine whether a juvenile is to be detained, to continue to be detained, or to be released, while juvenile proceedings are pending in his or her case.

Diagnosis or classification center. A functional unit within a correctional institution, or a separate facility, that holds persons held in custody in order to determine to which correctional facil-

ity or program they should be committed.

Dismissal. A decision by a judicial officer to terminate a case without a determination of guilt or innocence.

Disposition. The action by a criminal or juvenile justice agency that signifies that a portion of the justice process is complete and jurisdiction is relinquished or transferred to another agency or that signifies that a decision has been reached on one aspect of a case and a different aspect comes under consideration, requiring a different kind of decision.

Disposition, court. The final judicial decision, which terminates a criminal proceeding by a judgment of acquittal or dismissal or which states the specific sentence in the case of a conviction.

Disposition hearing. A hearing in juvenile court, conducted after an adjudicatory hearing and subsequent receipt of the report of any predisposition investigation, to determine the most appropriate disposition of a juvenile who has been adjudicated a delinquent, a status offender, or a dependent.

Disposition, juvenile court. The decision of a juvenile court, concluding a disposition hearing, that a juvenile be committed to a correctional facility, placed in a care or treatment program, required to meet certain standards of conduct, or released.

Diversion. The official halting or suspension, at any legally prescribed processing point after a recorded justice system entry, of formal criminal or juvenile justice proceedings against an alleged offender, and referral of that person to a treatment or care program administered by a nonjustice agency or a private agency, or no referral.

Driving under the influence—alcohol (drunk driving). The operation of any vehicle after having consumed a quantity of alcohol sufficient to potentially interfere with the ability to maintain safe operation.

Driving under the influence—drugs. The operation of any vehicle while attention or ability is impaired through the intake of a narcotic or an incapacitating quantity of another drug.

Drug law violation. The unlawful sale, transport, manufacture, cultivation, possession, or use of a controlled or prohibited drug.

Early release. Release from confinement before the sentence has been completed. Early release to supervision means less jail time and, with more rapid turnover, lower jail populations and capacity requirements. Early release may come about through parole, time off for good behavior or work performed, or modification of the sentence by the court. The last procedure is usually associated with sentences to jail with a period of probation to follow. Although there are some objections to its use, "probation with jail" is a common disposition in some jurisdictions. More often than not, these sentences are in lieu of a state prison term.

Embezzlement. The misappropriation, misapplication, or illegal disposal of legally entrusted property with intent to defraud the legal owner or intended beneficiary.

Escape. The unlawful departure of a lawfully confined person from a confinement facility or from custody while being transported.

Expunge. The sealing or purging of arrest, criminal, or juvenile record information.

Extortion. Unlawful obtaining or attempting to obtain the property of another by the threat of eventual injury or harm to that person, the person's property, or another person.

Felony. A criminal offense punishable by death or by incarceration in a state or federal confinement facility for a period of which the lower limit is prescribed by statute in a given jurisdiction, typically one year or more.

Field citation. Citation and release in the field by police as an alternative to booking and pretrial detention. This practice reduces law enforcement costs as well as jail costs.

Filing. The commencement of criminal proceedings by entering a charging document into a court's official record.

Finding. The official determination of a judicial officer or administrative body regarding a disputed matter of fact or law.

Fine. The penalty imposed on a convicted person by a court requiring that he or she pay a specified sum of money. The fine is a cash payment of a dollar amount assessed by the judge in an individual case or determined by a pub-lished schedule of penalties. Fines may be paid in installments in many jurisdictions.

Forgery. The creation or alteration of a written or printed document that, if validly executed, would constitute a record of a legally binding transaction, with the intent to defraud by affirming it to be the act of an unknowing second person. Defining features: Making or altering a written or printed document or record. Act being falsely attributed to an unknowing second person. Intent being to deprive illegally a person of property or legal rights.

Fraud. An element of certain offenses consisting of deceit or intentional misrepresentation with the aim of illegally depriving a person of property or legal rights.

Fugitive. A person who has concealed himself or herself or fled a given jurisdiction in order to avoid prosecution or confinement.

Group home. A nonconfining residential facility for adjudicated adults or juveniles or those subject to criminal or juvenile proceedings, intended to reproduce as closely as possible the circumstances of family life and at the minimum, providing access to community activities and resources.

Recommended conditions of use. Classify government facilities fitting this definition as *community facilities*.

Annotation. *Group home* is variously defined in different jurisdictions. Most of the facilities known by this name are privately operated, though they may be financed mainly from government funds. Classification problems unique to private facilities have not been dealt with in this terminology, although most recommended standard descriptors for publicly operated facilities are also applicable to the private sector. See *correctional facility* for recommended standard descriptors. The data collection questionnaire for the LEAA series "Children in Custody" defines *group home* as allows juveniles extensive contact with the community, such as through jobs and schools, but none or less than half are placed there on probation or "aftercare/parole." It is distinguished from *halfway house* in this series by the percentage of residents on probation or parole.

Halfway house. A nonconfining residential facility for adjudicated adults or juveniles or those subject to criminal or juvenile proceedings, intended as an alternative to confinement for persons not suited for probation or needing a period of readjustment to the community after confinement.

Recommended conditions of use. Classify government facilities fitting this definition as *community facilities*.

Annotation. *Halfway house* is variously defined in different jurisdictions. Most of the facilities known by this name are privately operated, though they may be financed mainly from government funds. Classification problems unique to private facilities have not been dealt with in this terminology, although most recommended standard descriptors for publicly operated facilities are also applicable to the private sector. See *correctional facility* for recommended standard descriptors. The data collection questionnaire for the LEAA series "Children in Custody" defines *halfway house* as has 50 percent or more juveniles on probation or aftercare/parole, allowing them extensive contact with the community, such as through "jobs and schools." It is distinguished from *group home* in this series by the percentage of residents on probation or parole.

Hearing. A proceeding in which arguments, evidence, or witnesses are heard by a judicial officer or administrative body.

Hearing, probable cause. A proceeding before a judicial officer in which arguments, evidence, or witnesses are presented and in which it is determined whether there is sufficient cause to hold the accused for trial or whether the case should be dismissed.

Homicide. Any killing of one person by another.

Homicide, criminal. The causing of the death of another person without justification or excuse.

Equivalent Terms
UCR term—for police-reporting level
Dictionary entry term Criminal homicide
Criminal homicide
Murder (often used as cover term for murder and nonnegligent manslaughter)
Murder
Nonnegligent manslaughter

Voluntary manslaughter
Equivalent Terms
Negligent manslaughter
Involuntary manslaughter
(Included in negligent manslaughter)
Vehicular manslaughter

Homicide, excusable. The intentional but justifiable causing of the death of another or the unintentional causing of the death of another by accident or misadventure, without gross negligence. Not a crime.

Homicide, justifiable. The intentional causing of the death of another in the legal performance of an official duty or in the circumstances defined by law as constituting legal justification. Not a crime.

Homicide, willful. The intentional causing of the death of another person, with or without legal justification.

Indictment. A formal written accusation made by a grand jury and filed in a court, alleging that a specified person(s) has committed a specific offense(s).

Infraction. An offense punishable by fine or other penalty, but not by incarceration.

Inmate. A person in custody in a confinement facility.

Institutional capacity. The officially stated number of inmates or residents that a correctional facility is designed to house, exclusive of extraordinary arrangements to accommodate overcrowded conditions.

Intake. The process during which a juvenile referral is received and a decision is made by an intake unit to file a petition in juvenile court, to release the juvenile, to place the juvenile under supervision, or to refer the juvenile elsewhere.

Intake unit. A government agency or agency subunit that receives juvenile referrals from police, other government agencies, private agencies, or persons and screens them, resulting in closing of the case, referral to care or supervision, or filing of a petition in juvenile court.

Jail. A confinement facility, usually administered by a local law enforcement agency, intended for adults but sometimes also containing juveniles, that holds persons detained pending adjudication and/or persons committed after adjudication for sentences of a year or less.

Jail (sentence). The penalty of commitment to the jurisdiction of a confinement facility system for adults, of which the custodial authority is limited to persons sentenced to a year or less of confinement.

Judge. A judicial officer who has been elected or appointed to preside over a court of law, whose position has been created by statute or by constitution and whose decisions in criminal and juvenile cases may only be reviewed by a judge or a higher court and may not be reviewed *de novo.*

Judgment. The statement of the decision of a court that the defendant is convicted or acquitted of the offense(s) charged.

Judicial officer. Any person exercising judicial powers in a court of law.

Jurisdiction. The territory, subject matter, or person over which lawful authority may be exercised.

Jurisdiction, original. The lawful authority of a court or an administrative agency to hear or act upon a case from its beginning and to pass judgment on it.

Jury, grand. A body of persons who have been selected and sworn to investigate criminal activity and the conduct of public officials and to hear the evidence against an accused person(s) to determine whether there is sufficient evidence to bring that person(s) to trial.

Jury, trial (jury, petit; jury). A statutorily defined number of persons selected according to law and sworn to determine certain matters of fact in a criminal action and to render a verdict of guilty or not guilty.

Juvenile. A person subject to juvenile court proceedings because a statutorily defined event was alleged to have occurred while his or her age was below the statutorily specified limit of original jurisdiction of a juvenile court.

Annotation. Jurisdiction is determined by age at the time of the event, not at the time of judicial proceedings, and continues until the case is terminated. Thus a person may be described in a given data system as a juvenile because he or she is still subject to juvenile court proceedings, even though his or her actual age may be several years over the limit. Conversely, criminal process data systems may include juveniles if the juvenile court has waived jurisdiction. Although the age limit varies in different states, it is most often the eighteenth birthday. The variation is small enough to permit nationally aggregated data to be meaningful, although individual states should note their age limit in communications with other states. UCR defines a juvenile as anyone under eighteen years of age. See *youthful offender.*

Juvenile court. A cover term for courts that have original jurisdiction over persons statutorily defined as juveniles and alleged to be delinquents, status offenders, or dependents.

Juvenile justice agency. A government agency, or subunit thereof, of which the functions are the investigation, supervision, adjudication, care, or confinement of juveniles whose conduct or condition has brought or could bring them within the jurisdiction of a juvenile court.

Juvenile record. An official record containing, at a minimum, summary information pertaining to an identified juvenile concerning juvenile court proceedings, and, if applicable, detention and correctional processes.

Kidnapping. Unlawful transportation of a person without his or her consent or without the consent of his or her guardian, if a minor.

Larceny (larceny-theft). Unlawful taking or attempted taking of property, other than a motor vehicle, from the possession of another.

Law enforcement agency. A federal, state, or local criminal justice agency of which the principal functions are the prevention, detection, and investigation of crime and the apprehension of alleged offenders.

Law enforcement agency, federal. A law enforcement agency that is an organizational unit, or subunit, of the federal government.

Law enforcement agency, local. A law enforcement agency that is an organizational unit, or subunit, of local government.

Law enforcement agency, state. A law enforcement agency that is an organizational unit, or subunit, of state government.

Law enforcement officer (peace officer, policeman). An employee of a law enforcement agency who is an officer sworn to carry out law enforcement duties or is a sworn employee of a federal prosecutorial agency who primarily performs investigative duties.

Law enforcement officer, federal. An employee of a federal law enforcement agency who is an officer sworn to carry out law enforcement duties or is a sworn employee of a federal prosecutorial agency who primarily performs investigative duties.

Law enforcement officer, local. An employee of a local law enforcement agency who is an officer sworn to carry out law enforcement duties or is a sworn employee of a local prosecutorial agency who primarily performs investigative duties.

Law enforcement officer, state. An employee of a state law enforcement agency who is an officer sworn to carry out law enforcement duties or is a sworn employee of a state prosecutorial agency who primarily performs investigative duties.

Level of government. The federal, state, regional, or local county or city location of administrative and major funding responsibility of a given agency.

Manslaughter, involuntary (negligent manslaughter). Causing the death of another by recklessness or gross negligence.

Manslaughter, vehicular. Causing the death of another by the grossly negligent operation of a motor vehicle.

Manslaughter, voluntary (nonnegligent manslaughter). Intentionally causing the death of another with reasonable provocation.

Misdemeanor. An offense usually punishable by incarceration in a local confinement facility for a period of which the upper limit is prescribed by statute in a given jurisdiction, typically limited to a year or less.

Model Penal Code. A generalized modern codification of that which is considered basic to criminal law, published by the American Law Institute in 1962.

Monitored release. Recognizance release with the addition of minimal supervision or service; that is, the defendant may be required to keep a pretrial services agency informed of his or her whereabouts, and the agency reminds the defendant of court dates and verifies the defendant's appearance.

Motion. An oral or written request made by a party to an action, before, during, or after a trial, that a court issue a rule or order.

Motor vehicle theft. Unlawful taking, or attempted taking, of a motor vehicle owned by another with the intent to deprive the owner of it permanently or temporarily.

Murder. Intentionally causing the death of another without reasonable provocation or legal justification, or causing the death of another while committing or attempting to commit another crime.

Nolo contendere. A defendant's formal answer in court to the charges in a complaint, information, or indictment in which the defendant states that he or she does not contest the charges and which, though not an admission of guilt, subjects the defendant to the same legal consequences as does a plea of guilty.

Offender (criminal). An adult who has been convicted of a criminal offense.

Offender, alleged. A person who has been charged with a specific criminal offense(s) by a law enforcement agency or court but has not been convicted.

Offense. An act committed or omitted in violation of a law forbidding or commanding it.

Offenses, Part I. A class of offenses selected for use in UCR, consisting of those crimes that are most likely to be reported, that occur with sufficient frequency to provide an adequate basis for comparison, and that are serious crimes by nature and/or volume.

Annotation: The Part I offenses are
1. Criminal homicide.
   a. Murder and nonnegligent (voluntary) manslaughter
   b. Manslaughter by negligence (involuntary manslaughter)
2. Forcible rape
   a. Rape by force
   b. Attempted forcible rape

3. Robbery
   a. Firearm
   b. Knife or cutting instrument
   c. Other dangerous weapon
   d. Strongarm
4. Aggravated Assault
   a. Firearm
   b. Knife or cutting instrument
   c. Other dangerous weapon
   d. Hands, fist, feet, etc.—aggravated injury
5. Burglary
   a. forcible entry
   b. Unlawful entry—no force
   c. Attempted forcible entry
6. Larceny-theft (larceny)
7. Motor vehicle theft
   a. Autos
   b. Trucks and buses
   c. Other vehicles

Offenses, Part II. A class of offenses selected for use in UCR, consisting of specific offenses and types of offenses that do not meet the criteria of frequency and/or seriousness necessary for Part I offenses.

Annotation: The Part II offenses are
Other assaults (simple,* nonaggravated)
Arson*
Forgery* and counterfeiting*
Fraud*
Embezzlement*
Stolen property: buying, receiving, possessing
Vandalism
Weapons; carrying, possessing, etc.
Prostitution and commercialized vice
Sex offenses (except forcible rape, prostitution, and commercialized vice)
Narcotic drug law violations
Gambling
Offenses against the family and children
Driving under the influence*
Liquor law violations
Drunkenness
Disorderly conduct
Vagrancy
All other offenses (except traffic law violations)
Suspicion*
Curfew and loitering law violations (juvenile violations)
Runaway* (juveniles)

Terms marked with an asterisk (*) are defined in this glossary, though not necessarily in accord with UCR usage. UCR does not collect reports of Part II offenses. Arrest data concerning such offenses, however, are collected and published.

Pardon. An act of executive clemency that absolves the party in part or in full from the legal consequences of the crime and conviction.

Annotation: Pardons can be full or conditional. The former generally applies to both the punishment ·and the guilt of the offender and blots out the existence of guilt in the eyes of the law. It also removes his or her disabilities and restores civil rights. The conditional pardon generally falls short of the remedies of the full pardon, is an expression of guilt, and does not obliterate the conviction. (U.S. Supreme Court decisions on pardons and their effects are directly contradictory, and thus state laws usually govern pardons.)

Parole. The status of an offender conditionally released from a confinement facility, prior to the expiration of his or her sentence, and placed under the supervision of a parole agency.

Parole agency. A correctional agency, which may or may not include a parole authority and of which the principal function is the supervision of adults or juveniles placed on parole.

Parole authority. A person or a correctional agency that has the authority to release on parole those adults or juveniles committed to confinement facilities, to revoke parole, and to discharge from parole.

Parolee. A person who has been conditionally released from a correctional institution before the expiration of his or her sentence and who has been placed under the supervision of a parole agency.

Parole violation. A parolee's act or a failure to act that does not conform to the conditions of his or her parole.

Partial confinement. An alternative to the traditional jail sentence, consisting of "weekend" sentences, that permit offenders to spend the work week in the community, with their families, and at their jobs; furloughs, which enable offenders to leave the jail for a period of a few hours to a few days for specified purposes—to seek employment, take care of personal matters or family obligations, or engage in community service; or work/study release, under which offenders work or attend school during the day and return to the detention facility at night and on weekends.

Penalty. The punishment annexed by law or judicial decision to the commission of a particular offense, which may be death, imprisonment, fine, or loss of civil privileges.

Percentage bail. A publicly managed bail service arrangement that requires the defendant to deposit a percentage (typically 10 percent) of the amount of bail with the court clerk. The deposit is returned to the defendant after scheduled court appearances are made, although a charge (usually 1 percent) may be deducted to help defray program costs.

Person. A human being, or a group of human beings considered a legal unit, which has the lawful capacity to defend rights, incur obligations, prosecute claims, or be prosecuted or adjudicated.

Personally secured bail. Security that is put up by the defendant or the defendant's family. This arrangement is generally out of reach of the less affluent defendant.

Petition (juvenile). A document filed in juvenile court alleging that a juvenile is a delinquent, a status offender, or a dependent and asking that the court assume jurisdiction over the juvenile or that the juvenile be transferred to a criminal court for prosecution as an adult.

Petition not sustained. The finding by a juvenile court in an adjudicatory hearing that there is not sufficient evidence to sustain an allegation that a juvenile is a delinquent, status offender, or dependent.

Plea. A defendant's formal answer in court to the charges brought against him or her in a complaint, information, or indictment.

Plea bargaining. The exchange of prosecutorial and/or judicial concessions, commonly a lesser charge, the dismissal of other pending charges, a recommendation by the prosecutor for a reduced sentence or a combination thereof, in return for a plea of guilty.

Plea, final. The last plea to a given charge, entered in a court record by or for a defendant.

Plea, guilty. A defendant's formal answer in court to the charges in a complaint, information, or indictment, in which the defendant states that the charges are true and that he or she has committed the offense as charged.

Plea, initial. The first plea to a given charge, entered in a court record by or for a defendant.

Plea, not guilty. A defendant's formal answer in court to the charges in a complaint, information, or indictment, in which the defendant states that he or she is not guilty.

Police department. A local law enforcement agency directed by a chief of police or a commissioner.

Police officer. A local law enforcement officer employed by a police department.

Population movement. Entries and exits of adjudicated persons, or persons subject to judicial proceedings, into or from correctional facilities or programs.

Predisposition report. The document resulting from an investigation by a probation agency or other designated authority, which has been requested by a juvenile court, into the past behavior, family background, and personality of a juvenile who has been adjudicated a delinquent, a status offender, or a dependent, in order to assist the court in determining the most appropriate disposition.

Presentence report. The document resulting from an investigation undertaken by a probation agency or other designated authority, at the request of a criminal court, into the past behavior, family circumstances, and personality of an adult who has been convicted of a crime, in order to assist the court in determining the most appropriate sentence.

Prior record. Criminal history record information concerning any law enforcement, court, or correctional proceedings that have occurred before the current investigation of, or proceedings against, a person; or statistical descriptions of the criminal histories of a set of persons.

Prison. A confinement facility having custodial authority over adults sentenced to confinement for more than a year.

Prisoner. A person in custody in a confinement facility or in the personal custody of a criminal justice official while being transported to or between confinement facilities.

Prison (sentence). The penalty of commitment to the jurisdiction of a confinement facility system for adults, whose custodial authority extends to persons sentenced to more than a year of confinement.

Privately secured bail. An arrangement similar to the bail bondsman system except that bail is provided without cost to the defendant. A private organization provides bail for indigent arrestees who meet its eligibility requirements.

Probable cause. A set of facts and circumstances that would induce a reasonably intelligent and prudent person to believe that an accused person had committed a specific crime.

Probation. The conditional freedom granted by a judicial officer to an alleged offender, or adjudicated adult or juvenile, as long as the person meets certain conditions of behavior. One requirement is to report to a designated person or agency over some specified period of time. Probation may contain special conditions, as discussed in the definition of suspended sentence. Probation often includes a suspended sentence but may be used in association with the suspension of a final judgment or a deferral of sentencing.

Probation agency (probation department). A correctional agency of which the principal functions are juvenile intake, the supervision of adults and juveniles placed on probation status, and the investigation of adults or juveniles for the purpose of preparing presentence or predisposition reports to assist the court in determining the proper sentence or juvenile court disposition.

Probationer. A person required by a court or probation agency to meet certain conditions of behavior who may or may not be placed under the supervision of a probation agency.

Probation officer. An employee of a probation agency whose primary duties include one or more of the probation agency functions.

Probation (sentence): A court requirement that a person fulfill certain conditions of behavior and accept the supervision of a probation agency, usually in lieu of a sentence to confinement but sometimes including a jail sentence.

Probation violation: An act or a failure to act by a probationer that does not conform to the conditions of his or her probation.

Prosecutor: An attorney employed by a government agency or subunit whose official duty is to initiate and maintain criminal proceedings on behalf of the government against persons accused of committing criminal offenses.

Prosecutorial agency: A federal, state, or local criminal justice agency whose principal function is the prosecution of alleged offenders.

Pro se (in propria persona): Acting as one's own defense attorney in criminal proceedings; representing oneself.

Public defender: An attorney employed by a government agency or subdivision, whose official duty is to represent defendants unable to hire private counsel.

Public defender's office: A federal, state, or local criminal justice agency or subunit of which the principal function is to represent defendants unable to hire private counsel.

Purge (record): The complete removal of arrest, criminal, or juvenile record information from a given records system.

Rape: Unlawful sexual intercourse with a female, by force or without legal or factual consent.

Rape, forcible: Sexual intercourse or attempted sexual intercourse with a female against her will, by force or threat of force.

Rape, statutory: Sexual intercourse with a female who has consented in fact but is deemed, because of age, to be legally incapable of consent.

Rape without force or consent. Sexual intercourse with a female legally of the age of consent but who is unconscious or whose ability to judge or control her conduct is inherently impaired by mental defect or intoxicating substances.

Recidivism. The repetition of criminal behavior; habitual criminality. *Annotation:* In statistical practice, a recidivism rate may be any of a number of possible counts of instances of arrest, conviction, correctional commitment, and correctional status changes, related to the numbers of repetitions of these events within a given period of time. Efforts to arrive at a single standard statistical description of recidivism have been hampered by the fact that the term's correct referent is the actual repeated criminal or delinquent behavior of a given person or

group; yet the only available statistical indicators of that behavior are records of such system events as rearrests, reconvictions, and probation or parole violations or revocations. It is recognized that these data reflect agency decisions about events and may or may not closely correspond with actual criminal behavior. Different conclusions about degrees of correspondence between system decisions and actual behavior consequently produce different definitions of recidivism, that is, different judgments of which system event repetition rates best measure actual recidivism rates. This is an empirical question, and not one of definition to be resolved solely by analysis of language usage and system logic. Resolution has also been delayed by the limited capacities of most criminal justice statistical systems, which do not routinely make available the standardized offender-based transaction data (OBTD) that may be needed for the best measurement of recidivism. Pending the adoption of a standard statistical description of recidivism and the ability to implement it, it is recommended that recidivism analyses include the widest possible range of system events that can correspond with actual recidivism and that sufficient detail on offenses charged be included to enable discrimination among degrees of gravity of offenses. The units of count should be clearly identified and the length of community exposure time of the subject population stated. The National Advisory Commission on Criminal Justice Standards and Goals recommends a standard definition of recidivism in its volume *Corrections* (1973):
Recidivism is measured by
(1) criminal acts that resulted in a conviction by a court, when committed by individuals who are under correctional supervision or who have been released from correctional supervision within the previous three years, and by
(2) technical violations of probation or parole in which a sentencing or paroling authority took action that resulted in an adverse change in the offender's "legal status." Neither of these formulations is endorsed as adequate for all purposes. Both limit the measure and concept of recidivism to populations that are or have been under correctional supervision. Yet the ultimate

significance of data concerning the repetition of criminal behavior often depends on the comparison of the behavior of unconfined or unsupervised offenders with the behavior of those with correctional experience.

Referral to intake. In juvenile proceedings, a request by the police, parents, or other agency or person that a juvenile intake unit take appropriate action concerning a juvenile alleged to have committed a delinquent act or status offense or to be dependent.

Release from detention. The authorized exit from detention of a person subject to criminal or juvenile justice proceedings.

Release from prison. A cover term for all lawful exits from federal or state confinement facilities primarily intended for adults serving sentences of more than a year, including all conditional and unconditional releases, deaths, and transfers to other jurisdictions, excluding escapes.
Transfer of jurisdiction
Release on parole
Conditional release
Release while still under jurisdiction of correctional agency, before expiration of sentence
Discretionary
Release date determined by parole authority
Mandatory
Release date determined by statute
Discharge from prison
Release ending all agency jurisdiction
Unconditional release
Discretionary
Pardon, commutation of sentence
Mandatory
Expiration of sentence
Temporary release
Authorized, unaccompanied temporary departure for educational, employment, or other authorized purposes
Transfer of jurisdiction
Transfer to jurisdiction of another correctional agency or a court
Death
Death from homicide, suicide, or natural causes
Execution
Execution of sentence of death
In some systems release on "parole" represents

only discretionary conditional release. It is recommended that mandatory conditional releases be included, as both types describe conditional releases with subsequent parole status.

Release on bail. The release by a judicial officer of an accused person who has been taken into custody, upon the accused's promise to pay a certain sum of money or property if he or she fails to appear in court as required, a promise that may or may not be secured by the deposit of an actual sum of money or property.

Release on own recognizance. The release, by a judicial officer, of an accused person who has been taken into custody, upon the accused's promise to appear in court as required for criminal proceedings.

Release, pretrial. A procedure whereby an accused person who has been taken into custody is allowed to be free before and during his or her trial.

Release to third party. The release, by a judicial officer, of an accused person who has been taken into custody, to a third party who promises to return the accused to court for criminal proceedings.

Residential treatment center. A government facility that serves juveniles whose behavior does not necessitate the strict confinement of a training school, often allowing them greater contact with the community.

Restitution. Usually a cash payment by the offender to the victim of an amount considered to offset the loss incurred by the victim or the community. The amount of the payment may be scaled down to the offender's earning capacity, and/or payments may be made in installments. Sometimes services directly or indirectly benefiting the victim may be substituted for cash payment.

Retained counsel. An attorney, not employed or compensated by a government agency or subunit or assigned by the court, who is privately hired to represent a person(s) in a criminal proceeding.

Revocation. An administrative act performed by a parole authority removing a person from parole, or a judicial order by a court removing a person from parole or probation, in response to a violation by the parolee or probationer.

Revocation hearing. An administrative and/or judicial hearing on the question of whether or not a person's probation or parole status should be revoked.

Rights of defendant. Those powers and privileges that are constitutionally guaranteed to every defendant.

Robbery. The unlawful taking or attempted taking of property that is in the immediate possession of another, by force or the threat of force.

Robbery, armed. The unlawful taking or attempted taking of property that is in the immediate possession of another, by the use or threatened use of a deadly or dangerous weapon.

Robbery, strongarm. The unlawful taking or attempted taking of property that is in the immediate possession of another by the use or threatened use of force, without the use of a weapon.

Runaway. A juvenile who has been adjudicated by a judicial officer of a juvenile court as having committed the status offense of leaving the custody and home of his or her parents, guardians, or custodians without permission and failing to return within a reasonable length of time.

Seal (record). The removal, for the benefit of the subject, of arrest, criminal, or juvenile record information from routinely available status to a status requiring special procedures for access.

Security. The degree of restriction of inmate movement within a correctional facility, usually divided into maximum, medium, and minimum levels.

Security and privacy standards. A set of principles and procedures developed to ensure the security and confidentiality of criminal or juvenile record information in order to protect the privacy of the persons identified in such records.

Sentence. The penalty imposed by a court on a convicted person, or the court decision to suspend imposition or execution of the penalty.

Sentence, indeterminate. A statutory provision for a type of sentence to imprisonment in which, after the court has determined that the convicted person shall be imprisoned, the exact length of imprisonment and parole supervision is afterward fixed within statutory limits by a parole authority.

Sentence, mandatory. A statutory requirement that a certain penalty shall be imposed and executed upon certain convicted offenders.

Sentence, suspended. The court decision postponing the pronouncement of sentence upon a convicted person or postponing the execution of a sentence that has been pronounced by the court.

Sentence, suspended execution. The court decision setting a penalty but postponing its execution.

Sentence, suspended imposition. The court decision postponing the setting of a penalty.

Shelter. A confinement or community facility for the care of juveniles, usually those held pending adjudication.

Sheriff. The elected or appointed chief officer of a county law enforcement agency, usually responsible for law enforcement in unincorporated areas and for operation of the county jail.

Sheriff, deputy. A law enforcement officer employed by a county sheriff's department.

Sheriff's department. A law enforcement agency organized at the county level, directed by a sheriff, that exercises its law enforcement functions at the county level, usually within unincorporated areas, and operates the county jail in most jurisdictions.

Speedy trial. The right of the defendant to have a prompt trial.

State highway patrol. A state law enforcement agency whose principal functions are the prevention, detection, and investigation of motor vehicle offenses and the apprehension of traffic offenders.

State highway patrol officer. An employee of a state highway patrol who is an officer sworn to carry out law enforcement duties, primarily traffic code enforcement.

State police. A state law enforcement agency whose principal functions may include maintaining statewide police communications, aiding local police in criminal investigation, training police, guarding state property, and patrolling highways.

State police officer. An employee of a state police agency who is an officer sworn to carry out law enforcement duties, sometimes including traffic enforcement duties.

Stationhouse citation. An alternative to pretrial detention, whereby the arrestee is escorted to the precinct police station or headquarters rather than the pretrial detention facility. Release, which may occur before or after booking, is contingent upon the defendant's written promise to appear in court as specified on the release form.

Status offender. A juvenile who has been adjudicated by a judicial officer of a juvenile court as having committed a status offense, which is an act or conduct that is an offense only when committed or engaged in by a juvenile.

Status offense. An act or conduct that is declared by statute to be an offense, but only when committed or engaged in by a juvenile, and that can be adjudicated only by a juvenile court.

Subjudicial officer. A judicial officer who is invested with certain judicial powers and functions but whose decisions in criminal and juvenile cases are subject to *de novo* review by a judge.

Subpoena. A written order issued by a judicial officer requiring a specified person to appear in a designated court at a specified time in order to serve as a witness in a case under the jurisdiction of that court or to bring material to that court.

Summons. A written order issued by a judicial officer requiring a person accused of a criminal offense to appear in a designated court at a specified time to answer the charge(s). The summons is a request or instruction to appear in court to face an accusation. As an alternative to the arrest warrant, it is used in cases on which complaints are registered with the magistrate or prosecutor's office.

Supervised release. A type of release requiring more frequent contact than monitored release does. Typically, various conditions are imposed and supervision is aimed at enforcing these conditions and providing services as needed. Some form of monetary bail also may be attached as a condition of supervised release, especially in higher-risk cases.

Suspect. A person, adult or juvenile, considered by a criminal justice agency to be one who may have committed a specific criminal offense but who has not been arrested or charged.

Suspended sentence. Essentially a threat to take more drastic action if the offender again commits a crime during some specified time period. When no special conditions are attached, it is assumed that the ends of justice have been satisfied by conviction and no further action is required, as long as the offender refrains from involvement in new offenses. Suspended sentences may be conditioned on various limitations as to mobility, associates, or activities or on requirements to make reparations or participate in some rehabilitation program.

Suspicion. Belief that a person has committed a criminal offense, based on facts and circumstances that are not sufficient to constitute probable cause.

Theft. Larceny, or in some legal classifications, the group of offenses including larceny, and robbery, burglary, extortion, fraudulent offenses, hijacking, and other offenses sharing the element of larceny.

Third-party release. A release extending to another person the responsibility for ensuring the defendant's appearance in court. This may be a person known to the defendant or a designated volunteer. Third-party release may be a condition of unsecured bail, with the third party as a cosigner.

Time served. The total time spent in confinement by a convicted adult before and after sentencing, or only the time spent in confinement after a sentence of commitment to a confinement facility.

Training school. A correctional institution for juveniles adjudicated to be delinquents or status offenders and committed to confinement by a judicial officer.

Transfer hearing. A preadjudicatory hearing in juvenile court in order to determine whether juvenile court jurisdiction should be retained or waived for a juvenile alleged to have committed a delinquent act(s) and whether he or she should be transferred to criminal court for prosecution as an adult.

Transfer to adult court. The decision by a juvenile court, resulting from a transfer hearing, that jurisdiction over an alleged delinquent will be waived and that he or she should be prosecuted as an adult in a criminal court.

Trial. The examination of issues of fact and law in a case or controversy, beginning when the jury has been selected in a jury trial, the first witness is sworn, or the first evidence is introduced in a court trial and concluding when a verdict is reached or the case is dismissed.

Trial, court (trial, judge). A trial in which there is no jury and a judicial officer determines the issues of fact and law in a case.

Trial, jury. a trial in which a jury determines the issues of fact in a case.

UCR. An abbreviation for the Federal Bureau of Investigation's uniform crime reporting program.

Unconditional discharge. As a posttrial disposition, essentially the same as unconditional diversion. No savings are obtained in criminal justice processing costs, but jail populations may be reduced; conditions of release are imposed for an offense in which the defendant's involvement has been established.

Unconditional diversion. The cessation of criminal processing at any point short of adjudication with no continuing threat of prosecution. This type of diversion may be a voluntary referral to a social service agency or program dealing with a problem underlying the offense.

Unsecured bail. A form of release differing from release on recognizance only in that the defendant is subject to paying the amount of bail if he or she defaults. Unsecured bail permits release without a deposit or purchase of a bondsman's services.

Venue. The geographical area from which the jury is drawn and in which trial is held in a criminal action.

Verdict. In criminal proceedings, the decision made by a jury in a jury trial, or by a judicial officer in a court trial, that a defendant is either guilty or not guilty of the offense(s) for which he or she has been tried.

Verdict, guilty. In criminal proceedings, the decision made by a jury in a jury trial, or by a judicial officer in a court trial, that the defendant is guilty of the offense(s) for which he or she has been tried.

Verdict, not guilty. In criminal proceedings, the decision made by a jury in a jury trial, or by a judicial officer in a court trial, that the defendant is not guilty of the offense(s) for which he or she has been tried.

Victim. A person who has suffered death, physical or mental suffering, or loss of property as the result of an actual or attempted criminal offense committed by another person.

Warrant, arrest. A document issued by a judicial officer that directs a law enforcement officer to arrest a person who has been accused of an offense.

Warrant, bench. A document issued by a judicial officer directing that a person who has failed to obey an order or notice to appear be brought before the court.

Warrant, search. A document issued by a judicial officer that directs a law enforcement officer to conduct a search for specified property or persons at a specific location, to seize the property or persons, if found, and to account for the results of the search to the issuing judicial officer.

Witness. A person who directly perceives an event or thing or who has expert knowledge relevant to a case.

Youthful offender. A person, adjudicated in criminal court, who may be above the statutory age limit for juveniles but is below a specified upper age limit, for whom special correctional commitments and special record sealing procedures are made available by statute.

Appendix B
National Policies on Corrections as Ratified by the American Correctional Association

National Correctional Policy on Classification

Introduction:

Classification is a continuing process basic to identifying and matching offender needs to correctional resources. This continuing process involves all phases of correctional management.

Statement:

Classification should balance the public's need for protection, the needs of offenders, and the efficient and effective operation of the correctional system. In developing and administering its classification system, a correctional agency should:

A. Develop written classification policies that establish criteria specifying different levels of security, supervision, and program involvement; establish procedures for documenting and reviewing all classification decisions and actions; describe the appeal process to be used by individuals subject to classification; and specify the time frames for monitoring and reclassifying cases;

B. Develop the appropriate range of resources and services to meet the identified control and program needs of the population served;

C. Base classification decisions on rational assessment of objective and

Source: The National Conference on Correctional Policy (College Park, Md: ACA, 1987), pp. 62–82. The most recent policies ratified are from Charlotte Nesbitt, Director, ACA National Correctional Policy Project, 1988. Reprinted by permission of the American Correctional Association and the National Institute of Corrections.

valid information, including background material (criminal history, nature of offense, social history, educational needs, medical/mental health needs, etc.) as well as information regarding the individual's current situation, adjustment, and program achievement;

D. Train all personnel in the classification process and require specialized training for those directly involved in classification functions;

E. Use the classification process to assign individuals to different levels of control on the basis of valid criteria regarding risk (to self and others) and individual needs, matching these characteristics with appropriate security, level of supervision, and program services;

F. Involve the individual directly in the classification process;

G. Assign appropriately trained staff to monitor individual classification plans for progress made and reclassification needs;

H. Objectively validate the classification process and instruments, assess on a planned basis the degree to which results meet written goals, and, as needed, refine the process and instruments; and

I. Provide for regular dissemination of classification information to all levels of correctional staff and to involved decision-makers outside of corrections as an aid in the planning, management, and operation of the correctional agency.

Public Correctional Policy on Health Care for Offenders _____

Introduction:

Correctional facilities and other correctional agencies that, either by law or as part of their stated mission, provide health care to accused and adjudicated offenders must provide health services that are appropriate and that reflect contemporary standards for health care. To ensure accountability and professional responsibility, these services should meet the policy guidelines set forth below and the health care standards of the American Correctional Association.

Statement:

Health care programs for offenders include medical, dental, and mental health services. Such programs should:

A. Be delivered by qualified health care professionals;

B. Provide to offenders, upon their arrival at a facility or at the beginning of their participation in a correctional program or service, both oral and written information concerning access to available health services;

C. Provide continuous, comprehensive services commencing at admission, including effective and timely screening, assessment and treatment, appropriate referral to alternate health care resources where warranted, and, if necessary, referral at discharge for continuing health problems;

D. Establish a system to identify and treat emergencies quickly and effectively;

E. Establish a formal program to treat and manage inmates with communicable diseases;

F. Provide appropriate health care training for all correctional staff and continuing education opportunities for professional health care providers;

G. Establish health education programs to encourage offenders to participate in their own health maintenance and prevention of communicable disease; and

H. Provide a medical records system for documentation of care and information sharing, consistent with privacy, confidentiality, and security concerns, to enhance continuity of service and professional accountability.

Public Correctional Policy on Employment of Women in Corrections _____

Introduction:

The American Correctional Association has a long-standing commitment to equal employment opportunity for women in adult and juvenile corrections.

Statement:

Women have a right to equal employment. No person who is qualified for a particular position/assignment or for job-related opportunities should be denied such employment or opportunities because of gender. Therefore, correctional agencies should:

A. Ensure that recruitment, selection, and promotion opportunities are open to women;

B. Assign female employees duties and responsibilities that provide career development and promotional opportunities equivalent to those provided to other employees;

C. Provide all levels of staff with appropriate training on developing effective and cooperative working relationships between male and female correctional personnel; and

D. Conduct regular monitoring and evaluation of affirmative action practices and take any needed corrective actions.

Public Correctional Policy on Employment of Ex-Offenders _____

Introduction:

Obtaining and maintaining employment is a primary step toward assuring the successful transition of offenders to law-abiding citizens in the community. The cooperation of government, business, industry, and volunteer agencies and organizations is essential in making employment opportunities available. In helping to implement this philosophy, correctional agencies should demonstrate their willingness to employ qualified ex-offenders.

Statement:

Ex-offenders should be given equitable consideration for employment. Correctional agencies should:

A. Implement and promote programs that will help offenders to prepare for, seek, and hold gainful employment in the community;
B. Develop and implement policy permitting qualified ex-offenders to be employed in correctional agencies in capacities that preserve the security and public safety mission of those agencies; and
C. Support legislation that will ensure that equal employment opportunities for ex-offenders are restored.

Public Correctional Policy on Correctional Research and Evaluation _____

Introduction:

Research and evaluation, and the use of the findings that result from such efforts, are essential to informed correctional policy, program development and decision-making.

Statement:

Correctional agencies have a continuing responsibility to promote, initiate, sponsor, and participate in correctional research and evaluation efforts, both external and internal, in order to expand knowledge about offender behavior and enhance the effectiveness and efficiency of programs and services. To encourage and support these research and evalution efforts, correctional agencies should:

A. Establish clearly defined procedures for data collection and analysis that ensure the accuracy, consistency, integrity, and impartiality of correctional research projects;

B. Conduct regular and systematic evaluation of correctional management, programs, and procedures and implement necessary changes;

C. Review and monitor correctional research to ensure compliance with professional standards, including those relating to confidentiality and the protection of human rights;

D. Prohibit the use of offenders as experimental subjects in medical, psychological, pharmacological, and cosmetic research except when warranted and prescribed for the diagnosis or treatment of an individual's specific condition in accordance with current standards of health care;

E. Make available to others the information necessary for correctional research and evaluation, consistent with concerns for privacy, confidentiality, and security;

F. Involve and train appropriate correctional staff in the application of correctional research and evaluation findings; and

G. Encourage the dissemination of correctional research and evaluation findings.

National Correctional Policy on Legal Issues and Litigation _____

Introduction:

Adherence to law is fundamental to professional correctional practice. This entails avoiding litigation through sound management, effective use of the adversarial process to resolve issues that are litigated, and professional compliance with judicial orders.

Statement:

Problems addressed through litigation, such as inadequate and insufficient facilities, services, procedures, and staffing, can often be remedied through professional correctional practice, supported by government officials and the public with the necessary capital and operational resources. To achieve sound management of legal issues, correctional agencies should:

A. Use the standards and accreditation process of the American Correctional Association and the Commission on Accreditation for Corrections as a method to develop and maintain professional practice;

B. Consult frequently with legal counsel to remain informed of current developments in the law and to anticipate and avoid emerging legal problems;

C. Train staff about legal issues and responsibilities and provide them with legal representation when appropriate;

D. Attempt to resolve potential legal problems through dispute resolution techniques such as administrative grievance procedures;

E. Negotiate and settle litigation when agreements can be developed consistent with professional correctional practice;

F. Litigate, when no professionally reasonable alternative is possible, with the best legal and correctional expertise available and with full preparation and development of the case; and

G. Implement court orders in a professional manner.

National Correctional Policy on Information Systems _____

Introduction:

Timely and accurate information is a basic requirement for effective management of organizations. Such information forms a basis for sound decision-making and provides for accountability in operations and program results.

Statement

For correctional managers to function effectively, they must have accurate and timely information. The design of correctional information systems must reflect combined efforts of both correctional professionals and information system specialists. To meet the diverse needs of a correctional agency, information systems should be designed that will support the management processes of the agency as their primary function, support service delivery functions by providing data relevant to their efficiency and outcome, and provide sufficient flexibility to support relevant research and evaluation.

To promote development of effective information systems, correctional agencies should:

A. Clearly define the desired scope of the system, consistent with a realistic assessment of anticipated resources and technologies;

B. Involve and train correctional managers in all stages of system development and operation to ensure managers' needs are met;

C. Prepare detailed and carefully monitored development plans to ensure systems are designed and implemented in a timely and cost-effective manner;

D. Require that the system include formal evaluation procedures to ensure the quality of system input and output;

E. Cooperate with correctional, law enforcement, and other public agencies to provide for mutual sharing of information, consistent with legitimate concerns for privacy, confidentiality, and system security;

      F. Ensure appropriate information needs of the public are met, consistent with legal requirements; and

      G. Advocate provision of resources to implement and update advanced information system technologies.

National Correctional Policy on Design of Correctional Facilities

Introduction:

The effectiveness and efficiency of correctional staff in maintaining security and delivering services can be either enhanced or limited by the physical plants in which they operate. Quality design has long-term cost and program advantages in assisting a correctional system to accomplish its mission.

Statement:

Correctional architecture is unique, involving the design of facilities that are functionally and environmentally supportive of the needs and activities of a confined society. The design of such facilities is a multidisciplinary process. To improve the design quality and operational adequacy of new and renovated correctional facilities, correctional agencies should:

      A. Define operations of correctional facilities prior to design, including written specifications of the facility's mission and functional elements, basic operating procedures, and staffing patterns so the design can fully support intended correctional operations;

      B. Select architects and engineers on merit, as demonstrated by either successful completion of prior correctional projects, or by successful completion of other projects combined with access to recognized correctional expertise;

      C. Design correctional facilities through a multidisciplinary process that directly involves correctional professionals, criminal justice planners, architects and engineers, and that also seeks the contribution of other groups and disciplines who have an interest in the facility's design, including those involved in the facility's day-to-day operations;

      D. Ensure that facility designs conform to applicable codes and nationally approved professional standards and that they encourage direct interaction in supervision of offenders, consistent with staff safety;

      E. Ensure facility design is sufficiently flexible to accommodate changes in offender population and in the facility's mission, operating procedures, and staffing;

      F. Maintain project oversight to assure design objectives are met;

G. Recognize the need for early selection of key staff who will be responsible for initial operation of the facility so they can participate in the design and construction process; and

H. Engage in an ongoing process of research and evaluation to develop, improve, and recognize the most successful design features, equipment technologies, and operating procedures.

National Correctional Policy on Purpose of Corrections

Introduction:

In order to establish the goals and objectives of any correctional system, there must be a universal statement of purpose that all members of the correctional community can use in goal setting and daily operations.

Statement:

The overall mission of criminal and juvenile justice, which consists of law enforcement, courts, and corrections, is to enhance social order and public safety. As a component of the justice system, the role of corrections is:

A. To implement court-ordered supervision and, when necessary, detention of those accused of unlawful behavior prior to adjudication;

B. To assist in maintaining the integrity of law by administering sanctions and punishments imposed by courts for unlawful behavior;

C. To offer the widest range of correctional options, including community corrections, probation, institutions, and parole services, necessary to meet the needs of both society and the individual; and

D. To provide humane program and service opportunities for accused and adjudicated offenders that will enhance their community integration and economic self-sufficiency, and that are administered in a just and equitable manner within the least restrictive environment consistent with public safety.

National Correctional Policy on Private Sector Involvement in Corrections

Introduction:

Although most correctional programs are operated by public agencies, there is increasing interest in the use of profit and nonprofit organizations as providers of services, facilities, and programs. Profit and nonprofit organizations have resources for the delivery of services that often are unavailable from the public correctional agency.

Statement:

Government has the ultimate authority and responsibility for corrections. For its most effective operation, corrections should use all appropriate resources, both public and private. When government considers the use of profit and nonprofit private sector correctional services, such programs must meet professional standards, provide necessary public safety, provide services equal to or better than government, and be cost-effective compared to well-managed governmental operations. While government retains the ultimate responsibility, authority, and accountability for actions of private agencies and individuals under contract, it is consistent with good correctional policy and practice to:

A. Use in an advisory and voluntary role the expertise and resources available from profit and nonprofit organizations in the development and implementation of correctional programs and policies;

B. Enhance service delivery systems by considering the concept of contracting with the private sector when justified in terms of cost, quality, and ability to meet program objectives;

C. Consider use of profit and nonprofit organizations to develop, fund, build, operate, and/or provide services, programs, and facilities when such an approach is cost-effective, safe, and consistent with the public interest and sound correctional practice;

D. Ensure the appropriate level of service delivery and compliance with recognized standards through professional contract preparation and vendor selection as well as effective evaluation and monitoring by the responsible government agency; and

E. Indicate clearly in any contract for services, facilities, or programs the responsibilities and obligations of both government and contractor, including but not limited to liability of all parties, performance bonding, and contractual termination.

National Correctional Policy on Offenders with Special Needs _____

Introduction:

The provision of humane programs and services for the accused and adjudicated requires addressing the special needs of certain offenders. To meet this goal, correctional agencies should develop and adopt procedures for the early identification of offenders with special needs. Agencies should also develop a plan for providing the services that respond to those needs and for monitoring the delivery of services in both confined and community settings.

Statement:

Correctional systems should assure provision of specialized services and programs to meet the special needs of offenders. To achieve this, they should:

A. Identify the categories of offenders who will require special care or programs. These categories include:
   1. Offenders with severe psychological needs, mental retardation, significant psychiatric disorders, behavior disorders, multiple handicaps, neurological impairments, and substance abuse;
   2. Offenders who are physically handicapped or chronically or terminally ill;
   3. Offenders who are elderly;
   4. Offenders with severe social and/or educational deficiencies, learning disabilities, or language barriers; and
   5. Offenders with special security or supervision needs, such as protective custody cases, death row inmates, and those who chronically exhibit potential for violent or aggressive behavior.
B. Provide specialized services or programs for those offenders who are identified as being in need of special care or programs. Such services and programs may be provided within the correctional agency itself, or by referral to another agency that has the necessary specialized program resources, or by contracting with private or voluntary agencies or individuals that meet professional standards;
C. Maintain specially trained staff for the delivery of care, programs, and services;
D. Maintain documentation of the services and programs provided;
E. Institute carefully controlled evaluation procedures to determine each program's effectiveness and the feasibility of its continuation or the need for adjustments; and
F. Provide leadership and advocacy for legislative and public support to obtain the resources needed to meet these special needs.

National Correctional Policy on Use of Appropriate Sanctions and Controls _____

Introduction:

In developing, selecting, and administering sanctions and punishments, decision-makers must balance concern for individual dignity, public safety, and maintenance of social order. Correctional programs and facilities are a costly and limited resource; the most restrictive are generally the most expensive. Therefore, it is good public policy to use these resources wisely and economically.

Statement:

The sanctions and controls imposed by courts and administered by corrections should be the least restrictive consistent with public and individual safety and maintenance of social order. Selection of the least restrictive sanctions and punishments in specific cases inherently requires balancing several important objectives—individual dignity, fiscal responsibility, and effective correctional operations. To meet these objectives, correctional agencies should:

A. Advocate to all branches of government—executive, legislative, and judicial—and to the public at large the development and appropriate use of the least restrictive sanctions, punishments, programs, and facilities;

B. Recommend the use of the least restrictive appropriate dispositions in judicial decisions;

C. Classify persons under correctional jurisdiction to the least restrictive appropriate programs and facilities; and

D. Employ only the level of regulation and control necessary for the safe and efficient operation of programs, services, and facilities.

National Correctional Policy on Community Corrections _____

Introduction:

Correctional programs operating in a community setting are an integral part of a comprehensive correctional system. These include community residential facilities, probation, parole, and other programs that provide supervision and services for accused or adjudicated juveniles and adults. Responsiveness to the needs of victims and offenders and to protection of the public is essential to the success of community programs and services.

Statement:

The least restrictive sanctions and controls consistent with public and individual safety and maintenance of social order require that the majority of offenders receive services in a community setting. It is the responsibility of government to develop, support, and maintain correctional programs and services in the community. A screening process to select offenders who can be safely maintained in the community is critical for placement in these programs. Those responsible for community corrections programs, services, and supervision should:

A. Seek statutory authority and adequate funding, both public and private, for community programs and services;

B. Develop and ensure access to an array of service, residential or non-residential, that adequately address the identifiable needs of offenders and the community;

C. Inform the public and offenders of the reasons for community programs and services, the criteria used for selecting individuals for these programs and services, and that placement in such a program is a punishment;

D. Ensure the integrity and accountability of community programs by establishing a reliable system for monitoring and measuring performance in accordance with accepted standards and professional practice;

E. Recognize that public acceptance of community corrections is enhanced by victim restitution and conciliation programs; and

F. Seek the active participation of a well-informed constituency, including citizen advisory boards and broad-based coalitions, to address community corrections issues.

National Correctional Policy on Correctional Industry _____

Introduction:

Correctional industry programs, whether operated by the public or private sector, aid correctional systems in reducing idleness, lowering costs, and providing opportunities for offenders to gain job skills, training, and economic self-sufficiency and to participate in programs of victim compensation and institution cost-sharing.

Statement:

Correctional industry programs, operating under sound management principles and effective leadership, should:

A. Be based on statutes and regulations that support the development, manufacturing, marketing, distribution, and delivery of correctional industry products and services;

B. Be unencumbered by laws and regulations that restrict access to the marketplace, competitive pricing, and fair work practices except as necessary to protect the offender and the system from exploitation;

C. Provide evaluation and recognition of job performance to assist in promoting good work habits that may enhance employability after release;

D. Provide training and safe working conditions, for both staff and offenders, similar to those found in the community at large;

E. Assure that the working conditions in an industry operated by public or private organizations are comparable with those in the industry at large, and that compensation to inmates is fair;

F. Recognize that profit-making and public service are both legitimate goals of an industry program;

G. Support reinvestment of profits to expand industrial programs, improve overall operations, maintain and upgrade equipment, and assist in the support of inmate training programs that enhance marketable skills, pre-release training and job placement services; and

H. Integrate industry programs, public or private, with other institutional programs and activities under the overall leadership of the institution's chief administrator.

National Correctional Policy on Use of Force _____

Introduction:

Correctional agencies administer sanctions and punishments imposed by courts for unlawful behavior. Assigned to correctional agencies involuntarily, offenders sometimes resist authority imposed on them, and may demonstrate violent and destructive behaviors. Use of legally authorized force by correctional authorities may become necessary to maintain custody, safety, and control.

Statement

Use of force consists of physical contact with an offender in a confrontational situation to control behavior and enforce order. Use of force includes use of restraints (other than for routine transportation and movement), chemical agents, and weapons. Force is justified only when required to maintain or regain control, or when there is imminent danger of personal injury or serious damage to property. To assure the use of force is appropriate and justifiable, correctional agencies should:

A. Establish and maintain policies that require reasonable steps be taken to reduce or prevent the necessity for the use of force, that authorize force only when no reasonable alternative is possible, that permit only the minimum force necessary, and that prohibit the use of force as a retaliatory or disciplinary measure;

B. Establish and enforce procedures that define the range of methods for and alternatives to the use of force, and that specify the conditions under which each is permitted. The procedures must assign responsibility for authorizing such force, assure appropriate medical care for all involved, and provide the fullest possible documentation and supervision of the action;

C. Establish and maintain procedures that limit the use of deadly force to those instances where it is legally authorized and where there is an imminent threat to human life or a threat to public safety that cannot reasonably be prevented by other means;

D. Maintain operating procedures and regular staff training designed to anticipate, stabilize, and defuse situations that might give rise to conflict, confrontation, and violence;

E. Provide specialized training to ensure competency in all methods of use of force, especially in methods and equipment requiring special knowledge and skills such as defensive tactics, weapons, restraints, and chemical agents; and

F. Establish and maintain procedures that require all incidents involving the use of force be fully documented and independently reviewed by a higher correctional authority. A report of the use of force, including appropriate investigation and any recommendations for preventive and remedial action, shall be submitted for administrative review and implementation of recommendations when appropriate.

National Correctional Policy on Conditions of Confinement

Introduction:

Correctional systems must administer the detention, sanctions, and punishments ordered by the courts in an environment that protects public safety and provides for the safety, rights, and dignity of staff, accused or adjudicated offenders, and citizens involved in programs.

Statement

Maintaining acceptable conditions of confinement requires adequate resources and effective management of the physical plant, operational procedures, programs, and staff. To provide acceptable conditions, agencies should:

A. Establish and maintain a safe and humane population limit for each institution based upon recognized professional standards;

B. Provide an environment that will support the health and safety of staff, confined persons, and citizens participating in programs. Such an environment results from appropriate design, construction, and maintenance of the physical plant as well as the effective operation of the facility;

C. Maintain a professional and accountable work environment for staff that includes necessary training and supervision as well as sufficient staffing to carry out the mission of the facility; and

D. Maintain a fair and disciplined environment that provides programs and services in a climate that encourages responsible behavior.

National Correctional Policy on Crowding and Excessive Workloads

Introduction:

Overpopulation of correctional programs and facilities can negate the effectiveness of management, program, security, and physical plant operations and can endanger offenders, staff, and the public at large. High population density within correctional facilities has been associated with increased physical and mental problems, more frequent disciplinary incidents, higher rates of assault and suicide, and decreased effectiveness of programs and services. When the population of a correctional program or facility exceeds capacity, maintaining safe and reasonable conditions of confinement and supervision becomes increasingly difficult, and may become impossible. Excessive workloads in institutional and community corrections dilute effectiveness of supervision and support services and threaten public safety.

Statement:

The number of offenders assigned to correctional facilities and community services should be limited to levels consistent with recognized professional standards. Correctional agencies should:

A. Establish and maintain safe and humane population and workload limits for each institution and service program based on recognized professional standards;

B. Develop, advocate, and implement, in coordination with the executive, legislative, and judicial branches of government, emergency and longterm processes by which offender populations can be managed within reasonable limits;

C. Anticipate the need for expanded program and facility capacity by using professional population projection methodologies that reflect both demographic and policy-related factors influencing correctional population growth;

D. Advocate the full development and appropriate use of pretrial/adjudication release, probation, parole, community residential facilities, and other community services that are alternatives to assigning offenders to crowded facilities or that reduce the duration of assignment of offenders to such facilities;

E. Develop, advocate, and implement plans for necessary additional facilities, staff, programs, and services.

National Correctional Policy on Offender Education and Training

Introduction:

Many accused and adjudicated juvenile and adult offenders lack basic educational, vocational, and social skills necessary to enhance community integration and economic self-sufficiency. These deficiencies may interact with other socioeconomic and psychological factors to affect the life choices made by offenders and may limit the legitimate financial and social opportunities available to these individuals.

Statement:

Education and training are integral parts of the total correctional process. Governmental jurisdictions should develop, expand, and improve delivery systems for academic, occupational, social, and other educational programs for accused and adjudicated juvenile and adult offenders in order to enhance their community integration and economic self-sufficiency. Toward this end, correctional agencies should:

A. Provide for assessment of academic, vocational, and social skills deficiencies of those under their jurisdictions;

B. Make available opportunities to participate in relevant, comprehensive educational, vocational, and social skills training programs and job placement activities that are fully coordinated and integrated with other components of the correctional process and the community as a whole.

C. Ensure programs provided are taught by certified instructors in accordance with professional standards and relevant techniques;

    D. Provide incentives for participation and achievement in education and training programs;

    E. Maximize use of public and private sector resources in development, implementation, coordination, and evaluation of education and training programs and job placement activities; and

    F. Evaluate the efficiency and effectiveness of program performance based on measurable goals and objectives.

National Correctional Policy on Juvenile Corrections _____

Introduction:

The juvenile corrections system must provide specialized care for young offenders in our society. Juvenile corrections, although sharing the same overall purpose as adult corrections, has significantly different processes and procedures and requires specialized care, services, and programs.

Statement

Children and youth have distinct personal growth and developmental needs and should be secure from any harmful effects of association with adult offenders. Juvenile corrections must provide a continuum of programs, services, and facilities for accused and adjudicated juvenile offenders that are separate from those for adult offenders. Services and care for the individual youth must be a primary concern, consistent with protection of the public and maintenance of social order. To achieve these goals, juvenile corrections officials and agencies should:

    A. Establish and maintain effective communication with all concerned with the juvenile justice system — executive, judicial, and legislative officials, prosecution and defense counsel, social service agencies, schools, police, and families — to achieve the fullest possible cooperation in making appropriate decisions in individual cases and in providing and using services and resources;

    B. Provide a range of community and residential programs and services to meet individual needs, including education, vocational training, recreation, religious opportunities, family, aftercare, medical, dental, mental health, and specialized programs and services such as substance abuse treatment;

    C. Involve the family and community as preferred resources and use the least restrictive appropriate dispositions in program planning and placement for juveniles;

D. Exclude from correctional systems all status offenders (those whose behavior would not be considered criminal if committed by adults);

E. Operate a juvenile classification system to identify and meet the program needs of the juvenile offender, while actively considering the public's need for protection; and

F. Support limitations on the use of juvenile records according to approved national standards, recognizing that the need to safeguard the privacy and rehabilitative goals of the juvenile should be balanced with concern for the protection of the public, including victims.

National Correctional Policy on Female Offender Services _____

Introduction:

Correctional systems must develop service delivery systems for accused and adjudicated female offenders that are comparable to those provided to males. Additional services must also be provided to meet the unique needs of the female offender population.

Statement:

Correctional systems must be guided by the principle of parity. Female offenders must receive the equivalent range of services available to other offenders, including opportunities for individualized programming and services that recognize the unique needs of this population. The services should:

A. Assure access to a range of alternatives to incarceration, including pretrial and post-trial diversion, probation, restitution, treatment for substance abuse, halfway houses, and parole services;

B. Provide acceptable conditions of confinement, including appropriately trained staff and sound operating procedures that address this population's needs in such areas as clothing, personal property, hygiene, exercise, recreation, and visitation with children and family;

C. Provide access to a full range of work and programs designed to expand economic and social roles of women, with emphasis on education; career counseling and exploration of non-traditional as well as traditional vocational training; relevant life skills, including parenting and social and economic assertiveness; and pre-release and work/education release programs;

D. Facilitate the maintenance and strengthening of family ties, particularly those between parent and child;

E. Deliver appropriate programs and services, including medical, dental, and mental health programs, services to pregnant women, substance abuse programs, child and family services, and provide access to legal services; and

F. Provide access to release programs that include aid in establishing homes, economic stability, and sound family relationships.

National Correctional Policy on Staff Recruitment and Development _____

Introduction:

Knowledgeable, highly skilled, motivated, and professional correctional personnel are essential to fulfill the purpose of corrections effectively. Professionalism is achieved through structured programs of recruitment and enhancement of the employee's skills, knowledge, insight, and understanding of the correctional process.

Statement:

Correctional staff are the primary agents for promoting health, welfare, security, and safety within correctional institutions and community supervision programs. They directly interact with accused and adjudicated offenders and are the essential catalysts of change in the correctional process. The education, recruitment, orientation, supervision, compensation, training, retention, and advancement of correctional staff must receive full support from the executive, judicial, and legislative branches of government. To achieve this, correctional agencies should:

A. Recruit personnel, including ex-offenders, in an open and accountable manner to assure equal employment opportunity for all qualified applicants regardless of sex, age, race, physical disability, religion, ethnic background, or political affiliation, and actively promote the employment of women and minorities;

B. Screen applicants for job-related aspects of physical suitability, personal adjustment, emotional stability, dependability, appropriate educational level, and experience. An additional requisite is the ability to relate to accused or adjudicated offenders in a manner that is fair, objective, and neither punitive nor vindictive;

C. Select, promote, and retain staff in accordance with valid job-related procedures that emphasize professional merit and technical competence. Voluntary transfers and promotions within and between correctional systems should be encouraged.

D. Comply with professional standards in staff development and offer a balance between operational requirements and the development of personal, social, and cultural understanding. Staff development programs should involve use of public and private resources, including colleges, universities, and professional associations;

E. Achieve parity between correctional staff and comparable criminal justice system staff in salaries and benefits, training, continuing education, performance evaluations, disciplinary procedures, career development opportunities, transfers, promotions, grievance procedures, and retirement; and

F. Encourage the participation of trained volunteers and students to enrich the correctional program and to provide a potential source of recruitment.

National Correctional Policy on Probation _____

Introduction:

The vast majority of adjudicated adult and juvenile offenders remain in the community. Probation is a judicial decision that assigns the responsibility for supervision and control of these offenders to community corrections.

Statement:

Probation is a frequently used and cost-effective sanction of the court for enhancing social order and public safety. Probation may be used as a sanction by itself or, where necessary and appropriate, be combined with other sanctions such as fines, restitution, community service, residential care, or confinement. Agencies responsible for probation should:

A. Prepare disposition assessments to assist the court in arriving at appropriate sanctions. The least restrictive disposition consistent with public safety should be recommended;

B. Establish a case management system for allocating supervisory resources through a standardized classification process;

C. Provide supervision to probationers and, with their input, develop a realistic plan to ensure compliance with orders of the court;

D. Monitor and evaluate, on an ongoing basis, the probationer's adherence to the plan of supervision and, when necessary, modify the plan of supervision according to the changing needs of the offender and the best interests of society;

E. Provide access to a wide range of services to meet identifiable needs, all of which are directed toward promoting law-abiding behavior;

F. Assure any intervention in an offender's life will not exceed the minimal amount needed to assure compliance with the orders of the court;

G. Initiate appropriate court proceedings, when necessary, if the probationer fails to comply with orders of the court, supervision plan, or other requirements so the court may consider other alternatives for the protection and well-being of the community;

H. Oppose use of the probation sanction for status offenders, neglected or dependent children, or any other individuals who are neither accused nor charged with delinquent or criminal behavior;

I. Establish an educational program for sharing information about probation with the public and other agencies; and

J. Evaluate program efficiency, effectiveness, and overall system accountability consistent with recognized correctional standards.

National Correctional Policy on Parole _____

Introduction:

Parole is the conditional release of an offender from confinement before expiration of sentence pursuant to specified terms and conditions of supervision in the community. The grant of parole and its revocation are responsibilities of the paroling authority. Supervision of the parolee is provided by a designated agency that ensures compliance with all requirements by the releasee through a case management process. Because the vast majority of those incarcerated will eventually be released into the community, the public is best protected by a supervised transition of the offender from institutional to community integration. Parole offers economic advantages to the public, the offender, and the correctional system by maximizing opportunities for offenders to become productive, law-abiding citizens.

Statement:

The parole component of the correctional system should function under separate but interdependent decision-making and case supervision processes. Paroling authorities should seek a balance in weighing the public interest and the readiness of the offender to re-enter society under a structured program of supervisory management and control. Paroling systems should be equipped with adequate resources for administering the investigative, supervisory, and research functions. Administrative regulations governing the grant of parole, its revocation, case supervision practices, and discharge procedures should incorporate standards of due process and fundamental fairness. To achieve the maximum cost-benefits of parole supervision, full advantage should be taken of community-based resources available for serving offender employment and training needs, substance abuse treatment, and other related services. The parole system should:

A. Establish procedures to provide an objective decision-making process incorporating standards of due process and fundamental fairness in granting of parole that will address, at a minimum, the risk to public safety, impact on the victim, and information about the offense and the offender;

B. Provide access to a wide range of support services to meet offender needs consistent with realistic objectives for promoting law-abiding behavior;

C. Ensure any intervention in an offender's life will not exceed the minimum needed to ensure compliance with the terms and conditions of parole;

D. Provide a case management system for allocating supervisory resources through a standardized classification process, reporting parolee progress, and monitoring individualized parolee supervision and treatment plans;

E. Provide for the timely and accurate transmittal of status reports to the paroling authority for use in decision-making with respect to revocation, modification, or discharge of parole cases;

F. Establish programs for sharing information, ideas, and experience with other agencies and the public; and

G. Evaluate program efficiency, effectiveness, and overall accountability consistent with recognized correctional standards.

National Correctional Policy on Standards and Accreditation

Introduction:

Correctional agencies should provide community and institutional programs and services that offer a full range of effective, just, humane, and safe dispositions and sanctions for accused and adjudicated offenders. To assure accountability and professional responsibility, these programs and services should meet accepted professional standards and obtain accreditation. The use of standards and the accreditation process provides a valuable mechanism for self-evaluation, stimulates improvement of correctional management and practice, and provides recognition of acceptable programs and facilities. The American Correctional Association and the Commission on Accreditation for Corrections have promulgated national standards and a voluntary system of national accreditation for correctional agencies. The beneficiaries of such a process are the administration and staff of correctional agencies, offenders, and the public.

Statement:

All correctional facilities and programs should be operated in accordance with the standards established by the American Correctional Association and should achieve and maintain accreditation through the Commission on Accreditation for Corrections. To fulfill this objective, correctional agencies should:

A. Implement improvement as necessary to comply with the appropriate standards specified or referenced in the following manuals and supplements:

- Standards for Adult Parole Authorities
- Standards for Adult Community Residential Services
- Standards for Adult Probation and Parole Field Services
- Standards for Adult Correctional Institutions
- Standards for Adult Local Detention Facilities
- Standards for Juvenile Community Residential Facilities
- Standards for Juvenile Probation and Aftercare Services
- Standards for Juvenile Detention Facilities
- Standards for Juvenile Training Schools
- Standards for the Administration of Correctional Agencies

B. Seek and maintain accreditation through the voluntary process developed by the Commission on Accreditation for Corrections in order that, through self-evaluation and peer review, necessary improvements are made, programs and services come into compliance with appropriate standards, and professional recognition is obtained.

National Correctional Policy on Victims of Crime _____

Introduction:

Victims of crime suffer financial, emotional, and/or physical trauma. The criminal justice system is dedicated to the principle of fair and equal justice for all people. Victims' rights should be pursued within the criminal justice system to ensure their needs are addressed.

Statement:

Victims have the right to be treated with respect and compassion, to be informed about and involved in the criminal justice process as it affects their lives, to be protected from harm and intimidation, and to be provided necessary financial and support services that attempt to restore them to their former position before the crime was committed. Although many components of the criminal justice system share in the responsibility of providing services to victims of crime, the correctional community has an important role in this process and should:

A. Support activities that advocate the rights of the victims;
B. Promote local, state, and federal legislation that emphasizes victim rights and the development of victim service programs in local communities;
C. Advocate funding and technical assistance to develop and expand victim service programs;
D. Promote and advocate the development of programs in which offenders provide restitution to victims, and compensation and service to the community;
E. Promote active participation of victims in the criminal justice process, including the opportunity to be heard;
F. Promote the use of existing community resources and community volunteers to serve the needs of victims;
G. Cooperate in the development of training programs, designed for criminal justice officials, that promote sensitivity to victims' rights and identify community services; and
H. Operate those victim assistance programs that appropriately fall within the responsibility of the field of corrections.

Index